INTERACTIVE
INDESIGN C

INTERACTIVE INDESIGN CC

BRIDGING THE GAP BETWEEN PRINT & DIGITAL PUBLISHING

MIRA RUBIN

Focal Press
Taylor & Francis Group

NEW YORK AND LONDON

First published 2014
by Focal Press
70 Blanchard Road, Suite 402, Burlington, MA 01803

and by Focal Press
2 Park Square, Milton Park, Abingdon, Oxon OX14 4RN

Focal Press is an imprint of the Taylor & Francis Group, an informa business

Notices

Knowledge and best practice in this field are constantly changing. As new research and experience broaden our understanding, changes in research methods, professional practices, or medical treatment may become necessary.

Practitioners and researchers must always rely on their own experience and knowledge in evaluating and using any information, methods, compounds, or experiments described herein. In using such information or methods they should be mindful of their own safety and the safety of others, including parties for whom they have a professional responsibility.

Product or corporate names may be trademarks or registered trademarks, and are used only for identification and explanation without intent to infringe.

Adobe®, Adobe Acrobat®, Adobe Bridge®, Adobe Content Viewer®, Adobe Digital Editions®, Adobe Dreamweaver®, Adobe Edge Animate®, Adobe Flash®, Adobe Illustrator®, Adobe InDesign®, Adobe Media Encoder®, Adobe Photoshop®, and Adobe Reader® are either registered trademarks or trademarks of Adobe Systems Incorporated in the United States and/or other countries. Apple® and Apple iPad® are trademarks of Apple Inc., registered in the US and other Countries. Pano2VR® is a registered trademark of Garden Gnome Software. Google®, GoogleMaps® and YouTube® are registered trademarks of Google, Inc. Microsoft Word®, Microsoft Excel®, Microsoft Office® are registered trademarks of Microsoft. All other trademarks are the property of their respective owners.

THIS PRODUCT IS NOT ENDORSED OR SPONSORED BY ADOBE SYSTEMS INCORPORATED, PUBLISHER OF ADOBE INDESIGN®.

Library of Congress Cataloging in Publication Data
CIP data has been applied for

ISBN: 978-0-415-66177-5 (pbk)
ISBN: 978-0-203-38521-0 (ebk)

Typeset in Futura Standard and Avenir LT Standard
By Mira Rubin, Joe Duffey and Katherine Veri
Printed in the US by RR Donnelley

SUSTAINABLE FORESTRY INITIATIVE

Certified Chain of Custody
At Least 20% Certified Forest Content
www.sfiprogram.org
SFI-01042

This book is dedicated to the power of mountains
to inspire their climbing
and of dreams
to inspire their fulfillment.

TABLE OF CONTENTS

ACKNOWLEDGEMENTS

This book was my Everest. Thank heavens I wasn't faced with making the climb alone because I never would have made it. Joe Duffey, renaissance man, business partner, and friend: your talent, insane persistence and relentless attention to detail got us to the summit. You took on the monumental task of tech editing the book with no idea what the journey would hold and hung in there through every unanticipated challenge. I can't thank you enough for your encouragement and support, the endless hours of editing, taking screen shots and reformatting; and the sheer will without which this project would never have been completed. It's your flag too at the top of that mountain.

Katherine Veri, you showed up out of nowhere when Joe and I were worn and weary. Like a magical Sherpa, you immediately became an essential part of the team, taking on whatever needed doing: tech editing, screen shots, reformatting. Thank you so much for the invaluable gift of your time, talent and dedication. It wouldn't have happened without you.

To Robin Sapossnek: dear friend, I'm so grateful to have you in my life. Thank you for your support on so many fronts. Without you, I don't know how I would have gotten through.

As an Adobe Certified Instructor, I've been immersed for years in the world of print and web design. However, when I began writing this book nearly a year and a half ago, I was relatively new to EPUB and DPS. PEPCON (the Print and ePublishing conference sponsored by David Blatner and Anne-Marie Concepción of InDesignSecrets.com) changed all that and got me off to a running start. Sincere thanks to David and Anne-Marie for producing the conference and for bringing together such a stellar brain trust. PEPCON 2012 woke me up to the power of InDesign Scripts and GREP which has been nothing short of life altering. How I managed to work in InDesign for so long without them I'll never know. In any case, thank you to Michael Murphy for your GREP tutorials and your beautifully esthetic and clear diagrams and to Erica Gamet, Anne-Marie and Mike Rankin for lists of scripts that redefine the meaning of the phrase "power-user." To the GREP and script writers who so generously share the fruits of their genius with the InDesign community notably Marc Autret, Kris Coppieters, Peter Kahrel, Gabe Harbs, Michael Murphy, and Marijan Tompa—thank you! We are all in your debt.

> **NOTE:** The EPUB Resources chapter begins on page 415 and the list of DPS resources starts on page 531.

A big thank you to the vital community of digital publishing experts for the rich resources you make available in print, online and in person. For a list of these folks and a good number of resources I found invaluable in the quest to provide a useful guide, check out the resource pages at the end of both the EPUB and DPS sections of the book.

Particular acknowledgement is due to Bob Bringhurst and Colin Fleming—both from Adobe. Thank you! Your DPS tutorials were absolutely indispensable.

With regard to EPUB, I owe a major debt of gratitude to Anne-Marie Concepción, Liz Castro and Gabriel Powell. Ann-Marie and Gabriel, your Lynda.com tutorials are brilliant and were essential to my education. Liz, your books and blog together formed the foundation of my EPUB understanding.

For all things InDesign, deep appreciation to the InDesignSecrets.com team, particularly Anne-Marie and David Blatner. Your site has taken on the role of trusted friend and advisor, with a scope that never ceases to amaze. Case in point, I recently learned how to set straight double quotes as a default preference through the Dictionary category of the Preferences panel. Who knew? Clearly you guys did! For that tip and so much more, thank you. I am deeply in your debt.

Thank you to the team at Garden Gnome Software for their awesomely cool Pano2VR software. Without you, I don't know how the magic of DPS panoramas would be possible.

To Alastair Onglingswan, Iris Chau, Stephen Chen and the GreenSoul Shoes team—you guys are an inspiration. You introduced me to the notion of social entrepreneurship and a triple bottom line—people, planet and profit. Thank you for the good work that you do and for allowing the use of your content. Your mission to shoe underprivileged children while building sustainable third world economies has inspired me to dream much bigger dreams. It's my fondest hope that the sharing of your story inspires the same in others and helps to bring the GreenSoul Shoes vision to fruition.

To Scott Bille, Daniel Helin, Katherine Houghton, and Shevi McNamara—you guys are the ones to "blame" for this book in the first place since you reviewed the initial proposal so many lifetimes ago. Thank you for your accolades. I may never forgive you.

Dad, you have my deep gratitude for helping to make yet another book possible. You've always been there for me. Mom, thank you for your confidence and encouragement. I love you both dearly.

Thank you to Barbara Ash, an enthusiastic reader of Interactive InDesign CS5 who volunteered some excellent recommendations for an improved reading experience. Barbara, the readers of this book are indebted to you for reducing their eyestrain.

Of course, if it weren't for Adobe and particularly the InDesign team, there wouldn't be anything to write about. I've had the privilege of meeting a bunch of you and came away from our conversations sincerely impressed by your deep commitment to make the product and the user experience the best it could be. Thank you for your dedication and the worlds of creativity you've put at our fingertips. Keep fighting the good fight. You guys are my heroes.

INTRODUCTION

Interactive InDesign: The Next Generation

Since Adobe's release of Creative Suite 5 in April of 2010, the digital media landscape has changed at a blinding speed and there's no indication of a slow-down any time soon. For a little perspective, it was also in April of 2010 that Apple released the very first iPad, forever changing media consumption habits worldwide.

InDesign CS5 ushered in a new era for designers by making it possible within the familiar InDesign environment to design not only for print but for digital media as well. All of a sudden it was possible to bring print projects to life with video, audio, interactive navigation, and even Flash animation. The movement from print to "printeractive" had begun with a roar.

Merely one year later in April of 2011, Adobe released Creative Suite 5.5 and Apple released the iPad 2. The unprecedented adoption of the iPad with it's lack of support for Flash, coupled with the rise of HTML5 signalled the beginning of the end for Flash. On November 11, 2011, Adobe announced that it was curtailing support for Flash on mobile devices. The Flash animation capabilities that had been so promising in

InDesign CS5 became significantly less relevant since there is still—as of 7/2013—no reliable way provided by Adobe to translate InDesign's Flash animation to HTML5, the new de facto standard for animation and video on mobile devices—and increasingly on the web.

Don't write Flash off completely however—at least not quite yet. It is still widely supported on the web by desktop browsers and can provide an excellent option for stand-alone executable presentations that rival the best of PowerPoint.

With InDesign animation and all things Flash being dealt a damaging blow, Adobe released Creative Suite 5.5 and its pièce de resistance: the Digital Publishing Suite (DPS.) Thus, as one door closed, another was flung wide open and InDesign became a viable tool to create digital magazines as apps that could be sold through the Apple App Store. New tools were added to enable all sorts of in-app interactivity and InDesign was off and running again, deep into the thick of the digital media frontier.

Once again in April, merely one year later in 2012, Adobe released Creative Suite 6 and Apple released the Retina Display iPad. Of course, the rest of the world wasn't standing still while Adobe and Apple were barrelling down the digital highway. In that same two-year window, Amazon released multiple versions of its Kindle eReader/tablet, the Barnes and Noble Nook saw multiple iterations, the Samsung Galaxy tablet carved out a name for itself, and Kobo became an eBook/eReader rising star. With tablets and eReaders an indisputable fact of life, InDesign CS6 rose to the challenge with greatly improved tools for digital content creation targeted to multiple devices.

And that brings us to the present with an invitation to join the mad migration to the largely uncharted digital frontier. The tools in InDesign CC will equip you well for the next leg of the journey and, if the pace of change over the last several years is any indication, it's going to be a wild ride.

About the Book

This book had its genesis in a moment of rapturous enthusiasm over the truly revolutionary, and evolutionary direction taken by Adobe with the release of InDesign CS5—a release that established InDesign as an application dedicated not just to print, but to digital publishing as well. InDesign CS5.5, CS6 and now InDesign CC have expanded on this ground-breaking shift of paradigm with support for a range of digital publishing options—from interactive PDF to eBooks and digital magazines, from apps for mobile devices to the ability to migrate content from InDesign to Flash Professional or Dreamweaver for further development. InDesign has become a truly "printeractive" application, enabling you to bring your print designs to life or your interactive designs to the printed page—all within the same robust and versatile interface. The truth is, the possibilities are so vast that if you don't yet use InDesign, now's the time to start. If you do use InDesign, now's the time to take it to the next level—and that's what this book is about.

The book is intended to be used both for reference and as a hands-on how-to manual. There's something here for everyone. If you're new to InDesign, the instructions and illustrations are concise enough that you should be able to follow along pretty easily. If you're a seasoned user, living daily in InDesign, not only will you learn about its interactive features, but you're bound to pick up lots of tips and tricks that will be a boon to your print work as well.

While you could most likely open to any exercise in any chapter and follow it, you'll get the most out of the book if you start at the beginning and work your way through to the end. Within the topic-based framework, tangential but relevant subjects are often discussed in the context of the exercise workflow. So, for example, a discussion about designing buttons might lead to discussion of effects, which then leads to a discussion of object styles. Each chapter builds on the last, and because there are all kinds of productivity gems sprinkled throughout, there's a lot you could miss by skipping around. Part 2 especially covers concepts and techniques essential to later topics.

The book is divided into seven parts:

Part 1: Interactive InDesign

This section provides all the preliminaries: an introduction to and comparison of each of InDesign's digital publishing options, discussion of interactive design concepts and considerations, and customization of the InDesign interface to best support your digital design workflow.

> DOWNLOAD: All the exercises files used throughout the book are available for download on the companion website: http://www.interactive-indesign.com.

Part 2: Document Layout & Navigation

This section lays the foundation for everything that follows. Starting with the basics, you'll cover topics that include formatting and threading text, as well as lesser known and more advanced type techniques like creating nested styles. You'll learn how to set up multi-page documents and work with master pages, and explore some of InDesign's fancier features including hyperlinks and cross-references, footnotes, and tables of contents. You'll even dig in to InDesign's graphic capabilities with an entire chapter dedicated to shapes and color. Whether you're a seasoned InDesign professional or a new user, this part has goodies you'll appreciate, and covers a number of tools and features you won't want to work without.

Part 3: Buttons

Buttons are at the heart of interactivity, and InDesign buttons have tremendous versatility and power that go well beyond simple interface navigation. In this section you'll discover the broad range of appearance options and functionality that you can build into your buttons. You'll start by modifying buttons from InDesign's Sample Buttons and Forms library and move on to building buttons of your own from scratch. Not only will you learn everything you need to know to make your buttons beautiful, but you'll put InDesign's button functionality to use to achieve unexpected and creative effects.

Part 4: Flash Animation and Output to SWF Animation

Despite the waning influence of Flash, the fact that you can create animation right in InDesign without writing code is pretty remarkable. Flash movies are still supported in Acrobat and Adobe Reader so you can include them in Interactive PDFs for desktop viewing. You can also transform your exported SWFs into executable files to make awesome stand-alone presentations. In this section, you'll learn how to work with animation presets, animate on a motion path, and set animation timing and triggers. Building on the basics, you'll expand your skills with advanced techniques and create complex, timed, interactive presentations and sequenced animations. As you play with animation in InDesign, you just might forget you're working in the industry's leading application for laying out print—it really is that terrifically cool!

Part 5: Interactive PDF

This section opens the door to the world of interactive PDF, from bookmarks to buttons; from incorporating animation, media, and page transitions to practical production strategies for creating interactive PDF forms. You'll become familiar with form fields including text fields, radio buttons, checkboxes, combo boxes, list boxes and signature fields. With tables to tailor your layout, you'll finish your form work in InDesign by using the Articles panel to touch-up tab order. You'll learn the ins and outs of interactive PDF export and wrap things up with some finishing touches in Acrobat Professional.

Part 6: EPUB

EPUB is a world unto itself and one that is defined by standards and technologies external to InDesign. An understanding of the EPUB landscape and its underpinnings is essential in order to use InDesign's EPUB creation features effectively. Think of this section as an EPUB field guide, first providing a map of the territory and then a primer on some of the survival skills and tools required to navigate its developing terrain. You'll go well outside the bounds of InDesign to collect eReaders and other software and scripts essential to EPUB production, learn HTML fundamentals—the underlying language of EPUB—and gain some experience with GREP—a tool that will revolutionize your InDesign long document workflow. Of course you'll also learn best practices for working with InDesign's tools and features to generate valid EPUBs. Wrapping up the section is an entire chapter dedicated to EPUB tools and resources—this chapter alone is worth its weight in gold.

Part 7: Digital Publishing Suite

The digital magazine-type apps you can generate using the Digital Publishing Suite (DPS) tools in InDesign are nothing short of spectacular. Similar to portions of the EPUB production workflow, the creation of a DPS app requires that you venture beyond InDesign to complete particular processes and collect required credentials. With a focus on creating Single Edition DPS apps for publication to the Apple App Store, you'll learn about the DPS subscription options, the Creative Cloud DPS benefit, and the steps needed to take your project to publication. You'll collect the peripheral tools necessary to preview and test your publications and then use InDesign's Folio Overlays panel to create the interactive elements in your articles. In the process, you'll discover that the artistry behind DPS overlays relies largely on the sometimes elaborate preparation of assets in tools external to InDesign. For a hands-on experience of a possible workflow, you'll make a quick jump to Photoshop and to Bridge and to another application called Pano2VR, to get briefly acquainted. You'll learn how to make your DPS content scroll and spin and zoom and swipe, and then you'll put it all together into a publishable DPS folio. And since the DPS and InDesign app horizon is morphing as rapidly as that for EPUB and the rest of the digital publishing landscape, this section too wraps things up with a list of resources to help you stay on top of the trends.

Conventions Used in the Book

The bulk of changes in InDesign CC have been made to things you'll never actually see—all the nuts and bolts under the hood have been retooled from the ground up for improved performance. That said, what you can't help but notice when you first open InDesign CC is the new dark interface designed to match the previously carbonized environments in Photoshop and Illustrator. In the interest of saving ink (and also in deference to our personal preference) the screenshots in the book were taken with the Interface Color Theme preference set to Light. To make your InDesign environment match the environment represented throughout the book, go to Edit > Preferences > Interface/InDesign > Preferences > Interface and select Light from the Color Theme dropdown. Then, deselect the Match Pasteboard to Theme Color checkbox.

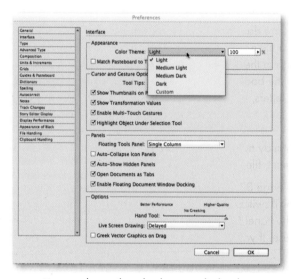

You can change the color theme applied to the interface through the Preferences panel.

Screenshots were taken using a Mac. In the interest of balance, for keyboard shortcuts and menu commands, Windows shortcuts are given first, followed by a slash, followed by shortcuts for Mac. A typical example is Ctrl+0/Command+0. The + sign in a shortcut means that the keys are additive rather than sequential; you need to hold them down at the same time. In other words, you hold down Ctrl or Command, add the 0, and then release the mouse before releasing the keys.

Menu commands are typically preceded by the words "Go to", followed by a hierarchy of menu names separated by a *greater than* sign (>).
EXAMPLE: Go to Window > Object & Layout > Align. In this example, "Window" is the parent menu, "Object & Layout" is a submenu and "Align" is the panel being opened.

There are frequent sidebars—tips are blue, notes are yellow, alerts are red, and links to downloadable files and supporting apps are green.

TIP: Tip sidebars are blue and contain the word TIP.

NOTE: Note sidebars are yellow and contain the word NOTE.

ALERT: Alert sidebars are red and contain the word ALERT.

DOWNLOAD: Download sidebars are green and contain the word DOWNLOAD.

Color-coded tips, notes, alerts and downloads appear in sidebars throughout the book.

There are lots of pictures too, to provide a visual reference. In the event that you're not in front of your computer when reading the book, in most cases you'll still be able to get a good idea of what's being discussed. Of course the exercises will make a lot more sense if you actually work through them in InDesign.

Exercise steps are dark blue, and conversational and explanatory text appears in black. Exercise file names are bolded. If a menu item, file name or button name is in lower case in the context of the application or file structure, it appears in lower case in the book. It was a toss-up as to whether to format such things in all lowercase letters, all initial capital letters or mixed for visual emphasis. We decided it made the most sense to stick to the capitalization conventions used in the application and actual file or object names. As a result, there are occasional sentences that may not make total sense until you identify the reference to an interface element, file, or object name.

In Chapter 3, page 33, you'll set up a customized workspace. Up until Chapter 25—when you'll switch to the [Book] workspace—exercises making reference to panels in the Panel Dock will assume that this customized workspace labeled **DigiPub** is in use. If you don't use the customized workspace, you may encounter references to panels that don't appear in the Panel Dock. Any panels missing from the Panel Dock can be opened from the Window menu.

Nearly every exercise has accompanying files that you can download from http://www.interactive-indesign.com. In most cases, an exercise has both a start and an end file so you can see the final result before going through the step-by-step lesson. Deconstruction of existing projects is a time-honored learning method and the "end" files are provided with that purpose in mind.

About QR Codes

An awesome new feature in InDesign CC is its ability to create QR (Quick Response) codes. QR codes encode information in a patterned graphical display that can be interpreted by dedicated decoding applications. You'll find several instances of QR codes in the book providing links that enable you to download supporting apps or documentation.

You should be able to find a number of applications for your device that can decode QR codes. Our current favorite for iPhone and iPad is NeoReader which actually reads a variety of barcode types.

DOWNLOAD: To view QR codes, download the NeoReader app from the iPhone iTunes App Store.

Using a QR Reader is really quite simple. Start the app and frame the QR code in the viewer window of your device ensuring that the squares at the top and lower left of the code are visible. Depending on your reader, you may have to adjust the position of your device to properly align the squares, then, capture the code. (Your app may do that for you automatically when it is able to interpret the image.) If the captured QR code contains a URL, your device should take you to that address. QR codes can also be used to send email, or text messages, capture contact information or convey plain text messages.

Since we're talking about QR codes, now is as good a time as any to take a quick side trip to learn how to make them.

Creating QR Codes in InDesign

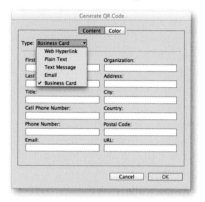

The Generate QR Code dialog.

To create a QR code with InDesign CC, go to Object > Generate QR Code, choose an option from the Type dropdown, and enter the desired information. To make the color of your QR code something other than black, click the color button at the top of the dialog and choose your color from the document color swatches. Click OK to load the QR code into your cursor then click to place it on your document. If you want your QR code to be a specific size, be sure to hold the Shift key while you drag your loaded cursor to the dimensions you want the code to be.

Editing an InDesign QR Code

Editing an existing QR code in InDesign is even easier than creating one. With the QR code selected, go to Object > Edit QR Code. When the Edit QR Code dialog opens, edit the information you want changed and then click OK to update the code.

Exporting QR Codes as Images

You can preserve your QR code for use in other documents by exporting it from InDesign as a PNG or JPEG. With your placed QR code selected, go to File > Export and choose PNG or JPEG as the file format. The trick to exporting only the QR code and not the entire document is to be sure to select the Selection option in the export dialog. You can choose the quality and resolution settings best suited to your destination but we recommend saving a high quality and high resolution PNG from which you can generate other versions of your QR code image as needed.

You can export your InDesign QR code as an image in PNG or JPEG format.

The Content and Exercise Assets

The flower, texture, animal and insect photographs used in the book and the accompanying projects were taken by Mira Rubin, with the exception of 3 purchased stock images (the turkeys, a loon, and birds playing in a bird bath) and four gorgeous flower images taken and generously contributed to the cause by Joe Duffey (the opening images for Chapters 5, 6, 25 and 26.) The Alice in Wonderland images and text used in the EPUB section were attained through Project Gutenberg and are in the public domain. There is an abundance of content throughout the book and exercises used by permission from GreenSoul Shoes which remains their property. All content was provided for the purpose of working through the exercises included with the book, and any distribution or commercial use is strictly prohibited without written consent.

It's our hope that in reading this book and working through the exercises, you will experience even a fraction of the excitement and enthusiasm about InDesign that brought the book into being. The excitement is about the worlds of possibility that InDesign puts at your fingertips. Enjoy, and create with abandon!

Part 1

INTERACTIVE INDESIGN

This section provides the foundation to get you up and running with the rich interactive capabilities of InDesign CC. You'll learn guidelines for interactive design, become acquainted with the interactive design tools, customize the interface, and get a taste of what you can really do when you put InDesign through its paces. Get ready for a wild ride! You're going to be amazed by the things you can do.

● Chapter 1

THE LAY OF THE LAND

You're going to be blown away by the rich variety of digital publishing options that InDesign puts at your fingertips. This chapter will help you navigate your options and provide you with a taste of what can be accomplished with this awesome tool. You'll tour some of the completed exercise files both in a browser and in Adobe Reader or Acrobat. You'll see video and animation in action, use dropdown menus, play slideshows and this is just the beginning. When it's all said and done, you'll have the rest of the book to learn how to do all of this and so much more.

The Stampede from Print to Digital Media

When speaking of the migration from print to digital media, we're reminded of the frenzy that must have characterized the days of the gold rush and the wild, wild west. These are indeed exciting times with emerging digital media technologies transforming the horizon almost minute-by-minute. While it would be wonderful to be able to provide a definitive set of instructions with explicit best practices, tried-and-true workflows and ultimately a reliable step-by-step guide, the fact is that the digital media landscape is changing so quickly that, at best, we can provide only a compass and some navigational aids to help you chart your travels.

So what exactly is it we mean when we talk about digital media? And how does InDesign factor into the mix? Known as the premiere layout application for magazine and print collateral, InDesign has been evolving to become an extremely powerful and versatile tool in the digital media space as well. As a creation tool for both static and Interactive PDF, Flash SWF, EPUB and apps that can be published for sale in various app stores, InDesign has been blazing a solid trail from print-to-interactive and helping to define the new Printeractive® paradigm.

As to the digital media side of things, sorting through all the possible digital destinations to choose the best option for your needs can be a little daunting. The fact is that the technologies and formats are morphing and converging at a staggering pace and what may be a clear distinction between them at this writing may not be so definitive in the near future. That said, let's take a look at the assortment of digital publishing options to help you better prepare for this wild and woolly journey.

PDF, Flash, EPUB, HTML or DPS?

Just as you wouldn't print a magazine when you needed a business card, or a billboard in lieu of a brochure, different digital modalities are best suited for different purposes. Understanding their strengths and weaknesses will go a long way toward helping you determine what direction to take as you navigate the evolving digital publishing frontier.

PDF

People just don't realize how sexy PDFs can be. When viewed in a desktop version of Adobe Reader or Acrobat (and other PDF readers with varied support), a PDF can contain bookmarks, hyperlinks, video, audio, Flash animation, interactive forms, navigational buttons, show/hide effects and page transitions. PDF functionality can be further extended in Acrobat Professional by adding form field calculations, custom JavaScript, attached files and more. You can even view PDFs in full screen mode for a more immersive interactive experience.

The development timeline for Interactive PDF can be minimal compared to other digital publishing options if you design your print assets to be able to accommodate media and interactive elements. Adobe Reader is widely adopted and freely available and you can easily distribute a PDF as an email attachment or a download from the web. One of the primary advantages to PDF is that your audience can zoom in and out as desired without compromising the precision or integrity of your layout—design elements stay where you place them and the fonts you chose are the fonts that appear in your publication. Your content can be viewed without an online connection, it's searchable, can be selected, annotated and secured. All in all, PDF has a lot going for it as a digital publishing platform.

For PDF as with anything else, some of its strengths can also be perceived as its weaknesses. Since its page dimensions are fixed, zooming and scrolling may be required in order to view content on a smaller screen making for a less pleasant user experience. If the viewing device is rotated, magnification may change but the orientation of the PDF page remains fixed, again possibly requiring that a user scroll to view it. And, like print, once published, the content in a PDF is fixed. Because Adobe Reader is available for free, and PDFs are so easily distributed, they are harder to monetize than eBooks and apps that have dedicated distribution channels. An even more significant downside at the time of this writing is the spotty mobile device support for interactive PDF features—including of course, lack of mobile support for Flash.

Flash

The rise of the iPad heralded the end of an era for Flash but Flash still has distinct advantages that make it worthy of consideration for specific types of interactive projects. The fact that you can output a fully animated Flash movie (SWF) that contains all manner of interactive elements, audio, and video directly from InDesign without writing any code is nothing less than extraordinary. InDesign will also generate the HTML page that's required for deployment of your content to the web. Flash movies retain layout integrity and support embedded fonts. The unfortunate thing of course is that Flash is unsupported on mobile devices. Several delivery mechanisms for Flash content still remain however: Desktop versions of Adobe Reader and Acrobat support Flash content, you can convert a Flash SWF to a stand-alone executable comparable to a self-contained PowerPoint presentation, and desktop browsers still support the free Flash Player.

EPUB

Flowable EPUB (EPUB 2.0.1) lends itself to long text-heavy documents with limited layout requirements. Particularly for novels and appropriate for many academic texts, EPUB 2 can flow to fit any screen. While options vary from one device to another, eReaders can provide the user with options to customize their reading experience by changing, among other things, page margins, page background color, font color, font face and font size. Supported by a growing number of eReaders, zoom-able images and audio and video can be added to your publication to further engage your EPUB audience. eReaders may also include enhancements such as search, bookmarking and annotation. Depending on the level of DRM (Digital Rights Management) applied, EPUB publications can either be freely shared or easily monetized through a number of established distribution channels such as Amazon, Barnes & Noble and Kobo.

On the down side, the types of documents appropriate for delivery as flowable EPUB are clearly limited. The fluidity and level of eReader customization that makes the EPUB experience so adaptable would wreak havoc on a document dependent on a design-intensive, precision-based layout. Also keep in mind that support for interactive features in flowable EPUB is substantially more limited than in Interactive PDF, Flash, HTML or DPS. Additionally, while you can export directly to EPUB from InDesign, the likelihood is that your publication will require some post-InDesign production work to get things to look exactly the way you want them. This means that you or your team will need some degree of fluency with HTML and CSS. (The HTML And CSS Fundamentals chapter, starting on page 347, will help you get going.) You'll also need to test your publication on all your target destination devices since supported features and their implementation can vary so widely. If you want to use established channels to distribute your eBook, you'll need to obtain the required credentials (which may include an ISBN— International Standard Book Number) and navigate the submission process.

Fixed Layout EPUB (EPUB 3.0) is an emerging standard that is well suited to documents such as cookbooks, comics and children's books that rely on more complex layout than is possible with EPUB 2.0.1. Since fixed layout EPUB incorporates HTML5, CSS3 and JavaScript, it can also include a broader spectrum of interactive capabilities. The standard is so new however, that devices that support it are few and far between and at this time, those that do, do so in a limited fashion. InDesign does have an Export to EPUB 3.0 option but it has not yet reached a level of maturity to make it a viable production option.

HTML

It shouldn't be news that HTML has a lot going for it as a digital delivery mechanism. It's easy to update, supports all sorts of dynamic content, media and interactivity, and can be accessed from nearly any device. Add to that the high level of layout customization made possible by CSS and you've got content that can adjust dynamically to accommodate nearly any screen.

You can actually export HTML from InDesign although the resulting HTML content will likely bear little resemblance to the appearance of your layout and would require substantial post production work to achieve a desirable result. While the book won't be addressing the InDesign to HTML workflow any further, we're mentioning HTML here because a discussion of digital publishing wouldn't be complete without it. After all, there are most certainly times when the web will prove to be the most effective method for digital delivery of your message.

Of course, the most obvious downsides to web content are first that it requires an internet connection and second that it must be viewed inside a browser. And then of course there's the code.

DPS (Digital Publishing Suite)

Being able to use InDesign to create apps that you can sell on an App store is just plain cool, there's no doubt about it. The apps you can create with DPS support a high level of interactivity with elements that can be made to scroll and spin and swipe and slide. Add audio and video, HTML animation and dual-orientation layouts, publish using PDF output and include high definition assets, and you've got an app that will perform nearly magical feats on any iPad as well as other devices—providing you've fulfilled the necessary licensing requirements. A huge advantage to DPS is that you can build the magic into your app directly in InDesign without writing a lick of code. Print assets can be readily repurposed and they retain their appearance on the page. You can easily add audio and video and get as crazy with other interactive elements as desired. Minor updates can be made to your app post-publication (within the publishing platform guidelines) and more dynamic changes can be made by strategically incorporating external HTML content (for which your audience would of course require an internet connection.) Your apps are built as a collection of articles in the model of a magazine and include a table of contents for ease of navigation. An obvious draw, apps are easily monetized and distributed through dedicated App stores.

There are a number of factors to take into account when considering DPS as a publishing platform. First, DPS is a subscription-based model that requires licensing through Adobe. The level of license you secure will determine the platforms through which you can distribute your app. (Your subscription to Creative Cloud includes unlimited Single Edition DPS licenses.) Before your app can be published, you'll also need to get squared away with your chosen distribution network, navigating its regulations and requirements, including the necessary licensing and certifications. Approval of your app will rely on the App Store so you'll want to be sure to understand their guidelines early in the app development process. Not a minor consideration is the fact that your apps will be platform-specific which, by definition, restricts distribution to an audience using specific devices. Apps created in InDesign are not yet searchable, nor can they be annotated. Given that DPS is so new however, who's to say what changes are on the horizon?

Key Questions

Now that you have a basic understanding of the strengths and weaknesses as they apply to the various publication platforms, answering a few key questions will help you determine which digital direction best meets your needs.

What's the intent of your content?

Is it sales-based, entertainment-based or informational? The demarkation between these categories is most certainly not clear-cut, however understanding the primary intent and feel for your publication is an important factor in making a media choice.

How important is the precise appearance of the page?

You've discovered that content is rendered differently depending on the digital platform you select. If your publication is graphically complex, flowable EPUB is easily eliminated from your options.

Will you be generating your digital content from scratch or repurposing collateral originally designed for print?

Determining how your document will be delivered before you begin designing can dramatically reduce your production time. Develop a design strategy that takes into account the conversion of your content to your desired destinations.

How long is your publication?

Generally not appropriate for short promotional pieces, EPUB and DPS are both better suited to more content-heavy publications. This is due in no small part to the steps required outside InDesign to get your content to the proper distribution channels.

How often will your content need updating?

At the moment, the web is by far the most responsive method of media delivery in that it enables instant updates. (You can incorporate live HTML in your DPS apps as a way to keep select content current in the otherwise fixed DPS environment.)

What kind of collateral do you already have and what would it take to convert it to the formats you're considering?

Asset creation, collection and conversion can be an unexpectedly costly endeavor. Proper planning during the asset creation and collection process can dramatically reduce what could otherwise easily become a crippling expense.

Who is your audience?

Understanding the demographics of your target audience will help you determine the most effective means to reach them. Are they iPad users? Do they use Android devices? When they use their devices, are they likely to have an internet connection?

What does your budget allow?

There are a number of budgetary factors to weigh when choosing to design for digital media. More complex by definition, merely conceptualizing an interactive project demands more time. You'll also need to allocate additional time and resources for the collection and preparation of assets for your project. What might have required merely one photograph in a print layout could easily call for a revolving image gallery or an instructional video for example. If you find it desirable to target your project to multiple devices and orientations, you'll face a corresponding increase in development time. And don't forget that the time and resources required for testing can also be considerable.

All these considerations aside, it's tremendously gratifying to see your designs come to life on the screen. The fact is, digital publishing is here to stay—and there's no time like the present to jump into the game.

With a clearer view of the differences between InDesign's digital publishing options and the considerations that can help guide you in choosing the best solution for your needs, it's time for a glimpse of some of the possibilities. For EPUB and DPS, you'll have to check out sections six and seven but for now, let's take a tour of some Interactive PDF and Flash content you'll be creating in the exercises to come.

Exercise 1.1: A Taste of Things to Come

1. Open your browser of choice, go to File > Open, and browse to the **chapter_1_exercises** folder. Open **interactive_indesign_end.html** and marvel at the images flying in from the left of the page. The animation was created entirely in InDesign!

This Flash movie HTML page contains interactive buttons, Flash animation, video, and audio.

2. Mouse over the large images to see the button rollovers and then mouse over the buttons on the navigation bar at the top of the page to see the dropdown menus. Click the upper left image of the tree bark to navigate to the Texture page.

3. Note the animation of the thumbnail images flying onto the filmstrip as the page loads. Mouse over the thumbnails to see the rollover effect on the buttons, and then click each thumbnail to display its corresponding large image.

4. Click the Flora button on the navbar (navigation bar) and explore the Flora About page. Mouse over the province names (below the "Pacific Ocean" text on the map) to highlight the Costa Rica provinces. Click the volcano names at the lower right of the page to display popups that tell you more about each volcano. When you're done, click the see Flora slide show text (yet another button) at the lower right of the page.

InDesign allows you to create rollovers and popups that translate to both Interactive PDF and SWF.

5. On the Flora Slide Show page, click the Next and Previous arrow buttons on either side of the flower images to cycle through the slide show. Click the fauna button on the navbar to navigate to the Fauna Scrap Book page.

6. Note how the scrap book images position themselves along an arc as the page loads. Click each of the thumbnail images, and when the large popup image appears, click to close it.

7. Mouse over the fauna button on the navbar to display the dropdown menu, and then click the slide show button. Click the thumbnail buttons on the scrolling navbar to display larger versions of the images.

InDesign's animation features can even be used to animate buttons.

8. From the fauna dropdown on the navbar, choose movie. This page includes Flash video and audio files. Play the movie slideshow by clicking on the photo of the flamingos. Click the gray buttons below the video to jump to preset cue points in the movie. Play each audio clip by clicking on the right-facing arrow below each photo.

Whether exporting to Flash SWF, Interactive PDF or DPS, you can include rich media in the documents you export from InDesign.

9. Click the Contact button on the navbar and mouse over the envelope on the page to see the rollover effect. Click to bring up your email client with a pre-addressed email, and then close your email application without sending.

10. Back in the browser, click the www.miraimages.com link. You'll likely receive an alert informing you that the browser has stopped a potentially unsafe operation. Close the alert and when you're done exploring, close the file but keep the browser open.

The rich media Flash SWF movie you've just seen is 100% InDesign, created with no external development, and not one line of code. The layout, the buttons, the animation—all of it was done directly in the foremost print layout application in the industry. With a few minor adjustments, the same file can be exported to Interactive PDF with similar results: the video, the audio, and even animation. But wait, there's more!

11. Still in the browser, go to File > Open, and from the chapter_1_exercises folder, open **banner_ad.html**.

Learn how to build Banner Ads, starting on page 231.

Banner ads are to web as print ads are to magazines and newspapers. Banner Ads, starting on page 231, teaches you how to create a banner ad with the proper dimensions and gives you the skinny on industry standards. The file size of the banners you can create in InDesign is too hefty for commercial placement, but might work perfectly for a local site. Whether you actually create banner ads or not, the skills and concepts you learn in this chapter will deepen your understanding of animation.

12. Close the banner ad, quit the browser, and open either Acrobat XI Standard or Professional, or Adobe Reader XI. Go to File > Open, navigate to the chapter_1_exercises folder, and open **flower_gallery.pdf.** When the alert pops up, click Yes to allow the file to display in Full Screen Mode. When the file opens, click the flower images to explore the gallery.

InDesign provides a wide assortment of page transitions you can apply to your projects and presentations with just a click.

In real life, you clearly wouldn't want a different transition on every page of a document, but this file is built for demonstration purposes to familiarize you with InDesign's wide assortment of Page Transitions.

13. When you're finished exploring the file, press Esc on your keyboard to exit Full Screen mode. Close the document and quit Acrobat or Reader.

The files you've just toured provided a taste, just a bit of a tease, and hopefully your mind is churning with ideas of how you might apply some of the effects you've seen to projects of your own. By the end of the book, you'll be able to do all this and so much more. So, without further ado, let the fun begin!

CHAPTER SUMMARY

This chapter got you up close and personal with a bunch of really remarkable results you can achieve with InDesign CC's interactive tools. You viewed documents exported to both Interactive PDF and Flash SWF that included interactive buttons, animation, audio, and video. You interacted with a full screen presentation complete with page transitions, and, hopefully, came away from it all awed and inspired by the possibilities of taking your print skills into the world of interactive design.

The next couple chapters provide a road map for navigating that world, and introduce you to the dynamic design tools in InDesign that make the journey possible.

Chapter 2

DESIGNING FOR INTERACTIVITY

If you're coming from the world of print, and migrating to the world of digital and interactive design, the landscape may initially feel somewhat upside down. Color model, image resolution, document dimensions, page orientation, font choices; the requirements for digital media are entirely different from those related to print. This chapter provides an orientation to the digital terrain and will get you started on the right foot as you begin your explorations into this exciting and expansive frontier.

Print vs. Web and Interactive

It's a good bet that if you're reading this book, you're probably a print designer. And like so many other print designers, you're probably being tasked to design beyond the printed page; for the web, tablets and other digital devices.

The thing is, print and electronic media are, by their nature, very different animals. To design effectively for both requires an understanding of the differences. You can then let these differences inform your design choices in order to create an optimal workflow.

Color: RGB vs. CMYK

In doing a point-by-point comparison, the obvious place to start is with color, or, more specifically, how that color is achieved. Color in print is obviously a function of ink on paper. In standard 4-color process printing, cyan, magenta, yellow, and black inks (CMYK) are combined to achieve a multitude of colors. The more ink is added, the darker the color becomes. Theoretically, if you add 100% cyan, 100% magenta, and 100% yellow ink together, you end up with black. In actuality, what you end up with is a muddy reddish brown, so black is added to make a true, rich black. Hence, CMYK rather than simply CMY.

In the world of digital communications, color is made of light. If you've ever seen light split through a prism, white light goes through the prism and the spectrum of colors comprising it are projected out. With projected light, the color white is achieved by combining 100% red, 100% green, and 100% blue light. This combination of red, green and blue is the foundation of what is known as the RGB color space. The exact opposite of ink: the more colored light that's added, the lighter the color becomes—until, when you've added all the color you can possibly add, the color disappears and what remains is pure white light.

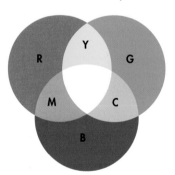

Opposites

Red	⟷	Cyan
Green	⟷	Magenta
Blue	⟷	Yellow
		K BlacK

Blue + Green = **C**yan (opposite **R**ed)

Red + Blue = **M**agenta (opposite **G**reen)

Red + Green = **Y**ellow (opposite **B**lue)

The RGB color space refers to color generated by light, while CMYK refers to color rendered in ink. RGB color is represented by an indexed scale from 0–255, where 0 = 0% light and 255=100% light. CMYK color is represented in ink percentages from 0%–100%.

CMYK is the color space applicable to print and RGB is the color space for devices that generate color through light. As you're discovering, the two color spaces are quite literally opposites. Red is actually the opposite of cyan, green is the opposite of magenta, and blue is the opposite of yellow. Should you want to reduce the amount of red in an image, you could achieve this by adding more cyan, its opposite. Similarly, to add yellow, you could reduce the amount of blue.

CMYK color is measured in ink percentages from 0%–100%. By contrast, RGB color is represented on an indexed scale of 0–255. On this scale, 0 equates to 0% light, and 255 equates to 100% light. While higher percentages of ink make color darker, higher index numbers in RGB color indicate a greater amount of light, and, generally, the more light, the lighter the color.

If you've been working in print, you know that, traditionally, you are expected to deliver your files to your print provider in CMYK color. It's useful to be aware that the RGB color space has a wider gamut than CMYK, meaning it encompasses a broader range of colors. When files are converted from RGB to CMYK, colors outside of the color space are irretrievably lost—switching back to RGB will not reclaim them. For this reason, even in a print workflow, it's best to stick with the RGB color space up to the last possible moment. In fact, Adobe has long recommended that files be kept in RGB until final print conversion to CMYK. If you're working with a commercial print provider, most modern RIPs (raster image processors) do an excellent RGB to CMYK conversion at the time of imaging. This means that most print providers can handle RGB files—making a strong case for maintaining an RGB workflow for both print and digital development.

If your print provider prefers CMYK content and they accept files in PDF format, you can typically do your RGB to CMYK conversion when you convert to PDF. This makes it feasible to repurpose the same RGB file for output to both print and digital documents.

Since you'll be working in RGB for digital documents, you'll want to be aware that there are a variety of RGB flavors to choose from. You can liken the variations in RGB color spaces to crayon boxes of different sizes. ProPhoto RGB is like the big, deluxe box of 128 crayons with more colors in it than you thought you could name. sRGB, on the other hand, is more like a crayon box with eight basic colors. Despite the fact that sRGB color is by no means the best possible RGB model, it is unfortunately the one in widest use and the one you will use when developing for digital devices. We have Microsoft to thank for its prevalence, since sRGB is used in Internet Explorer and the Microsoft Office Suite. Due to the ubiquity of these applications, Adobe has made sRGB the default RGB profile for the Creative Suite tools. This is a good thing for web or screen content in that it serves to maintain consistent color from one application to another. For high-end print, the more robust RGB flavors such as Adobe RGB (1998) or ProPhoto RGB are preferred. It used to be that, without employing color management, files created in Adobe applications would look terrible in Microsoft applications. Now, since the applications speak the same color language, results are more reliable.

Color management can be a complex topic but what it boils down to is making sure that your documents and the devices they interact with speak a similar enough language that the color in one translates reliably to another. If you ever have a situation where the color in a file becomes flat or washed out and you can't figure out why, it is most likely a case for color management.

When a document is created in any of the Creative Suite applications, a color profile that defines its color space is attached to it by default. When you convert a document from RGB to CMYK, or even between flavors within the same color model, you are in essence translating the color profile information from one language to another. The destination profile you choose will depend on the ultimate destination of the document. If you were to translate a poem from Italian to English, you'd want the translation to convey as much of the original poem's tone as possible. The words you'd choose would most certainly be different than if you were translating a scientific paper. Similarly, when translating from one document profile to another, the rendering intent you choose provides the rules that govern the way the colors are mapped to the new profile. Without getting into excessive detail, the thing to be aware of is that occasionally things may get lost in translation, resulting in a mismatch of color that can negatively impact your document. Sometimes, simply converting your document to the correct destination color space can correct such issues.

The destination color space is just that: the color space for the ultimate output destination of the document. If an image is destined to be on a digital device or the web, the destination color space would be sRGB. If it is destined to be printed, its destination color space would be determined by the type of press and paper to be used. Interestingly, the most common high-end print destination color space is now Adobe RGB 1998 or ColorMatch RGB rather than a flavor of CMYK. Check with your print shop, for recommendations on their preferred document profile.

Color management can get somewhat complicated but fortunately, by default, the Creative Suite applications are synchronized to pretty much handle it for you behind the scenes, particularly for onscreen or multimedia purposes. If you do want to learn more about color management—and there is quite a lot to know—do a search for it in InDesign Help. You'll find a wealth of information and resources at your disposal.

The growing adoption of a PDF workflow by commercial printers has dramatically simplified issues around RGB to CMYK conversion. It used to be that every placed image and element in an InDesign document destined for print had to be CMYK rather than RGB. Since digital images originate in RGB, that meant that each and every image had to be converted to CMYK, and document colors had to be carefully chosen to ensure they used the right color space. Now, with a PDF workflow, the tedious process of converting files placed in an InDesign document virtually disappears. You can rely on the PDF conversion process to do the conversion for you. You'll learn more about exporting to PDF on page 289.

Now that you've had a brief orientation to the concepts governing color management, let's get back to color basics. As mentioned earlier, CMYK colors are defined by the percentages of cyan, magenta, yellow and black inks that comprise them. RGB colors are defined in terms of an 8-bit index that goes from 0 to 255 for each of the 3 color channels: red, green, and blue. An index value of 0 indicates 0 light; in other words, black. At the other end of the spectrum, 255 represents 100% light in the channel—so, 255 in the red channel and 0 in the green and blue channels appears as the color red. An index value of 255 in each of the red, green, and blue channels appears as the color white.

In thinking of the web, you've most likely encountered the term "web-safe color." Web-safe color refers to a color palette of 216 colors that are universally supported across multiple operating systems. When computer monitors displayed 256 colors rather than the millions of colors more common today, using web-safe colors was the only way you could expect the cross-platform display of your graphics to come anywhere close to the appearance you intended.

One look at the web-safe color palette and it's clear that its colors were not chosen by designers. After all, how many shades of neon green does a designer really need? The fact is, the web-safe color palette was determined mathematically.

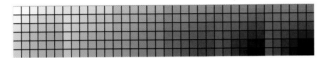

The colors of the web-safe palette are segmented into six groups, each containing a mathematical progression of hue.

Before proceeding with an explanation of how it all works, first a disclaimer. It is in no way essential that you understand the intricacies of how the hexadecimal web colors are defined or how the web-safe colors were determined. When you plug the numbers and letters in that define a hex color, they work, whether you understand exactly what they mean or not. That said, if you're a little queasy about math, feel free to skip this next little bit. (It's really simple math, though.) We just thought it was cool to be able to decode the puzzle and make some sense of those weird hexadecimal values.

To understand it all better, it's helpful to first understand the hexadecimal, or base 16, system. In a hexadecimal system, the value we know as 16 is represented as 10. Rather than going from 0 to 9 as our base 10 numbers do, additional "digits" are added to represent the values from 10–15. The count from 0 to 10 in base 16 would look like this: 0, 1, 2, 3, 4, 5, 6, 7, 8, 9, A, B, C, D, E, F, 10.

Web colors consist of three hexadecimal (base 16) values, one for each of the three color channels: red, green, and blue. The hexadecimal values are a translation of the value of the color index for that particular channel (0–255), and are always represented by two hexadecimal digits. As with the base 10 system, the first digit represents the number of times the base number, in this case 16, goes into the index value (between 0 and 255) and the second digit represents the remainder. (As an example, in base 10, 10 goes into 35, 3 times with a remainder of 5.) So if the index value for red were 255, to convert that value to a hex value, you would divide 255 by 16 to get 15 with a remainder of 15. 15 is represented in base 16 by the letter F, so the first digit in the hexadecimal pair would be F. With a remainder of 15, the second hex value would be F as well. Therefore, the hex representation of the index value of 255 works out to be FF.

Now that you know how the hex color values are calculated, if you're not too dizzy, we can take a look at how the web-safe colors were determined. Web-safe colors are always and only composed of combinations of the following paired hexadecimal digits: 00, 33, 66, 99, CC, and FF.

Here's how it breaks down:

index value	percentage of light	hex value
0	0	00
51	20%	33
102	40%	66
153	60%	99
204	80%	CC
255	100%	FF

Hexadecimal values as they relate to color index and percentage of light. The index value of all the web-safe colors are multiples of 51.

Nerdy but kinda cool, right? So, any time you see a hex value that has three identical hexadecimal pairs, you know it means the color has equal amounts of red, green, and blue and that, consequently, the color is a shade of gray.

hex value		Red	Green	Blue
#000000		00	00	00
#333333		33	33	33
#666666		66	66	66
#999999		99	99	99
#CCCCCC		CC	CC	CC
#FFFFFF		FF	FF	FF
#FF0000		FF	00	00
#00FF00		00	FF	00
#0000FF		00	00	FF
#FFFF00		FF	FF	00
#FF00FF		FF	00	FF
#00FFFF		00	FF	FF

Web-safe colors broken down by color channel.

To further reinforce the fact that the CMYK and RGB color models are truly opposite, note in the chart above that cyan contains no red, magenta contains no green and yellow contains no blue.

Image Resolution vs. Screen Resolution

Both image resolution and screen resolution are expressed in pixels (px.) A pixel is essentially a square of color with no inherent dimension. Pixel size is determined by the density of pixels squeezed into a given space.

Image resolution is measured in pixels per inch (ppi.) The print dimensions of the same image at 300 ppi will be less than one third the size of that image at 72 ppi. The greater the density of pixels, the smaller they are, the smaller the relative print dimensions of the image they combine to create.

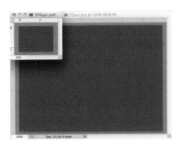

The same image at two different image resolutions. The resolution of the larger version of the image is 72 ppi and the resolution of the smaller version is 300 ppi.

Images destined for high-end print should have a resolution of no less than 300 ppi while the resolution of images destined for the web should be 72 ppi. When you add mobile devices to the mix, things get quite a bit more complicated since there is a vast assortment of devices representing many variations in screen size and aspect ratio.

NOTE: See Image Resolution, Image Compression, & File Size, starting on page 20 for more about preparing images for mobile devices.

While the number of pixels in an image is fixed, the resolution of a computer monitor is adjustable, within given parameters. Of course the monitor itself maintains its physical dimensions so the only thing that changes is the size and number of pixels displayed on the screen. The greater the density and number of pixels, the smaller the appearance of the elements displayed on the screen, the greater the area of content displayed.

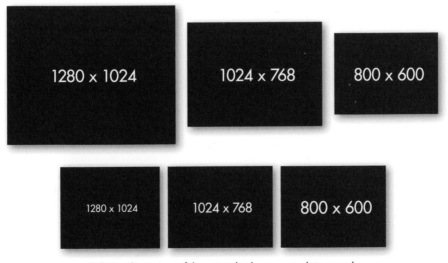

Relative dimensions of three standard screen resolutions and their appearance when displayed on the same monitor.

The diagram on the previous page illustrates the effect of screen resolution on content display. The top row of rectangles in the diagram represent the relative dimensions of three standard screen resolutions. The rectangles in the bottom row represent the relative appearance of content displayed at different screen resolutions on the same size monitor You can see that the text appears much smaller at the 1280 x 1024 resolution than it does at 800 x 600. At 1280 x 1024, more pixels encompassing a greater area are squeezed onto the screen making the content they render appear much smaller in size.

When working with images for the web or mobile devices, the print resolution of the image is actually irrelevant. It is the number of pixels in the image relative to the resolution of the screen on which that image will be displayed that determines if the image has too little data to produce a quality display or more pixels than are necessary to properly do the job. In situations where you want to provide your audience with an opportunity to zoom into an image, you will use image files that are larger than required to fill the destination display area. You should however still be conscious to use the smallest possible file size necessary to achieve your intended result. There are a number of reasons for being vigilant in policing the size of your image and project files. With digital content, file size impacts delivery and performance not to mention download time. File size constraints may also be imposed by distribution channels. As an example, at the time of this writing, Apple imposes a 50MB 3G download limit for any content from iTunes or the App Store. This means that if your content comes in at less than 50MB, potential customers will be able to download it directly to their phones or tablets, enabling you to benefit from impulse buys of your product. If your file is too large for 3G download, your potential customer will need to remember to download later through iTunes or the App Store which may result in lost sales and a negative impact on your bottom line.

Image Resolution, Image Compression, & File Size

Historically, the highest resolution images you would ever need to work with would be images destined for print at 300 ppi. The release in March of 2012 of Apple's Retina Display iPad heralds a rising challenge to that long-standing benchmark. With a screen resolution of 2048 x 1536 and image resolution of 264 ppi., it may not be long before images for the iPad and other mobile devices require a higher resolution than images for print! Of course with higher resolution comes more pixels and with more pixels comes larger file size and a greater need for attention to file optimization.

Image optimization is about finding a balance between quality and file size. The general rule for digital content is to use images with the lowest possible overhead—the lowest resolution, most highly compressed images that still maintain acceptable quality.

High resolution images can be optimized and downsampled in the DPS, EPUB, PDF, SWF, and HTML export process and you also have the option to set export preferences on an image-by-image basis. That said, it is at least theoretically feasible to design for output to print and multiple electronic destinations at the same time, letting InDesign downsample your images as necessary in the export process. Creating your source files using high resolution images and an RGB color space offers the greatest flexibility.

Page Orientation and Document Dimensions

While print layout most often employs a portrait orientation, the web typically calls for landscape, and mobile devices and tablets may call for both. You'll need to determine the screen dimensions of your target devices and calculate the actual viewing area of your document pages, taking into account the screen space consumed by navigational elements or browser chrome.

It's impossible to overemphasize the importance of identifying your target devices and delivery platforms before beginning your project. Different platforms have different development requirements and different devices have different dimensions. The number of devices out there is growing exponentially and there is simply no way to take a one-size-fits-all approach to designing for them. With this in mind, InDesign CC actually provides presets in its New Document dialog for iPhone, iPad, Kindle Fire/Nook and Android 10. The Retina Display iPad is conspicuously absent from the pre-populated list which just underscores the fact that when it comes to the mobile landscape, change is constant.

Font and Font Size

For the longest time, conventional wisdom had it that serif fonts were easier to read on the printed page than sans-serif fonts. While the controversy still rages in regard to print, it's pretty solidly accepted that, for general content, sans-serif fonts provide a better on-screen reading experience. For small text especially, the traditionally lower resolution of the screen makes the detail of serif text less intelligible. Serif fonts are fine for headers or typographical accents, but it's recommended that you stick with sans-serif fonts for the body of text on the page.

Serifs   Sans-serif (No serifs)

Serif and sans-serif fonts. Sans-serif font text is easier to read on screen.

> **TIP:** An em unit of measure is equivalent to the point size of the selected font.

What about font size? Well, check back to the monitor resolution diagram on page 19. The answer is, it depends. Like so many other aspects of designing for web and digital media, there's not one absolute and definitive answer. When developing for EPUB, your font size will best be expressed in relative units like ems or percentages. For DPS, PDF and SWF, the recommendation is that you test. In fact, that's the recommendation for any project you create for digital delivery. Test on multiple computers, multiple operating systems, multiple devices, multiple browsers. Testing your content is an essential part of designing for web and digital media, and that's just the way it is. There's simply no way around it.

Margins and Bleeds

To start, if you're designing for digital output only, you have license to forget about margins and bleeds entirely (though with DPS and EPUB, you'll want to make allowances for viewer scollbars and menus.) Margins can be useful as design guides but, unlike print where you may have concerns about staying within the printer margins, whatever you put within the page boundary of your digital design will appear in your finished product. If, however, you want to create a document for output to multiple destinations, the margins and/or bleeds you establish for print will have no negative impact on your digital output.

Interactive Design Guidelines

Certainly, an obvious use of InDesign's interactive capabilities is to bring life to existing print projects, but you can just as easily create digital projects from scratch. Regardless of the starting point, the design of any interactive project demands consideration of the factors that impact the user experience.

The quality of the user experience and the usability of the interactive interface are critical concerns when designing for interactivity. There are a number of things that contribute to the quality of this experience—some of which have been touched upon earlier in this chapter: file size as it influences delivery, and page and font size as they relate to your audience. The colors you choose, the layout of the page, the overall look and feel; these things too are obvious considerations for interactive design, as they are for projects of any type. Additionally, good interactive design requires attention to information design and information architecture.

The flow of information through your project, and the structure you establish to navigate it, are huge factors in defining the user experience. Unless specifically intended otherwise, the goal is to make the interface as user friendly and transparent as possible. It should be easy for your audience to find their way around visually, and logically, without having to put too much attention on figuring it out. You want folks to be able to find what they're looking for quickly and easily.

In service to this objective, before even starting design of the visuals, take some time to think through the intention of the project. Is it informational? Is it for entertainment purposes? What do you want people to come away with? Is there a call to action?

Identify your audience, and then get clear on the content you want to include. The next step is to flow-chart and storyboard the project. You can make these steps as detailed and formal as the project demands. You'll find that the effort you invest up front to work things out will reward you well when it comes time for the visual design.

A really valuable technique for working through the details of a project is to create a series of scenario-based case studies. Start with an objective, like finding contact information, and then itemize each step necessary to achieve it. Identify the menus used, the buttons clicked, etc. In the process, you'll identify the interface elements and the functionality you'll want to build into the project. You'll be surprised by the project requirements you'll expose with this procedural approach, and by how many wrong paths you can avoid by using it. Before getting too far along with filling in the visual details, test a skeletal structure of the project. Test it with people who are unfamiliar with it, to see if they can navigate it effectively. Since it's easy to get too close to a project and to miss otherwise obvious issues in site logic or concept, having outside testers is a really valuable way to get feedback.

If your interactive project has more than one page, you'll need to incorporate some sort of navigation. When designing navigation, make use of the fact that there are certain conventions, certain assumptions, that guide the experience of the audience engaging with your project. If you deviate from these conventions, do so in a

way that serves your overall objective. You don't want to burden your audience with having to figure things out, when what you really want is for them to retrieve information or take a particular action.

The first rule of navigation is to keep it consistent from page to page; in other words, don't change the location of navigational buttons from one page to the next. You don't want to distract your users from your content every time they get to a new page.

By convention, hyperlinks are identified by an underline and the color blue. Navigation bars or links are most often found at the top, bottom, and at either side of an interface (usually the left). Since computer users are generally acclimated to looking for navigation in these locations, it's pretty safe to remove the default underline from these links and to format them with an appearance other than the traditional link blue. If you have links elsewhere in the content, however, think carefully before removing the familiar underline and color. People are accustomed to these identifiers; if you use a different format, you run the risk of losing some of the click-through for which the link was intended.

It's important not to bury critical links where there's a risk they won't be found. Anything important should be easily accessible. Ideally, you want your visitors to be able to access significant site content in no more than two clicks—three at the most.

When using next and previous buttons for page navigation, people expect to find them on the lower right corner of a page, with the next button to the right of the previous button. If you decide to put them somewhere else, be consistent.

Color can be an excellent navigational indicator, providing a visual cue to help orient the user. This color-coding technique may be familiar from print design, where color is used to distinguish one section of a catalog from the next for example. Like a catalog, a product site would generally maintain a similar format from one section to another in order to present a consistent overall environment. While you might change color from one section of a site to another, you'll want to keep a consistent look and feel so your audience can be assured that they're still in the same site.

When there are interface features that aren't obvious, such as clickable elements that trigger pop-ups, for example, include a notation that provides necessary instruction. Remember, unless the site is deliberately meant to be an explorative experience, you want to give your audience as much assistance as you can to help them have the experience you designed the site to achieve.

Well, that about wraps up the guidelines. With a bit of a foundation under your belt, it's time to get to know the InDesign tools you'll use to bring your documents to life.

CHAPTER SUMMARY

This chapter provided you with an official introduction to the world of interactive design. You discovered a number of the considerations governing choices related to creating projects for digital output, including:

- Color models
- Document dimensions
- Image and screen resolution
- File size
- Font choices
- Project intent
- Planning a project
- Designing for user experience

Along the way, you learned about color models and color for digital output including:

- The difference between RGB and CMYK color
- Concepts around color management
- Hexadecimal color and how to interpret it
- Color in print-to-digital workflow

In considering the user experience, you learned the importance of:

- Testing
- Consistent navigation
- Using established conventions to inform your design

Having gained a solid orientation, the next step is to get familiar with the tools you'll rely on in your interactive work. Chapter 3 takes you on an extensive tour of the InDesign interface and provides all kinds of ways you can tailor it to the way you work. Whether you're a newbie or a seasoned professional, you're guaranteed to learn something useful and new.

Chapter 3

THE INTERACTIVE INTERFACE

This chapter will get you cozy with the tools in InDesign that make the magic possible. With two workspaces expressly dedicated to digital development, there are a plethora of panels to help you bring your projects to life. Once familiar with the panels, you'll learn to customize the workspace so you can always have just the tools you need right at your fingertips.

The Interactive Workspaces

NOTE: When you first open InDesign CC, the default interface has a dark appearance which can be changed by adjusting the Color setting in the Interface section of the Preferences panel. The screenshots throughout the book have been taken with the interface color to Light. See page xxviii of the Introduction to learn how to adjust the interface color.

NOTE: The Folio Builder and Folio Overlays panels will not appear in the Digital Publishing workspace panel dock until you run an initial software update to load the DPS tools into the InDesign interface.

InDesign CC has a multitude of panels and tools specifically geared toward digital and interactive design. In fact, there are two predefined workspaces expressly dedicated to this purpose. In case you're not familiar with workspaces, they are saved arrangements of panels and customized menu settings that make it easy to switch tools for one type of task to tools for another with only a click. InDesign CC is equipped with seven different task-based workspaces. You can also create your own, tailored perfectly to your needs. In fact, you'll be doing just that after you get a brief tour of the panels in the interactive workspace presets.

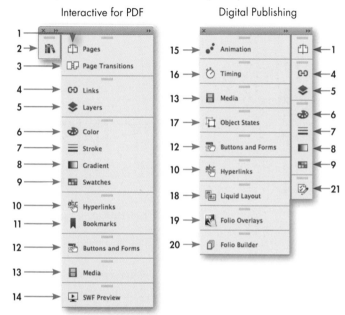

The Interactive for PDF and Digital Publishing workspace presets.
Click a panel name or icon to expand or collapse the view of a panel.

1) Pages
2) Sample Buttons And Forms Library
3) Page Transitions
4) Links
5) Layers
6) Color
7) Stroke
8) Gradient
9) Swatches
10) Hyperlinks
11) Bookmarks
12) Buttons and Forms
13) Media
14) SWF Preview
15) Animation
16) Timing
17) Object States
18) Liquid Layout
19) Folio Overlays
20) Folio Builder
21) Preflight

All of InDesign's panels can be found under the Window menu so you never need to worry about closing one by mistake and not being able to get it back. In the Window menu, some panels are hidden under submenus indicated by a black arrow to the right of the main menu item.

For example, there are ten panels found under the Window > Interactive submenu, all of which are dedicated specifically to InDesign's interactive functions. What follows is a brief introduction to each of those panels, in alphabetical order, as they appear in the menu.

Animation Panel

Now you can create Flash animation right in InDesign! From the animation panel, you can use any of a wide assortment of motion presets to make objects fade, bounce, zoom, rotate, and much more, simply with the click of a button. A preview window at the top of the panel shows the motion encoded in the selected preset to help you visually sort through the many choices. The motion presets in InDesign come directly from Flash, and are easily exchanged between the two applications. You can even create and save custom presets of your own directly in InDesign. To explore the possibilities and start animating, check out Part 4: Flash Animation and Output to SWF, starting on page 199.

Animation panel

Bookmarks Panel

Bookmarks are navigational links within a document that reside in the Bookmarks tab of Acrobat and Adobe Reader. Each bookmark jumps to a text anchor or document page. Bookmarks are a PDF-specific feature. Learn more about Bookmarks, starting on page 253.

Bookmarks panel

Buttons and Forms Panel

Buttons are at the very heart of interactivity in InDesign, enabling you to add page navigation, open URLs, control animation, and much more. With InDesign CC, the Buttons panel has expanded to become a Forms panel as well, making it possible to create and export fully functional interactive form fields directly to Interactive PDF. To learn more about buttons, check out Part 3: Buttons, starting on page 145. Learn about interactive forms in Chapter 18 starting on page 261.

Buttons and Forms panel

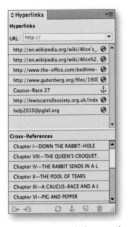

Hyperlinks Panel

The Hyperlinks panel does double duty, enabling you to create both links and cross-references to internal and external document destinations, as well as links to web URLs. Hyperlinks and cross-references export to EPUB, DPS, SWF and interactive PDF. For more on hyperlinks and cross-references, see page 99.

Hyperlinks panel

Liquid Layout panel

Liquid Layout Panel

Adapting content from one layout to another is now a nearly seamless endeavor with the combined features of the Page Tool and the Liquid Layout panel. You can apply scaling rules to entire pages or to individual page elements so they fluidly shift size and position to transform your layout from portrait to landscape or one size to another. Whether for print or digital media, if you're tasked with designing for multiple destinations, you'll find Liquid Layout to be an absolutely indispensable tool. Learn more about Liquid Layout on page 444.

Media Panel

Not only can you add video files to your InDesign document, you can actually preview those files in the Media Panel. The Media panel lets you scrub through your video and choose a poster (an image that appears on the page when the video isn't playing), as well as a controller that appears when it plays. You can add and test audio files too! For more on incorporating media into your documents, check out page 302 and page 472.

Media panel

Object States panel

Object States Panel

The Object States panel lets you create multi-state objects: slide shows that can include an unlimited number of slides. Each Object State can contain nearly anything you can put on a document page. Multi-state object slide shows export to both DPS and SWF. Learn more about Multi-state objects in Chapter 10, starting on page 147.

Page Transitions Panel

InDesign is great for creating full-screen presentations that work in both SWF and PDF, and page transitions can provide them with a little extra pizazz. The Page Transitions panel lets you choose from 13 pre-built transitions that you can preview in the panel. You can modify both the transition direction and speed, and then apply them to an entire document or to select pages. To see transitions in action, take a look at the Page Transitions chapter starting on page 281.

Page Transitions panel

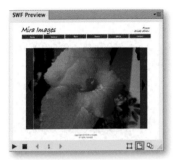

SWF Preview panel

SWF Preview Panel

The SWF Preview panel lets you preview your Flash content right in InDesign. Buttons work, animations play, and you can even watch included video. The SWF Preview panel lets you view a selection, a spread, or an entire document. An in depth introduction to the Preview panel begins on page 174.

Timing Panel

The Timing panel works with the Animation panel to keep your animations in proper order. Use it to change animations sequence, set delays, and group animations to play together. You won't be using this panel except for documents output to SWF, since InDesign animation doesn't translate to DPS, EPUB or Interactive PDF. Get familiar with the Timing panel on page 215.

Timing panel

Additional Panels for Digital Design

Included in the Digital Publishing workspace, the Preflight panel warrants an introduction as do some additional panels that you'll find especially useful when designing for interactivity.

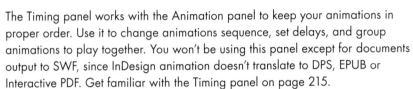

Preflight panel

Preflight Panel

For print or interactive design, the Preflight panel is a truly awesome tool for helping you keep your documents error free. It's absolutely indispensable for print work, but also provides a solid benefit for working with documents destined for the screen. It can help you keep track of overset text, image resolution, disproportionate scaling, and so much more. What's best about the Preflight panel is that it's dynamic, providing you with feedback as you go, so you don't end up with a host of unpleasant surprises when it's time to output your file. Check out page 44 in this chapter to learn more.

Align Panel

While InDesign's smart guides are tremendously useful, there are times when only the Align panel can do the job of aligning or distributing multiple objects. The Align panel is usually nested with the Pathfinder and Transform panels. Go to Window > Object & Layout > Align to open it.

Align panel

Effects Panel

The Effects panel provides an at-a-glance view of the effects applied to an object, its stroke, fill, and text. It enables you to set opacity and blending modes, isolate effects, and apply a knockout to an object group right in the panel. It also provides easy access to the Effects dialog. While you can also get to the Effects dialog through the Control panel, the visual feedback from the Effects panel makes it easier to decipher what's going on with your objects.

Effects panel

Object Styles Panel

The Object Styles panel enables the capture of all manner of object attributes that you can then apply at the click of a button. Object styles can incorporate paragraph styles, drop shadows, frame fitting options, and more. You'll find them invaluable in maintaining consistent appearances for buttons and other interface elements. Learn more about The Object Styles Dialog, starting on page 94.

Object Styles panel

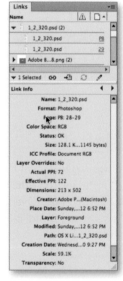

Links Panel

The Links panel is much more than a simple access point for managing placed files—rather it is an at-a-glance resource for important information. Twirl down the disclosure triangle at the bottom left of the panel to display a wealth of info for the selected file, including the page and layer on which the file was placed, content dimensions, effective resolution, color space, scaling percentage, and more. Learn more about the Links panel on page 47 of this chapter.

Links panel

Pathfinder Panel

The Pathfinder panel is a great aid in modifying paths and creating shapes that would otherwise be nearly impossible to draw. Its convenient all-in-one interface puts tools for paths, points, and shapes right at your fingertips. The Pathfinder panel is found under Window > Object & Layout > Pathfinder. Learn more about the Pathfinder panel on page 132.

Pathfinder panel

Tools for EPUB

We'll wrap up the tour of InDesign's interactive design panels with two panels that are especially useful in the specialized EPUB workflow.

Articles panel

Defining the sequence and flow of content in an EPUB can sometimes present a challenge. The Articles panel enables you to collect and sequence the objects that collectively create your EPUB so content flows predictably in your final publication. To learn more about the Articles panel, see page 323.

Articles panel

Scripts panel

Nearly anything you can do in InDesign can be automated with a script. From simple but tedious processes like removing extra white space to tasks as complex as generating a document index, scripts can be written to do it all. In fact, there's a good chance that a script already exists for the task you need to accomplish. The Scripts panel is pre-populated with an assortment of helpful scripts but that's just the beginning. There is an active community of InDesign developers who make scripts available for free or for fee. Check out the list of EPUB resources starting on page 415.

Scripts panel

Digital Publishing Suite Tools

Adobe Digital Publishing Suite (DPS) is a two-pronged technology with components both internal and external to InDesign. Its two content creation panels—Folio Builder and Folio Overlays—live in InDesign and interface with its external server-based digital publishing platform.

Folio Builder Panel

Like all magazines, a DPS publication is a collection of articles. The Folio Builder panel is where you collect the documents containing your portrait and/or landscape article layouts; and then assemble your articles to create the publication. Once complete, you use the panel to upload your document to the DPS server-side tools. Folio Builder is the communication bridge between InDesign and the external digital publishing platform. It communicates with the server-side of DPS to upload and download content and to keep current on required updates to the tools.

Folio Builder panel

Folio Overlays panel

Folio Overlays Panel

Consider the Folio Overlays panel to be like a command center where you wire up any and all interactivity to be included in your DPS publications. The panel provides controls for eight types of overlays, each accompanied by instruction on how to create it. You can create interactive 360° panoramas, slide shows, scrolling frames and more. And were that not enough, you can bring live web feeds from the likes of Twitter, Google Maps and YouTube as well as HTML5 animation right onto your digital page. The possibilities are truly endless! Learn more about the DPS platform, tools and workflow and start exploring the extraordinary things you can do in the Chapter 28 Intro to DPS, starting on page 427.

Setting Up a Custom Workspace

Having established a feel for some of the tools you'll be using, let's now take a couple minutes to create a custom workspace and make it even more conducive to the work of interactive design.

Custom Workspace.

The beauty of custom workspaces is that you can create as many as you need, tailored to the requirements of your various workflows. Since the workflow for EPUB is radically different from that for DPS, or for Flash or PDF interactivity, you may want to set up separate workspaces for interactive, DPS, and a third expressly for EPUB.

The Pages panel is a great tool for navigating from page to page, and full access to the Layers panel is extremely helpful for selecting and reorganizing objects in your document. We've found it useful to stack these two panels in a column of their own in the Panel Dock so they're always readily available. When working with Flash content, we've found it convenient to position the SWF Preview panel in a column to the left of the other panels, and to add the Align and Pathfinder panels to that column. It's great to have the Object Styles panel readily available, and you'll want the Character and Paragraph Styles panels close at hand as well. If you'll be doing a lot with Tables, you might as well add the Table and Cell Styles panels to the party. With so many panels in so little space, you can collapse most of them down to icons to conserve your screen real estate.

The following exercise walks you through the steps to create and save a custom workspace. The choice of panels and their arrangement is merely a suggestion based on what we've found useful. Once you know how, no doubt you'll find groups of panels that best suit your process and then you can create saved workspaces of your own.

TIP: While the panel icons may be unfamiliar at first, if you mouse-over a panel icon, a tooltip will pop up that displays the name of the panel.

Exercise 3.1: Setting Up a Custom Workspace

To complete this exercise, you'll begin with the Digital Publishing workspace and then customize the panel selection and arrangement.

1. Before we get started, if you're working on a Mac, you might want to turn on the Application Frame to enclose all the application interface elements in one moveable, scalable window. To do this, go to Window > Application Frame. You'll then be able to drag and reposition the application window, and all the tools and panels will travel with it. Also, if you click your desktop, your panels will still show. Without the Application Frame turned on, clicking outside InDesign makes the panels disappear.

   NOTE: For Mac users, the Application Frame is also available in Photoshop and Illustrator.

2. On the right side of the Application bar, at the very top of your screen, you should see the word "Essentials". This is the default workspace when you first open InDesign. Click the down arrow next to the word and choose Digital Publishing from the list of workspaces.

   DOWNLOAD: Exercise files for this chapter can be downloaded from http://www.interactive-indesign.com.

   When the workspace opens, you'll notice that one column of panels is collapsed to icons only, and the other displays both icons and the panel names. You're going to become very familiar with the interactive panels and their icons, so, in the interest of conserving space, you'll collapse the expanded column to show icons only. The Panel Icon Key on page 35 should serve as a reference for all the panels in the two interactive workspaces as well as the panels highlighted earlier in this chapter.

3. Position your cursor over the left edge of the expanded panel column. When you see the double-sided arrow, click and hold down the mouse, and drag to the right until the words in the column disappear. Keep dragging until the column snaps to the width of the icons.

Panels can be expanded and collapsed by dragging from their left edge. To open all the panels in a column, click the double arrow at the upper right of the column. To open an individual panel, click its icon.

Next, you'll drag the Pages and Layers panels into a new column.

4. Click and drag the Pages panel icon (⊡) to the left of the existing panel columns. When you see a blue line at the left edge of the column, release the mouse to dock the Pages panel in a column of its own.

To dock a panel in a new location, drag it to its new position and then release the mouse when you see a blue line.

5. Drag the Layers panel icon below the Pages panel icon and release the mouse when the blue line appears between them.

The stacked Pages and Layers panels.

6. Click the double arrow at the upper right of the panel column you just created to expand it.

The Pages panel can display document pages in two distinctly different views: side-by-side or by alternate layout. The Alternate Layout view of the Pages panel is tailored to digital publishing as it allows you to create, view, and compare multiple layouts (referred to as renditions) within the same document. This means that when designing for the iPad for example, you can create both landscape and portrait renditions, in the very same document, that together combine to create a single DPS article. You'll explore this feature along with a bunch of other great new innovations in the DPS section, starting on page 427.

InDesign defaults to the Alternate Layout view of the Pages panel when you open a new document using the Digital Publishing preset. The renditions are displayed side-by-side with the rendition pages displayed vertically.

If you are developing for a destination other than DPS and expect to have a large number of pages in your document, you may want to change the view of the Pages panel to display your pages and spreads side-by-side instead of vertically.

> NOTE: When the Pages panel is in Alternate Layout view, landscape pages are displayed in the H column (for horizontal) and portrait pages are in the V column (for vertical.)

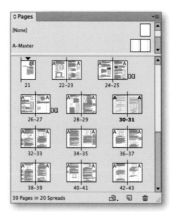

The Pages panel in Alternate Layout view with both landscape and portrait renditions of a two-page article and the Pages panel with pages arranged horizontally.

7. Click the menu button (▼≡) at the upper right corner of the Pages panel and choose Horizontally from the View Pages options.

To optimize the number of pages visible in the Pages panel, choose View Pages > Horizontally from the panel menu.

8. Go to Window > Interactive > SWF Preview. When the SWF Preview panel opens, drag it just to the left of the Pages panel and drop it when you see the blue line appear at the right edge of the SWF Preview panel.

9. Go to Window > Object & Layout > Align. The Align panel is grouped with the Pathfinder and the Transform panels. Click on the word "Align" and drag the Align panel directly below the SWF Preview panel icon. Release the panel when a blue line appears beneath the SWF Preview panel.

10. Drag the Pathfinder panel icon over the Align panel icon and this time, drop it when you see a blue outline around the entire icon. This will group the Align and Pathfinder panels into a panel group making them accessible through separate tabs in the same panel. Since you'll be able to do transformations from the Control panel, close the Transform panel.

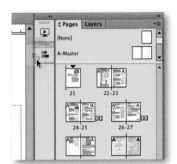

When you group panels in the dock, the panel icons have no dividing line between them. Each panel appears as a tab when the panel group is opened.

11. Go to Window > Styles > Paragraph Styles. Click and hold the dark gray bar at the top of the Paragraph and Character Styles panel group and drag it beneath the Preflight panel icon.

12. Go to Window > Styles > Object Styles and dock the Object Styles panel beneath the Paragraph and Character Styles.

13. Go to Window > Effects and dock the Effects panel just below the Object Styles panel.

14. If you'd like to add the Table and Cell Styles panels to the Panel Dock as well, go to Window > Styles > Table Styles to open the panels, and then dock them below the Paragraph and Character Styles panels.

    By default, InDesign's typical display uses a low resolution for placed files in order to conserve system resources and render the files more quickly. You may, on occasion, need to evaluate the quality and detail of a placed file, or, alternatively, choose to speed up page processing by displaying only placeholder images. The appearance of placed files on the page is controlled by the Display Performance settings, which are accessed either through a contextual menu or from the View or Object menus. To make the command easier to find, you'll highlight the menu item as part of your saved workspace.

15. Go to Edit > Menus. When the Menu Customization dialog opens, leave Category set to Application Menus and click the arrow to the left of the word "Object" in the Applications Menu Command section of the dialog.

PANEL ICON KEY	
Align	
Animation	
Articles	
Bookmarks	
Buttons and Forms	
Color	
Effects	
Folio Builder	
Folio Overlays	
Gradient	
Hyperlinks	
Layers	
Links	
Liquid Layout	
Media	
Object States	
Object Styles	
Pages	
Page Transitions	
Pathfinder	
Preflight	
Scripts	
Stroke	
Swatches	
SWF Preview	
Timing	

16. Scroll down until you see the words "Display Performance" and then click the word "None" to the right of the eye icon. This will display the menu highlight colors. Select a color and click OK to close the dialog. Go to the Object menu to see the Display Performance menu item highlighted in the color you selected.

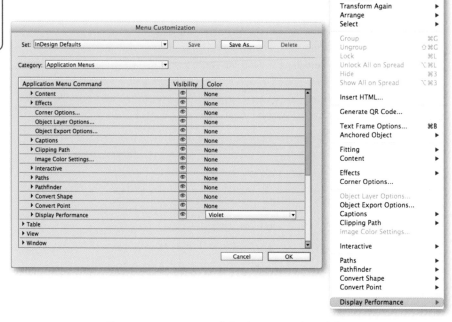

The Menu Customization dialog lets you set the visibility and highlight color for any InDesign menu.

The Menu Customization dialog makes it possible to assign colors to every menu in the application, and also to control menu visibility. Unless you're a very advanced InDesign user, familiar with the function of every menu item, we strongly encourage you to leave all menu items visible. There's no better way to learn the application than by digging into each of the available menus and tools. If you can't see them, you'll have no way of knowing what options are available. If you do decide to hide some menu items, you can still access them through the Show All Menu Items command at the bottom of any menu with hidden items. Alternatively, you can choose Window > Workspace > Show Full Menus to show all menus and hidden menu items for the active workspace.

Now that everything is in its place, it's time to save your workspace.

17. From the Workspace Switcher dropdown menu, or from Window > Workspace, choose New Workspace. Name your workspace "DigiPub" and check the Panel Locations and Menu Customization checkboxes.

Custom Workspaces can include both Panel Locations and Customized Menus.

In the course of your work, you may open or close panels and otherwise rearrange your workspace setup. InDesign retains the changes you make, assuming you want to keep your new workspace definition. To return to your saved workspace, select Reset (workspace name) from the Workspace dropdown.

Setting Application Preferences & Defaults

You can further customize InDesign by modifying application defaults to match your personal preferences. When you adjust your tool and/or menu settings with no document open, those settings become the defaults for all new documents. You can establish default settings in the other Creative Suite applications in the same way. If however, you have a document open when you change preferences or tools, most of your setting changes will become defaults that are specific only to that document.

You can capture your favorite font and text formatting as defaults as well. With no document open, just select the Type tool and enter your desired formatting in both the Character and Paragraph formatting sections of the Control panel. All the settings you choose will become the default definition applied to new text, including such things as Paragraph Rules, Keep Options, and Hyphenation.

You can establish defaults for fill and stroke color, stroke weight, object reference point, margins and columns, drop shadows and gradient colors; in short, any settings that you can change without an open document. A great use of this feature is to create a custom color palette—add colors to the Swatches panel with no document open and those swatches will be available in all new documents you create.

Setting Preferences in the Preferences Dialog

While there are at least three ways to do almost everything in Adobe applications, the Preferences dialog gives you access to a whole set of controls that are, in most cases, available nowhere else in the interface. Found under the Edit menu on a Windows machine and the InDesign menu on a Mac, the Preferences dialog is a parent–child type menu with categories on the left that relate to controls on the right. While it may appear a little overwhelming at first, and you'll never have cause to change the default settings for most of InDesign's Preferences, there are a couple settings that are worth adjusting in order to improve your workflow.

Exercise 3.2: Working with Preferences

In this exercise, you'll enable drag and drop text editing, turn on spell check, set the units of measure for your documents, and learn a very cool way to use the dynamic spelling feature to enhance efficiency.

When editing text, the ability to drag and drop text is an incredible efficiency enhancement. Since this feature not turned on by default, you'll enable it now in the Preferences dialog.

1. With no document open, go to Edit > Preferences (Windows) or InDesign > Preferences (Mac), and select Type from the Preferences submenu.

2. In the Drag and Drop Text Editing section of the dialog, check the Enable in Layout View checkbox.

You can set up drag and drop text editing in the Type section of the Preferences dialog.

Regardless of the length of your documents, it's probably a good idea to enable dynamic spelling, and possibly autocorrect. If you've used spell check in other applications, InDesign's spell check will make you feel right at home.

TIP: Misspelled words, uncapitalized words, uncapitalized sentences, and repeated words are indicated by a squiggly underline in whatever color you set when you enable dynamic spelling in the Preferences dialog.

3. Select Spelling from the column at the left of the Preferences dialog. Check the Enable Dynamic Spelling checkbox to turn on spell check. Then, choose colors you'd like to indicate misspelled words, uncapitalized words, uncapitalized sentences, and repeated words.

Autocorrection provides an additional spelling aid with its own dedicated Preferences category. If there are words you routinely misspell, you can add them to a customized dictionary. Additionally, you can extend Autocorrect to become a powerful efficiency tool for writing technical terms, company names, or any long words or phrases that you use regularly. Here's how.

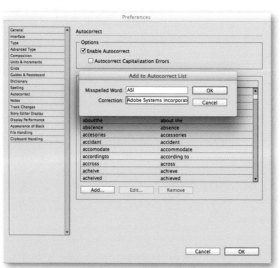

By being just a little clever with the Autocorrect feature, you can get InDesign to enter text for you automatically.

4. Select Autocorrect from the left column of the Preferences dialog. Check the Enable Autocorrect checkbox and click the Add button. In the Misspelled Word text field, type an easy-to-remember abbreviation for the word or phrase you would like to be able to enter more quickly. For example, enter ASI as an abbreviation for Adobe Systems Incorporated.

5. In the Correction field, type the full word or phrase you would like InDesign to enter automatically—in this case, Adobe Systems Incorporated. Click OK to close the Add to Autocorrect List dialog.

The next time you want to enter the word or phrase, just type the abbreviation you entered in the Misspelled Word field. InDesign will fill in the long version for you. Pretty cool, yes?

The spelling controls can also be accessed through the Edit menu and the text-specific context menu. To access the context menu, Right-Click/Ctrl+Click with the Type tool active in a text frame. From the Spelling menu option, you can choose Check Spelling, Dynamic Spelling, or Autocorrect. You can also access the User Dictionary or, if applicable, the dictionary specific to the active document.

The Units & Increments category of the Preferences dialog enables you to set the default unit of measure for your document to points, picas, inches, centimeters, millimeters, ciceros, agates, pixels, or even to a custom setting. For interactive design, the obvious choice is pixels. Truth is, pixels and points are effectively the same measure, since there are 72 of either in an inch (at least according to Adobe Postscript). In actual typesetting, there are 72.27 points per inch and, in fact, the Units & Increments dialog even offers a Traditional points/inch option that is true to that measure.

6. From the left column of the Preferences dialog, select Units & Increments. Choose Inches from both the Horizontal and Vertical dropdowns.

7. Click OK to close the Preferences dialog and complete the exercise.

> **TIP:** To remove a word from the Autocorrect word list, select the word and click the Remove button at the lower right of the dialog. To change an existing word in the list, select it and click the Edit button. Make your changes in the Edit Autocorrect List dialog and then click OK to close. To delete the entire list, select the first word in the list, hold down the Shift key, and click the last word in the list. With all the entries in the list selected, click the Remove button to delete them.

Creating a Document Preset

A couple minutes here and a couple minutes there can add up to hours and hours over the course of a project. Every little thing that cuts the time spent on routine tasks can result in huge long-term savings. Document presets fall into this time-saving category, capturing all the New Document settings in named and reusable presets that include the number of pages, page size, margin and column settings, ruler units, bleed, and slug. You can also choose from either print, web, or digital publishing intent, which automatically populate the Swatches panel with either CMYK or RGB colors, accordingly. Any presets you create stay in the preset list until you delete them or delete your application preferences. Also, any preset you use remains the default document preset in the New Document dialog, until you choose a different preset.

Exercise 3.3: Document Presets and Application Preferences

In this exercise, you'll set up a document preset, learn how to load and export saved presets, and learn how to set application defaults with no document open.

1. Go to File > New Document. In the New Document dialog, choose Digital Publishing from the Intent dropdown, leave Number of Pages set to 1, and ensure that the Primary Text Frame checkbox is checked. Enter 2048 for Width, 1536 for Height, and leave columns set to 1. Leave the margins set to the default of 36 px.

2. Click the disclosure triangle to the left of the words "Bleed and Slug" and ensure that all the Bleed and Slug values are set to 0.

3. Click the Save Preset button at the upper right of the panel (📥)and name the preset "iPad Retina". Click OK to close the Save Preset dialog, and then click OK to create your new document.

> **TIP:** When creating a new document for print, to set a bleed, click the disclosure triangle to the left of the words "Bleed and Slug" to access the settings.

> **TIP:** Click the Preview checkbox at the lower left of the New Document dialog to see what the layout of your new document will look like as you provide the settings.

You can create a new document and save a document preset all in one step from the New Document dialog.

You don't need to open a new document in order to create a document preset. InDesign has a Document Preset dialog where you can create, save, and edit presets or load any number of saved presets from an external file. In the next step, you'll load a collection of web presets.

As with other advertising media, web ads are most often sold in conventional sizes. The provided presets are representative of the most popular ad dimensions.

4. Go to File > Document Presets > Define. Click the Load button and browse to the chapter_3_exercises folder. Select the **web_banner_presets.dcst** file and click Open to add a collection of the most common web banner sizes to the list of saved presets. Click OK to close the Document Presets dialog.

The Document Presets dialog makes it possible to create, save, load, edit, and remove document presets.

The Document Setup dialog (File > Document Setup), which looks nearly identical to the New Document dialog, enables you to change the number of pages in an open document, the page orientation and dimensions, and the bleed and slug. Standard text frames already on your document pages won't be affected unless Layout Adjustment is turned on. Primary text frames will adjust to the new document dimensions. The settings you enter in the Document Setup dialog with no document open become the settings that appear in the New Document dialog when the [Default] document preset is selected.

5. Press Ctrl+−/Command+− once or twice to zoom out enough that you see the entire page and some of the pasteboard surrounding it. (If you zoom out too far press Ctrl++/Command++ to zoom back in again.)

6. Press Ctrl+R/Command+R to show the rulers if they're not already visible and note the document dimensions. (Pixels are the default unit of measure for documents created using web or digital publishing intent.)

7. Go to File > Document Setup. Choose iPad from the Page Size dropdown and note that the values in the Width and Height fields change to 1024 x 768. Click OK to apply the new dimensions to your document.

8. You should see the document jump to its new smaller size but check the rulers to confirm the change.

9. Using the Selection tool (▶), click the text frame on the page to select it. Mouse over the page badge at the upper left of the frame to see the popup tooltip indicating that the story is from the master's primary text flow.

10. Note that the text frame is inset from the edge of the page by 36 pixels as indicated by the X and Y coordinates displayed in the Control panel at the top of the screen. The X and Y coordinates confirm that the margin settings were maintained despite the changed document dimensions.

TIP: You can easily save and share a collection of document presets. If the presets you want to save are listed consecutively in the Document Presets dialog, click the first preset, hold down the Shift key, and click the last preset to select everything in between. (Hold the Ctrl/Command key and click to select non-consecutive items.) Then click Save, name your file, and click OK. The saved preset file will have a DCST extension.

TIP: When you create a new document with the Digital Publishing intent selected, the Pages panel display switches automatically to Alternate Layout view.

TIP: To turn on Layout Adjustment, go to Layout > Margins and Columns and check the Enable Layout Adjustment checkbox.

TIP: Hold down the Ctrl/Command key to temporarily switch to the Selection tool when any tool other than the Direct Selection tool is selected.

The position of the text frame on the page is indicated by
the X and Y coordinates displayed on the Control panel.

The Margins and Columns dialog, accessed through the Layout menu, enables
you to change the margin settings and the number of columns on a document
page or master page. When you change the margins and columns on a master
page, new pages based on that master reflect the new settings.

As with Document Setup, Layout Adjustment must be turned on for margin and
column changes to affect existing standard text frames. Layout Adjustment must
also be turned on in order for existing primary text frames to be affected by
changed margin and column settings.

Margins and Columns settings established with no document open become the
settings for the [Default] preset in the New Document dialog.

11. Double-Click the A-Master page icon in the top section of the Pages panel to
     display the A-Master page in the document window.

12. Go to Layout > Margins and Columns. When the dialog opens, click the link icon
     to unlock it (⚙)and to enable assignment of separate margin values.

13. Enter 144 for the top margin, 72 for the bottom, and change the number of
     columns to 3. Click OK to close the dialog.

     Note that the adjusted margins and columns are indicated on the page in
     magenta and purple. Note also that the text frame, indicated by a blue outline,
     is still in its original position on the page and has not updated to the new
     settings. You'll update it manually now.

14. Using the Selection tool, mouse over the sizing handle at the center of the upper
     edge of the text frame. When the cursor changes to a double-sided arrow, click
     and hold, and drag the frame edge down until it snaps to the top margin guide.

When Layout Adjustment is turned off, primary text frames are not affected by changes
made through the Margins and Columns dialog and require manual updating.

15. Drag the bottom edge of the text frame up to snap it to the bottom page margin.

16. To change the number of columns in the text frame, press Ctrl+B/Command+B
     (or go to Object > Text Frame Options.) In the Text Frame Options dialog, leave
     the Columns dropdown set to Fixed Number and set the number of columns to 3.
     Click OK to close the dialog.

17. To set the default font for your document, click the pasteboard to deselect the
     text frame. Select the Type tool and then choose Myriad Pro from the Font Family
     dropdown on the Control panel. Set the font size to 12 pt and, if necessary, set the
     font style to Regular.

Kerning is the space between a pair of adjacent characters. If the kerning is bad (we're looking at you, free fonts), the brain has to work harder to read each letter or word. Optical Kerning is an important and under-used InDesign feature that enhances readability by making letter spacing cleaner and more proportional. You can set Optical Kerning as the default for your type by redefining the [Basic Paragraph] style in the Paragraph Styles panel.

18. To reset the kerning of the [Basic Paragraph] style, go to Window > Styles > Paragraph Styles or click ( ) in the long first column of the Panel Dock. Right-Click/Ctrl+Click the style name in the panel and choose Edit "[Basic Paragraph]" from the contextual menu. When the Paragraph Style Options dialog opens, choose Basic Character Formats from the category list at its left. Choose Optical from the Kerning dropdown. Click OK to close the dialog and complete the exercise.

Customizing the Control Panel

In your customization of the InDesign interface, you can also choose to hide a number of the controls on the Control panel. Again, unless you are a very experienced user, and are certain that you don't want or need ready access to particular tools, we strongly recommend that you leave them showing. Then take some time to learn what they do.

The Customize Control Panel dialog is actually a good place for that learning to begin. It identifies each control by name, thereby providing a term you can investigate further if desired in InDesign's Help application. To open the dialog, choose the Customize option from the Control panel menu. Expand the categories and make note of any controls that are unfamiliar. It's a good bet that even if you're a seasoned InDesign user, you'll find things in the lists that you didn't even know existed.

> **TIP:** Click the ▾☰ icon at the far right of the Control panel to access the Control panel menu.

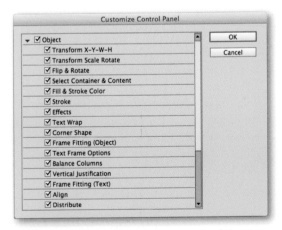

The Customize Control Panel dialog is a good place to familiarize yourself with all the Control panel controls.

Arranging Document Windows

You can have InDesign arrange multiple documents for you
from the Arrange option of the Window panel, or the
Arrange documents button on the Application Bar.

While not a persistent preference, you can also customize the way multiple
documents are displayed in the application window. By default, multiple
documents open in tabs that you can reorder by dragging. The tabs can also
be dragged away from the tab bar to float independently. You can then add
additional documents to the floating window. Each document you add will
have its own tab as part of the new document group.

TIP: To close the
windows for all open
documents, press
Shift+Ctrl+Alt+W/
Shift+Command+
Option+W.

Although you can manually arrange the windows, there are some handy
controls that can quickly arrange things for you. Go to Window > Arrange or
click the Arrange Documents button on the Application Bar and choose from the
available options.

The configurations available in the selection panel will depend on the number
of documents you have open. Just click an available layout to rearrange
your documents. To put all the files back into one window, go to Window >
Arrange > Consolidate All Windows or choose Consolidate All (■) from the
Arrange Documents selection panel (■▼).

Creating a Custom Preflight Profile

Whatever work you're doing in InDesign, be it for print, web, or interactive,
the objective is to smooth the workflow and make it as efficient and effortless
as possible. The Preflight panel is a great aid in that it can be set up to give
you dynamic feedback as you develop your document. The next exercise
explores some of the capabilities of the Preflight panel, and walks you through
establishing settings tailored specifically to interactive design.

Exercise 3.4: Customizing a Preflight Profile

TIP: To define a
Preflight profile,
you can also go to
Window > Output >
Preflight and choose
Define Profiles from
the panel menu, or
access the Preflight
panel by clicking
its icon (⮧) in the
Panel dock.

1. With the document open from the previous exercise, click the down arrow
   to the right of the Preflight Error Indicator at the bottom left of the document
   window. Choose Define Profiles from the Preflight menu.

Access the Preflight panel and the Define Profiles dialog by clicking the black arrow to
the right of the Preflight Error Indicator at the bottom left of the document window.

InDesign provides two preset profiles that appear at the left of the Preflight Profiles dialog. The [Basic] profile is applied automatically to documents created using the Print and Web document presets and the Digital Publishing profile is applied to documents based on the Digital Publishing document preset. Both profiles are set to detect missing, modified, and inaccessible links, overset text, missing fonts, and unresolved caption variables. While live feedback to inform you of these conditions is extremely useful, it's only the beginning of the benefits the Preflight panel has to offer.

NOTE: Live Preflight is active for all documents unless you deliberately turn it off.

Live Preflight dynamically checks your document against criteria you select.

There are many alerts you can set in the Preflight panel, depending on the requirements of your document. For purposes of this exercise, you'll add a few settings to the Digital Publishing profile that will greatly enhance its usefulness.

2. Click the New preflight profile button (⊞) at the bottom left of the Preflight Profiles dialog and when prompted, name the profile "Interactive".

3. Expand the Images and Objects section of the panel by clicking the arrow at the left of the category name, and check the Image Resolution checkbox.

4. Enter 225 as the minimum image resolution for color and grayscale images and 600 for 1-bit Image Minimum Resolution. Check the Non-Proportional Scaling of Placed Object checkbox.

You can set a Preflight Profile to check for minimum resolution and non-proportional scaling as well as other useful properties.

5. Scroll down to the Text section of the dialog, keep the default settings, and check the checkboxes for Glyph Missing and Dynamic Spelling Detects Errors. You may also choose to add a warning for minimum font size and non-proportional type scaling.

Text settings in a preflight profile can alert you to missing fonts
and glyphs, and check for spelling errors, disallowed font types,
non-proportional scaling, and minimum type size.

6. Click Save and then click OK to close the dialog.

   You can create as many preflight profiles as you like, tailored to the specifics of
   your output requirements. Now that you've created a new preflight profile, the
   next step is to apply it to your document.

7. Go to Window > Output > Preflight to open the Preflight panel. Choose Preflight
   Options from the Preflight panel menu, and when the dialog opens, choose your
   saved profile from the Working Profile dropdown. Leave the remaining default
   settings and click OK to close the dialog.

To switch preflight profiles, choose Preflight Options from the Preflight panel
menu and when the dialog opens, select the desired profile from the Working
Profile dropdown.

8. Close the document without saving to complete the exercise.

Customizing the Links Panel

The Links panel can be used in concert with the Preflight panel to help you keep on top of potential problems with placed files. While the Preflight panel provides an alert when there's an issue, the Links panel often provides additional detail that may be useful in straightening things out.

Clicking an item in the Links panel displays all manner of metadata (data about the selected file) in the panel's bottom pane. The best part of the panel though, is that you can customize it to display any of that metadata in the columns at the top of the panel. Then, at-a-glance, you can determine whether your linked images have the necessary image resolution, whether they are proportionally scaled, what color space they use, and so much more. The next exercise walks you through customization of the Links panel.

Exercise 3.5: Customizing the Links Panel

The first adjustment you'll make to the Links panel is to add a column that displays effective image resolution. Effective resolution is the actual output resolution of an image and is calculated by multiplying the original image resolution by the percentage the image has been scaled. For the web, any value under 72 ppi is going to create a problem with image quality. For DPS, a resolution of 108 ppi is recommended for content targeted to both standard and high-definition iPads. If you see that an image has two values in the Effective Resolution column of the Links panel, you know immediately that the image has been non-proportionally scaled.

The Links panel can also provide an at-a-glance view of image dimensions and scaling percentages, as well as object color space. Additionally, it can show the page and layer on which placed content occurs, making it easier to locate that content in your document. If a link is missing or its source file has been changed, the Links panel notifies you that action is required. A truly awesome tool, these are just some of the Links panel's many talents.

1. Go to Window > Links or click the 🔗 icon in the Panel Dock to open the Links panel.

2. Choose Panel Options from the panel menu. When the dialog opens, keep the default settings and, in the Show Column, check the checkboxes for Effective PPI, Dimension, Scale, and Layer. Click OK to close the dialog.

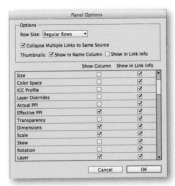

You can set a wide range of information to display in the Links panel through the Panel Options dialog.

Now that you've set the panel preferences, you'll adjust the columns to better see the information.

3. At the very top of the panel, position your cursor over the lines dividing the columns and when the cursor changes to a double-sided arrow, drag to adjust the column widths.

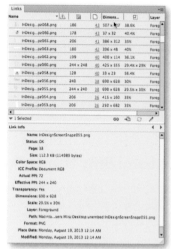

TIP: You can click a column header in the Links panel to sort the column contents. For example, click the Name header to sort the linked files alphabetically and numerically. Click again to switch between ascending and descending order.

The Links panel can be customized to display a wide variety of details about linked files. The two values in the Effective PPI and Scale columns for two of the files above indicate that they have been scaled non-proportionally.

Exercise 3.6: Correcting Preflight Errors

1. Open **ex3_6_start.indd** and save it as **ex3_6.indd**.

    A preflight profile named Web is embedded in the file. The Web profile checks for the same criteria you defined in the Interactive profile with one exception. Instead of images with a minimum resolution of 225 ppi, it checks for images with a resolution less than 72 ppi. Look at the Preflight Error indicator at the bottom left of the screen and note that five errors are present in the document.

2. Double-Click the red error indicator at the bottom left of your document window to open the Preflight panel. Twirl down the Images and Objects disclosure triangle and note that there are two issues with the problem object: resolution and non-proportional scaling. Twirl down the disclosure triangle for Image Resolution and click the blue page hyperlink (the number 1 at the right of the error entry) to select the image and jump to its location in the document.

3. With the image selected, click ⊖ in the Panel Dock to open the Links panel.

    The link is highlighted in the panel and you can see that the effective resolution of the image is 51 x 50, much too low to meet your minimum resolution requirements. The two resolution values, one for the horizontal and the other for the vertical, confirm that the image has been scaled non-proportionally. You can fix the resolution issue by exchanging the linked file for one with a higher resolution, but you'll need to fix the scaling issue manually.

4. Click the Relink button (⊖) at the bottom of top section of the Links panel and browse to the chapter_3_exercises folder. Select **CostaRicaProvinces.psd** and click Open to replace the existing file with a higher resolution image.

A look in the Links panel confirms that the new file has an effective resolution of at least 106, but the scaling issue is still unresolved. This next bit is a little tricky, in that the scaling percentages for the object that appears on the Control panel show 100% for both Width and Height. How can this be when you have multiple indicators that the object is non-proportionally scaled? Well, the dimensions and scale shown on the Control panel relate to the object frame, rather than the placed content. It's the scaling of the image inside the frame that needs to be corrected.

5. If necessary, click the hyperlink for the image in the Links panel to re-select it and isolate it from its frame. The image should be surrounded by a red bounding box. Note that the scaling percentages in the Control panel match those shown in the Links panel.

    For this particular image, it happens that the horizontal scale needs to be adjusted to match the correct vertical scale.

6. Click inside the Scale Y field on the Control panel and press Ctrl+A/Command+A to select the value (⬚ ⬆ 67.02120 ⬆). Press Ctrl+C/Command+C to copy it, and then select the value in the Scale X field. If necessary, click the link icon (⚙) to ensure that the scaling percentages are not constrained to scale proportionally. Press Ctrl+V/Command+V to paste the value in the Scale X field, and press Enter/Return to commit your change. Check the Scale and Effective PPI values in the Links panel to see that, now, they each display only one value. Check the Preflight panel to see that the Images and Objects errors have disappeared.

    You still have a couple of text errors to correct to make the document error-free.

7. In the Preflight panel, twirl down the Text arrow and then the arrow for Overset text. Click the blue 1 to the right of the first Text Frame error to jump to and select the overset text frame in your document. Note the red + sign at the lower right corner of the frame that indicates that the text is overset.

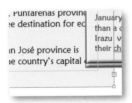

A red plus sign at the lower right edge of a text frame indicates that
the frame is not large enough to display all the text in the story.

8. With the Selection tool, position your cursor over the center adjustment handle on the bottom edge of the frame. When the double-sided vertical arrow appears, click and hold and drag down until the last line of text fits in the frame and the + sign disappears. Note that the first Text Frame entry in the Preflight panel disappears.

9. In the Preflight panel, Double-Click the remaining Text Frame item. Then, with the Selection tool, drag the lower right corner of the selected text frame to the right to widen it. Just that easily, another error bites the dust.

    Unfortunately, the Dynamic Spelling Problem error in the Preflight panel is a notification alert only, and does not link directly to the trouble spots in the document. Not a problem: you can locate the issues easily enough using the Check Spelling command.

Before doing so, however, you'll set some preferences to detect issues with spelling and repeated words and to ignore other error types.

NOTE: The interactive layouts you'll be working with are likely to have an assortment of buttons using lowercase names. Deselecting Uncapitalized Words and Uncapitalized Sentences from the Spelling Preferences will give you fewer false misspelling indicators.

10. On a Windows computer, go to Edit > Preferences > Spelling. On a Mac, go to InDesign > Preferences > Spelling. In the Preferences dialog, if necessary, deselect the checkboxes for Uncapitalized Words and Uncapitalized Sentences. If it's not already checked, check the Enable Dynamic Spelling checkbox and click OK to close the dialog.

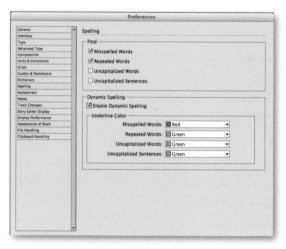

You can customize the type of errors detected by the Dynamic Spelling feature.

TIP: To access Spelling correction options, when the blinking Type tool cursor is active in a text frame, just Right-Click/ Ctrl-Click to open the contextual menu.

11. To detect and correct the spelling issue(s) in the document, go to Edit > Spelling, and choose Check Spelling (Ctrl+I/Command+I).

12. When the Check Spelling dialog opens, ensure that Document (not Story) is selected from the Search dropdown and click Start.

13. When the first misspelled word appears, choose "volcanoes" from the Suggested Corrections list, and then click Change. Change the next word to "characteristics" and then click the Done button to close the dialog.

14. Save and close the file to complete the exercise.

NOTE: The names of the volcanoes and provinces were added to the user dictionary which was then merged with the document. Had this not been done, each name would be targeted by Check Spelling as a misspelled word.

TIP: To embed the user dictionary in a document, from the Dictionary category of the Preferences panel, check the Merge User Dictionary into Document checkbox at the bottom of the panel.

The Check Spelling dialog enables you to check spelling in the remainder of the active Story, the entire Story, the Document, or All Documents.

Working with Bridge

Bridge is a great, but largely undiscovered, stand-alone application that installs with CC. Like Windows Explorer or File Browser on steroids, Bridge lets you visually browse much more than just image files. You can preview multi-page PDFs and multi-page InDesign files, native Photoshop and Illustrator files, video, audio, 3D files, SWF, FLV, and F4V files, as well as most files supported by the version of QuickTime that's on your computer. But Bridge does way more than browse files. It's also a user-friendly interface for keywording, filtering, sorting, and batch processing. In fact, you can use Bridge to batch rename files of any type, even Word docs! Bridge also contains a sophisticated image processing application called Camera Raw for non-destructive individual and batch correction of RAW, JPEG, and TIFF files. Impressive list of credentials, don't you think? Hopefully impressive enough to inspire you to take the time to learn more.

From Bridge, you can drag a file directly into your InDesign document or you can Right-Click/Ctrl+Click a file and choose Place > In InDesign from the context menu. Dragging a file either loads the Place cursor, or, if dragged over an existing frame, places the file.

By far, one of the coolest features of Bridge is that it can show you a virtual collection of all the files linked to any selected InDesign document. If you've ever been at a loss to remember where you stashed a particular image, but you remember the name of an InDesign file where you used it, locate that document in Bridge, Right-Click/Ctrl+Click on it, and choose Show Linked Files. Bridge will display the collected files in a single window for your viewing convenience.

Right-Click/Ctrl+Click the link icon at the upper right of a document thumbnail and choose Show Linked Files to view a virtual collection of all the links included in the selected file.

As with most things, the best way to get to know Bridge is to use it. In the next exercise, you'll get a feel for what it can do.

Exercise 3.7: An Introduction to Bridge

1. To open Bridge from InDesign, go to File > Browse in Bridge.

2. When Bridge opens, ensure that the Essentials workspace is selected from the Workspace Switcher dropdown at the upper right of the screen.

3. From the Favorites or Folders tab at the upper left of the interface, navigate to the **chapter_3_exercises** folder.

4. If necessary, scroll to locate **ex3_6_start.indd** and Right-Click/Ctrl+Click the link badge at the upper right of the file icon. Choose Show Linked Files.

   Bridge displays the **CostaRicaProvinces_low_res.psd** file that is linked to the document.

5. Click the back arrow (◀) at the upper left corner of the interface to return to the chapter_3_exercises folder.

   The breadcrumbs across the top of the panel display as much of the folder hierarchy as can fit across the width of the panel, with each folder name separated by a >. Click on a > to display a list of subfolders from which you can make a selection.

   > 💻 Computer > 🖥 Macintosh HD > 👤 Users > 🏠 Mira > 📁 CCExercises > 📁 chapter_13_exercises

   You can click a > on the Toolbar across the top of the
   Bridge window to access a list of selectable subfolders.

6. Click the rightmost > and then click "links" to open the links folder.

   A notation appears at the bottom left of the panel indicating that the folder contains 14 items.

7. If necessary, scroll to locate the **flower6.jpg** image thumbnail and click to select it. Press the Spacebar on your keyboard to open the image in Full Screen Preview mode and the image will fill the display window.

8. Click once on the image to zoom to 100% view, and then drag to inspect it. Click again to fit the image back in the window. Drag the mouse up and down to zoom in and out. You can also use the plus and minus keys on your keyboard to zoom.

9. Still in Full Screen Preview mode, navigate to the next and previous images in the folder using the right and left arrow keys on your keyboard. When you're done exploring, press Escape to close Preview mode and return to Bridge.

10. Click the Refine button (▣ ▾) at the upper left of the screen and choose Review Mode from the dropdown menu (Ctrl+B/Command+B.)

11. Use the right and left arrow controls at the lower left of the window (◆ ◆   ▾) to move through the images. When a non-insect image appears in the central viewing window, click the down arrow to remove it from the review. (You can also use the right, left, and down arrows on your keyboard.)

    Notice that when you move the mouse over the image in the central viewing area, the cursor changes to the Zoom tool (🔍).

TIP: In Bridge, a thumbnail displays a link icon at its upper right corner if the document contains linked files. Right-Click/Ctrl+Click the thumbnail and choose Show Linked Files from the context menu to display the collected linked files in a window of their own. Bridge will also provide an alert if files linked to the document are missing.

---

12. Click the image with the Zoom tool to open the Loupe, allowing you to inspect the image detail more closely. Use the + and – keys to zoom in and out. (Magnification percentages are displayed to the right of the filename below the selected image.) Click the Loupe to close it.

13. Using your arrow keys to navigate through the remaining images, Right-Click/ Ctrl+Click each image and add a star rating and/or label from the context menu. (You can also use the numbers 1–5 on your keyboard to assign a rating as you review.)

14. Click the New Collection button (▦) at the lower right of the window. In the New Collection dialog, enter the name "Insects". When you save the Collection, you'll get bounced out of Review Mode and back into Bridge.

TIP: Exit Review Mode in Bridge either by clicking on the X at the lower right of the Review window or by pressing Escape on your keyboard.

15. Click the Collections tab in the lower left column in Bridge and choose the Insects collection. The insect photos appear in the content window.

16. Click the back arrow at the upper left of the screen to return to the links folder. Drag the slider at the bottom right of the Content pod to zoom in and out on the thumbnails.

17. Click the boomerang icon (◖) at the upper left of the interface to return to InDesign.

18. Go to File > New > Document. Select the iPad Retina preset you created in Exercise 3.3: Document Presets and Application Preferences, starting on page 40. Click OK to open the new document.

19. Switch to Bridge and select eight of the images in the links folder by holding the Ctrl/Command key and clicking them with the Selection tool. Click and hold on one of the selected images and drag from Bridge to InDesign to load the multi-place cursor.

Loaded cursor transferring files from Bridge to InDesign.

20. Click the document with the loaded cursor and holding the mouse, drag on a diagonal down and to the right to draw a frame. Release the mouse to place your first image. Repeat for each of the remaining loaded images, drawing frames of different dimensions until the cursor has been emptied.

21. Save the file as ex3_7.indd in the chapter_3_exercises folder, and close it. Keep Bridge open for the next exercise.

TIP: Use the right and left arrows on your keyboard to cycle through the thumbnails for the images loaded into the cursor. A number on the thumbnail indicates the number of files loaded.

The Bridge Triple Play: Keywords, Advanced Search, and Smart Collections

Now that you and Bridge have had a chance to get acquainted, it's time to check out the awesome triple-play combination of three of its most useful and powerful facets: keywords, advanced search, and Smart Collections.

While we're not looking to do a deep dive into Bridge, the advanced search feature is just too wonderful a productivity tool to let it slip by without mention. What makes it so powerful is the phenomenally wide range of criteria on which you can base a search. From color space to aspect ratio and image resolution, to font face and swatch color, you can search for pretty much any metadata that can be encoded in a file. A search can contain as many criteria as you like so it can be as granular and specific as you could ever want.

One of the best applications of the search feature is when it's used in conjunction with keywords. Bridge makes it possible to create and apply keyword sets and subsets to your files that can then be leveraged as part of your search criteria. Used together, keywords and search are a tremendous productivity enhancer and their power is increased exponentially when you go one step further and save your search criteria as a Smart Collection. Smart Collections essentially enable an ongoing dynamic search. Every time you add a file to your system that matches criteria specified in a Smart Collection search, the file is added to the collection's virtual folder and appears the next time you access the collection—no matter where on your system the file is stored. We love this feature!

The organizational strategy of keywording your documents and creating saved searches in the form of Smart Collections can actually be life altering when it comes to your workflow. Just imagine the time you could save if you could actually find your files without having to dig through endless iterations to locate the specific version you're looking for. What a concept! Yes, it takes planning and an investment of some time to put it all together, but the time you'll save in the long run is truly incalculable. The next exercises provide an introduction—it's up to you to take it from there.

Exercise 3.8: Advanced Search in Bridge

1. In InDesign, go to File > Browse in Bridge. When Bridge opens, press Ctrl+F/ Command+F to open the Find dialog.

2. When the Bridge Find dialog opens, the Look in dropdown should be targeting the links folder that you had open from the previous exercise. Leave the links folder selected and expand the dropdown. You'll see a list of links to your recently visited folders, with a Browse link at the bottom.

3. From the first Criteria dropdown, choose Keywords, leave the word "contains" and enter "insects" in the fillable text field. If a second row appears in the Criteria list, click the ⊖ button at its left to delete it. Don't click Find yet.

    Keywords have been added to most of the files in the folder. The insect images have been tagged with two keywords: "Costa Rica" and "Insects". The flower images have been tagged with the words "Costa Rica" and "Flora". If you were to do a search for the keyword "Costa Rica", it would return photos of both the flowers and insects. To locate only the photos of insects from Costa Rica, you could define a search using the keywords "Insects" and "Costa Rica", and require that the search meet all criteria.

For this example, you want to locate only the insect images that have a width of 800 px. You could search for Width directly, since it's on the criteria list, but for the purpose of illustration, you'll search All Metadata for the number 800 instead.

4. Click the plus sign at the end of the first line to add back a second search criterion. Choose All Metadata from the criteria list, leave contains selected in the second dropdown and enter 800 in the value field. Don't click Find yet.

5. Ensure that the selected Match option is: if all criteria are met, and that both the include all subfolders and include non-indexed files checkboxes are checked.

Although rather unassuming in appearance, the Find dialog is an extremely powerful tool that lets you search based on any metadata encoded into your files.

6. Click Find to see the results of your search.

Note that the search returns only insect images. Click the files returned from the search to see that their dimensions are 800 x 600.

7. Click the Save as Smart Collection button to the left of the New Search button at the upper right of the Content pod. Name the collection "**Insects 800 x 600.**" Click Save to close the dialog and create the collection.

Smart Collections create virtual folders that update dynamically
to include all files that meet your search criteria.

NOTE: Pay particular attention to the folder you select when defining your Smart Collection, since the folder defines the scope of your search.

8. Mouse over the Smart Collection button again to see that its tooltip has now changed to Edit Smart Collection. Click the button and expand the Look in dropdown. If you see chapter_3_exercises in the list of recent folders, select it. Otherwise select Browse, locate and select the chapter_3_exercises folder, and click the Choose button. Click Save and the window will update immediately to include the additional file that matches your saved search.

9. Keep Bridge open and active for the next exercise.

If this exercise got your attention and your head is spinning with all the ways Smart Collections can revolutionize your workflow, you're probably eager to know how to add keywords to your documents. Check out the next exercise to learn just how easy it is.

Exercise 3.9: Working with Keywords

1. Still in Bridge, click the down arrow to the right of the word "Essentials" at the upper right of the interface and select Keywords from the Workspace Switcher dropdown menu.

2. In the Keywords workspace, the Keywords panel is located at the left of the Bridge interface. In the pod, you'll see some keyword sets for commonly used categories. Click to select any one of the insect images, and, if it wasn't already visible, the parent keyword "Costa Rica" appears with the child or sub keyword "Insects" nested below it.

The Bridge Keywords panel. When a file is selected, Keywords applied
to that file appear in the panel in italics if they weren't already included
in the list of existing keywords.

TIP: In Bridge, you can create a keyword to be used only for organizational purposes by enclosing the keyword in square brackets: [keyword]. Organizational keywords cannot be used to tag files.

3. To add a keyword, click the New Keyword button (🔲) at the bottom of the panel. Enter "Interactive InDesign" in the text field that pops up at the top of the panel and press Return/Enter to enter the name.

4. Select the "Interactive InDesign" keyword, click the New Sub Keyword button (🔲) and enter "[Photographs]" in the name field to create an organizational category name. Press Enter/Return to enter the keyword and keep it selected.

5. Click the New Sub Keyword button again, enter "Flora" and press Enter/Return.

6. With Flora selected, click the New Keyword button (⊞), enter "Fauna" and press Enter/Return. Repeat and enter "Texture" in the keyword field.

7. Using the path bar at the top of the Bridge window, navigate back to the chapter_3_exercises folder, Ctrl+Click/Command+Click to select **bug1.psd** and **CostaRicaProvinces.psd**, and check the Interactive InDesign keyword checkbox.

   Note that the keyword you've applied to the files appears with the file metadata in the Content pod.

8. Click once on **bug1.psd**, and check the "Fauna" keyword under Photographs to add it to the bug1.psd image.

9. Click the arrow to the right of the chapter_3_exercises folder in the path bar at the top of the Bridge interface, and choose **links** to open the folder. If you accidently click on the folder name instead of the arrow, you can get to the folder by typing "links" at the end of the path that appears in the window.

10. Apply the "Flora", "Fauna" and "Texture" keywords to the corresponding images in the folder.

11. Close out of Bridge and return to InDesign to complete the exercise.

CHAPTER SUMMARY

This chapter was all about getting acquainted with the InDesign interface, and then customizing both it and the application preferences to support a productive workflow. While getting familiar with the tools that you'll use in designing for interactivity, you also learned a lot about setting up the interface in ways that will serve you well for any type of project:

You were introduced to a number of the InDesign panels including:

- Align
- Animation
- Articles
- Bookmarks
- Buttons and Forms
- Effects
- Folio Builder
- Folio Overlays
- Hyperlinks
- Layers
- Links
- Liquid Layout
- Media
- Object States
- Object Styles
- Page Transitions
- Pathfinder
- Preflight
- Scripts
- SWF Preview
- Timing

You learned how to:

- Customize application menus
- Set preferences and defaults
- Create, load, and save document presets
- Customize the Control panel
- Customize Preflight Profiles
- Customize the Links panel
- Correct Preflight errors
- Work with Bridge to:

    - Navigate your files
    - Do advanced searches
    - Save Smart Collections
    - Use Keywords

In the process you:

- Set up Drag and Drop text editing and Dynamic Spelling
- Learned to automate Autocorrect to enter customized text
- Set Units & Increments
- Worked with the New Document dialog
- Set Document Setup and Margins and Columns preferences
- Worked with primary text frames
- Corrected overset text
- Used the Multiplace cursor to place multiple images

Now that the tools you'll need are handy and everything is in its place, it's time to get busy exploring the world of possibility that's literally at your fingertips. The next section provides a deep dive into Buttons, the very heart of interactivity for output to DPS, SWF and Interactive PDF.

Part 2

DOCUMENT LAYOUT & NAVIGATION

You'll find the tips and techniques in this portion of the book to be equally valuable in both your print and interactive work. You'll learn the fundamentals of working with text, how to flow and format it; you'll work with master pages and multi-page documents, hyperlinks, cross-references and footnotes; create and format a table of contents, learn all about InDesign's vast color resources, and employ its robust graphics tools to create compound shapes. The power-user tips in the next few chapters will take your InDesign skills to a whole new level and provide an arsenal of tools for your interactive endeavors.

Chapter 4

WORKING WITH TEXT

Getting familiar with the text formatting tools, managing text flow, spanning and splitting columns, flowing type on a path: these topics represent just a start to the goodies filling this chapter. You'll work with text wrap, create nested styles, convert print documents for on-screen display, work with anchored objects, and more. Count on it, the time you invest in working through this chapter will pay itself back with dividends!

Threaded Text Frames

NOTE: For more on primary text frames, see page 90.

All InDesign text resides in a text frame. If a primary text frame doesn't already exist on your document, you can create a new text frame in several ways. You can draw a text frame with the Type tool, you can place text from an external document, or you can convert an existing shape to a text frame by clicking it with the Type tool. Isolated text frames have their place, but there will no doubt be times when you want your content to flow across multiple text frames as well as multiple pages. This is easily done by threading text frames together to create what is known in InDesign as a story.

Text frames are threaded by linking the out port of one frame to the in port of another. Connecting lines called text threads span the distance between the frame ports and are a visual indicator of the flow of text through a document. You can toggle text thread visibility by going to View > Extras > Show (Hide) Text Threads (Alt+Ctrl+Y/Option+Command+Y). Even with text thread visibility turned on, a text frame must be selected with the Selection tool in order for the threads to be visible.

TIP: Go to View > Extras > Show Text Threads with no document open to make the setting an application default.

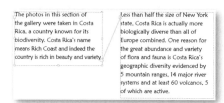

In order to see text threads, you need to select one of the text frames in a story with the Selection or Direct Selection tool. When a text frame is selected, it displays its in and out ports and its sizing handles. (In the image above, the frame on the left is selected.) When sizing a text frame, you need to be careful not to mistakenly click and drag a port instead of a sizing handle.

Threading text frames is easy, but there's one little trick to remember. You need to use the Selection tool rather than the Type tool to thread them. It makes sense if you think of text frames as boxes that contain text, each of which is independent until you connect them. To select an object—or a text box—you need to use the Selection tool. However, you're most likely to be using the Type tool when the need to thread text frames arises. You can hold down the Ctrl/Command key to temporarily switch from the active tool to the most recently selected Selection tool. This shortcut is handy for threading your text frames without requiring a trip to the Tools panel.

Exercise 4.1: Threading Text Frames

DOWNLOAD: Exercise files for this chapter can be downloaded from http://www.interactive-indesign.com.

In this exercise you'll see how easy it is to create threaded text frames.

1. Open **ex4_1_start.indd** and save it as ex4_1.indd.

    Note that the text in the paragraph starting with the words Costa Rica is overset, as indicated by the red plus sign (⊞) at the lower right of the text frame.

2. With the Selection tool, click once on the plus sign. The cursor should change to a loaded text cursor that displays the start of the actual text in the story.

    If the cursor doesn't load the first time, click again. Occasionally it doesn't register on the first try.

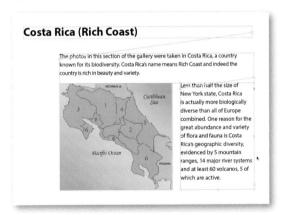

Costa Rica (Rich Coast)The photos in this section of the gallery were taken in Costa Rica, a country known for

The loaded Type tool cursor displays actual text from the beginning of your story.

3. With the loaded cursor, mouse over the empty text frame, below the title and above the Costa Rica map. When the symbol at the upper left of the cursor changes to a link (📎), click once to flow the text into the second frame.

   You'll notice that the second frame is also overset.

4. Click the red plus sign at the lower right of the second text frame to load the cursor once again. Mouse over the text frame to the right of the map, and click once when the link appears on the loaded cursor to flow the text into the frame.

   It would look better if the article title were separate from the body of the text. While you could have created a separate un-threaded text frame to hold the title, in this case you'll keep it connected to the story.

5. Position your cursor after the closing parenthesis in the title, and Double-Click with the Selection tool to activate the blinking Type tool cursor. Right-Click/Ctrl+Click, and, from the contextual menu, choose Insert Break Character > Frame Break to jump the text that's after the title into the next text frame.

   The text should now be flowing through all three text frames with the title text in a frame of its own. As the last refinement, you'll add a frame break to flow the second paragraph into the text frame to the right of the map.

> **TIP:** To reorganize content, copy and paste it within threaded text frames. Trying to rearrange the text frames themselves could result in an unmanageable rat's nest of tangled frames and mangled text.

Costa Rica (Rich Coast)

The photos in this section of the gallery were taken in Costa Rica, a country known for its biodiversity. Costa Rica's name means Rich Coast and indeed the country is rich in beauty and variety.

Less than half the size of New York state, Costa Rica is actually more biologically diverse than all of Europe combined. One reason for the great abundance and variety of flora and fauna is Costa Rica's geographic diversity, evidenced by 5 mountain ranges, 14 major river systems and at least 60 volcanos, 5 of which are active.

The appearance of the final layout.

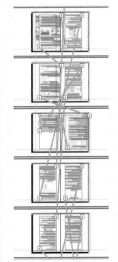

6. Position the Type tool cursor just in front of the word "Less" in the second text frame. Right-Click/Ctrl+Click , and from the contextual menu, choose Insert Break Character > Frame Break to jump to the last text frame.

7. Press Esc to select all the frames in the story and show the text threads linking them together. Save and close the file.

8. With no documents open, choose View > Extras > Show Text Threads to establish the setting as an application default. Going forward, whenever a linked text frame is selected, the text threads will be visible.

Managing Text Flow

In this section, you'll learn more about managing text flow and document pages, and take advantage of some of InDesign's productivity features.

In the last exercise, you learned how to manually thread text frames. If you're flowing a large volume of text across multiple pages, and you're not using a primary text frame, manually loading the cursor to thread each new frame can become tedious and time consuming. The next exercise introduces you to modifier keys that will save you some time by streamlining the text threading process.

Manually correcting overset text and empty pages that occur in the course of document editing can also take a good bit of time. You can let InDesign help by setting up a couple preferences that you'll cover in the next exercise as well. (Once again, setting the preferences with no document open will affect all new documents.)

Exercise 4.2: Managing Text Flow

The measurements in this exercise are given in pixels (px). As far as InDesign is concerned, points and pixels are equivalent. If your Preferences are set to use pixels, you won't need to change anything. Otherwise, you'll be changing the preference for units and increments later in the lesson. If you'd prefer to retain default ruler units other than pixels, you can type in the measurements we've supplied, followed by "px," and InDesign will do the unit conversion for you.

1. Go to File > New > Document and select Default from the Document Preset dropdown. If necessary, choose Print for Intent and Letter for Page Size. Be sure that the Primary Text Frame checkbox is deselected, leave the other defaults and click OK.

2. Press Ctrl+D/Command+D, navigate to the chapter_4_exercises folder, and Double-Click **advice_from_caterpillar.txt** to load it into the cursor.

3. Position the loaded text cursor somewhere in the middle of the page and click once to place the text.

   Notice that the text fills the page below the point where you clicked, and extends to the left and right margins of the page. When you place text by clicking, rather than dragging to define a text frame, the text frame boundaries automatically conform to the margin and column settings that you established in the Document or Margins and Columns dialogs. Had you specified multiple columns in your document setup, the placed text would have flowed to fill only the column in which you clicked.

   Note that each paragraph of the placed text is followed by two paragraph returns. In typography, this is a huge no-no, but removing the extra returns manually can be time consuming and annoying. Good thing InDesign can take care of it for you at the time the text is imported.

4. Press Ctrl+Z/Command+Z to undo the text placement, and then press Esc to clear the loaded text cursor.

5. Press Ctrl+D/Command+D again, but this time, check the Show Import Options checkbox at the bottom left of the Place dialog. Browse to and select the **advice_from_caterpillar.txt** file, and then click Open.

TIP: When you create a new document with the default Print Intent settings, pages are displayed in the Pages panel as two-page spreads, also known as facing pages. In a document with facing pages, page 1 starts on the right, as it would in a book, pages 2 and 3 are paired, as are 4 and 5, etc. This page arrangement can cause a bit of confusion should you try to scroll vertically from page to page in the document window. From page 1, you would scroll to page 3, for example. Navigating from one page to another by Double-Clicking a page in the Pages panel lets you target the page you want to go to without the frustration of scrolling up and down and left and right to position the desired page in the document window. Deselect the Facing Pages checkbox in the New Document dialog to set up a document with single page spreads.

---

6. In the Extra Carriage Returns section of the Text Import Options dialog, check the Remove Between Paragraphs checkbox. The file was created on a Mac, so, choose Macintosh Roman from the Character Set dropdown and choose Mac (Intel-based) from the Platform dropdown. Click OK to close the dialog.

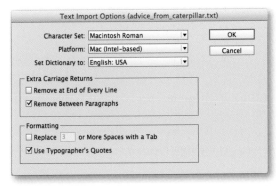

When placing text, InDesign can automatically remove extra returns between paragraphs as well as strip any formatting that was applied in Microsoft Word.

7. Position the loaded text cursor at the upper left margin of the page. This time, hold down the Alt/Option key and click once to place the text.

   When you hold down the Alt/Option modifier key, the text cursor icon changes to a broken squiggle ( ) (a technical term), indicating that you are about to semi-autoflow your text. Semi-autoflow places your text in the clicked column and then automatically reloads the cursor so you can selectively place the remaining text.

   Note that InDesign removed the extra paragraph returns from the placed text.

8. With the cursor loaded, click the Create new page button ( ) at the bottom of the Pages panel. When the empty page appears, hold down the Shift key and click at the upper left margin of the new page in the document window to autoflow the loaded text.

   In contrast to the semi-autoflow squiggle, the squiggle for the autoflow cursor is unbroken ( ). Autoflow flows the remaining text through your document, inserting additional pages as required.

   TIP: To add pages from the Pages panel menu, choose Insert Pages and then specify how many pages you want to add, where in the document you want to add them, and which master you want to apply to them.

9. Save the document as ex4_2.indd in the chapter_4_exercises folder.

   Next you'll set pixels to be the default unit of measure and set a preference to have InDesign automatically remove any empty pages that may occur in the course of editing.

10. Go to Edit > Preferences > Units & Increments (Windows)/ InDesign > Preferences > Units & Increments (Mac). Choose Pixels from the dropdowns for both the Horizontal and Vertical Ruler Units.

11. Select the Text category at the left of the Preferences dialog. Check the Smart Text Reflow and Delete Empty Pages checkboxes, uncheck Limit to Primary Text Frames and Click OK to close the Preferences dialog.

    TIP: Setting the Smart Text Reflow preference with a document open applies it to the active document only. To make Smart Text Reflow a global preference, set it with no documents open.

Control Panel Type Formatting Controls

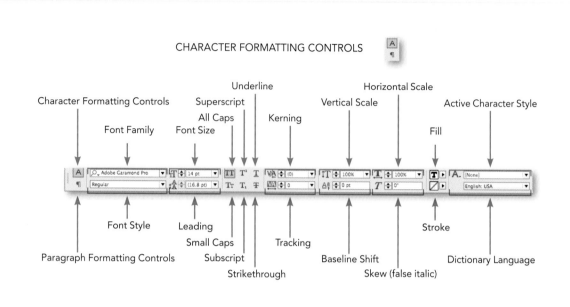

CHARACTER FORMATTING CONTROLS

Character Formatting Controls
Font Family
Superscript
All Caps
Font Size
Underline
Kerning
Vertical Scale
Horizontal Scale
Fill
Active Character Style

Font Style
Leading
Small Caps
Subscript
Tracking
Strikethrough
Baseline Shift
Skew (false italic)
Stroke
Dictionary Language
Paragraph Formatting Controls

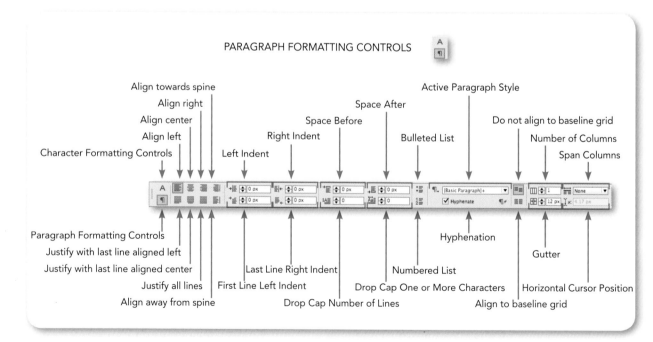

PARAGRAPH FORMATTING CONTROLS

Align towards spine
Align right
Align center
Align left
Character Formatting Controls
Left Indent
Right Indent
Space Before
Space After
Bulleted List
Active Paragraph Style
Do not align to baseline grid
Number of Columns
Span Columns

Paragraph Formatting Controls
Justify with last line aligned left
Justify with last line aligned center
Justify all lines
First Line Left Indent
Last Line Right Indent
Drop Cap Number of Lines
Numbered List
Drop Cap One or More Characters
Hyphenation
Align to baseline grid
Gutter
Horizontal Cursor Position
Align away from spine

Adjust just a few preferences, and InDesign will automatically add and remove pages for you as the amount of text in your document changes.

InDesign allows you to easily switch the setup of your document between single and facing pages at any point in the development cycle.

12. Go to File > Document Setup. When the dialog opens, deselect the facing pages checkbox.

13. Double-Click the words "A-Master" in the Pages panel to bring the master page into view. From the Pages panel menu, select Master Options for "A-Master." When the dialog opens, change the Number of Pages to 1 and click OK.

Should you need to make changes to margins and columns in an existing layout, Layout Adjustment provides a simple means of doing so for documents that don't rely on primary text frames.

14. With the master still active, go to Layout > Margins and Columns. First, check the Enable Layout Adjustment and Preview checkboxes. Ensure that the Make all settings the same link is linked. Enter 50 px in any of the Margins fields and press Tab. Unlink the link and enter 100 px in the Bottom margin field. Change the number of Columns to 2 and click OK to close the dialog.

Because A-Master is applied to all the document pages and Layout Adjustment is active, the new margin and column settings are applied throughout the document and the existing text frames are transformed from one column to two.

15. Double-Click on page 1 in the Pages panel. When the page appears in the document window, Double-Click the text frame on page 1 to switch to the Type tool. Press Ctrl+A/Command+A to select the entire story.

Note that there are four pages in the Pages panel.

16. With the Paragraph Formatting Controls active in the Control panel, add space after of 8 pt ( ) and deselect the Hyphenate checkbox. Switch to the Character Formatting Controls and format your text using Myriad Pro Regular, 10 pt with default leading.

TIP: You can highlight the content from the blinking Type tool cursor to the end of the text in a story (including overflow) by pressing Ctrl+Shift+End/ Command+Shift+End. On a Mac Laptop, press Command+Shift+FN+ right arrow.

NOTE: Introduced in InDesign CS6, Liquid Layout goes beyond Layout Adjustment to offer even more powerful and versatile capabilities. Learn more about Liquid Layout on page 444

NOTE: For more on
styles, see page 74

Note that there are now only three pages in the Pages panel. The number of pages in the document adjusted automatically to accommodate the reduction in font size.

17. With the text still selected, open the Paragraph Styles panel (Window > Styles > Paragraph Styles) and Alt+Click/Option+Click the Create new style button at the bottom of the panel. Name the style "body". Be sure to check the Apply Style to Selection checkbox, and then click OK.

18. Still on the first page, Triple-Click the first line to select the title "Advice from a Caterpillar" and style it as follows: Myriad Pro Regular 30 pt, all caps (**TT**), with tracking set to 75 () to give the title more emphasis. Make the font color green. With the "Advice from a Caterpillar" text still selected, press Shift+Ctrl+C/Shift+Command+C to center it.

Next to the column controls on the Paragraph formatting section of the Control panel are the Span Columns controls. Before span columns, if you wanted a header to span multiple columns, it was necessary to create a separate text frame for it. Span columns makes it possible to have a header span some or all the columns within a multi-column text frame. The Span Columns dialog actually has a dual function. In addition to spanning columns, it can split them too—creating 2, 3, and 4 columns of text, all within a single frame.

When you used Layout Adjustment to convert the document to two-column pages, the original singe text frame on each page was replaced by two threaded frames. To illustrate the Span Column feature, you'll convert the two threaded text frames on page 1 to a single two-column frame.

19. Switch to the Selection tool, select the rightmost text frame on the page 1 and delete it.

20. Because you enabled Smart Text Reflow, InDesign alerts you to the fact that it will add pages to prevent overset text.

With Smart Text Reflow enabled, InDesign will add and remove pages automatically to prevent overset text.

TIP: Another way to
set the number of
columns in a text
frame is through the
Column controls that
are available when the
Control panel
Paragraph Formatting
Controls are active.

21. Select the remaining text frame and mouse over the middle sizing handle on the right edge of the frame. When the cursor changes to a double-sided arrow, click and hold and drag right until the edge of the frame snaps to the right margin of the page.

22. Press Ctrl+B/Command+B to open the Text Frame Options dialog and set the Number of columns to two. Click OK to close the dialog.

Note that from the Text Frame Options dialog, among other things, you can set column width, the width for the gutter between columns, inset spacing, vertical justification, and you can balance columns as well.

23. Double-Click in the Advice from a Caterpillar paragraph to switch to the Type tool and then Quadruple-Click to select the entire title.

24. If necessary, switch to the Paragraph controls on the Control panel. Choose Span 2 from the Span Columns dropdown. Alt+Click/Option+Click the Span Columns icon (🏛) and add 20 px space after to the title paragraph to separate it from the body content.

From the Paragraph Formatting Controls on the Control panel, you can span and split columns within a single text frame.

Text wrap is another great feature to simplify the layout process, making text within a frame flow around other graphical elements. To illustrate this, you'll create a pull quote—content that is "pulled out" of the body content for emphasis.

25. Select the Rectangle tool and click once on the document. In the Rectangle dialog, enter 195 px for both width and height and click OK. Press V to switch to the Selection tool, and the rectangle should be selected automatically.

26. Click the arrow to the right of the Fill Swatch (☐) on the Control panel, and choose a fill color from the Swatches panel. If desired, adjust the tint at the top of the panel. (We chose a 30% green fill.) From the Control panel, choose a stroke color and stroke weight. We chose a 3 pt, 100% green stroke.

27. Select a corner style from the Corner Options dropdown on the Control panel and adjust the corner radius to 17 px. (If you don't see the controls for the Corner Options on the Control Panel, go to Object > Corner Options to apply your settings.)

You can set object corner options from the Control panel.

28. Double-Click in the body text to switch to the Type tool. Then, select the text in the third body paragraph on the first page that reads "at least I know who I was when I got up this morning, but I think I must have been changed several times since then." Press Ctrl+C/Command+C to copy, hold down the Ctrl/Command key to switch temporarily to the Selection tool and click the green rectangle. Release the modifier key and when you see the parentheses on either side of the Type tool cursor (🔲), click once to convert the shape to a text frame. Press Ctrl+V/Command+V to paste the quote into the rectangle.

29. Press Ctrl+A/Command+A to Select All and format the pull quote using Minion Pro Bold Italic, 16 pt, 30 pt leading, center-aligned. Press Ctrl+B/Command+B to bring up the Text Frame Options dialog and choose Center from the Vertical Justification dropdown. Click OK to close the dialog.

30. Using the Selection tool, drag the formatted text frame onto the document page and center it over the gutter between the text columns. You'll know the pull quote is centered when you see a magenta smart guide appear through the X marking the center of the frame as you drag.

TIP: The shortcut to toggle between Character and Paragraph Formatting Control views is Ctrl+Alt+7/ Command+Alt+7.

TIP: The stroke weight dropdown is just to the right of the fill and stroke swatches on the Control panel.

TIP: To set corner options directly on a selected rectangle, first click the yellow square at its upper right to activate the corner options. A yellow diamond appears at each corner of the object. Click and hold and drag a diamond to change the corner radius.

at least I know who I was when I got up this morning, but I think I must have been changed several times since then.

To affect an individual corner. Hold the Shift key while dragging. To change the corner style, hold the Alt/ Option key when you click a diamond. Hold both modifier keys to change the style of a single corner.

TIP: If you don't see a magenta guide as you drag an object over the center of the page, press Ctrl+U/Command+U to turn on smart guides. Alternatively, go to View > Grids & Guides > Smart Guides.

Align the X in the center of the pull quote to the
smart guide indicating both the center of the
page and the gutter between the columns.

31. To get the body text to wrap around the pull quote, go to Window > Text Wrap.
When the Text Wrap panel opens, choose the Wrap Around Object Shape
button and set the Offset to 18 pt. Leave Wrap To set to Both Right & Left Sides.

With Text Wrap, you can choose to wrap text around the
object bounding box or the object shape. You can also have
the text jump the object, or jump to the next column.

If you formatted your pull quote the way we did, you should have the
word "then" orphaned on a line of its own. There are two common ways
of rectifying this kind of situation. One way is to select the paragraph and
reduce the tracking to squeeze everything together just enough to jump the
isolated word up to the previous line.

The other option is to select the orphaned word and the word previous to it,
and add a No Break constraint.

32. With the Type tool, select the words "since" and "then" in the pull quote. Choose
No Break from the Control panel menu (at the far right of the Control panel) to
join both words on the last line of the paragraph.

33. Go to Window > Styles > Paragraph Styles. Right-Click/Ctrl+Click the body
style, and choose Edit "body" from the contextual menu. When the Paragraph
Styles dialog opens, select Basic Character Formats from the category list on the
left. Change the font size to 12 pt and the leading to 13 pt. Click OK to apply
your changes.

34. Double-Click page 2 in the Pages panel to activate it in the document
window. Go to Type > Show Hidden Characters (Alt+Ctrl+I/
Option+Command+I) and locate the Father William poem that begins in the first
column with the words: "'You are old, Father William,' the young man said."
Click with the Type tool before the first space at the beginning of the poem, hold
the Shift key and click just after the exclamation point at the end of the poem,
"down the stairs!" to select the entire poem.

TIP: Be judicious in
your use of tracking.
It doesn't take much
to have your type
look pinched or
to have too much
space between the
characters. -10 or +10
is generally pushing
the limits of what's
acceptable except in
special circumstances.

TIP: Hidden characters
are visual indicators
of spaces, paragraph
returns, tabs, etc.
They give you a little
bit of a look behind
the curtain so you can
see more of what's
actually going on in
your document. You
can find a free 5-page
guide to Hidden
Characters from
InDesignSecrets.com
at bit.ly/9qisMO.

Note that each paragraph of the poem starts with a number of spaces, making it tough to predictably control the global formatting of the text. You'll use InDesign's robust Find/Change feature to eliminate the extra spaces.

35. Press Ctrl+F/Command+F or go to Edit > Find/Change to open the Find/Change dialog. Select the GREP tab and choose Multiple Space to Single Space from the Query dropdown. Since you want to delete the spaces rather than replacing them, delete the \s from the Change to: field. Ensure that Selection is selected from the Search dropdown and click Find.

    InDesign finds and selects the first group of six consecutive spaces.

36. Click Change to confirm that the command deletes the extra spaces, and then click Change All.

37. An alert pops up to notify you that InDesign made 31 replacements. Click OK and then click Done to close the Find/Change dialog.

NOTE: To learn more about how InDesign's Find/Change features can revolutionize your workflow, see the chapter on GREP starting on page 379.

38. With the poem still selected and the Paragraph controls active in the Control panel, choose Split 2 from the Span Columns dropdown.

39. Change the poem font to Myriad Pro Italic, 11.5 pt, green and keep the text selected.

    In looking at the layout, the columns you just created could use a little adjusting. You can tune the spacing in the columns more finely through the Span Columns dialog.

40. From the Control panel menu, choose Span Columns. When the dialog opens, check the Preview checkbox. Set Inside Gutter to 13 px, and click OK to close the dialog.

TIP: You can Alt-Click/ Option-Click the Span Columns icon (▦) to access the Span Columns dialog.

Using the Span Columns dialog, when you split columns in a text frame, you can set the width for inside and outside gutters, as well as space before and space after the split.

Since so much of this document is quoted text, the alignment of the quotation marks inside the paragraph margins creates a really ragged appearance. You can easily fix that using InDesign's Optical Margin Alignment feature.

41. With the Type tool cursor active in the text frame, go to Type > Story. When the Story panel opens, check the Optical Margin Alignment checkbox and then set the overhang amount to the size of the volume of text used in the story: 12 pt.

TIP: When setting Optical Margin Alignment, it's generally recommended that you match the overhang setting to your font size.

The Story panel enables you to create hanging punctuation using Optical Margin Alignment which makes quotation marks, periods, commas, dashes, and the edges of letters such as "W" and "A" hang outside the text margins for a smoother appearance.

42. Save and close the file to complete the exercise.

Type on a Path

Flowing type in InDesign isn't restricted to enclosed frames; you can flow type on an open or closed path as well.

Exercise 4.3: Type on a Path

1. Go to File > New > Document, choose Digital Publishing from the Intent dropdown and iPad for Page Size. Leave the other default settings.

2. When the document opens, select the Ellipse tool (L). (Click and hold the Rectangle tool and then, when the tool submenu appears, click on the Ellipse tool to select it.)

.Click and hold the Rectangle tool to expose the hidden shape tools.

3. Close to the center of the document window, click and start dragging outward with the Ellipse tool. As you're dragging, hold down the Alt/Option key and then add the Shift key to draw a perfect circle from the center. When your circle is the size that you want it, be sure to release the mouse before releasing the modifier keys. Ensure that your circle has a stroke so you can see it on the page.

4. With the circle selected, set its width and height to 234 px in the Control panel. Alt-Drag/Option-Drag on the stroke to duplicate the circle.

5. Select the Type tool and mouse over the edge of the first circle. (Don't click.)

    Note the parentheses that appear on the Type tool cursor. The parentheses indicate that InDesign recognizes a closed path and will flow text into the contours of the shape if you click. ( ) (Don't click.)

6. In the Tools panel, click and hold the Type tool to expose the other tools it's hiding, and then select the Type on a Path tool ( ). Mouse over the path again and note that a little plus sign appears on the Type on a Path cursor to indicate that it recognizes the path ( ). Click to activate the path and type "Round and round."

7. Press Ctrl+A/Command+A to Select All, and then press Ctrl+D/Command+D. Browse to the chapter_4_exercises folder, select **path_text.txt,** and click Open to replace the existing text and flow the loaded text onto the circle.

8. If necessary, zoom in on the circle (Ctrl+/Command+) and switch to the Selection tool. With the circle selected and the Stroke swatch active, click the / key on your keyboard to set the stroke color to None.

    With type on a closed path, if the text is overset, the in and out ports of the text frame are positioned right on top of each other. A close look will reveal that there are two vertical lines indicating the text frame boundaries, each with its corresponding port. If you mouse over either line, your cursor will change to a line with a teeny tiny right- or left-facing arrow. Dragging the line shortens or lengthens the text path and, depending on which line you choose, repositions the beginning or end of the text on the path. As with any overset text, clicking the red plus sign loads your cursor allowing you to thread the text.

TIP: The little arrows throughout the interface are indicators that there are hidden tools or controls that you can click the arrows to discover. This is true for tools on the Tools panel, menus, and pretty much any other icon you may encounter that displays a tiny arrow, generally at the lower right

TIP: Holding the Shift key while drawing or scaling a shape constrains its proportions and constrains transformation angles to multiples of 45°. Holding Alt/Option while dragging to draw a shape draws the shape outward from the center. Holding the Spacebar while drawing a shape enables you to drag it to a new position.

TIP: With the exception of the Content Collector tool, as long as the Type tool is not active in a text frame, you can switch to a tool temporarily by holding its keyboard shortcut key.

When type is overset on a closed path, the in and out
ports of the text frame sit right on top of each other.

There is a third line, the center line, somewhat harder to locate, that indicates
the center of the text frame. On a closed path, it's always located directly
across from the in and out ports before they're repositioned. The center line
also acts as a control point to reorient the entire frame on the path. Dragging
the center line along the path repositions the frame. If you drag the line up
or down, you can flip the orientation of the text to the inside or outside of
the path.

Dragging the center line of the type on a path text frame
up or down flips the orientation of the type on the path.

9. Locate the right edge of the text frame, and, when you see the right-facing
    arrow, drag to the right to scale the text frame. Locate the center point of the
    frame and drag it in toward the center of the circle to flip the orientation of the
    text to the inside of your circle.

10. Click the out port (the red plus sign) and then mouse over the inside of the second
    circle. When you see the link icon on the cursor, click to place the remaining text
    inside the circle. Press Ctrl+B/Command+B, and, when the Text Frame Options
    dialog opens, adjust the Inset Spacing to 70 px and set Vertical Justification
    to Center.

    Next you'll relink the text, but first you need to break the existing link.

11. Click one of the out ports of the second circle and then position the loaded cursor
    somewhere over the inside of the circle. When the cursor icon changes to an
    unlocked link (see the screenshot), click to remove the threaded text from the
    circle. The out port of the original circle should display the red plus sign again.

To break a thread between text frames, use the Selection tool and click
a connecting port to load the text cursor. Then, mouse over the text
frame and when you see the broken link icon, click to break the
connection.

When the link is broken, the text will be overset again, and you'll need to
reload the cursor in order to thread it to another frame. Now you'll draw an
open path onto which you'll then thread the overset text.

12. Double-Click the Pencil tool to open the Pencil Tool Preferences dialog, and drag
    the Smoothness slider to around 80%. Leave the Keep Selected and Edit Selected

Paths checkboxes checked, and keep the default value of 12 in the proximity text field. Click OK to commit your settings and close the dialog.

The Pencil Tool Preferences let you control the rendering of free-form pencil paths. The lower the Fidelity, the more closely the path will follow the exact movement of your mouse as you draw, resulting in more points on the path. The higher the Smoothness, the smoother the curves. This does not necessarily result in a reduction of points, however. If you leave the Keep Selected checkbox checked, along with the Edit Selected Paths checkbox, you can keep redrawing the path until you get it the way you want it, as long as you start redrawing the path within the pixel distance specified in the slider.

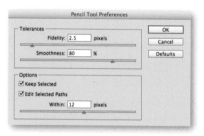

A path drawn with the Pencil tool and the Pencil Tool Preferences dialog.

13. Choose a stroke color and set the fill color to None. Click and drag with the Pencil tool to draw a curving path on the page.

14. Press Shift+T to select the Type on a Path tool, position the mouse over the path where you want the text to begin, and click when you see a plus on the Type tool cursor (⊥).

15. When the blinking Type cursor appears on the pencil path, hold the Ctrl/ Command key to switch temporarily to the Selection tool, and click to select the circle with the type on the path. Still holding the modifier key, click the red plus sign at the circle's out port to load the cursor.

16. With the overflow text from the circle loaded into the cursor, click the pencil path you just drew to thread the text from the circle to the curve. Don't worry if the text is still overset. This exercise was just for practice.

17. Save the file as ex4_3.indd in the chapter_4_exercises folder, and close it to complete the exercise.

Now you've explored a variety of ways to work with threading text—converting shapes to text frames and flowing text into shapes and onto open and closed paths.

Nested Styles

Nested styles are a wonderful time-saving feature when you have a volume of text that requires a pattern of repetitive formatting. Catalogs and directories are perfect candidates for nested styles, where each entry may require distinct formatting for each of its component elements.

Nested styles are really just an assemblage of character styles, separated by specific delineators and held in a paragraph definition. This being the case, it is easiest to create nested styles by first creating each component character style in the context of an example paragraph. When the character styles are all defined, you can then construct the paragraph style, compiling the assembly instructions in the Drop Caps and Nested Styles section of the Paragraph Styles dialog.

Exercise 4.4: Nested Styles

1. From the chapter_4_exercises folder, open **ex4_4.end.indd** and check it out. Open the Paragraph and Character Styles panels (Window > Styles > Character/Paragraph Styles) and Double-Click the style definitions to see how they're constructed. When you've finished investigating, keep the file open for reference. Open **ex4_4_start.indd** and save it as ex4_4.indd.

   The first step in creating a nested paragraph style is to set up each of its component character styles. In this example, you'll be setting up a total of three character styles: semi-bold, italic, and bold and green with caps.

2. With the Type tool, select the title of the book in the first paragraph (The Four Agreements: Toltec Wisdom Collection:), including both colons. Set the font to Myriad Pro Bold, 10 pt, 10 pt leading, All Caps (TT), and set the color to green.

3. With the text still selected, open the Character Styles panel and Alt+Click/ Option+Click the Create new style button at the bottom of the panel. Name the style "boldGreenCaps," check the Apply Style to Selection and Preview checkboxes, and click OK to close the dialog.

4. Select the byline (by don Miguel Ruiz), up to the opening parenthesis before the number of pages. Set the font to Myriad Pro Semibold 10 pt, 10 pt leading, black. Capture the formatting in a character style named "semibold."

5. Select the number of pages including both parentheses. Set the font to Myriad Pro Italic, 10 pt, 10 pt leading, black. Create a character style named "italic."

   That's it for the character styles you'll need. Now comes the part where you put it all together.

6. Position the Type tool cursor in the word "Publisher" in the second line of the book listing. Make sure that the font is set to Myriad Pro, 10pt, 10pt leading. Alt+Click/Option+Click the New Style button at the bottom of the Paragraph Styles panel. Name the new style "totalBook" and ensure that the Apply Style to Selection checkbox is checked. Keep the dialog open.

   InDesign captures style definitions based on the text format at the position of the Type tool cursor or from the first character of selected text. If the Type tool had been positioned in the book title when you created the paragraph style, the foundation paragraph style would have been bold, all caps and green.

7. Select the Basic Character Formats category from the list at the left of the panel.

   Notice that InDesign captured the attributes you set in the previous step. The font face should be set to Myriad Pro and the font style to Regular. Size and leading should be set to 10 pt with the case set to Regular.

8. From the Character Color category, select the Black color swatch. Select the Bullets and Numbering category, and set the List Type on the right to None. From the Indents and Spacing category, first set First Line Indent to 0, and leave Left Indent set to .25". Set Space After to .125. Keep the dialog open.

Here's where it all comes together. Now you get to assemble the Character styles to define the paragraph. The structure of the paragraph requires five nested styles in all.

9. Select Drop Caps and Nested Styles from the category list and click the New Nested Style button on the right. From the Character Style dropdown that appears in the Nested Styles section of the window, choose the boldGreenCaps character style.

   You get to choose whether to apply the style up to the delimiter or to style the delimiter as well. In this case, you want to apply the boldGreenCaps style to the colon as well as the preceding text so you'll leave the through option selected.

10. There are two colons that occur before you want the style to change, so select the number 1 and replace it with the number 2 in the number field. Since the colon is the delimiter, select the word "Words" in the last field of the first nested style and replace it by typing a colon.

TIP: A delimiter is a character or sequence of characters that mark the beginning or end of a measure of data. In the case of nested styles, colons, periods, spaces, etc. are all considered delimiters.

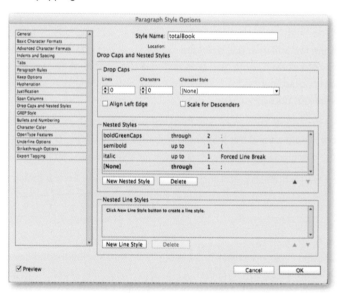

The Drop Caps and Nested Styles section of the Paragraph Styles dialog.

11. Click the New Nested Style button again, and set the character style to semibold. Since you want the semibold style to apply up to the parenthesis enclosing the number of pages, choose up to from the next dropdown, leave 1 selected, and type an opening parenthesis as the delimiter.

12. Add the remaining Character styles and settings to match the image below, and then click OK to close the Paragraph Styles dialog.

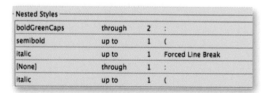

The five nested styles assembled to create the totalBook paragraph style.

13. To test your creation, select the next two paragraphs with the Type tool and apply the totalBook Paragraph style. Awesome, right?!

14. To test the style further, type the paragraph from the note at the right of this paragraph, which has the same delimiters. Be sure to end each line with a soft return (Shift+Enter/Shift+Return.)

    You could copy one of the paragraphs that are already in the exercise instead, but then you wouldn't get to see how cool it is that the styles change automatically as you type.

    The elaborate style you just built requires that each book entry be a single paragraph with the lines divided by soft returns. Another way to approach such a formatting challenge is to compose three separate nested Paragraph styles, one for each line of the book information. As part of a style definition, InDesign allows you to specify the style to apply to the paragraph that follows the paragraph being styled. Using this feature, you can sequence several nested Paragraph styles to achieve the same visual result as with the totalBook style.

15. With the Type tool cursor anywhere in the line of text that begins with "The Presence of the Past," Alt+Click/Option+Click the New Style button at the bottom of the Paragraph Styles panel. When the dialog opens, name the new style "book" and ensure that the Apply Style to Selection checkbox is checked. Be sure to select [No Paragraph Style] from the Based On: dropdown.

16. Select Drop Caps and Nested Styles, and then click the New Nested Style button. Format the style to match the following image:

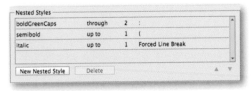

Nested styles for the book paragraph style definition.

17. Create another paragraph style based on [No Paragraph Style] and name it "publisher." Add the following nested styles:

Nested styles for the Publisher style definition

18. Create a third Paragraph style and name it "ISBN." Set the font to Myriad Pro Regular, 10 pt, 10 pt leading. Still in the Paragraph Styles dialog, select General, and choose book from the Next Style dropdown. Click OK to close the dialog.

19. In the Paragraph Styles panel, Right-Click/Ctrl+Click the book style and choose Edit "book" from the contextual menu. When the dialog opens, in the General section, choose publisher from the Next Style dropdown. Set the Next Style for the publisher style to ISBN.

NOTE: The Singularity Is Near: When Humans Transcend Biology: by Ray Kurzweil (672 pages)

[soft return]

Publisher: Penguin (Non-Classics); (September 26, 2006)

[soft return]

ISBN-10: 0143037889, # ISBN-13: 978-0143037880

TIP: The Next Style attribute of a paragraph style definition does not apply to styled text that has been broken with a return. A paragraph return in a paragraph that's already been styled generates a new paragraph with the same style.

To test the styles, you'll first strip the formatting you just applied.

20. Select all three paragraphs from the Sequential Nested Styles Paragraphs section of the document and click the [Basic Paragraph] style in the Paragraph Styles panel.

21. With the paragraphs still selected, Right-Click/Ctrl+Click the book style in the Paragraph Styles panel and choose Apply "book," then Next Style.

22. TaDa! Click with the Type tool in each of the three formatted paragraphs to confirm that the styles were indeed applied in the sequence you specified.

With lots of styles in your document, sorting through them to find the style you're looking for can get to be rather tedious. To keep things organized, you'll create a style group to keep the book styles together.

23. From the bottom of the Paragraph Styles panel, Alt+Click/Option+Click the New Style Group button (🗀). When the Style Group Options dialog opens, name the style group "bookStyles." Drag the book, publisher, and ISBN styles into the folder.

You can keep your styles organized by creating style groups (indicated by the folder icon), and dragging your styles into them. Alternatively, select all the styles you want included in a style group, Right-Click/Ctrl+Click , and choose New Group from Styles from the contextual menu.

In this exercise, you got a solid taste of how powerful nested styles can be. To dig even deeper into the possibilities that styles hold and to take them to an entirely new level, check out the chapter on GREP starting on page 379.

Anchored Objects

While anchored objects may not be a mainstay of your interactive work with DPS, Interactive PDF or Flash, they will most likely play a prominent role in your work with EPUB. EPUB is all about text flow, and anchored objects go with the flow— literally. Anchored to content rather than a static position, as your content flows, so flows an anchored object.

While not applicable to EPUB, by far the coolest aspect of anchored objects is that they also work with objects like sidebars, which can be made to flow from one page to the next and maintain their position relative to the document spine. Like everything else, the easiest way to understand anchored objects is to work with them, and that's what you'll do in the next exercise.

Exercise 4.5: Working with Anchored Objects

In this exercise, you'll place inline, above line, and custom-aligned anchored objects.

1. Open **ex4_5_end.indd** from the chapter_4_exercises folder. Note the images in the text frame on page 1. Click the next button at the lower left of the document

window to navigate to page 2, and note the position of the sidebar. If you like, keep the file open for reference.

2. Open **ex4_5_start.indd**. and save it as ex4_5.indd.

3. On page 1 of the document, click once on the image of the White Rabbit in the sidebar to select it. Click and drag from the blue square at the top right of the frame to the ellipsis after "then" in the sidebar.

4. You've just created your first anchored object. The White Rabbit will now go wherever the sidebar goes, and they'll both be relocating in short order.

5. Select the sidebar and drag from the blue square at its top right to the paragraph that begins "You are old...." (fourth line from the bottom of the second column).

A dashed line appears, connecting the sidebar text frame to the main content frame and the square that was at the top of the frame is replaced by an anchor badge.

TIP: If you don't see a dashed thread connecting a custom anchored object to the text in which it's anchored, go to View > Extras > Show Text Threads.

Anchored objects are indicated by an anchor badge at the upper right corner.

6. Alt+Click/Option+Click the anchor badge to open the Anchored Object options dialog. (Alternatively, go to Object > Anchored Object > Options.)

7. When the dialog opens, choose Custom from the Position dropdown and check the Preview and the Relative to Spine checkboxes. (Don't worry if the sidebar jumps to a new position. You'll get it back in line momentarily.)

8. Click the upper left corner of the right Anchored Object Reference Point proxy and the upper right corner of the right Anchored Position Reference Point proxy. Choose Page Margin from both the X Relative To and Y Relative To dropdowns and enter .175" in the X Offset text field. Click OK to close the dialog.

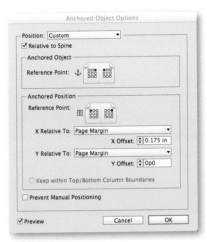

The custom settings view of the Anchored Object Options dialog.

The Anchored Object Options dialog can be a bit confusing at first glance but don't be intimidated. The first reference point refers to where on the anchored object the anchor is connected. In this instance, we've chosen the upper left corner and when the sidebar is selected, you can see that that's where the dashed anchor line connects. The second reference point refers to what the object is being anchored to. In this case we've chosen the page margin for both the X and Y reference points. To summarize, in hopes of making the settings more intelligible, we've aligned the upper left corner of the sidebar to the upper right corner of the page margin with .175" of horizontal space between them. OK, now's a good time to take a deep breath!

An anchored object can be positioned outside of a text frame and still travel with the text to which it's anchored.

You'll see the Relative to Spine alignment in action when you add the images to the body content—adding the images will push the text containing the anchor to the next page and the anchored object will flow right along with it.

9. Using the Selection tool, select the image of the Mad Hatter on the pasteboard. Shift-Drag from the anchor square at the upper right of the frame to the paragraph that begins "I'm afraid I am sir" near the top of the second column.

   The sidebar containing the White Rabbit does a disappearing trick (jumping to page 2) and the Mad Hatter is tucked cozily in the column as an inline anchored object.

10. Navigate to the second page of the document to confirm that the sidebar located itself on the page in the same position relative to the document spine that it had on page 1. Pretty smart sidebar, wouldn't you say? And a pretty fancy trick too.

11. Return to page 1 and select the image of Alice and the Caterpillar on the pasteboard. Shift-Drag the anchor square to the beginning of the second paragraph in the first column, which starts with "Who are you?"

    Alice has a nice new home, the Mad Hatter repositions himself, and the text to which he's anchored flows to make room for Alice.

12. Alt+Click/Option+Click the Anchor badge at Alice's upper right corner and when the Anchored Object Options dialog opens, select the Above Line radio button. Choose Center from the Alignment dropdown, set Space Before and After to 0p6. Click OK to close the dialog. Alice is centered in the column, with room to breathe both above and below. Save and close the file to complete the exercise.

That's it for anchored objects for now but if you're hungry for more, jump over to page 329 to learn about working with anchored objects for EPUB.

CHAPTER SUMMARY

This chapter was all about text: flowing it, formatting it, and making it conform to your design. To aid your typographical work, you made use of several helpful InDesign features including:

- The ability to show and hide text threads
- The ability to show hidden characters
- The robust Find/Change dialog

You flowed text through multiple text frames manually, and also used the autoflow and semi-autoflow modifier keys to speed the process. You then stepped outside the box to flow type onto closed and open paths, and learned to adjust the orientation of type on that path.

In your management of text flow and layout you

- Adjusted margins and columns on master pages
- Employed optical margin alignment
- Used the Text Wrap panel to wrap text around a pull quote
- Worked with the span columns dialog to span and split columns within a single text frame
- Set up the Smart Text Reflow preference to have InDesign add and remove pages automatically with the flow of text in your document
- Created character and paragraph styles and assembled multiple character styles to create complex nested paragraph styles
- Created inline, above line and custom anchored objects

In the course of your explorations you:

- Set application preferences by adjusting settings with no open documents
- Worked with the Pencil tool and set Pencil tool preferences
- Employed style groups to organize the definitions in the Paragraph Styles panel

Now that you have firm footing in your work with text, the next chapter provides a blueprint for developing multi-page documents. Employing the Pages and Layers panels, you'll establish a solid structure for any document you'll ever need to build.

Chapter 5

MULTI-PAGE DOCUMENT LAYOUT

This chapter covers the nuances of setting up a multi-layered, multi-page document and helps you to avoid possible pitfalls you may encounter in the process. The tools and techniques you'll learn in this chapter lay the groundwork for print and interactive documents alike.

Multi-page Layout

When creating multi-page interactive documents, it's easiest to keep track of things if you build your file with a separate named layer for each page. While all document layers are always visible in the Layers panel, the only sublayers that appear are for objects on the active document page. Because objects appear and disappear based on the active page, you will save yourself lots of time trying to figure out where things are if you create page-specific layers for your document contents. That way, all the objects on the active page will be visible in the Layers panel when the layer for that page is selected.

The InDesign Layers Panel

The InDesign Layers panel makes it possible to select individual objects within a layer (we'll call these object layers), change object stacking order and visibility, and lock individual objects to prevent any changes. Layers can be used as an organizational tool, like a containing folder for related objects. As with the objects they contain, the containing layers can be rearranged to change the stacking order of whole groups of objects at a time. When not in use, Layers can be collapsed to hide their object sublayers and de-clutter the panel display.

Understanding Layers and Object Layers

If the concept of layers is foreign to you, think back to an anatomy book you may have encountered when learning about the human body. In this book, the skeletal structure would have appeared on a white page, with transparent acetate pages overlaid for the various systems of the body. There may have been one sheet illustrating the internal organs, another showing the musculature, and yet another showing the vascular system. Think of each of these acetate sheets as layers, with the uppermost sheet representing the top layer in the stacking order.

To better understand the workings of the Layers panel, and InDesign altogether as an application, it helps to understand that, like Illustrator, InDesign is a vector-based application. For the uninitiated, this means that the objects created in InDesign are mathematically based and are defined by point coordinates, curve and corner angles, stroke and fill, etc. Very different from pixel-based artwork, which is resolution dependent, objects created in InDesign can be scaled and transformed nearly without limit and still remain crisp and clear.

There are some caveats to scalability however. While the vector objects created in InDesign are themselves resolution independent, the images placed within them are not. Therefore issues of resolution are still of primary concern when preparing an InDesign document for publishing.

Because of it's vector nature, each object created in InDesign is distinct. Having each object represented individually in the Layers panel makes it easy to select objects wherever they are in the document, regardless of how many objects may be stacked above them.

The Layers Panel Deconstructed

1) The default name (Layer 1) indicates a master layer. Clicking the disclosure triangle at its left expands and collapses the layer to display the object layers it contains.

2) The empty square in the visibility column indicates a hidden layer. Click in the square to show the object(s) on the layer.

3) The color bar reflects the color key for the master layer in which the object resides. Object bounding boxes are the color of the layer color key.

4) The eye in the visibility column indicates that layer objects are visible. Click the eye to hide the layer objects.

5) By default, a grouped object is indicated in the Layers panel by the word "<group>".

6) A text frame is indicated in the Layers panel by the text it contains.

7) A button's state is indicated in the Layers panel as a sublayer of the button. The button graphic is a sublayer of the button state.

8) A button is indicated in the Layers panel by its name. Each button has a unique name. The default name for a button is Button N, where "N" is a number.

9) The lock indicates that the layer or object is locked and cannot be moved or modified.

10) The grayed out lock indicates that a parent layer is locked, thereby locking its sublayers.

11) The active document page and the number of layers it contains is indicated at the bottom of the panel.

12) Layers panel menu button.

13) The Pen icon indicates that the current layer is active. New objects created will land on the layer displaying the Pen icon.

14) The small square in the selection column indicates that an object in a layer is selected, but the entire content of the layer is not. You can select an object by clicking in the selection column of the object layer. Shift+Click in the selection

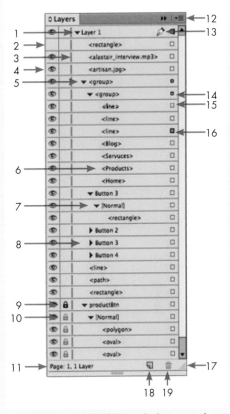

column to add additional objects to the selection.

15) A blue highlight indicates that a layer is active, although the objects it contains may not be selected. A layer must be highlighted in order to reposition it in the stacking order. You can move objects from one layer to another by highlighting and dragging the object layer. Shift+Click to select multiple layers.

16) The large square in the selection column indicates that the entire content of the layer is selected.

17) Click and drag the sizing control to change the height and width of the panel.

18) The New Layer button creates a new master layer.

19) The Delete Layer button deletes selected layers.

Working with Master Pages

Whether for print or interactive, master pages are an indispensable tool for designing multi-page documents that require certain consistent elements from page to page. Acting as a layout template, you can think of master pages in relation to the pages of a document as you would think of paragraph styles in relation to paragraph text. A master page contains objects and formatting that you can readily apply to any number of pages in your document. You can build one master page on another and you can have as many master pages as you like. Except for elements where overrides have been applied, changes to master pages globally change the child pages associated with them.

In the last chapter, you learned how by changing the master you can change margins and columns throughout a document. In this chapter, you'll use a master both to create a consistent interface from page to page and to populate your pages with design elements that you'll then modify as needed.

In working with master pages you may encounter a rather strange effect where items from a master page overlay items on a document page but don't appear in the Layers panel. Since they don't appear in the Layers panel, they can't be selected.

Items on master pages can obscure content on other layers as a
result of the object stacking order in the Layers panel.

This happens when objects on the master overlap objects on the active page and are positioned above them in the layer stacking order. This anomaly can be somewhat alarming if you don't know what's causing it. The best way to avoid the problem is to establish a separate layer for the master page objects, as for each of the document pages, and then position it appropriately in the Layers panel. Most often, the master page layer will best be positioned at the bottom of the layer stack. There are occasions, however, where some master page objects need to appear above the contents of the document pages, while other master page objects need to be positioned below them.

A perfect example of such a scenario is when you have a master page containing both a navigation bar with dropdown menus, as well as background interface elements. The background elements need to be positioned beneath the contents of the document pages but, in order for the dropdown menus to be visible, the navbar elements need to be positioned above them.

One way to resolve this issue is to create two layers for the master page objects: one for the background and one for the navbar. You would then position the navbar layer at the top of the layer stack, and the background layer at the bottom.

As an alternative, you might elect to use nested master pages. The foundation master could contain the background interface elements, while the child master would inherit the background, and then add the navigation buttons. The benefit to this approach is the clear separation created between the general interface and the navigation elements, allowing you to work on one without concern about inadvertently changing the other. You would still need to create two distinct layers, though, one for each of the masters, and they would still need to be appropriately positioned at the bottom and the top of the layer stack.

Exercise 5.1: Working with Master Pages

In this exercise you'll work with a multi-page document that uses nested masters— the A–Master provides the interface elements and the B–Master provides design elements. The interface master contains a dropdown menu so it needs to be at the top of the layer stack. The items on the design master will be used to build the contents of each page so its placement in the layer stack is not a critical factor. You'll set up named layers for each document page and customize some of the page content. Along the way, you'll create a grid of precisely sized and positioned rectangles and text frames; place and format text, place and scale images; work with the Gap tool; over-ride master page items; create and apply an object style and work with the align panel.

The exercise project: a multi-page document employing multiple master pages.

DOWNLOAD: Exercise files for this chapter can be downloaded from http://www.interactive-indesign.com.

NOTE: The document for this exercise is designed to be included in a DPS publication, hence the navbar. The navbar is a multi-state object converted to a Slideshow overlay. Learn all about multi-state objects, DPS and slideshow overlays starting on page 427 with Chapter 28.

1. Navigate to the chapter_5_exercises folder and open **ex5_1_end.indd** and explore it a bit. Check out the master pages in the Pages panel and the layer structure in the Layers panel. When you're done looking through the file, keep it open for reference.

2. Open **ex5_1_start.indd** and save it as ex5_1.indd.

3. If necessary, expand the Layers panel in the Panel Dock (⬥) and twirl down the disclosure triangle to the left of the master layer name. Notice that although you see content on the document page, the Layers panel displays no sublayers and there's nothing to select.

TIP: To create a nested master, Right-Click/ Ctrl+Click in the Master section at the top of the Pages panel and choose New Master from the contextual menu. When the dialog opens, name the new master and choose the desired parent master from the Based on Master dropdown. Click OK to create the master and close the dialog.
The new master appears in the document window and looks exactly like the first one. Try selecting any of the objects on the page, though, and you'll see that, like all master page items, the objects are locked by default.

When you base one master page on another, changes to the parent master update automatically in the children.

TIP: To change the name, number of pages or the Based On Master options for a master page, select Master Options for (Master Page Name) from the Pages panel menu.

TIP: To override and unlock a master page item on a document page, hold Ctrl+Shift/ Command+Shift and click the item.

4. If necessary, expand the Pages panel (⬚) in the Panel Dock and Double-Click "B–Design" in the Masters section at the top of the panel. (If necessary, mouse over the divider below the Masters section of the panel and when the cursor changes to a double-sided arrow, click and drag the divider down to expose the hidden master pages.)

You can confirm that the B–Master is active in the document window if the page name in the Pages panel is highlighted in black, the page icon is highlighted in blue and the page reference at the bottom left of the document window displays "B–Design."

5. With the Selection tool, click the objects on the page and note that the only objects you can select are the page header and the line beneath it.

The A-Interface master contains the elements that will remain consistent from page to page of the document. Because these elements are inherited by the B–Design master, they are locked by default, as are all master page objects when they're applied to an actual document page. Master page objects are indicated by a dotted outline.

6. Check out the Layers panel and notice that only the selectable objects on the Design master appear there. (If you want to explore the other objects, Double-Click the Interface master and dig around a bit.)

7. With the Design master active, select the Rectangle tool (M), and click the upper left square of the Reference Point proxy on the Control panel (⬚). Position the Rectangle tool crosshair at the intersection of the left margin and the first horizontal guide.

8. Click and hold and drag on a diagonal, down and to the right to draw a rectangle. Still holding down the mouse, press the up arrow on your keyboard four times to divide the frame into five equal frames. Release the mouse at the intersection of the first vertical guide and the horizontal guide at the bottom of the page.

You can create a grid of frames using the arrow keys on your keyboard to add and remove rows and columns.

9. Switch to the Type tool and position the tip of the arrow at the upper left of the cursor at the intersection of the second vertical guide and the horizontal guide at the top of the page. Drag down to the intersection of the bottom guide and the right page margin, pressing the up arrow to draw five uniformly sized text frames.

10. If necessary, go to View > Extras > Show Text Threads (Ctrl+Alt+Y/ Command+Option+Y) to see that the five frames are threaded together.

11. Switch to the Selection tool and mouse over the badge at the upper left of the topmost text frame. When the instructional tooltip appears, click to convert the story to the primary text flow.

12. Drag the B–Master icon onto the icon for page 1 in the Pages panel to apply the master and activate the primary text frames on the document page. Save the file.

    That's it for your work on the master, now you'll set up your layer structure, add content to the document pages and make some modifications to complete the layout of page 1.

TIP: You can apply a master to document pages by dragging the master icon onto the page icon in the Pages panel or, with a master selected, you can use the Apply Master to Pages command from the Pages panel menu.

13. Using the Create new layer button (⬚) at the bottom of the Layers panel, create three new layers. Click once to highlight the top layer then click the layer name to enter editing mode. Rename the layers from the top down: "management", "advisors" and "contributors" respectively. Drag the master layer to the top of the stack.

14. Double-Click page 1 in the Pages panel and press Ctrl+D/Command+D (File > Place.) Navigate to the chapter_5_exercises folder and select **team_text.txt**.

15. If the Text Options dialog opens, ensure that Character Set is set to Macintosh Roman and Platform is set to Mac (Intel-based.) Leave the other defaults and click OK.

16. Position the loaded Type tool cursor over the first text frame you placed on the page and click when you see parentheses around the icon at its upper left. The text flows through the threaded text frames and spawns a new page.

The loaded Type tool cursor displays parentheses around the flow icon at its upper left when positioned over a text frame.

Paragraph styles have been included in the document to make your page layout proceed more smoothly. The paragraph styles are built on top of one another so you'll be able to style multiple paragraphs at the same time. The teamName style definition includes a frame break which causes the text to start in a new frame. Initially, this may appear to be a problem but don't be alarmed. It all works out in the end.

17. With the Type tool, click and hold and drag to select the text beginning with the name "Alastair" and ending with "Toronto"—just before "Iris Chau."

18. In the Paragraph Styles panel, Right-Click/Ctrl+Click the teamName style and choose Apply "teamName" then Next Style.

Primary Text Frames

By default, a master page called A-Master is applied to all the pages of any document you create in InDesign. This master page captures the margin and bleed settings that you specify in the New Document dialog. If you check the Primary Text Frame checkbox in the New Document dialog, the A-Master will also contain a specialized text frame that then appears on all your document pages. This master page primary text frame has several special powers, the first of which is that it maintains connection with its document page counterparts. Thus, if the position or size of the primary text frame is changed on the master, the change populates automatically to unmodified primary text frames on the child pages. In cases where the primary text frame or story on a child page has been changed, reapplying the master reconfigures the child text frame while maintaining its content.

This is a **big** change from the behavior of master page text frames in earlier versions of InDesign. Previously, it was necessary to override a master page text frame on a document page in order to add content, and the connection to the master page text frame was lost in the process. Reapplying the master would duplicate the master text frame on the document page and leave the overridden text frame unchanged. In other words, changes to master page text frames had no effect on document text frames to which overrides had been applied. Any changes in text frame position or size made to the master would need to be made manually to the associated child pages. If you don't choose the Primary Text Frame option in the New Document dialog, this legacy behavior still applies.

Another special power of primary text frames is that they translate from one master to another. This means that if you apply a new master to pages in your document, the text frames connected to the first master's primary text

frame instantly conform to the configuration of the primary text frame in the new master. Primary text frames also recognize each other from one document page to the next, flowing seamlessly page to page, from one primary text frame to another regardless of the master applied.

Rather than becoming overset, when a primary text frame can hold no more content, it spawns a new page based on its master.

A primary text frame on a document page is live by default; you can just place your Type tool cursor in it and begin typing. This behavior too is quite different from previous incarnations of InDesign where you either had to draw a text frame on the page before you could start typing or override a master page text frame to unlock it before adding content.

Now that we've extolled the virtues of primary text frames, you might wonder what you can do if you neglected to check the Primary Text Frame checkbox in the New Document dialog. Not to worry; the page badge on the master page text frame acts as a toggle to switch between a standard text frame and a primary text frame. Start by Double-Clicking the A-Master in the top section of the Pages panel to make it the active page. Next, draw a text frame with the Type tool ([T]). Then, switch to the Selection tool ([↖]) and click the page badge that appears in the upper left of the frame to convert it to a primary text frame. If you're creating a document with multiple masters, you'll follow this procedure to add a primary text frame to the additional masters.

Be aware that there is a limit of one primary text frame story per master page.

Mouse over the page badge on a master page text frame and after the tooltip appears, click to toggle between primary and standard text frame behavior.

19. Repeat step 18 for the Iris Chau and Stephen Chen paragraphs noting that a portion of the text frame between Alastair and Iris ends up empty for the moment.

Now you'll place the photos for the management team.

20. Press Ctrl+D/Command+D and navigate to the chapter_5_exercises/team folder. The prefix "m_" identifies the management team images. Ctrl+Click/ Command+Click each of the three images to load them into the cursor.

The multi-place cursor displays a thumbnail of the file about to be placed. You can navigate through the loaded files using the right and left arrow keys on your keyboard.

21. With the loaded cursor, ensure that the thumbnail of Alastair is visible and then click the first placeholder frame in the column to the left of the text frames.

22. Place the images of Iris and Stephen in the next two placeholder frames.

23. Switch to the Gap tool (|↔|) and mouse over the space between the image and text frame columns, next to the photo of Iris. When the gap between the two columns is highlighted, click and hold and drag left to widen the text frames and narrow the image frames for Iris and Stephen. Release the mouse when the right boundaries of the image frames are aligned with the right edge of Alastair's photo in its frame.

The Gap tool enables you to shift and scale frames and the spacing between them.

24. Adjust the gap for the first-row column to match the gap for rows two and three. You can use smart guides to help with alignment. If the smart guides don't appear, press Ctrl+U/Command+U (View > Grids & Guides > Smart Guides.)

25. Position the Gap tool between the first and second rows and drag the gap down until all of Alastair's text just fits in the first-row text frame and Iris's text jumps into the text frame in the second row next to her photo.

26. Adjust the gap between the second and third rows so the text of Iris' bio fills the second-row text frame.

27. Adjust the gap between the third and fourth rows so that Stephen's bio fills the third-row text frame.

28. Press V to switch to the Selection tool then select and delete the bottom two text frames on the page. Click OK to dismiss the alert.

InDesign automatically adds pages instead of
allowing a primary text frame to become overset.

TIP: If a frame has
no fill, clicking inside
it will not select it.
You must click the
bounding box of an
object that has no fill
in order to select it.

29. Ctrl+Shift+Click/Command+Shift+Click on the border of each of the empty
    placeholder frames in the image column to unlock them from the master page.
    Delete both frames.

30. With the Selection tool, select Alastair's photo and mouse over its bottom border.
    When the cursor changes to a double-sided vertical arrow, click and hold and
    drag up to fit the frame to the photo.

31. If necessary, click to unlock the Constrain proportions link in the Height and
    Width controls on the Control panel. Select and copy (Ctrl+C/Command+C) the
    value in the Height field. Select Iris's photo and paste (Ctrl+V/Command+V) the
    copied value into the Control panel Height field.

The Width and Height Control panel controls
with the Constrain proportions link unlocked.

32. Select Stephen's photo and change its height to match the others by pasting the
    same copied value into the Height field on the Control panel.

NOTE: If you'd rather
not take the time to
create the object
style to format the
photos, you can apply
the dropShadow
style from the Object
Styles panel and
skip to step 37.

33. Select the photo of Iris, Right-Click/Ctrl+Click and choose Fitting > Fill Frame
    Proportionally. Click the *fx* button on the Control panel and choose Drop
    Shadow from the Effects dropdown. When the dialog opens, set Opacity to 40%.
    Leave the other default settings and click OK to close the dialog.

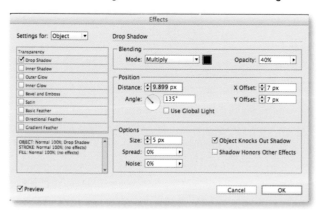

The settings for the effect applied to the photograph.

34. With the image still selected, click the Corner Options dropdown on the Control
    Panel (or go to Object > Corner Options), select rounded corners and set the
    corner radius to 20px.

    With the photo frame now styled, you'll capture the formatting as an
    Object Style.

35. Go to Window > Styles > Object Styles, or click the ⊡ button in the Panel Dock. When the Object Styles panel opens, Alt-Click/Option-Click the Create new style button at the bottom of the panel. In the New Object Style dialog, name the style "dropShadow2." Check the Apply Style to Selection and Preview checkboxes. Click the words "Frame Fitting Options"—not the checkbox—in the category list (you may need to scroll to see it) and when the options appear, ensure that all the Crop Amount values are set to 0. Click OK to close the dialog.

36. With the Selection tool, click the photo of Alastair, hold the Shift key and click the image of Stephen. In the Object Styles panel, click the dropShadow2 style to apply it.

37. Click and hold and drag the Selection tool from the pasteboard to the left of Alastair's photo through the photo and into the text frame with his bio and then release the mouse to select both objects. Click Alastair's photo to select it as the key object against which the other object will be aligned.

38. Expand the Align panel in the Panel Dock (▐) (or go to Window > Object & Layout > Align) and click the Align vertical centers icon (▐□). Press Ctrl+G/Command+G to group the objects

39. Repeat the procedure in steps 37 and 38 to group the photos and bios for Iris and Stephen.

40. Holding the Shift key to maintain alignment, drag Stephen's group down to the lower third of the page. Holding the Shift key, click Iris's and Alastair's groups to add them to the selection. Open the Align panel and click the Distribute vertical space button (═♣) in the Distribute Spacing section of the panel.

TIP: If they aren't already showing, you can display the Distribute Spacing options in the Align panel by choosing Show Options from the panel menu. To distribute space equally between selected objects, be sure to choose Align to Selection from the Align To dropdown.

41. Select the Line tool (\) and position the cursor on the left margin and between the first and second rows. Hold the Shift key to constrain the line, and click and hold and drag to the right margin of the page. Be sure to release the mouse before releasing the Shift key.

42. Switch to the Selection tool and Shift+Alt+Drag/Shift+Option+Drag to duplicate the line and position it between the second and third rows.

43. Select the three groups and the two lines and click the Distribute vertical space button in the Align panel.

44. Ctrl+Shift+Click/Command+Shift+Click the Management Team header to unlock it from the master.

Since all the objects on the page originated on the master page you'll move them now to the management layer.

45. Expand the Layers panel and pres Ctrl+A/Command+A to select all the objects on the page.

A square appears to the right of the layer names for all selected objects. In this case, the color for the layer is blue so the squares for the selected objects are blue.

46. Drag the blue square from the master layer to the management layer.

47. Twirl down the disclosure triangle at the left of the management layer name to show the repositioned object sublayers.

TIP: When you drag multiple items from one layer to another in the Layers panel, InDesign reverses their stacking order. If the stacking order of the objects in the layer is important, you can drag to reorder them within the layer or drag them to the new layer individually.

Working with Styles

Whether it be a Paragraph, Character, Cell, Table, or Object style, the easiest way to create a new style is to first format your text or object with the attributes you want the style to capture. Then, have InDesign save those settings for you in a style definition.

To create a new style, select your formatted object, hold down the Alt/Option key and click the Create new style button at the bottom of any of the Styles panels. When the style dialog box opens, enter a name for the style. If you forget to click the Alt/Option modifier key, InDesign will generate a new style with a numbered default style name, such as "Paragraph Style 1".

To apply a style, click the name of the style in the style panel with your object or text selected. You can Double-Click a style definition to open it for editing or Right-Click and choose Edit Style from the contextual menu. Double-Clicking a style name applies that style to anything that's selected, while opening the style dialog through the contextual menu enables you to edit the style without applying it

WARNING: Be aware that if you select a style with no object or text selected, that style will become the new default and will be applied to new text and/or new objects you create.

The Object Styles Dialog

The Object Styles dialog box.

Object styles can capture an extremely wide range of attributes, ranging from color and fill to Effects, Paragraph styles, Frame Fitting options, and more. They are particularly handy for maintaining consistency when formatting buttons and can increase your productivity exponentially.

The Object Styles dialog functions in much the same way as the Effects dialog, with a list of attribute categories on the left and corresponding controls on the right. Checking the attribute checkbox turns on the checked attribute, but you must click directly on the name of the attribute for its controls to appear on the right.

Be sure to pay attention to the Effect for section of the dialog since the selection you make here dictates how the settings are applied to your object. You can apply different settings to the object, fill, stroke and text of the same object by changing the Effect for option you select.

Managing Styles from the Control Panel

If you accidentally activate a style with no object selected, it becomes the new default and InDesign will apply that style automatically when new objects are created. Should you encounter behavior where text wraps or drop shadows or unexpected formatting of any type is applied to your objects or text, there are simple steps you can take to correct it. Ensure that nothing is selected in your document, and then set your Character and Object styles to [None] and your Paragraph style to [No Paragraph Style] or [Basic Paragraph.]

You can reset your styles from their individual panels or from the Control panel. There are Control panel dropdowns for Paragraph and Character styles that appear in the panel when the Type tool or Note tool is active. There is also a dropdown for Object styles that appears when any of the other tools are selected. Clustered with each of the styles dropdowns are all the controls and menu items you might require to manage your styles.

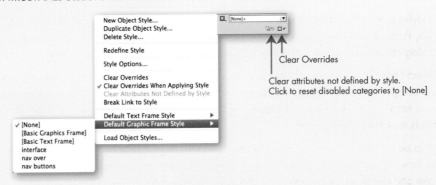

48. Click the visibility button at the left of the first group (👁) to determine which group the object layer contains. Stephen's information disappears from the page.

49. Click in the empty square in the visibility column to show Stephen's information and rename the layer "stephen."

50. Rename the groups for Alastair and Iris.

51. In the Layers panel, drag Alastair's layer to the top of the stack, followed by Iris, followed by Stephen.

    Your work with page one is complete and you have all the skills you need to complete the formatting for pages 2 and 3 if you'd like more practice. But let's take a moment to see how a change to a master page populates to all its associated child pages, and how issues of stacking order can occur with masters.

52. Double-Click the A-Interface master in the Pages panel and select the navbar at the top of the page.

53. Expand the Object States (📰) panel in the Panel Dock (or go to Window > Interactive > Object States.) Click the "team" state in the panel to show the navbar submenu. Double-Click the B–Design master in the Pages panel to make it the active page and to see the change it inherited from the A master.

    Note that the line below the page header overlays the dropdown menu. Since the objects reside on different masters and only the objects on the active page appear in the Layers panel, there is no way for you to simply reorder the layers to correct the issue. The solution is to create a separate layer for each master.

54. With the B–Master active, change the name of the "master" layer in the Layers panel to "designMaster."

55. Double-Click the A master in the Pages panel and press Ctrl+A/Command+A to select all. Create a new layer in the Layers panel and name it "interfaceMaster." Drag the square for the selected objects from the designMaster layer to the interfaceMaster layer.

56. Double-Click page 1 in the Pages panel to see that the navbar submenu now overlays the line below the header.

With you now a master of master pages, this chapter comes to a close.

CHAPTER SUMMARY

This chapter gave you what you need to know to set up a multi-page document using master pages. You learned how to:

- Create master and nested master pages
- Change master page options
- Apply a master to document pages
- Override master page items to unlock them on document pages
- Organize the Layers panel for multi-page documents

You gained an understanding of

- The Layers panel
- Weird layer visibility anomalies related to master pages
- Primary text frames
- Text and object styles

You also learned some new skills, including how to:

- Create a grid of uniformly sized frames
- Create, rename and reorder layers
- Manage styles from the Control panel
- Work with InDesign's Multiplace feature
- Work with the Gap tool to modify your layout
- Create precisely sized objects
- Customize and apply effects
- Work with the Align panel
- Create an object style

The next several chapters will acquaint you with features that are most often found in long print pieces but which can also be utilized selectively in digital design to add specialized navigation structures to your documents. We're talking about hyperlinks, cross-references, footnotes and tables of contents—lots of great information that is equally relevant to print and digital design.

● Chapter 6

HYPERLINKS AND CROSS-REFERENCES

In addition to buttons, you can also use hyperlinks and cross-references to add interactivity to your digital publications. Supported features and functions vary but hyperlinks and/or cross-references are applicable in some capacity to digital development for Interactive PDF, DPS, SWF and even EPUB—and cross-references are of course applicable to print documents as well.

Internal links, external links, links to text anchors or specific document pages— between hyperlinks and cross-references, they've got it covered. And by the end of this chapter, you will too.

Introduction

TIP: To ensure that the hyperlinks you create are included in your exported files, select the Include All Interactivity and Media option when exporting to SWF, and All Forms and Media when exporting to PDF.

InDesign hyperlinks bring to your interactive documents the familiar functionality you expect from hyperlinks on the web. You can create internal document links, links to related files and web pages, or trigger the opening of a mail client to send an email message. Sharing the panel with Hyperlinks, cross-references enable cross-linking of content within and between InDesign documents that is supported in output to EPUB, Interactive PDF and SWF in limited capacity. Not only can you create these links in InDesign, but you can test them too, without venturing outside the InDesign interface.

To open the Hyperlinks panel, go to Window > Interactive > Hyperlinks. The top half of the panel displays document hyperlinks and the bottom half displays cross-references. The panel controls and menu items provide everything you need to define and refine the source, destination, and appearance for any link you create.

NOTE: For DPS, Hyperlink overlays are supported only in scrollable frames and slideshows. To learn more about including hyperlinks in DPS publications, see the Hyperlinks section of Chapter 33 starting on page 502.

The Hyperlinks panel serves a dual purpose—it's command central for creating and managing both hyperlinks and cross-references.

About Hyperlinks

TIP: Hyperlinks can be applied to graphical elements as well as text. However, best practice dictates the use of buttons instead of hyperlinked graphics since buttons perform more reliably.

Cross-references specialize in internal links and links between InDesign book documents destined for output to EPUB, Interactive PDF, SWF or print. Hyperlinks have a broader reach, linking through any valid protocol: http, ftp, mailto, and file. You can create or select text to serve as your link text or you can let InDesign scour your document for URLs which it can then convert to hyperlinks for you.

To manually create a hyperlink, select the text you want to use as the hyperlink source and click the Create new hyperlink button ( ) at the bottom of the Hyperlinks panel. Choose a hyperlink type from the Link To dropdown and then complete the Destination information as required. The Hyperlinks dialog enables the creation of six different link types: URL, File, Email, Page, Text Anchor, and Shared Destination.

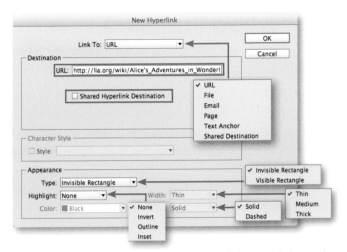

There are six types of hyperlinks you can create through the Hyperlinks panel but the most useful are URL, Email, Page and Text Anchor. The Appearance options at the bottom of the panel apply to Interactive PDF hyperlinks only.

While there are six types of hyperlinks you can create through the Hyperlinks panel, you'll find these four to be the most useful: URL, Email, Page and Text Anchor.

Applicable in specialized situations, the File hyperlink option enables you to create a link that opens an external file in its native application, providing that application is available on your system. InDesign links to external files work as long as the locations of the linked files always remain the same. The Link to File option creates something called an absolute rather than a relative path to the external file. An absolute path defines the location of the targeted file using an address that starts with the root of your hard drive or server. Relocating the file changes the path and causes the link to break. Try as we might, we've been unable to find a way around the absolute path that InDesign creates, limiting the usefulness of the Link to File option to files that will always remain in a fixed location.

Shared hyperlink destinations are essentially named anchors that can be referenced multiple times within the same file, or accessed between documents, and they too come with a cautionary note. Ideally, you could create a document with a complete list of hyperlink destinations for often-used links, and then reference that document to ensure that the paths for your links would always be correct. The unfortunate truth is that shared hyperlink destinations can result in quirky and unpredictable document behavior and are, for the most part, best avoided. The general rule is this: only use shared hyperlink destinations for links that will be used frequently in the same document, and don't rely on them for cross-document reference. Cross-document shared hyperlink destinations are sketchy when exported to PDF, and don't work at all when exported to SWF. The bottom line is, since it's checked by default, you want to be sure to deselect the Shared Hyperlink Destination checkbox whenever you create your hyperlinks. Should you mistakenly create shared hyperlink destinations, you can access and manage them through the Hyperlink Destination Options command in the Hyperlinks panel menu. Text anchors reside there as well, and you'll be getting acquainted with them all in the following exercises.

NOTE: In contrast to an absolute path, a relative path defines the location of linked files relative to each other rather than to the root of your system. The beauty of a relative path is that if the folder containing the linked files is moved, the paths between the files in the folder stay the same and therefore, the links between them remain intact.

NOTE: A hyperlinked file opens in its native application. E.g., a file with a .doc extension opens in MS Word.

ALERT: It's best to deselect the Shared Hyperlink Destination checkbox when you create your hyperlinks.

Exercise 6.1: Adding Hyperlinks

1. Open **ex6_1_end.indd** and if necessary, navigate to the Synopsis page: page 1.

2. Go to Window > Interactive > Hyperlinks or click the 🔖 icon in the Panel Dock.

3. Select the first URL link in the Hyperlinks panel and click the Go to destination button at the bottom of the panel ⇐ ⇒ to open your browser to the link URL.

4. Close your browser and return to the Hyperlinks panel in InDesign. Select the Caucus-Race link in the panel and click the Go to destination button to jump to the Chapter 3 text anchor.

5. Select the Caucus-Race link in the Hyperlinks panel and click the Go to source button to return to the synopsis page.

6. Select the email link (help2010@pglaf.org) in the Hyperlinks panel. Click the go to destination button to open your email client. Note the pre-populated email address and subject line.

7. Close your email client and close ex6_1_end.indd.

8. Now that you've seen them in action, it's time to make some hyperlinks of your own.

9. Open **ex6_1_start.indd** and save it as ex6_1.indd. If necessary, navigate to the Synopsis page: page 1.

10. From the Hyperlinks panel menu, select Convert URLs to Hyperlinks.

11. When the dialog opens, ensure that Document is selected from the Search dropdown. Check the Character Style checkbox, choose hyperlink from the Character Style dropdown and click the Find button.

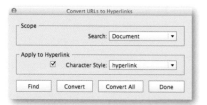

Select Convert URLs to Hyperlinks from the Hyperlinks panel menu to have InDesign detect and convert link text in your document to live hyperlinks.

InDesign highlights only a portion of the first web address in the footnote at the bottom of page one.

12. With the Type tool selected, hold down the Shift key and click after the ending "d" in "Wonderland" to select the entire URL. Click the Convert button. (InDesign converts only the portion of the URL it selected.)

13. Click Find and Convert six more times to convert the remaining URLs to hyperlinks. Click Done to exit the dialog.

Less than perfect, InDesign creates the hyperlinks and styles the portion of the addresses it captured with the "hyperlink" Character style that's been saved with the file.

While it's convenient to have InDesign do the heavy lifting for you, you saw that its results are not always reliable. An additional downside to this approach is that the links it creates are saved as, yep you guessed it, shared hyperlink destinations. So, now that you've got some, it's a good opportunity to show you how to delete them.

14. Choose Hyperlink Destination Options from the Hyperlinks panel menu. Your URLs will appear in the Destination dropdown. Click Delete All and then click OK to close the dialog.

When the destinations are deleted, the icons appearing to the right of the links in the Hyperlinks panel change from ⊕ to ▨, indicating that the link destinations are missing.

15. In the Hyperlinks panel, select the first broken link, hold down the Shift key on your keyboard and click the last broken link. Click the Delete button 🗑 at the bottom of the panel and then click Yes to dismiss the alert.

When a hyperlink is deleted, the hyperlink source text is converted to text and keeps the visual formatting that was applied to the hyperlink.

The link interactivity is removed from the text but the character style remains.

16. With the Type tool, select and copy the entire link text for the first link in the footnote on page 1 of the synopsis: http://en.wikipedia.org/wiki/Alice's_Adventures_in_Wonderland.

17. Click the New Hyperlink button (🔲) at the bottom of the Hyperlinks panel.

18. From the Link To dropdown, select URL and paste the copied web address into the URL field. Deselect the Shared Hyperlink Destination checkbox, and click OK to close the dialog. Repeat for the second hyperlink in the footnote.

19. Open the Hyperlinks panel menu.

Note that the Hyperlink Destination Options menu item is unavailable since the hyperlink you created wasn't saved as a shared hyperlink destination.

20. Navigate to the footnotes on page 2 of the document and select the first URL. Repeat steps 15–16 to add live links to the both web URLs on the page.

21. Still in the footnotes, select and copy the email address using the Type tool and click the Create new hyperlink button.

22. In the New Hyperlink dialog, choose Email from the Link To dropdown and paste the copied address into the Address field. Type "How can I get involved with Project Gutenberg?" for the Subject Line and deselect the Shared Hyperlink Destination checkbox. Style the link with the hyperlink Character Style and click OK to close the dialog.

ALERT: The New Hyperlink from URL option available through the Hyperlinks panel menu creates Shared Destinations and like the Convert URLs to Hyperlinks command is best avoided.

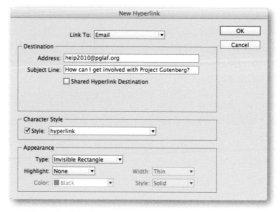

The Email hyperlink dialog includes an option to enter a Subject Line.

Now it's time to test your hyperlinks.

23. Select the first URL link in the Hyperlinks panel and click the Go to destination button ⇨ at the bottom of the panel.

    The browser should open and display the URL target. Pretty nifty, yes?

24. Test the remaining links and then close your browser and email client.

25. Navigate to the synopsis paragraph below the heading "Chapter III—A CAUCUS-RACE AND A LONG TALE" on page 1. Locate and select the words "Caucus-Race" that appear in blue.

26. Click the Create new hyperlink button and select Text Anchor from the Link To dropdown. The current document and the saved CaucusRace text anchor automatically populate the Document and Text Anchor dropdowns. Click OK to create the hyperlink and exit the dialog.

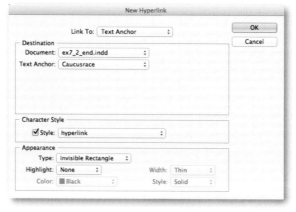

InDesign enables you to define and link to internal or external text anchors.

27. Test your link and then save and close the file to complete the exercise.

Adding and Formatting Cross-references

The real difference between a hyperlink and a cross-reference is that the link text for a cross-reference is dynamically generated. Cross-references can capture and display paragraph text or text from a predefined text anchor, page number, and/ or paragraph number, and are easily updated when the referenced text changes.

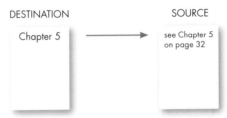

DESTINATION   SOURCE

Chapter 5   see Chapter 5
                               on page 32

CROSS-REFERENCE DESTINATION AND CROSS-REFERENCE SOURCE

The cross-reference destination paragraph text and its location (Chapter 5) provide the content for the link at the cross-reference source (see Chapter 5 on page 32.)

Like any other link, a cross-reference is composed of two parts, the source and the destination. The clickable cross-reference source text is dynamically populated by content from the destination. The cross-reference destination text is identified based on the paragraph style applied to it, or by a predefined text anchor saved as a hyperlink destination. InDesign provides an assortment of pre-built cross-reference format options which determine the actual content of the cross-reference source text. You can easily customize the formatting of the cross-reference text with a tiny bit of very simple code.

TIP: You can import cross-reference formats from other documents. Choose Load Cross-Reference Formats from the Hyperlinks panel menu and then navigate to and select the file containing the desired formats.

Exercise 6.2: Adding and Formatting Cross-References

In this exercise, you'll use cross-references to populate and update the titles for each chapter in the synopsis, create and edit cross-reference formatting, and create a text anchor that can be used as a hyperlink or cross-reference destination.

1. Open **ex6_2_end.indd** and if necessary, expand the Hyperlinks panel.

    Notice that the list of cross-references in the panel correspond to the chapter titles in the synopsis on pages 1 and 2 and that each chapter title in the document is prefixed with the word "chapter." Note also that there are no parentheses around the chapter titles. If you like, you can keep the file open for reference.

2. Open **ex6_2_start.indd**. Check out the Hyperlinks panel and explore the synopsis on pages 1 and 2.

    Notice that the chapter titles on the first page of the synopsis are quoted and begin with a Roman numeral chapter number. Each of these titles is populated by a cross-reference that appears at the bottom of the Hyperlinks panel. Note that the chapter titles on page 2 of the synopsis contain only the word "Chapter" followed by the chapter number. Next, you're going to define and edit cross-references to populate the chapter titles on page 2 and update the formatting of the titles on page 1.

NOTE: The first three pages of the ex6_2_start.indd file are numbered with lower case Roman numerals. Page 1 is actually the fourth page in the document.

NOTE: When you create a cross-reference to an external file, InDesign automatically opens the referenced file.

NOTE: "synopsis" is a custom cross-reference format created for these lessons that duplicates the default Full Paragraph format.

TIP: Though technically it requires that you work with "code," InDesign makes the process of customizing Cross-reference Formats as painless as possible with a slew of built-in hints to help you craft your cross-reference code correctly.

Click the icons at the right of the Cross-Reference Formats dialog for help in formatting your cross-references.

3. If necessary, go to Type > Show Hidden Characters or press Ctrl+Alt+I/Command+Option+I. Navigate to page 2 of the synopsis and select the words "Chapter 10" ensuring that you don't select the marker for the paragraph return.

4. Click the Create new cross-reference button ⚓ at the bottom of the Hyperlinks panel to open the New Cross-Reference dialog.

5. Choose Paragraph from the Link To dropdown.

   The list of paragraph styles in the document appear at the left of the panel. It is through these styles as they are applied to the document text that you will locate the destination text and define the source text for your cross-references.

6. Select the TitleCenterAllCaps paragraph style at the left of the dialog.

   Since the TitleCenterAllCaps paragraph style is applied to every chapter title, the contents of all the chapter title paragraphs appear at the right of the dialog.

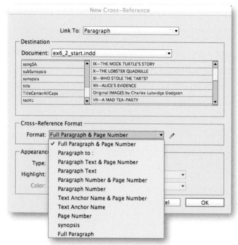

Cross-references are chosen based on the paragraph style with which the destination text is styled. The cross-reference format options then determine the content that InDesign generates for the source text that appears in the document.

7. Select "X—The Lobster Quadrille" from the paragraph list at the right of the dialog. Try out several options from the Format dropdown and notice how the cross-reference source text changes on the document page. Choose synopsis from the format list and note that your chapter title now looks like those on page 1. Click OK to close the dialog and create your cross-reference.

8. Create cross-references for Chapters 11 and 12 following the procedure in the previous steps. For Chapter 11, choose "XI—Who Stole the Tarts?" and choose "XII—Alice's Evidence" for Chapter 12.

   Now that you know how to create a cross-reference, you'll dig in a little deeper to modify the way it renders on the page. You'll remove the quotation marks from the source text and work some magic to further customize its content.

9. Double-Click the Chapter 12 cross-reference (XII—Alice's Evidence) in the Hyperlinks panel to open the Edit Cross-Reference dialog.

10. Click the ✏ button to the right of the Format dropdown to open the Cross-Reference Formats dialog.

11. With synopsis selected from the list of Formats on the left of the dialog, delete the quotation marks on either side of `<paraText />` in the Definition pane. Place your cursor in front of the opening < and type "Chapter" followed by a space. Click Save and then click OK to close the Cross-Reference Formats dialog. Click OK again to close the Edit Cross-Reference dialog.

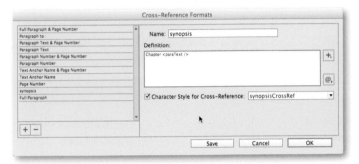

You can modify cross-reference formats to include custom text.

Note that all the chapter titles in the document have been updated to include the word "Chapter" before the chapter number and that the quotation marks have disappeared.

12. On page 2 of the synopsis, place the Type tool cursor in the empty paragraph just after the synopsis text for Chapter 12 and before the references.

13. Click the Create new cross-reference button on the Hyperlinks panel and select the TitleCenterAllCaps paragraph style. Select Original Images by Charles Lutwidge Dodgson from the list of paragraphs.

You can further customize the content captured in a cross-reference with just a little bit of simple code. Next, you'll use the customization options to limit the portion of the paragraph captured by the cross-reference.

14. From the Format dropdown, select Full Paragraph and click the ✐ button. When the Cross-Reference Formats dialog opens click the ➕ button directly below the format list. Name the new format "Paragraph to :"

15. In the Definition pane, after the **fullPara** text and before the /, type delim=":" Be sure to leave a space between the closing quotation mark and the forward slash (/). The final Format Definition should look like this: `<fullPara delim=":" />`

16. Click Save and click OK twice to create a cross-reference with the new formatting applied.

The code you've just written tells InDesign to include the text in the selected paragraph up to the colon and not beyond. If you wanted the cross-reference to include the colon as well, you would add **includeDelim="true"** after **delim=":"** The completed code would look like this: `<fullPara delim=":" includeDelim="true" />`

The end result is that only the chapter name populates the cross-reference on the page, rather than the entire text of the paragraph. Next, you'll employ a more traditional use of cross-references to create a page reference.

17. Place the Type tool cursor after the word "see" at the end of the last paragraph on page 2 of the synopsis.

> **NOTE:** To better understand the structure of the code, see the HTML Chapter starting on page 347. Structured in the same way as HTML, you can treat **fullPara** as you would an HTML tag selector, with **delim** and **includeDelim** as attributes having the attribute values of **:** and **true** enclosed in quotes.

18. Go to Type > Hyperlinks & Cross-References > Insert Cross-Reference to open the New Cross-Reference panel. Select "body" from the list of paragraph styles and the first or second entry in the paragraphs pane (they both reference the Lewis Carroll Society.) Choose Page Number from the Format dropdown to insert your page reference and click OK to close the dialog.

One of the beauties of cross-references is that they're dynamic in nature. When the cross-reference destination content changes, the Hyperlinks panel displays a hazard icon next to the changed link. You can then update the cross-reference with the click of a button.

19. Select the "Original Images" cross-reference in the Hyperlinks panel and click the Go to destination button (➡).

20. Change the word "Images" to "Illustrations" in the chapter title. Select the cross-reference again and click the Go to source button (⬅).

21. Note the hazard icon that appears to the right of the changed cross-reference in the Hyperlinks panel. Either Double-Click the hazard icon or click the ↻ button at the bottom of the panel to update the cross-reference on the page.

TIP: Like paragraphs, text anchors too can be employed as cross-reference destinations. To create a text anchor, select the anchor text and choose New Hyperlink Destination from the Hyperlinks panel menu. The destination name will auto-populate with the selected text and the destination Type will be automatically set to Text Anchor. A cross-reference to a text anchor is created in the same way as a paragraph cross-reference, except you choose Text Anchor instead of Paragraph from the Link To dropdown.

A hazard icon indicates a cross-reference that has changed. Click the Update button to render the change on your document.

Decoding the Hyperlinks Panel Hieroglyphics

The Hyperlinks panel provides an assortment of clues to help you manage your hyperlinks and cross-references.

⊕ means external link to page

🗋 means internal link to page

⚓ means internal/external text anchor

🌐 means web, email or file link

🗷 means broken destination

MP means the destination is on a Master Page

PB means the destination is on the pasteboard

HL means the destination is on a hidden layer

OV means the destination text is overset

⚠ means the destination text has changed

Formatting Hyperlinks and Cross-references

By applying the hyperlinks character style to your links, you provided a visual cue that distinguished them from the rest of the content on the page. As an alternative or complement to character style formatting (for output to Interactive PDF or SWF), InDesign gives you the option of outlining your hyperlinks with a thin, medium, or thick line that is solid or dashed. Additionally, you can choose an option for changing the link appearance when it is clicked. It can appear inverted, highlighted, inset, or, of course, it can display no change at all.

For output to Interactive PDF, hyperlinks and cross-references can be formatted with a solid or dashed outline and can appear inverted, highlighted, or inset when clicked.

Within InDesign, you can toggle the visibility of the hyperlink outlines by going to View > Extras > Show (or Hide) Hyperlinks. If multiple hyperlinks share the same appearance, you can change them all at once. Select the links you want to change in the Hyperlinks panel, choose Hyperlink Options from the panel menu, and make the desired changes.

CHAPTER SUMMARY

In this chapter you employed hyperlinks and cross-references as yet another means of adding interactivity to your digital documents. You worked extensively with the Hyperlinks panel to:

- Manage hyperlink destinations
- Add URL and Email links
- Create and link to text anchors
- Generate and format cross-references

You learned about absolute and relative paths and constraints that affect InDesign links to external files. In exploring InDesign's ability to locate and convert URLs to working links, you gained an understanding of shared hyperlink destinations: what they are, why they can be problematic, and how you can work around them when necessary.

You worked extensively with cross-references, using them to populate chapter titles and generate dynamic page references. Using customized cross-reference formats, you modified and updated existing cross-references, and learned to save and load formats from an external file.

After exploring the intricacies of hyperlink and cross-reference creation, you deciphered the cryptic icons that might appear in the Hyperlinks panel and learned how to format link appearances for export to Interactive PDF and SWF.

With your soup to nuts tour of hyperlinks and cross-references complete, the next chapter is about footnotes—another topic that crosses over the print to digital divide.

● Chapter 7

FOOTNOTES

What, you may ask, do footnotes have to do with interactive design? In fact, when exported to EPUB, footnotes and their reference numbers are automatically converted to links, adding yet one more way for users to navigate your document.

Whether imported with a placed Word file or added on the fly, InDesign makes creating and formatting footnotes a simple process. You'll find out just how easy it can be in the following pages.

Working with Footnotes

Similar to hyperlinks and cross-references, footnotes consist of two linked parts: the footnote reference number in the body of the document, and the footnote text that appears at the bottom of the page. When you export to EPUB, these two parts become live links, enabling your reader to jump back and forth between them. Not all the formatting you apply to footnotes translates to EPUB but you'll learn more about that in the EPUB chapter starting on page 309.

If you're composing directly in InDesign, you can create footnotes on the fly. If you're importing documents that originate in Word, you have the option to include footnotes when placing your files. You'll explore these options and more in the next exercise.

Exercise 7.1: Working with Footnotes

1. Navigate to the chapter_7_exercises folder, open **ex7_1_end.indd** and check out the way the footnotes and footnote references are formatted. Have a look at the paragraph and character styles and close the file when you're through.

2. Go to File > New > Document (Ctrl+N/Command+N), choose Digital Publishing from the Intent dropdown and Kindle Fire/Nook for the Page Size. Set the page orientation to Portrait, leave the other default settings and click OK to close the dialog. Save the file as ex7_1.indd.

3. Select the Type tool and click in the text frame to place the cursor.

4. Press Ctrl+D/Command+D, navigate to the chapter_7_exercises folder and select the **synopsis.docx** file. In the Place dialog, check the Show Import Options checkbox at the lower left of the window and click Open.

5. When the Microsoft Word Import Options dialog opens, note that the Include Footnotes checkbox is checked. Select the Custom Style Import radio button at the bottom of the dialog and then click the button labeled "Style Mapping."

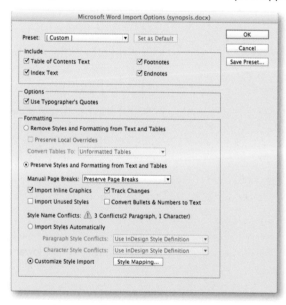

The Microsoft Word Import Options dialog.

When placing a Word file, the Style Mapping option lets you automate the conversion of the formatting in the Word doc to formatting specified in your InDesign file. If you don't have existing paragraph and character styles in your InDesign file, you have the option to create them on the fly. For this particular Word document, as is often the case with documents originating in Word, the formatting of the body copy was not captured in named styles. However, when the footnotes were created, Word generated several footnote-specific styles automatically. You'll create a character style to replace the footnote reference style from Word.

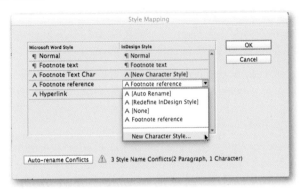

The Style Mapping dialog allows you to replace Word styles with paragraph and character styles defined in InDesign.

6. Click the InDesign Style dropdown to the right of the Footnote reference character style and then click the New Character Style option at the bottom of the dropdown list.

7. Name your character style "fnReference" and choose Basic Character Formats from the categories on the left of the dialog. Choose Superscript from the Position dropdown.

8. Choose Character Color from the categories list and change the font color to red. Click OK three times to exit the Import Options dialog.

    The text flows into the document and adds a second page (as long as you used the Digital Publishing preset which includes a primary text frame.)

9. Click around in the document with the Type tool to see how the character and paragraph styles were mapped to the footnotes and footnote references.

    You'll quickly discover that while InDesign visually formatted the footnotes and footnote references from Word, the fnReference style, and the Footnote text and Normal Word styles were imported but not applied; and the Hyperlink and Footnote Text Char styles simply disappeared. Were this a document with a huge number of footnotes, these circumstances might cause you a moment of panic—but, no need to worry—the problem is easily solved.

10. Go to Type > Document Footnote Options. In the Numbering and Formatting tab of the Footnote Options dialog, choose fnReference from the Character Style dropdown. If necessary, check the Preview checkbox at the lower left of the panel and you should see the footnote reference numbers turn red at the upper right of the "Synopsis" page header and the word "Dodo" at the end of the third line of the Chapter III—Caucus-Race summary. Keep the dialog open.

ALERT: If the Type tool cursor isn't active in the text frame before placing the file, the fnReference character style will be applied to the entire "Synopsis" header rather than just the footnote reference.

NOTE: Had you created character styles in InDesign that you then mapped to the Hyperlink and Footnote Text Char styles, those styles would have appeared in the Character Styles panel when the file was placed. Had you not created the fnReference style, the Footnote Reference style from Word still would have been imported into the document.

You may need to zoom in to see the "Dodo" reference number. Keep an eye on the document as you modify the footnote options to see how your changes affect the formatting.

11. In the Numbering section of the dialog, check the Restart Numbering Every checkbox and choose Section from the dropdown.

12. Check the Show Prefix/Suffix in checkbox and choose Footnote Reference from the dropdown.

13. Click the arrow to the right of the Prefix text field, click Hair Space (the characters representing the hair space: ^|), then click the parenthesis.

TIP: The caret (^) shares the 6 key on your keyboard. The pipe (|) shares the backslash key.

14. In the Suffix field, type a closing parenthesis followed by a caret, followed by a pipe: (Shift+6 for the caret: ^ and Shift+\ for the pipe:|.)

The hair space you added before and after the parentheses gives a little breathing room between the text and the reference. You can choose from the menus to have InDesign enter the metacharacters for you or, if you know them, you can type them in yourself.

TIP: If necessary, enter an appropriate number in the Start at field in the Numbering and Formatting pane of the Footnote Options dialog to continue footnote numbering across documents in an InDesign book. Otherwise, numbering of the footnotes will restart at 1 for each document in the book.

15. In the Footnote Formatting section of the dialog, choose Footnote text from the Paragraph Style dropdown. Delete the Tab separator (^t) and type a period. Click the button to the right of the Separator field to display the options menu and choose En Space. (The reference number in the footer should be followed by a period and the En space.)

NOTE: Try entering a value of 30 px in the Minimum Space Before Footnote field to see how text flow on the page is affected.

The footnote Numbering and Formatting options provide many options for customizing the appearance of your footnotes

With the paragraph and character styles now applied, you'll move on to format the footnote layout.

TIP: Space Before and Space After values in a footnote paragraph style only affect footnotes that contain multiple paragraphs.

16. Click the Layout tab of the dialog, enter a value of 12 in the Minimum Space Before First Footnote text field and a value of 6 in the Space Before Footnotes field.

17. In the Rule Above section of the dialog, change the Weight value to .5 pt and the Width to 100 px. Click OK to close the dialog.

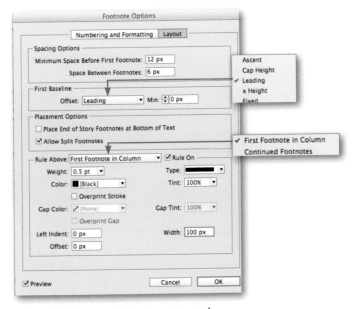

The Footnote Options Layout controls

Now that you've added some space between the body copy and the footnotes, and between the footnotes themselves, you'll refine the styling of the footnote text with a nested style to highlight the footnote reference number.

18. Place the Type tool cursor in the first footnote and open the Paragraph Styles panel. Note that the Footnote text style displays a plus sign indicating that there are overrides to the style definition. Mouse over the style to see a popup detailing the override.

TIP: Use the arrow keys on your keyboard to navigate from one footnote to another—even across pages.

19. Choose Redefine Style from the panel menu to incorporate the override in the style definition and make the override indicator disappear. Double-Click the style definition and when the Paragraph Style Options dialog opens, choose Drop Caps and Nested Styles from the categories list.

20. Click the New Nested Style button at the bottom of the panel and choose New Character Style from the nested style dropdown. Name the style "fnTextReference" and, in the Basic Character formats pane, set the font Style to Bold. In the Character Color pane, set the font color to Red, click OK and OK again to close the dialogs.

SYNOPSIS[1]

A Dodo[2]

Chapter VII—A MAD TEA-PARTY

Alice becomes a guest at a "mad" tea party along with the March Hare, the Hatter, and a very tired Dormouse who falls asleep frequently, only to be violently woken up moments later by the March Hare and the Hatter. The characters give Alice many riddles and stories, including the famous 'Why is a raven like a writing desk?'. The Hatter reveals that they have tea all day because Time has pun-

---

1. Synopsis from Wikipedia: http://en.wikipedia.org/wiki/Alice's_Adventures_in_Wonderland

2. Lewis Carroll (nom de plume of Charles Lutwidge Dodgson) is caricatured as the Dodo because Dodgson sometimes stuttered when he spoke- he sometimes pronounced his last name as Do-do-Dodgson http://en.wikipedia.org/wiki/Alice's_Adventures_in_Wonderland

The results of your footnote formatting efforts.

Next you'll add a footnote of your own.

TIP: To delete a footnote, delete the footnote reference number in the body of the document text. If you delete the actual footnote text, the structure of the footnote remains in the document.

21. Navigate to the last paragraph on page 2 of the document and place the Type tool cursor after the underlined text "Alice's Adventures Under Ground."

22. Right-Click/Ctrl+Click and choose Insert Footnote from the contextual menu (or go to Type > Insert Footnote.)

    InDesign inserts both the footnote separator and the footnote text reference, and relocates the Type tool cursor in readiness for entry of your footnote.

23. Type "The first version of the work later published as Alice's Adventures in Wonderland" for your footnote text.

24. Right-Click/Ctrl+Click in the footnote and choose Go to Footnote Reference from the contextual menu.

    InDesign jumps the Type tool cursor back to the origin of the footnote—a particularly great feature if you're composing in InDesign and creating footnotes on the fly.

CHAPTER SUMMARY

In this chapter you learned all about footnotes:

- How to import them with a placed Word document
- How to format them
- How to add and delete them

In the course of your explorations, you learned how to map styles from a Word document to InDesign character and paragraph styles.

You gave your footnotes more breathing room by adding space between the body copy and footnote text and between the footnotes as well. You applied character and paragraph styles to the footnote text and footnote reference and employed metacharacters for further customization.

Finally, you learned how to navigate your footnotes with key strokes and contextual menus.

Continuing with document layout and navigation, the next chapter takes you through building and formatting a table of contents. Relevant to your print work as well, a table of contents is an absolute requirement for EPUB production.

Chapter 8

CREATING A TOC

Common in long print documents, a table of contents is also an essential element in an eBook. In fact, you can't create a valid EPUB without one. When exported to EPUB, Interactive PDF, or SWF, an InDesign TOC is yet one more way to add interactivity to your digital documents and provide navigation hyperlinks to your referenced TOC destinations.

In this chapter you'll learn how to: create a table of contents, style its appearance on the page, adjust it for EPUB, and save a TOC style. Applicable to both print and digital production, what you learn about InDesign TOCs will expand your notion of what a TOC can do.

Building a Table of Contents

Similar to the way in which cross-references are generated, InDesign builds a table of contents based on paragraph styles. As you're coming to understand, particularly for long documents, styles are the foundation of an efficient workflow. If you've been consistent in applying them, your work creating a TOC is already half done. To create a table of contents, you'll open the Table of Contents dialog and choose the paragraph styles that are applied to the text you want in your TOC. You'll then set up some formatting rules and InDesign will do the rest, automatically generating a hyperlinked TOC.

NOTE: To learn all about working with InDesign book files, see Chapter 23, starting on page 339.

A table of contents is most often found in a long document. There are two ways to create long documents using InDesign—either as one large file or as a collection of documents assembled into an InDesign .indb book file. The book files can be synchronized to maintain proper pagination, share style definitions, master pages and more in order to maintain consistency from file to file. Whether your TOC is destined for a single document or a compiled InDesign book, the TOC creation process is pretty much the same. A TOC generated for an InDesign .indb, however, can actually be in its own file—as long as all the paragraph styles used in the book to style the TOC source content have been loaded into its Paragraph Styles panel. Should you want the TOC to include navigation to first and second level headers for example, the paragraph style definitions used in the book for the first and second level headers must also reside in the TOC file and the TOC must be included in the book.

Building a table of contents in InDesign is generally an iterative process. First, you define the content you want to include in the TOC, then you can concentrate on refining its appearance. Styling your TOC is often easiest if you create a first generation TOC with basic styling and then refine the formatting and style definitions from there. You can get very fancy if you like with options to assign distinct styling to each level of the TOC, to TOC page numbers and even to the leaders between the page numbers and the TOC entries.

In the next exercise, you'll create and format a TOC for inclusion in an existing InDesign book. Don't be fooled by the empty document page—the file already contains all the text styles required to generate the TOC.

Exercise 8.1: Building and Formatting a Table of Contents

NOTE: To see the layout of the completed TOC, go to the chapter_8_exercises folder and open ex8_1_end.indd. This file is no longer linked to the .indb file and is for illustration purposes only. It cannot be output to a hyperlinked TOC.

1. Duplicate the entire **chapter_8_exercises** folder for use in the exercise.

2. Go to File > Open (Ctrl+O/Command+O), and navigate to the resources folder inside the duplicated chapter_8_exercises folder. Double-Click **alice_in_wonderland.indb** to open it. If a warning alert pops up, click OK to dismiss the alert, click the menu button at the upper right of the Book panel and choose Automatic Document Conversion from the Book panel menu.

3. Don't be alarmed by any alerts that may appear in the panel. You'll be taking care of them momentarily. Click once on **ex8_1_start** in the book panel to highlight it, and choose Replace Document from the panel menu. Navigate to the chapter_8_exercises folder and Double-Click **ex8_1.indd** to add it to the book.

With replacement of the file, the book repaginates and any alert icons on the book documents disappear.

4. Double-Click ex8_1 in the book panel to open the file. Select the Type tool.

5. Go to Window > Styles > Paragraph Styles or expand the Paragraph Styles panel (⬚) in the Panel Dock to see the styles currently in the document.

   Throughout the other book documents, the TitleCenterAllCaps style is applied to the level one headers and the subSynopsis style is applied to the level two headers. You'll use these two styles to capture the content for your TOC entries.

6. Go to Layout > Table of Contents to open the Table of Contents dialog. If the bottom button at the right of the window reads "More Options", click to display additional TOC details.

   The Paragraph styles contained in the document are listed in the Other Styles section at the right of the Table of Contents dialog. You'll move the styles you choose to include in your TOC to the Include Paragraph Styles list on the left.

7. If necessary, click to select and highlight [No Paragraph Style] in the Include Paragraph Styles pane of the Table of Contents dialog and then click the Remove >> button to return the style to the Other Styles list at the right.

8. Select the TitleCenterAllCaps paragraph style from the Other Styles list and click the << Add button to move the style to the Include Paragraph Styles list.

9. Add the subSynopsis paragraph style to the Include Paragraph Styles list. Keep the dialog open.

   Notice that the subSynopsis style is automatically nested beneath the TitleCenterAllCaps style. With the subSynopsis style selected, the Level dropdown in the Style section of the dialog displays the number "2" indicating the second level of the TOC. InDesign automatically increments the TOC level for each paragraph style added to the TOC definition. Should your document have more than one style applied to content belonging at the same TOC level, simply select the style and select the appropriate number in the Level dropdown.

   You can style your TOC directly from the Table of Contents dialog by assigning existing styles to its component elements or by defining new styles on the fly. If defining new styles, your definitions will most likely require some massaging but that is easily accomplished after the TOC style is complete.

10. Select TitleCenterAllCaps, click the Entry Style dropdown in the Style section of the dialog, and choose New Paragraph Style from the very bottom of the list. When the New Paragraph Style dialog opens, name the new style "tocH1". Choose [No Paragraph Style] from the Based On dropdown, and click OK.

    This style will define the formatting for the Level 1 TOC entries. You'll edit it later to update the appearance of your TOC.

11. From the Style dropdown to the right of the Page Number dropdown, create a new character style called tocH1pageNum and ensure that [None] is selected in the Based On dropdown.

12. From the Style dropdown to the right of the Between Entry and Number dropdown, create a new character style called tocH1Leader based on [None].

13. Repeat the process in steps 10–12 selecting subSynopsis instead of TitleCenterAllCaps. Name your new paragraph style "tocH2." Name your character styles tocH2pageNum and tocH2Leader. Base tocH2 on tocH1, tocH2pageNum on tocH1pageNum, and tocH2Leader on tocH1Leader.

14. Type "Table of Contents" in the Title field at the top of the Table of Contents dialog. To style the TOC title, expand the Style dropdown to the right of the Title field and select the TOC Title paragraph style.

15. If necessary, check both the Create PDF Bookmarks and Include Book Documents checkboxes in the Options section at the bottom of the dialog. Click the Save Style button at the right of the dialog, name the TOC style "interior" and click OK.

16. Click OK to close the Table of Contents dialog and to load the cursor with the TOC. Click within the margins of the page to place the TOC on the page. Save your file and keep it open for the next exercise.

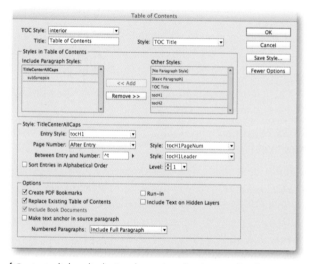

The Table of Contents dialog displaying the settings for the completed "interior" TOC style.

Formatting a Table of Contents

If you take a strategic approach to defining your TOC styles, you can create a foundation style that when changed, will change the font used throughout the entire TOC. Basing one paragraph style on the definition of another can streamline formatting changes and enable you to transform an entire document by updating a single style definition—update the foundation style and the change cascades through the hierarchy of dependent styles.

For a TOC, the likely candidate for a base style would be the style applied to the level 1 entry. In fact, in the last exercise, you established the dependency of the tocH2 style on the definition of tocH1.

Whether or not you use dependent styles, when you visually design a TOC, you may end up going back and forth a few times before you feel like you've got things looking just right. The time you spend won't be wasted however, since you can save the fruits of your labor in a named TOC style that can then be shared between documents.

Like other InDesign styles, a TOC style travels with the document in which it was created. When a TOC style is loaded from one document into another, its associated paragraph and character styles travel with it. In the next exercise you'll refine the paragraph and character styles for your TOC, save a TOC style, and then load the saved TOC style into a new document. Last but not least, you'll change the text style definitions to customize the appearance of the second TOC.

Exercise 8.2: Formatting a Table of Contents

In order to complete this exercise, you'll first need to complete exercise 8.1.

1. Position the Type tool cursor in the first TOC entry on the document page ("Synopsis") and expand the Paragraph Styles panel. Right-Click/Ctrl+Click tocH1 and choose Edit " tocH1" from the contextual menu. When the Paragraph Style Options dialog opens, format the text the way you'd like it to appear in the TOC. For the following categories we chose:

    Basic Character Formats:
    - Font Family: Adobe Garamond Pro
    - Font Style: Regular.
    - Size: 14 pt.
    - Kerning: Optical.
    - Case: All Caps.

    Indents and Spacing: Space After: 7 px.

    Character Color: 100% Black.

    Next, you'll format the tab between the TOC entry and the page number.

TIP: As long as there's enough room for the Tab panel to fit above the active text frame, you can click the magnet icon (🧲) at the right of the panel to align and snap it to the top of the frame.

2. Press Ctrl+0/Command+0 to fit the entire page in the document window. Scroll the page view so the pasteboard is visible at the top of the screen. Go to Type > Tabs (Shift+Ctrl+T/Shift+Command+T) to snap the Tab panel to the top of the frame.

    There are four options for the type of tabs you can create: left-justified, center-justified, right-justified, and a tab that's aligned to a particular character (the default character is a decimal point or period.) You can manually position a tab marker by selecting the type of tab you want to create, and then clicking in the white space above the ruler divisions to place it. You can then drag the tab indicator to reposition the tab, or you can enter a value in the X text field to position the tab precisely.

TIP: To remove a tab from the Tabs panel, click and drag it far up or far down and out of the panel.

You can click above the ruler markers in the Tabs panel to place a tab.

3. Select the Right-Justified tab, click in the white space above the ruler divisions, and enter 528 px in the X text field. In the Leader field, type a period and then a space to create the leader pattern. Press Enter/Return to set your tab and render the dot leaders on the page.

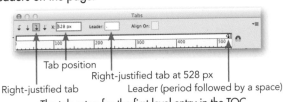

Tab position

Right-justified tab at 528 px

Right-justified tab

Leader (period followed by a space)

The tab setup for the first level entry in the TOC.

4. With the Type tool cursor positioned in the paragraph you just styled, if necessary, open the Paragraph Styles panel. The tocH1 style should be highlighted and display a + sign override indicator, since the style is already applied to the text and you've made changes to the fomatting. Choose Redefine Style from the panel menu to capture your changes and update all the entries on the page.

5. Open the Character styles panel (Window > Styles > Character Styles), Right-Click/Ctrl+Click tocH1Leader and choose Edit "tocH1Leader" from the contextual menu. When the Character Style Options dialog opens, select the Basic Character Formats category at the left of the dialog, change the Size to 16px and change the Font Style to Bold. In the Character Color category choose [Black] and set the Tint to 40%. Click OK to close the dialog.

6. Right-Click/Ctrl+Click tocH1pageNum in the Character Styles panel and choose Edit "tocH1pageNum" from the context menu. Change Font Style to Bold, Font size to 16 pt, Character Color to [Black] and Tint to 80%.

You've finished defining the styles for the level 1 TOC entries and now you'll use them as the foundation styles for level 2.

7. Place the Type tool cursor in the CHAPTER I entry and Double-Click tocH2 in the Paragraph Styles panel. Enter the following settings:
   Basic Character Formats: Size: 12 pt, Case: Normal
   Indents and Spacing: Left Indent: 30px
   Tabs: Right-justified tab: 500 px Leader: A period followed by a space
   Character Color: Tint: 60%

8. Back in the same TOC entry on the page, click to the right of the page number and open the Character Styles panel. The tocH2pageNum style should be highlighted in the panel. Double-Click the style name to open the Character Style Options dialog and apply the following settings:
   Basic Character Formats: Size: 12 pt
   Character Color: [Black], Tint: 60%

9. To complete the TOC level 2 styles, redefine the tocH2Leader style as follows:
   Basic Character Formats: Size: 14 pt
   Character Color: [Black], Tint: 40%

The last thing to style is the TOC title.

10. Position the Type tool cursor in the "Table of Contents" title and Double-Click TOC Title in the Paragraph Styles panel. Set Based On to tocH1, change Case to Small Caps in the Basic Character Formats category and click OK to close the dialog.

With basic formatting applied to all the TOC elements, now's the time to take stock and add any final touches or adjustments. The level 1 entries feel a little cramped and could use some extra space.

11. Place your cursor in one of the level 1 TOC entries and add 3 px space before in the Control panel. Redefine tocH1 from the Paragraph Styles panel menu to incorporate your change.

Because tocH2 is based on tocH1, adding the space before to tocH1 adds it to every entry in the TOC. You now need to remove the space before from the tocH2 style definition.

12. Place the type tool cursor in one of the level 2 TOC entries and change the value in the Space Before field on the Control panel to 0. Choose Redefine Style from the Paragraph Styles panel menu and save the file.

    With the styling for the TOC complete, now you'll see how easy it is to load your saved TOC style into another document.

13. Go to File > New > Document and choose Digital Publishing as the Intent. Choose Kindle Fire/Nook from the Page Size dropdown, set the orientation to Portrait and click OK.

    Even though there is nothing yet in the document, you can still import the Table of Contents style saved earlier in the exercise.

14. Go to Layout > Table of Contents Styles and click Load. Locate and Double-Click **ex8_1.indd**. Choose interior from the Table of Contents dialog and click OK to close the dialog and load the TOC style into your document.

15. To verify that the Table of Contents style has been added to your new, yet empty file, go to Layout > Table of Contents and choose interior from the TOC Style dropdown. Note that the whole TOC setup, as well as all the paragraph styles from the original TOC document, have been carried over to your new document. Click Cancel to close the TOC dialog.

16. Open the Character Styles panel and note that the character styles from the ex8_1.indd file have also been loaded into the file.

17. Save abd close the document to complete the exercise.

Creating an EPUB TOC

As mentioned in the beginning of this chapter, a table of contents must be included in an EPUB in order for it to pass validation. The interesting thing about this required TOC is that it doesn't appear within the actual pages of the EPUB. Instead, it is used by the eReader to provide navigation in much the same way that bookmarks function in a PDF, with each TOC entry hyperlinked to its respective section of the book. Since an EPUB TOC doesn't have a physical presence, you include a TOC in your InDesign-generated EPUB by way of a saved TOC style that you specify in the publication settings during export.

> NOTE: Check out Chapter 17, page 253 to learn all about bookmarks.

The continuous flow of an EPUB makes page numbers irrelevant, which greatly simplifies the formatting required for an EPUB TOC. Modifying an existing TOC style for use with EPUB is very simple—it merely requires that you exclude the page numbers and save the new style.

In the next exercise, you'll adapt the "interior" table of contents style that you created in the last lesson to create a new TOC style expressly for EPUB. You need to complete exercises 8.1 and 8.2 in order to have the file needed for exercise 8.3.

Exercise 8.3: Adapting a TOC for EPUB

1. Open the **ex8_1.indd** file that you saved in the last exercise and go to Layout > Table of Contents.

2. Select titleCenterAllCaps from the Include Paragraph Styles section of the panel and choose No Page Number from the Page Number dropdown.

Notice that when you choose No Page Number, the options for the page number and leader styles become grayed out.

3. Choose No Page Number for the subSynopsis paragraph style as well.

4. Press the Save Style button and name your new style EPUB. Click OK to exit the Table of Contents dialog. If you want to confirm that the page numbers are gone, click somewhere in the pasteboard with the loaded cursor to place the new TOC. Otherwise, press Escape to clear the cursor.

5. Save abd close the file to complete the lesson.

That's all there is to it—now you have an EPUB-ready TOC style. To learn how to include it in your published EPUB (and how to publish an EPUB in the first place) see Chapter 21 starting on page 309.

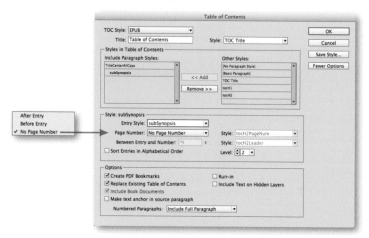

To create or convert a TOC for inclusion in an EPUB, be sure to choose No Page Number from the Page Number dropdown in the Table of Contents dialog.

TOC Innovations

At its core, a TOC is really nothing more than a specialized list. As such, it lends itself to of all sorts of creative list-building activities. As long as you've consistently applied the same paragraph style to the content you want to include in your list, the Table of Contents dialog will do the rest. You could compile a list of recipes in a cookbook for example; or a list of tips and tricks. Wouldn't that be a wonderful thing! Well, just to prove the point, and to provide you with a handy compendium of helpful hints, we've included just such a list at the back of the book, starting on page 535.

CHAPTER SUMMARY

In this chapter you learned the intricacies of creating a table of contents for a variety of document types. Whether for a single, long, stand-alone document, a compiled InDesign book file or a TOC for EPUB, the skills you learned apply to them all. And with a little outside-the-box thinking, you learned that a table of contents can contain more than traditional fare.

You learned how to set up, format, and update a TOC, and then save your work as a Table of Contents style for use in EPUB and future documents.

Your knowledge of InDesign wouldn't be anywhere near complete without an understanding of its graphical capabilities. The next chapter digs more deeply into some of InDesign's drawing tools, and then continues on into the rich and enchanting world of color.

● Chapter 9

SHAPES AND COLOR

To round out your work with layout, this chapter provides a taste, a tease, and an invitation to further explore the rich set of drawing tools and features InDesign has to offer. You'll make and assemble shapes, and indulge in the delicious feast of color you can whip up from InDesign's extensive collection of color resources. This chapter is purely a recipe for play; so, let the fun begin!

Creating Custom Shapes

An extraordinary layout application enriched by its capacity to create animation and interactivity, InDesign also possesses wonderful graphical capabilities that are all too often overlooked. Its robust selection of drawing tools include the shape tools, the Line tool, and the Pen, Pencil, Smooth and Erase tools. These tools, combined with the power of the Pathfinder panel, make it possible to do extensive graphical work directly in InDesign without the need for other applications.

InDesign's shortcuts for drawing with the shape tools will be quite familiar if you're already working with Photoshop and/or Illustrator: the Alt/Option key to draw a shape (Illustrator) or selection (Photoshop) from the center, the Shift key to constrain aspect ratio, and the Spacebar to reposition an object as you draw.

InDesign's Pathfinder panel makes it possible to combine multiple shapes to achieve complex results that would be nearly impossible to draw by hand. The Pathfinder buttons in InDesign function similarly to the Illustrator Pathfinder's Shape Modes buttons. With Pathfinder buttons to add, subtract, intersect and exclude, there's virtually no limit to the shapes it allows you to create. The big difference between the Illustrator and InDesign Pathfinder tools is that Illustrator makes it possible to maintain each of the combined shapes as editable objects—objects created with InDesign's Pathfinder are indivisible.

Exercise 9.1: Using the InDesign Drawing Tools

This exercise walks you through drawing a complex shape with InDesign, and puts together the pieces that make it possible to create elaborate graphics and logos.

Before getting to the work of drawing, you'll first enlist InDesign to set up guides which will assist you in creating your design.

NOTE: The Create Guides dialog enables you to fit guides to either the page dimensions or the area defined by the page margins. Since the exercise document has no margins, either setting has the same effect.

1. Go to File > New > Document and choose Web from the Intent dropdown. Set the page size to 900 x 700 and the margins to 0. Save the document as **ex9_1.indd** in the chapter_9_exercises folder.

2. Go to Layout > Create Guides, and, when the dialog opens, check the Preview checkbox so you can see what the guides will look like on the page. Set the Number for both Rows and Columns to 4, and set both Gutter values to 0. Press Return/Enter to close the dialog.

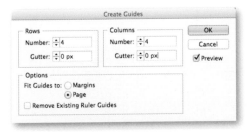

The Create Guides dialog enables you to set a custom grid of guides on your page. The image to the right shows the result of the settings in the dialog at the left.

3. Using the Selection tool, Double-Click the Fill swatch on the Control panel and choose any color from the Color Picker. We chose R: 255, G: 0, B: 0.

4. Press M on your keyboard to select the Rectangle tool, and then position the crosshair cursor at the intersection of the topmost horizontal guide and the leftmost vertical guide (X: 225 px, Y: 175 px.)

5. Hold down the mouse and start dragging down and to the right. Still holding the mouse, press the up arrow key on your keyboard once and then press the right arrow key once to create a total of four rectangles. Continue dragging to the intersection of the bottommost and rightmost guides, and then release the mouse.

6. Press V on your keyboard to switch to the Selection tool, and then press Ctrl+Shift+A/Command+Shift+A to deselect all. Select the upper right rectangle and click the yellow square at its upper right to turn on Corner Options. A yellow diamond appears at each corner of the rectangle. Hold down the Shift key, click and hold the diamond at the upper left corner, and drag to the right until the smart guide tooltip reads 40 px.

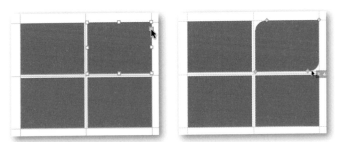

Click the yellow square at the upper right of a shape to turn on Corner Options. Hold down the Shift key and drag a diamond to shape an individual corner.

7. Select the lower right diamond on the same rectangle, hold down the Shift key, and drag left to set a radius of 40 px.

8. Select the lower right rectangle. If the Corner Options controls are visible on the Control panel, Alt+Click/Option+Click the ☐ icon. Otherwise, go to Object > Corner Options. When the dialog opens, ensure that the Make all settings the same link is unlinked. For the upper right and lower left corners, set the corner radius to 40 px, then click the ☐ ▼ dropdown and set the corner style to rounded. Set the upper left and lower right corner radius values to 0.

The Pathfinder Panel

The Pathfinder panel (Window > Object & Layout > Pathfinder) bundles a slew of useful commands into one nice, neat package. Although not identical, it bears a number of similarities to the Pathfinder panel in Illustrator. All the commands available through InDesign's Pathfinder panel can be found under the Object menu, but having them together on one panel can save you multiple trips to the Menu bar.

The Paths section of the panel makes it easy to connect points, open and close paths, and reverse path direction. The buttons in the Pathfinder section are great for slicing and dicing shapes. You can use them to create shapes that would be nearly impossible to draw by hand. The Convert Shape options enable you to change one shape into another, and provide a convenient visual reference. The Convert Point tools can be helpful when making adjustments to paths.

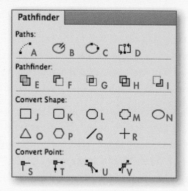

The Pathfinder panel.

A. Join Path: Connects two endpoints.
B. Open Path: Opens a closed path.
C. Close Path: Closes an open path.
D. Reverse Path: Reverses the direction of a path.
E. Add: Combines selected objects into one shape.
F. Subtract: Subtracts the frontmost objects from the backmost object.
G. Intersect: Creates a shape from the intersecting shape areas and deletes the rest.
H. Exclude Overlap: Creates a shape from all but the overlapping areas and deletes the rest.
I. Minus Back: Subtracts the backmost objects from the front object.
J. Rectangle: Converts the selected shape to a rectangle.
K. Rounded Rectangle: Converts the selected shape to a rounded rectangle based on the size of the current Corner Options radius.
L. Beveled Rectangle: Converts the selected shape to a beveled rectangle based on the size of the current Corner Options radius.

M. Inverse Rounded Rectangle: Converts the selected shape to an inverse rounded rectangle based on the size of the current Corner Options radius.
N. Ellipse: Converts the selected shape to an ellipse.
O. Triangle: Converts the selected shape to a triangle.
P. Polygon: Converts the selected shape to a polygon based on the current Polygon tool settings.
Q. Line: Converts the selected shape to a line.
R. Orthogonal Line: Converts the selected shape to a horizontal or vertical line.
S. Plain: Changes the selected point to have no direction handles.
T. Corner: Changes the selected point to have independent direction handles.
U. Smooth: Changes the selected point to be a smooth curve with connected adjustment handles.
V. Symmetrical: Changes the selected point to be a smooth curve with direction handles of equal length.

The Control Panel Transform Controls

To rotate or scale an object by a specific amount, you can use the Control panel Transform controls. If you click directly in a value field, you can use the up and down arrows to the left of the field or on your keyboard to incrementally increase and decrease the value. In Adobe applications, the up and down arrow trick works in 85% of the fields in dialogs and panels. Alternatively, you can enter a field value manually. To use a unit of measure other than the document default, type the unit abbreviation after the value: i or " = inches, px = pixels, pt = points, p = picas, mm = millimeters, c = centimeters. When using the "p" for picas and points, the placement of the letter determines the way the value is interpreted:

5p1 = 5 picas and 1 pt
p5 = 5 pts
5p = 5 picas

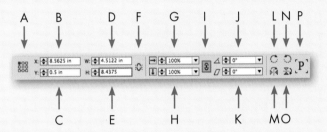

A. Reference point proxy

B. X coordinate based on selected reference point

C. Y coordinate based on selected reference point

D. Width

E. Height

F. Constrain width and height

G. Scale X: scales horizontal percentage

H. Scale Y: scales vertical percentage

I. Constrain proportions for scaling

J. Rotation angle

K. Shear X angle

L. Rotate 90° clockwise

M. Flip horizontal

N. Rotate 90° counter-clockwise

O. Flip vertical

P. Transform proxy: The P rotates and flips to reflect the transform on the object

You can set options for the individual corners of an object in the Corner Options dialog.

9. Select the upper left rectangle and round its upper right and lower left corners to a radius of 40 px.

10. Select the lower left rectangle and round its upper left and lower right corners to 40 px. Save your file.

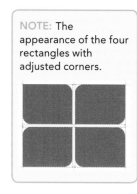

11. Press Ctrl+A/Command+A to select all four rectangles, and then press Ctrl+C/Command+C to copy them. Press Alt+Shift+Ctrl+V/Option+Shift+Command+V or Right-Click/Ctrl+Click and select Paste in Place from the contextual menu. With the duplicate rectangles still selected, click the arrow next to the Fill swatch on the Control panel and change the color to [Paper].

12. Deselect All, and then select the upper right and lower left white rectangles with the Selection tool. On the Control panel, check to be sure that the center point is selected in the Reference Point proxy and that the Constrain proportions for scaling link is locked for the scaling percentages. Enter 40 in the Scale X Percentage field and press Tab to uniformly scale the white rectangles and to center them on top of the colored rectangles.

13. Select the upper left rectangle, enter 60 in the Scale X field on the Control panel, and press Tab to scale the rectangle to 60% of its size. The white rectangle should be centered on the rectangle below it.

14. Select the lower right rectangle and scale it to 60% as well.

15. Select the Rectangle tool and click once on the document. When the Rectangle dialog opens, enter 10 for width and 190 for height, and then click OK or Enter/Return to exit the dialog.

16. Switch to the Selection tool and drag the rectangle to center it vertically between the rectangles on the left and the rectangles on the right. Mouse over a corner of the rectangle, and, when the cursor changes to a double-sided arrow, drag to rotate it to the left by 50°. Alternatively, enter 50 in the Rotation Angle field on the Control panel.

InDesign's drawing tools enable you to create and precisely transform shapes.

17. Hold down the Shift key and click on each of the four colored rectangles to select them. Open the Pathfinder panel by clicking the ▣ icon in the Panel Dock, or go to Window > Object & Layout > Pathfinder.

18. Click the first icon ( ) in the Pathfinder section of the panel (Add) to join the rectangles into a compound shape. Then click on the pasteboard to deselect it.

19. Shift+Click to select each of the five white rectangles (including the skinny one), and then join them using the Pathfinder Add command.

20. Select both the colored and the white compound paths, and click the second icon ( ) in the Pathfinder section of the panel (Subtract). The white shapes are subtracted from the colored shapes to create a new compound shape. Save the file and keep it open for the next exercise.

The moral of this lesson is that you don't have to be able to draw to create graphics with InDesign. If you can visually break objects into shapes, you can "draw." So let yourself play and see what kind of wonderful things you come up with.

The InDesign Color Palette

If you're looking for colors in InDesign, don't be fooled by the meager selection of colors in the Swatches panel. A bit misleading at first glance, the Swatches panel actually gives you access to a complete collection of swatch books with thousands of colors to choose from. While the swatch book colors are CMYK and are intended for use in print, they can easily be converted to RGB in the process of adding them to the Swatches panel. The color books can be likened to the sample paint chips you find at a hardware store when shopping for paint. Regardless of what you see on your screen, if you use the calibrated color book colors in your print document, your print provider will know the colors to match. Given the wide variability in color display from one computer monitor to another, the objective color standard provided by the color books is critically important to ensuring predictable output for print. In contrast, when creating documents for electronic delivery, you have greater freedom to choose any color you can create. With that flexibility in mind, for interactive design, you can take full advantage of the spectrum of color available through the Color panel. The Color panel enables you to choose your color model, build color by number, or visually select colors from a variety of color ramps.

InDesign's color resources don't stop with the Swatches and Color panels, though. Tucked away and out of view is the Kuler panel, with rich palettes containing enough color choices to boggle the mind. The Kuler panel (Window > Extensions > Kuler) provides access to thousands of 5-color themes shared by an online community of designers. A trip to the Kuler panel is like stepping into a kaleidoscopic time warp. Minutes melt away as worlds of color unfold. In other words, give yourself some time to play. Kuler is live and interactive, and you can transfer its colors directly to your Swatches panel. The colors and themes are completely editable, so you can use them as a jumping off point for themes of your own. If you'd rather "do it yourself," its Create panel lets you do just that, with a selection of six color harmony rules to assist in developing your palettes. Of course, if you're so inclined, you too can easily share your color themes with the Kuler community.

Exercise 9.2: Playing with Color

This exercise will familiarize you with the color resources in InDesign, and teach you how to use them. Perhaps even more important, it'll give you a chance to indulge in playing with color, just for the sheer fun of it.

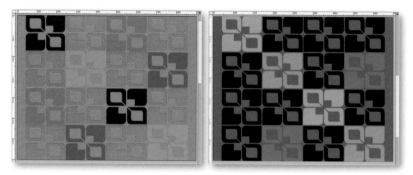

The palette of colors you can create in InDesign is virtually unlimited!

1. To get a sense of where this lesson is going, feel free to open **ex9_2_end.indd** from the chapter_9_exercises folder and check it out. In fact, if you want to jump straight to playing with color and don't want to mess with setting up the document, save it as ex9_2.indd and skip to step 21 of this exercise on page 139. Otherwise, if you don't have the file from the previous lesson open, go to the chapter_9_exercises folder and open **ex9_2_start.indd**. Whichever file is open, save it as ex9_2.indd.

   First, you'll set up a grid pattern with the shape you created in the previous lesson. You'll then save the page with the grid to a master page, so you can make as many pages to play with as you like. Then you'll get busy with color.

2. Switch to the Selection tool and, if necessary, unlock the Constrain proportions for width and height link in the Control panel. Select the shape on the page and change the width to 200 px and the height to 172 px in the Control panel.

3. Go to View > Grids & Guides > Delete All Guides on Spread.

4. With the shape still selected, select the upper left square of the Control panel Reference Point proxy and enter 0 for both the X and Y values. This will position the shape at the upper left corner of the page.

5. Go to Edit > Step and Repeat, and, when the dialog opens, check the Preview checkbox. Set the number of columns and rows to 4, the Vertical Offset to 177 px and the Horizontal Offset to 205 px. Check the Create as a grid checkbox to create a uniformly spaced 4 x 4 grid, and then click OK.

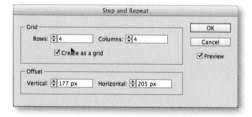

The Step and Repeat command enables you to duplicate objects with a specified offset.

6. Press Ctrl+G/Command+G to group the objects and, in the Align section of the Control panel, select the Align to Page option from the dropdown. Click the Align vertical centers and Align horizontal centers buttons to center your design, and then press Ctrl+Shift+G/Command+Shift+G to ungroup the objects.

TIP: If the Alignment tools aren't visible on the Control panel, go to Window > Object & Layout > Align to open the Align panel.

Align horizontal centers

Align to Page

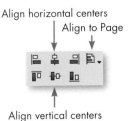

Align vertical centers

The Align controls on the Control panel.

7. To create a rectangle that will serve as the background, press M to select the Rectangle tool, and click once on the page. In the Rectangle dialog, enter 900 px for Width and 700 px for Height and then press Enter/Return to close the dialog.

8. If necessary, add a fill to your rectangle, and you'll see that it covers the other shapes. Press Shift+Ctrl+[/Shift +Command+[to send the rectangle to the bottom of the object stack. Alternatively, you could Right-Click/Ctrl+Click and choose Arrange > Send to Back from the contextual menu. Use the Align controls to center the rectangle on the page. Save your document.

Next, you'll start building your color palette from the color books, and then set up the color pattern for the design.

9. Click the ▦ icon in the Panel Dock or go to Window > Color > Swatches. To better see all the colors you'll be adding to the Swatches panel, choose Small Swatch from the panel menu. The swatches should appear as a collection of color squares, rather than as a list of named colors.

10. Next, choose New Color Swatch from the panel menu. From the Color Mode dropdown, choose Pantone Solid Coated. When the color book swatches appear, scroll through the list to find a color you like and Double-Click to select it. We chose Adobe Red: Pantone 485.

The name of the color book you choose will appear in the Color Mode dropdown.

11. If you wish to convert the color to RGB, choose RGB from the Color Mode dropdown. Ensure that Process is selected in the Color Type dropdown, and click Add to add the color to your swatches. Choose five more colors from any combination of the color books and add them to your swatches.

IMPORTANT! Do not choose randomly from the color books if you are creating CMYK documents for print. This workflow is for RGB documents only!

12. Click the second shape in the first row with the Selection tool. Hold the Shift key, and click every other shape as shown in the screenshot on the following page.

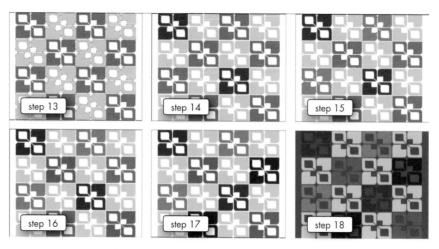

The color progression represented in steps 12-18.

13. Press Ctrl+G/Command+G to group the selected shapes, and then choose a fill color from one of the swatches you added. Feel free to try some colors we used, just to get things set up (R=192 G=196 B=204.)

NOTE: Feel free to work with a simpler 3-color palette and skip steps 14–17.

14. Deselect All, and then select the first shape in the first row and the third shape in the third row. Group them and apply a different fill color (R=88 G=69 B=99.)

15. Deselect All, and then select the third shape in the first row and the first shape in the third row. Group them and apply a third fill color (R=116 G=142 B=149.)

16. Deselect All, and then select the second shape in the second row and the fourth shape in the fourth row. Group them and apply a fourth fill color (R=114 G=107 B=129.)

17. Deselect All, and then select the fourth shape in the second row and the second shape in the fourth row. Group them and apply a fifth fill color (R=51 G=63 B=78.)

18. Deselect All. Click just to the left or right of the shapes to click on and select the background rectangle. Apply the sixth fill color (R=73 G=98 B=108.)

Don't get crazy about getting your colors perfect at this point. You've just begun to explore, and you'll be expanding your color selection shortly.

Before building out your palette, you'll first save your layout to a master page so you can create multiple pages for experimentation.

19. With page 1 highlighted in the Pages panel, from the panel menu, go to Master Pages > Save as Master. InDesign adds a new master page with a default name of B-Master, and it becomes the active page in the Pages panel.

NOTE: You need to Double-Click on page 1 to make it the active page in the document window, or else the pages you add will be added to the master page spread.

20. Double-Click on the page 1 icon in the Pages panel, and then select Insert Pages from the panel menu. Enter 3 in the Pages field, select B-Master from the Master dropdown, and then press Enter/Return to close the dialog. InDesign adds three color-coded pages to your document, each with your shape grid on it.

The Insert Pages dialog can be accessed from the Pages panel menu.

21. To unlock the master page objects so you can change the object colors, Right-Click/Ctrl+Click page 2 in the Pages panel and choose Override All Master Page Items (Alt+Shift+Ctrl+L/Option+Shift+Command+L). Do the same to unlock the objects on pages 3 and 4, and you'll be ready to go.

NOTE: When working with master pages, it's generally best to override page items on an item-by-item basis. The file for this exercise is a specialized case.

The sheer number of colors in the color books can be a little daunting, particularly when it comes to trying to choose an entire palette. As an alternative, Kuler is a phenomenal tool for finding ready-made palettes or for providing a starting point to create a palette of your own.

22. Go to Window > Extensions > Kuler, and, if necessary, click the Browse button at the top of the panel. Eye candy, right? This is just the beginning! Click the ◀ ▶ buttons at the upper left of the panel to scroll through the themes. If you want to look further, click the dropdowns just above the color swatches to choose a different theme category and sorting filter. When you find a theme you like, click to highlight it, and then click the Add selected theme to swatches button ( ) at the bottom of the panel. Add at least three themes to your swatches.

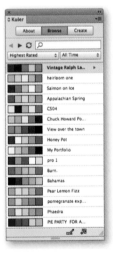

The Kuler panel is a feast for the eyes, and an awesome design tool for selecting colors.

TIP To access Kuler, you must be connected to the internet.

23. With one of your themes selected in the Kuler panel, click the Edit theme in Create panel button ( ) at the bottom of the panel.

If you've worked with Live Color in Illustrator, the Kuler Create panel should look familiar. You can use it to modify colors in a selected theme, or you can develop a theme from the fill or stroke color of a selected object. The Selected Rule dropdown lets you choose from six color harmony rules: Analogous, Monochromatic, Triad, Complementary, Compound, and Shades. You can also customize a color combination independent of the rules.

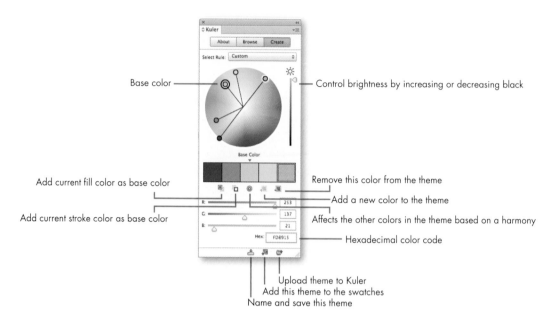

Base color

Control brightness by increasing or decreasing black

Add current fill color as base color

Remove this color from the theme

Add a new color to the theme

Add current stroke color as base color

Affects the other colors in the theme based on a harmony

R 253
G 137
B 21
Hex: FD8915

Hexadecimal color code

Upload theme to Kuler
Add this theme to the swatches
Name and save this theme

The Kuler Create panel.

24. Select any of the markers in the color wheel and drag to see the change in color. If you come up with a theme you'd like to keep, press the Add this theme to swatches button at the bottom of the panel.

25. Select a color other than the existing base color from the swatches under the color wheel, and then click the Affects the other colors in the theme based on a harmony button. This makes your selected color the new base color.

26. Select a color harmony rule from the Select Rule dropdown to create a new color theme. Then, save it to the Swatches panel.

27. Double-Click on page 2 in the Pages panel to make it the active page in the document window, and go to town! Just play for a bit and enjoy. When you've finished playing, there's even more to explore.

NOTE: For each new page of shapes, be sure to unlock all the objects on the page before trying to play with the colors. Choose Override All Master Page Items from the Pages panel menu.

28. Double-Click on page 3. After unlocking the master page items, press Ctrl+A/ Command+A to select everything on the page. Hold the Shift key and click the background rectangle with the Selection tool to deselect it. Press Ctrl+Shift+G/ Command+Shift+G to ungroup the shapes and then go to Window > Object & Layout > Pathfinder. Click the Add button to join all the shapes into one large compound shape.

29. With the new shape selected, go to Window > Color > Gradient or click the ▆ icon on the Panel Dock. Click just below the color ramp to activate the gradient and fill the shape. Select each of the gradient markers in turn, open the Swatches panel, and Alt+Click/Option+Click a color to assign it to the marker. Click just below the color ramp in the Gradient panel to add another color marker, and then assign a color to it as well. Choose Radial from the Type dropdown and drag the markers to shift the radius of the gradient colors. Drag the diamonds to shift the transition point between colors. When you're happy with your gradient, choose New Gradient Swatch from the Swatches panel menu. Name the gradient according to the colors you selected (RedPurpleRadial, for example) and click OK to add it to Swatches panel.

30. Select the Gradient tool (G) from the Tool panel, position the cursor in the center of the shape, and drag it to one of the corners. Experiment with dragging the gradient different lengths and from different starting points in the shape. Select Linear from the Type dropdown to see how it changes the look of the design.

31. Select the background rectangle on the page and create a gradient fill for it. If you settled on a Linear gradient for the compound shape, try a radial gradient for the rectangle. Add the gradient to the Swatches panel.

    Depending on your color selection, this could create something beautiful or a visual nightmare. Just remember, for now, it's about play and discovery.

32. Select the compound shape, click the arrow to the right of the Stroke swatch on the Control panel, and choose a stroke color. Adjust the stroke weight as you see fit.

    OK, we know we're pushing the boundaries of good design, or maybe we just made a plunge over the edge, but this is about the color. The point is to explore possibilities that you might not otherwise give yourself the freedom to explore. So let go of the preconceptions and have fun with it!

33. With the compound shape still selected, click the *fx.* button on the Control panel and choose Basic Feather from the Effects dropdown. When the Effects dialog opens, set Feather Width to 12 px, Choke to 21% and Corners to Rounded. Check the Preview checkbox and adjust the settings to your taste. Don't click OK yet.

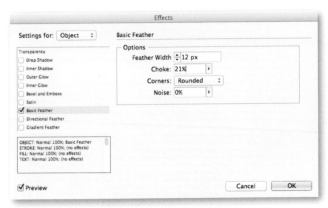

You can feather objects using the Effects dialog.

34. Click Transparency from the category list at the left of the panel and explore the different Blending modes. When you find a combination you like, click OK to close the dialog.

The color possibilities available in InDesign are truly
unlimited, so indulge yourself by taking some time to play.

You're probably starting to get the idea that the color variations available to you in InDesign are endless. And the truth is, there's still more. The Color panel lets you make precise refinements using separate color channel and tint controls for RGB, CMYK, and Lab color. You can also capture color from anywhere on your page with the Eyedropper tool (I). Two other little known InDesign color creation features are the Mixed Ink and Mixed Ink Group options, which let you develop individual colors or an entire palette by combining selected process and spot inks.

The next section of the exercise will familiarize you with these options.

35. Choose New Color Swatch from the Swatches panel menu, and then choose PANTONE+Solid Coated from the Color Mode dropdown. If you have a particular pantone color you need to find, you can type its number in the PANTONE field. Type in "2622" and click the Add button. Then, type in "3302" click Add and then click Done to close the dialog.

36. Choose New Mixed Ink Group from the Swatches panel menu. When the dialog opens, click in the square to the left of PANTONE 2622 C and PANTONE 3302 C to select the spot colors for the Mixed Ink Group. For both colors, enter 10 for the Initial ink percentage, 10 for Repeat, and 5 for Increment. Note that the number of swatches to be generated is 121. Press Preview Swatches to see the palette that will be generated, and then click OK to close the dialog and add the colors to the Swatches panel.

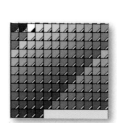
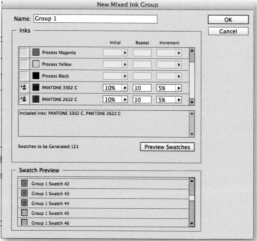

InDesign can generate custom palettes for you through the Mixed Ink Group dialog. Mixed Inks and Mixed Ink Groups can only be created using combinations of spot inks and the four process inks (CMYK).

Since the Swatches you just created were generated from spot inks and your document is destined for digital publication, you'll convert the colors to RGB.

37. Select the first spot color in the Swatches panel, hold down the Shift key, and click on the second spot color. Choose Swatch Options from the panel menu. Choose RGB from the Color Mode dropdown and Process from the Color Type dropdown. Click OK to convert the spot colors to RGB.

The mixed ink swatches are converted to CMYK when you convert the spot colors to RGB. Now you'll convert the mixed ink swatches to RGB too.

38. Select the first mixed ink color, hold down the Shift key, and select the last. Convert the Color Mode from CMYK to RGB in the Swatch Options dialog and click OK.

39. Double-Click on page 4 in the Pages panel to make it the active page in the document window, and use your color group swatches to color the pattern.

   The Color panel (Window > Color > Color) displays either the stroke or fill color of the selected object, depending on which one is active in the Tool panel. From the Color panel, you can change the color tint by clicking in the Tint Ramp, dragging the slider, or entering a value in the Tint Percentage field. If you're using the Color panel, it's likely you're looking to choose colors rather than to adjust a tint. For print, you're better off sticking with color book colors, since they're calibrated to an objective standard. For interactive and web design, the Color panel gives you access to a huge spectrum of color in a conveniently compact package.

40. With one of the object groups selected on the page, click the 🎨 icon in the Panel Dock or go to Window > Color > Color. Choose RGB from the Color panel menu to bring up the RGB color ramp. Select the value in the R, G, or B field and use the up and down arrows on your keyboard to change the value in the color channel incrementally.

   Alternatively, you can type a value in any of the fields, or click the color ramp to select a different color. You can also drag the individual color channel sliders. To choose a lighter or darker color, hold down the Shift key and drag one of the sliders to move all the sliders together. Right-Click/Ctrl+Click the ramp for quick access to the panel menu, and to add the selected color to the Swatches panel. Alt+Click/Option+Click the ramp to assign the selected color to the stroke if the fill is active or vice versa. Shift+Click the ramp to cycle through the RGB, CMYK, and Lab Color models.

41. Play to your heart's content, and, when finished, save and close your masterpiece to complete the exercise and the chapter.

NOTE: A number of the color books available from the New Color Swatch dialog are for spot colors (the Pantone Solid color books, for example) and you don't want to select them randomly since each spot color represents an additional plate that could add substantial cost to your print job.

While useful in creating RGB palettes, Mixed Ink and Mixed Ink Groups are especially relevant for print. They make it possible to create an entire palette by combining a spot color with another spot or any of the process colors. So, even with a 2-color job, you can have a broad spectrum of colors to use in your design.

CHAPTER SUMMARY

In this chapter, you dug deeper into InDesign's graphic capabilities and had an opportunity to play with shape and color. You learned to develop a color palette using:

- The Swatches panel
- Color books
- Kuler
- The Color Panel
- Mixed Ink Groups

You also became more familiar with master pages, the Pathfinder panel, and the Control panel transform controls. You learned how to:

- Save a page as a master page
- Override master page items
- Change the view of the Swatches panel
- Save and create themes in Kuler
- Work with blending modes
- Create gradients
- Work with the Basic Feather effect

Above all else, hopefully you had a lot of fun!

That wraps up the section on document layout and navigation. From text flow fundamentals to an exploration of InDesign's graphical capabilities, you now have an arsenal of tools to serve you in your work with InDesign whatever your output destination. Now that you have a solid foundation, the rest of the book focuses on interactive development and digital publishing.

With hyperlinks, cross-references, footnotes, and tables of contents you learned all about document structures that can add some level of interactivity and navigation to digital documents. As cool as these interactive features are, they have nothing on buttons! Buttons hold the key to interactivity and the next section of the book will divulge all their secrets.

Part 3

BUTTONS

For output to Interactive PDF, SWF and DPS, buttons are at the very heart of interactivity, and this section will teach you all about them. You'll learn about button appearances, button states, image-based buttons, multi-object buttons, button triggering events, and button actions. By the time you're finished, you'll be a button-making maestro, creating buttons for everything from basic interactivity, to image galleries, to popup tooltips, and more.

Chapter 10

ABOUT BUTTONS

Just wait until you see what you can do with buttons in InDesign. Not just for navigation, buttons open the door to creation of a rich, interactive user experience. This chapter lays the foundation for all the work you'll be doing with buttons—for SWF, Interactive PDF and DPS output—introducing you to button events, button states and appearances, and button actions. You'll become familiar with the Sample Buttons and Forms Library, learn to modify sample buttons, and, in the process, gain experience working with both the Layers panel and effects.

Introduction

Long requested and much anticipated, it's now possible to create and export Interactive PDF forms directly from InDesign! This is a major development and one that has been greeted with great enthusiasm by many a designer. But this is a chapter about buttons. "Why?" you may ask, is it starting off with a discussion of forms?

NOTE: InDesign's form fields are for Interactive PDF export only, while InDesign buttons function in Interactive PDF, SWF and DPS. Be aware though that On Roll Over and On Roll Off events are not applicable to tablet and device destinations.

Buttons and form fields share certain characteristics and they also share the Buttons and Forms panel in InDesign CC. This being the case, a discussion of one demands at least a nod to the other. Both buttons and forms are rich topics however, with each deserving its due. Therefore, this section of the book is about buttons, with forms to follow in a section of their own in Chapter 18, starting on page 261.

Anatomy of a Button

When you convert an object to a button in InDesign, you magically imbue it with superpowers. All of a sudden, it is transformed from a static graphic object that sits passively on a page, to an object with the ability to initiate and respond to a host of interactions. InDesign buttons can be made to display various appearances; navigate from one page of a document to another; play and stop sounds, video, animations; and more. Converting an object to a button can also enable it to respond to commands from other buttons, dramatically expanding the possibilities for interactivity.

There are three aspects of a button that combine to create its functionality. First is the button appearance, the aspect of the button actually seen by the viewer. Second is the mouse interaction, or event to which the button is programmed to respond. Last of course is the action the button initiates.

The area of the button that detects user interaction is called a hotspot. In InDesign, the button hotspot is defined by the rectangular bounding box of the button graphics, and includes whatever empty space is in the rectangle. In the case of a round button, for example, the hotspot includes the empty corners of the rectangle that encloses the button.

The hotspot area of the round button shown above is defined by its rectangular bounding box, indicated by the blue dashed line.

Button Events

Button functionality is triggered by user interaction. The interactions are referred to as events. InDesign buttons can be made to respond to six different events:

- **On Release or Tap:** The button action is triggered when the mouse is positioned over the button hotspot and released or the button is tapped. It's good practice to apply button actions to the on release event as opposed to a click. This makes it possible for users to change their minds after pressing but before releasing the mouse. In such a case, on release enables a user to drag the clicked mouse away from the button without triggering an action.

- **On Click:** The button action is triggered when the mouse is positioned over the button hotspot and clicked. The user needn't release the mouse in order to trigger the action.
- **On Roll Over:** The button action is triggered when the mouse is moved onto the button hotspot.
- **On Roll Off:** The button action is triggered when the mouse is rolled off of the button hotspot.
- **On Focus (PDF only):** The button action is triggered when the cursor is tabbed into the object.
- **On Blur (PDF only):** The button action is triggered when the cursor is tabbed out of the object.

Button Appearances

A change of appearance when the user's mouse is dragged onto or off of a button, or when a button is clicked, tapped, or released, can provide valuable visual feedback and create an enhanced user experience.

Typically, a button will be designed with at least two, and sometimes up to four, visual states:

- **Normal:** The default appearance of the button in its static state on the page.
- **Rollover:** The appearance of the button when the mouse is moved into the button hotspot.
- **Click/Down:** The appearance of the button when the mouse is clicked or the button is held down.
- **Disabled:** The appearance of the button when the button is unavailable for interaction.

InDesign makes it possible to design buttons with as few as one, and as many as three, different button appearances: Normal, Rollover, and Click.

Button Actions

A button makes certain functions available to the user. In InDesign, these functions are referred to as actions. Actions are assigned to the triggering events: On Release or Tap, On Click, On Roll Over, On Roll Off, On Focus, and On Blur. Some of InDesign's button actions apply across the board to SWF, PDF, and DPS documents while others apply to a specific platform only.

We'll be digging more deeply into the intricacies of button actions a little later but first, let's take a look at the Sample Buttons And Forms library.

Exploring the Sample Buttons And Forms Library

InDesign comes with a Sample Buttons And Forms library that contains a collection of pre-made buttons with actions and multiple visual states already defined. To access the Sample Buttons And Forms library, with the Interactive workspace selected, go to Window > Sample Buttons And Forms.

The Sample Buttons And Forms library contains an assortment of checkboxes and radio buttons, a pair of pre-populated month and day combo boxes, two navigation bars and eight button styles in five colors each. You can edit both the appearance and function of the sample form fields and buttons, so you're not limited by the preset definitions. If the samples don't meet your needs, you can easily use them as the jumping off point for creating an endless variety of form elements and buttons customized to your needs.

Exercise 10.1: Exploring Sample Buttons

NOTE: For more information on audio and incorporating it into your InDesign documents, see Chapter 31: Audio & Video Overlays, starting on page 471.

ALERT: Be sure to save the file to the chapter_10_exercises folder or your sounds will not play when you add the button action.

1. Open **ex10_1_start.indd** from the chapter_10_exercises folder.

    The file contains two placed audio files at the lower left of the page.

2. Check the Workspace Switcher at the upper right of your screen to ensure that the DigiPub workspace you created starting on page 34 is selected.

3. Go to Window > Sample Buttons And Forms to open the Sample Buttons And Forms library.

4. Select button 130 in the library panel and drag it onto your document. Note that the button icon (🖐) appears at the lower right of the button. (You may need to zoom in to see it.) Collapse the Sample Buttons And Forms library.

5. Go to File > Save As and save your document as ex10_1.indd in the chapter_10_exercises folder.

6. Click 🖱 in the Panel Dock at the right of your screen or go to Window > Interactive > Buttons and Forms to open the Buttons and Forms panel.

7. With the Selection tool, select and then Double-Click the button on the document to display the Appearance states in the Buttons and Forms panel.

    Note that the button has been given a default name.

8. Change the name of the button to "sampleBtn130" in the Name field at the top of the panel and press Enter/Return.

The Buttons and Forms panel display for sampleBtn130.
The sample button is built with both Normal and
Rollover states and has a default Go To URL action.

9. Click back and forth between the word "[Rollover]" and the word "[Normal]" in the panel, and watch the change in the button on the document. When you've seen both button states, be sure that you end with the Rollover state active and highlighted in the panel.

10. Note that the On Release or Tap event is selected in the Event dropdown, and the button has a Go To URL action applied to it. To make the action work, enter a complete web address in the URL field. We entered http://www.interactive-indesign.com.

11. Click the Event dropdown and select the On Roll Over event. The panel displays the message "[No Actions Added]."

12. Click the Add New Action button () near the top of the panel to the right of the word "Actions", and select Sound from the popup menu. The Sound action appears in the Buttons and Forms panel with the **click.mp3** audio file automatically assigned.

NOTE: InDesign automatically selected the **click.mp3** audio file because it was first alphabetically in the list of audio files available in the document.

13. Click the Sound dropdown and select **btnOver.mp3** to replace the audio file.

14. Note that Play is the default Options selection. Click the Options dropdown to see the other choices, and then ensure that Play remains the selected option.

The Buttons and Forms panel showing the Sound action set to play the btnOver.mp3 audio file on roll over.

15. Choose On Release or Tap from the Event dropdown and Sound from the Add New Action popup. The Sound dropdown is automatically populated by the **click.mp3** file and Play is automatically selected in the Options dropdown.

Multiple actions can be applied to a single event, as shown for the On Release or Tap Event for sampleBtn130.

Provided you have speakers or a headset, and an installed browser with an internet connection, you can preview your button, hear the sounds you just added, and follow the added URL.

ALERT: If the preview doesn't appear in the Preview panel, click the ▶ button at the lower left of the panel to refresh the view.

16. Click the Preview Spread button (▣) at the bottom left of the Buttons and Forms panel, or press Shift+Ctrl+Enter/Command+Shift+Return to open the Preview panel.

17. The button should appear in the Preview panel, but may be too small for you to easily see the rollover changes. To enlarge the Preview panel, mouse over its lower left corner. When the cursor changes to a double-sided diagonal arrow (⬋), click and drag down and to the left to expand the panel.

The Preview panel displaying sampleBtn130 in Preview Spread Mode.

18. Rollover the button to hear the sound and see the drop shadow rollover effect. Click the button and note that the sound plays when the mouse is released rather than pressed.

19. When your browser opens to the URL you entered, close it and return to InDesign. Click the double arrows at the upper right of the Preview panel to collapse it.

20. Open the Sample Buttons And Forms Library and drag button 101, the first navigation bar, onto your document. If the library is no longer available under the Window menu, you can access it from the Buttons and Forms panel menu.

    The navbar is actually a collection of objects. You'll group them to make them easier to manage.

21. With the newly placed objects still selected on your document, press Ctrl+G/ Command+G to group them (or go to Object > Group.)

    The round button and the first button in the navbar are both set to display the Rollover state. InDesign provides a convenient menu command to set all your buttons back to the Normal state, all at the same time.

22. Return to the Buttons and Forms panel and click the menu button (▾≣) at the upper right of the panel. Watch for the change in the button and navbar on the page and click Reset All Buttons to Normal State. The buttons should all display the Normal state appearance.

    You might find it easier to see the appearance of the button states in the Buttons and Forms panel if your enlarge the button thumbnails. This too can be done very simply.

23. From the Buttons and Forms panel menu, choose Panel Options. Click the radio button for the button Thumbnail Size that works best for you, and then click OK.

To change the size of the button thumbnails, choose
Panel Options from the Buttons and Forms panel menu.

Buttons can be converted back to plain objects with just a click. The converted object takes on the appearance of the active button state, and the contents of any other states are discarded.

24. On your document, Alt-Drag/Option-Drag sampleBtn130 with the Selection tool to duplicate it.

25. With the duplicate button selected, click the Convert to Object icon (➡️) at the bottom right of the Buttons and Forms panel. Click OK in the warning alert and note that you have just that easily, stripped that button of its superpowers. You've also made the graphic(s) available for inclusion in other buttons.

You can just as easily convert nearly any object to a button.

26. With the button graphic still selected, convert it to a new button by clicking the Convert to Button icon (➡️) at the lower right of the Buttons and Forms panel.

By default, your new button has a Normal state only, and no actions applied. Next, you'll add a Rollover state, which you'll give a distinct appearance in order to make your button more user-friendly.

27. To add a Rollover state, simply click the [Rollover] entry in the Appearance section of the Buttons and Forms panel.

The new Rollover state duplicated the Normal state appearance. Next, you'll make some changes to the Rollover state appearance to provide your audience with visual feedback.

28. With the Selection tool, Double-Click your new button, and then Double-Click the Fill swatch on the Control panel at the top of your screen to open the Color Picker.

A button acts like an envelope wrapped around the graphic objects that give it its appearance. A Double-Click takes you into the button envelope to access the objects inside.

29. Choose a new color and note that the Add Swatch button at the right of the panel is set by default to add an RGB swatch—as is appropriate for a digital document. Click the button to add the swatch and then click OK to close the dialog.

The new color is applied to the Rollover state of the button. Because you saved the new color to a swatch, it's easy to apply the same color to the Normal state.

30. In the Buttons and Forms panel, select the Normal state and Double-Click the button on the document with the Selection tool to access the Normal state graphic.

31. On the Control panel, click the right-facing arrow next to the Fill swatch to open the Swatches panel (▪▶).

32. Select the Rollover state swatch color you just saved to apply it to the Normal state of the button.

33. Save and keep the file open for the next exercise.

Editing Button Appearances Using Effects

Effects, which also include blending modes and transparency settings, influence the way an object visually interacts with other objects in a document. A robust set of features, InDesign effects include many of the same effects found in Photoshop and Illustrator. You can apply InDesign effects to an object, the object stroke, the object fill, and/or the text inside the object.

The Control panel features a set of effects tools that are grouped together for easy access. When applying effects from the Control panel, first click the Apply Effects To button and then choose the aspect of the object you would like to affect.

Click the Apply Effects to: button on the Control panel
to specify the target of an effect before you apply it.

To apply a Drop Shadow effect that uses preset shadow settings, simply click the Drop Shadow button (▢) on the Control panel. The Drop Shadow button acts as a toggle and displays its on-state (▣) when an object with a drop shadow is selected. To remove a drop shadow without straying from the Control panel, select the aspect of the object from which you want the shadow removed from the Apply Effects to dropdown, and then click the Drop Shadow button.

To adjust opacity from the Control panel, either click the right-facing arrow of the Transparency field and drag the slider, or type a value in the text field (▢ 100% ▶).

While InDesign provides several places where you can modify object opacity and blending mode, the setting controls for effects such as Drop Shadow and Outer Glow can only be accessed through the Effects dialog box. Click the *fx.* button (FX for Effects) on the Control panel or at the bottom of the Effects panel to open the Effects options menu and select from the list of available options. Alternatively, you can go to Object > Effects and make a selection from there that will then take you to the Effects dialog.

While the Effects tools on the Control panel provide quick and easy access, InDesign also provides a dedicated Effects panel. The Effects panel offers a more complete visual read of what's actually going on with an object than you can get from the Control panel. It's a particularly useful tool when working with buttons and multi-state objects. To access the Effects panel, go to Window > Effects or click the *fx.* icon in the Panel Dock.

The Effects panel displaying the settings for sampleBtn130.

You can use the blending mode and transparency controls at the top of the Effects panel to adjust transparency and blending mode for any of the four object variations. Choose either Object, Stroke, Fill, or Text; then select from the blending mode dropdown and make any desired opacity adjustments.

Access blending mode options from the dropdown at the top of the Effects panel.

The Effects panel also provides great visual feedback. If you mouse over the *fx.* icon at the right of the Object, Stroke, Fill, or Text entries in the panel, a tool tip pops up to tell you exactly which effects are applied to the object that's selected.

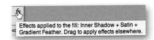

When you mouse over the *fx.* icon at the right of the Effects panel entries, a tooltip appears that details the applied effects.

The Effects panel also makes it easy to move an effect from one aspect of an object to another. For example, to move an effect from the object fill to its stroke, just drag the *fx* icon at the right of the Fill row up to the Stroke row. To duplicate an effect instead of moving it, Alt+Click/Option+Click and drag it to another aspect of the object.

Exercise 10.2: Button Editing & the Effects Panel

1. If you kept the file open from the last exercise, you're good to go. Otherwise, open **ex10_2_start.indd**. Save your open file as ex10_2.indd.

2. With sampleBtn130 (the green button) selected on the page, go to Window > Effects to open the Effects panel or click the *fx.* icon in the Panel Dock.

3. If you see the word "Group" displayed on the first line in the Effects panel, Double-Click the button on the page. The panel display should update to reflect characteristics of the object, rather than the group. If necessary, click the arrow to the left of the word "Object" in the panel to display the object details.

Working with the Effects Dialog

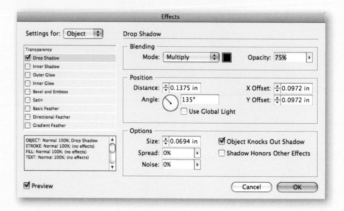

If you're already familiar with Photoshop or Illustrator, this dialog should make you feel right at home. If not, it's really pretty simple to navigate once you get the hang of it. The dialog is essentially split into two sections, with the list on the left providing access to the controls on the right for the different effects. The thing to be aware of is that you must click the effect name, rather than its associated checkbox, to make the controls for that effect appear on the right. If you click the checkbox instead, you'll turn on the effect with its default settings, and you won't gain access to the customization settings.

Different from the Effects dialog in Photoshop and Illustrator is the Settings for: dropdown at the upper left of the dialog window. The option you select from the dropdown dictates whether the effects you choose will be applied to the object, its stroke, its fill, or its text. To apply different settings to different object attributes, simply choose the first attribute, apply your settings, then choose the next attribute and repeat the process accordingly.

The Effects dialog is a place where people have been known to disappear for days without resurfacing, so immersed do they become in the visual magic and multitude of variations it makes available. The effects you can create are truly endless, so make a point to take some time to explore. The invested time will be well spent, since you can save the fruit of your efforts as object styles that you can use over and over again. For more on object styles, see Working with Styles on page 94.

Click the *fx.* button at the bottom of the Effects panel
and select an option to bring up the Effects dialog box.

Examine the effects settings for sampleBtn130 to see that it has a 100%
Normal blending mode applied to the object, stroke, and fill. Additional effects
are applied to the fill as indicated by the *fx.* on the Fill line of the panel.

4. To edit the effects applied to the fill of the button Normal state, ensure that the Fill
line of the panel is highlighted, and click the *fx.* button at the bottom of the panel.
Note that active effects are indicated by a check.

TIP: Changes made
to button instances
in your document do
not affect buttons in
the Sample Buttons
And Forms library.

5. Select Bevel and Emboss from the options menu. The Effects dialog opens to the
Bevel and Emboss controls and the Bevel and Emboss checkbox is checked.

6. If necessary, reposition the Effects dialog so you can see the button on your
document, and make sure that the Preview checkbox at the lower left of the panel
is checked.

7. Change the Style to Emboss and the Direction to Down. Play with adjusting some
of the other settings to see what they do, and then click OK to apply your changes.

8. Select the Rollover state in the Buttons and Forms panel and then Double-Click the
button on the page to get inside the button group.

9. Double-Click the Fill line in the Effects panel to open the Effects dialog and
then click the words "Bevel and Emboss" at its left. Click OK to apply the
default settings.

10. Toggle between the button states to test your button, and then save and close your
file to complete the exercise.

Replacing Missing Fonts

The font used in button 101, the first navbar in the Sample Buttons And Forms
library, is formatted using the [Basic Paragraph] paragraph style which uses a serif
font called Minion Pro by default. As you learned in Chapter 2, general wisdom
recommends that for smaller text especially, sans-serif fonts are easier to read
onscreen—a perfect opportunity to learn how to change fonts document-wide or to
replace fonts that are included in your document but missing from your system.

When InDesign opens a document containing references to a font that's not on your
system, it displays a Missing Font alert and a button for the Find Font dialog where
you can correct the issue. Missing fonts are indicated by a pink highlight appearing
on the affected text in your document.

The Missing Fonts alert (and text highlighted in pink) should never be ignored. You may choose to correct the issue later in your workflow, but missing fonts absolutely must be dealt with to ensure that your print documents print reliably, and that your electronic documents convert reliably to their output destinations.

In the next exercise, you'll learn all about how to use the The Find Font dialog to replace fonts throughout your document. It's important to know however, that Find Font is not the only, nor is it always the best way to cure missing fonts. Most often, missing fonts occur in documents inherited from other designers, but it's possible that a change to a paragraph style definition could cause fonts to go missing as well. If in the course of your work you all of a sudden find your document riddled with pink highlights, check the definitions of your paragraph and character styles. You may for example have defined a character style using an italic font and then changed the primary document font to a font family that contains no italic. In such a scenario, any text to which the italic character style is applied will display the dreaded missing font pink. In such a case, a simple adjustment to your italic character style will cure your missing font problem.

There is a Redefine Style When Changing All checkbox in the Find Font dialog that would appear to solve the missing font issue as it relates to styles (as described in the above scenario.) Unfortunately, the promise is not equalled by performance. Rather than redefining an offending style, overrides are applied to the text to which that style is applied. The style definition must then be manually updated to include the overrides.

One way to update the style definition to incorporate the overrides is to position the Type tool cursor in an instance of the styled text, Right-Click/Ctrl+Click on the name of the applied style in the Paragraph or Character Styles panel, and choose Redefine Style from the contextual menu. The plus sign after the style name will disappear and the style definition will be updated to include your new formatting.

Exercise 10.3: Using the Find Font dialog

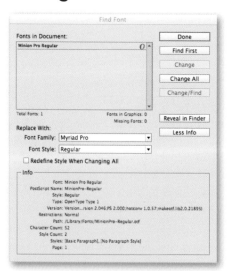

The Find Font dialog: Select the font you want to replace from the Fonts in Document pane and then specify the replacement font using the Replace With dropdowns.

1. Open **ex10_3_start.indd** and save it as ex10_3.indd.

    The ex10_3_start.indd file contains two versions of the Sample Button 101 navbar: one as it exists in the Sample Buttons And Forms library and the other expanded to show its component parts.

2. Go to Type > Find Font.

3. Select Minion Pro Regular in the Fonts in Document section of the dialog.

4. From the Font Family dropdown, select Myriad Pro.

5. Click Find First to select the first occurrence of the font in your document.

6. Click Change/Find.

    If the font were missing from your system, the pink missing font highlight would disappear from the selected text. Note that the name of your newly added font appears in the Fonts in Document section of the Find Fonts dialog.

7. Press what we call the "I'm feeling lucky" button, Change All. This replaces every instance of the Minion Pro font with Myriad Pro. Note that Minion Pro disappears from the list of document fonts.

8. If a warning alert pops up, it's because you have the Redefine Style When Changing All checkbox checked in the Find Font dialog. No cause for alarm; the alert is just making you aware that the font you've applied to the button text varies from the definition of the [Basic Paragraph] paragraph style that was applied to the buttons.

If the Redefine Style When Changing All checkbox is checked in the Find Font dialog, a warning dialog will pop up when you press the Change All button.

9. If necessary, click OK to dismiss the warning, and then click Done to close the dialog. Save the document and keep it open for the next exercise.

Deconstructing a Complex Button

Things are not always as they seem, and buttons are no exception. It's often the case that what looks like one object is actually an assemblage of component pieces. The navbar from the Sample Buttons And Forms library is a perfect example. The next exercise takes you behind the scenes to see how it all fits together and how to use effects to customize object appearances.

The sample button 101 navbar. Below the assembled navbar is an expanded view of its component pieces.

TIP: At the right of the Find Font dialog is a More Info button that exposes a wealth of information about the selected font in the document including: PostScript name, font type and version, licensing restrictions, where the font file is located on your system, the number and names of styles using the font, a character count and the pages on which it occurs in the document. (The button caption changes to Less Info when pressed.) There is also a Reveal in Finder/Reveal in Explorer button that locates and selects the font file on your system.

ALERT: The button text in the exploded view of the navbar doesn't show onscreen because the text color is white.

Exercise 10.4: Deconstructing Sample Button 101

1. If you don't already have the file open from the previous lesson, open **ex10_4_start.indd** from the chapter_10_exercises folder and save it as ex10_4.indd.

2. With the Selection tool, in the expanded view of the navbar, select the black rounded rectangle that serves as the button background. Click the arrow to the right of the Fill swatch on the Control panel and select Dark Blue from the swatches dropdown.

   Changing the color of the rounded rectangle will change the background color of the entire navbar when you put its pieces back together.

3. Select the long, highlight rectangle that's directly below the navbar background. Drag it up, onto the background, holding the Shift key as you drag to keep it aligned. Release the mouse when the top of the highlight is positioned a couple pixels from the top of the background. You can use the arrow keys on your keyboard to nudge the highlight into position.

4. With the Fill swatch active in the Tools panel, go to Window > Color > Gradient or click the ■ icon in the Panels dock to open the Gradient panel.

   When the Gradient panel opens, note that the object has a linear gradient fill going from white to black.

TIP: Gradient stops look like little houses positioned below the gradient ramp. When a gradient stop is selected it's "roof" turns black.

5. To see the effect more clearly, click the white gradient stop below the gradient ramp (⌂) to activate it, and then click the Swatches panel icon (▦) in the Panel Dock.

   When the Swatches panel opens, the Gradient panel closes.

6. Alt+Click/Option+Click the cyan swatch in the Swatches panel to replace the white color in the gradient.

   If you don't hold the Alt/Option key when you click the color swatch, the gradient in the navbar highlight will be replaced by solid cyan. If this happens, press Ctrl+Z/Command+Z to undo, and then start over by reselecting the white gradient stop in the Gradient panel.

TIP: For a linear gradient, the colors or transparency variations in the gradient are applied to an object sequentially, from left to right, as they appear on the gradient ramp. While linear gradients go from left to right, the variations in a radial gradient radiate outward from the center. The leftmost gradient stop on the gradient ramp represents the center of the radial gradient and its origin, while the rightmost gradient stop represents the outermost edge of the gradient definition.

7. Collapse the Swatches panel and note the change in appearance of the highlight bar on your document.

8. Click the *fx.* button on the Control panel to expand the list of effects.

9. Click the words "Gradient Feather" in the list of options to open the Effects dialog to the Gradient Feather controls.

   Previously a job reserved for Photoshop, InDesign's Gradient Feather effect can make an object fade out to full transparency. A Gradient Feather gradient goes from black to white, where the black gradient stop represents 100% opacity and the white stop represents full transparency. When applied to an object rather than its fill or stroke, you can swap out the contents of the object frame and still retain the transparency effect on its contents. This means you can use the Gradient Feather effect to fade images to transparency and then swap out the images on the fly. A truly awesome feature!

10. Click the black gradient stop under the gradient ramp to select it, and note that its opacity is set to 100%.

11. Click the white gradient stop and note that it's opacity is set to 0%. If necessary, check the Preview checkbox at the lower left of the panel. Then, with the stop still selected, click the arrow to the right of the Opacity text field and drag the Opacity slider to the right to increase the opacity percentage to about 15%.

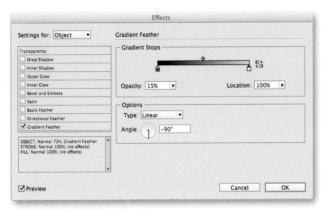

The adjusted settings in the Effects panel for the Gradient Feather applied to the navbar.

Note that the white gradient stop in the dialog changes to darker shades of gray when you increase the Opacity percentage, and the navbar highlight on the document becomes more solid in color.

The colors of the gradient stops in the Gradient Feather dialog represent opacity rather than color. A black swatch in the stop indicates that the selected object is completely opaque, white indicates that it is completely transparent, and shades of gray indicate degrees of opacity.

Note that the angle of the Gradient Feather is -90°, resulting in a gradient transparency effect that goes from opaque to transparent, from the top to the bottom of the object.

12. Drag the Angle pointer until the Angle value reads 90° and observe that the gradient on the highlight bar reverses direction. Type "-90" in the Angle field to return to your original setting.

A linear Gradient Feather effect at -90° goes from opaque to transparent; at 90°, it goes from transparent to opaque. You can change the gradient angle by dragging the Angle pointer or entering a value in the text field.

13. Note that there's a summary of applied effects in the box at the lower left of the Effects dialog, and then click OK to close the Effects dialog.

```
OBJECT: Normal 72%; Gradient Feather
STROKE: Normal 100%; (no effects)
FILL: Normal 100%; (no effects)
```

Effects panel summary of effects applied to the highlight bar.

14. Next, you'll modify the button text. With the Selection tool, click and hold and drag a selection marquee to intersect or surround the four rectangles and the three vertical lines that you've not yet moved onto the navbar. Shift-Drag the selected objects to center them on the navbar, and then use the arrow keys on your keyboard as necessary to nudge them into place.

15. With the Selection tool still active, Double-Click the word "Blog" to switch to the Type tool. Double-Click again to select the text, and change it to "Contact Us."

    Notice that the Control panel displays the Type controls and that the font used for the button text is Myriad Pro Regular.

<table>
<tr><td>ALERT: The button has no fill or stroke, so be sure to click on its edge rather than its interior to select it.</td></tr>
</table>

16. Press Esc to deselect your text and automatically switch to the Selection tool.

17. Select the button directly below the word "Home" from the row of remaining rectangles that you've not yet moved to the navbar. Open the Buttons and Forms panel.

    Notice that the default button name appears at the top of the panel. Note also that the button has a Go To Page action applied to the On Release event and is currently set to navigate to page 1 of the document.

ALERT: If the Appearance section of the Buttons and Forms panel is empty, Double-Click the button on the document to access the button states.

18. Select the Rollover state in the Buttons and Forms panel. There are two objects that combine to create this state of the button.

19. Double-Click the object with the gradient fill in the upper half of the button.

    The gradient should appear in the Fill swatches on the Toolbar and Control panel.

20. Open the Gradient panel to see the white to black gradient applied to the object. Select the black gradient stop, open the Swatches panel and Alt+Click/Option+Click the same Dark Blue you applied to the navbar background.

21. Return to the Gradient panel, select the gradient diamond above the gradient ramp and enter 45 in the Location percentage field to reposition the halfway point for the gradient transition. Leave the Angle set to -90°.

The black gradient stop replaced by dark blue,
and the Location percentage changed to 45%.

22. In the Effects panel, note that the opacity of the object is set to 81%. Double-Click the Object: Normal item in the panel to open the Effects dialog.

23. Click the black gradient stop at the right of the gradient ramp. Change the opacity percentage to 0 and then click OK to apply your changes and close the dialog.

24. Select the other object in the button's Rollover state and change its fill to the same Dark Blue you used in the gradient.

25. Select the second button with the Selection tool, hold down the Shift key, and click the two remaining buttons to add them to your selection. Press the Delete key on your keyboard to delete all three buttons. You'll duplicate your formatted button to create the other buttons on the navbar.

26. Hold down Alt+Shift/Option+Shift and drag the first button to the right. Release the mouse when you see a green vertical smart guide indicating that the duplicate button is aligned to the center of the Products text on the navbar above.

Alt+Shift+drag/Option+Shift+drag to duplicate the button
and constrain its horizontal position as it's dragged.

27. Repeat the procedure until you have a total of four buttons, each aligned under their respective text.

28. Drag a marquee selection around all four buttons with the Selection tool. Hold down the Shift key to constrain vertical movement, and drag the buttons straight up to center them on the navbar. If necessary, use your arrow keys to nudge the buttons into place.

29. Preview the Spread in the SWF Preview panel and roll over the buttons in both versions of the navbar. Save the file and keep it open for the next exercise.

The original sample button 101 navbar (top) and the edited version (bottom).

Selecting Stacked and Grouped Objects

Now that you've explored the inner workings of the component pieces of the navbar, let's take a look at various ways you can select them.

Buttons are essentially grouped objects. One way to select elements of a grouped object is to Double-Click the object in the group that you wish to select. This can be especially tricky with buttons, since some buttons may have no fill or stroke, and selecting them requires a precisely placed click on the button bounding box. If, as is the case with the navbar buttons, a text field is laid over the button, a Double-Click could easily activate the textbox rather than the button object. In instances such as these, trying to select the actual button using the Selection tool can become an exercise in futility. Thankfully, there is more than one way to approach the challenge.

The Select container and content tools on the Control panel enable you to access and navigate through stacked objects and objects in a group. The Layers panel is also an invaluable tool for locating and selecting any object in your file.

Exercise 10.5: Selecting Stacked and Grouped Objects

This exercise provides an introduction to the Select container and Select content tools. You'll learn to use these tools to select objects that elude selection using the Selection tool.

THE SELECT CONTAINER AND SELECT CONTENT TOOLS

A  C
B   D

A. Select container
B. Select content
C. Select previous object
D. Select next object

1. If you don't have the file open from the previous exercise, open **ex10_5_start.indd** and save it as ex10_5.indd.

2. Open the Layers panel (Window > Layers or click the ⬙ icon in the Panel Dock) and click the right-facing arrow on Layer 1 to show its object sublayers.

3. Expand the <group> object layer to show its component elements.

4. Expand and drag the Layers panel out of the Panel Dock.

5. Select the black navbar on the document using the Selection tool, and click the Select content button (⊕) on the Control panel to go inside the group.

   Note the large blue square at the right of the <group> object layer in the Layers panel indicating that the group is selected.

6. Click the Select next object button (⊞) four times on the Control panel and watch as the blue selection square in the Layers panel appears at the right of the <rectangle>, <path>, and <line> object layers, to end up at Button 38.

7. Notice that the Home button is selected on the document. Expand Button 38 in the Layers panel and then expand its Rollover state.

8. Click the Select content button again and note that the Rollover state of the button is selected on the document as indicated by the big blue square to the right of the [Rollover] object layer in the Layers panel.

You can click in the Layers panel selection column to select any object.

9. Click the Select content button yet again to select the button highlight.

   Note that the Fill swatches on the Control bar and Toolbar display the gradient fill that's applied to the highlight.

10. Click the Select next object button on the Control bar to select the button background object.

11. Now that you've learned how to select even the most elusive objects in a document, you can save and close the file to complete the exercise.

CHAPTER SUMMARY

You've covered a lot of territory in this chapter, learning the fundamentals of buttons, how they work, and how to change their appearance. Specifically you learned about:

- Button appearances
- Button events
- Button states
- Button actions
- The Sample Buttons And Forms Library
- The Buttons and Forms panel

As part of your exploration, you also become familiar with a number of the wonderful features and tools in InDesign. You got some experience with:

- The Find Font dialog
- Using the Control panel to work with effects
- The Effects panel
- The Gradient Feather effect
- Replacing a gradient color
- Selecting objects with the Select container and Select content buttons from the Control panel
- Radial and linear gradients and gradient angles
- Transparency

Now that you have a foundation, you're ready to build some buttons of your own. Chapter 11 will introduce you to simple buttons, and then you'll build from there.

Chapter 11

SIMPLE IMAGE-BASED BUTTONS

You can create buttons from any object, and a placed image is an obvious starting point. This chapter will have you creating elegant image-based buttons in no time, adding effects, and then using the buttons to control visibility of other objects in your document. Supported in both PDF and SWF export, making objects appear and disappear with user interaction is a fundamental part of the interactive magic you can create with InDesign. So, it's time to put on your top hat and get out your magic wand, and let the fun begin!

Introduction

While it's nice to have a starting point, and the Sample Buttons And Forms Library certainly provides that, it's also good to know how to design buttons of your own. The robust drawing tools in InDesign allow you to get as crazy as you like with shapes, highlights, and effects to create an unlimited variety of button appearances.

One simple and easy approach to button making is to create them from placed images. With an effect applied to the Rollover state, image-based buttons can be a simple and elegant solution to adding interactivity to your documentd.

Exercise 11.1: Simple Image-based Buttons

In this exercise, you will place multiple images, convert them to buttons, and add rollover appearances. You'll then add Show/Hide actions to the buttons to control the visibility of larger versions of the button images.

The buttons you create in this chapter can be used in projects output to Interactive PDF, SWF and DPS. The Show/Hide action is supported in Interactive PDF and SWF output but does not however translate to DPS. While the file requires some tweaking, and the buttons require different actions, you can actually accomplish a similar visual result with DPS using a multi-state object Slideshow overlay. Check out Chapter 34, Slideshow Overlays, starting on page 505 to learn how.

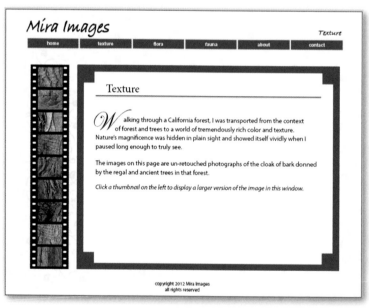

1. Open **ex11_2_end.indd** and press Shift+Ctrl+Enter/Shift+Command+Return to open the SWF Preview panel. (Be patient, this may take 30 seconds to a full minute to preview.) If necessary, click the Play button at the bottom left of the panel to generate the preview. Rollover and click each of the filmstrip thumbnails to see how they work.

2. Close the SWF Preview panel and explore the file. Open the Buttons and Forms panel and, with the Selection tool, Double-Click each of the texture buttons at the left of the page to see the events and actions applied to them.

3. Alt+Click/Option+Click the texture page 1 layer in the Layers panel to expand the layer and all its sublayers. Note the naming convention for the layers. When you've finished exploring, keep the file open for reference.

4. Open **ex11_1_start.indd** and save it as ex11_1.indd.

    First you'll zoom in on the filmstrip and then you'll add guides to help in your layout.

5. With the Selection tool selected, hold down Ctrl+Spacebar/ Command+Spacebar and note that the cursor changes to the Zoom tool. Position your mouse at the upper left of the filmstrip graphic and, still holding the modifier keys, drag diagonally, down and to the right, as if you were dragging a box around the entire filmstrip. Release the mouse and then release the keys on your keyboard to see the now zoomed-in view of the graphic. This is called a marquee zoom.

6. Place your cursor in the horizontal ruler at the top of the document window, and while holding down the mouse, drag down onto the page to drag a guide. Release the mouse when you see 141 px in the Y coordinate field on the Control panel.

    The coordinates of the guide update dynamically as you drag. If you release the guide before getting it properly positioned, you can select it with the Selection tool and enter the correct coordinate value in the Control panel.

    The Y coordinate field on the Control panel reflects the position of a guide as it is dragged from the horizontal ruler.

7. Drag a second horizontal guide to 630 px.

8. Drag guides from the vertical ruler to 81 px and 145 px.

    Next, you'll import the thumbnail images you'll use for the buttons.

9. Press Ctrl+D/Command+D or go to File > Place. Navigate to chapter_11_exercises > links. Click to select **texture1.jpg** and then hold down the Shift key to select **texture9.jpg**. Click Open to load your cursor with all nine images.

    In the upper left of the cursor thumbnail, you'll see a brush and a number representing the number of files loaded and ready to be placed.

    • Use the right and left arrows on your keyboard to navigate through the loaded files.
    • To remove a loaded file from the cursor, when its thumbnail is visible, click Esc on your keyboard.

    If you inadvertently replace the content of a selected frame with a file you've loaded in the cursor, press Ctrl+Z/Command+Z to undo. The loaded file will be removed from the page and loaded back into the cursor.

10. Position your cursor at the intersection of the guides at the upper left of the filmstrip. Hold down the mouse and drag down and to the right. Still holding the mouse, press the up arrow once on your keyboard and note the horizontal dividers that appear in the frame.

TIP: The lock icon at the upper left of the filmstrip graphic indicates that it is locked and cannot be selected or repositioned. To lock an object, select it and click Ctrl+L/Command+L or go to Object > Lock. To unlock an object, click the lock icon on the locked object.

TIP: If Rulers are not visible, press Ctrl+R/ Command+R or go to View > Show Rulers.

TIP: Hold the Ctrl/ Command key while you drag a guide to extend it across all pages of a multi-page spread. Dragging a guide from the ruler into the pasteboard rather than the page will also make the guide extend across the spread. To switch the direction of a guide between horizontal and vertical, hold down Alt/Option while dragging.

TIP: InDesign enables you to place a wide variety of file formats including: native Illustrator, Photoshop, and InDesign files, multi-page PDFs, as well as TIFF, JPEG, GIF, EPS, BMP, PNG, DOC, DOCX, TXT, RTF, XLS, XLXS, FLV, F4V, SWF, MP4, and MP3 files.

Before pressing the up arrow, you may have noticed that, as you dragged, the frame maintained the aspect ratio of the placed file. To override this default behavior, hold the Shift key while dragging, and InDesign will let you drag any size frame you like.

11. While still holding the mouse, press the up arrow a total of eight times to create nine uniformly sized frames. Drag the cursor to the intersection of the guides at the lower right of the filmstrip, and release the mouse. All nine loaded images should be placed and evenly spaced atop the filmstrip graphic.

    Since the aspect ratio of the frames doesn't exactly match the images, the images don't quite fill the frames. You'll fix that with InDesign's Fitting options.

12. With the Selection tool, click the first placed graphic, being sure not to click the target icon that appears in the center of the image when you roll the mouse over it.

    Clicking the target selects the object within the frame rather than the frame that contains it. When the object placed within the frame is selected, you can scale and transform it without affecting the frame.

When the mouse is rolled over a placed object, a target icon appears at its center. Clicking the target selects the content within the frame rather than the frame containing it.

13. Right-Click/Ctrl+Click the image and select Fitting > Fill Frame Proportionally.

    In order to streamline the process of applying the same fitting option to the other eight objects, you'll store the object settings in an Object style.

14. Go to Window > Styles > Object Styles (Ctrl+F7/Command+F7) to open the Object Styles panel or click the 🔲 icon in the Panel Dock.

15. Alt-Click/Option-Click the Create New Style button at the bottom of the panel to open the Object Styles dialog.

16. In the Style Name field of the New Object Style dialog, name your new style "ProportionalFit".

    It's good practice to name styles according to their function rather than appearance. This leaves you latitude to make changes in color or effect with the original name remaining an appropriate identifier.

17. In the Basic Attributes section of the dialog, click the Frame Fitting Options checkbox in the column at the left. (Be sure to click the checkbox and not the words to see that the parameter controls do not appear.)

    This incorporates the fitting settings from the selected object into the style definition.

18. Check the Apply Style to Selection checkbox at the lower left of the dialog.

19. Click the words "Frame Fitting Options" to display the Frame Fitting Options controls.

20. Check the Auto-Fit checkbox and choose the center square in the Align From reference point proxy to center the image in the frame. Ensure that the Crop Amount values are all set to 0.

TIP: The Auto-Fit feature enables you to scale the containing frame and its content as a unit, without the need to use modifier keys. Without Auto-Fit, you would need to hold Ctrl+Shift/Command+Shift while dragging in order to scale both the frame contents and the container frame together.

Frame Fitting Options for the ProportionalFit object style.

21. Click OK to close the dialog.

22. Select the second placed image, and, holding down the Shift key, click on each of the remaining images to add them to the selection.

23. Click once on ProportionalFit in the Object Styles panel to apply the style.

24. Deselect all the objects on the page by clicking on your pasteboard or pressing Command+Shift+A/Ctrl+Shift+A.

25. Select the first placed image (**texture1.jpg**) and open the Buttons and Forms panel. Click the Convert to Button icon at the bottom right of the panel.

26. Change the name of the button to "**texture_1_sm**."

27. Still in the Buttons panel, click the word "[Rollover]" to create and activate the rollover button appearance.

28. Open the Effects panel (Window > Effects) and note that the panel displays the word "Group". Double-Click the button on your document and Group is replaced in the Effects panel by Object, Stroke, and Fill.

29. Select Object in the Effects panel and click the *fx.* button at the bottom of the panel. Select Inner Glow from the Effects options.

30. If necessary, check the Preview checkbox at the lower left of the Effects dialog in order to preview your changes.

31. In the Blending section of the dialog, click the white color swatch to the right of the Mode dropdown. Choose RGB from the Color dropdown, and select a color for the Inner Glow. We chose an orange color: R=255 G=134 B=0.

32. Adjust the opacity as desired. We chose 42%.

33. Increase the Size setting to 25 px and then click OK to apply the effect and close the dialog.

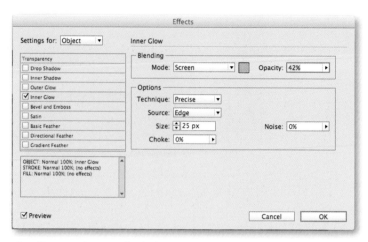

The Effects panel settings for the button Rollover state with Inner Glow applied.

34. With the button still selected and the Rollover state still active, Alt+Click/Option+Click the Create new style button at the bottom of the Object Styles panel and name your new style "**textureOver.**"

35. Convert each of the remaining filmstrip images to buttons and name them consecutively: "**texture_2_sm,**" "**texture_3_sm,**" etc.

36. For each button, create a Rollover state and apply the textureOver Object style.

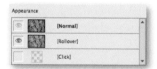

Button with textureOver Object style applied to the Rollover state

37. Press Ctrl+Shift+Enter/Command+Shift+Return to open the SWF Preview panel and then test your button rollovers.

38. After you've styled the Rollover state for all the buttons, and tested that they work, choose Reset All Buttons to Normal State from the Buttons and Forms panel menu. The orange highlight will disappear from all the buttons on the document.

39. Open the Layers panel and click the triangle at the left of the texture page 1 layer to expand it. Locate the textureDescription sublayer and click the eye icon to its left to hide the layer (the tool tip will say "Toggles visibility".) Press Ctrl+0/Command+0 to zoom out and fit the page in the window.

40. Save the file and keep it open for the next exercise.

Naming Conventions

If you explored the contents of the texture page 1 layer, you saw that the lesson file already contains large versions of the same nine images used to create your buttons and that the large images have been converted to buttons too.

In InDesign, for an object to talk to another object in order to send or receive commands, both objects must have unique names. Converting an object to a button enables you to name it. You can either keep the default name provided by InDesign or you can name it yourself, as you did earlier in this lesson.

Setting up reliable naming conventions and adhering to them will save you lots of time and aggravation as you develop projects containing potentially hundreds of objects, and numerous layers and styles. Naming objects, layers, and styles consistently also makes a project more decipherable to other designers and developers in a shared workflow. As an example, the large image buttons have names that correspond to the small image buttons to make them easy to pair—texture_1_sm corresponds to texture_1_lg.

Because InDesign files can be exported to Flash Professional for development, we've adhered to the rules for naming Flash variables when suggesting button names.

The standard rules for naming variables are:

- Start your variable name with a lower case letter or an underscore, not a number.
- Use only lowercase letters, numbers, dashes, and underscores in the variable name.
- Never use spaces or any crazy characters.

If you've chosen a button name that combines multiple words, use a lowercase letter for the first word and either begin the following words with an uppercase letter (myVariableName), or use an underscore or a dash to separate the words (my_variable_name).

Not to worry, it's unlikely that you'll break anything if you name your InDesign objects according to a different convention. Whatever convention you decide on, though, be consistent in using it. You'll find yourself spending much less time trouble-shooting and your workflow will move much more smoothly.

Getting Around in the SWF Preview Panel

THE SWF PREVIEW PANEL:
1) Play preview (Alt+Click/Option+Click to replay preview. 2) Clear preview. 3) Go to Previous Page. 4) Document page number (mouse over to see tooltip displaying file name and page number). 5) Go to Next Page. 6) Set Preview Selection Mode. 7) Set Preview Spread Mode. 8) Set Preview Document Mode.

The SWF Preview panel provides three modes for previewing your work: Selection, Spread, and Document.

The Preview Selection Mode enables you to preview selected objects, such as a specific button or buttons. The preview will display only the objects selected, so if there are internal links to other document pages, or actions controlling other objects that aren't selected, they will not be functional in this mode. Go To URL actions applied to the object will function as expected, however, enabling navigation to external web addresses and sending of email.

The Preview Spread Mode previews the entire spread. Actions affecting objects within the spread will work as will Go To URL actions. Any Flash animations in the spread will play as designed. Navigation to other pages in the document will not be active in this mode.

The Preview Document Mode generates a preview of the entire document that demonstrates the full functionality and Flash interactivity it contains. All navigation, internal and external, and all Flash animation, will perform as it will in the final SWF project. Navigate through the document pages by clicking the previous and next buttons, or any internal links you've established.

You may find that when the SWF Preview panel first opens, nothing but a blank screen appears. If this is the case, click the Play preview button at the lower left of the panel and then wait while InDesign generates the preview. Depending on the size of your document and the interactivity you've added, this can take a little while. However, it's well worth the wait to see your buttons functioning, links working, and animations playing.

If you've generated a preview in one mode and wish to switch to another, select the desired preview mode and click the Play preview button. InDesign will generate a new preview based on your selection.

To replay a preview from its start, hold the Alt/Option key and click the Play preview button.

Exercise 11.2: Using Buttons to Control Visibility

Next, you'll make the buttons you created in the previous exercise show a large version of their thumbnail image when clicked. This behavior is accomplished using the Show/Hide Button action found in the Actions section of the Buttons panel.

1. If you closed the file from the previous lesson, open **ex11_2_start.indd** and save it as ex11_2.indd Select the **texture_1_sm** thumbnail button, the first button on the filmstrip, and open the Buttons and Forms panel. With the default On Release or Tap event selected, click the plus icon next to the word "Actions" and select Show/Hide Buttons from the list of actions.

   In the Visibility section that appears in the Buttons and Forms panel, note that all the texture buttons have an X next to them.

2. Click once on the X next to **texture_1_lg** to make the large image show when the thumbnail button is clicked and the mouse is released.

   An open eye icon replaces the X. Alternatively, you can select the texture_1_lg item in the Visibility section and click the Show icon (👁) below the list.

3. Click twice in the Visibility column for **texture_2_lg** to hide that image when the texture_1_sm button is released.

   An eye icon with a slash through it indicates that the object will be hidden. Another way to set the object visibility would be to select the texture_2_lg item and click the Hide icon (👁) below the list.

> **TIP:** For the Show/Hide button Action, the X to the left of an object in the Visibility section of the Actions panel indicates that the object will retain its default visibility when the button is clicked. The 👁 icon indicates that the object will show and the 👁 icon indicates that the object will be hidden.

4. Hide the following buttons:

   textureDescription
   texture_3_lg
   texture_4_lg
   texture_5_lg
   texture_6_lg
   texture_7_lg
   texture_8_lg
   texture_9_lg

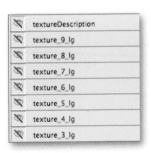

   Now, when the texture_1_sm button is released, the description and all the large images except texture_1_lg will be hidden, and the texture_1_lg image will show.

5. To test your work, click the Preview Spread icon (🖵) at the bottom of the Buttons and Forms panel.

6. When the SWF Preview panel opens, if you don't see the preview of your spread, click the Play button at the lower left of the panel. If necessary, enlarge the panel by dragging the lower left corner down and to the left.

7. Click on the texture_1_sm thumbnail to show the texture_1_lg image.

8. Close the SWF Preview panel and reopen the Buttons and Forms panel.

9. For each of the remaining thumbnail buttons, follow steps 2 through 6, naming the buttons and establishing the Show/Hide settings as follows.

Button Name	Show	Hide	
texture_2_sm	texture_2_lg	• textureDescription • texture_1_lg • texture_3_lg • texture_4_lg • texture_5_lg	• texture_6_lg • texture_7_lg • texture_8_lg • texture_9_lg
texture_3_sm	texture_3_lg	• textureDescription • texture_1_lg • texture_2_lg • texture_4_lg • texture_5_lg	• texture_6_lg • texture_7_lg • texture_8_lg • texture_9_lg
texture_4_sm	texture_4_lg	• textureDescription • texture_1_lg • texture_2_lg • texture_3_lg • texture_5_lg	• texture_6_lg • texture_7_lg • texture_8_lg • texture_9_lg
texture_5_sm	texture_5_lg	• textureDescription • texture_1_lg • texture_2_lg • texture_3_lg • texture_4_lg	• texture_6_lg • texture_7_lg • texture_8_lg • texture_9_lg
texture_6_sm	texture_6_lg	• textureDescription • texture_1_lg • texture_2_lg • texture_3_lg • texture_4_lg	• texture_5_lg • texture_7_lg • texture_8_lg • texture_9_lg
texture_7_sm	texture_7_lg	• textureDescription • texture_1_lg • texture_2_lg • texture_3_lg • texture_4_lg	• texture_5_lg • texture_6_lg • texture_8_lg • texture_9_lg
texture_8_sm	texture_8_lg	• textureDescription • texture_1_lg • texture_2_lg • texture_3_lg • texture_4_lg	• texture_5_lg • texture_6_lg • texture_7_lg • texture_9_lg
texture_9_sm	texture_9_lg	• textureDescription • texture_1_lg • texture_2_lg • texture_3_lg • texture_4_lg	• texture_5_lg • texture_6_lg • texture_7_lg • texture_8_lg

10. Preview your document again to ensure that each button is performing properly. Save and close the file to complete the lesson and the chapter.

CHAPTER SUMMARY

This chapter brought you deeper into the world of buttons and the power they have to transform a static document into one filled with life.

On this leg of the journey, you've learned all about:

- Converting objects to buttons
- Creating buttons from placed images
- Working with the Show/Hide action to control visibility
- Modifying effects
- Creating, editing, and applying Object styles
- Frame Fitting options and how to assign them

You became intimately familiar with the SWF Preview panel, an essential tool for testing your interactive work, and also learned about:

- Importable image formats
- Working with naming conventions
- Locking and unlocking objects
- Showing and hiding rulers
- Dragging a marquee selection
- Creating guides

In the next chapter, you'll venture further into the interactive landscape to expand your available design options with multi-object buttons.

Chapter 12

MULTI-OBJECT BUTTONS

When it comes to buttons, working with multiple objects multiplies your design options exponentially. In this chapter you'll create buttons from multiple objects, combining them to create the different button states, and then modifying or removing select objects to customize the button state appearances. You'll work with transparent button hotspots to activate areas of a static image and group multiple buttons to extend functionality. By the end of the chapter, you'll have a full repertoire of button-making techniques to employ when designing for interactivity.

Multi-object Buttons

While you can get lots of mileage from buttons consisting of only one object, your design options expand dramatically when you know how to make buttons from multiple elements. It's not all that tricky, but there are a few nuances that are good to know.

The first secret to creating a multi-object button is to group the objects you want to include in the button before you convert it. If you select and convert multiple objects without grouping them, InDesign creates an individual button from each object.

The best way to create a button with different multi-object appearances in its different states is to first select all the objects from all the states and group them. Create the button, and then create the Rollover state. Next, delete the extra objects from the state in which you don't want them to show and you're done.

Of course, there will be times when you have an existing button to which you want to add another object. This is when the Layers panel proves particularly useful. As mentioned earlier, a button is a group of sorts, and it appears in the Layers panel as an object sublayer, with a sublayer of its own that reflects the active button state.

Follow these steps to add an object to an existing button state:

1.   Select the object you want to add to the existing button.

2.   Expand the button layer in the Layers panel, and then expand the sublayer for the button state: [Normal], [Rollover] or [Click.]

3.   In the Layers panel, drag the object layer for the object you're adding into the button sublayer, and release it when you see a black line. Initially, you may need to drag the new object layer to the bottom of the button state layer stack. Once the new object is part of the button state, you can then drag it to its proper position in the stack.

The image below illustrates the <oval> layer being dragged into the [Normal] state of the button. The black line below the <rectangle> layer indicates where the <oval> layer will be positioned in the button stack when the mouse is released. Once within the [Normal] sublayer, the <oval> sublayer can then be dragged above the rectangle to the top of the [Normal] button stack.

The <oval> sublayer being dragged into the Button 1 Normal state.

Exercise 12.1: Creating Multi-object Buttons

You can create buttons from multiple objects to achieve
effects such as text appearing on rollover.

1. Open **ex12_1_end.indd** from the chapter_12_exercises folder.

2. To preview the file, open the SWF Preview panel, select Preview Document Mode
   (⬚) and then click the Play button.

3. In the SWF Preview panel, test each of the four image buttons on page one. After
   testing each button, use the page navigation buttons at the bottom left of the panel
   to return to page one from the interior document pages.

   ▶ ■ ◀   ▶

   Preview panel page navigation controls

4. When you've tested each button, collapse the Preview panel, returning to page 1
   of the document.

5. Select the upper left tree bark image with the Selection tool.

6. Expand the Buttons and Forms panel (🔲) in the Panel Dock and note that the image
   is part of a button called textureImage. Explore the other three image buttons and
   the actions assigned to them. Keep the file open for reference.

7. Open **ex12_1_start.indd** and save it as ex12_1.indd.

   The two images on the top row have been converted to buttons, and the
   images on the bottom row have not. You'll convert the bottom images to
   buttons, add text and style it for all four button Rollover states.

8. Open the Layers panel, select the home page layer, and twirl down the triangle at
   its left to expand it.

9. Select the Type tool and draw a small text frame approximately 140 px wide by
   40 px tall on top of the bird image. Type the word "Fauna" in the text frame.

10. Double-Click the word "Fauna" with the Type tool to select it and change the font
    face and size. We used Myriad Pro Bold, 22 px.

11. Select a color for your text. We chose the R=240 G=234 B=227 swatch from the
    Swatches panel (▦), a light cream color.

12. Click the **TT** button in the Character Formatting section of the Control panel to
    apply all caps.

NOTE: Be sure to
choose Preview
Document Mode to
preview the file or
the button Go To
Destination actions
won't work.

NOTE: New content
is added to the active
layer in the Layers
panel. To ensure that
the text appears above
the image button, be
sure the home page
layer is selected.

13. Click the ▾≣ button at the far right of the Control panel and choose Paragraph Rules from the panel menu. Apply the following settings:

- Click the Rule Above dropdown, choose Rule Below, check Rule On
- Weight: 5 pt
- Color: Text Color
- Width: Text (not Column)
- Offset: 2 px

14. Check the Preview checkbox at the lower left of the dialog to see your changes and then click OK.

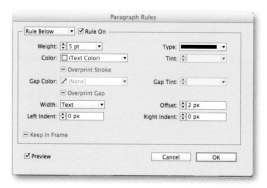

The Paragraph Rule settings for the Rollover state of the button titles.

TIP: Hold the Ctrl/Command key while any other tool is active to switch temporarily to the most recently selected Selection tool.

15. Hold down the Ctrl/Command key and Double-Click the lower right corner of the text frame.

   The text frame magically snaps to the size of your text.

16. If necessary, reposition the text frame on the image while still holding the Ctrl/Command key.

The Rollover state for the image button.

17. Double-Click the word "Fauna" to select it.

18. Open the Paragraph Styles panel and Alt+Click/Option+Click the Create new style button at the bottom of the panel. Name the style "homeRollover" and check the Preview and Apply Style to Selection checkboxes. Click OK to close the dialog.

19. With the Selection tool, select the bird image, and Shift-Click the Fauna text to add it to the selection. Press Ctrl+G/Command+G to group the two objects.

20. Right-Click/Ctrl+Click on the group and from the context menu, choose Interactive > Convert to Button.

Tips for Setting Font Face and Size

Like Illustrator and Photoshop, InDesign offers an assortment of ways to modify font face and size. The obvious approach, of course, is to select from the dropdown menu options. The font size dropdown provides only a limited number of options, however, and the size you want may not be among them.

If you know the name of the font face, or have a particular font size you want to use, you can select the font name or size in the Control panel and type in a new one. As you type the letters of a font name, InDesign jumps to the first name that matches those letters, so you rarely need to enter the entire name. For example, if you enter "Ari", InDesign jumps to Arial.

There are also a couple ways to style your text visually, in the context of your page. To change font size, select the text on the page you want to style, and then click in the Font Size field on the Control panel. Press the up and down arrows on your keyboard to increase and decrease the font size.

A similar approach can be used to select a font family. With your text selected on the document, click inside the Font field on the Control panel. Then, press the up or down arrow on your keyboard to move in alphabetical order through the fonts on your system. The text you've selected on the page will change to reflect the selected font as you cycle through the list.

Another, and more flexible way to modify font size is to first select either the text with the Type tool, or the text frame with the Selection tool. Then, while holding down the Ctrl+Shift/Command+Shift keys, press the > key on the keyboard to increase font size incrementally, or the < key to decrease it. Adding Alt/Option to the mix will result in incremental changes five times as large.

The default Preference setting for keyboard increments (the amount of change using the Ctrl+Shift+>/Command+Shift+> or Ctrl+Shift+</Command+Shift+< shortcuts) is 2 px if the ruler units are set to pixels. If you prefer a finer adjustment, you can go to Edit > Preferences > Units and Increments (Windows)/InDesign > Preferences > Units and Increments (Mac) and set the Size/Leading increment to 1. As is the case with other preferences, if set with no documents open, the setting becomes the preference for all new documents.

The Units and Increments section of the Preferences pane.

21. Open the Buttons and Forms panel and change the default button name to "faunaImage." Press the Enter/Return key to commit the change.

22. Still in the Buttons and Forms panel, keep the default On Release or Tap event, click the Add new action button to the right of "Actions" (**+**), and choose Go To Destination from the actions dropdown.

NOTE: Hyperlink Destinations are anchors built into a document which can be used as link destinations. For more on Hyperlink Destinations, see About Hyperlinks, starting on page 100.

23. Click the Destination dropdown to see that a destination has been created for each page in the document. Select the fauna destination and keep the other default settings.

24. Select the button you just created, and at the bottom of the Buttons and Forms panel, click the Preview Spread button (▣). In the SWF Preview panel, roll over the button to see that its appearance doesn't change. Close the panel.

25. With the faunaImage button still selected, add a Go To Destination action to its On Release or Tap event and select fauna from the Destination dropdown.

26. Click [Rollover] to add a Rollover state to the button and then switch back to the [Normal] state in the Buttons and Forms panel.

    You only want the text to appear when you rollover the button, so you'll delete the text from the button's Normal state.

27. With the Selection tool, Double-Click the button FAUNA text on the document to select the text frame within the button group. Delete the FAUNA text frame.

28. Select the Type tool and draw a text field on top of each of the three remaining images and enter the text as follows:

    - Upper-left image: Texture
    - Upper-right image: Flora
    - Lower-right image: About

29. Switch to the Selection tool, Shift+Click to select all three text frames, and then click homeRollover in the Paragraph Styles panel to style the text.

30. Click off the text frames to deselect them. Double-Click the lower right corner of each text frame to fit the frame to the text, and then position the text on the button images as desired.

31. Group the About text and its image, and then click the Convert to Button icon at the bottom of the Buttons and Forms panel. Name the button "aboutImage". For the Go to Destination action, choose "about" from the Destinations dropdown.

32. Create a Rollover state for the button and delete the text from the Normal state.

33. Next, you'll add text to the Rollover state of the existing textureImage button.

34. Select the textureImage button (upper-left on the document), and then select its Rollover state in the Buttons and Forms panel.

35. In the Layers panel, if necessary, expand the home page layer, the textureImage layer, and then the [Rollover] sublayer nested below it.

36. Locate the <Texture> text layer in the Layers panel and drag it into the [Rollover] sublayer of the textureImage button. If you dragged the text layer below <texture6.jpg>, drag to reposition it at the top of the button layer stack.

Dragging the <Texture> object layer into the
Rollover state of the textureImage button.

You should see the text on the thumbnail of the textureImage button Rollover
state in the Buttons and Forms panel.

37. Select the floralImage button on the document and then select its Rollover state in
the Buttons and Forms panel. In the Layers panel, drag the <Flora> text layer into
the expanded [Rollover] sublayer to complete the buttons on the Home page.

38. Open the SWF Preview panel, click the Preview Document Mode button and
click Play.

39. When the preview appears, test your buttons using the navigation controls at the
bottom left of the panel to return to the Home page.

40. Save and close the file to complete the exercise.

Invisible Buttons

Invisible buttons, also known as hotspots, are the perfect solution to a scenario in
which you'd like a pop up with additional content to appear when the user interacts
with a select area of a static image. Invisible buttons are ideal for setting up tooltips
that pop up to provide clarification or additional information. For situations that
don't lend themselves to the use of traditional buttons, laying an invisible hotspot
over existing content can provide an elegant means to add interactivity.

Because InDesign is vector-based, it's possible for an object to exist even without
the visible presence that a stroke or fill color provides. The mathematical definition
of the object exists despite the fact that you can't see it on the page. When an
object with no stroke or fill is converted to a button, it can be used to initiate actions
in the same way as any other button. Just like any other button, you can add a
rollover appearance to an invisible hotspot button to provide visual feedback to the
user when the hotspot is triggered.

Exercise 12.2: Invisible Buttons

In this exercise, you'll create invisible hotspot buttons on a map of Costa
Rica. When the user mouses over a button, its corresponding province on the
map will be highlighted in green. To create the highlights, the shape of each
province was traced with the pen tool and converted to a button. Each province
button was named with the province name appended by the word map; for
example, guanacasteMap.

Map of the provinces of Costa Rica with invisible hotspot buttons on
the province names and green highlighted buttons on the provinces.

1. Open **ex12_2_end.indd** from the chapter_12_exercises folder.

2. Press Ctrl+Shift+Enter/Command+Shift+Return to preview the file. Mouse over the province names below the words "Pacific Ocean" on the map to see the provinces highlighted in green. When finished exploring, close the SWF Preview panel and keep the file open for reference.

3. Open **ex12_2_start.indd** and save it as ex12_2.indd.

   When the document opens, the page is zoomed in to the list of Costa Rica provinces on the map and two vertical guides. You'll use the guides to define the width of the invisible buttons you'll create for the province names.

4. Select the Rectangle tool and position your cursor on the left guide, just below the number "1" in the list. Click and drag up and to the right to draw a rectangle 10 px high that covers the Alajuela text and extends to the guide on the right.

   The dimensions should appear in the smart guides display as you drag. If necessary, after dragging the rectangle, you can change its height by entering "10 px" in the H field of the Control panel. Before entering the height value, be sure that the constrain proportions link is unlocked.

   Provinces of Costa Rica
   1) Alajuela
   2) Cartago

   Rectangles with no fill or stroke will be converted to invisible hotspot buttons for each of the Costa Rica province names.

5. If you need to, reposition the rectangle so its bottom edge is centered between list entries 1 and 2. You can use the arrow keys on your keyboard to nudge it into place.

6. Switch to the Selection tool, hold down Alt+Shift/Option+Shift, and drag a duplicate rectangle straight down until its top edge meets the bottom edge of the original rectangle. Release the mouse before releasing the modifier keys.

   The Shift key keeps the duplicate rectangle vertically aligned as you drag.

   You need a total of seven buttons, and you could easily repeat the above process a total of five more times. However, InDesign provides a set of wonderful commands that enable you to repeat a transformation on single or multiple objects. Go to: Object > Transform Again to see these commands.

It's debatable as to whether it's more efficient in this specific case to manually duplicate the buttons, or to repeatedly select the menu command. A third option is to streamline the process by creating a custom keyboard shortcut to automate the task.

7. Go to Edit > Keyboard shortcuts, and choose Object Menu from the Product Area dropdown.

8. Scroll through the list of Commands to find Transform Again: Transform Again and select it. Note that there is no shortcut currently assigned to the command.

9. Place your cursor in the New Shortcut field at the bottom left of the window and press Shift+Ctrl+D/Shift+Command+D on your keyboard.

You will see a notation saying that the shortcut is currently assigned to Links. You could try other key combinations to arrive at one that's not in use; but since the Links panel is readily accessible, you'll overwrite the existing shortcut.

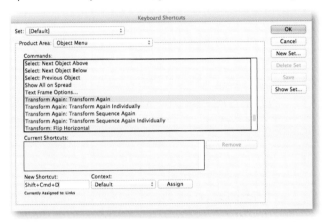

You can create or edit a keyboard shortcut for any InDesign menu command. Go to Edit > Keyboard Shortcuts, choose a Product Area and choose a Command. Then place your cursor in the New Shortcut field and press the desired shortcut key sequence on your keyboard.

10. Click Assign to accept the new shortcut and click Yes on the alert that reads: "Cannot modify the default set. Create a new set based on the Default set?"

11. Name the new set "Interactive" and click OK.

12. Click the Set dropdown to see that you now have four sets of shortcuts to choose from: InDesign's default, Shortcuts for PageMaker 7.0, Shortcuts for QuarkXPress 4.0 and the Interactive set you just created. Click OK to exit the Keyboard Shortcuts dialog.

13. With the newest rectangle selected and your new keyboard shortcut set up and ready to go, hold down the Shift+Ctrl/Shift+Command keys and press D, five times to automatically duplicate and position the required buttons.

14. With the Selection tool, click and drag through all seven rectangles to select them. If the rectangles have a fill and/or stroke color, press the / key on your keyboard, press the X key to swap focus between the stroke and fill, and then press / again to remove the color.

Your rectangles should now be invisible, save for the bounding boxes that appear in InDesign's Normal view mode.

Selected invisible hotspot rectangles with no stroke or fill color.

15. Open the Buttons and Forms panel, select the first rectangle, and convert it to a button. Name the button "**alajuelaBtn**" and add a Rollover state.

16. With the Rollover state active, click the arrow to the right of the Fill swatch on the Control panel to open the Swatches panel. Choose the R=232 G=232 B=232 color swatch, a very light gray color.

17. Double-Click the button with the Selection tool to access the button rectangle, and click the *fx.* icon on the Control panel. Choose Transparency from the Effects options.

18. Select Overlay from the Mode dropdown in the Effects dialog and click OK.

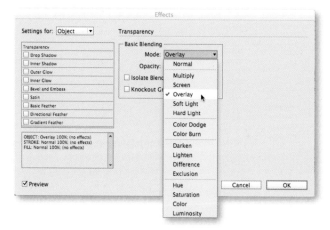

Add an Overlay Transparency effect to the Rollover state of the hotspot.

19. Open the Object Styles panel, Alt+Click/Option+Click the Create new style button at the bottom of the panel, and name the new style "provincesOver." Be sure to apply the style to your button.

20. Return to the Buttons and Forms panel and change the event to On Roll Over.

21. Add a Show/Hide Buttons and Forms action and turn on visibility for the alajuelaMap button.

22. When the user rolls over the alajuelaBtn, the action you just added will make the green highlight on Alajuela province show.

23. Change the button event to On Roll Off and add a Show/Hide Buttons and Forms action to hide the alajuelaMap button.

When you preview your button in the next step, you'll note that, while your button works properly, the alajuelaMap button is visible when the page first loads, and only disappears when you roll off the alajuelaBtn hotspot. You'll need to set the province buttons to be hidden until they are triggered by the hotspots.

24. Preview your page in the SWF Preview panel, roll over and roll off the alajuelaBtn hotspot, and then close the Preview panel.

25. In the Layers panel, expand the flora page 1 layer, unlock the provinces sublayer and expand it.

26. Click in the selection column to the right of the alajuelaMap sublayer in the Layers panel to select the button. Then, in the Buttons and Forms panel, check the Hidden Until Triggered checkbox at the lower left of the Appearance section of the panel.

27. Set each of the remaining six province buttons to Hidden Until Triggered so they are hidden when the page first loads.

NOTE: If you select all the provinces buttons, you can check the Hidden Until Triggered checkbox to change the setting for them all at the same time.

28. Convert each of the remaining hotspot rectangles to buttons, add a Rollover state, and then apply the provincesOver object style. Name the buttons and target their actions as follows:

Button Name	Show/Hide Target
cartagoBtn	cartagoMap
guanacasteBtn	guanacateMap
herediaBtn	herediaMap
limonBtn	limonMap
puntarenasBtn	puntarenasMap
sanjoseBtn	sanjoseMap

29. Preview the page to check that each of your buttons is functioning properly.

30. Select all seven buttons and group them (Ctrl+G/Command+G.) You may find it easiest to select the buttons by Shift+Clicking the selection column for each of them in the Layers panel rather than selecting them on the page.

By grouping the buttons, you create a sublayer in the Layers panel that helps to keep things organized.

31. Note that the button group appears as a sublayer in the Layers panel with the default name of <group>. Click once on the sublayer name, pause very briefly, and click again to activate the name field. Rename the sublayer "provinces hotspots."

Notice that the province buttons appear in the Layers panel in the order in which you created them, with alejuelaBtn at the bottom of the stack. You may find navigating the layers in the panel easier if they reflect the position of the buttons on the document. Rearranging the object stacking order is quite simple, just select and drag each object layer to a new position.

32. Select the alajuelaBtn object layer and drag it to the top of the provinces hotspots group in the Layers panel.

33. Rearrange the remaining province buttons to reflect the order of provinces in the list below the map.

The province buttons in the Layers panel arranged
to reflect their order on the document.

34. Save and close the file to complete the exercise.

Compound Multi-button Groups

The fact that buttons continue to function when part of a group is particularly useful when you need an object with richer functionality than one simple button can provide. In such a case, you can create a grouped object that contains multiple buttons, each with their own functionality.

Exercise 12.3: Compound Multi-button Groups

In this exercise, you'll create pop-up buttons from text objects that contain information about the active volcanoes in Costa Rica. The buttons will be hidden when the page loads, and will appear when you release the mouse after clicking a hotspot on the corresponding volcano name. You will also add a Close button to each volcano pop-up to create a compound button group that appears as a single object.

The volcano pop-ups are triggered when a hotspot over the volcano name
is clicked and released. The Close button and the volcano popup are
separate buttons that are grouped to appear as a single object.

1. Open **ex12_3_end.indd** and press Ctrl+Shift+Enter/Command+Shift+Return to preview the file. Click each volcano name to display the corresponding volcano pop-up. When necessary, use the Close button to hide the open pop-up. Close the SWF Preview panel and, if you like, leave the file open for reference.

2. Open **ex12_3_start.indd** and save it as ex12_3.indd**.

3. Go to View > Entire Pasteboard to see the objects to the left of the spread that you'll use to create the pop-ups.

4. Press and hold Ctrl+Spacebar/Command+Spacebar and, when the Zoom icon appears on the cursor, drag a rectangular marquee around the objects to zoom in on them. Release the mouse before releasing the modifier keys.

5. Open the Buttons and Forms panel, select the object on the page that contains the Arenal Volcano text, and convert it to a button. Name the button "**popupAV**" and check the Hidden until Triggered checkbox at the bottom of the panel.

6. Convert the remaining text objects to buttons and check the Hidden until Triggered checkbox for each. Name the buttons as follows:

- Irazu Volcano text object: **popupIV**
- Poás Volcano text object: **popupPV**
- Turrialba Volcano text object: **popupTV**
- Rincón de la Vieja Volcano text object: **popupRVV**

Since the buttons you just created will act as pop-ups, you won't be adding any functionality to them directly. Instead, you'll create an additional button that will be grouped with each pop-up and that will serve to close it.

7. Go to File > Open and open **lib12.indl** from the chapter_12_exercises folder.

8. Select the popupAV button on the pasteboard, and then drag the Close button graphic from the Library panel onto its upper right corner.

9. With the Close button graphic selected, open the Buttons and Forms panel and convert it to a button.

10. Name the button "**closeAV**" and, with the On Release or Tap event selected, add a Show/Hide Buttons and Forms action. Hide popupAV and closeAV and check the Hidden Until Triggered checkbox at the bottom left of the panel.

11. Select both pop-upAV and the closeAV button with the Selection tool. On the Control panel, click the ▤▾ button and choose Align to Selection. Click the Align top edges and Align right edges buttons to align the Close button to the upper right of the pop-up.

> NOTE: The pop-up buttons have been strategically positioned so they overlap the left edge of the document. A button must at least touch the document page, in order to appear in the list of objects that can be affected by a Show/Hide action.

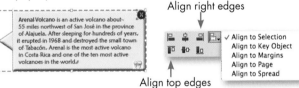

The Pop-up and Close buttons aligned using the Control panel alignment tools.

12. Alt+Shift+Drag/Option+Shift+Drag the closeAV button onto the popupIV button to create a duplicate while keeping the duplicate button vertically aligned. (Be sure to release the mouse before releasing the keys on your keyboard.)

Don't rename the duplicate button just yet. You'll do that after you've created the close buttons for the other pop-ups.

13. To repeat the transform using the keyboard shortcut you set up in steps 7–11 of the previous exercise (page 187), hold down the Shift+Ctrl/ Shift+Command keys and click the D key three times. You should now have four duplicates of the closeAV button, all vertically aligned and automatically renamed.

14. Select popupIV and its Close button, and then click once on the popup button. A bold outline surrounds the popup object indicating that it is the Key Object to which the other selected object(s) will align. Click the Align top edges icon on the Control panel.

15. Select each remaining pop-up and its Close button, and align their top edges.

InDesign Libraries and Snippets

The .indl library item extension stands for "InDesign library." A library is a standalone file that enables you to store page elements for later use. Library items can include text, graphics, animation, audio, video, folio overlays, grids and guides; anything you can include on a document page. Identical in format and function to the Sample Buttons and Forms Library, you can add elements from a page or spread, even an entire page layout, to an InDesign library. In fact, anything you can add to an .indl file, you can add to the Sample Buttons And Forms Library as well. There is nothing in the structure of the Sample Buttons And Forms Library that restricts it to containing only buttons and form elements.

To create a library, go to File > New > Library, name your library file, and save it in a location of your choosing. The new library will open in InDesign, and a panel displaying its contents will appear in the Panel Dock. All libraries, including the Sample Buttons and Forms Library, display the same panel icon, and libraries you create display the file name at the top of the panel. You can open as many libraries as your computer memory can handle at any given time.

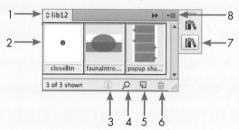

OBJECT LIBRARY

1. Library file name. 2. Object thumbnail and name. 3. Library Item Information button. 4. Show Library Subset button. 5. New Library Item button. 6. Delete Library Item button. 7. Library panel icon. 8. Library panel menu.

Library items travel with all their formatting including Character, Paragraph, Object, Cell and Table styles, as well as swatches for each of their colors.

So, if you were to save a formatted table to a library, not only would the table maintain its styling when placed from the library into your document, it would actually populate the Style panels with the definitions for all the styles applied to it. And, while you can drag library items to any position on a page, if you use the Place Item(s) command from the Library panel menu instead, the library item will be automatically positioned at its original x,y page coordinates.

There are a number of ways to add items to a library:

- Select and drag the items from your document into the Library panel.
- Select the items and click the New Library Item button at the bottom of the panel.
- Add selected items using any of the Add options in the panel menu.

With each of these methods, the item is added to the library with a default name of "Untitled." This could become problematic as the number of items in your library grows.

The Library panel menu.

The library's Show Subset feature enables you to filter library items based on item name, creation date, object type, and description. Of course, you must first enter a name and description in order to take advantage of this organizational feature. Holding the Alt/Option key while clicking the New button will add your new item to the library, and also open the Item Information dialog where you can enter a name and description. For an existing library item, double click the item to access the dialog. Note that the Creation Date and Object Type are entered automatically.

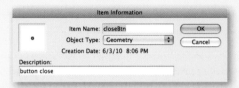

Alt+Click/Option+Click the New Library Item button or Double-Click an existing library item to access the Item Information dialog.

To filter the objects appearing in your library, click the Show Library Subset button at the bottom of the panel. The Show Subset dialog provides the option to search the entire library, or only the items that are currently visible in the panel. You can choose any combination of search parameters to create any level of granularity for your search. When you press OK, only the items conforming to your search criteria appear in the panel. To restore the view of the complete library collection, choose Show All from the panel menu. You can also sort the visible items based on name, description, type, and creation date from the panel menu.

Select search parameters in the Show Subset dialog to display only the library items that match your criteria.

Snippets

Snippets are essentially library items without the Library panel. Just like library items, Snippets can include any item or collection of items on a page or spread. To create a Snippet, select the objects you want to include and go to File > Export. Choose InDesign Snippet from the Save As Type (Windows) or Format (Mac) menu dropdown in the Export dialog. Save the file to your preferred location.

You place a Snippet just as you would place any other file; go to File > Place (Ctrl+D/Command+D) and browse to the desired file. Like library items, Snippets can remember their original page coordinates. If you go to Preferences > File Handling, you can set the behavior for placed Snippets to be positioned at either the cursor location or their original page coordinates. Regardless of the default, you can override it and invoke the opposite behavior on a case-by-case basis by holding down the Alt/Option key when you click to place a Snippet on the page.

Format dropdown from the Export dialog.

The file extension for InDesign CC Snippets is .idms, but was .inds in versions previous to CS5. InDesign CC Snippets are backward compatible to InDesign CS4, and cannot be opened in earlier versions of the program.

16. Select the closeAV button and position your cursor after the text in the X coordinate field at the far left of the Control panel. Type "-6"and press Enter on your keyboard to subtract 6 from the existing coordinates

    InDesign does the math for you and subtracts 6 from the X coordinate to reposition the button on the document.

17. Tab to the Y text field and type "+5" after the Y coordinate to move the close button down 5 px on the page.

18. Select the Close button on popupIV and Shift+Click to select the Close buttons on popupPV, popupTV, and popupRVV.

19. Go to Object > Transform Again > Transform Sequence Again Individually. Ta-da! Like magic, all the Close buttons are precisely and uniformly positioned atop their respective pop-ups.

20. Select the Close button for popupIV, rename it "**closeIV**" and press Tab to commit the change. Update the Show/Hide action to hide popupIV and closeIV.

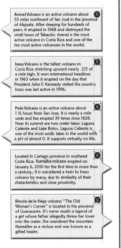

InDesign may already "know" which Close button you want to hide, but you will still need to manually set the pop-up visibility.

21. Select the Close button for popupPV and rename it "**closePV**." Change its Show/Hide action to hide popupPV and closePV.

22. Select the Close button for popupTV and rename it "**closeTV**." Change its Show/Hide action to hide popupTV and closeTV.

23. Select the Close button for popupRVV and rename it "**closeRVV**." Change its Show/Hide action to hide popupRVV and closeRVV.

24. Group each of the pop-ups with their respective Close buttons.

25. Select and rename each pop-up group in the Layers panel with its volcano name appended by the word "popup." ("Arenal popup," "Irazu popup," etc.)

26. Position the first three pop-ups on the document so their arrows point to the appropriate volcano names. Use the arrow keys on your keyboard to nudge them into place as necessary.

27. When you're happy with the placement of the volcano pop-ups in the first column, hide them in the Layers panel and position the remaining two pop-ups.

The two columns of volcano popups positioned next to their corresponding volcano names.

28. Show the hidden pop-ups in the Layers panel, select all five pop-ups, and group them. Rename the group sublayer "**volcano popups**" and hide it in the Layers panel.

29. Draw a rectangle with no fill or stroke over the underlined Arenal Volcano text at the lower right of the page. Convert the rectangle to a button and name it "**btnAV**." Add the following to a Show/Hide action on the On Release or Tap event:

Show:	**popupAV and closeAV**
Hide:	popupIV and closeIV
	popupPV and closePV
	popupTV and close TV
	popupRVV and closeRVV

30. Make four duplicates of btnAV and position one over each of the remaining volcano names. Name each button and add Show/Hide actions as follows:

Button Name	Show	Hide
btnIV	popupIV and closeIV	popupAV and closeAV popupPV and closePV popupTV and close TV popupRVV and closeRVV
btnPV	popupPV and closePV	popupAV and closeAV popupIV and closeIV popupTV and close TV popupRVV and closeRVV
btnTV	popupTV and closeTV	popupAV and closeAV popupIV and closeIV popupPV and closePV popupRVV and closeRVV
btnRVV	popupRVV and closeRVV	popupAV and closeAV popupIV and closeIV popupPV and closePV popupTV and closeTV

31. Select the five invisible hotspot buttons and group them. Name the group "volcano buttons" in the Layers panel.

32. Show the volcano pop-ups sublayer and preview the spread to check your work.

33. Save and close the file to complete the chapter exercises.

The files you worked with in this chapter are built for output to Interactive PDF or SWF. Show/Hide actions do not translate to DPS nor do rollover appearances or rollover and rolloff events. Despite these differences, it is often possible to use the same assets and rework a file to achieve similar visual results using DPS slideshows. To learn more about slideshows, check out Slideshow Overlays, starting on page 505.

While the available button actions are not all supported for output to Interactive PDF, SWF and DPS, the actual buttons are—so the techniques for creating button appearances are applicable to all your InDesign interactive endeavors.

CHAPTER SUMMARY

In this chapter you took your button-making skills to the next level. You learned to create buttons using multiple objects and to differentiate button states by using different combinations of objects to define them. In the process, you learned to:

- Create buttons from multiple objects
- Add and remove objects from existing button states
- Work with the Layers panel to add objects to existing buttons

You also deepened your experience with text formatting and gained experience with:

- Applying all caps formatting to text
- Formatting paragraph rules
- An assortment of ways to set font face and font size

In addition, you got better acquainted with the Preferences dialog by taking a side trip to set units and increments.

At this point, you've got all the fundamentals of button-making under your belt. The next chapter takes you a bit outside the box to explore some of the less obvious ways you can employ buttons in your interactive projects.

Part 4

FLASH ANIMATION AND OUTPUT TO SWF

The introduction of Flash animation in InDesign CS5 opened a new vista of possibility for creating stand-alone presentations and engaging interactive experiences. In this portion of the book you'll learn everything there is to learn about creating animation in InDesign, how to output it, and where and how best to use it.

Chapter 13

INTRODUCING: ANIMATION IN INDESIGN!

Animation is a natural if not essential factor in creating an engaging user experience. What better way to bring a document to life than with movement—from simple cross-fades to objects that perform mobile antics on the page.

In this chapter, you'll combine animation of rotation, scale, and opacity with existing animation presets, as well as set triggering events, duration, sequence, and timing delays. You'll learn to animate objects on a path called a motion path, and then apply all these skills to captivating your audience with the compelling experience of a document in motion.

Introduction

Before digging into InDesign's awesome animation tools let's first take a moment to talk about Flash—past, present and future.

Not that long ago, just about three years in fact, Flash was king. It was the standard for animation on the web, the vehicle of choice for delivery of online video, and it was well integrated with a multitude of mobile devices. It seemed that Flash would live forever.

Concurrent with the release of Creative Suite 5 in April of 2010, the very first iPad burst upon the scene and changed the digital landscape forever. Lack of support for Flash on the iPad and the adoption of HTML5 signalled the beginning of the end for Flash on mobile devices. At the time of this writing HTML5 is rapidly displacing Flash for delivery of video and animation on the desktop as well, making imminent the king's demise.

BUT, despite the seemingly inevitable outcome, the king has not yet drawn a final breath. There is still wide-spread support for the Flash player in desktop browsers and you can still create stand-alone executable Flash files that make a great solution for dynamic presentations (if you have the free Flash Player.)

That said, the next several chapters are devoted to exploring the animation tools in InDesign and then, how to output your interactive masterpieces to SWF (the format for compiled Flash files.) Who knows, maybe by the next release of InDesign the animation tools will be reconfigured to output to HTML5 instead of SWF. Adobe, are you listening?

InDesign makes it extremely easy to animate any object, including placed files, text boxes, graphics, and even buttons. There are three panels around which all your animation work will revolve: the Animation panel, the Timing panel and the SWF Preview panel. You'll set all the parameters for your animations using the Animation panel and then use the Timing panel to control the sequence of play and timing delays. When you're ready to see everything in action, you'll preview and test your creations in the SWF Preview panel.

The Animation Panel

The Animation panel is chock full of controls, all in one neat little package. You can find it with all the other interactive panels at Window > Interactive > Animation.

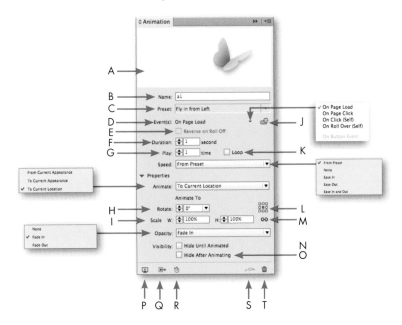

A. Animation Preset preview.

B. Name field.

C. Preset dropdown

D. Events triggering animation.

E. Reverse on Roll Off: available when Roll Over Self event is applied; reverses animation.

F. Duration of animation.

G. Number of times to play animation.

H. Degrees of rotation to animate.

I. Width and height scale percentages to animate

J. Create Button Trigger.

K. Loop animation.

L. Reference point for animation of rotation and scale.

M. Lock to scale proportionately or unlock to scale disproportionately.

N. Hide object until animated.

O. Hide object after animating.

P. Preview Spread

Q. Show Animation proxy.

R. Open Timing panel.

S. Convert path to Motion Path.

T. Remove animation.

Working with Motion Presets

Motion presets provide a starting point for most if not all of the animations you'll create in InDesign. These presets are the very same as those found in Flash Professional. When you select a motion preset in the InDesign Animation panel, a proxy of the selected animation is displayed at the top of the panel. That little pink butterfly takes the guesswork out of choosing a preset by demonstrating the animation for you right in the preview window. Be aware, however, that the butterfly is for presets only. Once you make a change to the preset parameters, the butterfly disappears.

The first field in the Animation panel is the Name field. In your investigation of buttons, you learned that in order to be controlled by actions and events, an object must have a name. Under the hood, InDesign animations are controlled programmatically, and therefore, they, like buttons, require names. InDesign obliges by automatically providing a generic name for each animation. As with buttons, it's good practice to name your animations deliberately and descriptively. This is particularly helpful If your document contains multiple animations and you need to make adjustments to sequence or timing. A descriptive name makes it easier to know which animation is which.

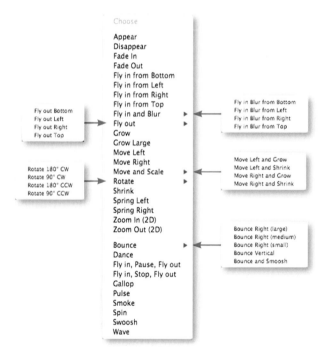

Animation presets are accessed from the Presets dropdown in the Animation panel.

The easiest way to get started with animation in InDesign is to select an object you want to animate, open the Animation panel, and choose a motion preset. InDesign does the rest. Of the multitude of motion presets that ship with InDesign, more than a quarter of them animate changes in scale, rotation, opacity, and/or speed. The controls on the Animation panel make it possible to modify existing presets or to create similar types of animations from scratch. The remaining motion presets are complex animations that go beyond what can be created directly in InDesign.

Exercise 13.1: Easing, Duration, & Motion Presets

As "Hello world!" is to programmers, the bouncing ball is to animators. Animating a bouncing ball has long been the traditional initiation into the world of animation. In homage to this hallowed tradition, naturally, your first InDesign animation has to be a bouncing ball.

1. Go to File > New > Document and, in the New Document window, choose Web as the Intent. Leave the other defaults settings and click OK.

2. Select the Ellipse tool (L). Hold down the Shift key and drag to create a small, perfect circle. Release the mouse before releasing the Shift key.

3. Switch to the Selection tool. With the circle still selected, click the Stroke swatch at the bottom of the Tools panel and set the color to None. Then, select the Fill swatch at the bottom of the Tools panel to ensure that it's active, and open the Gradient panel (Window > Color > Gradient.)

4. Choose Radial from the Type dropdown and then click the black gradient color stop to select it. Open the Swatches panel and Alt-Click/Option+Click any color to replace the black in the gradient. If you don't hold down the Alt/Option key, the gradient will be replaced with the solid color of the swatch you selected.

5. With the circle still selected, go to Window > Interactive > Animation or click the ✦ icon in the Panel Dock to open the Animation panel.

6. Type "ball" in the Name field to replace the default name of "circle."

7. Near the bottom of the Preset dropdown, choose Bounce > Bounce and Smoosh.

8. Press Ctrl+Shift+Enter/Command+Shift+Return to preview the animation.

    With the animated ball selected, you'll notice an animation indicator at the lower right of the ball and a green line with dots and an arrow, pointing in the direction of the animated motion. The green line is called a motion path, and the dots on it indicate duration. The more dots there are on the path, the more time the animation takes to play.

    In the image to the left, the duration of the first ball animation is the  Bounce and Smoosh preset default of 3.125 seconds. The second instance of the animation was set to a duration of 1 second. As you can see, the motion path for the shorter animation has fewer dots. Notice, too, that the dots are not spaced evenly on the motion path—the changing density of the dots indicates easing. The closer the dots, the less distance is traveled, the slower the motion. The farther apart they are, the more distance is traveled, the faster the motion. For this particular preset, you can see that the velocity of the ball is variable, starting out slow, accelerating, then alternately slowing and accelerating with the bounce. This preset incorporates a sequence of transformations in scale and easing that are beyond what you can create in InDesign. You can, however, make modifications to the preset to incorporate changes of rotation, scale, and opacity.

9. Alt-Drag/Option-Drag the ball with the Selection tool to duplicate it. Rename the duplicated animation "ball2."

DOWNLOAD:
Exercise files for this chapter can be downloaded from http://www.interactive-indesign.com.

TIP: The Ellipse tool is hidden under the Rectangle tool (not the Rectangle Frame tool). Click and hold the Rectangle tool to expose the Ellipse tool so you can select it.

	Rectangle Tool	M
	Ellipse Tool	L
	Polygon Tool	

TIP: Easing: Transitions in animation speed are referred to as easing. InDesign has six easing options:
From Preset: Inherits easing from Preset.
None: No easing.
Ease In: Starts slowly and increases in speed to give the impression of acceleration.
Ease Out: Starts fast and slows down to give the impression of deceleration.
Ease In and Out: Starts fast, slows in the middle, and speeds up at the end.

---

10. With ball2 selected on the document, and the Digital Publishing workspace active, drag the Preview panel to a column of its own in the Panel Dock. Open the panel and drag the lower left corner to enlarge it.

11. Open the Animation panel. If necessary, twirl down the Properties arrow at the bottom of the panel to display additional controls. Both the Preview panel and the Animation panel should be visible and accessible, with the Animation panel overlapping the Preview panel.

12. Preview the animation again to see that the first animation plays through before the second animation begins. By default, InDesign animations play in sequence based on the order in which they were created.

With the Preview panel open, you can change the animation properties of a selected object in the Animation panel, and then click the Play button in the Preview panel to refresh the animation.

13. With both panels still open, change the Duration of the ball2 animation to 1 second. Set Opacity to Fade Out. Make sure the Constrain the Scale Value link icon is linked (⬚) (to the right of Scale Height), and enter "50" in the W field. Tab to populate the H field with the same value.

14. Click the Play button on the Preview panel to refresh the animation preview.

    Easing can give your animation a more realistic feel, conveying a sense of momentum or deceleration. While sometimes subtle, appropriate use of the Speed options can lend authenticity to movement on the screen.

15. Delete the second ball. With the remaining ball selected, choose Fly in From Top from the Preset dropdown in the Animation panel. Change the Duration to 3 seconds.

16. Alt-Drag/Option-Drag to duplicate until you have a total of five balls. In the Animation pane, name each of the ball animations: **"ball1"**, **"ball2"**, **"ball3"**, **"ball4"**, **"ball5."**

17. Position one ball near the left margin and another near the right margin, with the other three balls in between. Select all five balls and go to Window > Object & Layout > Align to open the Align panel.

    While there are Align controls on the Control panel, the Distribute Spacing commands are only available through the Align panel.

18. From the Align panel menu, choose Show Options to display the Distribute Spacing commands. Confirm that Align to Selection is chosen and then click the Distribute Horizontal Space button.

Align to Selection

Align to Key Object

Align to Margins

Align to Page

Align to Spread

The Align To options of the Align panel and a highlight on the Distribute Horizontal Space button.

19. Choose Align to Page from the Align to dropdown and then click the ⬛ button to align the vertical centers of the objects to the vertical center of the page. This will enable you to see the entire animation.

20. Select the first ball and ensure that the Speed option in the Animation panel is set to From Preset. Select the second ball and set the Speed to None, the third to Ease In, the fourth to Ease Out, and the fifth to Ease In and Out.

21. At the bottom of the Animation panel, press the ⏱ button to open the Timing panel.

22. Select the first item in the list, hold the Shift key, and select the last. With all the items selected, click the Play Together button (⬛) at the bottom of the panel.

23. Click the Preview Spread button at the bottom of the Timing panel. In the preview, note the differences in the animations due to the ease settings. Save the file as ex13_1.indd in the chapter_13_exercises folder and then close the document to complete the exercise.

Working with the Pen Tool

The Pen tool in InDesign is the same tool found in Illustrator and Photoshop. It's a tool that people just love to hate. If you're one of those folks who want to tear their hair out at the mere mention of the Pen tool, take heart. With a few simple pointers and a little bit of practice, you'll be on your way to mastery.

Working efficiently with the Pen tool entails use of several keyboard shortcuts. The first of these shortcuts is the Ctrl/Command key. When you have the Pen tool selected, holding the Ctrl/Command key switches temporarily to the Direct Selection tool. When you release the key, the Pen tool returns. You'll be placing points as you draw with the Pen tool, and there will be times when you'll need the Direct Selection tool to select and manipulate those points so the shortcut comes in very handy.

In order for the Pen tool to function as intended, ensure that the Corner Options controls at the far right of the Control panel are set to None. (The Corner Options controls are available when any tool other than the Type tool or the Note tool is selected.)

open path · closed path

Ensure that Corner Options are set to None on the Control panel before drawing with the Pen tool. (If you don't see the controls on the Control panel, go to Object > Corner Options.)

Hold down the Ctrl/Command key and click off a path to deselect it. To close an active, open path, mouse over the first point on the path, and click when the Pen tool cursor displays a little circle.

Drawing straight lines with the Pen tool is simple. Just click where you want to place a point, and then release without dragging. When you click and release to place a second point, the two points will be connected by a straight line segment. Holding the Shift key when you place a point constrains its placement to an angle that's a multiple of 45° from the previous point. To draw a path that is perfectly horizontal or perfectly vertical, hold the Shift key when you click to place a point, and then release the mouse without dragging, before you release the Shift key.

To terminate an open path, hold the Ctrl/Command key to switch temporarily to the Direct Selection tool and click off the path to deselect it—or press P on your keyboard. P is the shortcut for the Pen tool, and pressing it when a path is active deselects the path and readies the Pen to start again, as indicated by an asterisk at the lower right of the Pen tool cursor.

To draw curves with the Pen tool, it helps to think of a rubber band that you're stretching in the direction you want the curve to go. When you click with the Pen tool to place an anchor point, and then drag while still holding the mouse, direction lines appear that enable you to shape a curve. The trick is to drag the direction line in the direction you want the curve to go. Drag up when you want the curve to move upward, and drag down when you want the curve to flow down.

When drawing curves with the Pen tool, drag the direction handles in the direction you want the curve to flow.

You can draw straight lines at angles in multiples of 45° by holding the Shift key when clicking with the Pen tool.

As a general rule, the fewer the points, the smoother the curve—when it comes to working with the Pen tool, less is more. To change the direction in which a curve is flowing, you must convert the anchor point of the curve to a corner point. The Convert Direction Point tool is made for this very purpose. While dragging a direction line with the Pen tool, hold the Alt/Option key to temporarily switch to the Convert Direction Point tool and drag the direction line in the direction you want the new curve to flow.

Hold the Alt/Option key to switch temporarily to the Convert Direction Point tool and then drag the direction line to change the trajectory of a curve.

The Convert Direction Point cursor of the Pen tool.

When you mouse over a newly placed anchor point with the Pen tool, the cursor changes to display the icon for the Convert Direction Point tool. Click the anchor point to remove the second direction line in order to make a corner for a straight path.

The Pen tool provides visual feedback through contextual indicators that appear at the lower right of the pen icon on the cursor. When the cursor displays an asterisk, no path is being drawn. When a path is being drawn, the cursor displays only the pen. When hovering over an existing and active path, but not over an anchor point, the cursor displays the Add Anchor Point plus sign. Clicking when this cursor is visible adds an anchor point to the path. Conversely, if you hover over an existing point on an active path, the cursor displays the minus sign for the Delete Anchor Point tool. Clicking when this cursor is showing removes the anchor point from the path. In all, there are nine variations on the Pen tool cursor, each with its own story to tell. As small as the indicators are, learning their language is necessary to mastering the tool. All nine variations are illustrated below.

A   B   C   D   E   F   G   H   I

The many faces of the Pen tool cursor: A) Ready to draw a new path. B) A path is being drawn. C) Click an endpoint on an existing path to pick up and continue drawing. D) Click to close the path. E) Click to snap to guide—only available when Snap to Guides is turned on. F) Add anchor point. G) Delete anchor point. H) Convert direction point. I) Join anchor points.

Exercise 13.2: The Pen Tool

Mastery of the Pen tool takes a bit of practice, but it's a truly useful skill. Once you have it down, you'll be able to modify any vector graphic, create perfect tracings, and, drawing motion paths for your animations will be a no-brainer.

This exercise provides an introduction to the basic skills you'll need to develop your Pen tool chops.

1. From the chapter_13_exercises folder, open **ex13_2_start.indd** and save it as ex13_2.indd.

2. Choose a stroke color from the Tools panel and set the fill color to None.

3. Select the Pen tool (P) and position the cursor over the center of the first red target (⊙) on path A1. Click once and release without dragging to place the first point of the path.

---

4. Hold down the Shift key, and click once on each of the red targets on the path, releasing after each click without dragging. (The Shift key constrains the path to angles that are a multiple of 45°. After you click the last target, release the Shift key, hold the Ctrl/Command key, and click off the path to deselect it (or press P.)

5. In path A2, click and release each of the targets consecutively starting with target 1. This time, don't hold down the Shift key. After you click target 7, position the Pen tool over point 1. When you see the close path cursor for the Pen tool (✎₀), click to close the path.

6. For path B, click the first red target and, still holding down the mouse, drag a direction line up to the first red dot and release. (Always drag direction lines in the direction you want the curve to go.)

7. For each of the remaining targets in path B, click and hold and drag the direction line to follow the curve, and then release the mouse at the red dot.

8. After dragging the direction line for the last target, press the P key on your keyboard to terminate the path.

9. For path C, click the first target and drag the direction line up to the first red dot. Click the second target and drag down to the second red dot. Keep holding the mouse! Press the Alt/Option key and drag the direction line up to the first yellow dot. Be sure to release the mouse before releasing the Alt/Option key.

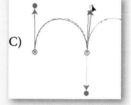

You can change the direction of a curve using the Convert Direction Point tool to create a corner point. Drag the adjustment handle to define the trajectory of the new curve.

10. After dragging the direction line for the last target on the path, hold the Ctrl/Command key and click off the path to deselect it.

11. For path D, click the first target, drag up to the red dot, and release the mouse. Click the next target and drag down to complete the curve. Then, release the mouse and position your cursor over the point you just placed. When you see the Convert Direction Point cursor of the Pen tool (✎ᵥ), click and release to create a corner point. The second direction line is automatically removed.

12. Hold down the Shift key, click the next target, and release the mouse. By holding the Shift key, you keep the points in horizontal alignment.

13. Position your cursor over the point you just placed, and when the Convert Direction Point cursor appears, click and drag down to the red dot to start the next curve.

14. Continue the process outlined above, dragging the direction lines to create curves and Shift+Clicking to draw straight lines. For each point you place, convert the anchor point by clicking with the Convert Direction Point cursor of the Pen tool.

15. After placing the last point, hold the Ctrl/Command key and click off the path to deselect it.

16. Save and close the file to complete the exercise.

Working with Motion Paths

As you saw in Exercise 13.1, motion paths determine the path travelled by an animated object. You can edit the path used in a motion preset or you can create a motion path of your own. The motion path is actually distinct from the object being animated and must be manipulated independently. You can make changes to a motion path using the Selection tool and the Transform tools but for changes in the actual shape of a path, you'll need to use the Pen and Direct Selection tools.

Exercise 13.3: Modifying Preset Motion Paths

1. Open **ex13_3_end.indd** from the chapter_13_exercises folder and preview the document (Ctrl+Shift+Enter/Command+Shift+Enter). Note the text frames flying in from the left sequentially. Click the purple polygon at the left of the first row to watch it trace the motion path to the center. Click the purple polygon at the right of the second row to see it travel to the center as well. Click the purple polygon in the middle of the last row to see it travel to the right, away from the center. Close the Preview panel.

   The polygon animations demonstrate the three destination options available through the Animate dropdown in the Animation panel. The animation for all the objects, including the text, started with the same motion preset: Fly in From Left. For the text frames, the motion paths were scaled to cover a greater distance, and for the polygons, the contour of the paths was changed.

2. With the Selection tool, select each object on the page in turn, and inspect the settings in the Animation panel. When you're done exploring, keep the file open for reference.

3. Open **ex13_3_start.indd** and save it as ex13_3.indd.

4. Select the Polygon tool (nested under the Rectangle tool) and click once on the document. When the Polygon dialog opens, enter 61 px for Width, 53 px for Height, 8 for the Number of Sides, and ensure that the Star Inset is set to 0. Click OK to create the polygon and then position it on top of the yellow polygon in the top row of the background image.

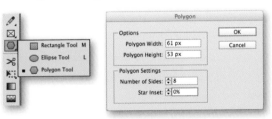

> NOTE: The Tools panel displays the icon for the most recently used shape tool so it's a good idea to get familiar with the icon for each of the tools.

The Polygon and Ellipse tools are hidden under the Rectangle tool. Click and hold the visible tool to display the other shape tools. With the Polygon tool selected, click once on the document to open the Polygon dialog.

5. Select the polygon with the Selection tool and, if it doesn't already have one, give it a fill. We chose purple. Open the Animation panel and choose Fly in From Left from the Preset dropdown. Click the Show animation proxy button (▣→) at the bottom of the panel. This displays a ghost of the animated object at the starting point of the animation.

6. Alt-Drag/Option-Drag the polygon you created straight down to copy it, and align it on top of the middle polygon in the background image. Copy it again and position it on the bottom polygon.

7. Shift-Click on each of the text frames to select them and apply the Fly in From Left motion preset from the Animation panel.

8. Save and preview your document. Note that the animations play sequentially. Note also that the order in which the text frames play is incorrect.

    The text frame animations originate directly on the page. You will edit them so the animations begin from outside the page boundaries.

9. Zoom in on the left edge of the text frames, go to View > Grids and Guides, and confirm that Snap to Guides is checked. Switch to the Selection tool.

10. Click once on the first text frame to select it. Note the green line of the motion path running through the text, with a dot at either end.

•• A number of the InDesign Animatio

Selected text frame with motion path applied.

11. Mouse over the motion path until you see a tooltip saying "Motion Path, click to edit." Click the motion path to select it.

> NOTE: When the cursor changes to a double-sided arrow, click and drag to the left to lengthen the motion path.
>
>

12. Mouse over the left edge of the motion path. When the cursor changes to a double-sided arrow, drag left to the vertical guide located on the pasteboard.

13. Preview the spread and note the apparent acceleration of the first text frame as it travels along the motion path. Collapse the SWF Preview panel and confirm that the animation rather than just the motion path is selected on the page. Expand the Animation panel in the Panel Dock and note that Duration is still set to 1.

14. From the Animation panel menu, select Save. When the Animation Preset dialog appears, enter "Fly In Text" in the Name field and click OK.

15. Select the remaining text frames and open the Animation panel. Select Fly In Text from the top of the Preset dropdown to apply your new motion preset.

16. Deselect the text frames and then reselect only the second text frame. Notice that the motion path extends to the right rather than the left. A peek at the Animation panel reveals that the selected Animate option is set to From Current Appearance.

17. Reselect the text frames and choose To Current Location from the Animate dropdown. Preview and save the file.

    Next, you'll edit the motion paths for the polygons.

18. With the Selection tool, click once on the top-most polygon to select it, and then select its motion path.

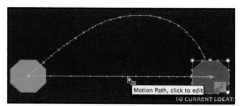

Editing a motion path with the Pen tool.

19. With the motion path selected, press P to switch to the Pen tool. Mouse over the point in the middle of the path, and, when you see the plus sign appear at the lower right of the Pen tool cursor, click once and release to add a point to the path.

20. Hold down the Ctrl/Command key (to switch temporarily to the Direct Selection tool), and drag the point to the apex of the curve, as shown below. Release the mouse and then release the Ctrl/Command key.

Reposition the point you added to the motion path with the Pen tool.

21. Holding down the Alt/Option key (to switch temporarily to the Convert Direction Point tool), click and hold the point you placed and drag down and to the right, extending the direction line in order to round out the curve. Release the mouse.

Converting a corner point to a curve with the Convert Direction Point tool.

22. Select the polygon, and, from the Animation panel menu, choose Save. Name the preset "Arch". Select the remaining two polygons and apply the Arch preset.

23. Select the second polygon and, in the Animation panel, choose To Current Appearance from the Animate dropdown to change the direction of the animation. Choose Fade Out from the Opacity dropdown in the Properties section of the panel. Save, preview, and close the file.

Timing, Triggering Events, and Buttons

By default, animations are triggered by the On Page Load event—playing automatically when the page loads, in the order they were created. In addition to On Page Load, there are four other events you can select in the Animation panel to trigger your animations. Each of them rely on user interaction: On Page Click, On Click (Self), On Roll Over (Self), and On Button Event. The On Button Event is only available from the Animation panel Event dropdown if there is already a button in the document with an action targeted to an existing animation. You can use the On Button Event option to make a button trigger an animation using any of the four button events: On Click, On Release, On Roll Over, and On Roll Off.

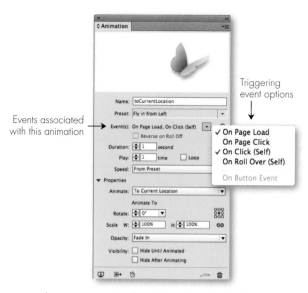

Events associated with this animation

Triggering event options

The events associated with the selected animation are listed in the Events section of the Animation panel.

Just below the Preset dropdown on the Animation panel, you'll find the list of events associated with the selected animation. To add or remove events, press the little arrow (⬇) to the right of the listed events, and select or deselect the desired event.

The same event can be applied to multiple animations, and any animation can be triggered by multiple events. When multiple animations are set to play On Page Load, On Page Click, and/or On Button Event, you can use the Timing panel to change the order in which the animations play.

In the Timing panel (Window > Interactive > Timing), changing the animation sequence is as simple as dragging the animation name to the desired position in the play list. You can group animations to have them play simultaneously, and you can add delays to customize the timing.

In the Timing panel, drag animation names up or down in the stack to change the order in which they play.

To set animations to play together, Shift-Click on each animation you want to include in the animation group, and click the 🖮 button at the bottom of the panel. To remove an animation from the group, select it and click the Play separately button (🖮).

To play animations together, select them in the Timing panel
and click the link button at the bottom of the panel.

The events available from the Timing panel Event dropdown are determined by
the triggering events established for each animation in the Animation panel. To
adjust the timing for animations associated with a particular event, you must first
select the event in the Timing panel. To show animations triggered by the On Page
Click event, first select On Page Click from the Event dropdown. All the animations
associated with that event will appear in the panel, and you can set their timing.
For the Timing panel to show animations triggered by button events, the triggering
button must be selected on the document. If a button has multiple events that trigger
animations, such as On Roll Over and On Roll Off you can choose the triggering
event from the Timing panel Event dropdown when the button is selected on
the document.

You can apply a Play Animation action to an existing button right from the
Animation panel. Select the animation on your document and then click the Create
button trigger button (🔘) in the Event section of the panel. Next, just click the
button to which you want to add the action. The Button panel opens, allowing you
to make any adjustments. The default button event is On Release, but you can, of
course, add actions to other events.

Exercise 13.4: Timing, Triggering Events, & Buttons

1. Open **ex13_4_end.indd** from the chapter_13_exercises folder and preview the file
    (Ctrl+Shift+Enter/Command+Shift+Return.) Be sure to select Set Preview Document
    Mode at the far lower right of the Preview panel, since this is a multi-page
    document. Use the next and previous arrow buttons at the lower right of the pages
    to navigate through the document. When you're done exploring, you can close the
    Preview panel and keep the file open for reference.

2. Open **ex13_4_start.indd**, save it as ex13_4.indd and preview the file in
    Document Mode. Close the Preview panel and ensure that you are on page 1 of
    the document.

    As you saw in the preview, the text animations on the first and second pages
    need to be reordered.

3. Go to Window > Interactive > Timing or click the ⏱ icon in the Panel Dock to
    open the Timing panel. Since the text animations are automatically named with the
    text they contain, they are easy to identify. Select the animation that starts with "A
    number..." and drag it to the top of the stack of text animations.

---

4. Select the text animation that starts with "You can also..." and drag it to the bottom of the stack.

The text animations ordered in the proper sequence in the Timing panel.

For a little variety and more interactivity, you'll set the polygon animations on page 1 to be triggered when clicked rather than by the On Page Load event. You'll add text to the polygon objects that instruct the user to click the buttons to play the animations.

5. With the Type tool selected, type the words "click to play" in the second and third polygons on page 1. Don't worry about formatting the text just yet; although, if necessary, you can make it smaller to fit in the shape.

6. With the Type tool active in one of the polygons, press Ctrl+B/Command+B (Object > Text Frame Options) to open the Text Frame Options dialog. Choose Center from the Vertical Justification Align dropdown and click OK.

TIP: With your text or text frame selected, hold down the Shift+Ctrl/ Shift+Command keys and press the > key to increase font size, or the < key to decrease it.

7. Press Ctrl+A/Command+A to select the text and then press Shift+Ctrl+C/ Shift+Command+C to center it. Choose a typeface and font size. We chose Myriad Pro and set the size to 10 px.

8. When you're satisfied with the appearance of the text, select the Eyedropper tool and click the text to capture its formatting. You'll see that the Eyedropper fills up half way with black ink. Click and drag the loaded Eyedropper across the text in the other two polygons to apply the formatting.

The Eyedropper captures the formatting of the text but not of the text frame. We've created an Object style to handle the vertical centering of the text in the text frame, to save you a few steps.

TIP: A triple click in the middle of a line of text with the loaded Eyedropper tool applies the formatting it's captured to the entire line.

9. Select all three polygons. From the Object Styles panel, click the buttonText style to apply it.

There's no necessity to apply the Object style to the first polygon other than to keep the objects uniform. This puts you in a good position later, should you decide that you want to make a universal change in appearance.

10. With the polygons still selected, open the Animation panel. Click the ⏷ button to access the trigger events and deselect On Page Load to stop the animation from playing automatically when the page is displayed. Click the button again and choose On Click (Self). Notice that the On Click (Self) event appears in the panel next to the word "Event(s)."

The On Click (Self) event applied to multiple
animations. Notice that the Name field is empty.

11. Save the document and preview the spread. Notice that the text flies in in the proper order, and the buttons don't play until clicked. Close the SWF Preview panel.

12. Navigate to page 2 of the document and open the Timing panel. Rearrange the text animations to reflect their order on the document.

13. Select all three polygons and apply the Fly in from Left motion preset. Choose From Current Appearance from the Animate dropdown.

14. Click off to deselect and then reselect the first polygon. In the Animation panel, set the Duration to 1.5 seconds, and set the Rotate value to 90°.

15. Select the second polygon and set the Duration to 2 seconds. Set both W and H to 175%.

16. Select the last polygon, leave the default duration of 1 second, and choose Fade Out from the Opacity dropdown.

   Note that there are three text buttons sitting just within the left page margin, one for each of the polygons. You can add a Play Animation action to each of the buttons from the Buttons panel, but it's easier to use the Create Button Trigger button on the Animation panel.

17. Select the polygon with the rotate animation, and, in the Animation panel, click the Create Button Trigger button to the right of "Event(s)". Then, click on the click to play button to the left of the animation. The Buttons panel pops open to display the Animation action and the default On Release or Tap event. Note that each of the buttons have been named with reference to the animations they will trigger.

18. Drag the button onto the rotate polygon, select both objects, and press Ctrl+G/ Command+G to group them.

19. Repeat steps 17 and 18 for the two remaining polygons, adding the text buttons to their respective animations. Save and preview the spread to confirm that the animations play as expected. Leave the SWF Preview panel open.

20. Navigate to page 3 of the document and preview the spread. Note that all the animations on the page are triggered by the On Page Load event and that they all play sequentially. Close the Preview panel.

21. Select all six polygons on page 3. In the Animation panel, remove the On Page Load triggering event.

TIP: When you click the Create Button Trigger button in the Animation panel, the cursor changes to a target until you click the button that you want to use to trigger the animation.

22. Deselect, and then reselect the first large polygon. In the Animation panel, click the Create Button Trigger button, and then click the playDelay1 button (the button to the left of the first set of polygons).

23. Select the two remaining large polygons and, once again, click the Create Button Trigger button and then click the playDelay1 button.

24. Note that clicking on a button with the Create Button Trigger button selects the button. With the playDelay1 button thus selected, open the Timing panel. Note that only the animations associated with the button appear in the panel, and the event displayed is the On Release event. Note also that the animations have been named to make them easier to identify.

25. Select delay1b in the Timing panel and set the Delay to 1 second.

26. Select delay1c in the Timing panel and set the Delay to 2 seconds. Preview your animation and click the first click to play button to activate the animation. Close the Preview panel.

27. Select the three small polygons, open the Animation panel, and click the Create Button Trigger button. Then click the button to the left of the small polygon group (the playDelay2 button) to set it as the trigger button.

28. With the button still selected, open the Timing panel and Shift-Click on each of the animations to select all three. Click the up arrow next to the Delay field to set the delay to .25 seconds.

   The up and down arrows of the Delay field initially increment the delay value by .25 seconds. However, if you hold an arrow down for several seconds worth of increments, the values begin to shift by whole seconds. If you prefer, you can instead click in the Delay field and type in a value.

29. Select the playDelay1 button and drag it on top of the first large polygon. Drag through the polygon with the Selection tool to select both the polygon and the button, and press Ctrl+G/Command+G to group them.

30. Select the playDelay2 button and drag it on top of the first small polygon. Drag through the polygon and the button with the Selection tool to select both objects, and press Ctrl+G/Command+G to group them as well. Click off the group to deselect.

31. In the Timing panel, Shift-Click to select all the text animations and click the ⬗ button at the bottom of the panel to set them to play at the same time.

32. Save and preview the file to check the timing of your animations.

33. Close the SWF Preview panel and return to the Timing panel. Select the first text animation in the list and set its delay to 1 second. Set the delay for the second text animation to 2 seconds, the third to 3, and the fourth to 4.

34. Save and preview the document, paying particular attention to the effect of the timing settings you established. Close the SWF Preview panel, and then save and close the file to complete the exercise and the chapter.

CHAPTER SUMMARY

This chapter laid the foundation for every animation you'll create in InDesign. Starting with the Animation panel, you explored the provided motion presets and then proceeded to customize them by modifying their parameters. In making adjustments to the default settings, you gained an understanding of:

- How to interpret the markings on a motion path
- The differences between the Animate options:
  - From Current Appearance
  - To Current Appearance
  - From Current Location
- How to set the duration of an animation
- Using the easing options to control the appearance of acceleration and deceleration:
  - Ease In
  - Ease Out
  - Ease In and Out
  - From Preset
- How to save and apply a custom motion preset
- How to set triggering events for your animations including:
  - Choosing a trigger event from the Event dropdown options
  - Creating a button trigger
  - Using the On Click (Self) event

With multiple animations in your document, you then explored the Timing panel and learned how to:

- Set the sequence of your animations
- Set animations to play together
- Set animation delays

Peripheral to your animation work, you gained a solid foundation in use of the Pen tool and learned to draw straight and curved paths, streamlining the process with the use of modifier keys. You got an in-depth view of the Corner Options controls, set parameters for the Polygon tool and became familiar with the Align panel features. You also employed the Eyedropper tool to capture and apply formatting.

With the essentials of InDesign animation solidly in place, you're ready to innovate. The next chapter takes you well beyond the basics to create advanced animation effects that will make you proud.

Chapter 14

GETTING FANCY WITH ANIMATION

Now that you've got the fundamentals down, let's start looking at what kinds of effects you can achieve with a little bit of creativity and some inspired sleight of hand. This chapter opens up whole new vistas for what's possible with animation in InDesign, and then takes that knowledge to another dimension, literally, to create the illusion of objects moving through 3-D space.

Custom Motion Paths, and Cool Effects

Once the creative juices start flowing, you'll likely surprise yourself with all the animation ideas that will fill your head. Animation doesn't have to be complicated to enrich the texture of a project or page. Just a little bit of motion can go a long way. One caution about interactive design and animation that demands careful consideration is this: before you fill your pages with gratuitous animations of all shapes and sizes, remember—just because you can, doesn't mean you should. If a little is good, more is not necessarily better. A simple transition, maybe some title animation, possibly text that flies in or buttons that animate on rollover: all good. The truth of the matter is, animation for animation's sake can get old pretty quickly. Better to go for simple elegance over bells and whistles that jangle and clang. If your animation serves to engage and enhance, great. If it's there simply because you thought it was cool, it may be best to think again.

That said, this chapter is about cool stuff you can do. And while the actual examples may not necessarily represent the pinnacle of elegance, they should serve to stimulate some ideas and prime that creative pump. With new tools in your toolbox, it'll be up to you to find elegant ways to employ your expanded skills.

While you've been working with the motion paths built into InDesign's motion presets, you can also make motion paths of your own. You can even combine motion presets with custom motion paths to take your animations to the next level. You can nest animations one inside another, animate buttons—the list goes on and on.

When it comes down to it, it's all about creating a convincing illusion, so pull out your wand and let's make some magic.

Intro to Custom Motion Paths

They say the quickest way to get from point A to point B is a straight line. The same holds true for motion paths. There's a lot you can do with just a straight line of motion when it comes to animation, beyond objects flying onto and off of a page. Whether a straight line or an elaborate path with twists and turns, the process of connecting that path to an object in order to set it in motion remains the same.

Animating on a custom motion path is accomplished in three basic steps: 1) Create the object you want to animate. 2) Create the path. 3) Connect them. It really is that simple.

> **TIP:** When attaching a custom motion path to an object, the path must be above the object in the layer stacking order.

Moving through 3D Space...But Not Really

Animation is all about illusion. Add a little extra smoke and mirrors to the techniques you already know and you can make it seem like objects are moving through 3D space. You're not going to believe how easy this really is.

Pure and simple, the trick is to hide the animated object as it travels certain portions of the motion path. The objects masking the animated object just need to be above it in the Layer stacking order. In many cases, the most challenging part is to create a convincing path for the object to travel.

Exercise 14.1: Moving through 3D Space

In this exercise, you'll create the illusion of one object spiralling around another.

1. To see the effect in action and to get a peek under the hood, navigate to the chapter_14_exercises folder, open **ex14_1_end.indd** and preview the file. Dig around a bit to see how it all works and keep the file open for reference.

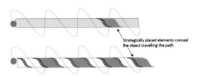

By strategically placing masking objects over portions of the motion path, you can make one object appear to spiral around another.

2. Go to File > New > Document, set the Intent to Web, leave the default settings and click OK. Save the file as ex14_1.indd in the chapter_14_exercises folder.

3. Select the Ellipse tool (L) and, holding down the Shift key, draw a small circle about 20 px in diameter. Give it a fill and no stroke.

4. Switch to the Selection tool, deselect your circle, and Press Ctrl+D/Command+D. Open the chapter_14_exercises folder. Select **candy_cane.idms** and then hold down the Ctrl/Command key and click **red_green_stripe.idms** to add it to the selection. Click OK to load your cursor.

5. Click twice anywhere on the page to place the two Snippets.

    You will load a motion preset that was exported from InDesign and use it to make the ball appear to revolve around the candy cane. You'll use the red and green stripes to hide the ball as it travels portions of the path.

6. Choose Manage Presets from the Animation panel menu. When the Manage Presets dialog opens, click the Load button and navigate to the chapter_14_exercises folder. Select **horizontal_spiral.xml** and click Open. Click Done in the Manage Presets dialog to load the motion preset and close the dialog.

7. Select the circle on your page. In the Animation panel, choose horizontal-spiral from the custom presets in the top section of the Presets dropdown.

8. Position the animation on top of the candy cane with the ball just outside its left edge and the path centered vertically over it. The lines of the motion path should fall halfway between the candy cane stripes. You can use your arrow keys to nudge the circle animation into place if necessary.

9. Preview the animation and note that the ball is traveling either entirely behind or entirely in front of the candy cane, depending on the layer stacking order. If the motion path and ball are behind the candy cane, Right-Click/Ctrl+Click on the ball and choose Arrange > Bring to Front to bring the animation to the top of the stack.

10. Drag the green and red stripe pair onto the candy cane and align its red stripe with the first red stripe at the right of the candy cane. With the stripe pair still selected, hold down the Alt/Option key and drag to the left to duplicate the stripes. Skipping one red stripe on the candy cane, align the red stripe from the

---

NOTE: For more on snippets, see InDesign Libraries and Snippets, starting on page 192

TIP: To create a custom motion preset, select the animation you want to capture and then choose Save from the Animation panel menu. Enter a name for your preset and click OK.

TIP: To export a motion preset to share with other InDesign or Flash users, choose Manage Presets from the Animation panel menu. Select a Preset and click Save As. The Save dialog will appear with the preset name appended by the .xml extension. Browse to where you'd like to save the file and click Save.

---

stripe pair with the next red stripe. Nudge the stripe pair into place with your arrow keys if necessary. Repeat to fill the candy cane with alternating stripes and a total of 5 stripe pairs. The last pair of stripes will cover the ball.

Alt-Drag/Option-Drag to duplicate the stripe on the candy cane.

11. Hold down the Shift key and click each pair of stripes you placed on the candy cane. Then, Right-Click/Ctrl+Click, and, from the context menu, choose Arrange > Bring to Front (or press Shift+Ctrl+]/Shift+Command+]) to ensure that the stripes are positioned above the candy cane in the stacking order.

12. Preview your file again and pat yourself on the back! You've created a convincing illusion of an object looping through space.

Motion Path Previews

To create a preview for a custom motion preset, with a completed animation on your page, go to File > Export and browse to the animation panel's custom preset folder.

In Windows, the path to the folder is
C:\Users\<username>\AppData\Roaming\Adobe\InDesign\Version 7.0\en_US\Motion Presets

On a Mac, the path is

Mac/Users/[username]/Library/Preferences/Adobe InDesign/Version 7.0/en_US/Motion Presets

In the Save dialog, set the Format dropdown to Flash Player (SWF) and click OK.

In order for the preview to show properly in the preview section of the Animation panel, it works best to scale the motion path and the object so their total dimensions do not exceed a width of 250 px and a height of 100 px. Center the animation on the page and then export it. Anything in the 250 px by 100 px window will show in the Preset preview.

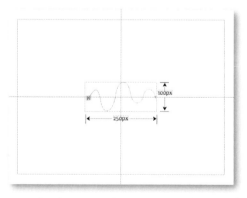

To capture an animation as a motion preset, center it in your document window in an area no more than 250 px wide by 100 px high.

Continuous Loops

The next project is both elegant and practical. The idea is pretty straightforward. Start with a bar or banner that loops from one edge of a page to the other, and then put things on the banner like buttons, animation, text, etc. In the exercise example, there are image thumbnail buttons on the banner that show a larger image when clicked. You could use the same idea to create navigation for an entire Flash site or presentation if you were to put the button banner on a Master page. There are lots of exciting possibilities to play with, so let's show you how.

You have nearly all the pieces you need already. You know how to make buttons and how to animate with motion presets and custom motion paths. You know how to add Show/Hide actions, and how to set the animation timing to make all your animations play together. The only piece that's missing, and this is the piece that makes or breaks the entire effect, is how to get the animation to loop seamlessly. Now that, dear reader, is the secret you'll soon discover.

When you add a motion path to animate an object From Current Appearance, the path attaches to the center of the object. The object moves the distance of the motion path; so, in order for an animation to appear to loop, the appearance of the object at each end of the path needs to match seamlessly. You can see how this works in the diagrams below. Look at the green squares in the first example and the yellow squares in the second; in each case, the motion path starts halfway into one square and ends halfway through the other. If you were to paste together the ends of the graphic spanning the motion path, you would have the seamless loop that we're looking for. But that's literally only half the story. The motion path pulls the animated object to the right a distance equal to its length. The remainder of the object it's dragging needs to be at least the length of the path, or it will leave a portion of the viewing window empty. In other words, the animated object must be at least twice the length of the path. Again, in order to make it seamless, the end of the animation must match up with the beginning. Therefore, the pattern in the graphic defined by the motion path must be repeated in order to complete the loop.

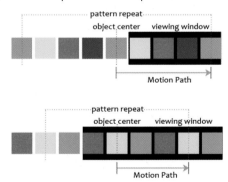

To create a continuous loop, the animated object must
be at least twice the length of the motion path.

There's no better way to learn than by doing. The next exercise gives you a chance to see exactly how it works when you put all the pieces together.

Exercise 14.2: Continuous Scroller

1. Open **ex14_2_end.indd** and preview the file. Be sure to select Set Preview Document Mode ([image] .) Take a look at the second page to see the example of the scroller in action. Keep the file open for reference.

2. Open **ex14_2_start.indd** and save it as ex14_2.indd. Navigate to page 2 of the document.

3. Go to File > Place (Ctrl+D/Command+D) and select all six flower files in the **links** folder in the chapter_14_exercises folder. Click Open to load the cursor.

Scrolling navbar created using a continuous loop animation.

4. Position the loaded cursor at the upper left corner of the large, red rectangle and click six times in the same spot to place the six flower images at their full size.

5. Press Ctrl+A/Command+A to select all the flower images (the black background rectangle is locked so it won't be selected.) In the Buttons and Forms panel, click the Convert to Button icon at the bottom of the panel and, if necessary, expand the Layers panel in the Panel Dock.

6. Rename the first button in the Layers panel "**f1Big**" and click the visibility button to the left of the layer to hide it.

7. Repeat step 6 for the remaining flower images, using the same naming convention and naming them consecutively (**f2Big**, **f3Big**, **f4Big**, **f5Big**, **f6Big**). When all the images are converted to buttons, you can turn their visibility back on.

8. Press Ctrl–/Command– to zoom out until you see the placement guide at the lower right of the pasteboard. Press and hold Ctrl+Spacebar/Command+Spacebar and click and drag a rectangle around the placement guide to zoom in on it. Release the mouse, and then release the keys to center the guide in view.

9. Again, load all six flower files for placement on the page. Position the loaded cursor at the upper left corner of the guide, click, and begin dragging slightly down and to the right. Still holding down the mouse, press the right arrow key five times to divide the frame into a total of six individual frames on the horizontal axis. Continue dragging to match the contours of the placement guide, and then release the mouse. The six placed thumbnail images are of uniform size and are equidistant from one another.

> **TIP:** Objects on hidden layers will not be visible when you preview the document or when it is exported.

10. Select the first small flower image on the right and convert it to a button in the Buttons panel. Name the button "**f1Btn**," click the 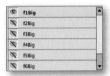 button, and add a Show/Hide Buttons and Forms action to the On Release or Tap event. Show f1Big and hide f2Big through f6Big.

11. Repeat step 10 for each of the remaining thumbnails naming each button consecutively (f2Btn, f3Btn, etc.) and adding a Show/Hide action. Show the corresponding Big button and hide the other five Big buttons.

For each button, show its corresponding Big button and hide the others.

12. Go to View > Entire Pasteboard. Select all six small buttons with the Selection tool and press Ctrl+G/Command+G to group them. Hold down the Alt+Shift/Option+Shift keys and drag to the left to duplicate the buttons and position them to the left of the originals. Repeat to make a third set of buttons, again placing them to the left of the existing buttons.

13. Zoom in enough on the buttons to visually adjust the space between the button groups, holding the Shift key to constrain movement to the horizontal if you need to drag a group to the left or right. The spacing between the groups needn't be exact; just eyeball it for now. You'll refine it in just a minute.

14. Fit the page in the window and select all the thumbnail buttons. Press Shift+Ctrl+G/Shift+Command+G to ungroup them.

15. With the buttons still selected, expand the Align panel in the Panel Dock (or go to Window > Object & Layout > Align.) If necessary, choose Show Options from the Align panel menu to display the Distribute Spacing controls.

TIP: If you ever want to turn off the target that selects the placed image inside a frame, go to View > Extras > Hide Content Grabber.

To access the Distribute Spacing controls on the Align panel, choose Show Options from the panel menu.

16. Select Align to Selection from the Align To dropdown and then press the second button on the last row (Distribute Horizontal Space) to space the buttons evenly across the bar. Press Ctrl+G/Command+G (Object > Group) to group the buttons.

Because you copied the buttons as you did, InDesign named and ordered them appropriately in the Layers panel. Unfortunately, the Show/Hide Actions are not copied with the buttons. For this example, due to the width of the viewing window, the scrolling bar needs to be at least 15 thumbnails wide. You wouldn't actually know that from the beginning, though, so let's go through the process of figuring it out. You'll want to determine how many thumbnails you need before spending the time adding Show/Hide actions to buttons you might end up deleting.

17. Select the Line tool and position your cursor over the center of the rightmost button. Holding down the Shift key, click and drag left across the first six button images. Release the mouse at the center of the first button image that matches the one where you started the path and then release the Shift key. The path you just created will become your motion path.

TIP: Motion paths snap to the center of the object being animated. Before connecting them, center the origin of the path on the object so when the motion path snaps to the object, the object maintains its position.

18. With the path still selected, switch to the Selection tool (V) and Shift-Click to select the thumbnail group. Click the Convert to motion path button (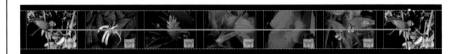) at the bottom of the Animation panel and name the animation "**scroller**". Check the Loop checkbox and, for now, leave the Duration set to 1 second, so you don't have to wait too long to see whether or not the motion path needs to be adjusted.

The line for the motion path was drawn from the center of an image at the right to the center of the first matching image to its left. Because the path was drawn from right to left, the default flow of the animation is right to left as well.

19. Preview the animation.

Because you drew the path from right to left, you need to reverse the direction of the motion path to get the animation to travel in the proper direction.

20. Select the animation with the Selection tool, hover over the path and click when you see the tooltip that says "Click to Edit." In the Pathfinder panel (Window > Object & Layout > Pathfinder), click the Reverse Path button ( ).

Reversing the path automatically repositions the animation.

21. Align the right edge of the button group with the right edge of the large, solid black rectangle on the page.

Before previewing the file, take note of the placement of the motion path on the graphic. Remember, the path always connects to the middle of the animated object when it is set to animate From Current Appearance. You know the path is the right length since it goes from the center of a thumbnail to the center of its first duplicate. Now it's just a matter of, first, seeing if the animation works, and second, determining if some of the thumbnail buttons can be eliminated.

22. Preview your file to see if the scroller scrolls continuously.

Congratulations! You've got that part handled. Now let's eliminate some of the buttons and adjust the timing. In shortening the scroller, you need to ensure that you include at least three duplicates of the same thumbnail—one for the beginning, one for the middle, and one for the end of the loop. You also need to ensure that the length of the graphic to the left of the origin of the motion path is at least the length of the Path. The last thing to keep in mind is that, as you change the length of the scroller, the attachment point for the motion path shifts to the new center of the object. InDesign makes this shift automatically. Taking one of the thumbnails from the left shifts the motion path to the right.

23. With the Selection tool, Double-Click on and then delete the last three thumbnails at the left of the scroller. Test your animation again to see that it still works.

    Awesome, right?! At this point, you've accomplished the main intention of the exercise. There are just a few things to do to wrap up the project.

24. For each of the remaining button thumbnails, add a Show/Hide action. Hide all the large image buttons except the one associated with the thumbnail and show the large version of the thumbnail image.

25. Adjust the timing so the scroller moves at a comfortable pace. We chose 15 seconds.

26. Save and test your file, pat yourself on the back, and close it when you're done.

You've learned the fundamentals of animation in InDesign and gone beyond, to learn some techniques that should provide a solid foundation for further exploration and discovery. Now it's time to see what's involved in outputting your interactive content to Flash SWF.

> **TIP:** When exporting to SWF and Interactive PDF, buttons may break when they come in contact with transparency. If you encounter strange behavior in files containing buttons and objects with applied effects, removing the effects may effectively resolve the issue.

CHAPTER SUMMARY

This chapter expanded your animation skills to include more advanced animation effects. You learned how to:

- Create custom motion paths

- Connect objects to custom motion paths

- Reverse path direction to reverse the direction of your animation

- Load and export motion presets

- Create a motion path preview

- Create the illusion of objects moving through 3D space

- Animate a continuous scroller with interactive buttons

By now you've learned pretty much everything there is to know about how to animate in InDesign. In the next chapter you'll create a banner ad—a practical application of your skills.

Chapter 15

BANNER ADS

The Web is riddled with them. Love 'em or hate 'em, they're here to stay. While InDesign can't generate banner ads that meet commercial file size guidelines, don't let that stop you from creating banners for your own site and possibly for other non-commercial venues. Whether or not you use them in creating banner ads, the technique you'll learn in this chapter—for sequencing animations and controlling timing—can be carried forward into any animation project you do.

Introduction

Web banners, like any advertising medium, are governed by specific guidelines. In Exercise 3.3: Document Presets and Application Preferences, starting on page 42, you loaded a collection of document presets that represent a number of standard banner dimensions. File size is another significant factor in the preparation of commercial web banners, with an acceptable standard range between 10k and 40k. As a point of reference, and to clearly illustrate why InDesign is not yet web-banner worthy, we'll share the results of a simple test. An InDesign document that was 234 px x 60 px, with no animation, and only a rectangle on the page, resulted in a file that was 112K when exported to SWF at the highest compression. OUCH! Not ready for prime time, at least not for commercial advertising. As we said earlier though, you may have occasion to create banners for sites without such rigorous file size restrictions.

If you want to learn more about commercial banner ad specifications, by far the best resource is the IAB (Interactive Advertising Bureau) website. Founded in 1996, the IAB is a group of over 460 media and technology companies that together sell somewhere in the neighborhood of 86% of all U.S. online advertising. The IAB is an advocate for, and provides education about, the interactive advertising marketplace. Together with its member companies, the IAB makes recommendations for standards and practices for interactive advertising. You can find a comprehensive chart for banner dimension and additional guidelines on the IAB website at:

http://www.iab.net/iab_products_and_industry_services/508676/508767/Ad_Unit.

Exercise 15.1: Creating a Banner Ad

DOWNLOAD:
Exercise files for this chapter can be downloaded from http://www.interactive-indesign.com.

1. Open **ex15_1_end.indd** from the chapter_15_exercises folder and preview the file. Take a look at the animations on the objects and check out the Timing panel to see how things are put together. When you're finished, keep the file open for reference, open **ex15_1_start.indd,** and save it as ex15_1.indd.

   The animation takes place in two parts. The first part is composed of three lines of text that fly onto the page in sequence. The second part is one three-line message, as well as a triangle and text that fly in from the corner.

TIP: You can apply separate animations to a group and to the objects within that group.

2. If necessary, open the Layers panel (Window > Layers) and expand the Layer1 layer. The four hidden layers contain the objects for the second phase of the animation. Click the triangle at the left of the messagesGroup layer to show the individual text object layers. Click in the Selection column to the right of <Learn Photography>. Hold down the Shift key and click in the Selection column for both <A Rewarding Hobby> and <A Colorful Career> to add them to the selection.

Select the objects within a group rather than the group itself to animate each object separately.

By selecting the objects separately, when you apply an animation, it applies to each of the selected objects individually, with only one click.

3. If necessary, open the Animation panel (Window > Interactive > Animation) and select Fly in from Right from the Preset dropdown. If necessary, twirl down the disclosure triangle to the left of Properties and choose None from the Opacity dropdown. Keep the other default settings.

4. Open the Timing panel (Window > Interactive > Timing) and if necessary, arrange the animations so that Learn Photography is at the top of the stack, followed by A Rewarding Hobby. Select A Rewarding Hobby and change the value in the Delay field to .5 seconds. Do the same for A Colorful Career.

The text objects properly ordered in the Timing panel with a .5 second Delay applied.

5. With the Selection tool, click the page background to deselect and then click the text on the page to select the messagesGroup object. Open the Animation panel and choose Fade Out from the Preset dropdown. Set the Duration to .5 seconds.

You want the viewer to have time to read the animated text before the next part of the message appears. Since you've already set a delay of a half-second for the second and third lines of text, another 2 seconds before the message fades out should provide ample time for your audience to read it.

6. Go to the Timing panel, select messagesGroup, and set the Delay to 2 seconds.

7. Hide the messagesGroup layer in the Layers panel and show the motion path, <Click now to enroll...>, corner, and <Register Now> layers.

8. Select <Click now to enroll...> in the Layers panel selection column and return to the Animation panel. Choose Fade In from the Preset dropdown and set the Duration to .5 seconds.

You're going to animate the corner graphic and the Register Now text separately, but you want both animations to fly in at the same angle. Before converting the path to an actual motion path, you'll duplicate it so you can be assured that the animation angle of the two objects will match.

9. In the Layers panel, click and drag the motion path layer down onto the Create new layer button at the bottom of the panel. When you see the plus sign on the cursor, release the mouse to duplicate the layer.

You can duplicate a layer in the Layers panel by dragging it
onto the Create new layer button at the bottom of the panel.

10. Click the selection column for one of the motion path layers in the Layers panel,
    hold down the Shift key, and click in the selection column for the corner layer to
    add it to the selection.

11. In the Animation panel, click the Convert to motion path button ( ) at the
    bottom of the panel. From the Animate dropdown, choose To Current Location
    and set the Duration to .5 seconds.

12. Return to the Layers panel and select the second motion path and the
    Register Now text object.

13. Return to the Animation panel and click the Convert to motion path button at the
    bottom of the panel. Select To Current Location from the Animate dropdown and
    set the Duration to .5 seconds.

14. Open the Timing panel, select corner, and set its delay to .5 seconds. Hold down
    the Shift key and click Register Now and Click Now to Enroll. Click the Play
    together button at the bottom right of the panel ( ).

    The point of a banner ad is to get the viewer to take action—to click the banner
    for more information. For that to happen, they need something to click. You'll
    wrap up the exercise, and the banner, by creating an invisible button that
    effectively converts the entire banner into a link.

15. Switch to the Rectangle tool (M) and drag a rectangle from the upper left corner
    of the banner all the way down to its lower right corner. Set both the fill and the
    stroke to None. Go to the Buttons panel (Window > Interactive > Buttons), and
    press the Convert to button icon ( ) at the bottom of the panel. Name the
    button "registerBtn," and add a Go to URL Action to its On Release event. Enter
    "http://www.interactive-indesign.com" in the URL field.

16. Turn on the visibility of the messagesGroup layer in the Layers panel and press
    Shift+Ctrl+Enter/Shift+Command+Return to open the SWF Preview panel and
    preview the animation on the page.

17. Feel free to play with the timing to see how it can change the feel of the
    animation. Then, save and close your file to complete the lesson and the chapter.

CHAPTER SUMMARY

In this chapter, you were introduced to the IAB (Interactive Advertising Bureau), one of the organizations that develop the specifications governing web advertising. You learned that for commercial purposes, the file size of Flash web banners must fall within a standard range of 10–40k and that, while InDesign Flash files cannot be made small enough to be commercially acceptable, you can still employ them effectively on your own website(s).

Your work with the web banner served largely to reinforce skills related to animation sequence and timing. In the course of the exercise, you applied custom motion guides, rearranged the sequence of animated elements and set durations and delays. You also created an invisible button with a Go to URL action to make your banner an effective call to action.

Congratulations! You can now consider yourself an InDesign animation pro. Just add your imagination to the host of animation tricks and techniques up your sleeve and you can't help but make the magic happen.

Your next trick, and the one that will make all the difference, is getting the animation rabbit out of the InDesign hat and into the world. Next up: output.

Chapter 16

SWF OUTPUT

The mechanics of actual output, whether to Interactive PDF, SWF, or FLA for Flash Professional, are relatively straightforward. You just need to be aware of what the various export settings mean, as well as their implications and some of the standard conventions. This chapter walks you through all those details so the export process itself will become the easiest part of your workflow.

NOTE: Depending
on who you talk to,
the SWF acronym
stands either for
Shockwave Flash
or small web file.

NOTE: InDesign
also enables you
to publish a file in
the FLA format for
further development
in Flash Professional.
The topic of export
to FLA is outside the
scope of this book.

Introduction

Your project is finished, you've tested it throughout the development process, and now it's ready for export. This is the easy part, once you understand the options in the export dialog. This chapter shepherds you through, and provides recommendations and guidelines for the output of your projects to SWF.

All exports start by going to File > Export. The Format dropdown at the bottom of the window gives you quite a few options from which to choose, but to create interactive Flash files, you'll choose Flash Player (SWF).

```
Adobe InDesign Tagged Text
Adobe PDF (Interactive)
Adobe PDF (Print)
EPS
✓ EPUB
Flash CS6 Professional (FLA)
Flash Player (SWF)
HTML
InCopy Document
InDesign Markup (IDML)
JPEG
PNG
Rich Text Format
Text Only
XML
```

To export your interactive Flash file go to File > Export and then choose Flash Player (SWF) from the Format dropdown at the bottom of the dialog.

Export to SWF

NOTE: For information
on how to get your
SWF and HTML page
onto your site, check
in with your hosting
service. They should
be able to provide the
guidance you need.

Before jumping directly into the details of SWF export, we should probably take a few minutes to explain how SWF files are displayed on the web. To view a SWF file in a browser, it needs to be embedded in an HTML page. The HTML page and the SWF file will ultimately reside on the server where your website is hosted. When you export your interactive document to SWF, you can choose to create only the SWF, or you can have InDesign generate both the SWF and the HTML page to contain it. This is great, since the page InDesign generates checks to see which version of the Flash player is being used in the browser, and provides a message if the user needs to update to a newer version. It's also great because it means you don't have to figure out how to make the page yourself! While helpful that InDesign does the work for you, in some instances you may want to adjust the position of the SWF on the page, or possibly change the HTML background color. You'll want to check out Adjusting a SWF HTML Page, starting on page 245 to learn how to tweak a couple lines of HTML code to get your page looking the way you want it.

Since you'll be dealing with multiple files when you export your SWF for the web, you must be certain to keep the related files together. Along with the primary SWF and its associated HTML page, separate files for each SWF, audio, video, and SWF video controller you've included in your document will be exported to a folder called "resources." This folder needs to travel with the SWF and HTML page, and the relative position of all these files in the file hierarchy needs to be maintained in order for things to play properly. This means that you must resist any temptation to add subfolders to the resource folder, or to rename any of the associated files after the fact. You can create a folder to contain the SWF, HTML page, and the resource folder, as long as you take that folder into account when linking the HTML page in your site. The only file you can safely rename without breaking your project is the

HTML file itself. If you intend to use your interactive project as the home page of your site, you'll need to rename your HTML page index.html (all lower case). The index page needs to be placed direct to the top level folder in your site in order to be recognized by the browser as your home page. This means that you can't use the containing folder mentioned above if you want your home page to be found.

As for the export itself, you may remember, that in the second chapter we made mention of the balancing act between quality, performance, and speed that is a constant consideration when developing for the web. Speed is inversely proportional to file size: the smaller a file, the faster it downloads, the speedier the delivery. You can impact file size by adjusting the export settings for compression and resolution of the images you use in your file. The goal is to achieve the smallest possible file size, using the greatest possible compression, while maintaining acceptable quality.

When working with Flash, file size is not the only factor to influence performance; the complexity of the animation in a file can also have a dramatic impact. Some animations require more processing power than others, putting so much demand on the system to perform all the necessary calculations that the movie may not play smoothly. This is just one more reason to test your projects on multiple machines with different capabilities to ensure that you don't encounter unanticipated and unpleasant surprises. If you're having issues with the performance of your file, you may need to simplify the animations you've employed in your project. Unfortunately, this may mean changing or even eliminating some of your animation. You'll have to make the call as to whether the trade-off is warranted.

When exporting your Flash file, frame rate is another consideration that can affect both performance and file size. Remember that video and animation are really a series of still frames shown in rapid sequence to create the illusion of motion over time. The number of frames per second (fps) is referred to as the frame rate. The higher the frame rate, the greater the demand placed on the processor. Back in the day, 12 fps was the default Flash frame rate, but, as processors have improved, there is hot debate as to whether a frame rate of 24 fps or 30 fps is preferable. 35 mm movie cameras use a standard exposure rate of 24 frames per second, and it's arguable as to whether there is a perceptible difference in smoothness of play between 24 fps and 30 fps. Much of the animation you'll create in your projects won't require a frame rate that high. If your animations are complex enough to tax a processor, frankly, it won't matter what frame rate you set; the processor will only play the frames at the rate it can process them. Also, higher frame rates may translate to larger files, since the file requires more frames to fill each second, which may translate to more keyframes. Once again, we're back to the balance between quality and performance. A good rule of thumb when you need to optimize your project is this: use the lowest frame rate that delivers an acceptable result.

It's important to know that, despite all the steps you take to optimize your Flash export, the SWF files generated by InDesign are bloated in comparison to what you could achieve directly in Flash Professional. Sad, but true. Adobe's focus was on adding all kinds of cool InDesign animation features, and not especially on optimization of file size. Hopefully, at some point, the animation will export to HTML5 and we'll see improvement in file optimization as well.

Now that you have a basic understanding of some of the considerations surrounding your export choices, let's get on with the business of the actual export. There are lots of controls in the SWF Export dialog, but there's no reason to get overwhelmed. It's really very simple and, most likely, you'll find a group of settings that work for you and use them pretty routinely. The rest of the settings are good to know about for the occasion when your reliable standards don't get the job done to your satisfaction.

The Export SWF dialog has two tabs. When it first opens, it displays the General tab, and its settings are pretty self-explanatory.

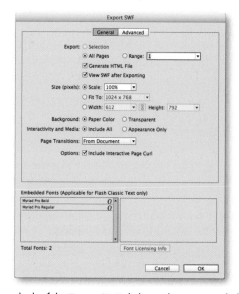

The General tab of the Export SWF dialog with recommended settings.

NOTE: To learn how to incorporate SWF files in Interactive PDFs, see page 295 in Chapter 20.

You'll note that Selection is one of the options in the Export section of the dialog. This option allows you to export a portion of your project or a specific animation to a SWF that can then be used in other contexts or even placed back in an InDesign document for export to Interactive PDF. You also have the option to export All Pages in the document, or a Range of pages you specify. This section of the panel is also where you choose whether to have InDesign generate an HTML page, so you can display your SWF in a browser. It's always a good idea to check the View SWF after Exporting checkbox, so you can see right away if there are any issues you need to address. The View SWF after Exporting checkbox only appears if you choose to generate the HTML page.

In the Size section of the dialog, the Scale value of 100% renders your project with the original document dimensions. You can elect, instead, to scale the movie to fit any of the standard predefined web dimensions in the Fit To dropdown, or set a width or height of your own. InDesign will scale your document proportionally, so whatever value you enter in the Width field will dictate the value for the Height field and vice versa. You want to be careful that you don't scale your document up to a point where the image resolution ends up being less than 72 ppi. Scaling your document down won't pose resolution issues, but if you shrink your page by too great a percentage, the image quality may suffer, and text could become very hard to read.

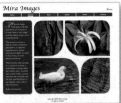

| 1280 x 800 | 100% | 800 x 600 | 300 x 234 |
| (328 KB) | (307KB) | (270 KB) | (160 KB) |

You can modify the output size of your document in the export dialog. For an image-heavy document, you can see that page size has a big impact on SWF file size.

Of all the options on the General tab, perhaps the most obscure are the Background choices. The default Background setting is Paper Color. Typically, the paper color in an InDesign document is white. Be aware, though, that you can change the paper color in InDesign, just as you would change any other swatch color. Just Double-Click the [Paper] swatch in the Swatches panel to access the color controls, and make your changes in the Swatch Options dialog. With Paper Color selected for the Background option in the Export SWF dialog, whatever the paper color is in your document will be the background color of your exported SWF.

The Transparent background option is a bit more curious. You can actually export your SWF as if it had no background, with all its content floating freely atop the HTML page that contains it. Choosing the Transparent option disables Page Transitions and the Interactive Page Curl (which you'll learn about shortly.) The default HTML page background color is gray. You'll learn how to change that when you tweak the HTML code.

Exported with paper color background.

Exported with transparent background. (The default HTML page background color is gray.)

The gray color in the transparent SWF on the right is the background color of the HTML page showing through the semi-transparent background graphic in the SWF.

In the Interactivity and Media section of the dialog, you'll want to be sure to select the Include All radio button. The Appearance Only radio button wipes out all the interactivity in your file, which kind of defeats the whole purpose of creating an interactive document in the first place, right? It captures the Normal state appearance of any buttons, posters from included videos, and the state of any animated elements as they appear in the layout at the time of export. The Appearance Only button is activated when the Rasterize Pages and/or Flatten Transparency options are selected on the Advanced tab of the dialog.

NOTE: To learn more about adding media to your files, see Audio & Video Overlays, starting on page 472.

The Page Transitions dropdown allows you to override any Page Transitions you applied to your document, and apply the selected transition to every page instead. The From Document option exports the document with the selection of Page Transitions you applied manually in the development process.

The last checkbox enables you to add an interactive page curl. You can add this effect regardless of whether you include other page transitions. Learn more about page transitions on page 281 and the Interactive Page Curl on page 245.

Outside of the document dimension settings, all the options that impact the size of your final file reside on the Advanced tab of the Export SWF dialog.

THE ADVANCED TAB OF THE EXPORT SWF DIALOG

The 24 fps default is suitable for most SWF files, and matches the default frame rate found in Flash Professional. Higher frame rates create smoother animations, but may increase the file size of the exported SWF. The duration of your animations will not change if you modify this setting.

Removes live transparency in the SWF, but preserves the appearance of transparent objects. This will cause all interactivity to be dropped from the SWF.

List of embedded fonts with Font Vendor for selected font appearing in the pane at the right. The Font Licensing Info button connects to a web resource providing licensing details.

Maintains InDesign text as actual text in the SWF file. This is the best option for keeping file size to a minimum.

Converts InDesign text to vector paths in the SWF file.

Converts InDesign text to raster images in the SWF file.

Turns each exported page into an image. This removes interactivity from the SWF file, and increases file size.

JPEG: Best choice for smallest file sizes, or for using the Quality setting to control the level of compression.

PNG: Best choice for high-quality images (uses compression without loss of data).

Automatic: Chooses image compression on a per-image basis.

Controls the tradeoff between image quality and file size.

Higher values create larger file sizes, but allow for zooming in on images in the SWF with less visual degradation.

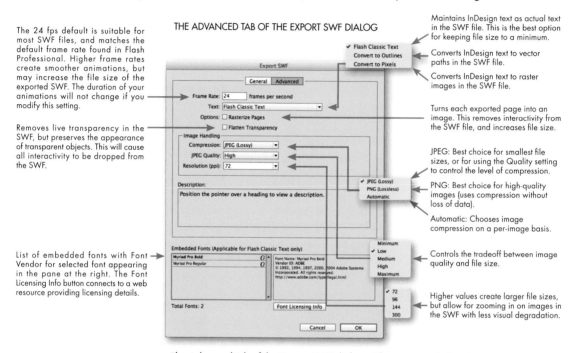

The Advanced tab of the Export SWF dialog with recommended settings.

The default frame rate for export is 24 fps, which is the same as the default for Flash Professional. In many cases, changing the frame rate will have no impact at all on the size of your exported SWF. Of course, it doesn't hurt to do a little experimentation, since every little bit of optimization counts. Since processor demand is also an important consideration, even if the file size isn't affected, the rule of thumb is to use the lowest possible frame rate that produces an acceptable result.

For the Text options, typically your best choice will be Flash Classic text. This is true for a couple reasons. First, this option results in the smallest file size. Second, the text is searchable and can therefore be picked up by search engines.

Rasterize Pages and Flatten Transparency both wipe out the interactivity in your file. Obviously not the choice for exporting an interactive file.

We did some testing to determine the effect of frame rate and image compression on file size to provide a real-life reference for the impact of the different options. While the results will most likely vary from one file to another (this is a fact of life in web and interactive development) for the one file we tried, we found no change at all in file size due to change in frame rate from 12 fps to 24 and 30 fps.

As you might expect, our testing proved the file size to vary quite dramatically in image-heavy SWFs exported using the assorted compression options. We found the Automatic compression option to produce the best results most consistently. With Automatic selected, the biggest factor to impact the size of the SWF file was the level of JPEG compression. For image-laden files, we recommend starting with Low to see if the quality of the output is acceptable. If it looks fine to you, the next step would be to try Minimum to see if the result is workable. Remember, you want the smallest possible file that passes the quality test. If the output from the Low setting isn't usable, try Medium next, going up the ladder until you achieve an acceptable result.

NOTE: For a file containing only vector content, changing the JPEG compression options has no effect at all.

Compression Option	SWF File Size
PNG	3.1 MB
Auto: JPEG Maximum	1.4 MB
Auto: JPEG High	401 KB
Auto: JPEG Medium	311 KB
Auto: JPEG Low	262 KB
Auto: JPEG Minimum	201 KB

Export to SWF Auto: JPEG compression settings—file size comparison. The exported file was a one-page, 900 px x 700 px, image-heavy document.

The export resolution you choose for the images in your document will also impact file size. While image resolution cannot be increased regardless of the export settings, high resolution images will be downsampled to match the selected setting. Obviously, higher resolution images result in larger files but the up side is that they permit the ability to zoom in on an image without a loss of image quality—another tradeoff to weigh in your development process. Remember that 72 ppi is the standard resolution for images published to the web, and the optimal resolution for SWF export with regard to the balance of quality and file size.

Exercise 16.1: Exploring the SWF Export Options

This exercise takes you on a tour of files that demonstrate the various export options.

1.   From the chapter_16_exercises folder, open **ex16_1_start.indd** and save as ex16_1.indd. Go to File > Export and choose Flash Player (SWF) from the Format dropdown at the bottom of the dialog. Navigate to the chapter_16_exercises folder, name the file **home_low.swf** in the Save As field, and click Save.

2.   In the Export SWF dialog, select the following settings on the General tab: All Pages, Generate HTML File, View SWF after Exporting, Scale: 100%, Paper Color, Include All. Since this is a single-page document, you can ignore the transitions and interactive page curl. Of course, given that the document is only one page, the links won't work.

3.   Switch to the Advanced tab and apply the following settings: Frame Rate: 24 fps, Flash Classic Text, Compression: Automatic, JPEG Quality: Low, Resolution: 72 ppi. Click OK to export your SWF.

DOWNLOAD: Exercise files for this chapter can be downloaded from http://www.interactive-indesign.com.

4. An HTML page with your exported SWF opens in the browser. Note the quality of the images in the file, and keep the file open. Keep the browser open for the rest of the exercise.

    Not so tough, right? Like we said, the export is the easy part. Now you'll look at files exported using different compressions to see how they differ in appearance.

5. From the browser, go to File > Open File. Navigate to the **chapter_16_exercises > output > compression_options** folder, and select **home_auto_min72.html**.

6. When the file opens in the browser, observe the quality of the images. This file is more compressed than the file you exported, and the quality of the images is definitely not passable. If you have enough screen real estate, you might want to arrange the browser windows so you can compare the files side-by-side. Close home_auto_min72.html if necessary to make room, but keep the browser and your exported file open.

    As you're evaluating the quality of the files, be aware also of their file sizes as listed in the sidebar to the left.

NOTE: As a point of reference, long before high speed connections were standard fare, the rule of thumb was that a web page with all its component elements should total no more than 35K in file size.

SWF FILE SIZE COMPARISON

compression_options folder	swf size
home_auto_medium72.swf	308 KB
home_auto_min72.swf	202 KB
text_options folder	
home_flash_txt_auto72.swf	263 KB
home_outline_txt_auto72.swf	280 KB
home_raster_txt_auto72.swf	264 KB

7. In your browser, go again to File > Open. Browse to the chapter_16_exercises > output > compression options folder and open **home_auto_medium72.html**.

8. Compare this file to the file you exported to decide if the difference in quality justifies the difference in file size (approximately 50KB).

9. Close the HTML files, but keep the browser open.

    Now that you've had a chance to see the effects of compression on your SWF file, you'll take a few minutes to look at the results of the different text export options.

10. From the chapter_16_exercises > output > text_options folder, open **home_raster_txt_auto72.html, home_outline_txt_auto72.html**, and **home_flash_txt_auto72.html** in your browser. You should have three files open, each representative of one of the text export options. Compare the appearance of the text in the files to see if you detect a difference.

    Lastly, you'll take a look at a file that was exported with a transparent background.

11. From the chapter_16_exercises > output folder, open **transparent.html**. Note the default gray of the HTML page background showing through the background of the SWF.

12. Close the open HTML files, quit the browser and return to InDesign. Close the ex16_1.indd file to complete the lesson.

Adjusting a SWF HTML Page

Don't know about you, but we're not big fans of the default gray background color in the HTML page that's generated when exporting to SWF. We also find it somewhat disconcerting that sometimes the SWF appears at the upper left corner of the page, and when the interactive page curl is applied, it's located in the middle with space above it. No worries, the fix is actually easy, if working with code doesn't make you too squeamish. You can make a few really simple adjustments to get things to look just the way you want them to.

If you have Dreamweaver, you'll be able to play around and see your results as you work. If not, you can use any text editing application, and then test your HTML page in the browser. It'll take a little more back and forth with a text editor, but the result will be the same. Before your HTML page will open in a text editor however, you may first need to replace the .html extension with .txt, in order for it to display properly as plain text. You'll make your corrections, and then re-save your result with the .html extension. The portion of the code you need to change is toward the bottom of the page, so it's easy to find.

Exercise 16.2: Adjusting a SWF HTML Page

In this exercise, you'll export two SWFs, one with and one without page curl, to see the difference in the resulting HTML code. You'll then modify the code to change both the position of the SWF on the page, and the document background color. In the process, you'll see how easy it is to include a page curl in your exported SWF.

1. Open **ex16_2_start.indd** from the chapter_16_exercises folder. Go to File > Export (Ctrl+E/Command+E) and choose Flash Player (SWF) from the Format dropdown at the bottom of the Export dialog. Name the file ex16_2.swf.

2. In the Export SWF dialog, for the first export, choose All Pages, Generate HTML file, View SWF after Exporting, Scale 100%, Paper Color, Include All, From Document, and check the Include Interactive Page Curl checkbox. Keep the default Advanced settings and click OK.

    When the page opens in the browser, note that the movie is offset from the top and left edges of the browser window.

3. Right-Click/Ctrl+Click on the gray area of the HTML page and choose View Page Source or View Source, or Source, etc.—different browsers use somewhat different commands. If the View Source command isn't available in the context menu, you may be able to find it in the View menu located in your browser's tool bar. OK, it's a lot of code, but don't sweat it. The part you're concerned with is really simple. Scroll down to the bottom of the page.

4. Before deconstructing the code to understand the changes you can make, leave the source code open and return to InDesign to export the file a second time. Use the same settings except this time, be sure to deselect the Include Interactive Page Curl checkbox. Save the file as ex16_2_no_curl.swf.

5. When the second page opens in the browser, note that the SWF is aligned to the upper left of the page. View the source code, scroll down to the bottom of the page, and position the two pages of code side-by-side for comparison.

NOTE: The exercise file is a perfect demonstration of page transitions gone terribly wrong—remember, just because you can doesn't mean you should! Actually, it's intended to be a sampler of the page transitions you can apply to your document in InDesign. To learn more about page transitions and how to apply them, check out Page Transitions, starting on page 281.

TIP: To check out the page curl, mouse over a page corner. The page corner will automatically curl, just a little bit. When you see the curl, click and drag to begin turning the page. If you drag so that just over half the height of the page is curled, and then release, the page will flip as if you were turning a page in a book.

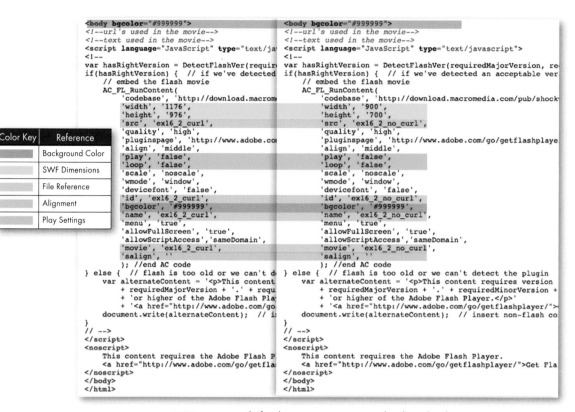

```
<body bgcolor="#999999">                                <body bgcolor="#999999">
<!--url's used in the movie-->                          <!--url's used in the movie-->
<!--text used in the movie-->                           <!--text used in the movie-->
<script language="JavaScript" type="text/ja             <script language="JavaScript" type="text/javascript">
<!--                                                    <!--
var hasRightVersion = DetectFlashVersion(requir         var hasRightVersion = DetectFlashVer(requiredMajorVersion, re
if(hasRightVersion) {  // if we've detected             if(hasRightVersion) {  // if we've detected an acceptable ver
    // embed the flash movie                                // embed the flash movie
    AC_FL_RunContent(                                       AC_FL_RunContent(
        'codebase', 'http://download.macrom                     'codebase', 'http://download.macromedia.com/pub/shock
        'width', '1176',                                        'width', '900',
        'height', '976',                                        'height', '700',
        'src', 'ex16_2_curl',                                   'src', 'ex16_2_no_curl',
        'quality', 'high',                                      'quality', 'high',
        'pluginspage', 'http://www.adobe.co                     'pluginspage', 'http://www.adobe.com/go/getflashplaye
        'align', 'middle',                                      'align', 'middle',
        'play', 'false',                                        'play', 'false',
        'loop', 'false',                                        'loop', 'false',
        'scale', 'noscale',                                     'scale', 'noscale',
        'wmode', 'window',                                      'wmode', 'window',
        'devicefont', 'false',                                  'devicefont', 'false',
        'id', 'ex16_2_curl',                                    'id', 'ex16_2_no_curl',
        'bgcolor', '#999999',                                   'bgcolor', '#999999',
        'name', 'ex16_2_curl',                                  'name', 'ex16_2_no_curl',
        'menu', 'true',                                         'menu', 'true',
        'allowFullScreen', 'true',                              'allowFullScreen', 'true',
        'allowScriptAccess','sameDomain',                       'allowScriptAccess','sameDomain',
        'movie', 'ex16_2_curl',                                 'movie', 'ex16_2_no_curl',
        'salign', ''                                            'salign', ''
    ); //end AC code                                        ); //end AC code
} else {  // flash is too old or we can't d             } else {  // flash is too old or we can't detect the plugin
    var alternateContent = '<p>This content                    var alternateContent = '<p>This content requires version
        + requiredMajorVersion + '.' + requ                        + requiredMajorVersion + '.' + requiredMinorVersion +
        + 'or higher of the Adobe Flash Pla                        + 'or higher of the Adobe Flash Player.</p>'
        + '<a href="http://www.adobe.com/go                        + '<a href="http://www.adobe.com/go/getflashplayer/">
    document.write(alternateContent);  // i                     document.write(alternateContent);  // insert non-flash co
}                                                       }
// -->                                                  // -->
</script>                                               </script>
<noscript>                                              <noscript>
    This content requires the Adobe Flash P                     This content requires the Adobe Flash Player.
        <a href="http://www.adobe.com/go/getfla                     <a href="http://www.adobe.com/go/getflashplayer/">Get Fla
</noscript>                                              </noscript>
</body>                                                  </body>
</html>                                                  </html>
```

Color Key	Reference
	Background Color
	SWF Dimensions
	File Reference
	Alignment
	Play Settings

HTML source code for the same SWF exported with and without interactive page curl. The width and height values for the SWF (highlighted in orange) are different, even though the same movie was exported for both files. The color key in the image above is used throughout the following explanation, so you can easily identify the referenced portions of the code.

The highlighted sections of the code above are the portions you can modify to change the background color of the page and the size and color of the block containing the SWF. As you can see, the dimensions that InDesign allocates for the SWF are different depending on whether or not the interactive page curl is selected in the export settings (see the ▯ highlighted section on the image above.) Strange! In the exercise example, the original SWF was 900 x 700. When exported with the page curl, the size of the block containing the SWF is instead, 1176 x 976. Regardless of the dimensions of this SWF block, the SWF is centered in it by default, contributing in part to the offset of the movie from the top of the page. You can change the dimensions of the SWF block to reposition the SWF on the page.

The midtone gray background color (bgcolor in the code above and highlighted in blue ▮) is applied to both the block containing the SWF (toward the bottom of the code) and the HTML page background (at the top of the code) You can alter either or both of the background color values to change the appearance of the page. If you change both the color and the dimensions of the block containing the SWF, you can create the appearance of a partial frame around your movie either on the top and bottom or on either side.

By changing background colors and the dimensions of the block containing the SWF in your HTML page, you can create the appearance of a partial frame around your Flash movie.

To change a background color, enter a hexadecimal value for either or both of the bgcolor options. (For a reminder about Hex colors, check out the explanation starting on page 14.) Or, maybe we can save you some time by reminding you that the hexadecimal value for white is #FFFFFF and black is #000000.

The last thing we'll mention is that, if you ever need to swap out the SWF in an HTML file, you can just replace all the references to the file (shown in the code example highlighted in green:). There's an additional file reference in the title tag that isn't shown in the code example that you'll probably want to change as well. The title tag has nothing to do with whether your SWF plays or not, but it is seen by your audience at the top of the browser window when they open your page, and it becomes the title of saved bookmarks or favorites. It would be best to enter a name you want people to see as opposed to the default page title assigned by InDesign, which is generated from the file name. If you swap out one movie for another in an HTML page, you'll also want to be sure to change the dimensions of the SWF block to accommodate the dimensions of the new movie.

To save you the time working with the code, we've provided an example HTML page where the background colors and the size of the SWF block have already been changed.

6. In your browser, go to File > Open and browse to the chapter_16_exercises folder. Open **ex16_2_end.html** and view the source code. Scroll to the bottom of the page to check out the changes to the code. The page title has been changed as well, to "Flower Gallery." Scroll up to the top of the page inside the opening <head> tag to see the <title> tag.) When you've finished perusing the code, close the file, quit the browser and return to InDesign to complete the exercise.

Creating a Stand-alone Flash Projector

The Flash animation tools in InDesign make it possible to create rich and engaging content that lends itself perfectly to presentations and self-guided interactive experiences. Aside from posting such content on the web, another way to share it is through a Flash projector file.

A Flash projector file is a platform-specific executable that includes the Flash Player in the file package. In other words, as long as the projector is created for the appropriate platform, anyone can view it with a simple Double-Click—no need for a browser, nor for any other software. If the file is small enough, you can email it, or you can burn it to disk or distribute it in any other way you see fit.

If you have the stand-alone Flash Player (it's included in any CC package that includes Flash), you can create a projector from your InDesign SWF content literally with the click of a button. Here's how it works:

1. Open Flash Player.
2. Go to File > Open File and open the SWF you want to convert to the projector.
3. Go to File > Create Projector.

And that's all there is to it!

There are two Flash projector files in the chapter_16_exercises folder for you to check out if you like, one for each platform.

Cautions

Just a couple pointers to wrap things up...

Be aware that objects using certain animation presets don't play well with page transitions or the interactive page curl. For example, an object with a Fade in animation will show when a page is being turned or while a page transition plays. This behavior occurs with the following animations: Appear, Fade In, the Fly-in presets, Zoom in 2D and Swoosh.

You'll also want to take precautions against allowing objects with transparency to overlap interactive elements as it may cause interactivity to be lost when the file is exported to SWF.

TIP: Depending on the version of Flash Player you are using, you may find that the Create Projector menu option is grayed out. So far, the only work-around we've been able to come up with is to use a different version of Flash Player. You can find archived versions of the player at http://helpx.adobe.com/flash-player/kb/archived-flash-player-versions.html#Flash%20Player%20archives.

CHAPTER SUMMARY

This chapter took you from your finished InDesign document to a finished Flash movie. You learned how to export to SWF, and how to create a Flash projector as another way to share your content.

In the process, you gained an understanding of:

- The difference between the JPEG, PNG and Automatic compression options
- The difference between the Flash Classic Text, Convert to Outlines, and the Convert to Pixels export options
- Factors that affect file size
- The tradeoff between file size, quality and performance

You also learned how to customize the appearance of the HTML page generated by InDesign by changing:

- The background color of the page and the block containing the SWF file
- The dimensions of the SWF block
- The title of the HTML page
- The SWF displayed in the HTML page

Additionally, you discovered a couple potential problems and how to avoid them.

This chapter wraps up the section on Flash animation and output to SWF. Next, you'll learn all about Interactive PDF, another excellent vehicle for sharing dynamic digital content.

Part 5

INTERACTIVE PDF

It's probably not a stretch to say that pretty much everyone who uses a computer has at least encountered a PDF a one time or another. Yet, as ubiquitous as PDF technology is, we would venture to say that its interactive capabilities are probably the best kept secret ever.

In this section of the book, you'll discover how to bring your PDFs to life with animated page transitions, buttons, bookmarks, interactive forms and media. From workflow tips to post-production pointers, the next pages provide everything you'll need to take your PDFs from static to fantastic.

Chapter 17

BOOKMARKS

Bookmarks are exclusively a PDF feature. While traditionally used to navigate long print documents exported to PDF, they can be effectively employed in navigating Interactive PDFs as well. Bookmarks can be generated automatically by InDesign when you create a table of contents, or you can add them manually through the Bookmarks panel. The skills you'll learn in this chapter for creating bookmarks efficiently and effectively will translate equally well to projects for print and digital publishing.

Why Bookmarks?

Before InDesign was even a glimmer in Adobe's eye, bookmarks were a well-established feature in Acrobat and what was then Acrobat Reader. Particularly useful for navigating long documents, bookmarks can be created directly inside Acrobat Standard or Professional. Residing in a dedicated panel, PDF bookmarks are similar in function to hyperlinks in that they jump to a specific document location. When created in Acrobat, they can hone in on a particular area of a page at a specified magnification. Bookmarks created in Acrobat can also be tied to actions in much the same way as buttons in InDesign, and they possess similar functionality. They can be used to play sounds and video, open files and web links, reset forms, and more.

As far as we can tell Acrobat is one of the most widely adopted and most under-used applications on the market. Few people are really aware of what it can do, but many of the interactive features you can now develop in InDesign have been part of Acrobat for years. Do yourself a favor and take a serious look at the awesome Acrobat feature set. You'll be amazed at what you can do with it. There are currently three flavors of Acrobat to choose from; you can check them out at this link: http://www.adobe.com/products/acrobat/matrix.html.

Enough about Acrobat, let's get back to bookmarks and InDesign! InDesign has a dedicated panel just for bookmarks. The panel allows you to create and manage your bookmarks, and also provides the convenience of being able to test them right in the InDesign environment.

TIP: The bookmarks you create in InDesign export with navigational capabilities only but, you can modify them in Acrobat to add actions, set zoom levels and apply limited formatting.

The bookmarks you create manually in InDesign can be targeted to a page, selected text, or a selected object. InDesign can also automatically generate PDF bookmarks based on entries in a table of contents. Whether created manually or through a TOC, bookmarks can be arranged hierarchically into multiple levels. By default, TOC-generated bookmarks are appended to those you create manually. Once created, you can reorder your bookmarks by dragging them into position in the Bookmarks panel.

Adding Bookmarks

If you've created a table of contents for your document, InDesign can do the tedious work of creating bookmarks for you. You learned all about building a table of contents in Chapter 8, starting on page 119. That means you've already got the hard part handled.

If you're creating an Interactive PDF where you want the bookmarks but not the TOC, the trick is to put the TOC on the last page of the document. Then, just omit the last page when you export the document as an Interactive PDF, and you have bookmarks for navigation without the TOC. Pretty nifty little trick, right?

The exercise file already has a TOC on its last page as well as the bookmarks the TOC generated. You'll first experiment with adding some bookmarks manually and then you'll make some adjustments to the file so that InDesign creates the desired bookmarks for you. When all is said and done, you'll take the file into Acrobat or Reader to take your bookmarks for a spin.

Exercise 17.1: Adding Bookmarks and a TOC

1. Launch Acrobat or Adobe Reader and go to File > Open. Browse to the chapter_17_exercises folder and open **ex17_1_end.pdf**. If necessary, scale the document window so the entire page is in view. The Bookmarks panel should be visible at the left of the window with the bookmarks for each page listed in sequence and appropriately nested to reflect the hierarchy of pages in the document.

   You can also use the buttons in the document to get around, of course. But for now, note that the only animation that carried over from InDesign was the multi-state object on page 4 of the document. The animation of the large image buttons flying onto the home page was lost in conversion to Interactive PDF. InDesign animation does not translate to PDF so we did some fancy footwork to include the multi-state object in the project. First, we selected the multi-state object, and then we exported it to SWF, choosing Selection from the export dialog. The SWF file was then placed back in InDesign. Since interactive PDF supports SWF files (the Flash Player is incorporated into both Acrobat and Reader), the end result is a PDF page that includes a seamless rendering of the animation, all generated directly from InDesign. Way cool!

2. When you've finished exploring, close Acrobat or Reader and return to InDesign. Open **ex17_1_end.indd** from the chapter_17_exercises folder. Use the navigation controls at the bottom left of the document window to browse through the document pages. Go to page 4, select the SWF (multistate.swf) with the Selection tool, and open the Media Panel (▥ in the Panel Dock or go to Window > Interactive > Media.) Note that the Play on Page Load option is selected and the Poster dropdown is set to None.

   The effect is that, when the page is opened in Acrobat or Reader, the animation plays and the flower image grows to nearly fill the page. The previous and next buttons in the SWF move you through the object states. Export of InDesign animation to SWF and subsequent placement of the SWF back in InDesign is a workaround that enables you to make the user experience of your Interactive PDF and SWF output more consistent.

3. Press Ctrl+J/Command+J, enter 9 in the text field, and click OK to jump to page 9.

   This is where you'll find the phantom TOC that generated the bookmarks. You may recall that the PDF you explored had only nine pages. When the file was exported to PDF, the last page was simply excluded.

4. Go to Window > Workspace > [Interactive for PDF] or choose Interactive for PDF from the Workspace Switcher at the upper right of the interface.

5. Open the Bookmarks panel (Window > Interactive > Bookmarks, or click the ▌ icon in the Panel dock). If necessary, twirl down the arrows next to the Flora and Fauna bookmarks to see the bookmarks nested below. Notice how the bookmarks follow the same hierarchical structure reflected in the TOC. Select any one of the bookmarks and choose Go to Selected Bookmark from the panel menu.

> **DOWNLOAD:** Exercise files for this chapter can be downloaded from http://www.interactive-indesign.com.

> **NOTE:** You'll learn all about multi-state objects in Chapter 34: Slideshow Overlays, starting on page 505.

> **NOTE:** For a refresher on exporting to SWF, see Chapter 16: SWF Output, starting on page 237.

> **NOTE:** See Exercise 19.1: Working with Page Transitions, starting on page 282 to learn your way around the SWF workaround.

The Bookmarks panel displaying bookmarks for
each of the main site pages and their sub-pages.

6. When you've finished exploring, keep the file open for reference and open
ex17_1_start.indd. Save it as ex17_1.indd.

7. Navigate to page 9 to see the table of contents and compare the TOC entries to
the bookmarks.

Note that the TOC contains an entry for each of the document pages but all
the entries appear on the same level rather than with some page references
nested beneath others as they are in the final exercise file.

Note also that there is a bookmark for each of the TOC entries—and like
the TOC entries, they are all on the same level. The next step is to group the
bookmarks for the Flora and Fauna pages and nest them under an appropriate
section name.

There are two ways to accomplish this objective, and determining which is best
in real life will depend on the specific requirements of your project and your
workflow. The first option, and the one that might initially seem most obvious,
would be to manually add the top level bookmarks to the Bookmarks panel.
You could then drag the second level bookmarks below the bookmarks with
their respective section names. The only problem with this approach arises
if you then need to update the TOC. If you add or remove pages and then
regenerate the TOC, the bookmarks get updated too. All the manual changes
you made will be lost and you'll need to start over from scratch.

An alternate approach involves tricking InDesign into auto-generating the
nested bookmarks for you. By taking advantage of the TOC option to include
hidden text, you can use invisible text frames to flesh out your TOC. In the
exercise example, you'll add title text to the first Flora page and the first Fauna
page, style the titles with the section Paragraph style and hide them. This will
generate the top level bookmarks (Flora and Fauna.) A duplicate of the section
Paragraph style (section2) has already been applied to the pages you'll be
nesting within the sections. You'll then redefine the TOC to have a second level
and InDesign will do the rest.

It sounds more complicated than it actually is. It'll all make sense, though,
as you work through the rest of the exercise. While it may take a little more
planning up front to get InDesign to generate your bookmarks, it's worth
the effort if you're working a large document or you expect the TOC to
change routinely.

You'll first experiment with the manual approach to nesting the bookmarks.

8. Navigate to page 3 of the document and select the Flora: About page title with the Selection tool. Open the Bookmarks panel. Click the Create new bookmark button at the bottom of the panel. Type "Flora" for the bookmark text and press Enter/Return.

9. Navigate to page 5. With the Type tool, select just the word Fauna from the page title. Click the New Bookmark button and note that the bookmark takes on the selected text as its name. Note also that an (⚓) icon appears to the left of the bookmark indicating that it's tied to a text anchor. What's cool about this is that if the text flows to another page, the bookmark destination flows with it.

TIP: If you have text selected when you create a bookmark, InDesign captures both the text and the document location in the bookmark definition.

10. In the Bookmarks panel, drag the Flora bookmark above Flora: About and release the mouse when you see a black line under Texture that extends to the left edge of the bookmark icon.

You can drag to rearrange and nest bookmarks in the Bookmarks panel.

11. Drag the Fauna bookmark above Fauna: Slideshow.

12. Mouse over the two new bookmarks, and you should see tooltips displaying the destination page number and the bookmark name. Double-Click the Flora bookmark to jump to its page in the document.

13. Still in the Bookmarks panel, select Flora: About, and drag it onto the Flora bookmark. When the hand cursor appears over the word Flora, release the mouse to nest Flora: About below it.

Nesting a bookmark.

14. Twirl down the arrow to the left of the Flora bookmark and select Flora: Slide Show. Drag it up and to the right, under Flora: About, until a black line extending to the left edge of the Flora: About icon appears. Note that the line is indented compared to the line that appeared under Flora.

More rearranging of bookmarks

15. Use the same technique to nest the two Fauna bookmarks under Fauna.

Now that you've spent all that time rearranging the bookmarks, let's see what happens when you update the TOC.

16. Navigate to page 9 and place the Type tool in the text frame containing the TOC. Go to Layout > Update Table of Contents, and you should get a message confirming that it has been updated successfully. Now take a look at the Bookmarks panel.

    You're pretty much back to where you started, with all the bookmarks at the same level, and all your nesting gone. Shift+Click to select both the Flora and Fauna bookmarks and click the Delete button at the bottom of the panel. Now you're truly back at square one.

    This time you'll make changes to the document and the TOC to achieve the desired bookmark hierarchy which will then be retained when the TOC is updated.

NOTE: The reason for positioning the duplicated page titles above the originals in the page layout is so that InDesign will render both the TOC entries and the bookmarks in the proper order. Since both titles reside on the same page, the text frame appearing first on the page appears first in the TOC.

17. Switch to the Selection tool and go to page 3 of the document. Click once on the Flora: About text frame to select it, then press Ctrl+C/Command+C to copy. Go to Edit > Paste In Place and drag the duplicated text frame up on the page to position it above the original

18. Double-Click the text to activate the Type tool, and delete the colon and the word "About." Expand the Paragraph Styles panel in the Panel Dock. (If necessary, go to Window > Styles > Paragraph Styles to open it.) Apply the section paragraph style to the word Flora and then hide the layer in the Layers panel. (For the purpose of the exercise, the section2 paragraph style has been applied to the original text.)

19. Go to page 5 and then select and duplicate the Fauna: Slideshow text frame. Position it above the original text on the page, apply the section Paragraph style and delete the colon and the word "Slideshow." Hide the layer in the layers panel.

    Now you get to see where all this was heading.

20. Navigate back to page 9 and go to Layout > Table of Contents to bring up the TOC definition dialog. Select the section2 paragraph style from the left of the panel, then click the More Options button to the panel's right. In the Style section, change the level value to 2. If you'd like the second level entries in the actual TOC to have a distinct appearance, you can assign the TOC2 paragraph style from the Entry Style dropdown. Click OK to update the TOC.

21. Check out the Bookmarks panel again to see the neatly nested bookmarks.

NOTE: By setting the export page range from 1–9 you are omitting the last page that contains the TOC. Even though the TOC is not included, the bookmarks carry over to the PDF.

22. Save the file and then go to File > Export. In the Export dialog, choose Adobe PDF (Interactive) from the Format dropdown and navigate to the chapter_17_exercises folder. Click Save, and, in the Export dialog, choose the Range radio button and type "1–9" in the text field. Set the View dropdown to Fit Page and check the View After Exporting checkbox. Leave the other default settings, and click OK to export the file.

    As the export begins, dismiss the alert and proceed. The export will take a little while, so this is probably a good time to take a break and stretch your legs.

Adobe InDesign

One or more interactive elements are clipped in ways that PDF files cannot reproduce. Those elements will be adjusted in the exported PDF.

[Cancel] [OK]

For this particular file, you can safely dismiss the alert. Be aware that when you encounter these alerts, you may find your PDF file exhibiting all sorts of strange behaviors. (More on that in PDF Peculiarities, starting on page 297.)

While your document contains the bookmark structure you built, the bookmarks will not show when the PDF is opened unless you explicitly set the initial view of the PDF to display them. Unfortunately, this is something you need to do directly in the full version of Acrobat. Reader doesn't have the capability to set initial view preferences.

23. To ensure that your audience can take advantage of the bookmark navigation you've established, open your document in Acrobat, go to File > Properties and choose the Initial View tab in the Document Properties dialog.

> ALERT: You must have a full version of Acrobat (not Adobe Reader) to set the initial view for a PDF.

The Adobe Acrobat Document Properties window.

24. From the Navigation tab dropdown, choose Bookmarks Panel and Page. Page layout should be set to Single Page and Magnification to Fit Page. Be sure to deselect the Open in Full Screen mode checkbox. Click OK and then save and close the file.

25. Still in Acrobat, go to File > Open Recent File and select **ex17_1.pdf** from the file list. When the PDF opens, the Navigation panel should be open to the Bookmarks pane. Click each bookmark to test it out and when you're finished, quit Acrobat, return to InDesign and close the file the complete the exercise and the chapter.

CHAPTER SUMMARY

This chapter showed you how to use a table of contents, a feature traditionally employed in long print documents, to create bookmark navigation in your interactive PDFs.

In your creation of bookmarks, you employed the Bookmarks panel to:

- Manually add bookmarks targeted to specific objects and text
- Reorder existing bookmarks in the panel
- Create a hierarchical structure of nested bookmarks

Additionally, you learned how to set up your PDF in Acrobat to be certain that your audience can easily access your bookmark navigation structure.

One of the coolest things you learned, outside of bookmarks specifically, is how to add SWF content to your interactive PDF. Who knew?!

The next chapter introduces Interactive PDF forms, one of the most passionately requested features ever.

Chapter 18

INTERACTIVE PDF FORMS

With InDesign CS6, the rich design and layout environment in InDesign got richer with new capabilities to create text fields, radio buttons, checkboxes, list boxes, combo boxes, and signature fields—all of which become interactive, fillable form fields when exported to PDF. You heard that right—you can now create fillable PDF forms right from InDesign! If you've never worked with fillable PDF forms, this chapter provides the perfect introduction—and if you're already a seasoned pro, you'll especially appreciate learning how you can customize your form components. Plus, you'll pick up all sorts of tips to ease your form-building workflow. So, enough with the prelude, let's get started!

About Interactive Forms

Tools to create interactive PDF forms were first introduced in Adobe Acrobat 3.0. Since that time, fillable PDF forms have become a mainstay for collecting and transmitting information across organizations large and small.

Prior to the release of InDesign CS6, the traditional workflow for interactive PDF form development required two distinct steps. Using a layout application like InDesign, designing the appearance of the form and exporting it to PDF was step one. Step two required a trip to Acrobat Professional where you would add the fields to make the form interactive. Once complete, you could then enable the form for Adobe Reader in Acrobat Professional and, last but not least, distribute it. (Enabling a form for Reader makes it possible for users viewing it in Reader to save and print a completed form.)

While it is still necessary to jump over to Acrobat Professional to fine tune certain aspects of your InDesign forms and to enable them for Reader, the bulk of your development can be accomplished without the need to venture outside of InDesign. Developing your forms in InDesign enables you to customize your form elements to some degree and give your forms some flair, add tooltips, set tab order and more. The best part is that you get to use the rich InDesign feature set to do it. With the bulk of your work complete, a quick jaunt to Acrobat for some finishing touches is all you'll need to have a form that's ready to roll.

Interactive Form Basics

In your exploration of buttons (starting with About Buttons starting on page 147), you learned that an object must have a unique name in order to initiate or be targeted by an action. Unique names are required for form fields as well. In the case of an electronic form, when the form is submitted, the information is transmitted as a series of name/value pairs—the name is the name you give to the form field object and the value captures the user entry. As an example, if a user were to enter a phone number (222-333-4444) in a text field called "phone," the name/value pair transmitted by the form would be: phone:222-333-4444.

If you've ever worked with Microsoft Excel, you should be familiar with the basic concept of a database. Each row of information in an Excel spreadsheet represents a record, and each column contains a bit of data related to that record. The data from a PDF form can be imported into an Excel spreadsheet as a record where the names from the name/value pairs map to the spreadsheet column names and the values populate the corresponding columns in the record.

The column names identify the record data in a meaningful way that makes it possible to interpret the information in the record. After all, data is only as good as the ability to interpret it, and a solid naming strategy is key. Of course, this is the case for any data, whether it be in Excel or data collected using a PDF form.

If you develop a consistent naming convention, you'll be able to repurpose both the form fields you create as well as the information they collect and transmit. In fact, you can use InDesign's Snippet and Library features (page 192) to save named form fields for just such repurposing.

Form Field Types

InDesign provides for the creation of seven different types of form fields through use of the Buttons and Forms panel.

Buttons

Everything you learned about buttons in the previous chapters is applicable to the buttons you'll use in forms. In fact, the show/hide techniques you learned can come in quite handy in your forms work for creating pop-up tooltips with invisible button hotspots (see how to make an invisible button on page 234.) Outside of the fancy tricks they can do, buttons perform three essential functions in an interactive form: they can submit a form, clear a form, and print a form.

Checkboxes

While they often appear on a form as part of a group, a checkbox can be checked or unchecked without affecting other checkboxes. Typically, each checkbox has a unique name with an assigned value of "yes."

Combo Boxes

Combo boxes are dropdown lists that display multiple options from which a user can select only one. A combo box can be made sortable and can be enabled to allow user input.

List Boxes

Similar to combo boxes, list boxes display multiple choices either in a dropdown or, depending on the number of available options, a scrolling visible list. Unlike combo boxes, list boxes can provide the option to select multiple responses. List boxes cannot accept user input but they can be made sortable.

Radio Buttons

Radio buttons provide multiple options from which the user can make only one selection. To get the buttons to work as a group, each radio button is given the same name but a unique value that is passed when the form is submitted. Once a radio button is selected, it can only be cleared by choosing another radio button or by resetting the form.

Signature Fields

Signature fields enable a user to digitally sign a document. If you click a digital signature field in a PDF form and a digital signature already resides on your system, a Sign Document dialog pops up allowing you to choose a signature. If you don't have a digital signature stored on your system, you are prompted to create one. When the signature is applied, Acrobat opens the save dialog so you can choose a location to save the signed version of the document.

Signatures are an integral part of Acrobat-based security, an involved topic that is beyond the scope of this book. To learn more about digital signatures and Acrobat security search Adobe Community Help.

> **TIP:** An identifying badge appears at the lower right corner of every form field indicating the type of form field it is.
>
> | | |
> |---|---|
> | ▾ | **Combo Box** |
> | ☑ | **Check Box** |
> | ⦿ | **Radio Box** |
> | ▥ | **List Box** |
> | ⊡ | **Text Field** |
> | ✍ | **Signature Field** |
> | ☝ | **Button** |

> **TIP:** You can convert an object to a form field either through the Buttons and Forms panel or, go to Object > Interactive and choose from the available options.
>
> Convert to Button
> Convert to Check Box
> Convert to Combo Box
> Convert to List Box
> Convert to Radio Button
> Convert to Signature Field
> Convert to Text Field
>
> Convert to Object
> Convert to Motion Path
> Set Tab Order...

Text Fields

By far the most commonly used type of form field, text fields can be single or multi-lined, scrollable or static. You can also designate a text field as a password field and while not actually encrypted, the field will display asterisks in place of the entered text. If taken into Acrobat Professional for further manipulation, you can require that the value entered in a text field conform to certain characters and patterns such as a phone numbers or zip codes.

Any type of form field you create can be designated as a required field.

Exercise 18.1: Exploring PDF Form Fields

1. Open Acrobat or Adobe Reader, navigate to the chapter_18_exercises folder and open **ex18_1_start.pdf**.

2. Notice that the checkboxes and radio buttons have a drop shadow in their inactive state and that the shadows disappear when the form fields are clicked. Notice also that the other forms fields have no shadows.

3. Take some time to interact with each of the form fields. Click the radio buttons and checkboxes, enter text in the text fields and select options from the combo and list boxes. (You can use the up and down arrows on your keyboard to move through the list of items in the combo box.) Don't place a signature just yet.

4. Click the Reset button to clear the fields in the form.

5. Ctrl+Click/Command+Click to select multiple options in the expanded list box.

6. Click the signature field and follow the prompts to add a signature. Save the signed form as **ex18_1_signed.pdf**.

7. Close the file, quit Acrobat or Reader and return to InDesign.

8. From the chapter_18_exercises folder, open **ex18_1_start.indd**.

    Note that although each of the fields in the form display a drop shadow, it only appears on the radio buttons and checkboxes in the PDF form.

9. Expand the Buttons and Forms panel in the Panel Dock (🗃) or go to Window > Interactive > Buttons and Forms.

10. With the Selection tool, click the combo box on the document and scroll through the list items in the Buttons and Forms panel.

11. Click each of the list boxes and explore their list items as well.

12. Click through each of the checkboxes and radio buttons noting how they are named and the values assigned to them.

13. Explore the remaining fields and be sure to notice the action on each of the buttons.

14. When you're finished checking everything out, close the file without saving to complete the exercise.

Exercise 18.2: Form Layout

Form design is a discipline in and of itself guided by a number of user experience considerations. Fields should be labeled in a way that provides clear direction to the person filling out the form, the placement of form labels should make it clear which fields they apply to, and the data requested should be organized into logical information blocks. If you have complex forms to create, you might consider making a study of existing forms from organizations like the IRS whose forms are used by millions of people.

Like anything else that involves user interaction, testing your forms for usability is strongly recommended. Things that may appear obvious or intuitive to you may not be as apparent to those in your audience.

When it comes to form layout, InDesign tables provide the perfect foundation for a structured yet flexible design. Add guides to the mix for added precision and you've got a winning formula (pun intended.)

Since you can't really add form fields without a foundation to put them on, the next exercise presents an approach to form layout that's applicable to even the most complicated forms.

TIP: Click and hold the Screen Mode icon on the Control panel or at the bottom of the Tool panel and choose from the options to change the screen display mode. Alternatively, press the letter "W" on your keyboard to toggle between Normal and Preview Mode.

1. To see a form that includes elements from the exercise, navigate to the chapter_18_exercises folder and open **ex18_2_example.indd**. This form is not an actual order form—it is simply for illustrative purposes and is decidedly more involved than the form in the exercise. If you'd like to take the PDF version for a test drive, open **ex18_2_example.pdf** in Acrobat or Reader and explore. (There are no calculations in the form although you can add calculations in Acrobat Pro.)

2. The InDesign version of the form opens in Preview mode. To see the way the form is built, make sure that nothing is selected on the page and press the letter "W" on your keyboard to switch to Normal mode.

   In Normal mode, you can see the table that provides the foundation structure of the form and the form fields laid over the table cells. A number of the cell borders were given a stroke weight of zero in order to achieve the final appearance.

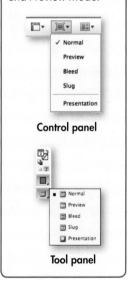

Control panel

Tool panel

3. Press Ctrl+;/Command+; to toggle the visibility of the grid of guides on the page or go to View > Grids & Guides > Show Guides.

   The guides were used to set up the height of the table rows, and to precisely position and size the form fields.

4. When you've finished exploring the form, close the file without saving to complete the exercise.

NOTE: To see a finished version of the actual layout you'll be creating in the exercise, check out **ex18_2_end.indd** in the chapter_18_exercises folder.

Name				
Street address				
City			State	Zip
Phone		Email		Add me to the mailing list
Visa MC AMEX Discover	Credit card number		Expiration date	CVV

Instructions

The end result of the layout you'll complete in this exercise.

NOTE: Despite choosing Print for the document intent, the finished form will be exported as an Interactive PDF.

5. Go to File > New > Document and choose Print from the Intent dropdown. Choose Letter from the Page Size dropdown, deselect the Facing Pages checkbox, and check the Primary Text Frame checkbox. Leave the remaining default settings, and click OK to exit the dialog and to create your new document.

6. When your new document opens, go to Layout > Create Guides and check the Preview checkbox. In the Create Guides dialog, set the Number of Rows to 31 and the Gutter for the Rows to 0.125 in. (Don't click OK yet.)

7. Set the number of columns to 6 and the Gutter for the Columns to 0. Ensure that the Margins radio button is selected and click OK to add the guides to the page. Go to View > Grids & Guides > Lock Guides (Ctrl+Alt+;/Command+Option+;)

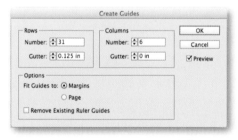

Go to Layout > Create Guides to add a custom grid of guides to your page.

Next you'll build the table that will serve as the foundation of your form.

TIP: Tables always reside in a text frame. If you want to have a stand-alone table, you must first create a text frame in which to insert it.

8. Place your Type tool cursor in the primary text frame on the page and go to Table > Insert Table.

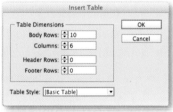

The Insert Table dialog enables you to define the number of rows and columns for your table, the number of header and footer rows, and also provides the option to assign a table style.

9. Set the value for Body Rows to 10 and the value for Columns to 6. Leave the remaining default settings and click OK to add your table to the page.

10. With the Selection tool, mouse over the upper border of the text frame and when you see a double-sided vertical arrow, click and hold and drag down to snap to the second horizontal guide (the upper edge of the gutter between the guides.)

The distance between the horizontal guides on the page alternates from gutter to row, gutter to row. You'll expand the table so that each table row aligns to a gutter and row pair.

11. Position the Type tool cursor at the bottom of the table (not the bottom of the text frame) so that the cursor changes to a double-sided vertical arrow. Count down 10 gutter/row guide pairs from the top of the text frame, and click and hold and drag the bottom of the table to snap it to the bottom guide of the tenth pair.

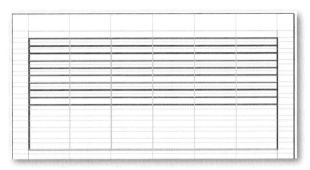

The combined power of tables and guides
provides an ideal framework for form design.

12. Position the Type tool cursor at the upper left corner of the table and when the cursor changes to a double-sided diagonal arrow, click to select the entire table.

The table turns blue when selected.

13. Go to Table > Distribute Rows Evenly to align the table rows to the guides.

14. With the table still selected, set the font size to 7 pt in the Control panel.

The [Basic Table] style is applied to the table by default with inset spacing of 0.0556" and text aligned to the top of the table cells. This inset provides the perfect margin for the labels you'll apply to the form fields.

15. Position the Type tool cursor in the first cell of the table and type "Name" to label the cell.

- Press the Down Arrow key on your keyboard to move the cursor to the second row of the table and label the cell "Street address."
- Press the Down Arrow again and label the cell "City."
- Press the Tab key four times and label the cell "State."
- Tab again and label the cell "Zip."
- Tab again to the next row of the table and label the cell "Phone."
- Tab two times and label the cell "Email."
- Tab three times and label the cell "Add me to the mailing list."

16. Tab to the next row and label the cell "Visa." On the Control panel click the Justify all lines button (▤) to set the text alignment for the cell. With the Type tool cursor still positioned after the "a" in Visa and the letters of the word stretched across the cell, Right-Click/Ctrl+Click and choose Insert White Space > Flush Space from the contextual menu. The letters of the word space themselves normally and the word aligns to the left of the cell. Type "MC" and add another Flush Space. Type "AMEX" and add a third Flush Space followed by the word "Discover."

TIP: Using a Flush Space between entries on a line in a paragraph that has alignment set to "Justify all lines" distributes the entries evenly across the line.

Visa   MC   Amex

About Tables

The table creation tools in InDesign provide a wide range of customization options that include granular controls for cell borders and background; cell height and insets; text styling and rotation; table formatting and more. Your settings can be captured as table styles which are built on cell style definitions that can include paragraph styles as part of their formatting options. While this might sound a bit complicated, let it instead be an indicator of the level of control you can exercise over the design and layout of your InDesign tables. Search Adobe Community Help to learn how to create table and cell styles.

When you create a table with the default [Basic Table] settings, inset spacing of 0.0556" is applied to the interior of each cell, cell content is left and top aligned, and each cell border has a solid stroke with a stroke weight of 1 pt. With the defaults as your jumping off point, when you know how to employ the tools, there's virtually no limit to the way you can customize your tables.

You can format a table using either the Control panel or the Table panel. Both panels contain the same controls with additional tools in the Control panel for customizing cell borders.

CONTROL PANEL TABLE FORMATTING CONTROLS

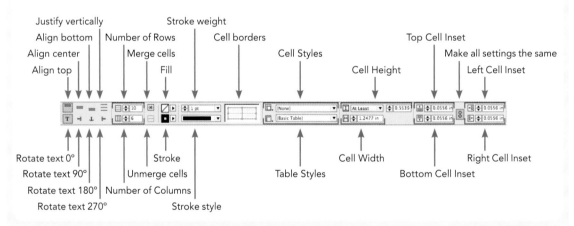

At first blush, the controls for refining cell borders may seem somewhat counter-intuitive. In truth, they're pretty easy to manipulate once you know how. When a border is selected in the cell border proxy it turns blue and the weight displayed in the stroke weight dropdown is applied to it. To remove a stroke from individual borders of a table cell, make sure those borders are blue in the proxy and then set the cell weight to zero.

Table panel

To select a table cell (or cells) for formatting, click and drag through the cell(s) with the Type tool cursor to highlight the entire cell. When a cell is selected, the cell formatting controls appear in the Control panel and the cell background turns blue. To select an entire row or column, position the Type tool cursor to the left of the row or at the top of the column. When the cursor turns to a black arrow, click to select the row or column.

To resize a column or row, position the Type tool cursor over the border dividing the cells, and when the cursor changes to a double-sided arrow, click and hold and drag. The width or height of the entire table shifts as a row or column border is repositioned. To maintain the existing width or height of the table and affect only the rows or columns on either side of the active border, hold the Shift key while dragging.

17. Tab to the next cell and label it "Credit card number."

    - Press Tab two times and label the cell "Expiration date."
    - Tab twice and label the cell "CVV."
    - Tab once, press the Down Arrow once, and label the cell "Instructions".

18. Save the file as ex18_2.indd.

    That completes the entry of the form labels—now you're ready to format the cells.

19. Position the Type tool cursor outside and to the left of the cell with the "Name" label and when the cursor changes to a right-pointing arrow, click to select the table row. Click the Merge Cells button on the Control panel. ([⊠])

20. Repeat step 19 for the row with the "Street address" label.

21. Click in the cell labeled City and holding down the mouse, drag into the third cell to its right so that all four cells turn blue. Merge the cells.

22. Merge the cells related to the labels "Phone", "Email" and "Credit card number."

    If you were to merge the two rows that you'll allocate for the "Instructions" section of the form, the two rows would collapse into one. Instead, you'll employ a little bit of smoke and mirrors to hide the strokes between the cells and give the appearance of one large cell. You'll use the same technique to create visual separation between the contact information section of the table and the instructions.

23. Click and drag through the cells in the row following the credit card information. In the Cell Border Proxy, click each of the lines in the figure as necessary so the vertical lines turn blue and the horizontal lines turn gray. Set the stroke weight to 0.

    Stroke weight settings affect the blue borders in the Cell Border Proxy while gray borders are unaffected. In the figure above, with a stroke weight of zero, the vertical borders of the selected cells will be hidden

24. Click and drag the Type tool cursor to select the row containing the cell label "Instructions" and the row below it. In the Cell Border Proxy, click to turn the interior cell borders blue and the exterior borders gray. Set the Stroke Weight to 0.

    You'll delete the extra two rows at the bottom of the table to wrap up the table formatting.

25. Select the bottom two rows of the form and go to Table > Delete > Row.

26. To see the fruit of your labors, switch to the Selection tool and press W on your keyboard to switch to Preview mode.

27. Save the file and keep it open for the next exercise.

With the layout of the form complete, in the next exercise, you'll add the form fields that will bring it to life.

Creating Form Fields

As with buttons, you can convert almost any object to a form field. Don't be fooled into thinking that this means your form fields can be customized in the same way that buttons can however. InDesign actually is a bit of a tease in this regard, allowing you to think that the fancy corners, effects, gradients and even images you convert to form fields will be maintained in the transition. But alas, with the exception of checkboxes and radio buttons, which like standard buttons can take pretty much anything you throw at them, it's all an illusion. While beautiful to behold in InDesign, when you export your meticulously designed form fields to PDF, you're in for a bit of a shock. Images and gradient strokes and fills simply disappear as do drop shadows. Fancy corners also bite the dust, patterned strokes are reduced to a solid line, and transparency is converted to solid color. The up side is that solid stroke color and weight are maintained for all field types as is fill color and tint. So, for any field types other than buttons, checkboxes, and radio buttons, keep your strokes and fills solid with no transparency and steer clear of stroke and corner options as well as effects.

Exercise 18.3: Adding Form Fields

1. If you have the file open from the previous exercise, you're good to go. Otherwise, navigate to the chapter_18_exercises folder, open **ex18_3_start.indd** and save it as ex18_3.indd. Make sure the document display is set to Normal mode and that the guides are visible on the page.

2. If necessary, expand the Layers panel in the Panel Dock ( ) and change the name of Layer 1 to "Form layout." Lock the layer.

3. Click the Create new layer button ( ) at the bottom of the panel and name the new layer "Form fields." Zoom in to the form so its width fills the screen.

4. Align the arrow at the upper left of the Type tool cursor to the lower left corner of the cell containing the label "Name." Drag up and to the right until the text frame snaps to the horizontal guide within the cell and the cell's right edge. Press the Escape key on your keyboard to switch to the Selection tool and to select the text frame.

Settings in the Buttons and Forms panel for the Name text field.

5. Expand the Buttons and Forms panel in the Panel Dock (or go to Window > Interactive > Buttons and Forms) and click the Convert to Button (◄▭) button at the bottom of the panel. At the top of the panel, select Text Field from the Type dropdown and name the text field "name." In the Description field, type "Enter your name" and if necessary, deselect the Scrollable checkbox. Select the value in the Font Size field and type in the number 9.

Now that you have a text field with the desired properties and of the appropriate height, you'll duplicate it to create the other text fields in the form.

6. Hold down the Alt/Option key on the keyboard and with the Selection tool, click and hold and drag the Name text field straight down to snap the bottom of the duplicated field to the bottom of the cell with the "Street address" label. Rename the field "addressStreet" in the Buttons and Forms panel.

7. Duplicate the addressStreet text field and snap the lower edge of the duplicated field to the bottom of the cell with the label "City." Rename the field "addressCity." Mouse over the right edge of the addressCity field and when the cursor changes to a double-sided horizontal arrow, click and hold and drag left to snap the edge of the field to the right edge of the City cell.

8. Repeat the duplication process to create, name and position the following fields:

Cell Label	Field Name
Zip	addressZip
Phone	contactPhone
Email	contactEmail
Credit card number	ccNumber
CVV	ccCVV
Instructions	instructions

Size the instructions field to stretch vertically from the guide just below the cell label to the bottom of the last row of the table and then check the Multiline checkbox in the Buttons and Forms panel.

9. Select the Rectangle tool from the Tool panel (▢) and, holding the Shift key to constrain the proportions of the shape, draw a square in the field with the "Add me to the mailing list" label. Give the square a black stroke and a white fill.

10. With the square selected, go to Object > Interactive > Convert to Check Box. In the Buttons and Forms panel, name the checkbox mailingList and leave the Value at the bottom of the panel set to "yes." (When the checkbox is checked, its name value pair will be mailingList: yes.)

Note that the check box has two states by default: [Normal On] and [Normal Off] and that InDesign automatically applies a check mark to the On state. As with any button, you can create rollover and click states and provide the states with distinct appearances. (For more on setting button appearances, see page 149.)

11. Go to File > Open, navigate to the chapter_18_exercises folder, and open **Forms.indl**.

There are two combo boxes saved to the library: one is a list of state abbreviations, and the other is list from 1–12 for the months of the year. There is also a radio button group that you'll put to work for the selection of credit card type. Additionally, there is a set of three buttons that you'll use to print, reset and submit the form.

12. Shift+Click to select the two combo boxes and the radio buttons in the library and drag them onto your document. Position the month combo box and its label in the Expiration Date cell. Position the state combo box in the State cell and position the radio buttons in the cell with the credit card labels. With the radio buttons still selected, name them "cc" in the Buttons and Forms panel.

The state combo box is missing an entry for the state of Wisconsin. You'll correct that error next.

NOTE: If you want to save the updated state combo box for future use, simply drag it into the Sample Buttons and Forms Library. To name it, Double-Click the item in the library and fill out the Item Information fields as desired.

13. Select the state combo box and if necessary, expand the Buttons and Forms panel. Type "WI" in the List Items field and click the ➕ button to add the entry. If necessary, scroll to the bottom of the list to locate the WI list item and then drag it into its proper position between Washington and West Virginia.

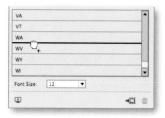

Simply drag to reorder list items in a Combo box or List box.

14. In the Expiration date field duplicate the "Month" text frame, change the text in the duplicate frame to "Year" and position it to the right of the combo box in the cell.

15. Draw a text frame about the size of the combo box with the Type tool. Give it a 10% black fill and no stroke. Select Combo Box from Type dropdown in the Buttons and Forms panel and name the combo box "ccExpYear." Add List Items for each year from 2014 through 2020. Position the combo box to the right of its label.

16. Select all three combo boxes and set the Font Size to 9 pt.

17. Select the radio button under the Visa label and enter "visa" in the Button Values field at the bottom of the Buttons and Forms panel. Enter Button Values that correspond to the labels for each of the remaining radio buttons and ensure that for each, the Selected by default checkbox is deselected.

While the form you've created will be fillable when exported to Interactive PDF, and your users will be able to print the completed form, a Submit button is required in order to transmit the form data electronically. As a courtesy to your user, you may also want to include a Reset button to allow them to clear the form of its data and start over. Last but not least, you may also choose to include a Print button as an added convenience. These buttons have been provided for you in the Forms library file located in the chapter_18_exercises folder. They already have names and rollover states so you'll just need to add the appropriate actions.

18. If necessary, press Ctrl+;/Command+; to show the guides. From the Forms library, drag the reset, print, and submit button group to your document and position the buttons to the lower right of the form, aligning them to the guides. Deselect the buttons.

19. Select the print button and in the Buttons and Forms panel, apply the Print Form action.

20. Add the Clear Form action to the reset button.

21. Shift+Click to select all three buttons on the document and then deselect the Printable checkbox in the Buttons and Forms panel.

22. Select the submit button and in the Buttons and Forms panel, apply the Submit Form action. Type **mailto:** followed by your email address in the URL field.

That completes the fields for your form and it's almost ready to go. The last thing you need to do before export is set the Tab order—and you'll do just that in the next exercise.

TIP: Since buttons are only functional in the digital version of the document, there's no reason to include them in a printed version of a form. To prevent buttons from printing, deselect the Printable checkbox in the Buttons and Forms panel.

Tab Order

When filling out a form, it's common practice to use the Tab key to move from field to field. The order in which the fields receive focus is called tab order. While a convenience for someone filling out a form, tab order, as a reflection of the underlying document structure, is essential for people using assistive technologies in that it makes the content accessible to their devices.

There are two ways to set tab order in InDesign: either through the dedicated Tab Order panel or through the Articles panel. To access the Tab Order panel, go to Object > Interactive > Set Tab Order. Simply drag the field names into the proper order in the panel or use the Move Up and Move Down buttons to rearrange them.

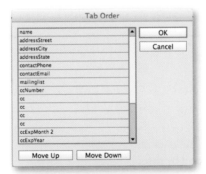

Go to Object > Interactive > Set Tab Order to access the Tab Order panel.

As an alternative, the Articles panel is a powerful tool for setting reading order and document structure for export to EPUB, HTML and Accessible PDF. It performs a similar function to the XML Structure panel but with a much more intuitive interface. As an additional benefit, the Articles panel is an effective tool to establish tab order for Interactive PDF forms.

You'll learn more about using the Articles panel with EPUB in Exercise 22.1: Setting Sequence with the Articles Panel starting on page 323. For now, you'll use the Articles panel in the next exercise to set the tab order for your form.

Exercise 18.4: Setting Tab Order

1. Open **ex18_4_start.indd** from the chapter_18_exercises folder.

2. Press Ctrl+A/Command+A to select the form fields on the page. (The table layer is locked so you don't have to worry about selecting it.)

3. Go to Window > Articles and when the Articles panel opens, drag all the form fields into the panel. Alternatively, you can press the + button at the bottom of the panel to create an article from the selection.

4. Name the article "Form Fields", ensure that the Include When Exporting checkbox is checked and click OK.

Articles provide a way to set up reading
order for forms as well as for EPUB.

5. The labels for the combo boxes, indicated by a **T** icon in the Articles panel, were included in the Article along with the form fields. To remove them from the article Ctrl+Click/Command+Click the two label names and press the delete button at the bottom of the panel.

6. Drag to arrange the field names in the Articles panel to match the sequence of fields on the form (and in the screenshot below.)

You can use the Articles panel to create multiple articles each of
which can contain multiple elements. You can drag articles as
well as the content within them to adjust the reading order.

7. To ensure that the tab order you established in the Articles panel translates reliably when the form is converted to PDF, choose Use for Reading Order in Tagged PDF from the Articles panel menu. Save the file.

In order for the reading order established in the Articles panel to carry over to PDF, you must select Use for Reading Order in Tagged PDF from the Articles panel menu.

Now comes the moment of truth where you get to export your form to Interactive PDF and test the result of your efforts.

8. Go to File > Export and choose Adobe PDF (Interactive) from the Format dropdown. Save the file to a location of your choosing. When the Export to Interactive PDF dialog opens, be sure that both the Create Tagged PDF and Use Structure for Tab Order checkboxes are checked.

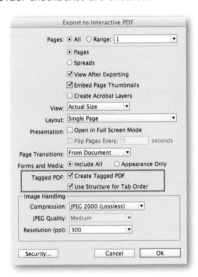

Check both Tagged PDF checkboxes to have InDesign to include the structure you established in the Articles panel in the exported PDF.

9. If necessary, check the View After Exporting checkbox and click OK.

10. If your form does not open automatically in Acrobat Professional, but you have the application on your system, open the form file in Acrobat Professional now. If you don't have Acrobat Professional on your system, you won't be able to complete the next part of the exercise.

> **ALERT:** Acrobat Professional is required to complete the remainder of the exercise.

By default, when an Interactive PDF form is viewed in Adobe Reader, it can be filled out and printed but the completed form cannot be saved. If you have Acrobat Professional, you can add Adobe's "special sauce" to your form to enable Reader users to save their data. Be aware however that the free special sauce comes with a limit of 500 servings. You can only distribute

> **NOTE:** Acrobat XI Pro was used for the instructions and screenshots in this exercise.

500 enabled forms. After that, you'll need to contact Adobe to determine the catering fee.

11. With your form open in Acrobat Professional, go to File > Save As > Reader Extended PDF > Enable Additional Features.

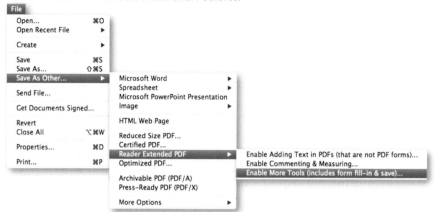

You can add usage rights to your PDF forms that enable up to 500 users to save their form data.

Acrobat displays an alert to inform you of the rights that will be assigned to the form and the editing limitations that will result from saving the Reader Enabled document.

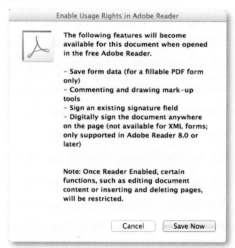

Usage rights for Adobe Reader users can be extended in Acrobat Professional to support the saving of form data, commenting and markup, and digital signatures.

12. Save the file and test out your form. Tab from field to field, filling in the information as you go. Try the reset and print buttons and when you've finished filling out the form, try the submit button.

13. When you press the submit button, the Select Email Client dialog pops up asking whether you would like to use your desktop mail application or internet mail. Choose your preference and send the email.

When submitting a form to email, Acrobat or Reader give you the option of using your local email application or internet mail.

InDesign auto-populates the email subject line. For the form from the exercise, the subject line was: Form Returned: ex18_4_end.pdf. The completed PDF form is sent as an attachment to the email. Alternatively, you could have entered a web URL directed to an online script for processing the form data. CGI scripts and the like are outside the scope of this book but a simple web search will provide you with a wide variety of resources.

14. Close your email client and close out of Acrobat. Return to InDesign and close the exercise file to complete the lesson.

Sizing Form Fields Uniformly with Object Styles

Have we got a trick for you! A shout out to Keith Gilbert for his awesome post on InDesignSecrets.com: "Make an Object Style specify frame width." In reading the post, a light bulb went off—if you can use an object style to specify frame width, why not create one to control the width of your form fields? In any case, it was just too cool a tip not to share, so...

Exercise 18.5: Controlling Form Field Width with Object Styles

1. Open a new document. Any settings are fine. With the Type tool—this won't work if you use a non-type object—drag out a text frame for your text field.

2. Press Esc on your keyboard to select the frame and to switch to the Selection tool.

3. In the Buttons and Forms panel, convert the frame to a text field and name it—for the example, any name will do.

4. Expand the Object Styles panel in the Panel Dock or go to Window > Styles > Object Styles. With the text frame selected, Alt+Click/Option+Click the new button at the bottom of the panel and name the new style "FormField."

5. Select the Text Frame General Options category at the left of the Object Style Options panel and choose Fixed Width from the Columns dropdown at the right. Leave the Number of columns set to 1 and enter a value in the Width field. Optionally, enter values for Inset Spacing and change the Vertical Justification Align value to Center. Click OK to close the dialog and then click the style name in the Object Styles panel to apply it to the form field.

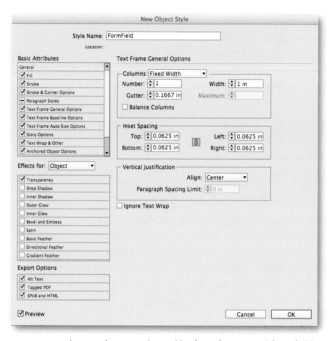

You can use object styles to set the width of text frames and form fields.

By default, the Object Style definition captures all the formatting applied to the text field, including stroke and fill. If you'd like to be able to apply the style without affecting specific object properties, deselect the category checkboxes for those properties at the left of the Object Style Options dialog.

6. To update the width of all form fields to which an existing style is applied—in this case we'll call the style "FormField"—Right-Click/Ctrl+Click the style name in the Object Style panel and choose Edit "FormField" from the contextual menu. Ensure that the Preview checkbox at the lower left of the dialog is checked. Select the Text Frame General Options category and change the Width value. TA DA! The width of the styled form field(s) updates to reflect your changes. Awesome, right?

What's beautiful about this technique is that it works for any type of form field (or text frame), including buttons, check boxes and radio buttons. A cautionary note however—buttons, checkboxes, and radio buttons have multiple states and the object style must be applied to each state in order for their sizes to remain congruent.

And that concludes our fabulous foray into forms!

CHAPTER SUMMARY

This chapter included form basics and beyond, providing solid principles and techniques applicable to development of even the most complex forms You started by gaining an understanding of name/value pairs and the importance of establishing a solid naming convention for your form fields. You learned about the seven types of form fields and the properties that distinguish them from one another:

- Buttons
- Checkboxes
- Combo Boxes
- List Boxes
- Radio Buttons
- Signature Fields
- Text Fields

Combining the power of InDesign's layout guides with its robust table features you employed a scalable layout strategy to create the appearance of your form. In your work with tables you learned

- All about the Control panel Table Formatting tools
- How to add a table to a document
- How to resize columns and rows
- How to select, merge, and format cells and cell borders

After laying out the table, you went on to add form fields, positioning them precisely and naming them strategically. Additionally, you learned about the significance of document structure and reading order and became familiar with two techniques for setting tab order—using the dedicated Tab Order panel and the Articles panel. You then applied settings in both the Articles panel and the Export to Interactive PDF dialog to ensure that the document structure you established would translate properly in the export process.

You then took a trip to Acrobat Professional and added Adobe's "special sauce" to extend usage rights for Adobe Reader users, enabling them to save the data in their completed forms.

Last but not least, you got an awesome tip for using object styles to set the width of form fields and text frames.

So far, you've learned how to add bookmarks and form elements to your interactive PDFs. The next chapter is all about page transitions—an easy and potentially elegant way to add just the right amount of animation to your interactive publication.

Chapter 19

PAGE TRANSITIONS

Page transitions are a quick and easy way to add visual interest to a project. With a few simple clicks, you can make your document pages flip, fade, wipe, or dissolve, and put an otherwise static document into motion.

This chapter discusses best practices for using transitions, how to apply and remove them, and how to publish them to PDF (and SWF.) You'll also take a quick trip to Acrobat to experience the chapter project in full screen mode.

Working with Page Transitions

Adding page transitions is the easiest way to add animation to a multi-page document. Supported in both Interactive PDF and SWF, a fade or wipe from one page to the next can add just the right amount of spice to your project. Everything in moderation, though—and page transitions are no exception to this rule. Used sparingly, they can help to bring your project to life. Too many different transitions, however, like too many different fonts on a page, create a visual cacophony that cheapens even the most beautifully designed document.

Transitions can be applied on a page-by-page basis or document-wide, and there is a dedicated panel to manage them. Go to Window > Interactive > Page Transitions (or click ⊞ in the Panel Dock) to get to it. With 12 categories, and variations in direction and speed available for most of them, there is a plethora of transitions from which to choose. This is both a blessing and a curse; a blessing in that you have so many choices, a curse in that you might feel compelled to choose too many of them. The likelihood is that you'll play for a while, and then choose a couple of favorites upon which you'll come to rely.

With that notion in mind, the next exercise lets you get some of that playing out of your system. At the same time, it's designed to get you familiar with the available page transition options. So for now, throw caution (and good design principles) to the wind, and for the next little bit, just use this opportunity to experiment and play.

Exercise 19.1: Working with Page Transitions

1. Open **ex19_1_end.indd** from the chapter_19_exercises folder and preview the file to get familiar with how it works. When you're done previewing, check out the Pages panel and note the transitions icon next to each of the pages. When you're done exploring, you can keep the document open for reference.

So you have a feel for how the document was set up, here's a little overview. Hyperlink destinations were established for each of the document pages and named with the associated page number. The images on the first page are buttons. Each button has a Go to Destination action targeted to the page that displays a larger version of the button image. The document master for these pages has an invisible button laid over the large photo in the center of the page, with a Go to Destination action targeted to page 1.

NOTE: You were introduced to the file used in this exercise in Chapter 16: SWF Output, starting on page 237

2. Open **ex19_1_start.indd** from the chapter_19_exercises folder and save it as ex19_1.indd.

The document has nine pages so you've got a lot of opportunity to play with the different transition options.

3. Go to Window > Interactive > Page Transitions or click the ▱ button in the Panel Dock to open the Page Transitions panel. Ensure that page 1 is highlighted in the Pages panel.

4. To get an experience of all the transitions you can choose from, select Choose from the Page Transitions panel menu.

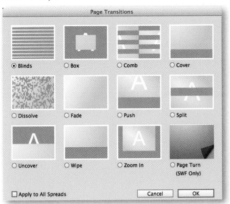

The Page Transitions dialog lets you preview 12 different page transitions all in the same place. From this dialog, you can apply a transition to only the page that is active in the Pages panel, or to all the spreads in your document.

5. Mouse over each transition to get a feel for how it works. Ensure that the Apply to All Spreads checkbox at the lower left of the dialog is unchecked. Then, select the Blinds radio button and click OK to assign the transition to page 1.

6. When the Page Transitions dialog closes, the default settings for the Blinds transition are active in the Page Transitions panel. Mouse over the preview at the top of the panel to play the animation. Select Vertical from the Direction dropdown and preview the transition again. Try each of the speed settings and choose the settings you prefer.

Be aware that page transitions are applied to the highlighted page in the Pages panel, regardless of the page showing in the document window. For this reason, be sure to first select a page in the Pages panel before applying your transition.

7. In the Pages panel, mouse over the page transition icon next to page 1. A tooltip pops up that says "Page Transition Applied."

The ▱ icon next to a page in the Pages panel indicates that a page transition has been applied to it.

8. Double-Click on page 2 in the Pages panel and choose Box from the Transition dropdown in the Page Transitions panel. Choose a direction and speed.

9. Assign a different transition to each page, exploring the options for each transition along the way. Skip the Page Curl—that is a feature exclusively for output to SWF. You saw it in action in SWF Output, starting on page 237.

Although the focus in this chapter is on Interactive PDF, page transitions are also supported in export to SWF. Since this is the case, the SWF Preview panel provides an excellent way to preview and test your transitions in InDesign—without requiring that you export to Interactive PDF until you're satisfied with the result.

NOTE: The Interactive Page Curl is definitely cool, but, unfortunately, it doesn't work when you export to PDF.

10. Open the Preview panel (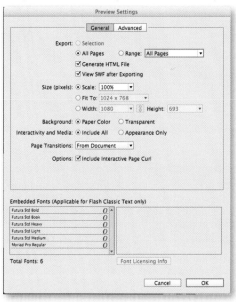 in the Panel Dock) and choose Edit Preview Settings from the panel menu. From the General tab of the Preview Settings dialog, confirm that the All Pages radio button is selected. If necessary, check the Generate HTML file and View SWF after Exporting checkboxes. Leave the other default settings and check the Include Interactive Page Curl checkbox at the bottom of the dialog. Click Save Settings to close the dialog.

The Preview Settings dialog is identical in content to the Export SWF dialog which you learned about in Chapter 16: SWF Output, starting on page 237. The settings you enter in this dialog are applied to both the movie displayed in the Preview panel and the file that's generated when you choose the Test in Browser option from the Preview panel menu.

11. In the Preview panel, click the Preview Document Mode button ( ) and then click the Play Preview button. When the preview appears, click each button on the home page to jump to the enlarged version of the button image. Then click the large image to return to the home page.

When previewing the document, you saw that, rather than enhancing the presentation, the many transitions served to overpower and distract from the content.

TIP: To clear all the page transitions from a document at once, choose Clear All from the Page Transitions panel menu.

12. In the Page Transitions panel, select Fade from the Transition dropdown and make a selection from the Speed dropdown. Click the Apply to All Spreads button ( ) at the bottom right of the panel and preview the file again.

13. Go to File > Export and choose Adobe PDF (Interactive) from the Format dropdown. Click Save and assign the following export settings:

- Check the View After Exporting checkbox
- Check the Open in Full Screen Mode checkbox
- Check the Flip Pages Every checkbox
- Enter "3" in the seconds field.
- Choose From Document from the Page Transitions dropdown
- Confirm that Include All is selected
- Assign compression settings of your choosing.

14. Click OK to export the PDF.

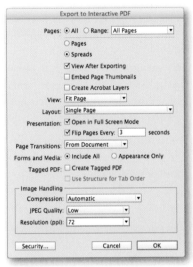

The Export to Interactive PDF dialog.

15. When the export is complete, Acrobat or Reader should open and the Full Screen alert should appear. Click the Remember my choice for this document checkbox and then click Yes to allow the document to open in full screen mode.

> NOTE: If you check the Remember my choice for this document checkbox, you won't need to deal with the Full Screen alert again for this file, as long as you don't change the file name.

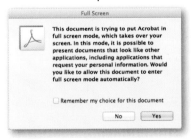

Interactive PDF page transitions can only be viewed in full screen mode.

16. Click through the pages. When you've finished viewing the document, press Escape to exit full screen mode. (Ctrl+L/Command+L will also toggle in and out of full screen mode.) Close the document, quit Acrobat or Reader and return to InDesign to complete the lesson.

If you have Adobe Reader configured as your default application for viewing PDFs, you will see the same alert that appears in Acrobat, and you can use the same keys to control full screen mode.

> NOTE: If you use an application other than Acrobat or Reader to view PDFs, it's likely that the features you add to your Interactive PDF won't work.

Page Transition Tips

If you add, remove or rearrange pages in a document containing page transitions, InDesign will present you with the following alert:

If your document contains spreads with facing pages, unless you specify otherwise, the pages will get rearranged, or "shuffled" from one spread to another when pages are added or removed. This causes any page transitions applied to the altered spreads to be removed.

Transitions are applied to an entire spread rather than individual pages, so, for documents with facing page spreads, shuffling pages from one spread to another results in page transitions being lost. You can pretty much disregard this message entirely if your document doesn't use facing pages or manual spreads.

To remove transitions from your entire document at once, go to the Page Transitions panel menu and choose Clear All. Alternatively, from the Pages panel menu, go to Page Attributes > Page Transitions > Clear All.

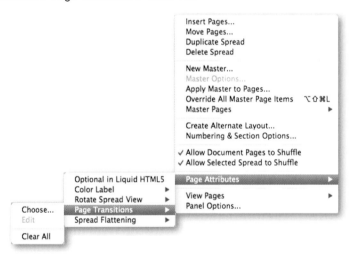

You can remove all the page transitions in your document from the Pages panel menu.

CHAPTER SUMMARY

Page transitions are an incredibly easy way to add sparkle to a multi-page document. However, you learned that when it comes to page transitions, less is more—that too many transitions can be visually distracting. You also learned

- How to add transitions to document spreads using the Page Transitions panel

- How to customize the default page transition settings by changing transition direction and speed

- How to identify spreads with page transitions in the Pages panel

- How to set up a document to export to Interactive PDF in Full Screen mode

- How to clear all page transitions from your document

In order to see your page transitions in action, you made modifications to the Preview panel settings and previewed your document in InDesign You also took a trip to Acrobat or Adobe Reader and viewed the Interactive PDF version of your document in full screen mode to see the impact of your efforts.

You definitely want to check out the next chapter—it's chock full of tips for navigating the sometimes bizarre behaviors you may encounter in your Interactive PDF development process. You'll also learn how to optimize and output your files, and wrap it all up with a bow.

Chapter 20

PREPARING FOR PDF EXPORT

This chapter is critical to your interactive PDF production, providing tips and workarounds for known issues with PDF export, and helping you to avoid problems before they arise. While you've been learning how to push the boundaries of InDesign's interactive features, this chapter spells out some limitations and helps you work them to your best advantage.

Export to Interactive PDF

You may have noticed that whenever we've referred to PDF, we've used the term Interactive PDF as distinct from the term PDF. The primary reason for this is that InDesign has two separate PDF export dialogs—one for print and a second that's dedicated expressly to Interactive PDF. Adobe's choice to separate print from interactive PDF export is a good thing, particularly because the Interactive PDF export options are fewer and much simpler to navigate than those for print. As with print, export to Interactive PDF provides the choice of whether to output to spreads or individual pages. It also provides a range of compression options similar to those in the SWF export dialog. To access the Export to Interactive PDF dialog, go to File > Export and choose Adobe PDF (Interactive) from the Format dropdown at the bottom of the dialog.

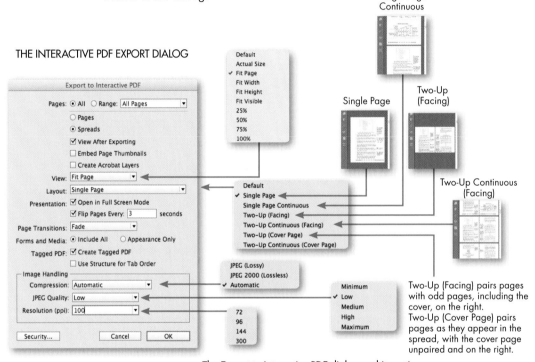

The Export to Interactive PDF dialog and its options.

The choices you'll make in the top half of the dialog have more to do with the display of the document than with optimization. You can choose to export your entire document, or a range of pages. It's always a good idea to check the View After Exporting checkbox so you can verify that your document exports as expected and so you can give it a final check. Page thumbnails add to file size, so, if file optimization is a priority, you won't want to include them in your file. If you check the Create Acrobat Layers checkbox, the primary layers in your InDesign document carry over to your PDF, and you can add Show/Hide actions in Acrobat Professional to turn the layer visibility on and off. A number of the interactive capabilities in InDesign actually existed first in Acrobat, including media support and buttons, as well as tools to create interactive forms. You can in fact, extend a PDF exported from InDesign, using any of the interactive tools in Acrobat. But that's for another book.

Continuing with the export dialog, you'll want to check the Create Tagged PDF checkbox. As you learned in the discussion of tab order for Interactive PDF forms (starting on page 274), tagging your PDF provides it with additional structure. The added structure makes the document accessible to screen readers and, therefore, compliant with the Americans with Disabilities Act (section 508). The additional structure provided by tagging also helps resolve a number of quirky typographical issues that might otherwise arise in the conversion process.

The export dialog provides a host of options for page view and layout. For an Interactive PDF, it's a safe bet that you'll want your entire page to fit in the document window, so, for View, choose Fit Page. For Layout, Single Page will most likely be your best option, since it shows one page (or one spread) at a time. You may choose to check the Open in Full Screen Mode checkbox, but be forewarned: before a document set to Full Screen Mode opens, it first puts up an alert to warn of potential danger. It could be a little scary to someone opening your document who isn't familiar with the drill.

Before a PDF set to Full Screen Mode opens,
Acrobat and Reader display the above alert.

If you choose to have your document open in full screen mode, you can set it up so the pages flip automatically every couple seconds. Just check the Flip Pages Every checkbox, and enter a number in the Seconds field. Perfect for a self-running presentation—you can just set it and forget it.

The page transition options are the same for Interactive PDF as they are for SWF export. You can use the transitions you set in the document, or choose a single transition that plays for every page. For the Forms and Media option, you'll want to choose Include All or you'll lose all the interactivity you set up in your document.

NOTE: Learn about page transitions starting on page 281.

When exporting to Interactive PDF, just as with SWF, file size is an important consideration—particularly if you intend to deliver your document via the web. The principles governing your compression choices are the same—choose the highest possible compression that produces an acceptable result. For Compression, you can choose Automatic, JPEG (Lossy), or JPEG 2000 (Lossless). The JPEG quality settings are the same as in the SWF export dialog.

When optimizing an Interactive PDF, your choice of image resolution depends on how much you want to allow your user to zoom in on the document without losing image quality. Zooming beyond the limits of the image resolution (beyond 100% magnification for a file with images at 72 ppi) results in degradation of image quality and ultimately in pixelization. Therefore, to maintain image quality and enable zooming above 100%, a resolution higher than 72 ppi is required. As you've no doubt anticipated, the increase in resolution comes at the price of a larger file. Once again, you're confronted with the tradeoff between file size and quality. You need to weigh how much you want your audience to be able to zoom in against the time the larger file takes to download. If you want people to be able to zoom, a good rule of thumb is to choose a resolution somewhere between 100 ppi and 150 ppi. As an alternative to the preset resolution settings, you can type your preferred value in the Resolution field.

Exercise 20.1: Exporting to Interactive PDF

DOWNLOAD:
Exercise files for this chapter can be downloaded from http://www.interactive-indesign.com

In this exercise, you'll set print preferences for buttons, export an Interactive PDF, and then compare several files that were exported with different compression options.

1. Go to the chapter_20_exercises folder and open **ex_20_1_start.indd.** Save it as ex_20_1.indd**.**

2. Go to File > Export, and choose Adobe PDF (Interactive) from the Format dropdown at the bottom of the Export dialog. Browse to the chapter_20_exercises folder and save the file as **ex20_1_low_100.pdf**.

3. In the Export to Interactive PDF dialog, choose the following settings:

    *   Pages: All
    *   Pages
    *   View After Exporting
    *   Deselect Embed Page Thumbnails
    *   Deselect Create Acrobat Layers
    *   View: Fit Page
    *   Layout: Single Page
    *   Open in Full Screen Mode
    *   Flip Pages Every 3 Seconds

    *   Page Transitions: Fade
    *   Forms and Media: Include All
    *   Create Tagged PDF (optional)
    *   Use Structure for Tab Order (optional)
    *   Compression: Automatic
    *   JPEG Quality: Low
    *   Resolution: 100

The export settings for ex21_1_low_100.pdf.

TIP: When applying Security settings in PDF export, the passwords to open the document and to change permissions cannot be the same.

4. Click the Security button at the bottom of the dialog. Check Require a password to open the document, and enter "1234" in the Document Open Password field. Check Use a password to restrict printing, editing and other tasks and enter "5678" in the Permissions Password field. Choose None from both the Printing Allowed and Changes Allowed dropdowns, and deselect Enable copying of text, images and other content. Leave the other two check boxes checked and click OK to export your PDF.

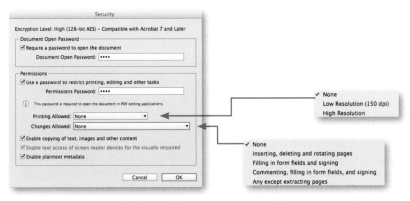

The Security dialog enables you to set passwords for opening and making changes to the document. If you apply both a Document Open Password and a Permissions password, the Permissions password can do double duty and can be used to open the document as well. The Document Open Password, however, works only to open the document.

5. Enter "1234" in the first Password dialog and click OK. Then enter "5678" in the second Password dialog and click OK. Click OK in the Export Interactive PDF dialog to generate your PDF.

Before InDesign exports the document, it asks you to confirm the security passwords.

6. Before Acrobat Professional or Adobe Reader opens, you are prompted to enter a password to open the document. Enter "5678," the Permissions password—which also acts as a master password—and click OK.

The Permissions password can be used both to open the document and to change the document Security settings.

7. The Full Screen alert pops up to scare you. Check the Remember my choice for this document checkbox, and click Yes to open the document.

8. The document opens in Full Screen Mode, and the pages change with a Fade transition every three seconds until the end of the presentation is reached. Press Esc, or Ctrl+L/Command+L on your keyboard to exit Full Screen Mode.

9. Press Ctrl+/Command+ to zoom in as many times as necessary to reach a magnification of at least 150%. You should see the magnification percentage displayed in the Select and Zoom toolbar, located at the top of your screen. You can also press the + button on the toolbar, manually enter a zoom value in the magnification percentage field, or click the tiny black arrow to its right to choose a predefined percentage. The images should still be crisp and clear at 150% magnification. Close the file and return to InDesign.

The Select and Zoom toolbar in Acrobat XI Professional.

10. If you'd like to compare the results of the different compression options for yourself, go to the chapter_20_exercises > output > folder and open **ex20_1_low_72.pdf**, **ex20_1_med_72.pdf** and **ex20_1_max_72.pdf**.

11. Go to Window > Tile > Vertically to arrange all three documents side-by-side. Click the same flower button on each document to go to a large flower image and, If necessary, select 100% from the preset magnifications for each window. If you need to reposition the flowers, select the Hand tool (🖑) and click and drag so that all three windows display the same view. Compare the quality of the images and when you're done, close all three documents.

| Auto: Low | Auto: Medium | Auto: Maximum |
| 505 KB | 671 KB | 4.7 MB |

Comparison of image quality at 100% magnification in PDFs exported with different compression settings.

The comparison of the three files should bring home the balancing act between quality and file size that is a constant consideration in digital development.

12. Still in Acrobat or Reader, navigate to the chapter_20_exercises > output folder. Hold down the Ctrl/Command key and click to select **ex20_1_low_72.pdf**, **ex20_1_low_96.pdf**, **ex20_1_low_144.pdf**, and **ex20_1_low_300.pdf**. Go to Window > Tile > Vertically to arrange the documents and compare the image quality at different magnification percentages.

| Auto: Low: 72 ppi | Auto: Low: 96 ppi | Auto: Low: 144 ppi | Auto: Low: 300 ppi |
| 505 KB | 720 KB | 1.3 MB | 2.9 MB |

Comparison of files exported with the same compression settings but different resolutions.

13. When you're finished exploring, close all the files, quit Acrobat or Reader and return to InDesign. Close the ex_20_1.indd file to complete the lesson.

Workarounds

While it would be ideal to be able to create one interactive document that would function equally well for print, SWF, Interactive PDF, DPS and EPUB, the fact is they are different animals, with different applications and different strengths and limitations. While it is indeed possible to incorporate a number of workarounds in your file that accommodate assorted output requirements, you may find it more efficient to create separate versions of the file, specific to an output destination. Whichever approach you choose, knowing the destination-specific quirks you may encounter can inform your design process and maximize the cross-functionality you can achieve throughout the development process.

Adding Animation to an Interactive PDF

You should already be aware that animation you create in the InDesign Animation panel doesn't carry over when you export your document to Interactive PDF. This is not as much of a crisis as it might first appear, since export of your InDesign files to Interactive PDF does support export of placed SWF files. How do you get the SWF files? You learned in Chapter 17, starting on page 253 that you can actually export the animation you create in InDesign to SWF, and then place that SWF back in InDesign for export to Interactive PDF. In the next exercise, you'll get hands-on experience of the process.

Exercise 20.2: Adding Animation to an Interactive PDF

Depending on the complexity of the animation on the page, you can export an entire spread to SWF and then place it back in InDesign, or you can export and place only the animated elements. In this exercise, you'll export a multi-state object to SWF along with the buttons that control it, place the SWF back in the InDesign spread, and then export the document to Interactive PDF.

1. Navigate to the chapter_20_exercises folder, open **ex20_2_start.indd,** and save it as ex20_2.indd.

2. The multi-state object on the page is grouped with the buttons that control it. Select the group with the Selection tool.

3. Go to File > Export and choose Flash Player (SWF) from the Format dropdown at the bottom of the Export dialog.

4. Save the file as **multistate.swf** in the chapter_20_exercises folder.

5. When the Export SWF dialog opens, select the Selection radio button and deselect the Generate HTML File checkbox. Leave the other default settings on the General tab, and switch to the Advanced tab.

6. Set Compression to Automatic and JPEG Quality to Low. Leave Frame Rate set to 24 fps, set Resolution to 72, and leave the other checkboxes unchecked. Leave Flash Classic Text selected and press OK to export.

7. When the export is complete, if necessary, open the Layers panel in InDesign (Window > Layers), click once on the flora page 2 layer to highlight it, and click

the Create New Layer button ( ) at the bottom of the panel. Double-Click the layer name and rename the layer "SWF" in the Layer Options dialog.

8. Press Ctrl+D/Command+D (File > Place), browse to the chapter_20_exercises folder (or wherever you saved the SWF), and select **multistate.swf**.

9. With the SWF layer highlighted in the Layers panel, click once with the loaded cursor on the upper left corner of the multi-state object group to place the SWF.

The Place cursor displays a filmstrip icon
when loaded with the Flash SWF.

The placed SWF is indicated by a Flash icon at its upper left.

If a placed SWF is not set to play on page load, and you haven't assigned a poster to customize its appearance on the page, the SWF icon in the upper left corner will display in the exported PDF. Not pretty. Since this animation zooms in to fill the page, you'll want to set it to play on page load and therefore, it won't need a poster. Time for a trip to the Media panel to set things up.

10. With the SWF still selected, go to Window > Interactive > Media or click the ⊞ button in the Panel Dock to open the Media panel. Check the Play on Page Load checkbox, and, from the Poster dropdown, choose From Current Frame. (Although it will never be seen for this particular animation, there's no harm in setting a poster—if only for practice in this case.)

Set the SWF to Play on Page Load and
choose From Current Frame for the poster.

11. In the Layers panel, click the eyeball icon to the left of the flora page 2 layer to hide it.

Since PDFs don't understand multi-state objects, they capture the first state of a multi-state object as a poster. If you don't hide the layer containing the multi-state object before exporting to Interactive PDF, the poster representing it will show during the initial portion of the SWF animation, when the flower grows to fill the screen.

12. Go to File > Export and choose Adobe PDF (Interactive) from the Format dropdown at the bottom of the Export dialog. Browse to the chapter_20_exercises folder and save the file as ex20_2.pdf.

13. When the Export to Interactive PDF dialog opens, be sure that the Pages radio button is set to All and the View After Exporting checkbox is checked. If necessary, choose Fit Page from the View dropdown, uncheck Open in Full Screen Mode and set Page Transitions to none. Also be sure that Include All is selected in the Forms and Media section of the dialog. Set Compression to Automatic, JPEG Quality to Low, and Resolution (ppi) to 72. Click OK to export the file.

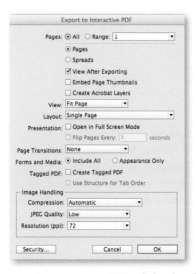

The export settings to test your PDF with the placed SWF.

14. When the ex20_2.pdf file opens in Acrobat XI or Adobe Reader XI, click the animation to activate it. Click the buttons to the left and right of the image to navigate the slideshow. Close the file and keep Acrobat or Reader open for the next exercise.

The Fit Page setting you used in export ensures that the PDF page, and therefore the SWF it contains, are scaled to fit in the document window. Scaling the document automatically scales the SWF.

PDF Peculiarities

Show/Hide actions are a mainstay of interactivity, and you've already had a good amount of experience with them. One of the strange behaviors you may encounter when exporting your interactive document to PDF is with objects that should be hidden making an uninvited appearance on top of other visible elements. You'll check out a file that exemplifies this behavior so you can see what we mean and how to fix it.

It's possible that this anomaly occurs due to a problem in processing objects with transformations, such as rotation and scaling, in combination with transparency, when converting to PDF. The folks at Adobe were as perplexed by the behavior as we were. In any case, we figured out a workaround, which is what you'll explore in the next exercise.

Exercise 20.3: PDF Show/Hide Anomalies

1. Switch to Acrobat Professional or Adobe Reader and open **ex20_3_start.pdf** from the chapter_20_exercises folder. Click the thumbnail image buttons on the arc to see what happens.

   While the Flash version of the file plays as expected, the PDF presents some problems. You quickly discover that when the thumbnail buttons should hide, they remain visible, overlaying the enlarged images when they appear. In this exercise, you'll learn how to eliminate this anomalous behavior.

2. Close the file, leave Acrobat or Reader open, and return to InDesign.

3. Navigate to the chapter_20_exercises folder, open **ex_20_3_start.indd**, and save it as ex20_3.indd

4. If necessary, press F7 to open the Layers panel (or go to Window > Layers.) Twirl down the disclosure triangle for the fauna page layer and then for the fauna images layer to see each of the image button sublayers.

5. Click in the selection column of the faunaImg2 sub-layer to select the first large image button. If necessary, open the Buttons and Forms panel to see the button details. Scroll through the Visibility list in the Buttons and Forms panel to see that when the button is tapped or released, it's set to hide only itself. The Visibility thumbnail buttons are set to "Ignore" (✖) which means they inherit the default visibility.

6. In the Layers panel, click the eyeball to the left of the fauna images layer to hide it, and then click the first thumbnail image button on the document to select it. Scroll through the Visibility list in the Buttons and Forms panel. You'll see that the button is set to hide all the large images, with the exception of the image that matches its thumbnail.

   The strange visibility behavior can be resolved by explicitly hiding everything that shouldn't show, including the thumbnails, rather than leaving the thumbnail buttons set to "Ignore." Then, when a large image button is clicked, it needs to hide itself and show all the thumbnail buttons.

7. With the first thumbnail still selected, in the Visibility section of the Buttons and Forms panel, click to highlight faunaBtn9. (You may have to scroll to the top of the list to find it.) Hold down the Shift key and click faunaBtn2 to select it and all the buttons in between. Click the Hide button just below the list to hide all the thumbnails.

In the Buttons and Forms panel, select all
the thumbnail buttons and hide them.

8. Select the next thumbnail image button on the document, and with faunaBtn9–faunaBtn2 still selected in the Visibility section of the Buttons and Forms panel, click the Hide button.

9. Repeat for each button thumbnail and then show the fauna images layer in the Layers panel. If necessary, expand the fauna images layer and click in the Selection column to select faunaImg2.

NOTE: The thumbnail motion path is an additional indicator of which thumbnail is selected.

10. In the Visibility section of the Buttons and Forms panel, note that all the thumbnail buttons are still selected. Click the Show button at the bottom of the panel.

11. Show the thumbnail buttons in the Buttons and Forms panel for each of the remaining faunaImg buttons and then save the document in the chapter_20_exercises folder.

12. Go to File > Export and choose Adobe PDF (Interactive) from the Format dropdown at the bottom of the Export dialog. Name the file **ex20_3.pdf** and verify that Compression is set to Automatic, JPEG Quality to Low, and Resolution to 72 (ppi). The View After Export checkbox should still be checked. Click OK to export the file.

13. An alert will pop up to warn you of a potential issue. Click OK to dismiss it and complete the export.

> Adobe InDesign
>
> One or more interactive elements are rotated or sheared in ways that PDF files cannot reproduce. Those elements will be adjusted in the exported PDF.
>
> Cancel   OK

InDesign will alert you if there are objects in your file
with features that are not supported in PDF export.

14. When the file opens in Acrobat, test the buttons to see that the issue of the floating thumbnails has been resolved. Close out of Acrobat, return to InDesign, and close the open file to complete the lesson.

The moral of the story is, for PDF export, if you want to take advantage of Show/Hide actions, deliberately hide everything in the document that shouldn't be seen, and don't "ignore" any interactive elements.

Buttons and PDF File Size

Since file size is an important consideration for Interactive PDFs, it's important to know that buttons on master pages are repeated on every spread of an exported PDF as independent objects. To decrease file size and eliminate unnecessary overhead in your file, you can take advantage of the interactive form capabilities in Acrobat Professional to create multiple instances of the same button by duplicating it onto multiple pages.

To prepare your file, you'd remove all buttons from the master page in InDesign, and position them instead on the first page of your document. When the export to Interactive PDF is complete, you would then distribute the buttons across the document pages using the Duplicate command in Acrobat Professional. As mentioned earlier, the form features in Acrobat (which include buttons) have been supported for many versions. Keep in mind, though, that if you've included Flash media in an Interactive PDF exported from InDesign, you must use Acrobat or Adobe Reader 9 or later for the media to play.

Exercise 20.4: Optimizing Buttons in an Interactive PDF

The file for this exercise has been specially prepared for export to Interactive PDF by removing the navbar buttons from the master page and placing them on the first page of the document. In this lesson, you'll export the file and then duplicate its buttons in Acrobat Professional.

1. Open **ex20_4_start.indd** from the chapter_20_exercises folder. Click through the pages using the Next Page button at the bottom left of the document window to see that the navbar buttons appear on only the first page. If necessary, open the Buttons and Forms panel and click each of the buttons on page 1 to see that they each have a Go To Destination action applied to them.

2. Go to File > Export (Ctrl+E/Command+E) and choose Adobe PDF (Interactive) from the Format dropdown at the bottom of the dialog. Name the file **ex20_4.pdf** and save it in the chapter_20_exercises folder.

3. In the Export to Interactive PDF dialog, be sure that View File After Exporting is selected and choose your other export settings. Click OK to export the file.

4. With the file open in Acrobat XI Pro, use the Next and Previous buttons just above the document window to click through the document pages, and then return to page 1. Note that page 1 is the only page in the document with buttons displayed across the top.

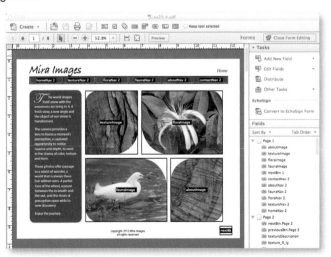

You can use the up and down arrows in Acrobat to navigate through the document pages.

5. Click "Tools" at the right of the Toolbar at the top of the screen to show the Tools pane and then click "Forms." In the Forms pane, click "Edit" to enter Form Editing mode.

Form Editing mode in Acrobat XI Professional. The form fields are highlighted and selectable with the Forms Tasks appearing on the right. The Fields pane lists all the form fields in the document.

Beneath the Form Editing Tasks pane is the Fields pane which displays a list of the form fields in the document sorted according to tab order and the page on which the fields appear. You'll notice that when you switch to Form Editing mode, a bounding box appears around each button on the document page with the button name appearing inside.

TIP: In Acrobat Professional, form fields can be sorted in the Fields pane alphabetically or based on tab order.

6. Click contactNav2 in the Fields pane, hold down the Shift key, and click homeNav2 to select both buttons, and all the buttons in between. (You could also select the buttons directly on the document.) Right-Click/Ctrl+Click on one of the selected button names and choose Duplicate Across Pages from the contextual menu.

7. In the Duplicate Field dialog, select the From radio button. Enter 2 in the first text field. The number 8 should already be in the second text field. Click OK to duplicate the buttons.

In Acrobat Pro, Right-Click/Ctrl+Click a field name in the Fields pane to access the Duplicate Field dialog.

8. Click Close Form Editing at the upper right of the Form Editing pane, and test your buttons.

9. Save the file as **ex20_4_end.pdf,** close out of Acrobat Pro, and return to InDesign. Close the open file to complete the exercise.

Adding Audio for Export to PDF (and SWF)

Adding audio to your document is quite similar to adding video, but with fewer controls to manage. While you have an option in the Media panel to add a poster as a visual indicator of audio, the poster shows only in an exported Interactive PDF, and not in an exported SWF. To optimize the development cycle, you'll want to conserve your time and focus your efforts on a workflow that serves multiple platforms as effectively as possible. With that objective in mind, and to maintain as much visual consistency as possible across output destinations, you can use a placed image instead of the sound poster to indicate your audio file and leave the built-in poster blank.

ALERT: In order for sound to play when exported to Interactive PDF, the placeholder for the audio file must be placed on the document page in InDesign and not on the pasteboard.

The Media panel lets you choose between the standard poster (🔊), a poster using an image you select, or no poster at all. You would think that if you were to choose no poster, the sound would play without visual representation on the page. While this is indeed the case for an exported SWF, you're not so fortunate with an Interactive PDF. When the sound is activated in Acrobat or Reader, a controller matching the dimensions of the sound placeholder in the InDesign document pops up, regardless of whether you assigned a visible poster to that sound or not.

The controller pops up above any non-button content on the page—regardless of where the sound placeholder, with or without a visible poster, was located in the stacking order in InDesign. The only way to stop the controller from making an unwelcome appearance is to cover the sound placeholder completely in InDesign with a button placed above it in the layer stacking order.

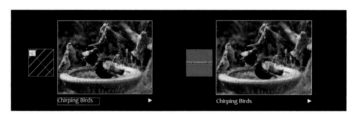

On the left is the "invisible" placeholder poster for the sound placed in InDesign; on the right is the controller on the default gray background that pops up when the audio is activated in Acrobat or Adobe Reader.

Placing such a button also serves to eliminate another potentially undesirable behavior. Unless there's a button covering it, when you mouse over a sound poster in Acrobat (even if it's invisible), a tooltip pops up with an instruction to click to activate the audio. Click, and then the controller appears.

The controller isn't an entirely bad thing. Even if it's very small, its controls are actually functional. If you want your audience to be able to rewind, fast forward, pause, and mute the sound, you could choose to eliminate any other Play buttons, pick a poster image and let the controller pop up in Acrobat or Reader. Once activated, the controller replaces the initial poster graphic. The tooltip appears when the poster is moused over and sounds play through, playing over each other if activated in close enough succession. Unlike a controller which controls only its specific sound, a button can be made to stop other sounds so that the sound it plays, plays alone. However, buttons having both play and stop actions generate yet another strange behavior in Acrobat and Reader. The first sound button to be clicked activates all the sounds on the page at once, resulting in quite a cacophony.

After this initial, potentially problematic outpouring of sound, the buttons seem to work as intended.

NOTE: To learn how to add video in InDesign, see page 471.

What it boils down to is that there are some trade-offs to make if you elect to include multiple sounds on a single page in an Interactive PDF exported from InDesign. You can choose a poster for your sound and allow the PDF controller to replace it when it pops up, or you can cover the placeholder with a button which prevents activation of the controller as well as its tooltip. If you do include buttons, you can set them with only a Play action, or with both Play and Stop actions in which case all the sounds on the page will play at once when the first button is clicked. Your call. In the next exercise, you'll choose a dummy controller image for the sound posters so there will be no visible change when they are replaced by the actual controllers. You'll also add actions to buttons already on the page, setting them to play a sound and stop other sounds that might be playing. True, when the first button is clicked, all the sounds will play at once, but there are only three sounds and they're all of birds singing. Change things up if you like to get a feel for which options suit you best.

Exercise 20.5: Adding Sound for Export to PDF (and SWF)

1. Open **ex20_6_start.indd** from the chapter_20_exercises folder and save it as ex20_5.indd.

2. Expand the Audio layer in the Layers panel and take a look at how the document is structured.

    There is a sequence of sublayers specific to each bird: a button, followed by a placeholder rectangle, followed by the bird image, followed by the caption. You'll place your sounds in the placeholder rectangles and use the dummy controller image for the sound posters.

    When output to Interactive PDF, hidden layers are omitted from export. After adding the sounds and posters, you may choose to experiment with hiding the button sublayers to see if you prefer having only the controller in the final output.

3. Press Ctrl+D/Command+D and navigate to chapter_20_exercises > sounds. Ctrl+Click/Command+Click to select the following files: **bird_sings_in_the_morning.mp3**, **gobbler.mp3**, and **loon.mp3**. If you selected the files in the order listed, they will be in the same order as the birds on the page. Position the multi-place gun over the placeholder rectangle for the first bird and click when you see parentheses around the cursor icon. Repeat for the second and third placeholder rectangles on the page.

The multi-place gun displays parentheses around the cursor icon when it recognizes the placeholder rectangle beneath it.

4. Select the placeholder for the Chirping Birds sound (the one at the top), and confirm in the Layers panel that **bird_sings_in_the_morning.mp3** is positioned with the chirping birds sublayers. Check the other two sounds to be sure that they're also positioned in the Layers panel with the appropriate sublayers.

5. Select the **bird_sings_in_the_morning.mp3** sound again, and open the Media panel. Choose From File from the Poster dropdown, navigate to the chapter_20_exercises > **links** folder, and select **controller.psd**. Check the Stop on Page Turn checkbox and click the Play button in the panel to test the sound.

6. Double-Click the sound poster graphic on the document with the Selection tool. Mouse over the bottom of the green bounding box that appears for the sound and, when the cursor changes to a double-sided arrow, click and hold and drag it up to snap it to the bottom border of the rectangle placeholder.

7. Mouse over the right border of the poster image and when the cursor changes to a double-sided arrow, click and hold and drag it to the right until it snaps to the right border of the placeholder rectangle.

8. Last but not least, Right-Click/Ctrl+Click the poster image and choose Fitting > Fit Content Proportionally.

   The adjustments you've made to the poster graphic make it mimic the appearance of the controller that pops up in Acrobat or Reader to create a seamless transition.

The steps for scaling the poster bounding box to fit the controller graphic.

9. Repeat steps 5 through 8 for the other two sound posters and save the document.

   Next, you'll set up the buttons.

10. Select the white triangular play button to the right of the sound poster below the first bird photo. In the Buttons and Forms panel, add a Sound action to the On Release or Tap event. From the Sound dropdown, choose **gobbler.mp3** and choose Stop from the Options dropdown. Add a second Sound action to stop **loon.mp3**. Add a final Sound action to play **birds_sings_in_the_morning.mp3**.

11. Select the triangular play button associated with the image of the Turkeys. Add Sound actions to stop **birds_sings_in_the_morning.mp3** and **loon.mp3**. Add a third Sound action to play **gobbler.mp3**.

12. Select the button for the Loon image. Add Sound actions to stop **gobbler.mp3** and **birds_sings_in_the_morning.mp3**. Add a third Sound action to play **loon.mp3**.

13. Save the file and go to File > Export. Choose Adobe PDF (Interactive) from the Format dropdown, and navigate to the chapter_20_exercises folder. Save the file as **ex20_5.pdf**.

14. Since the document is only one page, some of the export options are irrelevant. Do check the View After Exporting checkbox, though, and set the View to Fit Page. For Image Handling, set Compression to JPEG2000 (Lossless) (since the images are already compressed), and leave the Resolution at 72 ppi. Confirm that the Include All radio button is selected in the Forms and Media section of the dialog, and then click OK to export the file.

   With the View set to Fit Page, the full document page will display regardless of the window size in Acrobat or Adobe Reader.

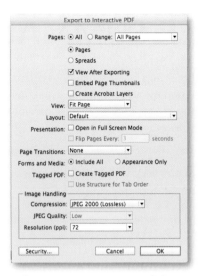

The Export to Interactive PDF dialog.

15. When the document opens in Acrobat or Reader, mouse over one of the controller proxy images. A Click to activate tooltip should pop up. Instead of clicking the proxy image, click one of the white triangular buttons to hear all three bird clips in concert, and to see all the controllers appear. Click the white buttons in turn to note that each button turns off the other bird sounds when its own sound starts to play. When you've finished exploring, close the file, quit Acrobat or Reader, and return to InDesign.

16. Save and close the file to complete the lesson and your exploration of the sometimes strange behaviors you may encounter when outputting to Interactive PDF.

CHAPTER SUMMARY

....

This chapter was about tying together the loose ends related to Interactive PDF production and addressing some of the issues you may encounter in the process. You learned how to properly prepare your files for output, and covered topics in InDesign including:

- The ins and outs of the Interactive PDF export dialog
- Acrobat and Reader page layout options
- PDF Security export settings
- File size as it relates to compression and image resolution
- Exporting animation from InDesign
- Adding animation to a document for output to Interactive PDF
- Resolving Interactive PDF show/hide anomalies
- Adding audio for export to Interactive PDF (and SWF)
- Working with posters for audio controllers
- Navigating audio controller behaviors

In the course of your Interactive PDF adventures, you also got some exposure to Acrobat XI Professional. Specifically, you:

- Learned about document open and permissions passwords
- Learned how to duplicate buttons in an Interactive PDF to minimize file size
- Worked with Form Editing mode

What you've learned in this section should have you well prepared to take your PDFs from static to dramatic. Both PDF and SWF output lend themselves to self-contained presentations and neither output destination requires interface with external organizations or technologies for publishing or distribution.

The next two sections of the book focus on Adobe Digital Publishing Suite and EPUB. While the road to both these digital destinations may originate in InDesign, your travels will take you well beyond its bounds to other technologies and paths to publishing. So gear up and let's go! New vistas await.

Part 6

EPUB

This section is your EPUB primer. Starting with an introduction to the structure of EPUB and its peculiarities, you'll learn how to design and style your InDesign documents for the greatest versatility. You'll gather and work with EPUB tools that are essential to an efficient workflow, learn the intricacies of InDesign EPUB export, and then dig deep into the internal EPUB files to further tailor the appearance of your finished product. When all is said and done, you'll have the tools and resources you need to publish an eBook for online retail distribution.

Chapter 21

EPUB ANATOMY

While InDesign certainly plays a major role, it is by no means the only tool you'll need in the course of your work with EPUB. This chapter provides an orientation to the peripheral skills and supplemental tools that are essentials in an EPUB workflow. You'll get a look at an EPUB file as it appears on an eReader and then pop the hood to see just what makes the whole thing tick. You'll learn about EPUB validation and adding metadata, and have the experience of your first EPUB export. After finding that the scary stuff isn't all that scary, you'll be well on your way to EPUB production.

About EPUB

An important distinction, the terms eBook and EPUB are not synonymous. Technically, an eBook is simply a book that can be read on an electronic device—that means interactive iBooks and books in PDF, EPUB, and Kindle formats all fall under the eBook umbrella. EPUB, short for electronic publication, refers to a free and open standard for eBooks developed by the International Digital Publishing Forum (IDPF.)

Like the rest of the digital publishing landscape, the world of EPUB is changing minute by minute. Things are shifting so rapidly in fact that by the time you read this, there's no doubt that some of the information in this section will be obsolete. Therefore, rather than attempting to provide a comprehensive and absolute how-to we hope you'll view this section more as a jumping off point that provides a foundation for your further EPUB adventures.

At the time of this writing, EPUB is transitioning from the EPUB 2.0.1 specification to EPUB 3.0 with eReader support for EPUB 3.0 features not yet broadly supported. To gain a better understanding of what this might mean to your digital development options as time progresses, a little bit of background might be in order.

At its heart, EPUB is actually HTML, the very same stuff of which web sites are made. In fact, an EPUB file is simply a zip archive with an .epub extension that contains XHTML content pages, at least one Cascading Style Sheet that defines formatting, and certain EPUB-specific XML files that define the EPUB sructure. If all these acronyms just sound like alphabet soup, don't fret—the chapter on HTML and CSS starting on page 347 will help you make some sense of it all. One of the beauties of HTML, and what makes it ideal for EPUB, is that HTML content naturally reflows to fill its viewing window. This means that someone reading a flowable EPUB can customize their reading experience by changing the font or font size in their eReader, and the book content will automatically reflow to accommodate the new settings. The EPUB 2.0.1 specification is all about flow.

The introduction of the iPad in 2010 brought about a dramatic surge in the use of electronic devices for the consumption of all flavors of digital media. People became more acclimated to apps with high levels of interactivity and all sorts of new devices appeared on the market with a growing number of bells and whistles. The introduction of HTML5 and CSS3 brought with it new formatting features and easier inclusion of rich media on the web. With the increase in digital readership came an increase in demand for eBooks requiring more precise layout—like cookbooks and comic books. The IDPF recognized the need to expand the EPUB specification to include media support and an option for fixed layout, as well as support for other new HTML and CSS features. Thus was the EPUB 3.0 specification conceived. OK, a bit of an over simplification, but you get the idea. What's interesting is that as the supported EPUB feature set expands, the line between eBooks and apps is becoming less distinct. In fact, it's conceivable that we may see a complete convergence of these technologies in the not-so-distant future.

InDesign's EPUB export function is awesome. Yes, you really can export an EPUB directly from InDesign. But, while it's simple to choose the EPUB export option, it's important to understand that there's more to it if you want to create an EPUB that is optimally configured for distribution or sale. To ensure that your EPUB will open

---

DOWNLOAD: The EPUB 3.0 support grid developed by BISG (Book Industry Study Group) provides an at-a-glance view of the supported EPUB 3.0 features on various devices and reading systems. You can download it at: bit.ly/ObMe7S

TIP: Though you may see it written in a variety of different ways, "EPUB" is preferred, per the IDPF.

NOTE: Fixed layout EPUB and EPUB 3.0 are topics outside the scope of this book. For lots of information on both topics, check out Liz Castro's books and website: www.pigsgourdsandwikis.com, Anne-Marie Concepción's excellent tutorials on www.Lynda.com and the wealth of information available at www.indesignsecrets.com and www.epubsecrets.com.

on various reading systems and devices, it must validate—meaning its structure and component files must meet specific criteria. The good news is that as long as you provide it with the necessary pieces, InDesign will do most of the heavy lifting for you, creating the required file structure, writing the necessary code, and ultimately generating a valid EPUB. YAY!

That said, once generated, it's very likely that you'll want to dig into your EPUB to make some adjustments to the document's appearance by tweaking the cascading style sheet responsible for your book's formatting, or to make your eBook Kindle worthy for example. In order to gain access to the inner sanctum—to the collected files in the EPUB wrapper—you'll need to venture out of the InDesign environment. To access the underlying files, if you're using a Windows machine you can change the .epub extension to .zip and then simply unzip the file. If you're on a Mac, you'll need a separate application or a script to crack open your EPUB to access the goodies inside. The fact is, if you're serious about working with EPUB, it's essential that you gather some tools and develop some skills that go beyond your work with InDesign.

NOTE: While you can read an EPUB on most eReaders, Amazon's Kindle devices require that your eBook be in Amazon's proprietary .mobi or KF8 format. See page 408 to learn how to convert your EPUB to the proper format for Kindle.

Gathering the Tools

Rather than detail all the recommended EPUB tools and resources right here, you'll find a list at the end of this section starting on page 417. Following is a short list of the types of extras you'll need to get down and dirty with your EPUB production.

Let it be said yet again that at this moment in time, digital publishing is a journey through largely uncharted territory. In such circumstances, fellow travelers who can help decipher the trail are a cherished resource. If you are not currently a Twitter follower, and are truly serious about EPUB, you must—yes MUST—follow #eprdctn. All about EPUB, these folks are the down-in-the-trenches, real-deal, cutting-edge professionals. They are the best real-time EPUB resource you're going to find—bar none. Now that that's settled, let's look at other tools and resources your EPUB production will require.

- **Must have:** At least one eReader to view your exported EPUBs. Since different devices and reader applications display differently, it's advisable that you download a variety of reader applications (that you can view on your computer—either stand-alone or in a browser), and collect a variety of reader devices, to test the rendering and performance of your EPUBs. Reminiscent of the bad old days of the browser wars on the web, you can't be assured that just because your EPUB looks great on one device or reader app that it will render acceptably on another.

- **Must have:** If you're on a Mac, you'll need a way to crack open and recompile your EPUBs. You can download the zip and unzip scripts at http://bit.ly/QbqR77 or use an application that also serves as a code editor, some of which are listed in the resources section starting on page 418.

- **Must have:** You need an application to edit the HTML, CSS and XML code in the EPUB files. At the most bare-bones level, this could be a plain text editor. On the other end of the spectrum, you might want to use an application like Dreamweaver or oXygen that has all kinds of extra features to make code editing easier and more efficient.

- **Must have:** At least a basic knowledge of HTML and CSS. Not to worry—we've got you covered. Check out HTML And CSS Fundamentals, starting on page 347.
- **Nice to have/Must have:** Scripts. When working with long documents, scripts enable you to perform complex processes on an entire document with the click of a button. Without scripts, some documents might be nearly impossible to tackle. See page 416 in Chapter 27 to learn about working with scripts.
- **Nice to have/Must have:** GREP expressions. Similar to the power placed at your fingertips by scripts, GREP expressions enable you to make global document changes at the click of a button. Again, without GREP expressions, the time you'd have to invest in editing certain documents would make their conversion to EPUB completely impractical if not impossible. Get your feet wet with GREP starting on page 379.

If you're a person who likes having all your tools at hand before digging in to a project, head on over to the resources section starting on page 415 and get busy downloading and installing the scripts and applications that will become essential elements in your EPUB workflow. If you'd rather grab what you need as you need it, hang in there and keep reading, and we'll let you know when the time is right.

Anatomy of an EPUB

Since it's likely that you'll want to make changes to your EPUB once it's created, it's important that you understand what's actually inside. You can take our word for it and follow along with the explanation, or if you'd rather see for yourself, skip to Exercise 21.2: Cracking Open Your First EPUB, starting on page 316. After you've opened the EPUB, you can head back here for the guided tour.

Don't get too crazy about the code at this point. You'll learn what you need to in the chapter on HTML And CSS Fundamentals, starting on page 347. This section is merely for informational purposes and to shine some light inside the mysterious EPUB black box.

An EPUB document includes the following folders and files:

1. The META-INF folder: The META-INF folder generally contains a single file: container.xml. The same META-INF folder can be used for all your EPUBs as long as the container.xml is always placed inside it. If you embed fonts or apply digital rights management (DRM) to your EPUB, an encryption.xml file is also included in the META-INF folder.

    The entire contents of the container.xml file looks like this:

    ```
    <?xml version="1.0" encoding="UTF-8"?>
    <container xmlns="urn:oasis:names:tc:opendocument:xmlns:container" version="1.0">
     <rootfiles>
     <rootfile full-path="OEBPS/content.opf"
            media-type="application/oebps-package+xml"/>
     </rootfiles>
    </container>
    ```

    The full-path attribute in the rootfile element should point to the content.opf file. The path as written indicates that the content.opf file is inside the OEBPS folder (the OPS folder in the figure on the next page). If you don't change the location of the content.opf file, you should never have to change this file.

2. The mimetype file: The purpose of the mimetype file is to identify the document as an EPUB. The mimetype file is always titled "mimetype" and it is the same for every EPUB. It is a simple text file and contains only this text: application/epub+zip.

3. The OEBPS folder: OEBPS stands for Open eBook Publication Structure. Referred to as OEBPS, the folder contains:

   a. The toc.ncx XML file: a required file that is used by eReaders to generate a navigational table of contents, the .ncx extension is an abbreviation for Navigational Control file for XML. This file is auto-generated by InDesign and, as long as your TOC style is up to date, you shouldn't have to edit it directly.

   b. The content.opf XML file: a required file that contains four sections:

      i. Required: the <metadata> section contains the required title, publication date, unique identifier (could be the ISBN number but doesn't have to be,) copyright, language, description, and keywords; in short, any metadata included in the EPUB.

      ii. Required: the <manifest> lists all the XHTML files included in the eBook and all the resources referenced in your XHTML pages.

      iii. Required: the <spine> defines the proper order of the XHTML documents in the EPUB.

      iv. Optional for EPUB (Required for Kindle, recommended by Apple): the <guide> describes the role played by each XHTML file in the book. Choices include cover, title-page, toc, index, glossary, acknowledgements, bibliography, colophon, copyright-page, dedication, epigraph, forward, loi (list of illustrations), lot (list of tables), notes, preface, and text (first page of actual content such as Chapter 1.)

   c. XHTML content files: the actual content of the book

   d. Formatting instructions in the form of CSS file(s)

   e. An images folder containing all the images that appear in the book

   f. A fonts folder if your EPUB has specified fonts

   g. Media files such as audio or video if they're included in the book.

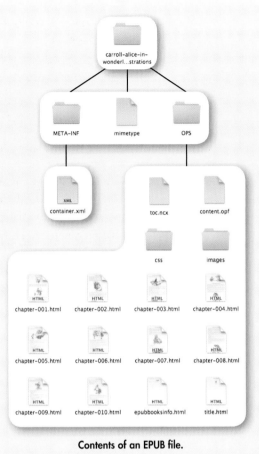

Contents of an EPUB file.

TIP: Colophon: publisher's emblem or information related to the printing and publication of the book, including some or all of the following: date and place of publication/printing, name of the printer, name of the publisher, possibly name of a proof-reader or editor and other book-related references.

Exercise 21.1: Viewing Your First EPUB

In this exercise you will add a book to the Adobe Digital Editions 2.0 eReader application and get familiar with how the reader works. If you don't already have it on your computer, you can download Adobe Digital Editions 2.0 (ADE) at: http://www.adobe.com/products/digital-editions/download.html.

1. Open the Adobe Digital Editions 2.0 (ADE) application. Go to File and choose Add Item to Library from the dropdown menu. Navigate to the chapter_21_exercises folder, select **alices_adventures_in_wonderland.epub** and click the Add button.

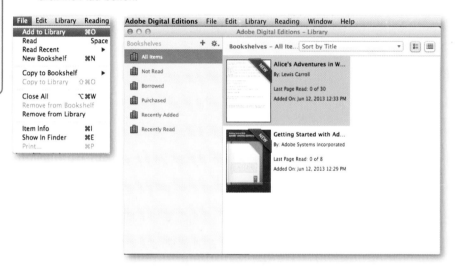

Choose Add Item to Library from the File dropdown menu to add a book to the Adobe Digital Editions reader application.

A thumbnail for the book appears in the pane at the right of the interface.

2. Double-Click on the book thumbnail to open the eBook.

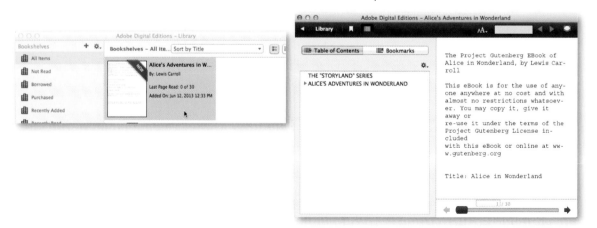

Double-Click thumbnail to open the eBook.

Digital Editions switches to READING mode and the book content appears in the display window.

---

3. If the Navigation pane isn't showing, go to READING in the application toolbar menu and choose Show Navigation Pane from the dropdown menu.

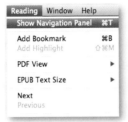

The Reading dropdown provides options to show and hide the Navigation pane, to increase and decrease text size, to navigate the pages of the selected eBook and more.

4. Click the arrow to the left of the book title in the Navigation Pane to access the TOC hyperlinks. Click the hyperlinks to navigate to different chapters in the book.

The Navigation Pane provides access to the navigational TOC for the EPUB.

5. Click the left and right arrows on the scroll bar at the bottom right of the interface to navigate the "pages" of the eBook or drag the scroller.

Use the controls at the top of the screen to go to a specific "page," place a bookmark, change font size, enter search criteria and search the book.

6. Close ADE to complete the exercise.

Exercise 21.2: Cracking Open Your First EPUB

The process for cracking open and recompiling an EPUB is different if you're using a Mac than if you're using a Windows machine.

DOWNLOAD: A shortened version of the link to the zip/unzip script: http://bit.ly/QbqR77

For Mac Users:

If you're on a Mac you'll need to download a couple easy-to-use scripts.

1. Go to http://www.mobileread.com/forums/attachment.php?attachmentid=60210&d=1288043085 (You may need to sign up for a free account.)

2. Unzip the script archive and save the folder where it's easy to access for your EPUB work.

3. To crack open an EPUB, just drag the EPUB file onto the **EPUB UnZip 1.0 script**.

    The script generates a folder with the same name as the EPUB but without the .epub extension.

For Windows Users:

1. Navigate to the chapter_21_exercises folders and select **alices_adventures_in_wonderland.epub**. Duplicate the file. (One way to duplicate the file is to select it and press Ctrl+C to copy and then Ctrl+V to paste the copy. Windows will automatically rename the file.)

2. Select the .epub file extension of the duplicated file and change it to .zip. Double-Click the zip file to unzip it.

Exercise 21.3: Examining the File Structure

The EPUB you've cracked open was created by Project Gutenberg, a volunteer-based organization with a stated mission to encourage the creation and distribution of eBooks. Project Gutenberg offers over 40,000 free titles previously published by bona fide publishers. You can learn more about Project Gutenberg at http://www.gutenberg.org.

The explanation of EPUB structure beginning on page 312, should be regarded as a guideline rather than a universal rule. While some elements remain constant, it's likely that you will also encounter variations in file names and file structure from EPUB to EPUB. In exploring the Alice in Wonderland EPUB files, you'll discover some of those variations.

1. From the chapter_21_exercises folder, expand the **alices_adventures_in_ wonderland** folder and its subfolders in Windows Explorer or Finder.

    Notice that the images are placed directly in the OEPBS folder rather than in an images subfolder. Notice also that this EPUB has three CSS files: 0.css, 1.css and pgepub.css.

    Further examination reveals that there are only two HTML files, one contains the Project Gutenberg copyright notice and the other the entire content of the book. You'll also notice that in addition to container.xml the META-INF contains two other files: signatures.xml and sinf.xml.

    Next you'll check out the EPUB to see if it passes validation.

EPUB Validation

As mentioned at the beginning of this chapter, EPUB 2.0.1 and EPUB 3.0 are eBook standards established by the IDPF. These standards comprise a large body of rules that define a valid EPUB. Many vendors require that EPUBs submitted to them for distribution and sale comply with these rules and pass validation.

When you export to EPUB, InDesign generates most of the information and content necessary to create an EPUB that will validate. The one exception—a title—must be entered manually. InDesign will then include the title in the metadata section of the .OPF file. While adequate to pass validation, the auto-generated InDesign information is hardly optimal. Fortunately InDesign makes it possible to replace its generic information with custom content that will improve both the user experience and the likelihood of trouble-free uploads.

Creating an EPUB that passes validation and looks the way you want it to is an iterative process. If you don't have all the custom elements in place, it's best to start by exporting your file with the InDesign defaults, ensure that it passes validation, and then validate again each time you make a substantial change. As with every file destined for digital delivery, the golden rule is: Test early and test often. The same applies to EPUB validation. Frequent validation means early detection of issues with your files and therefore makes troubleshooting infinitely easier.

You can find links to validation scripts and online validation utilities on page 416. For now, you'll get your feet wet with one of the free online validation tools in the next exercise.

Exercise 21.4: Validating an EPUB

1. Open your browser of choice and navigate to http://validator.idpf.org.

2. Click the Choose File button, navigate to the chapter_21_exercises folder and select **alice_in _wonderland.epub**

3. Click the Validate button.

   Your EPUB fails validation due to a missing title.

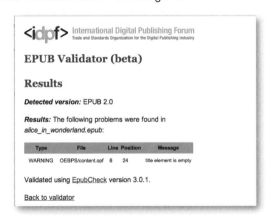

If your EPUB fails to pass validation the ePub Validator generates an itemized error report.

4. Leave the browser open and return to InDesign.

DOWNLOAD: You can find the complete EPUB 2.0.1specification at http://idpf. org/epub/201.

NOTE: Although not technically supported in the EPUB 2.0.1 specification, some eReaders (like iBooks and Nook Color) do support "enhanced EPUBs" that use HTML5 tags to include audio and video. Outside the scope of this book, you might want to get a hold of Liz Castro's "Audio and Video in EPUB miniguide" which you can learn about at http://www. pigsgourdsandwikis. com/2011/05/ audio-and-video- in-epub-new- straight-to.html.

5. In the chapter_21_exercises folder, navigate to the **AliceChapters** folder and Double-Click **alice_in_wonderland.indb** to open the book file.

6. Double-Click front_matter in the Book panel and when the file opens, go to File > File Info. If necessary, choose the Description tab at the top left of the dialog. Type "Alice's Adventures in Wonderland" in the Document Title field and click OK to close the dialog.

To create a valid EPUB, the only required field in the File Information dialog is the Document Title. The more metadata you provide however, the easier it will be for prospective readers to locate your publication.

7. In the Book panel, if necessary, click in the square to the left of the synopsis file to set it as the style source for the book.

The style source for a book is indicated by an icon in the column to the left of its file name in the Book panel. Both the Document Title and the TOC style must be defined in the style source or the EPUB won't pass validation.

The document title is defined in front_matter.indd but synopsis.indd is set as the style source. You'll export the file to EPUB and run it through the validator to see what happens.

8. From the Book panel menu, choose Export Book to EPUB.

9. Save the file in the chapter_21_exercises folder with the default file name of **alice_in_wonderland.epub**. When prompted, click Replace to overwrite the existing file.

10. In the EPUB Export Options dialog, confirm that EPUB 2.0.1 is selected from the Version dropdown and that Cover is set to Rasterize First Page. Choose TOC Style from the Navigation dropdown with [Default] for the selected style. Set the Margins to 0, leave the other default settings, and confirm that the View EPUB after Exporting checkbox is deselected. Click OK to export your EPUB.

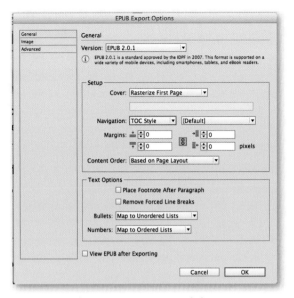

The EPUB Export Options dialog.

11. Return to the ePub Validator in your browser. If necessary, scroll down to locate the Choose File button below both the FAIL message and the Email Report Now button. Browse to the new **alice_in_wonderland.epub** file and click the Validate Now button.

   Once again, the EPUB fails to validate.

12. Leave the browser open and return to InDesign.

13. In the Book panel, set front_matter as the style source and repeat steps 8–11.

   This time, because the TOC style is defined in the front_matter document and the file is set as the style source, the EPUB passes validation.

14. Close the browser, return to InDesign and close all open files.

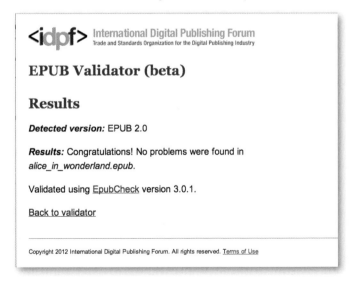

CHAPTER SUMMARY

In this chapter you've broken the EPUB black box wide open and hopefully discovered that it's not that scary inside. You made distinctions between eBooks and EPUBs, learned about the different EPUB specifications and got to use some tools of the trade. In fact, you got a first introduction to a number of the processes that will become the mainstay of your EPUB workflow including:

- Viewing your EPUB in an eReader

- Cracking open an EPUB

- Validating an EPUB

- Exporting an EPUB

- Adding document metadata, specifically a title (which is required for EPUB validation)

You traversed the internal EPUB structure and were introduced to its component elements including:

- The OEPBS (Open eBook Publication Structure) folder with its content.opf, toc.ncx, XHTML and CSS files as well as optional image, font and media folders

- The META-INF folder with its container.xml file

- The mimetype file

You downloaded and got acquainted with Adobe Digital Editions, adding an eBook to the Library and navigating its pages. And, you even got a first look at some of the code that makes the magic happen—which will by the way, become much less scary as you learn more about it in the next few chapters.

We hope to have whet your appetite because there's lot's more to come. Bon Apétit!

● Chapter 22

IMAGES, OBJECTS & THE FLOW

Your first experiences exporting to EPUB may feel like you've been transported to a world of the weird, with things all askew and not much of anything remaining quite where you left it. In this chapter you'll become familiar with the peculiarities of flowable EPUB—exercising control where you can and going with the flow where you can't. Anchored images and objects, the Articles panel and custom rasterization will all prove invaluable as you learn to navigate this often unpredictable terrain.

EPUB vs. Print: Through the Looking Glass

To a print designer, stepping into the world of EPUB may be comparable in some ways to Alice's tumble down the rabbit hole—nothing is quite as it appears to be. When exported to EPUB from InDesign, objects may appear in an entirely different arrangement than on the page you prepared, and sometimes they don't appear at all. When viewed on an eReader, text can be made to grow larger and smaller and even change face based on the reader's whim. Positioning of objects on the page changes as one page flows into the next and page breaks can vary from one device to another, or change with a change in font size. In other words, when designing for EPUB, the precise control that is the foundation of professional print design must give way to a more fluid approach—you must literally learn to "go with the flow."

In the realm of flowable EPUB, sidebars and pull quotes don't exist as elements that are separate from the main document content. Everything: images, captions, tables, sidebars, and stories occur in the context of a single document flow. Truth is, there are certain types of documents that lend themselves to EPUB and others that most certainly do not. Flowable EPUB is a wonderful medium for long, text-heavy documents such as novels. For documents with an elaborate graphic-heavy layout, flowable EPUB will deliver a decidedly disappointing result. While there are definite design constraints inherent to flowable EPUB as a medium, thankfully there are some steps you can take to make your EPUB documents render more predictably.

Anticipating the Flow

The objects in your document are rendered in a very specific sequence when exported to EPUB as determined by their position on the InDesign page. Starting at the top left, InDesign scans the page, from top to bottom, left to right, identifying and exporting the next consecutive leftmost object.

The figure on the following page illustrates that when converted to EPUB with InDesign's default export settings, some elements in your layout may render quite differently than anticipated, or may actually disappear altogether. Without some fancy footwork, native InDesign graphics are completely ignored in EPUB export. The same anomaly applies to the background color in text frames containing a background fill. These rather unusual export behaviors can make for an unpleasant surprise, resulting in an EPUB that potentially bears little resemblance to your meticulously designed InDesign layout.

Fortunately, InDesign offers several ways to influence both the appearance and the order of things in your exported EPUB. Anchored objects and the Articles panel provide a means to exercise greater control over content flow. Custom rasterization settings in the Object Export Options dialog make it possible to render InDesign graphics as images, and thereby overcome the disappearing object dilemma. If your EPUB-destined document contains images, expect to become quite chummy with the Object Export Options dialog. Its interface provides essential options to properly prepare your file for EPUB conversion. You'll become familiar with all these features and more as you proceed through the chapter.

TIP: When publishing to EPUB, an InDesign story (including all its linked text frames) is treated as a single object, regardless of interspersed text or graphics or how many pages it may span.

NOTE: Overset text is always included in EPUB export as is content that may be hidden by stacking one object on top of another.

NOTE: As an alternative to the Articles panel and anchored objects, you can use XML to affect EPUB content flow. The InDesign XML workflow does however have its quirks and limitations. To learn more about XML as it applies to EPUB, check out David Blatner's excellent article at http://indesignsecrets.com/structure-pane-versus-page-order-for-epub-export-from-indesign.php.

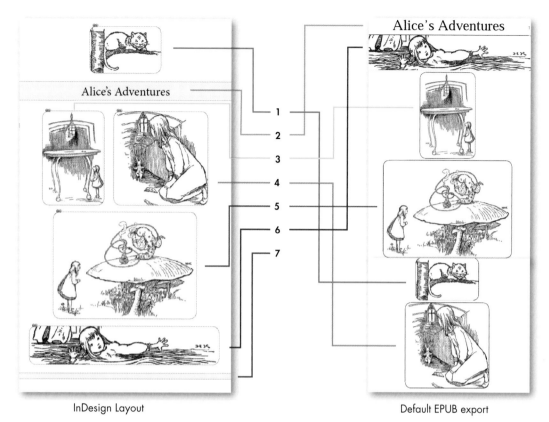

InDesign Layout   Default EPUB export

The EPUB export sequence starts with the object closest to the top left of the page and proceeds through each consecutive leftmost object from top to bottom. The resulting EPUB may have little resemblance to the original InDesign layout.

Exercise 22.1: Setting Sequence with the Articles Panel

1. Navigate to the chapter_22_exercises folder and open **ex22_1a.indd**. Make note of the sequence of the objects on the page and go to File > Export.

2. Choose EPUB from the format dropdown at the bottom of the Export window and save the file as ex22_1a.epub. In the EPUB Export Options dialog ensure that the View EPUB after Exporting checkbox is checked and then click the Image category at the left of the dialog. Confirm that Fixed is selected in the Image Size dropdown. Leave the other default settings and click OK.

3. If it doesn't display your EPUB automatically, open Adobe Digital Editions (ADE) and go to File > Add to Library (Ctrl+0/Command+0). Navigate to and open **ex22_1a.epub**.

4. Still in ADE, Double-Click the thumbnail for **ex22_1a.epub** to display it in the reader and scroll through to see that the image sequence is quite different from the original layout in InDesign.

    The green background in the Alice's Adventures text frame disappeared completely, as did the green bar that had been at the bottom of the InDesign document page. Additionally, the images are so large that they are distributed

DOWNLOAD: Exercise files for this chapter can be downloaded from http://www.interactive-indesign.com.

TIP: Seeing frame edges makes it easier to anticipate the export order of objects in your EPUB. Go to View > Extras > Show Frame Edges to turn them on.

over multiple pages rather than fitting on a single page as they did in the source document.

5. Scale the viewing window to see what happens to the page layout. When you're finished inspecting the EPUB, leave ADE open and return to InDesign.

6. Go to Window > Articles to open the Articles panel. Using the Selection tool, select the Cheshire Cat image at the top of the document page. Drag the image to the Articles panel and release the mouse when the cursor displays a grabber hand with a plus sign (✋). Type "Alice's Adventures" in the name field of the New Article dialog, leave the Include When Exporting checkbox selected, and click OK.

The New Article dialog.

The <cheshire_cat.jpg> item appears in the list of article items below the highlighted article name.

7. Position the Selection tool at the left margin of the page between the Cheshire Cat image and the Alice's Adventures text. Click and hold and drag down to the bottom right of the page to select the other objects on the page. With the article name highlighted in the Articles panel, click the plus sign at the bottom of the panel to include the selected objects in the article.

Articles and the objects they contain can be rearranged
in the Articles panel to help control EPUB content flow.

Notice that to the right of each new object in the Articles panel is a blue square similar to the selection column squares in the Layers panel. As is the case in the Layers panel, the squares indicate objects that are selected.

8. Click in the empty gray area beneath the list in the Articles panel to deselect all the objects in the article.

9. Click the Alice's Adventures text in the document window and confirm that a selection square appears to the right of the <Alice's Adventures> item in the Articles panel.

Note that the order of the items in the Articles panel doesn't match the sequence of objects on the page. Next, you'll drag the article items into correct position.

10. Click and hold <Alice's Adventures> in the Articles panel. Drag up and release the mouse when you see a black line beneath <cheshire_cat.jpg>.

11. Double-Click <alice_and_key.jpg> in the Articles panel to select the image on the document page. Confirm that the position of the object in the Articles panel reflects its position on the page. Confirm that the <white_rabbit.jpg> object is also in the correct position in the panel list.

12. Double-Click <pool_of_tears.jpg> in the Articles panel and note that it should be positioned lower in the list in order to match the layout. Click and hold and drag the item down in the list until a black line appears above the <rectangle> item. Release the mouse.

13. Click through the objects on the document page to confirm that the order of the objects in the Articles panel matches the sequence of objects on the page. Save the file as **ex22_1b.indd**.

14. Go to File > Export, choose EPUB, and save the file as **ex22_1b.epub** in the chapter_22_exercises folder.

15. In the EPUB Export Options dialog, choose Same as Articles Panel from the Content Order dropdown and click OK.

16. If it doesn't open automatically, open the exported EPUB in ADE.

    Notice that while the images now appear in the proper sequence, the green background is still absent from the title text and the second and third images do not appear side-by-side. This time however, by virtue of being included in an article, the green bar at the bottom of the InDesign page has made it into the EPUB.

17. Return to InDesign.

18. In the Articles panel, click on <alice_and_key.jpg>, hold down the Shift key and click on <white_rabbit.jpg> to select both items. Click the trash can icon at the lower right-hand corner of the panel to delete the items from the panel.

19. Use the Selection tool to select the two side-by-side images below the Alice's Adventures text frame and press Ctrl+G/Command+G to group them.

20. Click and hold and drag the image group into the Articles panel so that a black line appears between <Alice's Adventures> and <caterpillar.jpg>. Release the mouse and the word "group" appears in the Articles panel with a disclosure triangle and a special group icon (▶ ⬜ <group>) at its left. Click the triangle to show the objects contained in the group.

    Thus far, when exporting the document to EPUB you've left the default image settings unchanged. The exported images appeared in the EPUB, at their actual size and remained unchanged when the EPUB display was scaled.

    Next, you'll apply custom rasterization settings to the images to enable the EPUB to better approximate the original.

21. Click and drag with the Selection tool from the upper left corner of the document page to the bottom right to select all the objects on the page. Go to Object > Object Export Options and when the dialog opens, click the EPUB and HTML button at its upper right. Check the Custom Rasterization checkbox and choose Relative to Page Width from the Size dropdown. If necessary, set Resolution to 150 and leave the other default settings. Click Done to close the dialog.

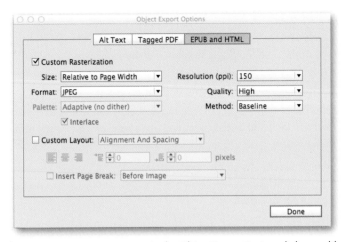

The Custom Rasterization options in the Object Export Options dialog enable you to choose whether images and objects scale with the EPUB page display and to specify the rasterization format and resolution.

22. Export the document to the chapter_22_exercises folder as **ex22_1_c.epub**. Ensure that Content Order is set to Same as Articles Panel and that the View EPUB After Exporting check box is checked. Click the image category at the left of the dialog and ensure that resolution is set to 150 with Image Size set to Relative to Page. Leave the other default settings and click OK to export the file.

23. When the document opens in Adobe Digital Editions, scale the viewing window and notice that the images scale with it. Notice too that when scaled small enough, all the images fit on the "page" with an appearance similar to the original InDesign document. The green background appears behind the Alice's adventures text and the green bar at the bottom of the page stretches from edge to edge.

24. Exit ADE and return to InDesign. Close all open files to complete the exercise.

Adding Alt Text

Alt text is alternate text that appears in lieu of an image with a broken link or that's read by a screen reader in an exported EPUB (or HTML page.) It is coded in HTML as an attribute of the **<img>** tag and is factored into the algorithms used by search engines to establish website ranking. While you'd never see it unless you cracked open your EPUB, Alt text is required for Section 508 compliance (Americans with Disabilities Act) and is meant to be read by assistive devices for the visually impaired. Since it's required for a valid EPUB, InDesign automatically generates Alt text for you from the file name of placed images. While this is great in case you forget to enter it, Alt text should actually be descriptive of the image content as opposed to containing a nondescriptive file name. Luckily, InDesign makes it possible to customize Alt text through the Object Export Options dialog. The dialog enables you to enter descriptive text manually or, if you're inspired to take the time to add it, you can have InDesign pull content from XMP metadata that you can enter in Bridge.

Exercise 22.2: Adding Alt Text

1. Navigate to the chapter_22_exercises folder, open **ex22_2_start.indd** and save it as ex22_2.indd.

2. With the Selection tool, click the Cheshire cat image at the top of the page and go to Object > Object Export Options.

3. Click the Alt Text button at the upper left of the dialog and choose Custom from the Alt Text Source dropdown. Click in the white text area and type "The Cheshire Cat."

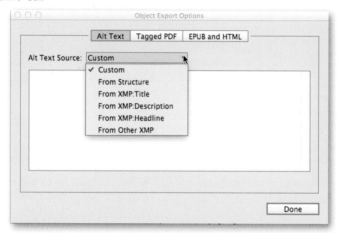

The Custom option in the Alt text section of the Object Export dialog allows you to enter Alt text manually. Alternatively, you can elect to have InDesign populate the Alt text from XMP metadata or use the actual file name (when the From Structure option is selected.)

4. With the dialog still open, select the Alice's Adventures text frame on the document.

   In order to render the green background, you'll have InDesign convert this text frame to an image; so you'll want to enter the appropriate Alt text.

5. Choose Custom from the Alt Text Source dropdown and type "Alice's Adventures" in the text area of the dialog.

6. Click the image group below the Alice's Adventures text with the Selection tool. If necessary, choose From Structure from the Alt Text Source dropdown so you will be able to see an example of InDesign's auto-generated Alt text in the exported EPUB. Click Done to close the Object Export Options dialog.

   You were first exposed to XMP metadata in Exercise 3.9: Working with Keywords, starting on page 56. Next you'll take another quick side trip to Bridge to enter metadata that InDesign will use as Alt text.

7. Select the image of Alice and the caterpillar and expand the Links panel in the Panel Dock. Right-Click/Ctrl+Click **caterpillar.jpg** in the panel (it should be highlighted) and choose Reveal in Bridge from the contextual menu.

The IPTC Core section of the Bridge METADATA panel enables you to add custom metadata, which can then be used by InDesign to generate Alt text.

8. When Bridge opens, ensure that the ESSENTIALS workspace is active. If necessary, scroll to locate the IPTC Core section of the METADATA panel at the right of the interface. Click the disclosure triangle to the left of the words "IPTC Core" to expose the editable metadata fields and locate the Headline field.

9. In the Headline text field, enter a description you would like to use as the Alt text for the image. (We entered "The hookah-smoking caterpillar.") After completing your description, click the image and when Bridge asks if you want to apply the changes to the metadata, click Apply .

10. Return to InDesign and note the hazard icon on the image and in the Links panel next to the file name. Click the icon on the image to update the file.

TIP: A change in metadata registers as a change to the related file. Such a change prompts the appearance of an out of date alert icon on the modified image on the page and to the right of the file name in the Links panel. Click the icon on the image or Double-Click the icon in the Links panel to update the link.

A hazard icon appears at the upper left of an image that's been modified outside of InDesign. Click the icon to update the link.

11. With the image still selected, go to Object > Object Export Options and click the Alt Text button. From the Alt Text Source dropdown, choose XMP Headline.

    InDesign populates the Alt text field with the text you added to the Headline metadata field in Bridge.

12. Select the image of Alice in the pool of tears and add Alt text as in step 11.

    The Headline metadata that's already been added to the pool_of_tears.jpg file populates the Alt Text field.

NOTE: You may elect to have InDesign generate image captions as well as Alt text from XMP data. However you choose to generate it, out of courtesy to those relying on assistive devices, choose Alt text with different content from your captions.

13. Select the green bar at the bottom of the page and choose Custom from the Alt text source dropdown. Type "empty" in the text field. Click Done to close the Object Export Options dialog.

It is recommended in the EPUB accessibility guidelines that "empty" be used as the Alt text for purely decorative elements. The "empty" Alt text value is ignored by reader applications and eliminates extraneous content for those using assistive devices.

14. Export the file to EPUB as **ex22_2.epub** and save it in the chapter_22_exercises folder. Crack open the file (see page 316 for instructions,) and open **ex22_2.xhtml** from the OEBPS folder in your HTML editing application. If you're using Dreamweaver, switch to Split View if necessary, and click one of the images in Design view to highlight the corresponding code. If you're using a text editor, do a search for: alt=".

The Alt text you entered appears in the alt attribute of the <img> tag.

15. Click the Alice's Adventures image in Design view and observe the alt attribute in the HTML code. The apostrophe character has been replaced by the following code: ' Select the code and replace it with the apostrophe character.

16. Locate the <img> tag for the grouped images and note that InDesign converted the two images to one and named the resulting image **1321.jpg**. Note also that the Alt text for the images duplicates the file name. Select the Alt text and replace it with descriptive text of your choosing. We entered "Alice spying a tiny key through a glass table top," and "Alice watching the White Rabbit scurry away down a corridor."

17. Locate the <img> tag for the green decorative bar at the bottom of the document window. Note that "empty" appears as the Alt attribute value.

18. Save the XHTML file and close it.

19. Return to InDesign. Save and close ex22_2.indd to complete the exercise.

> **NOTE:** If you'd prefer not to export and crack open your EPUB, you can take a look at the code in the **ex22_2.xhtml** file instead. In the chapter_22_exercises folder, go to ex22_2/OEBPS to find it.

> **NOTE:** For a list of HTML/XML/EPUB editing tools, see page 418.

Anchored Objects

Another way to influence the flow of the elements in your document is by using anchored objects. You started learning about anchored objects on page 78, but the next section is targeted specifically to an EPUB workflow. For text heavy documents with occasional images, using in-line or above-line anchored objects to incorporate your images produces the most predictable results. It's best to create a paragraph style specifically for adding such elements. Inline elements aren't limited to images; they can just as easily be InDesign graphics or text elements such as pull quotes.

Exercise 22.3: EPUB Anchored Objects

1. Open **ex22_3_start.indd** from the chapter_22_exercises folder and save it as ex22_3.indd.

2. Go to Window > Text Wrap to open the Text Wrap panel. Using the Selection tool, click through the graphical elements on the page to see that text wrap is applied to the image of Alice and the White Rabbit as well as the star and the first green bar toward the bottom of the page.

You're going to anchor the image of Alice and the caption in the flow of the story along with the other graphical elements on the page. In order to sequence things properly using the Articles panel you'd have to break the single story text frame into multiple, un-threaded frames. Using anchored objects instead, you can keep the single text frame and maintain your document layout by embedding the objects directly in the document flow.

One way to anchor an object in the document flow, is to drag the colored square at the upper right of its frame to the anchor text. An uppercase T appears on the cursor as it's dragged. A colored anchor icon ([⚓]) replaces the colored square at the upper right of the image to indicate that the object has been anchored.

3. Click to select the image of Alice and the White Rabbit positioned in the green text frame on the pasteboard.

   A blue square appears toward the upper right of the image frame.

4. Click and hold and drag from the blue square at the upper right of the image to just in front of the caption text, and release the mouse to anchor the image in the caption.

   The caption disappears (hidden by the image) and the blue square is replaced by a blue anchor badge.

5. Hold down the Alt/Option key and click the anchor badge at the upper right of the image. When the Anchored Object Options dialog opens, choose Inline or Above Line from the Position dropdown and select the Above Line radio button. Ensure that the Preview checkbox at the lower left of the dialog is checked and choose Center from the Alignment dropdown. Change the Space After value to 18 px and click OK to close the dialog.

Above Line anchored object settings to anchor the image to the caption text.

6. Switch to the Type tool, and click to position the cursor in the text frame on the page just in front of the words "Third paragraph." Press Enter/Return.

7. Press Escape to switch back to the Selection tool and select the green text frame on the pasteboard. Hold the Shift key and drag from the blue square at its upper right corner to the pilcrow for the new paragraph to anchor the text frame inline.

TIP: The backwards P symbol that indicates a paragraph is called a pilcrow.

8. Switch back to the Type tool (T) and click to position your cursor in front of the newly anchored frame. Go to Window > Styles > Paragraph Styles or click the Paragraph Styles icon in the Panel Dock ( ). Alt+Click/Option+Click the New Style button at the bottom of the panel.

9. Name the new style "anchor" and select [No Paragraph Style] from the Based On dropdown. Ensure that the Apply Style to Selection checkbox is checked. From the Basic Character Formats category at the left of the dialog, ensure that Auto is chosen from the Leading dropdown.

   Parentheses surrounding the leading value indicate that the default auto leading of 120% of the font size is applied (unless you've changed your preferences.) With leading set to auto, the paragraph expands to accommodate the height of the anchored object, and the image and caption pop into place between the second and third paragraphs of the text frame. You could then add space before and space after to create some breathing room between the in-line anchored object and the surrounding content. You can further customize spacing around images and anchored objects through settings in the Object Export Options dialog.

10. Still in the New Paragraph Style panel, choose the Indents and Spacing category. Set Alignment to Center and set Left, Right and First Line Indent to 0. Enter 25 px for Space Before and 20 px for Space After. Leave the other default settings and click OK.

11. Add a return between paragraphs four and five and apply the anchor style.

12. Switch to the Selection tool and select the first green bar below the text. Hold the Shift key and drag from the blue square at the upper right of the bar to the pilcrow for the new paragraph.

   The green bar jumps into position in the paragraph.

13. Select the star graphic and drag from the blue square at its upper right to just in front of the words "Third paragraph." If necessary, reposition the star so the text flows around it to your liking.

   Even when an object is anchored and text wrap is applied, InDesign needs some extra help to translate the wrapping of the text to the EPUB HTML code. That's easily accomplished in the Object Export Options Dialog.

14. With the star still selected, go to Object > Object Export Options and click the EPUB and HTML button. Check the Custom Layout checkbox and choose Float Right from the dropdown. Click Done to close the dialog.

   Float Right places the image to the right and wraps the text to its left. Float Left positions the image to the left and wraps the text around it to the right.

15. Using the Selection tool, drag from the blue square at the upper right of the green bar at the bottom of the page to the end of the last paragraph to anchor it.

16. Save the file as **ex22_3_b.indd** and export it to EPUB. Save the EPUB to the chapter_22_exercises folder as **ex22_3.epub**.

17. In the EPUB Export Options dialog, click the Image item in the category list at the left. If necessary, check the Preserve Appearance from Layout checkbox, set Image Size to Relative to Page, and check the Settings Apply to Anchored Objects checkbox. Leave the other default settings and click OK to export the file.

When exporting to EPUB, check the Settings Apply to Anchored Objects checkbox to affect objects anchored with Custom selected from the Position dropdown in the Anchored Objects dialog.

18. If necessary, open the EPUB in ADE to see how InDesign integrated the anchored objects in the document flow. When you're finished exploring, close out of ADE and return to InDesign.

19. Close all open documents to complete the exercise.

Image Optimization Guidelines

With so many eReaders out there, it's impossible to target your documents specifically to each one. That said, there are some image creation guidelines that can help you prepare your eBooks to perform as well as possible across the board with some tweaks for the more popular devices.

As you've come to understand, image optimization is always a trade-off between image quality and file size. When it comes to digital publishing, file size can often impact performance. The higher the number, quality, and resolution of your images, the larger your document will be; the longer it will take to download.

InDesign image optimization for EPUB is not entirely a black and white issue. While you could opt to apply global optimization settings, as you saw earlier in the chapter, InDesign also makes it possible to assign optimization settings on an object-by-object basis. When certain images or objects require special attention, you have the option to export them at a different resolution, quality, and format than specified in the more general EPUB Export Options dialog.

To set rasterization options for individual objects or images, select the object(s) and go to Object > Object Export Options. The custom rasterization options appear in the EPUB and HTML section of the panel. Any type of object can be rasterized (converted to an image): tables, grouped objects, and InDesign graphics. Converting objects to images ensures that they will render predictably in your EPUB. This is an especially useful option should you have groups of objects that collectively comprise a diagram, for example.

THE EPUB AND HTML OBJECT EXPORT OPTIONS DIALOG

The Custom Rasterization options available in the Object Export Options dialog are dependent on the Option selected in the Format dropdown. The Resolution (ppi) option is always available regardless of which format is selected. There are no PNG-specific options.

- Fixed images remain the same size regardless of the size of the display area.
- Relative to Page Width results in an image that scales with the size of the display area.

Fixed
√ Relative to Page Width

Selecting GIF activates the Palette dropdown

√ JPEG
GIF
PNG

√ Adaptive (no dither)
Web
System (Win)
System (Mac)

- Float left floats the image to the left and wraps text around it to the right.
- Float right floats the image to the right and wraps the text to its left.
- Selecting Alignment And Spacing activates the alignment and spacing controls

Float Left
Float Right
√ Alignment And Spacing

72
96
√ 150
300

Selecting JPEG format activates the Quality, and Method dropdowns

Low
Medium
√ High
Maximum

Progressive
√ Baseline

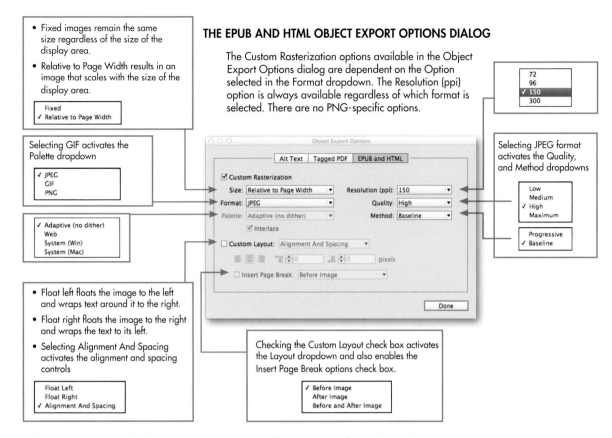

Checking the Custom Layout check box activates the Layout dropdown and also enables the Insert Page Break options check box.

√ Before Image
After Image
Before and After Image

InDesign supports EPUB export to three image formats, any of which can be exported with a resolution of 72, 96, 150 or 300 ppi:

JPEG: JPEG stands for Joint Photographic Experts Group. It's a compression algorithm developed expressly for photographs having millions of colors like sunrises and sunsets. JPEG is a lossy format. This means that every time a JPEG is saved, it throws away what it considers to be extraneous information. InDesign offers four quality options for JPEG compression: low, medium, high, and maximum with low quality resulting in the smallest file size. The progressive JPEG option renders the image line-by-line to fade it in gradually. The baseline option handles the image as a whole. For most images, you won't go wrong if you set your Custom Rasterization settings to High Quality Progressive JPG at 150 ppi.

GIF: GIF stands for Graphical Interchange Format. It supports a maximum of 256 colors and is best applied to images and objects with solid colors such as logos. The GIF palette can be based on operating system colors, web-safe colors, or an adaptive palette generated from the actual colors in the image or graphic. The dither option blends the 256 colors to create the appearance of additional colors.

PNG: PNG (pronounced "ping") stands for Portable Network Graphics. The PNG format supports transparency. Illustrator vector graphics that include transparency are converted to PNG when exported to EPUB. InDesign does not apply compression when converting to PNG.

The export alignment options enable you to left-, right- or center-align an object and assign specific spacing before and/or after it. Custom Layout spacing options provide a handy way to add space around images and objects. As you saw in the previous exercise you can apply the float left or float right option to approximate text wrap. Float left floats the image to the left and wraps the text to the right. Float right floats the image to the right and wraps the text to its left.

Managing page breaks is another of EPUBs ongoing challenges. The Insert Page Break options in the Object Export Options dialog are great in that they make it possible to insert a page break to force an image to the beginning of a new page. Alternatively, to make an image the last element on a page you can insert a page break after. You can even make an image the sole object on a page by inserting page breaks both before and after.

Resolution is a bit of a thorny issue since new devices with higher resolutions haven't yet supplanted the old, and proprietary specifications haven't evolved at pace with the technology. That aside, a good general rule of thumb is to set an export resolution of 150 ppi. However, the Kindle guidelines recommend using high quality and high resolution images (300 ppi) if you intend to use KindleGen to convert from EPUB to a Kindle format. Another possible exception to the 150 ppi guideline might be vector art where you may choose to up the resolution to 300 ppi for a crisper result or to allow for zooming in an iBook. Regardless of your export resolution, it's important to realize that InDesign will not up-sample your images. If the effective ppi is lower than the export resolution, the images will be exported at the effective ppi. For example, an image with an effective resolution of 72 ppi will remain at 72 ppi despite an export resolution setting of 150 ppi. (You can create a custom preflight profile for Live Preflight to detect minimum image resolution and you can also identify the effective resolution of an image in the Links panel.) Another place you can check effective ppi is in the preflight details displayed when InDesign runs its Package function. Go to File > Package and when the Package dialog opens, select Links and Images from the category list at the left. Click a link in the top section of the panel to see the Effective ppi value in the details pane below.

You can check effective ppi in the Links and Image section of the Package dialog when InDesign runs the Package function.

TIP: Effective resolution is the resolution of an image after it's been scaled. If the image is scaled up, the effective ppi will be less than the actual ppi. If the image is scaled down, the effective ppi will be greater than the actual ppi.

NOTE: See page 49 to learn about customizing the Links panel to display effective ppi See page 46 to learn about creating a custom preflight profile.

Understanding the Relative vs. Fixed Size Options

When you choose Relative to Page Width for EPUB image export, InDesign calculates the image size as a percentage of the frame or column into which the image is anchored or relative to the width of the page. This percentage then appears as the width value in the EPUB CSS. Objects wider than their container are assigned a CSS width of 100%. When the font size is changed in the eReader or the viewing window is scaled, objects with percentage-based widths scale with the change.

For images that shouldn't be scaled such as icons for example, choose Fixed from the Object Export Options Custom Rasterization Size dropdown. If the Preserve Appearance from Layout option is selected in the EPUB Export Options dialog, images without individually defined export options will export at the same size and with the same transforms they possess on the InDesign page.

NOTE: See page 333 for an overview of the EPUB Export Options dialog.

Creating an EPUB Cover Image

While we all know that you can't judge a book by its cover, we'd be naive to think that people don't. In other words, a compelling cover can be a significant factor in boosting your EPUB sales. There are actually a couple ways to create a cover image right in InDesign. You can export selected content or pages to JPG or PNG format or you can have InDesign rasterize the first page of your document during EPUB export.

TIP: InDesign uses the PNG format when rasterizing the first page of a document during EPUB export.

If you intend to distribute your book through Amazon or the Apple iBookstore, there are some guidelines to keep in mind with regard to images, and cover images in particular. Both Amazon, with its mobi and KF8 specifications for Kindle, and iBookstore accept documents with JPEG or PNG cover images.

eBooks created for Kindle require both an internal content cover image and a marketing cover image. The Amazon Kindle Publishing Guidelines Version 2012.5 require that the marketing cover image be a minimum of 1000 pixels on the longest side with 2500 pixels preferred. Covers with less than 500 pixels on the smallest side will upload without an error message but will not be displayed on the website. If the internal cover image doesn't meet the above size criteria, the book will fail Amazon quality assurance. Cover images can't contain pricing or promotional offers. It's also important to be aware that each image in a publication for Kindle must be no larger than 127 KB.

At this writing, iBookstore requires that cover images use RGB color mode and be at least 1400 pixels along the shorter axis with 2400 pixels recommended (1400 X 1873 minimum size.) The iBookstore upper limit of two million pixels per image does not apply to cover images. Regarding the two million pixel limit, clearly the Retina iPad has brought a wrinkle to the rules and the specifications haven't quite caught up yet. The dimensions of the Retina iPad display are 2048 px by 1536 px. As the rules currently stand, an EPUB containing an image with these dimensions will be rejected by iBookstore since the image would contain 3,145,728 pixels. This being the case, we can only hope that by the time you're reading this, Apple will have made some adjustments to their parameters. Ahh, growing pains...

TIP: Multiply the pixel values for height and width to establish the total number of pixels in an image.

In any case, for iBookstore, cover images must be high-quality JPEGs (quality of 85 is recommended) with a .jpg extension or PNGs with a .png extension. The title on the cover must match the metadata title and the image must be crisp and clear. It mustn't reference materials that aren't included in the eBook (such as a CD) nor may it contain prices. It also may not contain advertisements or links to competing sites or products, or up-sell to a more complete version of the product.

With all the rules out of the way, actually creating the cover is the easy part, as you'll discover in the next exercise.

Exercise 22.4: Creating an EPUB Cover Image

1. Navigate to the chapter_22_exercises folder and open **ex22_4_start.indd**.

   This file is a one-page document with dimensions that comply with the current iBookstore and Kindle minimum specification for a marketing cover image—it is 1632 pixels along the vertical axis and 1224 pixels along the horizontal— totaling under two million pixels.

2. Go go File > Export (Ctrl+E/Command+E) and choose JPEG from the Format options at the bottom of the dialog. Save the file in the chapter_22_exercises folder as **cover_max.jpg**.

3. When the JPG Options window opens, you can leave Range set to All since the document has only one page and you want the entire page as your cover image. Change Quality to Maximum, leave the other default settings and click Export.

You can specify a selection or the specific page or pages
you want to export in the Range text entry box.

4. Repeat steps 2–3 but this time, save the exported JPEG as **cover_high.jpg** and set the export image Quality to High.

   Next you'll compare the file size and quality of the two images you just exported.

5. After the export, expand the Pages panel in the Panel Dock and click the Create new page button at the bottom of the panel twice to add two new pages.

6. Press Ctrl+D/Command+D and navigate to the chapter_22_exercises folder. Select both images that you just exported to load them into the Place Gun.

7. Double-Click the page 2 icon in the Pages panel to display it in the document window.

8. Position the Place Gun cursor at the upper left of the page and click to place the first image.

9. Double-Click the page 3 icon in the Pages panel and place the remaining image.

10. Right-Click/Ctrl+Click the placed image and mouse over the Display Performance option in the contextual menu. Choose High Quality Display from the submenu.

11. Set Display Performance for the image on page two to High Quality as well.

12. Press Ctrl+1/Command+1 to zoom in to 100% magnification, and compare the quality of the two placed images.

13. Expand the Links panel in the Panel Dock (**G⊃**). If necessary, click the disclosure triangle at the lower left of the panel to expand the Link Info section. Click the cover image link items and note the file size listed in the Link Info section of the panel.

    Notice that the image exported at maximum quality is close to twice the size of the one exported at high quality. Both files are much larger than the maximum allowable image size for Kindle.

CHAPTER SUMMARY

This chapter took you deeper still into the weird and wonderful world of EPUB. You gained an understanding of how to anticipate and exert some control over the flow of your exported document in several ways:

- Sequencing document contents using the Articles panel
- Inserting anchored objects in the document flow
- Adding a page break before and/or after images

In working with the Articles panel, you learned how to:

- Create an article
- Add, delete and reorder article objects

You discovered the Object Export Options dialog and became quite familiar with:

- The EPUB and HTML pane with its custom rasterization and custom layout options
- The Alt Text pane with its Custom, Structure and XMP option

As part of your work with Alt text, you took a side trip to Bridge to enter XMP data. For purely decorative page elements, you learned to set the Alt Text value to empty. You then cracked open the EPUB and had a look at the resulting code and did some editing to the HTML while you were at it.

You learned all about custom rasterization options and how you can use them to render InDesign graphics in your EPUB, also gaining some understanding of the JPEG, GIF, and PNG image formats. You learned the difference between images exported at a fixed as opposed to relative size and how that difference is rendered in the EPUB CSS.

Last but not least, you learned how to create a cover image directly in InDesign and had an introduction to some of the Amazon and iBookstore image and cover image guidelines.

In this chapter you learned some ways to affect a degree of control over EPUB document flow and pagination. The next chapter provides you with additional strategies for controlling page breaks and for compiling multiple documents into one final EPUB.

● Chapter 23

CREATING AN INDESIGN BOOK

Regardless of the individual pages you establish in InDesign, EPUB documents flow continuously, ignoring the pagination of your layout. For longer documents that contain multiple chapters or sections, one way to ensure that each new chapter begins a new page is to divide the chapters into separate documents. You can then use an InDesign book file to compile the chapters and export them collectively as a single EPUB. The InDesign book panel has a number of features that are equally applicable to print documents, so the skills and techniques you learn in this chapter will serve you well in both print and digital development.

Working with InDesign Books

As you are no doubt coming to understand, one of the greatest challenges faced by designers in controlling the flow of flowable EPUB is in keeping specific blocks of content together and controlling page breaks. The Object Export Options dialog provides a way to control page breaks around images, but when there are no images in the mix, InDesign provides two other ways to inject page breaks where you want them.

NOTE: Jump over to page 367 to learn more about Export Tagging.

The Export Tagging category of the Style Options dialogs enables you to make some choices about how styles are mapped to the HTML and CSS in your EPUB. One of those choices is whether to split the EPUB at a given paragraph style. If you apply a paragraph style called chapterHeader to the title of each chapter of your book for example, by including the Split Document option in the style definition, you can ensure that each new chapter will be preceded by a page break.

Another way to ensure that each chapter begins on a new page is to create separate InDesign documents for each chapter and then compile them in an InDesign book file. The documents included in the book can be synchronized to share text styles and object styles, swatches, master pages and more. When exported to EPUB (or PDF) the combined files create one unified and consistently formatted document. The book workflow is ideal for projects where team members work in tandem on separate sections of a longer document, and working with smaller files can also make them easier to edit. Long documents destined for EPUB should to be broken into smaller pieces anyway, since no single HTML file in the EPUB should exceed 300K.

Exercise 23.1: Creating an InDesign Book

DOWNLOAD: Exercise files for this chapter can be downloaded from http://www.interactive-indesign.com.

1. Go to File > New > Book, navigate to the chapter_23_exercises folder and save the book file as **ex23.indb**.

   You can add documents to a book file one-by-one or, if they're already collected in a single location, you can add multiple files all at the same time.

2. Either click the Add documents button at the bottom of the Book panel (**+**) or choose Add Document from the Book panel menu. Navigate to chapter_23_exercises > chapter23_resources. With the files displayed alphabetically, click the **chapter001.indd** file, hold the Shift key and click **synopsis.indd** to select both files and all those in between. Click Open.

   A book file manages the formatting of the documents it contains as well as page numbering. While not relevant for an eBook, the page numbering feature is awesome for long print documents. For that reason, we're going to take a side trip to show you how to make the most of it.

   If you take a look at the populated Book panel, you can see that the page numbers begin at 1 and progress consecutively until they restart with the synopsis file at the bottom of the document stack. For every new document you create in InDesign, the first page automatically marks the beginning of a new section. A document can have as many sections as it does pages, and each section provides the opportunity to choose page, section, and chapter naming and numbering options. If you add page and section markers to a master page, you can have page numbers and section names appear dynamically on all the pages in your document to which that master page is applied.

Master pages elements do not export to EPUB but that shouldn't stop you from using them in your layout if you intend to output your document to print as well.

The synopsis.indd file already has two sections: the TOC on the first page and the synopsis section which makes up the balance of the document. The TOC page has the [None] master page applied to it so the section marker and page numbers that you'll be setting up in the exercise won't appear on that page. Visible page numbering for the book will start with the synopsis section and its pages will be numbered with lower case roman numerals. You'll then set up the Chapter 1 file to restart numbering at page 1 with arabic numerals.

3. In the Book panel, Double-Click the **synopsis** file at the bottom of the document stack to open it.

If you open a document you've included in a book and the Book panel isn't open, the next time you open it, the Book panel displays a warning icon indicating that the document was modified outside of the book. To avoid having to clear the warning, it's best practice to open files contained in a book directly from the panel.

The Book panel showing: the documents included in the book file, the document page numbers, an open document icon (●), a warning icon (⚠) indicating a file that was opened outside of the book, and a missing document icon (❓).

While it appears that the first page of the synopsis document is empty except for the Table of Contents header, there is already a TOC style defined and applied to the page. Later in the exercise, you will update the table of contents to reflect the contents of the book file.

4. In the Pages panel, Double-Click the black section indicator above the second of the two pages numbered 1 to open the Numbering & Section Options dialog.

5. The page numbering of the section is already set to start at page 1. Choose lower case Roman numerals from the Page Numbering Style dropdown and type "Synopsis" in the Section Marker text field. Click OK to close the dialog.

The Numbering & Section Options dialog displaying the settings for the second section of the synopsis.indd document.

Notice how the page numbers in the Books panel update to reflect the new number style. The combination of the arabic and lower case roman numerals reflect the different numbering styles for the two sections in the document.

The page numbers in the Book panel reflect the
numbering styles applied to the document sections.

Next you'll add page number and section markers to the master page so they appear on the document pages.

6.   Double-Click the A-Master icon at the top of the Pages panel to make it active in the document window. Select the Type tool and beginning at the bottom left margin of the page, drag down to the intersection of the guide and the right margin.

7.   Press Ctrl+B/Command+B to open the Text Frame Options dialog. Choose Bottom from the Vertical Justification Align dropdown and then click OK.

8.   Press Shift+Ctrl+C/Shift+Command+C to center-align the text and then, if necessary, activate the Character Formatting Controls on the Control panel.

9.   Choose Adobe Garamond Pro from the Font Family dropdown and Regular from the Font Style dropdown to match the formatting of the rest of the document.

10. Right-Click in the text frame and choose Insert Special Character > Markers > Section Marker. After the section marker, type a colon, a space, the word "page" and a space.

11. Right-Click in the text frame again and choose Insert Special Character > Markers > Current Page Number.

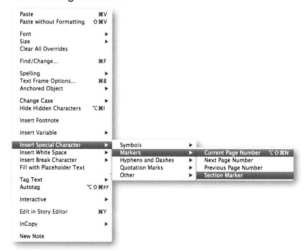

The contextual menus for adding section markers and page numbers.

12. Double-Click the page 1 icon in the Pages panel and note the section name and page number that appear at the bottom of the page in the document window.

Next, you'll correct the order of the documents in the Book panel.

13. In the Book panel, click **front_matter**, hold the Shift key and click **synopsis** to select both files. Release the Shift key and drag the files to the top of the document stack. Release the mouse when you see a black line above the chapter001 file.

The files in the Book panel automatically repaginate
when dragged into a different sequence.

14. Select the Type tool and place the cursor in the Table of Contents text frame on the
first page of the document. Go to Layout > Update Table of Contents.

InDesign magically compiles the information from the collected book files and
when complete, displays an alert stating: "The Table of Contents has been
updated successfully."

The TOC style attached to the document is designed for output to EPUB and,
therefore, the page numbers were not included in the style definition. If you'd
like to include the page numbers in the TOC, everything is already set up for
you. With the Type tool cursor active in the Table of Contents text, just go to
Layout > Table of Contents, select chapterTitle in the Include Paragraph Styles
pane, and choose After Entry from the Page Number dropdown. Repeat
for subTitle and then click OK. The TOC will regenerate with page numbers
displayed.

NOTE: For an in-depth
explanation of how
to create a Table of
Contents, see Chapter
8: Creating a TOC,
starting on page 119.

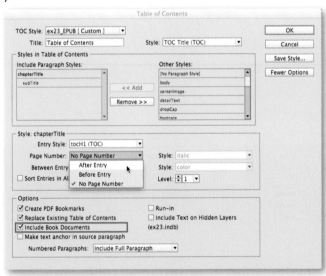

The Table of Contents dialog. When creating a TOC for a book file, be sure to
check the Include Book Documents checkbox at the bottom left of the dialog.

To complete the page numbering portion of the exercise, you'll change the start
page of chapter one so that it begins on page one rather than on page three.

15. In the Book panel, Double-Click **chapter001** to open the document and then Double-Click the section indicator above the first page icon in the Pages panel. In the Numbering & Section Options dialog, click the Start Page Numbering at radio button and enter 1 in the page number text field. Ensure that arabic numerals are chosen for the number style, and note that the chapter title has already been entered for you in the section marker text field. Click OK to close the dialog.

    Next, you'll compare the current state of a couple of the book files and then synchronize the book to make the style definitions and master pages consistent throughout.

16. With **chapter001.indd** active in the document window, take a look at the Paragraph Styles panel and note that it contains five styles in addition to the [Basic Paragraph] style.

17. Place the Type tool cursor in the chapter title on the document, and note that the font size is 20 pt and the font color is black. Also note that there is no section marker or page number at the bottom of the page.

18. Click the document tab for **synopsis.indd** (just below the Control panel) to switch documents, and check out the Paragraph Styles panel again. Note that there are nine styles in the panel and a TOC style group containing three more styles specific to the Table of Contents.

19. Place the Type tool cursor in the word "Synopsis" and note that the font size is 30 pt and that the font color is green. The document also contains a master page that provides the footer you want to appear throughout the book.

20. In the Book panel, click the empty square to the left of the synopsis item to set **synopsis.indd** as the style source for the book.

21. Choose Synchronize Options from the Book panel menu and ensure that the Master Pages checkbox is checked. Click OK to close the dialog.

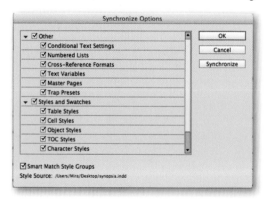

The Synchronize Options dialog enables you to choose which features you want to share across the documents included in a book file.

22. Click the empty gray area below the file list in the Book panel to deselect all the book files. (You may need to drag the bottom of the panel down to show the space below the list.) Choose Synchronize Book from the Book panel menu.

    InDesign displays a message to let you know that the synchronization was successfully completed.

23. Click the document tab for **chapter001.indd** and notice that the formatting of the chapter title on the page has been updated to match the style definition in the synopsis file. The footer appears at the bottom of the page and a look at the Paragraph Styles panel reveals that the styles from the synopsis file have been added.

24. Click the Save the book button (⏏) at the bottom of the Book panel.

The Book panel menu offers a number of commands that are invaluable for both print and digital development. As you've seen, you can arrange and synchronize book documents and you can export your book to EPUB. The Book panel also enables you to export to PDF, preflight, package, and print the entire book or only selected documents. Additionally, the Book panel provides access to the Section & Page Numbering Options dialog for individual book files as well as page numbering options for the compiled book.

NOTE: The table of contents style for the EPUB must be included in the document you've designated as the style source for your book. When you synchronized the book, the TOC style was synchronized with the rest of the styles and is therefore accessible from any of the book files making any one of them a possible candidate for the style source.

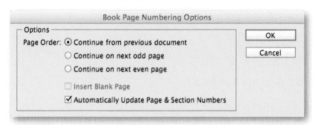

You can access Book Page Numbering Options from the Book panel menu.

25. Close all open files to complete the exercise and the chapter.

CHAPTER SUMMARY

In this chapter, you learned a sure-fire way to create page breaks in your EPUB by assembling multiple documents in an InDesign book file for EPUB export. Useful for both print and EPUB, this chapter took you through the ins and outs of working with InDesign books. Working with the Book panel, you learned how to:

- Add documents
- Arrange documents
- Replace missing documents
- Set a style source
- Set book synchronization options
- Synchronize a book
- Interpret Book panel indicator icons
- Update page numbering

In the process, you worked with individual book documents to:

- Set up Numbering and Section options
- Add page number and section markers to a document master
- Adapt a TOC to work with a book file

Using InDesign book files can potentially streamline workflow by making it possible for multiple team members to develop content concurrently. For print and EPUB both, InDesign books make it easier to rearrange, edit and manage long documents.

The next chapter takes you ever deeper into the EPUB domain with an HTML and CSS field guide to help you better navigate the territory. With map in hand, you'll find that what may have first appeared as ominous terrain is more akin to a walk in the park.

● Chapter 24

HTML AND CSS FUNDAMENTALS

If you're serious about working with EPUB, you simply have to have at least a foundation knowledge of HTML and CSS. This chapter is intended to provide you with fundamentals that will help you make sense of the Export Tagging and EPUB Export options available in InDesign and demystify some of the anomalies you may encounter in your exported EPUBs. Who knows, by the time you're done, you may even be surprised to find yourself with a new appreciation of and curiosity for the code itself.

Why HTML and CSS?

As you learned at the beginning of this section, when you export to EPUB from InDesign, your document content is converted to a collection of HTML pages (with an XHTML extension) and your style information—based on the export settings you've chosen—is captured in a CSS (cascading stylesheet) file.

The choices you make in InDesign when you define and assign styles directly affect the code that's exported to your EPUB. So, even if you have other EPUB team mates who will edit the final EPUB HTML, CSS, and XML code (and it's likely that you'll choose to make at least minor edits to create an optimal result), a basic knowledge of HTML and CSS will help you make the most of the available InDesign export options and better navigate its quirks.

This chapter is intended as a rudimentary introduction to HTML and CSS and is in no way intended to provide exhaustive coverage of the topic. The hope is that we can provide you with a strong enough foundation that you'll be able to:

1. Work effectively with InDesign's paragraph style export tagging options to generate the best code for your EPUB
2. Identify and remove extraneous code from your exported EPUB HTML
3. Make simple refinements to the final style definitions in the EPUB CSS

If you already have a working knowledge of HTML and CSS, you can skip over to InDesign's EPUB HTML & CSS, starting on page 364 for some insight into InDesign-generated EPUB HTML code.

Introduction to HTML and CSS

HTML stands for Hypertext Markup Language. HTML markup is all about containers—boxes inside boxes. Think Tupperware—containers with fitted lids that you can stack and arrange. You can even nest smaller containers inside larger ones. Imagine that these Tupperware containers are somewhat specialized, where the type of container you use is specific to what you're storing in it. Desserts go in dessert containers, main courses go in main course containers; you get the idea. That's pretty much how it is with HTML—the containers define the logical role of the elements within the page. Paragraphs go in paragraph containers—called tags in HTML—tables go in table tags, etc.

While HTML provides the logical structure of a web or EPUB page, cascading stylesheets (CSS) define the way the HTML elements appear on the page. In the context of the Tupperware metaphor, you can think of CSS loosely as labels that include the recipe for what's inside the container. CSS governs the appearance of HTML elements in the same way that paragraph, character, object, table, and cell styles govern the appearance of content in your InDesign documents. In fact, depending on your export settings, the style definitions you create in InDesign are translated as closely as possible to a cascading stylesheet that's generated for inclusion in your exported EPUB.

To get a more intuitive grasp of the inner workings of HTML, it helps to understand its origin. HTML began as a medium through which scientists could share their research. A scientific research paper has its own internal logic and typically contains a hierarchical structure of headers, bulleted lists, numbered lists, definition lists, blockquotes, figures, captions, tables, paragraphs, citations, abbreviations, etc. True to its academic origins, these logical elements are all included in the lexicon of HTML tags.

HTML started out as a loose and forgiving markup language. It didn't really care if tags were properly closed. It wasn't case-sensitive. It didn't care if attributes—descriptors inside the tags—were in quotations or not. Back to the Tupperware idea; you can imagine what would happen if you didn't bother to put the right size lids on your containers or even put lids on at all. Things could get messy pretty quickly if you wanted to collect some of those containers to take dinner to a friend.

As the web evolved and mobile devices began to hit the scene, the messy container problem became an issue for HTML as well. In order to transport content between devices, the code needed to be packaged more reliably, and thus a new standard called XHTML was developed with more rigorous rules. XHTML requires that tag selectors be written in lowercase, that every element have a closing tag, that attributes be written in lowercase and quoted, and that only certain elements be nested inside other elements.

There are a few additional rules, but for the most part, even in its stricter XHTML form, you'll see that HTML markup is still pretty simple to navigate.

HTML Page and Tag Structure

Like anything else that's new and unfamiliar, your first glance of HTML markup could be a little daunting. Not to worry; breaking it into its component pieces is easy and makes it quite approachable. The structure of the code is consistent so once you understand how its built, you'll be able to find your way around quite comfortably.

An HTML page is composed of three fundamental parts:

1. **The HTML container:** Defines the start and end of the HTML content. All the other HTML elements in the document are contained within the opening and closing HTML tags.

2. **The HEAD:** Appears at the top of the document directly after the opening HTML tag. In much the same way that we hold information in our heads that is unseen, the **<head>** section of an HTML document holds information that is not directly seen on the page. The **<title>** tag is nested between the opening and closing **<head>** tags, as are **<meta>** tags which contain information about the document itself. Code for scripts and CSS, or links to external scripts and external CSS may also be found in the **<head>** of the document.

3. **The BODY:** The **<body>** container holds everything that is actually seen on the page. The opening **<body>** tag appears after the closing **</head>** tag. The closing **</body>** tag appears just before the closing **</html>** tag.

The skeleton structure of an HTML page looks something like the figure below which includes some optional goodies in the **<head>** section of the page.

With no content in the body tag, the skeleton HTML code shown above would display in a browser as a blank page.

With the exception of the **meta** and **link** tags, you'll notice that each tag has a separate closing tag. The forward slash that indicates the close of the tag tells the browser to stop interpreting that tag.

Generally, the opening tags used in XHTML have a specific structure that follows this format:

The selector is the name of the tag like **p** for a paragraph or **a** for an anchor tag as you see above. A property or attribute is something that further describes the tag. A tag may or may not include properties but if it does, the property value will appear in quotes. Note that the entire tag is written in lowercase.

A stand-alone closing tag contains only the selector preceded by a forward slash:**</a>.** The structure for self-contained XHTML tags (no separate closing tag) looks like this:

The closing of the tag is achieved by adding a space after the tag contents, followed by a forward slash, followed by the closing chevron.

Default Formatting

HTML is whitespace-insensitive. Regardless of how many spaces or tabs or returns you enter in your code, one space and only one space will render on the display. Overall, this is a good thing in that it allows you to format the code in a way that makes it easier to read and troubleshoot. You can indent nested tags and put any number of returns between the lines of your code for visual clarity. To add additional spaces between words that actually render on the page, you need to use the Unicode character for a non-breaking space: **nbsp&;**.

Many HTML elements have default appearance attributes. For example, they may be bold or italicized. They may be centered, or have an inherent size, or put space between themselves and other content on the page. All these attributes can be changed using CSS but it's useful to be aware of the default properties so you can define your styles appropriately. We'll be discussing these default attributes when we introduce you to some of the more common HTML tags.

Block Level and Inline Elements

HTML elements fall into two primary categories: block level elements and inline elements. HTML block level elements create a line break between themselves and other elements. Headers, paragraphs, blockquotes, lists and list items are all examples of HTML block level elements.

Inline elements create no break between themselves and surrounding content. By default, a link is an inline element—it exists in the flow of the paragraph or other containing element. The **<em>** and **<strong>** tags are also examples of inline elements.

> **TIP:** The content of an HTML <em> tag generally appears italicized while the default appearance for the <strong> tag is bold.

The difference between block level and inline elements becomes particularly relevant when defining and assigning CSS styles. Just as you can define a paragraph style in InDesign to include font formatting along with indents and spacing before and after the paragraph, you can apply similar styling to HTML block level elements with CSS. In contrast, styling an HTML inline element would be more like applying an InDesign character style, where only select characters within a paragraph are affected.

HTML4 Block Level Elements

h1 – Level-one heading
h2 – Level-two heading
h3 – Level-three heading
h4 – Level-four heading
h5 – Level-five heading
h6 – Level-six heading
table – Table
thead – Table head
tbody – Table body
tfoot – Table foot
tr – Table row
th – Table header cell

td – Table data cell
ul – Unordered list
ol – Ordered list
li – List item
dl – Definition list
dd – Definition description
dt – Definition term
div – Generic container
hr – Horizontal rule
blockquote – Block quote
p – Paragraph
pre – Preformatted text

*Not a comprehensive list

HTML 4 Inline Elements

a – Anchor	**q** – Short quotation
abbr – Abbreviation	**samp** – Sample output
acronym – Acronym	**span** – Inline container
cite – Citation	**strong** – Strong emphasis
code – Computer code	**sub** – Subscript
dfn – Defined term	**sup** – Superscript
em – Emphasis	**tt** – Teletype text
img – Inline image	**var** – Variable
input – Form input	*Not a comprehensive list*

Writing HTML and CSS code

Although there are many tools available to make the process easier, you can actually write HTML and CSS code in any plain text editor. If written correctly and saved with a **.html** or **.xhtml** extension, your code will render properly in a browser or an eReader if it's part of a properly packaged EPUB. A CSS file is also a plain text file—saved with a **.css** extension. While working in a plain text editor is certainly an option, Dreamweaver, included in the Creative Cloud suite of applications, is an awesome tool for managing files and writing and editing HTML and CSS. You'll be getting a cursory introduction to Dreamweaver in the code editing exercises later in this section.

In choosing a code editor, look for one that offers a robust Find/Change feature. It's likely that you'll be doing a bit of code cleaning and tweaking as part of your EPUB development and the right tool can make the difference between an easy and efficient workflow and a tediously frustrating experience. Save yourself a lot of headaches and check out the list of EPUB Editing Tools, starting on page 418.

Exercise 24.1: HTML: A first look

Now that you have a bit of background, it's time to have a look at some code.

1. Navigate to the chapter_24_exercises folder and locate **html_sampler.xhtml**. Right-Click/Ctrl-Click the file and choose a browser from the Open With menu option.

2. When it opens in your browser, scroll through the page to explore its various elements. Note that the headers are bold and that they decrease in size as the level of the header increases—H2 headers are smaller than H1 headers. Note the space between the paragraphs, the lists and the table, and that the table headers are bold and centered. Notice the paragraphs containing the bold and italicized text and the content that appears in orange. Also notice that the hyperlink on the page is blue.

   With the exception of the orange text and the formatting applied to the **<div>** tag which you'll learn about shortly (the box bounded by the orange border), the elements on the page display their default appearances. The sizing, the spacing and font style, the blue color of the link, are all default attributes of the HTML elements on the page. You can change the default appearance of any HTML element by applying a CSS rule that explicitly redefines its properties. (You'll learn more about CSS later in this chapter, starting on page 360.)

3. Look at the very top of the browser window and note that the page title "HTML Sampler" appears there.

4. When you've finished looking through the page and have identified its various elements, Right-Click/Ctrl-Click on the body of the page in the browser. When the contextual menu appears, if it's available, choose the command that enables you to view the document source code. It should say something like "View page source."

5. If necessary, scroll down in the code to the opening **<body>** tag.

   Following the **<body>** tag, you'll see the code for the six HTML header tags.

6. Scroll down through the page source, reading the notations and getting familiar with the tags:

   <h1>Header level 1</h1>
   <h2>Header level 2</h2>
   <h3>Header level 3</h3>
   <h4>Header level 4</h4>
   <h5>Header level 5</h5>
   <h6>Header level 6</h6>

   <p>Paragraph </p>

   <ol> stands for ordered list which is also known as a numbered list. Each list item is enclosed by an opening and a closing **<li>** tag. Only content within the **<li>** tags is visible on the page.

   <ol>
       <li>List Item</li>
       <li>List Item</li>
   </ol>

   <ul> stands for unordered list also known as a bulleted list. Like an ordered list, only content within the **<li>** tags is visible on the page.

   <ul>
       <li>List Item in an Unordered (bulleted) List</li>
       <li>List Item</li>
   </ul>

   The code below creates a basic table with two rows and two columns. Only the content in the **<th>** and **<td>** tags appears in the table cells on the page. The **<table>** tag and the **<tr>** tags (for table rows) simply set up the table structure. The first of the two table rows in the example is a header row and the **<th>** that defines its cells stands for table header By default, content in a **<th>** tag is bold and centered. The **<td>** tags (for table data) define the body cells of the table. Note that each cell has its own distinct border when displayed on the HTML page.

   <table>
       <tr>
           <th>Table Header (table cell)</th>
           <th>Table Header (table cell)</th>

NOTE: For more on the Object Export Options dialog and InDesign's options for adding Alt text, see page 327

NOTE: The code class="orange" and class="box" in the span, div and p tags to the left are CSS class assignments. Learn more about CSS starting on page 347.

```
        </tr>
        <tr>
            <td>Table Data (table cell)<td>
            <td>Table Data (table cell)<td>
        </tr>
</table>
```

```
<em>Emphasis (italic by default)</em>
```

```
<strong>Strong (bold by default)</strong>
```

```
<p><span class="orange">Span: </span>The span tag is an inline
element that allows you to style the string of characters enclosed by
the tag using CSS. In this case a CSS class called "orange" is applied to
the span.</p>
```

```
<div class="box">
    <p class ="orange">Div is something of a magic tag in that you can
    store pretty much anything in it. It is a block level element and can
    contain any number of other elements including other divs. In this
    example, the div contains a single paragraph to which the orange
    class is applied.</p>
</div>
```

The **img** (image) tag is self contained—it doesn't have a separate closing tag. Its **src** attribute provides the path to the image file displayed on the page. As you learned in Chapter 22, the **alt** attribute should contain descriptive information about the image. Required for EPUB validation, **alt** text is used by assistive technologies to make content accessible to people with disabilities. The **img** tag may or may not include image width and height attributes. InDesign incorporates image dimensions into a CSS rule rather than coding them into the HTML when it exports to EPUB.

```
<img src="images/cheshire_cat.jpg" alt="The Cheshire Cat" width="316"
height="213" />
```

A definition list has two visible elements that alternate on the page: the term being defined <dt> and the definition of that term <dd>. Being block level elements, they appear on separate lines with the <dd> element slightly indented from the <dt>. The collection of terms and their definitions are wrapped in opening and closing <dl> tags indicating the start and termination of the list.

```
<dl>
    <dt>This is a definition term in a definition list </dt>
    <dd>This is a definition definition in a definition list</dd>
    <dt>This is a second definition term</dt>
    <dd>This is a second definition definition</dd>
</dl>
```

```
<pre>     This is preformatted text (contained in the &lt;pre&gt; tag)

    By default, preformatted text uses a monospaced font.
        Preformatted text also respects
                white space (spaces, returns and tabs&#8212;
        although tabs are not always rendered reliably
                on the page.)</pre>
```

```
<p>This is a paragraph that contains <!--beginning of the code tag- an
inline element--><code>content inside the code tag.</code><!--end of the
code tag--> Note the default monospaced font.</p>
```

```
<blockquote>
    <p>This content is contained in a paragraph within a blockquote tag.
    The blockquote tag is used to set off a long quote and is traditionally
    rendered as an indented block with default right and left margins of
    about 40 pixels each.</p>
</blockquote>
```

A tour of your first HTML document wouldn't be complete without a look at the opening lines of code on the page. This and the code inside the **<head>** tag are probably the most intimidating in the entire HTML document. Don't be too concerned about them though. InDesign adds them for you automatically when it converts your InDesign document to EPUB and it's unlikely that you'll need to make any edits to them other than possibly changing a link to a stylesheet. Here's what the initial lines of the document look like:

```
<?xml version="1.0" encoding="UTF-8"?>
<!DOCTYPE html PUBLIC "-//W3C//DTD XHTML 1.1//EN"
"http://www.w3.org/TR/xhtml11/DTD/xhtml11.dtd">
```

This code precedes the opening HTML tag and is actually XML rather than HTML. It's obviously not written in lowercase but the opening and closing chevrons as well as the quoted attributes are characteristic of both the XML and HTML markup languages.

While it looks somewhat impenetrable, the code is really just identifying the flavor of HTML being used in the document and which set of standards-based rules govern its structure. In the case of XHTML documents, the first line explains that the rules originate in xml version "1.0." XML stands for Extensible Markup Language. UTF-8 encoding means that any character in the Unicode character set can be represented in the document.

> **NOTE:** The EPUB 2.0.1 specification is based on XHTML. XHTML is a hybrid of XML and HTML. The EPUB 3.0 specification is based on HTML5.

Next comes the DOCTYPE declaration saying this is an HTML document that follows the rules and patterns established in the XHTML 1.1 DTD (Document Type Definition.) The next portion of the code is the URL where the actual DTD can be found. This "pre-HTML" code is required in order for your HTML or EPUB 2.0.1 documents to validate.

The next line of code is also required and, thankfully, it's more code written by InDesign that you won't have to edit. It looks like this:

```
<html xmlns="http://www.w3.org/1999/xhtml" xml:lang="en">
```

This is actually the opening HTML tag. As you can see, it has a bit more information than the skeleton HTML tag shown in the earlier example but it follows the standard tag structure illustrated on page 349. As discussed earlier, it tells the browser to start interpreting HTML.

xmlns stands for XML Name Space and is followed by a link to the W3C which is the organization that developed and maintains the standards for HTML and CSS.

xml:lang="en" tells the browser that the document is written in English.

The next code block is the **<head>** of the document and while it might vary somewhat from EPUB to EPUB, it will look something like this:

```
<head>
    <title>HTML Sampler</title>
    <link href="html_sampler.css" rel="stylesheet" type="text/css" />
</head>
```

Inside the **<head>** container is the **<title>** tag. Remember that the contents of the **<title>** tag appear in the browser title bar rather than on the actual page.

Following the **<title>** tag in this document is the **<link>** tag which links to an external stylesheet. The **"href"** attribute (hypertext reference) points to a stylesheet named **html_sampler.css**.

"rel", the second attribute in the link tag, defines the relationship of the linked file to the document—in this case, the linked file is a stylesheet. The third and last property of the link tag, the **"type"** property, identifies the type of file targeted by the link as a css text file.

Note that the link tag doesn't have a separate closing tag. Its information is self-contained and the tag is terminated by a space and a forward slash followed by the closing chevron.

The head of the document may also contain **<meta>** tags that provide additional information about the document itself.

7. When you've finished perusing the code, close out of the browser and return to InDesign to complete the exercise.

Links

Links are at the very foundation of HTML—connecting everything on the web to everything else and enabling interactivity. Like buttons, the genius of links is that they can detect an assortment of user interactions—triggering events such as when a mouse is moved onto or off of a link or when the mouse is depressed (poor mouse) or released. Also like buttons, the user events can be tied to any number of actions—from the familiar opening of another page to on-page events such as showing or hiding content on the page.

Links rely on two components—the link itself and its destination. An HTML link destination can be to an anchor in the same document or to another document entirely. Using a # sign as the link destination, you can create a link that in fact goes nowhere at all, but that can still detect and trigger actions in response to user interaction.

The HTML link or hotspot on the page is wrapped in an opening and closing anchor tag like this:

```
<a href="http://www.interactive-indesign.com">Check out the Interactive InDesign book</a>
```

The **a** stands for anchor and **href** stands for hypertext reference, which is the path to the link destination. **http** stands for hypertext transfer protocol and it's telling the browser to interpret the document at the destination as a hypertext document. The entire web address is representative of what is commonly known as a URL—a Uniform or Universal Resource Locator—in other words, an absolute path.

Paths come in two flavors: absolute and relative. Think of an absolute path as comparable to geographic coordinates. If given the latitude and longitude for a specific location, you can locate that destination on a map regardless of where you yourself might be. For example, the latitude and longitude of Austin, TX—30° 16′ 0″ N / 97° 44′ 34″ W—would be comparable to an absolute path.

In contrast, a relative location is expressed relative to the document where the link originates. In geographical terms, we could say that Austin is 1663 driving miles southwest of Philadelphia. In such an example, unless you know where Philadelphia is, it's unlikely that you'd find your way to Austin. Most often, links within a site are described using relative paths with absolute paths reserved for external pages.

A relative path to a file named contact_us.html that is located in the same folder as an html page that links to it would look like this:

<a href="contact_us.html">Get in touch</a>

Paths: Relatively Speaking

Tracing a path from one document to another often requires jumping in and out of multiple folders.

A hierarchy of files that a link may be required to navigate.

Based on the file hierarchy in the previous figure, to display the mi_logo.gif image in the index.html page, the image tag would look like this:

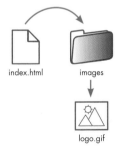

<img src="images/logo.gif">

The / after the images folder name indicates that the link from the index page must jump inside the images folder to locate the logo file.

If the linked file were located inside a hierarchy of folders, the name of each nested folder would be separated by a forward slash like this:

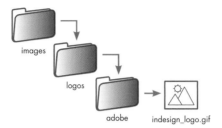

images/logos/adobe/indesign_logo.gif

The path above indicates that it's necessary to jump into a folder called "images" and then into a folder named "logos," and finally into a folder called "adobe" in order to link to the image file called indesign_logo.gif.

Use ../ in a path when it's necessary to jump out of a folder to get to another file. Continuing with the previous example, the code for the tag that would make the indesign_icon.gif image appear in the indesign.html document would look like this:

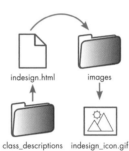

<img src="../images/indesign_icon.gif">

The path would first have to jump out of the class_descriptions folder and then jump into the images folder to locate the indesign_icon.gif file.

A link from indesign.html to index.html, would have to jump out of the class_descriptions folder to reach the index page. With the word "home" appearing as hypertext on the page, the anchor tag would look like this:

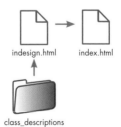

<a href="../index.html">home</a>

To turn the mi_logo.gif image in the indesign.html document into a link to the index.html page, the anchor tag for the link would have to wrap around the image tag and the HTML would look like this:

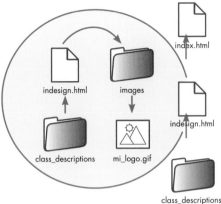

```
<a href="../index.html">
    <img src="../images/mi_logo.gif" alt="Mira Images logo" />
</a>
```

In contrast, a link on indesign_icon.gif from index.html page to indesign.html would look like this:

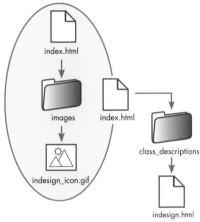

```
<a href="class_descriptions/indesign.html">
    <img src="images/indesign_icon.gif" alt="InDesign icon" />
</a>
```

For long, scrolling document pages, it's often helpful to provide a link from the bottom of the page back to the top. To link within an HTML document, you must first create a destination anchor. Destinations can be created in one of two ways. You can create a code anchor on the page that has no visible appearance like this:

```
<a name="top" id="top"></a>
```

Or, you can assign an ID to an existing element on the page which you could then target as a destination:

```
<p id="top">This paragraph is named top</p>
```

The reference to an internal anchor is indicated by a # sign and looks like this:

```
<a href="#top">This is a link to the anchor named top</a>
```

Styling with CSS

NOTE: Cascading style sheets are so named because of the way properties are inherited between elements and the styles applied to them. For example, formatting applied to the body element is inherited by all the elements it contains, unless they are explicitly styled otherwise. An <em> tag inside a <p> tag inside a <div> tag could actually inherit formatting from styles applied to the <body>, <div>, <p> and <em> tags. As you might imagine, things can get a little complicated if you don't have a way to keep track of what's affecting what. Dreamweaver's CSS panel is a great tool for tracing the style cascade as it affects the elements in your document.

CSS style definitions can reside in the body of your HTML code, in the head of the HTML document, in a linked external stylesheet, or any combination of the three. When you export to EPUB from InDesign, it generates an external stylesheet and links that document to every HTML page in the EPUB. This is a wonderful thing in that you can make a global change to your EPUB simply by changing the rules in the stylesheet. There is no restriction on the number of stylesheets you can attach to a page and InDesign does have a provision to add stylesheets of your choosing. Be aware however that multiple stylesheets bring with them additional complexity and may cause unpredictable results. That said, given that certain eReaders render code very differently from others, you may elect to develop multiple stylesheets, each tailored to the idiosyncrasies of specific target devices. If you want to get fancy after exporting, you can add some code to direct various eReaders to pull their styling from the appropriate stylesheet using something called a media query.

It's important to be aware that the formatting you apply in InDesign is unlikely to translate perfectly when exported to EPUB HTML. This is partly a result of the inherent differences between print and CSS/HTML styling, partly due to the way InDesign maps (or doesn't map) its style definitions to CSS and partly due to the display limitations of various eReaders. Learning how InDesign translates style definitions to EPUB, and then how the CSS styles are rendered (or not) in target eReaders is critical to producing an EPUB that performs according to your expectations. As with any other digital development workflow, testing early and often is absolutely essential.

In the HTML examples earlier in the chapter, you were introduced to the syntax for assigning a class to an HTML tag, i.e., **class = "className"** is inserted after the HTML tag selector and before the close of the tag. The resulting code looks like this: **<div class="box">** Classes are essentially a CSS version of InDesign styles, capturing and applying formatting in the same way that style definitions do in InDesign. A wonderful feature of CSS class rules is that the same rule can be applied to pretty much any HTML element. Depending on the element properties, however, the style attributes may or may not have a visible effect.

NOTE: For a rather academic explanation of media queries and how to work with them, check out what the folks who wrote the rules have to say at: http://www.w3.org/TR/css3-mediaqueries/

In the last exercise, you saw that the same **"orange"** class was applied to both the **span** element and to the paragraph nested inside the **div**. In both cases, the text to which the class was applied turned orange on the page. In the example file, the **"orange"** style rule is defined in a linked external CSS stylesheet called **html_sampler.css**. When you export to EPUB from InDesign, you can instruct InDesign to export your paragraph, character and object style definitions to rules in an external stylesheet—similar to the external style sheet containing the **"orange"** rule—and apply the rules to your HTML content. While classes are not the only way to apply CSS styling to HTML elements, the code that InDesign generates relies on them almost exclusively.

CSS Syntax

As with HTML, the basic syntax for writing CSS is quite simple. Unlike HTML, no "introductory" code is required before launching into the actual style definitions.

Each CSS rule begins with a selector. There are a variety of selector types you may encounter in your post-InDesign code editing so we've outlined them below.

Following the selector, a CSS style rule can contain multiple declarations, with each declaration consisting of a single property and value pair terminated by a semicolon. The collected declarations are enclosed in curly braces and together with the selector combine to define the rule.

CSS Rule Examples

Selector Types	Selector	Declaration
HTML element	p	{font-family:"Futura Std Light", sans-serif; font-size:1em;}
Multiple elements	th, td	{borderstyle:solid; border-width:1px;}
Descendent	li a	{color: #F39; text-decoration: none;}
Class	.orange	{color:#F63;}
ID	#box	{padding:15px; width:50%; border:thin solid #F63;}

HTML Element: CSS can be used to globally redefine the appearance of an HTML selector. A rule that formats the **<p>** tag for example, automatically applies to every **<p>** tag on every page to which the stylesheet containing the rule is applied.

Multiple Elements: You can apply the same CSS formatting to multiple elements at the same time by separating the element selectors with a comma.

Descendent: A descendent selector references a nested element and is more specific than a rule formatting a single element on its own. Rather than affecting all anchors in the site, the descendent rule **li a** only targets anchors occurring within a list.

Class: Classes always begin with a period and can be applied to any element. You can also apply the same class to multiple elements. In the code example on page 354 for instance, the "orange" class was applied to both a <span> and a <p> tag. Unlike CSS rules using HTML elements as selectors, CSS classes must be explicitly assigned to the elements they style. The code to assign a class looks like any other property value pair: **<p class="orange">my paragraph</p>**

ID: When you explicitly assign a name to a page element (see the link anchor example on page 359) you are assigning an ID. IDs are generally used to identify elements that appear only once on a page such as a **<div>** that might be used as a sidebar or footer.

Each CSS rule begins with a selector. Since InDesign works primarily with class selectors, we'll focus our attention on classes for now. In a stylesheet, a class selector always starts with a period followed by the selector name. The collected rule declarations are enclosed by curly braces and each declaration in the rule is terminated by a semicolon.

To make your code more readable and easier to trouble shoot, you might choose to separate your style declarations onto multiple lines. The declarations in the .box class defined below are the same as those in the #box ID example on the previous page. It makes no difference whether you write your rules in one line or many as long as you're sure to terminate each declaration with a semi-colon.

```
.box {
    padding: 15px; /*padding is a CSS version of InDesign's text frame inset
    spacing. Inset spacing in an anchored InDesign text frame does translate
    to CSS.*/
    width: 50%;
    margin-right: auto;
    margin-left: auto;
    border: thin solid #F63;
}
```

The CSS Box Model

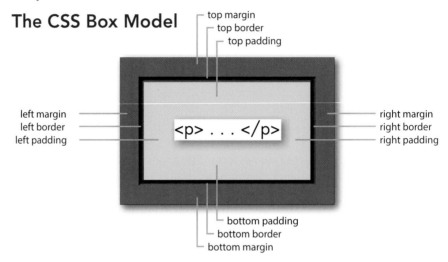

One of the things that makes CSS such a powerful formatting tool is the imaginary
box it imposes on each HTML element. With the ability to set separate values for
top, right, bottom and left, the element is surrounded by and separated from the
bounds of its box by padding. A border surrounds the box and the box is offset
from the surrounding content by outside margins.

CSS Padding would equate to inset spacing set in InDesign through the Text Frame
Options dialog. InDesign maps inset spacing values to CSS padding only if the
object with the inset is an anchored object. If you want space between the border
of an unanchored text frame and its contents, you'll need to manually add padding
in your stylesheet. When specifying box properties, reference to the box sides is
made in several ways. If assigning a value to each side of the box individually, you
start with the top and then proceed clockwise. The sequence is always top, right,
bottom, left. To assign one value to the top and bottom and another value to the
right and left, you could use two values—the top and bottom value first, followed
by the value for the right and left. If you want all the values to be the same, you can
assign just that one value.

```
.box {
    padding: 5px 20px;/*top and bottom padding:5px,
    right and left padding:20px*/
    margin: 0px 20px 15px 30px;/*top margin:0px, right margin:20px,
    bottom margin:15px, left margin:30px*/
    border: thin solid #F00;/*all borders thin, solid and red*/
}
```

Specificity

Assuming that you include styles in your EPUB export, when you map an InDesign style to an HTML tag and also apply a class, a separate CSS rule is created for each InDesign paragraph style. For example, if you were to map an InDesign style to an **h1** tag and apply a class named **magenta**, InDesign would generate a rule with an **h1.magenta** selector. The rule would then apply only to **<h1>** tags to which a **magenta** class were assigned. Similarly, an InDesign style mapped to a **p** tag with a **magenta** class would result in a **p.magenta** rule that would affect only **<p>** tags to which a **magenta** class were applied. The inclusion of the HTML tag in the CSS selector gives the rule greater specificity than a rule with a selector defined by the class name alone. Despite sharing the same class name, the rules could have entirely unrelated definitions.

The more specific a rule, the greater the strength it has to override other rules in the cascade of style properties. For example, in a stylesheet with both an **h1.magenta** rule and a plain **.magenta** class, an **<h1>** tag with a **.magenta** class assignment will employ the **h1.magenta** rule. This is because, in relation to the **<h1>** tag, the **h1.magenta** rule has a greater specificity than the **.magenta** rule.

Should you want the option of applying a common attribute—such as a magenta color—to multiple elements, a less specific class rule provides the perfect solution. The same **.magenta** class defining only the color property could be used to change the color of **em**, **strong** and **a** elements for example and, unless additional styling were otherwise applied, the default formatting of the elements would be retained. The contents of each element would be colored magenta but the **em** content would be italicized, the **strong** content would be bold and the **a** content would be underlined. Since InDesign's export tagging feature associates all class definitions to specific selectors rather than generating more generic class rules, you would need to edit your EPUB CSS after export to create a stand-alone class.

Relativity

InDesign translates font size from paragraph and character styles to ems in the CSS rules it generates. An em is a relative unit of measure originally defined by the width of a capital M in a given typeface. One em is now generally understood to be equal to the point size of a font. As text is scaled in an eReader, anything that's sized with ems is scaled along with it. Since flowable EPUB is all about scalability, it's recommended that you use ems and percentages rather than pixels or points to specify font-size, text-indent, line-height, width, height, margin and padding. To scale elements relative to the display instead of font size, use percentages rather than ems.

In the CSS it generates during EPUB export, InDesign translates font sizes to ems.

12 pt = 1em	20 pt = 1.5em
14 pt = 1.167em	22 pt = 1.833em
16 pt = 1.333em	24 pt = 1.833em
18 pt = 1.5em	

Line-height is expressed in percentages. InDesign's default auto leading of 120% appears in the CSS as **line-height: 1.2;**

InDesign's EPUB HTML & CSS

TIP: Having InDesign export your EPUB with your custom stylesheet rather than adding it to your publication after the fact saves you the trouble of updating other files that itemize the EPUB contents.

NOTE: You'll learn more about export tagging starting with page 367 of this chapter.

When you export from InDesign to EPUB or HTML you can map your paragraph, character, and object styles to HTML tags and optionally assign classes to those tags. In the Export Tagging category of the Paragraph Style Options dialog, you can choose the **p** tag or any of the six headers from the Tag dropdown list, or you can manually enter your choice of tag selector instead.

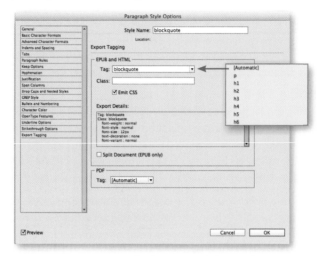

You can map your paragraph, character and object styles to HTML tags from the Export Tagging section of the Styles panels.

InDesign's default list of export tagging selectors for Character styles includes:

    <strong> (bold by default)

    <em> (italic by default) and

    <span> (no inherent default formatting)

InDesign CC also enables you to map object styles to **div** or **span** tags.

When you use InDesign's Export Tagging feature to map a style to an HTML tag but don't also assign a class, no CSS rule corresponding to that InDesign style is generated in the CSS stylesheet. As a result, any special formatting associated with the mapped InDesign style will not be translated to your EPUB and the default HTML formatting will prevail. This can be a good thing if you prefer to code your CSS rules yourself. In fact, if you really are a do-it-yourselfer, one of the big improvements in InDesign CC is that it allows you to export your EPUB without any stylesheet at all or with only a stylesheet (or multiple stylesheets) of your choosing. This is really quite a good thing in that it supports an iterative workflow where you can go back and forth between InDesign and your code editor to perfect your CSS. Once you have InDesign styles and a stylesheet that perform to your standards, you can use that stylesheet as a jumping off point for future EPUB publications. Huzzah!

If you'd prefer to have InDesign do the heavy lifting and translate your InDesign styling to CSS—or at least provide you with an initial stylesheet to which you can make your refinements—add a class name when you make your tag assignment in Export Tagging. When you export your file to EPUB, be sure to check the Generate CSS checkbox in the Advanced tab of the EPUB Export Options dialog to have InDesign do its magic.

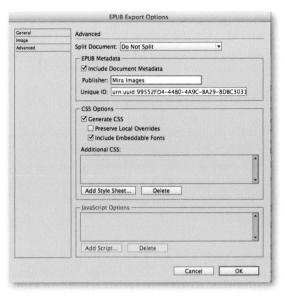

The Advanced tab of the EPUB Export Options allows you to choose whether to have InDesign translate your style definitions—to the best of its ability—to a CSS stylesheet in your exported EPUB, and/or to add a stylesheet(s) of your own.

While InDesign can generate a usable and valid EPUB, it's just a fact of life that the HTML and CSS code it writes won't necessarily provide exactly the results you're looking for. Knowing the nuances of InDesign's code export can help you:

- Define, name, and apply styles in InDesign in a way that makes editing of the exported HTML and CSS code easier.

- Understand how and why certain exported elements render the way they do and how to change the code to adjust their appearance.

InDesign-Generated EPUB HTML & CSS

Now that you've had a chance to see what the default HTML elements look like, and have checked out the underlying HTML code, you're in a better position to recognize some of the possible issues you may encounter as a result of InDesign's default CSS.

When you select the Generate CSS option in the EPUB Export Options dialog, InDesign generates a stylesheet with five default style rules—whether or not you've applied styles to your InDesign document or even if the InDesign document you export to EPUB is literally a blank page. You'll explore those five rules and what they do in the following exercise.

Exercise 24.2: Exploring the EPUB Style Sheet

1. Navigate to the chapter_24_exercises folder and **open ex24_2_start.indd**.

   The exercise file is a copy of the default style rules InDesign exports with every EPUB for which it generates a stylesheet. The color highlights have been added to make the code easier to decipher. The selectors, curly braces and semicolons are highlighted in magenta, the attributes in dark blue and the attribute values in light blue.

2. Take a look at the rules to understand their syntax and the following explanations of what they do.

```
body, div, dl, dt, dd, h1, h2, h3, h4, h5, h6, p, pre, code, blockquote {
    margin:0;
    padding:0;
    border-width:0;
}
```

The first rule in the stylesheet (shown above) strips out the default margins and padding around a number of block level HTML elements. This is actually common practice when setting up a stylesheet in that it allows you to start from scratch and apply white space to page elements as needed. The effect is illustrated below in the comparison of header tags shown with and without the InDesign stylesheet applied.

Default HTML formatting for <h> elements with no styles applied.

Appearance of <h> elements as exported from InDesign with InDesign's default style sheet. Notice that the default margins and padding have been stripped.

TIP: To generate the cleanest possible code when exporting to EPUB, ALL your InDesign styling should ALWAYS be applied using saved styles.

The second style rule applies a one pixel border to all table cells. Regardless of any table or cell styles you've applied or manual adjustments you've made in InDesign, the stroke settings you apply to table cells do not at this time carry over to an exported EPUB. Cell insets do translate however, and will appear in the stylesheet with the cell style name you've assigned in InDesign—or as a style override if you've styled the cell manually and have checked the Preserve Local Overrides in the EPUB Export Options dialog. The style rule responsible for the one pixel table cell border looks like this:

```
td, th {
    border-style:solid;
    border-width:1px;
}
```

To change the weight or appearance of the borders of the table cells, you would need to edit this rule, and possibly create new style rules to apply different appearances to different cells. Remember that the CSS box model enables you to assign individual values to top, right, bottom, and left margins, padding, and borders.

```
table {
    border-collapse:collapse;
}
```

The third rule (above) collapses the cell borders for adjacent table cells to a single line rather than displaying separate borders for each cell.

```
body {
    -epub-hyphens:auto;
    -webkit-hyphens:auto;
}
```

For devices that support it, the fourth rule (above) is intended to enable hyphenation throughout the EPUB.

```
@page {
    margin : 20px 20px 20px 20px;
}
```

The @page selector in the fifth and final default rule defines a page block. The rule sets the margins of the page block according to the margin values you specify in the EPUB export dialog.

3. When you've finished exploring the rules, close the document without saving to complete the exercise.

Export Tagging

InDesign makes it possible to map styles on a style-by-style basis through the paragraph, character and object styles panels or you can map multiple styles at the same time through the Edit All Export Tags dialog. In the next exercise, you'll become familiar with InDesign's export tagging feature and gain some insight into working with CSS classes.

Exercise 24.3: Export Tagging and CSS Classes

1. Navigate to the chapter_24_exercises folder, open **ex24_3.start.indd** and save it as ex24_3.indd.

   A paragraph style named "h1" is applied to the header and a style named "body" is applied to the body text. There are three character styles defined in the document:

   - **magenta**: sets the character color to magenta
   - **strong**: bolds the text and sets the character color to magenta
   - **em**: italicizes the text and sets the character color to magenta

   You'll use InDesign's export tagging feature to map your styles to HTML tags—taking advantage of the default HTML formatting—and assign the magenta class to those tags.

2. Position the Type tool cursor in the document header and click the 🔲 icon in the Panel Dock to expand the Paragraph Styles panel (or go to Window > Styles > Paragraph Styles.) Right-Click/Ctrl-Click the highlighted h1 paragraph style and choose Edit "h1".

3. Choose Export Tagging from the categories list at the left of the Paragraph Style Options dialog.

   With the Export Tagging Tag option set to [Automatic], when the document is exported to EPUB, InDesign assigns a <p> tag with a class called **h1** (from the paragraph style name) to content styled in InDesign with the h1 paragraph style. Scroll through the Export Details to see the complete rule for the h1 class.

> NOTE: If you enter the tag selectors manually in the Export Tagging Tag field, you can export from InDesign to other tags including **blockquote**, the **code** tag or preformatted text. The **blockquote** and **pre** selectors can be mapped to a paragraph style and the **code** selector can be mapped to a character style. These tags are also included in the HTML Sampler in Exercise 24.1 (along with a definition list) so you can see what they look like.

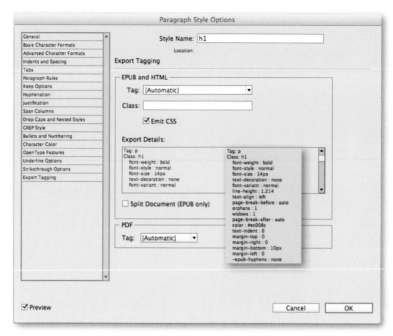

When exporting to EPUB, InDesign's default behavior is to assign a <p> tag and a class with the same name as the InDesign paragraph style.

The CSS rule for the class is unnecessarily long since a number of its declarations make no change to the default formatting. In exercise 24.5 you'll remove the extraneous declarations to refine the rule.

4. Choose h1 from the Tag dropdown and if necessary, check the Emit CSS checkbox.

    If you wanted to map the paragraph style to the <h1> tag without a class assignment, you would leave the Emit CSS checkbox unchecked.

5. Type "magenta" in the Class: text field and press Tab to register your change.

6. Click OK to close the Paragraph Styles panel.

7. Position the Type tool cursor in the "bold and magenta" text on the document and expand the Character Styles panel (A in the Panel Dock.) Double-Click the strong character style to open the Character Style Options dialog and then choose Export Tagging from the category list at the left.

8. Select strong from the Tag dropdown, type "magenta" in the Class text field and if necessary, check the Emit CSS checkbox. Press Tab to commit your changes and then click OK to close the dialog. (Remember that by default, content of the strong element is displayed on the HTML page in bold.)

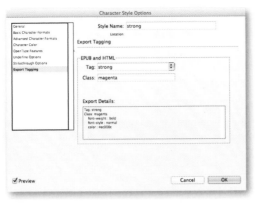

The same CSS class name can be applied to a variety of HTML elements.

9. From the Character Styles panel menu, choose Edit All Export Tags.

10. Assign a **<p>** tag to the body style and a **<span>** tag to the magenta style. For the remaining styles, match the tag to the style name: h1 to h1, em to em—text in the HTML em tag is italicized by default—and strong to strong. Assign a class called "body" to the **<p>** tag and a class called "magenta" to all the other tags. Deselect the Emit CSS checkbox for the [Basic Paragraph], [Basic Graphics Frame] and [Basic Text Frame] styles. Click OK to apply your settings and to close the dialog.

You can set the export tagging options for multiple paragraph, character and object styles at the same time from the Edit All Export Tags dialog.

11. Press Ctrl+E/Command+E to open the Export dialog. Choose EPUB from the Format dropdown at the bottom of the dialog and navigate to the chapter_24_exercises folder. Save the file as **ex24_3.epub**.

When the Preserve Local Overrides checkbox is deselected, manually applied formatting and style overrides are not included in the exported EPUB code.

12. When the EPUB Export Options dialog opens, if it's not already checked, check the View EPUB after Exporting checkbox. Select Advanced from the category list at the left of the dialog and deselect both the Preserve Local Overrides and Include Embeddable Fonts checkboxes. Enter your name in the Publisher text field and click OK to export the EPUB.

While InDesign CC allows you to assign the same class name to different HTML elements, it generates an alert to inform you of the collision of class definitions before proceeding with the EPUB export:

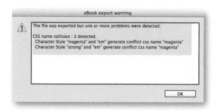

The file was exported but one or more problems were detected: CSS name collision: 2 detected. Character Style "magenta" and "em" generate conflict css name "magenta." Character Style "strong" and "em" generate conflict css name "magenta."

Whereas InDesign CS6 would take it upon itself to automatically rename conflicting style rules, if you have mapped the same tag and class to multiple styles, InDesign CC simply generates multiple rules using the same selector.

13. After viewing the EPUB in your default eReader to see that the magenta elements are properly styled, close the reader, return to InDesign, and close the InDesign file.

Editing InDesign HTML and CSS

Next you'll check out the HTML and CSS code InDesign created in the last exercise and learn how to streamline it a bit. We'll be using Dreamweaver CC to work with the code. If you don't have Dreamweaver, you can use a code editor of your choosing or even a plain text editor to make your changes—just be careful to dot all your i's and cross all your t's and, most of all, put all your quotation marks in the proper places.

Exercise 24.4: Tweaking InDesign HTML

1. If you feel inspired to work with the EPUB you just exported, crack it open now. If you'd rather just use the files we've provided, navigate to the chapter_24_exercises folder, and drill down through the **ex24_3_start** and **OEBPS** folders to locate the **ex24_3.xhtml** file. If you have Dreamweaver or another code editor on your system, use that to open the file, otherwise, use a plain text editor—not Word (since it may add a bunch of extraneous code.)

If you're editing the code outside of Dreamweaver, skip to page 374.

2. At the upper left corner of the Dreamweaver document window are four buttons: Code, Split, Design and Live. Click the Split button to display the HTML source code at the left of the window and the design view of the document at the right. Mouse over the vertical divider between the two windows and when your cursor changes to a double-sided arrow, drag right or left to adjust the relative size of the windows.

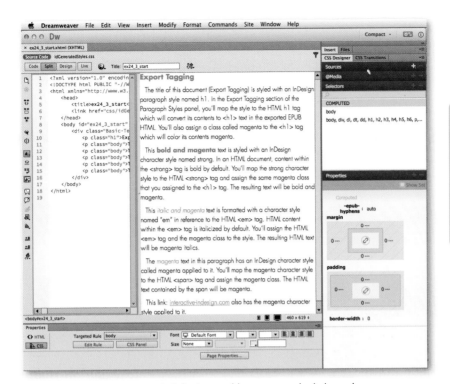

Dreamweaver's Split view enables you to see both the code
and the appearance of your HTML page at the same time.

NOTE:
Dreamweaver CC. was used for the Dreamweaver screenshots in this chapter but while the interface looks somewhat different, earlier versions of Dreamweaver work just as well for purposes of this exercise.

InDesign actually did a great job with the EPUB export and generated clean HTML code according to the tag and class assignments made in the export tagging dialog. The only changes we'll make to the HTML is to remove the body class from the paragraphs, assign the magenta class directly to the anchor tag and remove the extraneous span tag in the anchor. Is this change to the code in any way essential? Absolutely not. The EPUB would function perfectly well as it is. The only visual difference will be that by assigning the magenta class directly to the anchor tag, the underline color of the link will change from the default blue to magenta.

3. In the design window, Double-Click the word "Export" in the document header to select it. Look at the code view pane to see that the word "Export" is highlighted and that the code for the corresponding **<h1>** tag reads as follows:

<h1 class="magenta">Export Tagging</h1>

TIP: In Dreamweaver, selecting content in the design window selects the same content in the code window.

4. Click through the other magenta text in the design window and check out the HTML code to see how the magenta style is applied to the tags. Then, in Design view, select the magenta link text. Click the Live View button (in the group of 4 View buttons) at the upper left of the document window to see the link underline turn blue.

When viewed in the eReader, the link underline was blue. In Dreamweaver's design view however the link underline is magenta. To get a more accurate view of the way the page will truly render, it's always a good idea to check out the page in Live View.

The link text is contained by a **<span>** tag to which the magenta class is applied. You're going to apply the class directly to the **<a>** tag.

TIP: Press Ctrl+X/ Command+X to cut selected text. This shortcut works across many applications including but not limited to Adobe and Microsoft programs.

5. With your cursor in the link text in the design window, go to Edit > Find and Replace.

6. Ensure that Current Document is chosen from the Find in: dropdown and choose Specific Tag from the Search dropdown. If the word "span" doesn't automatically appear in the field to its right, type it there now. If the dialog displays a dropdown on the next line that says With Attribute, click the ➖ at its left to delete it. Choose Strip Tag from the Action dropdown.

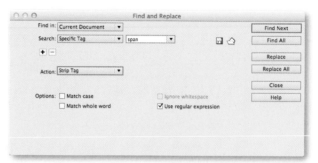

Dreamweaver has a very robust Find and Replace feature that makes it an excellent tool for tweaking and cleaning EPUB code exported by InDesign.

7. Click the Find Next button at the right of the dialog.

The span tag formatting the paragraph text with the magenta class is selected.

8. Click the Find Next button again to select the **<span>** tag that's nested in the anchor tag. Click the Replace button and then click Close to exit the Find and Replace dialog.

The **<span>** tag is removed, along with the magenta class, and the link turns blue in the design view window. Now you'll apply the class directly to the anchor tag.

NOTE: Even though InDesign did not generate a CSS rule for the Basic-Text-Frame style per your instruction, it still assigned the non-existent class to the div tag that wraps contents of the page.

9. Position your cursor in the link text in the design view window.

At the lower left of the document window is a sequence of HTML tags that reflect the location of the anchor in the document structure. In this case, the anchor tag is nested inside a paragraph styled with the body class, which is inside a div styled with the Basic-Text-Frame class which is inside the **<body>** tag.

`<body#ex24_3> <div.Basic-Text-Frame> <p.body> <a>`

Dreamweaver displays a hierarchy of tags at the bottom of the document window that reflect the placement of selected content within the document structure.

NOTE: The underline of the anchor tag was initially blue because the magenta class was applied to the text within the span rather than to the anchor itself. After assigning the class to the anchor, it remains its default color due to the way the rules in the stylesheet are defined. You'll make the necessary adjustments to the stylesheet in the next exercise.

10. Click the **<a>** in the tag hierarchy to select the code for the anchor tag.

Located by default at the bottom of the Dreamweaver interface is the Properties panel which contains many essential controls and is comparable in function to the InDesign Control panel. You'll use the Properties panel to assign the magenta class to the anchor tag.

11. With the HTML button active at the far left of the Properties panel, choose magenta from the Class dropdown. Save the document and be sure to keep the file name the same (File > Save.)

One way to assign an existing class in Dreamweaver is to select the tag you want to target and then choose from the Class dropdown in the Properties panel.

Next, you'll use Find and Replace to strip the extraneous **body** class from the **<p>** tags.

12. Press Ctrl+F/Command+F to open the Find and Replace dialog. Set Find In: to Current Document and set Search to Specific Tag: p. Click the ⊞ button to add a search criterion and choose With Attribute from the dropdown. Type "class" in the attribute field, leave the = sign and type "body" in the field for the attribute value. Set the Action to Remove Attribute and type "class" in the attribute field to its right. Your settings should match the screenshot below.

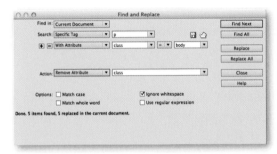

The Find and Replace settings that will remove the extraneous class assignments.

13. Press Find All and just above the Properties panel, Dreamweaver displays the Search panel with a list of all five instances of the <p> tag that meet your search criteria. Inspect the list to confirm that you want to change the targeted elements and then click Replace All in the Find and Replace dialog.

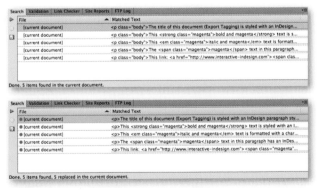

Dreamweaver's Find All command returns a hyperlinked list of your search results for you to review before making global changes.

14. Double-Click the Search tab to collapse the results pane.

15. Select and delete **class="Basic-Text-Frame"** from the <div> tag that immediately follows the opening body tag, and save the file. (Ctrl+S/ Command+S.) Keep the file open in Dreamweaver for the next lesson.

If editing the code outside of Dreamweaver...

1. Select and cut: **class="magenta"** from the **<span>** tag. Position your cursor after the closing quotation mark of the href attribute value in the anchor tag code and type a space. Paste the copied code (Ctrl+V/Command+V.)

   The resulting anchor tag should look like this:

   <a href="http://www.interactive-indesign.com" class="magenta" >

2. Select and delete the opening and closing **<span>** tags nested inside the **<a>** tag.

3. Select and delete **class="Basic-Text-Frame"** from the **<div>** tag that immediately follows the opening body tag.

4. To finish editing the HTML, select and delete: **class="body"** from each of the five instances of the **<p>** tag. Save the file with the same name and keep it open.

Exercise 24.5: Tweaking InDesign CSS

One of the awesome things about Dreamweaver, and there really are quite a few, is that it gives you easy access to linked code files such as stylesheets, includes, and external scripts. With code or split view active, you can click the name of a linked file at the top left of the document window and the code in the linked file is displayed for editing. If you'd rather not edit the code manually, Dreamweaver also has a rich set of WYSIWYG tools you can use to create and edit your CSS; but for now, you'll make a couple simple manual changes to the code to see how easy it really is.

1. If you're editing outside of Dreamweaver, navigate to chapter_24_exercises > **ex24_3_start > OEBPS** and locate **idGeneratedStyles.css**. If you're using Dreamweaver, click idGeneratedStyles.css at the upper left of the document window, (just above the four View buttons) to show the stylesheet in the code window.

Dreamweaver makes it easy to access and edit linked code files through clickable tabs across the top of the document window.

2. Scroll to the bottom of the stylesheet if necessary in order to see the h1.magenta style and the other magenta rules below it.

   Notice that InDesign created separate rules for each of your InDesign paragraph and character styles. As they're defined, each rule is specific to the tag to which it's applied. As you can see, this allows each rule to be defined differently despite the use of the same class name. The **h1.magenta** rule applies only to **<h1>** tags to which the magenta class is assigned. Likewise with the other magenta rules—the way the selectors are named makes each rule tag-specific.

   In this particular example, with the exception of the **<h1>** tag, the objective is to have each tag retain its default attributes but to be magenta in color. The beauty of CSS classes is that the same class can be applied to multiple HTML elements. You'll rewrite the CSS code to make it all work.

3. Select and delete the **p.** that precedes **body** in the **p.body** rule. Delete the extraneous declarations in the body rule so that the resulting rule looks like this:

```
body {
    font-family:"Myriad Pro", sans-serif;
    font-size:1em;
    line-height:1.417;
    margin-bottom:10px;
    orphans:1;
    text-indent:13px;
    widows:1;
}
```

Since everything in the document occurs within the body tag, the rule applied to the body will be inherited by other elements on the page (depending on their default formatting) unless otherwise explicitly defined.

4. Select and delete the entire **strong.magenta** rule including the closing curly brace.

5. Select and delete the entire **em.magenta** rule.

6. Select and delete the word "span" from the **span.magenta** rule. Be sure to leave the period untouched.

7. Select and delete the period and the word "magenta" from the **h1.magenta** rule.

The **h1.magenta** rule applies only to **h1** tags to which the **.magenta** class is assigned. By removing the class, the **h1** rule applies to any and all **h1** tags on any page to which the CSS file is linked. In effect, you've created a new default appearance for the tag. Next you'll take a minute to clean up the **h1** rule.

8. Select and delete the extraneous portions of the h1 rule so the resulting rule looks like this:

```
h1 {
    font-size: 1.167em;
    line-height: 1.214;
    margin-bottom: 10px;
    text-indent: 0;
}
```

Notice that InDesign translated the font size to ems. Notice also that the **margin-bottom** value of both the **body** and the **h1** rules are set in pixels.

9. Replace the **10px** value for the **margin-bottom** property in both the **body** and **h1** rules with a value of **1em** (no space between the 1 and the e.)

10. Save both the HTML and CSS files. If you're feeling ambitious, you can recompile your EPUB and view the result in an eReader. Alternatively, you can open and view the **ex24_3.xhtml** page in a browser.

11. Experiment with setting the **margin** and **text-indent** values in the **body** rule to **ems**, previewing your changes as you go. When you've finished playing, save and close the files to complete the exercise.

NOTE: If you're in split or design view in Dreamweaver, when you remove the word "span" from the span.magenta rule, you should see the link text on the page turn from blue to magenta, including the underline.

TIP: To add space before to an HTML element, assign a value to the margin-top property in the appropriate CSS rule: **margin-top: .5em;** Likewise, to add space after, assign a value to the margin-bottom property **margin-bottom: .5em;**

Why Style?

Now that you've got a sense of how the code works, and what clean code looks like, you're in a better position to understand why we so strongly admonish you to deliberately style everything that is style-able in InDesign before exporting to EPUB. The Advanced tab of the EPUB Export Options dialog provides you with three options for handling conversion of your InDesign styling to EPUB

1. You can avoid CSS conversion of your InDesign styles entirely by deselecting the Generate CSS checkbox.

2. You can convert only those styles for which you have checked the Emit CSS checkbox in the Export Tagging category of their style definitions by selecting the Generate CSS checkbox and deselecting the Preserve Local Overrides checkbox.

3. You can allow InDesign to convert the styles you marked in export tagging and to generate its own style definitions for elements with local styling—any elements with style overrides or without explicit style definitions—by checking both the Generate CSS and Preserve Local Overrides checkboxes.

The third option is the one to avoid because it makes a mess of your code if you've applied local overrides. In its attempt to retain the appearance of your pages, InDesign generates a potentially ginormous amount of extraneous code that can clog up both the HTML and CSS in your EPUBs. You've seen how much unnecessary code InDesign adds to a CSS rule in trying to retain the original styling as reliably as possible. Multiply that one hundred fold for a document with lots of local styling and you can imagine the mess that results. The moral of the story? Style everything! Avoid style overrides and, the simpler you can keep things the better.

If you need to see what we're talking about to believe it, you can go to chapter_24_exercises > **overrides > OEBPS** and check out **html_sampler.xhtml** and **idGeneratedStyles.css** (in the css folder.) This is from a one-page InDesign document (overrides.indd: also in the chapter_24_exercises folder) to which no styles have been applied. It's not meant to be a thing of beauty, just to prove a point.

InDesign-generated styles are named as follows according to the types of overrides they represent:

INDESIGN-GENERATED CSS CLASS PREFIXES	
CharOverride-#	Character Attribute override
ParaOverride-#	Paragraph Attribute override
TableOverride-#	Table Attribute override
CellOverride-#	Cell Attribute override
ObjectOverride-#	Object (PageItem) Attribute override
_idGenParaOverride-#	To deal with CSS property inheritance (such as left indent)
_idGenCharOverride-#	To deal with CSS property inheritance (such as point size)
_idGenDropcap-#	To make the dropcap look more like InDesign
_idGenBNMarker-#	To make the Bullet & Number characters look more like InDesign
_idGenTableRowColumn	To support alternating table strokes and fills
_idGenPageitem-#	To carry the width and height of the PageItem/Object

Font Embedding

While the ability to customize the reading experience is a boon for the eBook audience, it's anathema to designers. After all, the fonts you choose for your publication, particularly for long documents, set the entire tone of the experience. Prior to InDesign CC, fonts embedded by InDesign were unrecognized by iBooks reader, and the wide selection of iOS device fonts were inaccessible to your EPUB without post-InDesign machinations. InDesign CC has made big strides to palliate this pain so that embedded fonts are now honored, and referenced iOS fonts are now accessible for inclusion in your publication. Embedded fonts won't unfortunately prevent your reading audience from overriding your preferences but at least you'll get to determine the initial presentation of your publication. Unfortunately, support for embedded fonts is by no means universal so don't presume that they'll be seen just because they're included in your EPUB. At the time of this writing for example, embedded fonts are still unsupported by Kindle. The pace of change is fast and furious however, so who's to know what tomorrow may bring.

TIP: For a comprehensive list of iOS fonts, check out http://iosfonts.com.

Embedded fonts are included in your EPUB when you check the Include Embeddable Fonts checkbox in the Advanced tab of the EPUB Export Options dialog. A folder containing the fonts is added to your EPUB package and the fonts are referenced in the CSS with **@font face** rules like so:

```
@font-face {
    font-family:"Minion Pro";
    font-style:normal;
    font-weight:bold;
    src : url("../font/MinionPro-Bold.otf");
}
```

The named font is then referenced by the style rules like so:

```
p.Basic-Paragraph {
    color:#000000;
    font-family:"Minion Pro", serif;
    [etc.]

}
```

Well, for now, that about wraps up the conversation about EPUB HTML and CSS. We encourage you to think of EPUB, and digital publishing in general, as a journey rather than a destination. HTML is evolving from XHTML to HTML5, CSS is transitioning to CSS3, and the EPUB 2.0.1 specification is being supplanted by EPUB 3.0. Add to that the rapid evolution of devices for reading eBooks and you have a field in which the only reliable constant is change. The good news is that there are lots of great resources available to help you along the way. You'll want to explore the more complete list of EPUB resources starting on page 417, but for code-specific information we recommend that you check out Liz Castro's books and website: http://www.pigsgourdsandwikis.com/. Liz's EPUB books provide concise treatment of many essentials of EPUB production including lots of specifics on working with EPUB code, and her most recent HTML and CSS book: HTML5 & CSS3 Visual QuickStart Guide, provides in-depth coverage of the code at the very heart of the EPUB 3.0 specification. ... And no, we don't receive commissions on Liz's books, nor does she have any idea that we're making these endorsements (but we're guessing she'll be happy we did!)

CHAPTER SUMMARY

This chapter provided a pretty intensive dive into the fundamentals of HTML and CSS. Given the tremendous amount of territory you covered, here are some of the highlights. Regarding HTML, you learned:

- About HTML page structure
- The basics of HTML markup including
    - Proper nesting of tags
    - Formatting: lower case, quoted attributes
    - HTML terminology: selector, attribute/property, attribute values
- A number of HTML tags including

    - <h1>–<h6>
    - <p>
    - <ol>, <ul>, <li>
    - <em>
    - <strong>
    - <blockquote>
    - <pre>

    - <code>
    - <table>, <tr>, <th>, <td>
    - <dl>, <dt>, <dd>
    - <img>
    - <a>
    - <div>
    - <span>

- The difference between block level and inline elements
- Default formatting and style assignment

You were also introduced to CSS and become familiar with:

- CSS syntax:
    - Classes begin with a period
    - Rules are contained in opening and closing curly braces
    - Rules can contain multiple declarations and each declaration includes a property followed by a colon and a property value, and is terminated by a semicolon
- CSS Editing
- Specificity and the style cascade
- Font embedding and the @font face rule

You employed Export Tagging to map your styles to HTML tags and assigned CSS classes to those tags.

You even took a side trip to Dreamweaver (if the application was on your system) or another text editor to modify your files.

In summary, this chapter has served as a foundational guide to the twists and turns of the EPUB HTML and CSS terrain. They say the hardest part of a journey is the first step. Now that you've taken that step and rounded the first bend, you've got a firm foot on the unfolding EPUB frontier.

Chapter 25

GREP

General Regular Expressions entirely redefine the capability of InDesign's Find/Change feature and open a whole new world of possibility for cleaning up and formatting long documents. Essential to an efficient EPUB workflow, GREP targets pattern rather than fixed content, making it possible to effortlessly remove extraneous spaces, tabs and returns, locate and reformat phone numbers, email addresses and URLs—in fact, anything with a definable pattern is fair game for GREP. In this chapter, you'll gain a solid introduction to GREP, using it to supercharge paragraph style definitions as well as Find/Change queries. Be assured that GREP is a total game-changer—harnessing its power will forever alter your workflow.

What is GREP?

TIP: Originally developed for the UNIX operating system, the term GREP comes from the command g/re/p (global/regular expression/print) which would print all lines that matched a specified pattern.

GREP (Global Regular Expression Parser) is an extraordinarily powerful tool for locating and formatting document content based on pattern—zip codes, email addresses, and phone numbers are just a few of the most obvious types of GREP targets. GREP also can be used to find the first letter or word of a sentence, multiple spaces and returns and SO much more—in short, pretty much any pattern you can define, GREP can help you find. Without GREP, it would be nearly impossible to process certain documents due to their length or complexity but with the magic of GREP, you can process the very same document automatically in a matter of clicks. If you'll be working with large volumes of text, for EPUB or otherwise, being able to harness the power of GREP is absolutely essential to an efficient and reliable workflow. GREP is typically used to create Find/Change queries but InDesign also enables you to incorporate GREP expressions in paragraph style definitions to expand their usefulness exponentially.

Creating and Testing a GREP Expression

NOTE: GREP is also supported by a number of code editing tools (including Dreamweaver) and is essential to a streamlined EPUB development and editing workflow.

The intelligence you can build into InDesign paragraph styles using GREP is like building nested styles on steroids. There's no limit to the number of GREP styles you can include in a paragraph style definition, and for each GREP style, you can assign a character style that formats the targeted text.

The characters used to write GREP expressions are called metacharacters. At first glance, a string of GREP metacharacters can look like an unintelligible jumble but after some practice, and with InDesign's help, you'll be able to craft GREP expressions of your own that absolutely transform your workflow.

TIP: Lost in space? Here's a key:
em space: fixed-width space equal to the size of the font. Often used to create a one-em indent at the beginning of a paragraph.
en space: fixed-width space that is half the width of an em space.
flush space: used at the end of a fully justified paragraph to position an end of story character flush right.
hair space: fixed-width space that is 1/24th the width of an em space.
nonbreaking space: width of space created with the Spacebar, prevents a line break between words. Fixed width does not expand or compress with justified text.

The example below comes with InDesign and is a saved expression in the Find/Change dialog. It finds any instance of two or more consecutive spaces of any type.

$$[\sim m \sim > \sim f \sim | \sim S \sim s \sim < \sim / \sim . \sim 3 \sim 4 \sim \% \ ]\{2,\}$$

When you break it down, it's not quite as impenetrable as at first it might seem. The square brackets define a character set that includes all the different white space variations available in InDesign. The 2 and the comma in the curly braces say that the expression is looking for any combination of two or more characters that are contained in the character set.

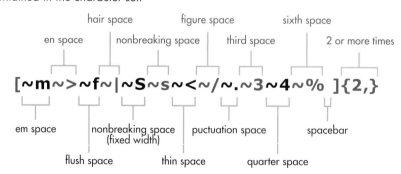

A GREP expression designed to capture any sequence of two or more consecutive spaces.

If you're still a bit intimidated, the good news is that InDesign provides a series of menus in plain language to help you assemble your GREP expressions—both for

Find/Change and GREP paragraph styles. With just a little bit of clarification on how the menu options work, you'll be on your way to writing your own expressions and really taking advantage of the richness GREP can offer.

Exercise 25.1: Creating a character style for GREP testing

You'll be developing your first GREP expression in the GREP Styles section of the Paragraph Styles panel. Before you begin with the GREP code, it's a good idea to set up a character style that provides visual feedback showing the results of your GREP expression as it evolves. You'll create a character style to highlight the targeted text and that looks something like this:

jane@example.com

Jane.Doe@example.com

Jane-Marie.Doe@example.com

Jane_Marie.G.Doe@dept-3.com

Jane-Marie.G.Doe123@dept-3.com.edu

To test your GREP expressions, it's helpful to create a character style that highlights the target text.

1. Go to Window > Workspace and choose [Book.]

2. Navigate to the chapter_25_exercises folder, open **ex25_1_start.indd** and save as ex25_1.indd.

3. With the Type tool, click in the text frame containing the email addresses and press Ctrl+A/Command+A to select all the text in the frame.

4. Expand the Paragraph Styles panel at the lower right of the Panel Dock (⌸).

5. Alt+Click/Option+Click the Create New Style Button (⌸) at the bottom of the panel.

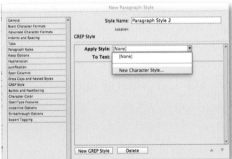

You can create and assign a character style to your GREP Style directly from the New Paragraph Style dialog.

6. Select the GREP Style category at the left of the Paragraph Style Options window.

7. Click the New GREP Style button at the bottom of the GREP style window and delete any text that appears in the To Text: text field.

8. Click [None] to the right of Apply Style: and choose New Character style from the bottom of the dropdown menu.

Spaces continued:
thin space: fixed-width space that is 1/8th the width of an em space.
figure space: a space the width of a figure in the given font.
punctuation space: a space the width of a period, colon, or exclamation point in the given font.
third space: fixed-width space that is 1/3rd the width of an em space.
quarter space: fixed-width space that is 1/4th the width of an em space.
sixth space: fixed-width space that is 1/6th the width of an em space.

DOWNLOAD: Exercise files for this chapter can be downloaded from http://www.interactive-indesign.com.

TIP: You can develop and test GREP expressions in the Find/Change dialog or in the GREP Style section of the Paragraph Styles panel. We prefer using the GREP Styles dialog because of the instant visual feedback you can receive using character styles to format the captured content.

9. Name the character style grepTest.

10. From the Basic Character Formats category of the New Character Style dialog, check the No Break checkbox.

11. Select Underline Options from the character style options list and check the Underline On check box. Set the Weight of the underline to 10 pt. Set the Offset to -3 pt to move the underline behind the text.

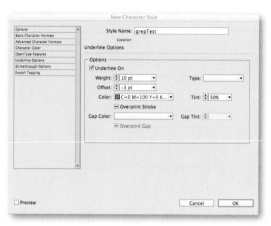

You can use the Underline option to create a character style that highlights the text.

12. Click the Color dropdown and select a highlight color. (We selected Magenta.) Set the tint to percentage to 50%. Click OK to return to the New Paragraph Style dialog.

13. Name the paragraph style "body" and click OK to close the Paragraph Styles panel. Ensure that the paragraph style is applied to the selected text.

14. Place the Type tool cursor in the text frame below the email addresses (the frame containing the filler text), and press Ctrl+A/Command+A to select all. Click the body style in the Paragraph Styles panel to apply it to the text.

15. If the text frame becomes overset when you apply the style, resize the frame by dragging its bottom sizing handle.

16. Save the document as **ex25_1.indd** and keep it open for the next exercise.

Using GREP to Capture Email Addresses

Before actually tackling a GREP expression it's important to first identify the structure or pattern you want to target. Every email address is constructed of the following components:

- Addressing name: can contain one or more upper and lowercase letters, numbers, dashes, underscores, and periods
- @ symbol
- Domain name: can contain one or more upper and lowercase letters, numbers, dashes, underscores, and periods
- Domain extension: follows a period and can contain a minimum of 2 and a maximum of 4 upper or lowercase letters
- Optional second domain extension: follows a period and can contain a minimum of 2 and a maximum of 4 upper or lowercase letters

While quite varied in appearance, the following email addresses all adhere to the structure outlined on the previous page. The object is to craft a single expression that captures them all but won't capture variations that don't conform to the proper syntax.

jane@example.com

Jane.Doe@example.com

Jane-Marie.Doe@example.com

Jane_Marie.G.Doe@dept-3.com

Jane-Marie.G.Doe123@dept-3.com.edu

Exercise 25.2: Capturing and styling email addresses with GREP

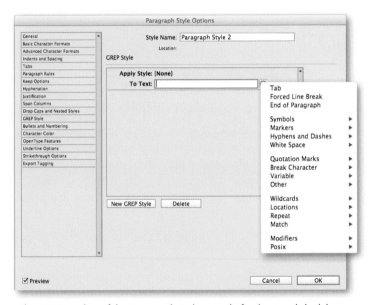

The GREP window of the Paragraph Styles panel after having clicked the New GREP Style button, deleted the default GREP expression, and clicked the @ symbol to bring up the Special characters for search menu.

1. If the file from the last lesson isn't open, navigate to the chapter_25_exercises folder and open **ex25_2_start.indd**.

2. Position the Type tool cursor in the email text frame and Double-Click the body style in the Paragraph Styles panel. When the Paragraph Style Options dialog opens, select GREP Style from the category list at the left of the panel.

3. With your cursor in the To Text field of the GREP Styles window, click the @ symbol to open the Special characters for search menu.

   You first want InDesign to look for the upper and lowercase letters, numbers, dashes, underscores, and periods that may be present in the addressing name. There is a GREP wildcard that looks for any word character including upper and lowercase letters, numbers and underscores. You will create a collection of characters called a character set that will include the Any Word Character wildcard, periods and dashes.

4. Choose Match > Character Set from the menu.

5. InDesign places two empty square brackets in the GREP composition field. Move your cursor between the two brackets and choose Wildcards > Any Word Character from the Special characters for search menu.

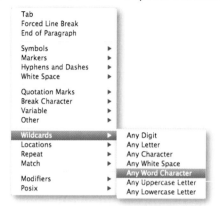

A GREP wildcard is a single symbol used to represent an assortment of characters.

The code in the field should look like this: [\w] with the Any Word Character wildcard placed between the square brackets that define the character set.

You should notice that with the exception of the dashes, periods, and @ symbols, the text of the email addresses is highlighted in the underline color you chose for the grepTest character style. If you don't see the highlight, ensure that the Preview checkbox at the lower left corner of the Paragraph Style Options window is checked. The next step is to add dashes and periods to the character set.

6. Move your cursor to just inside the opening bracket of the character set and type a dash followed by a period.

This should result in the email addresses being completely highlighted with the exception of the @ symbol. Your code should now look like this: [-.\w]

Note that the backslash before the w is part of the any word character wildcard—the backslash distinguishes the symbol from the actual letter "w." Since a period is also a wildcard metacharacter when it's not in a character set (the period wildcard represents any character), adding the period and the dash at the beginning of the character set spares InDesign any confusion.

Per the structure you've outlined, an email addressing name can contain one or more characters and, therefore, any of the characters in the character set can repeat 1 or more times.

7. Move your cursor outside the closing square bracket in the composition field and choose Repeat > One or More Times from the Special characters for search menu.

InDesign adds a plus sign at the end of your expression. So far, you've captured all the relevant characters in the first part of the email addresses, however, the expression targets those same characters throughout all the content styled with the body paragraph style. Next, you'll refine the expression to limit its scope to just the first portion of the addresses and the @ symbol.

---

8. Since the first set of characters in the email address is followed by the @ symbol, simply type the @ symbol after the plus.

   The grepTest highlight appears on the email addressing names and the @ symbol, and the code should look like this: [-.\w]+@

   The next step is to capture the domain name that follows the @ symbol. This section of the address has the same allowable characters as the addressing name so you can just copy and paste the code you've written thus far.

9. Place your cursor in the beginning of the composition field and drag to select the existing code. Press Ctrl+C/Command+C to copy.

10. Position your cursor after the existing code in the composition field, and press Ctrl+V/Command+V to paste the copied code.

    Once again, the expression captures the remainder of the email characters while you want it to capture only up to the period preceding the domain extension. You need to constrain the scope of the code and eliminate the possibility of capturing an additional @ symbol.

11. Delete the @ symbol at the end of the code and then the period located in the second character set (contained by the square brackets).

    The code should now look like this: [-.\w]+@[-\w]+ and everything up to the period preceding the domain extension should be highlighted in the email addresses.

    As mentioned earlier, when not included in a character set, the period serves as a wildcard metacharacter that represents any character. To target a literal period outside a character set, you need to "escape it" by preceding it with a backslash like so: \.

12. Place your cursor after the second plus sign in the composition field and type \. to target the period preceding the domain extension.

    Domain extensions can have a minimum of two upper or lowercase letters and a maximum of four. You'll create a new character set using wildcards for the upper and lowercase letters and then define the number of times these characters can appear.

13. With your cursor after the period, choose Match > Character Set to enter the character set square brackets at the end of your expression.

14. Move your cursor between the brackets and select Wildcards > Any Uppercase Letter from the Special characters for search menu. Then choose Wildcards > Any Lowercase Letter.

    The code should now look like this: [-.\w]+@[-\w]+\.[\u\l] and the first character of each email domain extension should be highlighted.

15. Type {2,4} at the end of the expression.

    The first domain extension in each of the email addresses should now be highlighted and the code should look like this: [-.\w]+@[-\w]+\.[\u\l]{2,4}

    Unfortunately, the InDesign GREP Special characters for search menu doesn't offer any option to indicate a specific number of allowable characters or

> **TIP:** To indicate a specific number of times a criterion should be met, enclose that number in curly braces. To indicate a repeat range, enter the minimum number followed by a comma, and then the maximum number. {2,5} means 2,3,4, or 5.

repeats. In the above example, the curly braces are used to specify the number of allowable characters from the preceding character set. In this case, the number "2" followed by the comma and then the number "4" means a minimum of two, possibly three, or a maximum of four of the character set characters are allowed.

Last but not least, you need to target the optional second domain extension. The code for this extension will be the same as for the first, however, since it is optional, you will contain it in parentheses and follow it with a Match modifier to indicate that it can appear zero or one time.

16. Place your cursor after the second plus sign in the composition field. Select the code beginning with the \. and ending with the }. Press Ctrl+C/Command+C to copy the code.

17. Place your cursor at the end of the existing code, after the closing curly brace, and type an opening parenthesis. Paste the code and then type a closing parenthesis. The code should look like this: [-.\w]+@[-\w]+\.[\u\l]{2,4}(\.[\u\l]{2,4})

If you update your preview, you'll notice that now only the last email address with the double domain is highlighted. This is because you have not yet specified that the second domain is optional.

18. To complete the expression, with your cursor at the end of the code, choose Repeat > Zero or One Time from the Special characters for search menu. Refresh your preview to see that all the email addresses are now highlighted.

The final code should look like this: [-.\w]+@[-\w]+\.[\u\l]{2,4}(\.[\u\l]{2,4})?

19. Save your file as **ex25_2.indd** and keep it open for the next exercise.

Now that you know your GREP style works, you could create and assign a new character style to it to better format the email addresses in the document.

Congratulations, you've compiled your first GREP expression! Below is a complete diagram of the code.

Email GREP Query

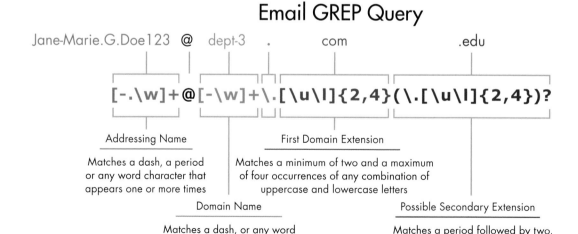

Jane-Marie.G.Doe123   @   dept-3   .   com   .edu

`[-.\w]+@[-\w]+\.[\u\l]{2,4}(\.[\u\l]{2,4})?`

Addressing Name
Matches a dash, a period or any word character that appears one or more times

First Domain Extension
Matches a minimum of two and a maximum of four occurrences of any combination of uppercase and lowercase letters

Domain Name
Matches a dash, or any word character that appears one or more times

Possible Secondary Extension
Matches a period followed by two, three, or four upper or lowercase letters that may appear zero or one time.

Saving A GREP Query

Since you've expended substantial effort in crafting your GREP expression, it would be a shame to have to do it from scratch ever again. You can preserve any expression you write by saving it as a query in the GREP section of InDesign's extremely robust Find/Change dialog.

The great news about saved queries is that they are saved as XML files and can be shared with other users. Depending on your operating system, the location for stored queries is:

Mac: UserFolder > Library Preferences > Adobe InDesign > [Version] > en_US > Find-Change Queries > GREP

Windows XP: Documents and Settings > [username] > Application Data > Adobe > InDesign > [Version] > Find-Change Queries > GREP.

Windows Vista and Windows 7: Users > [username] > AppData > Roaming > Adobe > InDesign > [Version] Find-Change Queries > GREP.

Exercise 25.3: Saving a GREP Query

1. If the file isn't open from the last exercise, navigate to the chapter_25_exercises folder, open **ex25_3_start.indd** and save as ex25_3.indd.

2. With the Type tool cursor in the text frame containing the email addresses, Double-Click the body paragraph style in the Paragraph Styles panel to open the Paragraph Style Options dialog.

3. Select the GREP Style category at the left of the dialog to open the GREP Styles pane. Click in the To Text field to select the expression and then press Ctrl+C/Command+C to copy it.

4. Close the Paragraph Styles panel and go to Edit > Find/Change (Ctrl+F/Command+F.)

5. Select the GREP tab at the top of the window, position the cursor in the Find what: field, and press Ctrl+V/Command+V to paste the expression.

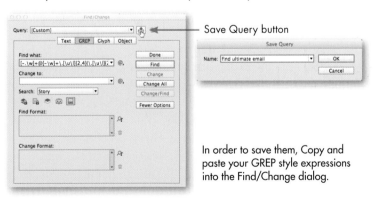

Save Query button

In order to save them, Copy and paste your GREP style expressions into the Find/Change dialog.

6. Click the Save Query button at the top of the window. Name the query "find ultimate email".
7. Click the Query dropdown to confirm that your query appears in the list of saved queries.

Saved GREP queries appear in the Query dropdown of the Find/Change dialog.

8. Close ex25_3_start.indd without saving to complete the lesson.

InDesign comes with a list of saved queries in the Find/Change dialog. The top section of the list displays saved text queries, the middle section shows saved GREP queries, and the bottom section shows saved object queries.

You'll find the GREP queries for multiple returns and spaces and trailing whitespace to be especially useful in your work with EPUB and long documents.

Exercise 25.4: Transforming Data Using GREP Find/Change

If you're not already wowed by what GREP can do, this exercise should make a believer out of you. You'll develop a GREP expression that removes extraneous content, and rearranges what's left according to your specifications. Using GREP Find/Change, you'll reformat the arrangement of each entry in a list of State Representatives and their respective states.

NOTE: The exercise file already contains the paragraph and character styles you'll use to test your GREP expressions and format the content.

1. Navigate to the chapter_25_exercises folder, open **ex25_4_start.indd** and save as ex25_4.indd.

It's a good strategy to develop your GREP expressions incrementally as modules, testing as you go. This is a particularly useful approach given the limited space in the GREP composition field. You can then assemble the tested GREP code modules, adjusting as necessary to achieve your final result. With the modular approach in mind, you'll start with an expression to capture the various name patterns.

NOTE: The original list is numbered with each representative's name appearing last name first, preceded by their state. You'll remove the list numbers, move the state after the name, and display the names with first name first.

While the specific patterns of the names may vary, each name consists of two essential pieces: the last name which precedes the comma, and the first name which appears after the comma. This makes things surprisingly easy. Remember the wildcard for any character?

1	Alabama	Bonner, Jo
2	Alabama	Sewell, Terri A.
3	Alaska	Faleomavaega, Eni F. H.
4	Colorado	DeGette, Diana
5	District of Columbia	Norton, Eleanor Holmes
6	Florida	Young, C.W. Bill
7	Florida	Ros-Lehtinen, Ileana
8	Louisiana	Boustany Jr., Charles W.
9	Maryland	Van Hollen, Chris
10	Massachusetts	McGovern, James
11	Missouri	Clay Jr., William "Lacy"

The list in the original format.

2. Zoom out if necessary to see the pasteboard at the left of the document window. With the Type tool, click in the text frame containing the list of names.

3. Go to Edit > Find/Change (Ctrl+F/Command+F) and click the GREP button at the top of the dialog.

4. If necessary select More Options from the right hand side of the panel to access the Find and Change Format fields. At the bottom of the window, to the upper right of the Change Format pane, click the Specify attributes to change button (⚙).

5. When the Change Format Settings window opens, ensure that Style Options is selected from the category list at the left and choose grepTest from the Character Style dropdown. Click OK to close the window and to add the character style to the Change Format pane.

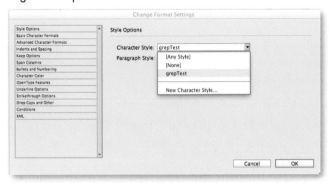

InDesign's Find/Change makes it possible to reformat content document-wide based on content identified using GREP.

6. Delete any content in the Find what: field, click the @ symbol and choose Wildcards > Any Character from the Special characters for search menu (or type a period.) Choose Story from the Search dropdown.

7. Click Find several times to see that each character in the text frame is selected one by one.

8. Type + after the period to indicate that the character should be repeated one or more times.

9. Click Find several times to see that the simple change in code now targets the contents of each paragraph—the entire name—up to the paragraph return.

10. Position your cursor at the end of the GREP expression after the plus sign and type a comma followed by \s into the field to search for a comma followed by a space.

    The code should now look like this: .+,\s

11. Click Find several times and note that just that easily, you've limited the targeted content to every last name variation as well as the comma and the space by which it's followed.

    Since you want to reverse the order of the content before and after the comma and space, you need to capture these pieces separately as marked subexpressions, excluding the comma and space from the targeted text.

12. Position your cursor before the period and type an opening parenthesis. Move the cursor after the plus sign and type a closing parenthesis.

    The code should now look like this: (.+),\s

13. Click Find again to see that nothing seems to have changed. The query still targets the last name, the comma, and the space.

    While the targeted content appears to be the same, the way it is targeted is actually quite different. The parentheses define a marking subexpression that is your first manipulable code module. Next you'll create a module that targets the first name.

TIP: Surrounding GREP code with parentheses defines that code as a marked subexpression. You can reference marked subexpressions by number and use them to reorder document content.

14. Position your cursor after the \s and then choose Match > Marking Subexpression from the Special characters for search menu.

    InDesign adds an opening and closing parenthesis to the code.

15. Move your cursor inside the parentheses and type .+ to indicate any character, one or more times.

    The code should now look like this: (.+),\s(.+) and should capture each individual name. With just a very few characters, you've managed to target every name variation on the list.

    Now, let's see what it takes to reverse the order of the names.

16. Place your cursor in the Change to: field, click the @ button, and choose Found > Found 2 from the Special characters for search menu. The code in the Change to field should look like this: $2

    Found 2 represents the second of the two marking subexpressions you created. Specifically, Found 2 represents the captured first name characters following the comma and space.

17. Click Find and then click Change/Find a couple times.

    The last names disappear, as do the commas and spaces, leaving the highlighted first names in their place. You're half way there. Pretty cool, right?

18. Press Ctrl+Z/Command+Z as many times as necessary to undo your changes to the list. Place your cursor after the 2 in the Change to field and type \s$1 to add a space followed by the last name which you captured in the first marking subexpression.

    The code in the Change to field should look like this: $2\s$1

19. Position the Type tool cursor at the beginning of one of the names and test the query once again using Find and then Change/Find to see that you've succeeded in reordering the names in the list. Save and close the file and keep the Find/Change dialog open for the next lesson.

The Find/Change dialog with the first "module" of the name change query.

GREP Expression Development Tips

As you saw with the email query, GREP code can easily get rather unwieldy. As the code gets longer, it's impossible to see it in its entirety in the limited space provided by the GREP composition field. In order to keep track of things, you may find it helpful to create a scratch pad of sorts where you copy the code from the GREP composition field and paste it as text onto your document pasteboard or even into a separate document that you use as a "scratch pad." You could then display your working document and the scratch pad document side-by-side in 2-up view.

It's a good idea to annotate your code as you develop it to help you remember exactly what it was meant to do. It's also advisable to keep the code examples in sequence so you can return to a previous iteration if necessary.

Be aware that when you paste the code copied from the GREP composition field into a text frame, InDesign may convert some of the GREP characters. For example, \s renders as a literal space in your pasted text, \r renders as a paragraph return, \n renders as a soft return and \t renders as a tab. In such cases, ensure that Show Hidden Characters is turned on (Ctrl+Alt+I/Command+Option+I), and replace the rendered characters with the appropriate GREP metacharacters in your code.

TIP: To view two documents side-by-side, choose the first 2-up view from the Arrange Documents dropdown at the upper left of the InDesign interface.

Find what (to capture last name, first name)

(.+),\s(.+)

- any character one or more times (last name)
- followed by a comma and a space
- followed by any character one or more times (firstname)

GREP "scratch pad" example

Exercise 25.5: Non-marking Subexpressions

InDesign supports a maximum of nine marking subexpressions in any single GREP expression. Instead of wasting precious marking subexpressions, you can use non-marking subexpressions to target content you want to remove from the document flow.

For the list of House of Representatives members, you want to dispose of the number and tab before the name of the Representative's state. A non-marking subexpression is the perfect way to contain and remove this unwanted content.

The tabs in each paragraph provide a useful breakpoint for content capture. You'll capture the characters up to and including the tab preceding the state name, and since these characters will be eliminated from the document flow, you'll capture them with a non-marking subexpression. You'll then capture the state name, the last name, and the first name in separate marking subexpressions and build the new version of the list section-by-section.

1. Navigate to the chapter_25_exercises folder and open **ex25_5_start.indd**.

2. Position the Type tool cursor in the first line of the list of representatives and, if it's not already open, press Ctrl+F/Command+F to open the Find/Change dialog. Clear any existing code from the Find what: and Change to: fields and ensure that the grepTest character style appears in the Change Format pane.

3. Position your cursor in the Find what: field and choose Match > Non-marking Subexpression from the Special characters for search menu.

The code should look like this: **(?:)**

The **\d** metacharacter identifies any digit. You'll use it to target the numbers at the beginning of each paragraph.

4. Move your cursor inside the closing parenthesis and after the colon, and choose Wildcards > Any Digit from the Special characters for search menu. Since some of the numbers contain more than one digit, type a plus sign after the \d (or choose Repeat > One or More Times from the Special characters for search menu.)

The code should look like this: **(?:\d+)**

5. Click Find several times to see what's targeted.

6. To add the tab that follows the numbers to the non-marking subexpression, position your cursor before the closing parenthesis in the Find what: field and type \t (or choose Tab from the Special characters for search menu.)

Next you need to capture the state name that follows the tab. Since you'll want the name of the state to appear after the representative's name, you'll capture it in a marking subexpression so you can move it around.

In order to capture all the state names, including all three words of District of Columbia, you'll work with the Any Word Character wildcard.

7. Position your cursor after the closing parenthesis and choose Wildcard > Any Word Character. Type a plus sign after the \w since you want to capture more than one character. Click Find to test.

The code should look like this: **(?:\d+\t)\w+**

The expression captures the beginning of each list entry through the first word of the state name. Only the word District is captured in the name District of Columbia. Since you want to make allowances for multiple words separated by a space, you'll capture the pattern for the additional words in a marking subexpression.

8. With your cursor positioned at the end of the expression in the Find what: field, type an opening parenthesis to begin the marking subexpression. Choose Wildcards > Any White Space from the Special characters for search menu and then type \w+) after the \s entered by InDesign.

The code should now look like this: **(?:\d+\t)\w+(\s\w+)** and should capture through the words District of on line five and through McGovern on line ten. The reason McGovern is captured is that the state name is followed by a single tab which is being interpreted by InDesign as a single instance of white space. The other state names are not captured because you haven't yet specified that the additional words are optional. You can take care of that easily by adding the correct metacharacter.

9. Position your cursor outside the closing parenthesis in the Find what: field, and choose Repeat > Zero or More Times from the Special characters for search menu. An asterisk is added to the expression. Test again.

The code should look like this: **(?:\d+\t)\w+(\s\w+)***

This time, the expression captures each of the state names but you still have the problem with line ten, and now the last name has been added to the state name on line five. This is not an issue; you just need to refine the expression to recognize the tab(s) that follow the state name.

10. Place your cursor after the asterisk in the Find what field and type \t+ to indicate one or more tabs. Once again, test the expression.

You've succeeded in limiting the range of the expression to the content preceding the last names. Now it's time to add the code you developed to capture the names, and that will nearly finish the Find portion of the code.

11. Open **ex25_scratchpad.indd** in the Chapter 25 exercise folder, place the Type tool cursor in the very first line of code and drag to select it. Press Ctrl+C/Command+C to copy it. Position your cursor after the existing code in the Find what: field and press Ctrl+V/Command+V to paste the copied code. Press Find several times to test the expression.

The code should look like this: **(?:\d+\t)\w+(\s\w+)*\t+(.+),\s(.+)**
In just a moment, you'll be moving on to the Change to: portion of your query. With that in mind, take a close look at the code to determine if it's appropriately segmented into marking subexpressions for the first name, the last name and the state name.

The first set of parentheses defines a non-marking subexpression, and this is fine since you'll be removing its contents from the document flow. The next bit of code: **\w+(\s\w+)*** targets the state names. In order to reference the text that it targets, the entire state name expression must be wrapped in parentheses to make it into a marking subexpression. Once created, this new subexpression will be referenced as Found 1 (**$1**) in the Change to: field since it is the first marking subexpression to appear in the code.

12. Position your cursor before the first \w in the code and type an opening parenthesis. Position your cursor after the asterisk and before the \t and type a closing parenthesis. Now pat yourself on the back and take a deep breath. You're finished with the hard part!

The final Find what: code should look like this:
(?:\d+\t)(\w+(\s\w+)*)\t+(.+),\s(.+)

The code you've written contains four marking subexpressions The first refers to the state names and the second is included in the first. While it's important to count it as the second marking subexpression, you won't be referring to it directly when you reorganize the document content.

The third and fourth marking subexpressions represent the last names and first names respectively. They will be referenced as **$3** and **$4**. When you reorganize the list contents, the first name will be first, followed by a space, the last name, a colon and a space, and then the state name. The reorganized list entries will look like this: **William "Lacy" Clay Jr.: Missouri**

13. Now for the Change to: portion of the query. Place your cursor in the Change to: field and choose Found > Found 4 from the Special characters for replace menu. Click Find and then click Change to test your expression.

14. The entire listing for the representative is replaced by their first name which is formatted with the grepTest character style. Now to add the last name.

15. Press Ctrl+Z/Command+Z to undo the formatting changes you've made to the document.

16. Position your cursor after the 4 in the Change to: field. Type \s$3 to enter a space followed by the last name.

    The code should look like this: $4\s$3

17. Click Find and then Change/Find a couple times to test and confirm that the query now captures the first and last names.

18. Undo your changes, position your cursor after the 3 in the Change to: field and type :\s$1 This adds a colon, followed by a space, followed by the representative's state. Test it.

19. Congratulations! You've successfully used GREP to rearrange the contents of the list and have completed the lesson!

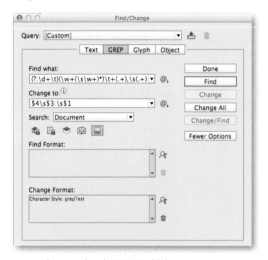

The completed GREP Find/Change query.

GREP Resources

While this chapter has provided a solid introduction to GREP and the possibilities it offers, there's certainly more to learn if you want to dig in deeper. The GREP diagram and metacharacter table on the next two pages put a whole bunch of information all in one place for your reference. We've also provided a number of excellent resources at the end of this section starting on page 415). From further training, to downloads developed by veritable GREP wizards willing to share the fruits of their genius, you'll find the GREP resources to be worth their weight in gold. Enjoy!

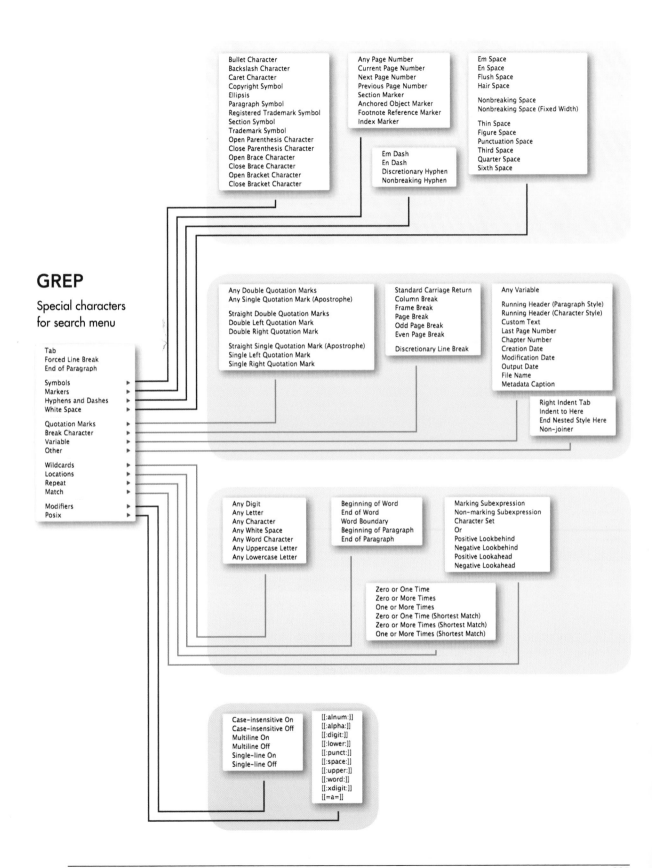

GREP

Special characters for search menu

- Tab
- Forced Line Break
- End of Paragraph

- Symbols ▶
- Markers ▶
- Hyphens and Dashes ▶
- White Space ▶

- Quotation Marks ▶
- Break Character ▶
- Variable ▶
- Other ▶

- Wildcards ▶
- Locations ▶
- Repeat ▶
- Match ▶

- Modifiers ▶
- Posix ▶

Symbols:
- Bullet Character
- Backslash Character
- Caret Character
- Copyright Symbol
- Ellipsis
- Paragraph Symbol
- Registered Trademark Symbol
- Section Symbol
- Trademark Symbol
- Open Parenthesis Character
- Close Parenthesis Character
- Open Brace Character
- Close Brace Character
- Open Bracket Character
- Close Bracket Character

Markers:
- Any Page Number
- Current Page Number
- Next Page Number
- Previous Page Number
- Section Marker
- Anchored Object Marker
- Footnote Reference Marker
- Index Marker

White Space:
- Em Space
- En Space
- Flush Space
- Hair Space

- Nonbreaking Space
- Nonbreaking Space (Fixed Width)

- Thin Space
- Figure Space
- Punctuation Space
- Third Space
- Quarter Space
- Sixth Space

Hyphens and Dashes:
- Em Dash
- En Dash
- Discretionary Hyphen
- Nonbreaking Hyphen

Quotation Marks:
- Any Double Quotation Marks
- Any Single Quotation Mark (Apostrophe)

- Straight Double Quotation Marks
- Double Left Quotation Mark
- Double Right Quotation Mark

- Straight Single Quotation Mark (Apostrophe)
- Single Left Quotation Mark
- Single Right Quotation Mark

Break Character:
- Standard Carriage Return
- Column Break
- Frame Break
- Page Break
- Odd Page Break
- Even Page Break

- Discretionary Line Break

Variable:
- Any Variable

- Running Header (Paragraph Style)
- Running Header (Character Style)
- Custom Text
- Last Page Number
- Chapter Number
- Creation Date
- Modification Date
- Output Date
- File Name
- Metadata Caption

Other:
- Right Indent Tab
- Indent to Here
- End Nested Style Here
- Non-joiner

Wildcards:
- Any Digit
- Any Letter
- Any Character
- Any White Space
- Any Word Character
- Any Uppercase Letter
- Any Lowercase Letter

Locations:
- Beginning of Word
- End of Word
- Word Boundary
- Beginning of Paragraph
- End of Paragraph

Match:
- Marking Subexpression
- Non-marking Subexpression
- Character Set
- Or
- Positive Lookbehind
- Negative Lookbehind
- Positive Lookahead
- Negative Lookahead

Repeat:
- Zero or One Time
- Zero or More Times
- One or More Times
- Zero or One Time (Shortest Match)
- Zero or More Times (Shortest Match)
- One or More Times (Shortest Match)

Modifiers:
- Case-insensitive On
- Case-insensitive Off
- Multiline On
- Multiline Off
- Single-line On
- Single-line Off

Posix:
- [[:alnum:]]
- [[:alpha:]]
- [[:digit:]]
- [[:lower:]]
- [[:punct:]]
- [[:space:]]
- [[:upper:]]
- [[:word:]]
- [[:xdigit:]]
- [[=a=]]

TEXT AND GREP METACHARACTERS FOR FIND/CHANGE AND GREP STYLES

Description	Text	GREP
Tab Character	^t	\t
Forced Line Break	^n	\n
End of Paragraph	^p	\r

Symbols		
Bullet Character	^8	~8
Backslash Character	\	\\
Caret Character	^^	\^
Copyright Symbol	^2	~2
Ellipsis	^e	~e
Paragraph Symbol	^7	~7
Registered Trademark Symbol	^r	~r
Section Symbol	^6	~6
Trademark Symbol	^d	~d
Open Parenthesis Character	(	\(
Close Parenthesis Character	)	\)
Open Brace Character	{	\{
Close Brace Character	}	\}
Open Bracket Character	[	\[
Close Bracket Character	]	\]
Tilde	~	\~

Markers		
Any Page Number	^#	~#
Current Page Number	^N	~N
Next Page Number	^X	~X
Previous Page Number	^V	~V
Section Marker	^x	~x
Anchored Object Marker	^a	~a
Footnote Reference Marker	^F	~F
Index Marker	^I	~I

Hyphens and Dashes		
Em Dash	^_	~_
En Dash	^=	~=
Discretionary Hyphen	^-	~-
Nonbreaking Hyphen	^~	~~

White Space		
Em Space	^m	~m
En Space	^>	~>
Flush Space	^f	~f
Hair Space	^|	~|
Nonbreaking Space	^s	~s
–	^S	~S
Thin Space	^<	~<
Figure Space	^/	~/
Punctuation Space	^.	~.
Third Space	^3	~3
Quarter Space	^4	~4
Sixth Space	^%	~%

Quotation Marks		
Any Double Quotation Mark	"	"
Any Single Quotation Mark	'	'
Straight Double Quotation Mark	^"	~"
Double Left Quotation Mark	^{	~{
Double Right Quotation Mark	^}	~}
Straight Single Quotation Mark	^'	~'
Single Left Quotation Mark	^[	~[
Single Right Quotation Mark	^]	~]

Break Character	Text	
Standard carriage return	^b	~b
Column Break	^M	~M
Frame Break	^R	~R
Page Break	^P	~P
Odd Page Break	^L	~L
Even Page Break	^E	~E
Discretionary Line Break	^k	~k

Variable		
Any Variable	~v	^v
Running header (paragraph style)	^Y	~Y
Running header (character style)	^Z	~Z
Custom text	^u	~u
Last page number	^T	~T
Chapter number	^H	~H
Creation date	^S	~S
Modification date	^o	~o
Output date	^D	~D
File name (lowercase L)	^l	~l
Metadata Caption	^J	~J

Other		
Right Indent Tab	^y	~y
Indent to Here	^i	~i
End Nested Style Here	^h	~h
Non-joiner	^j	~j

Wildcards		
Any Digit	^9	\d
Any character that is not a digit		\D
Any Letter	^$	[\l\u]
Any Character	^?	.
Any White Space (or tab)	^w	\s
Any character that is *not* a white space		\S
Any Word Character		\w
Any character that is *not* a word character		\W
Any Uppercase Letter		\u
Any character that is *not* an uppercase letter		\U
Any lowercase letter		\l
Any character that is *not* a lowercase letter		\L

Locations		
Beginning of Word		\<
End of Word		\>
Word Boundary		\b
Opposite of Word Boundary		\B
Beginning of Paragraph		^
End of Paragraph [location]		$
Beginning of Story		\A
End of Story		\z

Repeat		
Zero or One Time		?
Zero or More Times		*
One or More Times		+
Zero or One Time (Shortest Match)		??
Zero or More Times (Shortest Match)		*?
One or More Times (Shortest Match)		+?

Match	GREP
Marking Subexpression	( )
Non-marking Subexpression	(?:)
Character Set	[ ]
Or		
Positive Lookbehind	(?<=)
Negative Lookbehind	(?<!)
Positive Lookahead	(?=)
Negative Lookahead	(?!)

Modifiers		
Case-insensitive On	(?i)
Case-insensitive Off	(?-i)
Multiline On	(?m)
Multiline Off	(?-m)
Single-line On	(?s)
Single-line Off	(?-s)

POSIX	
Any alphanumeric character	[[:alnum:]]
Any alphabetic character	[[:alpha:]]
Any digit	[[:digit]]
Any lowercase character	[[:lower:]
Any punctuation character	[[:punct:]]
Any space	[[:space:]]
Any uppercase character	[[:upper:]]
Any word	[[:word:]]
Any hexadecimal digit character 0–9, a–f, and A–F	[[:xdigit:]]
Any character of a certain glyph set, such as a, à, á, â, ã, ä, å, A, À, Á, Â, Ã, Ä and Å	[[=a=]]
Any blank character: space or tab	[[:blank:]]
Any control character	[[:control:]]
Any graphical character	[[:graph:]]
Any printable character	[[:print:]]
Any character whose code is greater than 255	[[:unicode:]]

Change to Other		
Clipboard Contents, Formatted	^c	~c
Clipboard Contents, Unformatted	^C	~C

Change to Found	
All Found Text	$0
Found Text (specifies the number of the grouping found, such as $3 for the third grouping; groupings are enclosed in parentheses)	
Found 1	$1
Found 2	$2
Found 3	$3
Found 4	$4
Found 5	$5
Found 6	$6
Found 7	$7
Found 8	$8
Found 9	$9

CHAPTER SUMMARY

Another jumping off point, we're hoping we've ignited some sparks with this chapter that will fire you up to learn more. You got your feet wet with InDesign's built-in GREP features, using them to amplify the power of paragraph styles and to take Find/Change to a whole new level. Essential to efficient EPUB production, the GREP skills you learned, with minor adaptations, are portable to a number of code editing applications and will also prove invaluable for cleanup of your EPUB HTML files.

In your work with GREP you

- Were introduced to InDesign's saved GREP queries

- Analyzed content to identify patterns you could target with GREP

- Used a character style to provide visual feedback during GREP development and testing

- Created an awesome GREP expression to target email addresses

- Learned your way around some of the GREP Special characters for search menu options

- Learned how to save and share GREP queries

- Used GREP Find/Change to extract and reorganize document content

Additionally you became familiar with

- GREP Wildcards

- Repeats

- Marking subexpressions

- Non-marking subexpressions

Sure there's more, but with InDesign's help you definitely know enough to be dangerous. And to fan the flame just a bit, think about using GREP in your paragraph styles to eliminate widows and orphans, and to automatically format certain words or types of phrases the same way every time they appear such as email addresses, phone numbers, twitter handles—the possibilities are literally endless!

The next chapter pulls together all the pieces that play a part in EPUB production. It gives you everything you need to put a bow on it, so, let's wrap things up.

● Chapter 26

EPUB EXPORT & PUBLISHING

This chapter will help you put the finishing touches on your EPUB and to ready it for prime time. You'll learn the ins and outs of InDesign's EPUB export options and how to convert your file to Mobi format—a requirement if you intend to sell your book on Amazon. With your eBook ready to launch, you'll learn how you can actually get it out into the world, exploring some options, learning what to watch out for and getting started on the right foot.

Before Exporting to EPUB

TIP: Go to File > File Info and complete the Document Title metadata field on the Description tab to add a title to your document for export to EPUB.

With information it gathers from your document and the default EPUB export settings, along with some additional fancy footwork, InDesign does an admirable job of generating an EPUB that complies with the 2.0.1 standard. It rasterizes the first page to use as a cover image, employs file names as image Alt text, adds a creation date and a navigational table of contents (with a single navigation point), specifies the language of the document, and generates the required unique identifier. As long as you've kept your end of the deal and added a title, barring any peripheral issues, the final product should indeed comply with the letter of the law. If you intend to distribute your eBook commercially however, the resulting EPUB is, shall we say "less than optimal," and may not pass muster when you try submitting it to online stores.

Not to worry, you've already become familiar with most of what you need to know to design and create a sales-worthy EPUB.

NOTE: For Kindle and iBookstore cover image guidelines, see page 408.

- You've learned how to optimize images and objects using custom rasterization, add appropriate Alt text, and create a cover image that meets established guidelines (Chapter 22: Images, Objects & The Flow, starting on page 321.)

- You've generated a TOC for EPUB and saved a TOC style (Chapter 8: Creating a TOC, starting on page 119.)

- You've used export tagging to map your InDesign paragraph and character styles to HTML tags and CSS classes (Chapter 24: HTML And CSS Fundamentals, starting on page 347) and made edits to the resulting code.

- You've anchored objects (page 329) and/or used the Articles panel (page 323) to control document flow .

- You've learned three ways to implement page breaks: defining breaks before and/or after objects through Object Export Options, splitting a document based on paragraph style, and compiling multiple documents into a single book file.

- You've learned how to add metadata that will help your audience find your eBook.

You're almost ready to put it all together but first we must emphasize yet again the importance of proper file naming when it comes to publishing digital content. The best way to stay out of trouble is to use only lower-case letters, numbers and underscores in your file names, no spaces or crazy characters, and only begin a file name with an underscore or lower-case letter. With EPUB, this convention should be applied to your InDesign source file, any of its linked content, folder names and the name of the EPUB itself. Files have been known to fail the upload process due to naming problems so devoting the proper attention up front can save you a boatload of troubleshooting on the back end. You're best off staying away from spaces and crazy characters in your style names as well, and keep them unique to avoid confusion in the CSS style cascade.

Now that you have all the pieces, you're in a better position to make the most of the EPUB export options. You've seen that without much attention to the options, you can export your document to EPUB for testing purposes at pretty much any point in your workflow. This enables you to tweak your layout and make modifications as necessary to achieve your desired appearance and flow. You can even take advantage of this iterative approach to develop a customized style sheet for inclusion during export or to use as a replacement for the default InDesign CSS when the final export is complete.

The EPUB Export Options Dialog

You've already had a glance at it but now we'll take a few minutes to make sense of the options in the EPUB Export Options dialog. The dialog is divided into three tabs: General, Images and Advanced.

The General tab

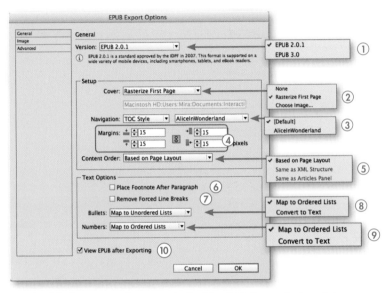

The default settings in the General tab of the EPUB Export Options dialog.

1. Version: For flowable EPUB choose EPUB 2.0.1. EPUB 3.0 supports fixed layout as well as a number of additional features and is outside the scope of this book.

2. Cover: Required for a valid EPUB. If you choose the Rasterize First Page option, ensure that the resulting file conforms to the requirements of your target platform.

3. Navigation: For all the details of creating and saving a TOC style see Chapter 8, starting on page 119.

4. Margins: The margin settings entered here will appear in the CSS in an @page rule with margin values specified in pixels like so:
   @page{
       margin : 0px 0px 0px 0px;
   }
   Not all eReaders respect margin settings.

5. Content Order: When Based On Page Layout is selected, InDesign scans the page from left to right and top to bottom to determine reading order. XML tagging can also be used to determine content order however it's not without

its limitations. See David Blatner's article at http://indesignsecrets.com/
structure-pane-versus-page-order-for-epub-export-from-indesign.php
to learn more. If you've created articles to control content order choose Same
as Articles Panel. Only articles that are checked in the panel will be included
in export.

6. Place Footnote After Paragraph: If selected, footnotes will be place after the
paragraph. Otherwise, footnotes will be converted to endnotes.

7. Remove Forced Line Breaks: Removes all soft returns.

8. Bullets: Either maps bulleted lists to HTML <ul> tags or to <p> tags if Convert to
Text is selected.

9. Numbers: Either maps ordered lists to HTML <ol> tags or to <p> tags if
Convert to Text is selected. We were unable to discern a difference between
the results of the Ordered Lists and Static Ordered Lists options.

10. View EPUB after Exporting: Generally a good idea since it provides yet
another opportunity to catch errors that may have otherwise been overlooked.

The Image tab

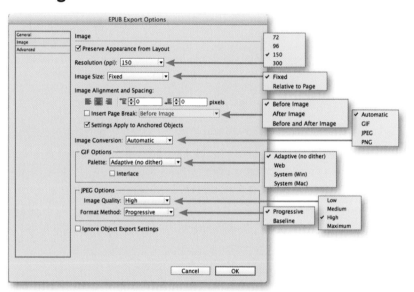

The default settings in the Image tab of the EPUB Export Options dialog.

The options on the Image tab of the EPUB Export dialog should for the most part be
quite familiar. They are largely the same as the EPUB and HTML options provided in
the Object Export Options dialog explored in Chapter 22 (page 333.)

The Preserve Appearance option at the top of the dialog is an instruction to
InDesign to rasterize images so the appearance of any transformations and effects
you've applied—scale, rotation, drop shadow, etc.—is maintained. This option
does not pertain to InDesign graphics and text frames to which effects have been
applied. If you leave the box unchecked, images without custom rasterization
settings will render at their original dimensions without transformations or effects.

The Settings Apply to Anchored Objects option applies alignment and spacing options to custom anchored objects and not objects anchored inline or above line.

The Ignore Object Export Settings checkbox enables you to override the export options applied to individual objects in favor of the settings in the EPUB Export Options dialog.

The Advanced tab

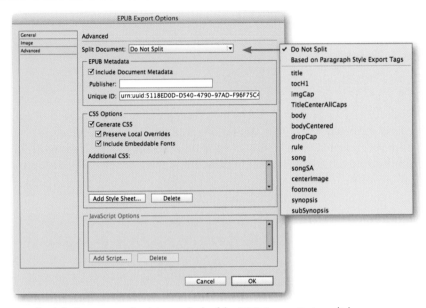

The default settings in the Advanced tab of the EPUB Export Options dialog.

Split Document: Based on the option you choose, InDesign will either split the document based on the export tags you've applied to individual paragraph styles, ignore those settings and not split the document at all, or split it based on a style you select from the Split Document paragraph styles dropdown in the dialog.

EPUB Metadata: You don't want to deselect the Include EPUB Metadata checkbox if you want a valid EPUB. A Unique ID is required for EPUB validation and iBookstore requires a Publisher name (as well as an ISBN for the Unique ID.) In other words, including metadata is non-negotiable.

NOTE: For more on ISBNs, see page 407.

CSS Options: The Include Style Definitions checkbox determines whether or not the formatting choices you capture in saved InDesign styles are carried over to style definitions in the EPUB CSS file. If deselected, classes assigned in Export Tagging are included in the HTML code but the class rules will be absent from the style sheet. Because InDesign includes nearly every possible property in the CSS it generates, you may opt not to include style definitions in the EPUB export and instead create your own CSS rules in a code editor after the fact.

If Preserve Local Formatting is selected, along with the Include Style Definitions option, any style overrides or manual styling you've applied in InDesign is converted to class rules in the CSS and applied to the corresponding HTML tags. This can make for extremely messy code with a separate style rule created for each variation in formatting. Therefore, if you're going to include style definitions in your export, it's strongly recommended that you style all content explicitly with saved styles. Even with Preserve Local Formatting deselected, paragraphs to which no paragraph style has been applied still generate a **p.No-Paragraph-Style** rule in the CSS.

Choosing to Include Embeddable Fonts will not by any means guarantee that the fonts you used in your InDesign document will appear in your EPUB. There are a number of reasons why selected fonts may not show up—from font licensing restrictions, to the way the font is encoded in the eBook, to lack of support for embedded fonts on a given device. For further insights, see Gabriel Powell's excellent discussion of the topic at http://indesignsecrets.com/forum/epub-and-ebook/embedding-fonts-in-epubs-most-of-mine-wont-embed.

The Add Style Sheet option enables you to include custom style sheets in your EPUB, which is a wonderful thing. You can write your own style sheet from scratch or crack open your EPUB and change the InDesign CSS to achieve your desired appearance, being sure to save the resulting style sheet with a unique name. If you include your customized style sheet in the EPUB export and deselect the other CSS export options, InDesign generates its default style sheet (which also includes rules that define the dimensions of every image in the file), and your custom style sheet sets the appearance for everything else.

In order to make this work, be certain to match the names of the CSS classes in your custom style sheet to the class names you assign to the paragraph and character styles in InDesign. InDesign assigns the classes to the appropriate tags during export so you shouldn't have to edit the HTML.

Of course you could just as easily crack open your EPUB and modify the InDesign CSS and HTML after the fact. This is fine if you don't want the option of returning to InDesign for further edits. The thing you don't want to do is add supplemental style sheets to your EPUB in the post-InDesign HTML editing phase—unless you make sure to update the manifest in the content.opf file that is. This isn't really that big a deal—just a simple line of code with the right file path for each CSS file: e.g., `<item id="additional.css" href="css/additional.css" media-type="text/css" />` but adding the CSS in InDesign can spare you the extra effort.

EPUB Workflow

There's a lot to remember in the process of creating a valid EPUB and we figured that a checklist might come in handy. There's really no absolute sequence to follow as long as you cover all the bases. Use the list as a starting point to refine your workflow. We've included an InDesign file of the list in the chapter_26_exercises folder so you can adapt it to your needs (**epub_workflow_checklist.indd**.)

EPUB Workflow Checklist

	Ensure that all linked content files are properly named
	Ensure that all paragraph, character, object, cell and table styles have unique names
	Use GREP Find/Change to remove extraneous white space: multiple spaces, tabs and returns as well as non-breaking spaces
	Apply paragraph, character, object, table, and cell styles to all document content
	Assign HTML tags and CSS classes to paragraph and character styles with Export Tagging
	Anchor images in document content and/or set document flow using the Articles panel
	Apply custom rasterization and layout options to images and placed objects
	Add Alt text to all images and rasterized objects
	Create a cover image
	Create and save a TOC style (with no page numbers)
	Add a document title and other metadata
	If compiling documents in an InDesign book file, choose a style source file that contains the TOC style and document title. Synchronize the book.
	Preflight your document and correct any errors (Run Check Spelling)
	Package the book (at least for archival purposes)
	Export the book (add Publisher name and optionally replace auto-generated unique ID with ISBN)
	Validate the EPUB
	Test the EPUB on target devices
	Make changes as necessary to InDesign source file
	Optional: Crack open the EPUB and tweak the HTML and CSS
	Repackage the EPUB
	Test and validate again
	Convert your EPUB for Kindle

Next steps

So now that you've got an EPUB complete with all the fixings, how do you get it out into the world? Well, there are several approaches you can take. The most time and energy intensive option is to distribute your eBook on your own and handle all the sales and promotion yourself. Unless you're a brilliant marketeer with lots of time and resources, it might be best to consider this as a supplemental strategy rather than a primary approach.

On the opposite end of the spectrum are companies called aggregators that specialize in eBook distribution. For a fee or possibly a percentage, aggregators submit your publication to an assortment of retailers, often completing any conversion required to meet vendor specifications. Here's an alphabetical list of some aggregators and their websites for your further investigation:

- Author Solutions
  http://www.authorsolutions.com/authorservices.aspx

- BookBaby
  http://www.bookbaby.com/

- EBookIt
  http://www.ebookit.com/index.php

- FastPencil
  http://www.fastpencil.com/

- Infinity Publishing
  http://www.infinitypublishing.com/additional-book-publishing-services/ebook.html

- LibreDigital
  http://marketplaces.libredigital.com/

- Lulu (Also print on demand)
  https://www.lulu.com/s1/ebook_publishing

- SmashWords
  http://www.smashwords.com/about/how_to_publish_on_smashwords

- XinXii
  http://www.xinxii.com/gd_cms.php/en?page=publish_en

The list is not intended as endorsement of the included companies. Please use it as a jumping off point to learn more about the workings of the industry and to explore some of the available options.

Not all the aggregators distribute to the same retailers. Some will get your book into the Amazon store and some won't. The same holds true for Apple iBookstore. You may choose to use an aggregator to handle one set of retailers while you set up accounts to handle others directly. There are many ways to go and you'll need to do your homework to determine what works best for you. As a cautionary note, take care to read the fine print. Confirm which retailers are included in an aggregator's bundle, what the fees are, how you get paid, and keep an eye open for exclusivity clauses.

A third option is to deal directly with the majors. Whether through aggregators or direct accounts your hit list should include Amazon, Apple iBookstore, Barnes & Noble Nook Store, Kobo Bookstore and Sony Reader Store—although the major players may very well change by the time you read these words.

Again, don't overlook the fine print. For example, Amazon's KDP Select currently includes a three-month exclusivity clause. Check commission structures carefully since percentages may vary depending on the price point of your publication. There may also be some hoops to jump through to meet retailer requirements. Some retailers require that you have a Tax ID and a US bank account—not having either of these may be a good reason to consider an aggregator. Amazon requires that your eBook be in their proprietary KF8 or Mobi7 format and Apple iBookstore requires that you use a Mac to upload to iTunesConnect. The point is, the landscape is in constant transition with lots of quirky hills and valleys so its beholden to you to do your due diligence.

NOTE: To learn more about converting to Kindle formats see page 408.

Now that you've been properly cautioned, you'll find extensive resources on the publishing portals that provide step-by-step guidance. Here are links to get you started:

- Amazon KDP (Kindle Direct Publishing
  https://kdp.amazon.com/self-publishing/signin

- Apple iTunes Connect
  http://www.apple.com/itunes/content-providers/book-faq.html

- Barnes & Noble PubIt!
  http://pubit.barnesandnoble.com/pubit_app/bn?t=pi_reg_home

- Kobo Writing Life
  http://www.kobobooks.com/kobowritinglife

- Sony Reader Store
  https://ebookstore.sony.com/publishers/

To ISBN or not to ISBN...

ISBN stands for International Standard Book Number. An ISBN enables your publication to be listed in third-party databases of available eBooks and it can serve as the unique identifier required to meet the EPUB specifications. Apple and Kobo require ISBNs, while Amazon and Barnes & Noble do not. In fact, Amazon assigns an ASIN (Amazon Standard Identification Number) which it uses instead of an ISBN to identify your eBook. Aggregators often provide an ISBN as part of their service. Be aware however that while assignment of an ISBN has no implication of rights ownership, the owner of the ISBN does become the publisher of record. Some aggregators make provisions for you to use your own ISBN.

While ISBNs are international, they are distributed regionally. In the United States, ISBNs are available for purchase from Bowker Identifier Services at https://www.myidentifiers.com. Yup, believe it or not, they are the only company in the entire country from which you can actually purchase your own ISBN. Strange, right? In any case, at this writing you can purchase one ISBN for $125, ten for $250, one hundred for $575 and one thousand for $1000. Unfortunately, you cannot sell or reassign them—each block of ISBNs is always and forever bound to the purchasing publisher. If the ownership of the publishing company is transferred, the ownership of the ISBNs can however be transferred with it.

An ISBN can be used only once and each version and format of a publication requires an ISBN of its own. A hard-bound book, the soft-bound version, the EPUB, the audio book, even EPUB versions with significantly different DRM (Digital Rights Management) settings must each have unique ISBNs.

So, the question is, "To ISBN or not to ISBN?" Before you make that determination you'll need to do your research, and then decide based on the choices you make about distributing your EPUB.

Converting your EPUB for Kindle

At this time, Amazon is the leading eBook retailer, which makes it a necessity that your book be in Kindle format if you want the widest possible distribution. Fortunately, there are several options for getting your EPUB converted for Kindle. One way is to upload your EPUB to Amazon KDP and they can run it through the conversion for you. A number of aggregators also handle Kindle conversion as part of their service. If you'd rather do the conversion yourself, there are a couple tools direct from Amazon that can do the trick.

- You can download KindleGen which is a command line tool available for Mac, Windows and Linux.
  http://www.amazon.com/gp/feature.html?ie=UTF8&docId=1000765211

- If you'd rather steer clear of the command line thing, but still want to generate your own Mobi file from an EPUB, download and install Kindle Previewer. http://www.amazon.com/kindleformat/kindlepreviewer Kindle Previewer converts EPUB, HTML, or OPF files to Mobi and also emulates both Kindle e-Ink (black & white reader), Kindle Fire (color tablet), and iOS (iPad and iPhone) devices so you can get a reasonable idea of what the final product will look like.

- Alternatively, you can download and install the Kindle plugin for InDesign, which makes it possible to export to Kindle directly from InDesign without requiring that you first export to EPUB
  http://www.amazon.com/gp/feature.html?ie=UTF8&docId=1000765271

Exercise 26.1: EPUB to Kindle Conversion

1. Download and install Kindle Previewer. (http://www.amazon.com/kindleformat/kindlepreviewer)

2. Once installed, open Kindle Previewer and familiarize yourself with the initial screen. Notice that the Help links include a link to the Kindle Publishing Guidelines. Notice also that there is a link to the Kindle Plugin for InDesign in the Miscellaneous section of the screen (currently only supported in CS4, CS5, CS5.5 and CS6.) Ensure that Kindle Paperwhite is chosen from the Set Default Device Mode dropdown

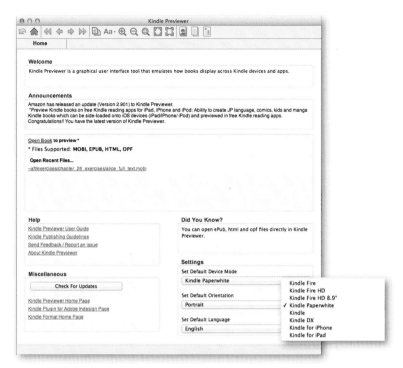

Kindle Previewer serves a dual function as a previewer for Kindle devices and reader apps, and an EPUB to Mobi converter.

3.   Go to File > Open Book, navigate to the chapter_26_exercises folder and select **alice.epub**. When Kindle Previewer finishes compiling the book, click OK.

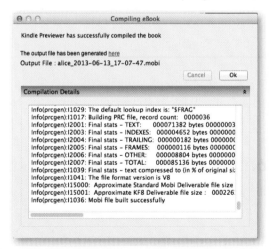

Click the arrows below the OK button to see the eBook compilation details.

Kindle Previewer generates a folder called Compiled-alice.epub to contain the new Mobi file. The name of the Mobi file includes the original file name followed by the date and time the file was generated. Kindle Previewer displays the book using the Kindle Paperwhite device profile you chose when you converted the file.

4. Use the arrows at the upper left of the window to navigate through the file.

Just above the document display are buttons for the device profiles in the selected category—the Kindle e-Ink category includes Kindle Paperwhite, Kindle, and Kindle DX. The other categories are Kindle Fire and Kindle iOS.

5. Click through the e-Ink device profiles above the document window to compare the different displays. To check out the other device categories, go to Devices and choose another option from the dropdown menu.

6. When you've finished exploring the appearance of the book on the different devices, go to File > Close Book and click the Home icon at the upper left of the screen. Keep the application open for the next exercise.

Exercise 26.2: The Kindle Plugin for InDesign

ALERT: We've included this exercise in hopes that by the time you have a chance to work with it, the Kindle Plugin for InDesign will be updated to be compatible with InDesign CC.

1. In Kindle Previewer, click the Kindle Plugin for Adobe InDesign link.

As long as you have an internet connection, the plugin download page should open.

2. Scroll down as necessary to the Downloads section of the page, agree to the terms of use, and choose the download appropriate for your operating system.

If you're using a Mac, it's recommended on the site that you also download and install a VeriSign certificate. Links to the certificate and instructions are right on the page. The certificate install is quick and easy.

3. Ensure that InDesign is closed before installing the plugin. The installer walks you through the steps. When the install is complete, reopen InDesign.

NOTE: When you install the Kindle plugin for InDesign an Export Book For Kindle option is added to the InDesign Book panel menu and an Export for Kindle option is added to the File menu.

The Kindle Plugin for InDesign installer walks you explicitly through the install process.

4. In InDesign, go to File > Open, navigate to the chapter_26_exercises folder and open **alice_full_text.indd**.

NOTE: Embedding of audio or video files is not currently supported by the plugin.

5. Go to File > Export for Kindle and when prompted, save the file in the chapter_26_exercises folder as **alice_full_text.mobi**.

The Kindle Plugin presents a series of dialogs with options quite similar to InDesign's EPUB Export Options.

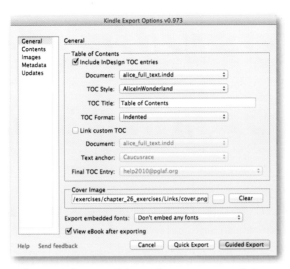

The General options of the Kindle Export Options dialog.

6. In the General pane of the Kindle Export Options dialog, check the Include InDesign TOC entries and choose AliceInWonderland from the TOC Style dropdown. Click the square to the left of the Clear button and navigate to the links folder inside the chapter_26_exercises folder. Select **cover.png**. Choose Don't embed any fonts from the Export embedded fonts dropdown and check the View eBook after exporting checkbox.

7. Select the Contents category at the left of the dialog and deselect the checkboxes for Preserve consecutive white space and new lines and Preserve forced line breaks.

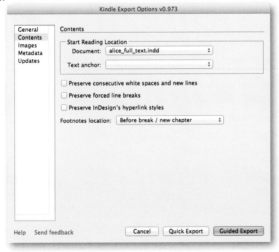

The Contents options of the Kindle Export Options dialog.

8. Select the Images category of the Kindle Export Options dialog and note the similarity to the Image options in the InDesign EPUB Export dialog. Leave the default settings.

The Images category of the Kindle Export Options dialog.

9. Select the Metadata category of the Kindle Export Options dialog. Complete each of the fields with the exception of the ISBN field.

The Metadata category of the Kindle Export Options dialog.

10. Select the Updates category of the Kindle Export Options dialog and optionally deselect the Switch on auto-updates and Join the Plugin Usage Improvement Program checkboxes.

The Updates category of the Kindle Export Options dialog.

11. Click the Guided Export button. When the Select drop caps style dialog appears, leave the default settings and press Continue.

Mobi7 doesn't support the CSS float property used to create the appearance of drop caps but KF8 does. The Select drop caps style dialog enables you to assign drop cap font size and margins supported in KF8, and font size for an initial cap in lieu of a drop cap for Mobi7.

Had you elected to export embedded fonts, you would have also been presented with an opportunity to choose which fonts to include and which to omit from your file.

When you choose to export embedded fonts using Guided Export, you will have an opportunity to specify which fonts you want to embed in the Mobi file.

12. When the conversion is complete, the Export for Kindle dialog appears to notify you of any warnings or errors. Warnings alert you to potential problems but it is not mandatory that they be corrected. Errors must be corrected or your file risks rejection by Amazon. When you've finished exploring, close the file to complete the exercise.

Had you chosen to export embedded fonts with the exercise file, the Export for Kindle dialog would have alerted you to possible issues related to font display.

CHAPTER SUMMARY

The intention of this chapter was to help you put all the pieces together and to provide a solid notion of how to proceed with getting your eBook out into the world. To keep things straight, a workflow checklist itemized the many tasks and components that factor into EPUB development—proper file naming among them.

You explored the intricacies of the EPUB Export dialog, reviewing the options on each of its three tabs:

- The General tab
- The Image tab
- The Advanced tab

Next was a conversation about publishing and distribution options and you were introduced to a selection of aggregators and retailers. You learned to look for contract details that may include

- The list of retailers included in an aggregator package
- Aggregator services that may include
  - Formatting
  - File conversion where required
  - Inclusion of an ISBN
- Fees and royalty rates
- Royalties based on publication pricing
- Special requirements that may be necessary to establish an account

In the process of exploring your publishing options you learned about ISBNs:

- What they are for
- Where to buy them
- How much they cost
- Where they're required

Last but not least, you learned multiple ways to generate Kindle Mobi files for launch on the Amazon store:

- KindleGen command line utility
- Kindle Previewer
- Kindle Plugin for InDesign

As we've said again and again, EPUB (and digital publishing in general) is a journey rather a destination. The next chapter provides you with tools and resources that will help to make it a more rewarding trip.

Chapter 27

EPUB RESOURCES

From production to publishing, the resources in this chapter will help you in all dimensions of your EPUB adventures. You'll find a wide selection of scripts to ease your workflow, eReaders for testing, eBook aggregators and retailers to bring your eBooks to market and a collection of websites and EPUB experts to help keep you up to date with the latest and greatest in the EPUB arena. The goodies in this chapter are pure gold. Mine them well and enjoy!

Scripts

InDesign scripts, like GREP expressions are a phenomenal tool to automate tasks that would be impossibly time consuming without them. InDesign includes a built-in collection of useful scripts and there are also several extremely talented developers who generously share the fruits of their genius with the InDesign community. In just a couple pages, you'll find the treasure trove of resources we've been promising. Before that however, you'll learn how simple it is to work with scripts.

Modifying a Script

The FindChangeByList script—included in the JavaScript folder inside the Samples folder in the Scripts panel—is one you may find particularly useful in your work with EPUB. With the help of an associated text file called FindChangeList.txt, the script performs a sequence of GREP Find/Change commands that replace the following:

NOTE: The FindChangeList.txt can be found in the FindChangeSupport subfolder in the Scripts panel.

- all double spaces with single spaces
- all returns followed by a space with single returns
- all returns preceded by a space with single returns
- all double tabs with a single tab
- all returns followed by a tab with single returns
- all returns preceded by a tab with single returns
- all double returns with single returns
- all space-dash-space with an en dash
- all dash-dash and replace with an em dash

Since the flow of text in your EPUB changes with changing font size, you may also want to replace non-breaking spaces with punctuation spaces. You can accomplish this with a simple edit to the text file.

Exercise 27.1: Modifying a Script

DOWNLOAD: Exercise files for this chapter can be downloaded from http://www.interactive-indesign.com.

1. Go to Window > Utilities > Scripts.

   There are two folders in the Scripts panel: the Application folder and the User folder. The Application folder contains a Samples folder that contains AppleScript (Mac only) and JavaScript subfolders. Initially, the User folder is empty and, like the Application folder, can be used to store scripts you load into InDesign yourself. The User folder is stored in your preferences and the Application folder is in the InDesign application folder. You can find the exact location of the script folders on your system through the Scripts panel menu.

2. Click the disclosure triangles to expand the Application folder, the Samples folder, the JavaScript folder and the FindChangeSupport folder. Right-Click/Ctrl+Click the **FindChangeList.txt** file and choose Reveal In Explorer (Windows) or Reveal In Finder (Mac OS).

3. Copy and save the file with a different name—just in case—and open the original in a plain text editor. Expand the text frame so you can view the full script.

4. Select and copy the third line from the bottom of the text and paste it just below

the line you copied.

The code you copied can be broken into four pieces separated by tabs:

DOWNLOAD:
http://indesignsecrets.
com/resources/plug-
ins-and-scripts

- **The find type:** grep
- **The findWhat GREP code:** {findWhat:"\r\r+"} (two or more returns)
- **The changeTo GREP code:** {changeTo:"\r"} (a single return)
- **The Find/Change options:** {includeFootnotes:true, includeMasterPages:true, includeHiddenLayers:true, wholeWord:false}
- **Add a description:** Find all double returns and replace with single returns.

5. Change the findWhat GREP code to
   {findWhat:"[~s~S]"} (fixed-width nonbreaking space or nonbreaking space)

6. **Change the changeTo GREP code to**
   {changeTo:"~."} (punctuation space)

7. Leave the The Find/Change options unchanged and edit the description to read:
   "Find all nonbreaking spaces and replace with punctuation spaces."

```
character and replace with single returns.
grep    {find what:"\t\r"}     {change to:"\r"}      {include footnotes:true, include master
pages:true, include hidden layers:true, whole word:false}      Find all returns followed by a tab
character and replace with single returns.
grep    {find what:"[~s~S]"}    {change to:"~."}      {include footnotes:true, include master
pages:true, include hidden layers:true, whole word:false}      Find all nonbreaking spaces and
replace with punctuation spaces.
text    {find what:" - "}      {change to:"^="}      {include footnotes:true, include master
pages:true, include hidden layers:true, whole word:false}      Find all space-dash-space and
replace with an en dash.
text    {find what:"--"}       {change to:"^_"}      {include footnotes:true, include master
pages:true, include hidden layers:true, whole word:false}      Find all dash-dash and replace with
an em dash.
```

8. Save the script, close the text editor and return to InDesign to complete the exercise.

Exercise 27.2: Running a Script

1. Go to File > Open, navigate to the chapter_27_exercises folder and open ex27_2_start.indd. Save the file as ex27_2.indd.

   Before running the corrective script, if you want take a minute to confirm some of the issues with the file, use GREP Find/Change and check for multiple returns, multiple spaces, multiple tabs, nonbreaking spaces, a tab followed by a return, a return followed by a tab, a double dash and a dash space dash sequence.

   NOTE: For details on how to work with GREP Find/Change, see Chapter 25 about GREP, starting on page 379.

2. To run the script, Double-Click **FindChangeByList.jsx** in the Script panel. If you check the document again, you'll find that all the issues have been corrected.

   Don't be concerned if your receive an error message. It doesn't seem to impact the performance of the script.

3. Close the file to complete the exercise.

Installing a Script

Installing a script is as easy as running one. Simply download and unpack it, and then add the .jsx file to the appropriate folder—which you can locate through the options in the Script panel context menu.

Now that you know how to install and run scripts, you're all set to take full advantage of the goodies to follow.

Resources

At long last, the resources we've been promising! By no means an exhaustive list, before installing, please confirm that any scripts, plugins, or other applications you choose are compatible with your system and the version of InDesign you are running. Otherwise, it's possible you may experience unintended and potentially undesirable results.

eReaders

Adobe Digital Editions
http://www.adobe.com/products/digital-editions/download.html

Azardi: Supports EPUB 3
http://azardi.infogridpacific.com/

Barnes & Noble Nook
http://www.barnesandnoble.com/u/free-nook-apps/379003593

Calibre
http://calibre-ebook.com/download

Kindle Previewer:
Visual interface for KindleGen also doubles as a Kindle device and application emulator
http://www.amazon.com/kindleformat/kindlepreviewer

Readium™, a project of the International Digital Publishing Forum (IDPF). Supports EPUB 3
http://readium.org/

Sony Reader
http://ebookstore.sony.com/download/

EPUB Editing Tools

BB Edit:
Professional HTML and text editing software. Inexpensive big brother to Text Wrangler, BB Edit is also Mac-only Comparison of BB Edit to Text Wrangler:
http://www.barebones.com/products/bbedit/

Calibre:
Calibre is a free tool for reading, creating, editing, and converting eBooks to and from a variety of formats including ePub and Mobi.
http://calibre-ebook.com/

Adobe Dreamweaver:
Awesome tool for writing, editing, and validating HTML and CSS (as well as other code languages) through both WYSIWYG and code-based environments. Also an excellent site management tool and FTP application.
http://www.adobe.com/products/dreamweaver.html

KindleGen:
Command line tool available for Mac, Windows and Linux.
http://www.amazon.com/gp/feature.html?ie=UTF8&docId=1000765211

Kindle Previewer:
Visual interface for KindleGen also doubles as a Kindle device and application emulator
http://www.amazon.com/kindleformat/kindlepreviewer

Kindle plugin for InDesign:
Alternative to Kindle Previewer, you can download and install the Kindle plugin for InDesign that will permit you to export to Kindle direct from InDesign without having to export first to EPUB
http://www.amazon.com/gp/feature.html?ie=UTF8&docId=1000765271

Notepad ++:
Free Windows-only code editor and Notepad alternative.
http://notepad-plus-plus.org/

XML Author:
Primarily an XML editing tool, Oxygen allows you to access and update all the internal EPUB files without requiring that you crack open (and then re-package) your EPUB. It also includes ePubcheck validation and the ability to drag/drop files (including images.)
http://www.oxygenxml.com/

Sigil EPUB Editor:
> Free multi-platform EPUB ebook editor.
> http://code.google.com/p/sigil/downloads/list

Text Wrangler:
> Free Mac-only code and text editing software
> http://www.barebones.com/products/textwrangler/download.html

Zip/Unzip Scripts (for Mac users)

Scroll to the second post (#18 by Dan Rodney) and download EPUB-Zip-and-UnZip.zip. (You will have to create a free account with a login and password for the link to work.)
> http://www.mobileread.com/forums/attachment.php?attachmentid=6021
> 0&d=1288043085 (http://bit.ly/QbqR77)

EPUB Validation Tools

Validates uploaded DRM-free EPUB documents with epubcheck 3.0b5-pre.
> http://www.epubconversion.com/ePub-validator-iBook.jsp

Validates uploaded EPUB documents that are10 MB or less
> http://validator.idpf.org/

EPUB validator for Windows, Mac and Linux
> http://code.google.com/p/flightcrew/

(Mac only tool)
> http://www.macupdate.com/app/mac/35031/epubchecker

Command line tool
> http://code.google.com/p/epubcheck/

eBook Aggregators

Author Solutions: http://www.authorsolutions.com/authorservices.aspx

BookBaby: http://www.bookbaby.com/

EBookIt: http://www.ebookit.com/index.php

EPUB Direct: http://www.epubdirect.com/

FastPencil: http://www.fastpencil.com/

Infinity Publishing: http://www.infinitypublishing.com/additional-book-publishing-services/ebook.html

LibreDigital: http://marketplaces.libredigital.com/

Lulu (Also print on demand): https://www.lulu.com/s1/ebook_publishing

SmashWords: http://www.smashwords.com/about/how_to_publish_on_smashwords

XinXii: http://www.xinxii.com/gd_cms.php/en?page=publish_en

eBook Retailers

Amazon KDP (Kindle Direct Publishing)
> https://kdp.amazon.com/self-publishing/signin

Apple iTunes Connect
> http://www.apple.com/itunes/content-providers/book-faq.html

Barnes & Noble PubIt!
> http://pubit.barnesandnoble.com/

Kobo Writing Life
> http://www.kobobooks.com/kobowritinglife

Sony Reader Store
> https://ebookstore.sony.com/publishers/

GREP Resources

Michael Murphy: Prolific GREP master.
- blog at http://www.theindesigner.com/blog/category/grep
- InDesign CS4: Learning GREP with Michael Murphy at Lynda.com
- Article: GREP in InDesign CS3

EPUBSecrets.com: excellent EPUB resource
http://epubsecrets.com/grep-cleanup-of-indesign-to-epub-files-from-ron-bilodeau.php

InDesignSecrets.com: is a wealth of information for everything InDesign. You'll find a resource page dedicated entirely to GREP at
http://indesignsecrets.com/grep

Peter Kahrel, InDesign scripter and GREP wizard extraordinaire
http://www.kahrel.plus.com/indesign/script-info.html

Scripts

A whole page of links to a collection of scripts
created by Peter Kahrel
http://www.kahrel.plus.com/indesignscripts.html

Another whole page of links to a collection of scripts
created by Harbs at in-tools.com
http://in-tools.com/products/scripts/

Showing Text Formatting Overrides
Adds a menu item below Show Hidden Characters in the Text menu to show a strike-through on text with character-level overrides and a vertical line next to text with paragraph-level overrides.
created by Harbs: In-Tools.com
http://in-tools.com/article/scripts-blog/showing-text-formatting-overrides/

The Hidden Way to Highlight Styles
Shows applied paragraph and character styles in color based on color coding that you assign
created by Marc Autret: Indiscripts.com
http://www.indiscripts.com/post/2012/05/the-hidden-way-to-highlight-styles

ePubCrawler
(InDesign Fixed Layout ePub Assistant) helps convert from InDesign to fixed layout ePub. In the process, it generates a skeleton ePub folder, css files, xhtml files, and linked images. Extensive features and instructions.
created by Kris Coppieters: Rorohiko.com
http://www.rorohiko.com/wordpress/manuals/fixed-layout-epub-assistant-in-indesign-epubcrawler/

TomaxxiLinkRename
Renames linked files to match their page numbers
created by Marijan Tompa
http://tomaxxi.com/downloads/

Share My Screen:
Adds a Share My Screen option to the File menu to restore access to Acrobat.com
created by Marijan Tompa
http://tomaxxi.com/downloads/

Enable/disable GREP expressions
InDesign panel extension that enables you to toggle GREP Paragraph expressions on and off.
created by Marijan Tompa
http://tomaxxi.com/2011/08/panel-tomaxxigrep/

tomaxxiResizeEach
Enables you to resize selected objects to a size you specify
created by Marijan Tompa
http://tomaxxi.com/downloads/

StorySplitter
Removes threading between text frames of a selected story without reflowing the text. Provides an option to either split all fames of the story or to split the story thread into two separate stories before or after the selected text frame. Great for breaking a story into separate frames to sequence article elements in the Articles panel.
Included in the collection of scripts in the InDesign Script panel Sample folder

Convert Multicolumn Text Frames to Individual Frames Script

Breaks the columns of a multicolumn text frame into separate threaded text frames

created by Steve Wareham

http://indesignsecrets.com/convert-multicolumn-text-frames-to-individual-frames-script.php

A GREP Editor

Excellent GREP editing tool with resizeable window that supports multiline entries and comments, automatically highlights matches, and allows you to load and save queries.

created by Peter Kahrel

http://www.kahrel.plus.com/indesign/grep_editor.html

Merge Text Frames Extension for Adobe InDesign

Merges multiple text frames into one, maintaining paragraph styles and enabling control of the size of the resulting textframe

created by Justin Putney and AJ Petersen

http://ajarproductions.com/blog/2008/11/28/merge-textframes-extension-for-adobe-indesign/

Easy Catalog

Not just for catalogs, Easy Catalog provides database publishing solutions for InDesign

Created by 65bit Software Limited.

http://www.65bit.com/products/easycatalog/overview/overview.shtm

Apply Nested Styles

Converts nested styles into actual applied character styles

created by Harbs at in-tools.com

http://in-tools.com/products/scripts/

FindChangeByList

Can be used to quickly clean up a document for EPUB export. (see Exercise 27.1 for details.)

Included in the collection of scripts in the InDesign Script panel Sample folder

Perfect Prep Text

Creates and applies character styles to locally formatted text

created by Theunis DeJong, aka "Jongware." and Peter Kahrel

http://indesignsecrets.com/perfectpreptext-a-smart-way-to-style-local-formatting.php

Show/Hide Local Formatting:

Indicates character style overrides with red strikethroughs and paragraph style overrides with a red vertical bar at the left of an overridden paragraph.

created by Marc Autret

http://www.indiscripts.com/post/2010/05/show-local-formatting-in-indesign-cs4

Websites

http://code.google.com/p/epub-samples/

EPUB 3.0 examples. (Click the Downloads link on the top navbar.)

http://ebookninjas.com

Podcasts. (Joshua Tallent, Toby Stevenson, and Chris Casey are the eBook Ninjas.)

http://epubzengarden.com/

Lots of example epubs with downloadable HTML, CSS and asset files.

http://www.adobe.com/jp/devnet/digitalpublishing.html

Adobe Digital Publishing Technology Center

http://www.mobileread.com

MobileRead Forum. (Free membership required.)

http://epubsecrets.com

Awesome EPUB resource site created by David Blatner and Anne-Marie Concepción, and hosted by Matthew Diener.

http://indesignsecrets.com/

All InDesign, all the time: David Blatner and Anne-Marie Concepción

http://www.pigsgourdsandwikis.com

Liz Castro

http://www.theindesigner.com

Michael Murphy

http://www.instantindesign.com

Gabriel Powell and Chad Chelius

http://www.lynda.com/

Massive subscription-based video training library

http://idpf.org/
> International Digital Publishing Forum: Trade and standards organization for the digital publishing industry

http://www.bisg.org/
> Book Industry Study Group: Provides information relevant to the book industry

https://twitter.com/search?q=%23eprdctn
> #eprdctn: Twitter e-Production group of in-the-trenches professionals

Embeddable Fonts

Google Web Fonts
> http://www.google.com/webfonts

SIL International fonts
> http://scripts.sil.org/cms/scripts/page.php?cat_id=FontDownloads

Scientific and Technical Information Exchange (STIX) font project
> http://sourceforge.net/projects/stixfonts/

Adobe Edge Web Fonts through the Creative Cloud (Typekit)
> https://typekit.com/

EPUB and EPUB Resource Gurus (Alphabetical)

Marc Autret: http://www.indiscripts.com/

David Blatner and Anne-Marie Concepción: http://indesignsecrets.com

Ron Bilodeau: http://silvadeau.wordpress.com/about/

Laura Brady: http://www.bradytypesetting.com

Liz Castro: http://www.pigsgourdsandwikis.com/

Kris Coppieters: http://rorohiko.blogspot.com/

Colleen Cunningham: http://twitpic.com/photos/BookDesignGirl

Matthew Diener: http://epubsecrets.com

Harbs (Gabe Harbs): http://in-tools.com/

Cari Jansen: http://carijansen.com

Peter Kahrel: http://indisnip.wordpress.com/tag/peter-kahrel/

Michael Murphy http://www.theindesigner.com

Gabriel Powell and Chad Chelius: http://www.instantindesign.com/index.php?view=391

Joshua Tallent, Toby Stevenson, and Chris Casey: eBook Ninjas: http://ebookninjas.com/

Joshua Tallent: eBook Architects: http://ebookarchitects.com/resources/

Marijan Tompa: http://tomaxxi.com/

CHAPTER SUMMARY

This chapter wraps up the section on EPUB. With guidebook in hand and the companionship of seasoned travelers to help chart your way, you're well equipped for a foray into the EPUB frontier.

As EPUB evolves, incorporating more media and interactivity, the boundaries between eBooks and apps will undoubtedly continue to blur. Complement or competition—who's to say? We can't know with any certainty which technology will "win" or what disruptive new medium may emerge—which is what makes this digital migration such a wild ride. That said, a discussion of digital publishing with InDesign wouldn't be anywhere near complete without an in-depth look at DPS—Digital Publishing Suite—the topic of the next, and last section of the book.

Part 7

DIGITAL PUBLISHING SUITE

Adobe Digital Publishing Suite (DPS) is yet one more landmark development in the evolution of InDesign from print layout application to "printeractive" development platform. With DPS, you too can create immersive interactive experiences like the Wired magazine and Martha Stewart Living apps now available in the Apple iTunes store. With InDesign tools and features specifically tailored to meet the specialized demands of mobile design, you'll be completely awed by the possibilities these tools will open to you.

Chapter 28

INTRO TO DPS

This chapter provides an overview of DPS—what it is and how it works. You'll gain an understanding of the DPS publishing process and the steps you'll need to take to get up and running. With the big picture in view, you'll be well equipped to further explore this awesomely cool technology.

Digital Publishing Suite: The Big Picture

There are no two ways about it; being able to use the same tried and true print application that you have come to know and love to build an actual App Store-worthy app is pretty mind blowing. This section of the book will teach you how to do just that. You'll learn how to create slideshows and panoramas, and how to integrate audio and video and even web content in your app. Along the way, you'll also learn some very powerful tips and tricks to maximize the possibilities that DPS and InDesign's tools present. That said, it's important to realize that building your app and getting it into an App Store are two different things. The primary focus of this section is on the process of creating the content for your app but we'll also point you to some excellent resources to help you navigate the technical details of getting your app to market. Fact is, when it comes to creating and publishing a DPS app, InDesign is but one piece of a bigger puzzle, so let's take a look at the pieces and how they fit together.

First off, DPS is actually an Adobe subscription service with several enrollment options. (It's not necessary however to have a subscription in order to use the DPS tools to design your app in InDesign. You only need the subscription or the Single Edition license when you're actually ready to publish your app.) At this writing, you can create one-off Single Edition apps to distribute through the Apple App Store exclusively (not Amazon Kindle Fire Newsstand or Android Marketplace) for a one time fee to Adobe of $395 per app. A Single Edition app is ideal for transforming publications like brochures, catalogs, portfolios, yearbooks, or annual reports into interactive experiences.

The good news, and we think this is REALLY good news if you're psyched about DPS, is that one of the benefits of paid Creative Cloud membership is an unlimited number of DPS Single Edition licenses. That means no $395 fees. Since this book is about InDesign CC, you're no doubt familiar with the fact that unless you've limited your subscription to specific applications, Creative Cloud enables you to download any/all of the software included in what used to be the Adobe Master Collection: Photoshop, Illustrator, InDesign, Acrobat, Dreamweaver, Fireworks, Flash, Premiere, After Effects, Audition, and more. In addition to these applications, and included in a free Creative Cloud membership, is a selection of software tools and services available only through Creative Cloud. At the time of this writing, Edge Animate, a tool for creating HTML5-based animation is one of the applications included in the free membership for example. You'll be hearing more about Edge Animate later in this section. Monthly fees for Creative Cloud range at this time from $19.95 to $69.95 depending on whether you want to license a single app or the entire collection, what existing software licenses you have, and whether you are a single user or part of a team. If you intend to publish Single Edition DPS apps, subscribing to Creative Cloud is a no-brainer. To learn more about what Creative Cloud has to offer, check out the FAQ at http://www.adobe.com/products/creativecloud/faq.html.

We've already made mention of DPS Single Edition but there are two additional DPS subscription levels to choose from: Professional Edition and Enterprise Edition. These subscription levels enable you the option to expand the reach of your app beyond the Apple App Store to include Android Market Place and Amazon Kindle

Fire Newsstand. Both subscription models provide access to analytics and greater customization options as well as the ability to create multi-folio applications like magazines with monthly issues. For a comparison of features and pricing, take a look at these links:

Digital Publishing Suite, Professional and Enterprise Edition:
http://www.adobe.com/products/digital-publishing-suite-pro/buying-guide.html

Digital Publishing Suite, Single Edition:
http://www.adobe.com/products/digital-publishing-suite-single/buying-guide.html

Digital Publishing Suite FAQ:
http://www.adobe.com/products/digital-publishing-suite-enterprise/faq.html

In discussing DPS throughout the following chapters, the focus is exclusively on Single Edition publications. The underlying assumption therefore is that the files you create are destined for viewing exclusively on the iPad. Which brings us to the next piece of the puzzle: becoming an Apple Developer.

> **NOTE:** While you must use a Mac in order to submit your app to the App Store, you are free to develop your application using InDesign's DPS tools on both Mac and Windows platforms.

To develop and distribute iOS apps, you must have an Intel-based Mac running Mac OS X Snow Leopard or later, and you must be enrolled in the Apple iOS Developer Program. While it's free to register as an Apple Developer, in order to access some of the essential tools and to actually distribute your apps on the App Store, you must pay a $99 annual enrollment fee. Learn more about the program here: https://developer.apple.com/programs/ios/.

You must have an Apple ID, be enrolled in the Apple iOS Developer program and have an Intel-based Mac running Mac OS X Snow Leopard or later to develop and distribute iOS and Mac apps. If enrolling as a company or an organization, you'll need to provide a legal entity name and a D-U-N-S® Number.

Don't get yourself crazy over the process; just keep putting one foot in front of the other and follow the steps laid out on the Apple Developer website. There are FAQs and all kinds of support materials to help and if there's a problem with your application, Apple's pretty good at following up to assist in getting things sorted out.

Once you get your enrollment squared away, in order to publish your app, at some point you'll need to create an App ID, certificates, mobileprovisioning

---

files, icons and screenshots. Don't be daunted. An excellent and essential step-by-step guide to the application process and to assembling all the required supporting assets and documents can be found at this link: http://help.adobe.com/en_US/ppcompdoc/Step_by_step_guide_to_dps_se.pdf. Download it before you get started. It'll step you through exactly what you need to do to get your DPS app from InDesign to the App Store and it's kept current with any changes made by Apple or Adobe.

So, now that you've had full disclosure and all the possible monsters under the bed have been exposed, just know that the thrill of seeing your app in the App Store completely justifies the effort of getting it there.

Setting Up for DPS

DOWNLOAD: If for some reason you are unable to download the DPS tools by updating InDesign, you can access the downloads here:

Mac: http://www.adobe.com/support/downloads/detail.jsp?ftpID=5377

Windows http://www.adobe.com/support/downloads/detail.jsp?ftpID=5376

If you've never used DPS in InDesign, the first thing you'll need to do is download and install the DPS tools. Not to worry, this is a really simple process. Go to Help > Updates (for both Windows and Mac) and the update should proceed automatically. After the update, the Folio Overlays and Folio Builder panels should appear in the Digital Publishing workspace Panel Dock and also be available from the Windows menu. The update will also install Adobe Content Viewer—an AIR application (Adobe Integrated Runtime) that enables you to preview folio files on the desktop. AIR is a runtime-environment created by Adobe for the development of Internet-based applications that can be run on the desktop or on mobile devices. Periodically, you may be prompted to update the version of AIR running on your computer. Run the updates to ensure support for the latest version of Adobe Content Viewer, which you'll need in order to preview your DPS content.

The DPS tools are updated frequently so don't be alarmed if you receive notification that you must update the software before you can proceed with your work. Of course, you'll need an internet connection to do so.

An Adobe ID is required in order to access Folio Producer and App Builder for Mac, an online service that helps you ready your DPS app for publication. You'll also need an Adobe ID to access Creative Cloud, regardless of whether you are a free or paid subscriber.

At some point in the development of your Single Edition app, you'll need to interface with Folio Producer and App Builder for Mac, the online DPS interfaces that help you ready your app for publication. At that point, you'll need an Adobe ID that's specific to the app you're creating. Setting up an Adobe ID is simple, requiring nothing more than an email address and password. Go to https://www.adobe.com/account/sign-in.adobedotcom.html and click the "Don't have an Adobe ID?" link to get to the registration screen.

As alluded to earlier, a really cool feature of DPS is that it enables you to preview your app on an iPad directly from InDesign. To do so, however, you need to download the free Adobe Content Viewer app from the App Store and install it on your iPad. You can search the App Store for Adobe Content Viewer through iTunes, use the QR code at the right, or follow this link:

https://itunes.apple.com/gb/app/adobe-content-viewer/id389067418?mt=8

DOWNLOAD: Link to Adobe Content Viewer app.

To view DPS content directly on your device, download the free Adobe Content Viewer from the App Store and sync through iTunes to install the app on your iPad.

DOWNLOAD: Exercise files for this chapter can be downloaded from http://www.interactive-indesign.com.

NOTE: For explicit instructions on creating a customized workspace, see Setting up a custom workspace starting on page 33.

Exercise 28.1: Customizing the DPS Workspace

Before getting started, it's worth taking just a few minutes to customize InDesign's default Digital Publishing workspace to better serve your work with DPS.

1. Go to Window > Workspace > [Digital Publishing].

2. First, close the Animation and Timing panels since InDesign animation is not supported by DPS. Next, we recommend that you drag the Pages and Layers panels into their own shared column and then open and dock the following panels to approximate the screenshot:

   - Paragraph Styles
   - Character Styles
   - Text Wrap
   - Object Styles

   - Effects
   - Align
   - Pathfinder
   - Transform

DPS Workspace

3. Choose New Workspace from the Workspace Switcher dropdown at the upper right of the application window, name the new workspace **DPS,** and click OK to close the dialog.

Folios, Articles and Overlays, Oh My!

NOTE: As an alternative to using two separate documents in a dual-orientation article, a more convenient workflow using alternate layouts makes it possible to combine both a portrait and landscape layout in a single document. Learn more about alternate layouts starting on page 449.

Folio is Adobe's name for the assemblage of articles that collectively comprise the contents of an app. Articles can be composed of up to two documents; one each for the horizontal and vertical orientations of the iPad. Like a magazine, a folio can contain any number of articles. Also like a magazine, an article can range from one to an unlimited number of pages. Folios and articles are assembled in the Folio Builder panel. An example folio might look like this:

A folio example with four articles. Each folio article can include up to two documents, one for the horizontal and one for the vertical iPad layout. It's also possible to create a single article that contains both horizontal and vertical layouts using InDesign's Alternate Layout option. The articles in the image above have one layout for each article.

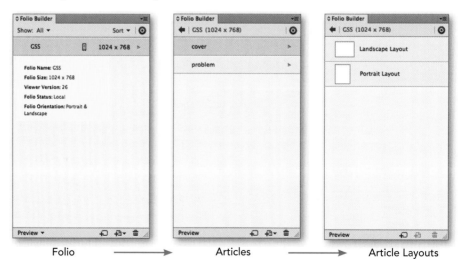

Articles are assembled into a folio in the Folio Builder panel. Articles can contain portrait, landscape, or both portrait and landscape layouts, but, the orientation(s) of all the articles in the folio must be consistent. Each folio can contain an unlimited number of articles. Click the arrow to the right of a folio or article name to move to the next pane in the panel. Click the arrow at the upper left to move to the previous view.

Creating a Folio

In order to define an article, you must first create a folio to contain it. You'll need to decide up front whether you'd like your folio to have horizontal, vertical or dual orientation and eventually, you'll need to provide the appropriate cover image(s). You'll also need to decide on the default format for the articles in your folio. You can choose from JPEG, PNG or PDF or let InDesign choose for you by selecting Auto as the Default Format. PDF is the best choice if you want your folio to perform well on both standard and high-definition iPads. The pros and cons of the PDF format compared to the other options are discussed in some depth starting on page 442. Your choice of orientation and default article format can't be changed after the initial folio setup. You can however change the cover image(s) through the Folio Properties panel which you can access from the Folio Builder panel menu.

> **ALERT:** To complete the exercises in this section, at the very least, you will need to have run an initial InDesign update to install the DPS tools (which include Adobe Content Viewer for the desktop.) Ideally, you will also have an iPad onto which you have installed the free Adobe Content Viewer app downloaded from the Apple App Store so you can preview content on the device.

New Folio panel

Identifies the folio in the Folio Builder panel. It is not visible to readers in the Viewer. Required

Determines the earliest version of the viewer in which the folio can be viewed. Click the version number to access the version options.

Choose a size/target device and orientation for the folio. Right edge binding displays articles in the viewer from right to left rather than from left to right.

Choose from JPEG, PNG or PDF or select automatic to have InDesign select the default article format for you. Choosing PDF will preserve vector graphics and reduce file size.

Selecting a higher JPEG quality will result in increased folio file size.

Sets the preview images used for the folio in the library. Folio previews should be JPEG or PNG files using the same dimensions as the folio.

Creates the folio locally so it can be worked on when no network connection is available.

The New Folio panel

Exercise 28.2: Creating a DPS Folio

In this exercise, you'll create a dual-orientation folio and add two existing dual-orientation articles to it.

1. Navigate to the chapter_28_exercises and Double-Click to open **gss_problem.indd**.

2. Expand the Folio Builder panel (🗇) in the Panel Dock and click the Create new folio button at the bottom of the panel.

3. When the New Folio dialog opens, type "GSS" in the Folio Name field and click on the highlighted number next to Viewer Version to choose version 26 from the dropdown.

> **ALERT:** The DPS Viewer Version at the time of this writing is v26. The DPS tools and Viewer are updated quite frequently so it's likely you'll have more current versions to choose from. We're recommending you choose version 26 simply for the sake of consistency with the exercise.

4. Choose Apple iPad from the Target Device dropdown, and in the Orientation section of the panel, click to select the Portrait and Landscape Folio button. Choose PDF from the Default Format dropdown.

5. Click the folder icon to the right of the word "Vertical" in the Cover Preview section of the panel, and navigate to the chapter_28_exercises folder. Double-Click **gss_cover_v.png** to load the vertical cover image.

6. Click the folder icon for the Horizontal cover, navigate to the chapter_28_exercises folder and Double-Click **gss_cover_h.png** to load the landscape cover image.

7. Check the Create Offline Folio checkbox and click OK to create the folio.

The Folio Builder panel jumps to its Article pane and invites you to add an article.

After creating a folio, the panel directs you start adding articles.

8. Ensure that the **gss_problem.indd** file is active in the document window. Click the Add Article button at the bottom of the Folio Builder panel and choose Add Open InDesign Document.

The New Article panel settings for a dual-orientation article.

9. When the New Article dialog opens, name the article "problem" and set the Article Format dropdown to PDF. The Portrait and Landscape Layout dropdowns auto-populate with the appropriate layouts from the document. Click OK to close the dialog and create the article.

10. Navigate to the chapter_28_exercises folder and Double-Click **gss_cover.indd**.

11. When gss_cover.indd opens in InDesign, click the Add Article button at the bottom of the Folio Builder panel and choose Add Open InDesign Document. Name the article "cover" and set the Article Format to PDF. Leave the other default settings and click OK to exit the dialog.

12. In the Folio Builder panel, click and hold and drag the cover article up to position it as the first article in the folio. Release the mouse when the line above the problem article turns dark gray.

13. With the cover article selected in the Folio Builder panel, click the arrow to the right of the article name to display the thumbnails for its landscape and portrait layouts. (You can add or delete layouts from this pane of the panel.)

The Folio Builder panel enables you to manage and navigate folios, the articles within them and the layouts within the articles.

TIP: Smooth scrolling is only for DPS articles containing one long continuous page. (Pinch and zoom will not work with smooth scrolling articles and applies only to snap-to-page articles exported in PDF format that have no interactive elements.)

14. Click the dark gray arrow at the upper left of the panel to navigate back to the cover article.

   Now that you've created your folio, you'll need to add metadata for each of the articles. Keep the article files open for the next exercise.

Article Properties

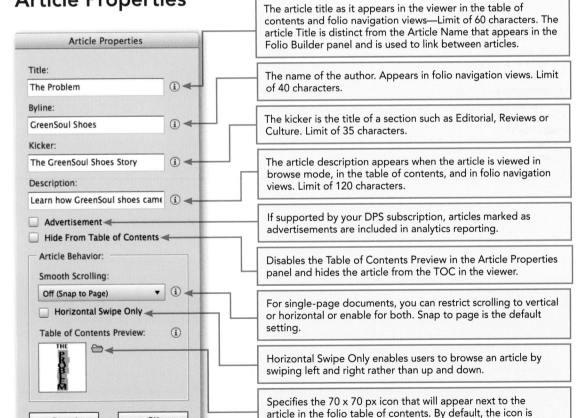

The article title as it appears in the viewer in the table of contents and folio navigation views—Limit of 60 characters. The article Title is distinct from the Article Name that appears in the Folio Builder panel and is used to link between articles.

The name of the author. Appears in folio navigation views. Limit of 40 characters.

The kicker is the title of a section such as Editorial, Reviews or Culture. Limit of 35 characters.

The article description appears when the article is viewed in browse mode, in the table of contents, and in folio navigation views. Limit of 120 characters.

If supported by your DPS subscription, articles marked as advertisements are included in analytics reporting.

Disables the Table of Contents Preview in the Article Properties panel and hides the article from the TOC in the viewer.

For single-page documents, you can restrict scrolling to vertical or horizontal or enable for both. Snap to page is the default setting.

Horizontal Swipe Only enables users to browse an article by swiping left and right rather than up and down.

Specifies the 70 x 70 px icon that will appear next to the article in the folio table of contents. By default, the icon is automatically generated from the first page of the article. For a customized image, create a 70 x 70 px PNG.

You'll need to add metadata to the articles in your folio to serve as reference in the TOC and to determine how the article is treated in the folio. One way to add article metadata is through the Article Properties dialog which is available from the Folio Builder panel menu when its Articles pane is active and an article is selected.

Three of the four Article Properties fields can also be populated automatically with metadata entered in the InDesign File Information dialog.

Exercise 28.3: Adding Article Properties

In this exercise, you'll set properties for the folio articles you created in Exercise 28.1.

1. With both **gss_problem.indd** and **gss_cover.indd** open in InDesign, click the tab for **gss_problem.indd** to make it the active document. Go to File > File Info to open the File Information pane and display the document metadata. Note the contents of the Title, Author, and Description fields and click OK to close the dialog.

The contents of the Document Title, Author and Description fields in the InDesign File Information dialog automatically populate the corresponding fields in the Article Properties dialog.

2. If necessary, expand the Folio Builder panel, click the arrow to the right of the gss folio entry and then click the problem article to select it. Click the menu icon at the upper right of the panel and choose Article Properties from the menu options.

3. Notice that the Title, Byline and Description fields contain the metadata from the File Information dialog. Type "The GreenSoul Shoes Story" in the Kicker field.

4. Click the folder icon in the Table of Contents Preview section of the panel and navigate to the chapter_28_exercises folder. Double-Click **gss_problem.png** to select it as the article icon for the TOC and then click OK to exit the panel.

5. Select the cover article in the Folio Builder panel and choose Article Properties from the panel menu options.

NOTE: For more information about managing article metadata, go to http://helpx. adobe.com/digital-publishing-suite/help/create-articles.html

6. Enter "Cover" for the Title, "GreenSoul Shoes" for the Byline, "Cover" for the Kicker, and "GreenSoul Shoes Cover" for the Description. Click the folder icon in the Table of Contents Preview section of the panel, navigate to the chapter_28_exercises folder and Double-Click **gss_problem.png** to set it as the article icon. Click OK to exit the dialog.

7. Click the arrow at the upper left of the Folio Builder panel to navigate back to the folio pane. With the GSS folio selected, click the Preview button at the bottom of the panel, pause and click Preview on Desktop. Swipe to navigate between the articles and press Ctrl+R/Command+R to toggle between horizontal and vertical orientations. When you're done exploring, return to InDesign.

8. Save and close the files to complete the exercise and the chapter.

CHAPTER SUMMARY

This chapter provided you with a broad view of DPS—the publishing process, document structure, and some of the tools and technologies required for production.

You were introduced to the three levels in the current DPS subscription model:

- Single Edition (Included with a paid Creative Cloud Subscription)
- Professional Edition
- Enterprise Edition

You learned about the DPS Single Edition benefit that's included with a paid Creative Cloud subscription and how to create additional Adobe IDs for your DPS publications.

You discovered how to begin the process of becoming an Apple Developer and learned that you must have a Mac that meets Apple's specifications in order to actually publish your completed DPS app (currently an Intel-based Mac running Mac OS X Snow Leopard or later.)

Perhaps most importantly, you learned how to download the DPS tools and viewers for both desktop and iPad.

Second only to the tools themselves, the most valuable thing in the chapter may be this link: http://help.adobe.com/en_US/ppcompdoc/Step_by_step_guide_to_dps_se.pdf. If you haven't downloaded this incredibly helpful step-by-step DPS publishing guide, don't wait a minute longer. **DO IT NOW!** We highly recommend that you read the entire guide before you get too deeply into production so you don't find yourself scrambling with peripheral details when you're ready to publish your project.

Last but not least, foreshadowing what's yet to come, you gained an understanding of DPS anatomy—that DPS overlays are built in layouts that are nested inside articles that combine to create a folio.

With the preliminaries out of the way, now comes the fun part! In the next couple chapters you'll get to dig in deep with the various overlay types and go well beyond the basics—and even the beyond the bounds of InDesign itself.

Chapter 29

DESIGNING FOR DPS

When it comes to DPS, overlays are where the action is—literally. The very lifeblood of DPS interactivity, overlays make it possible for your audience to scroll through content on a page, to view slideshows and video, take a 360° virtual tour, connect to external content and more.

This chapter introduces the various types of overlays and their underlying structures, InDesign's responsive design tools, and some of the workflow and design considerations you'll face in DPS development. In short, this chapter sets the stage for your work with DPS—so let the show begin!

Understanding Overlays

Overlays are the interactive components that you can include in your DPS articles. They're called overlays because they actually lay over—or on top of—the static content on the page. Any number of overlays can be added to an article, or for that matter, to a single document page.

The bulk of time you'll invest in creating overlays will largely be spent with preliminary work—preparing the overlay elements in InDesign and in some cases, doing extensive work outside of InDesign to develop the assets your overlays require. Once everything is ready to go, the transformation of your content into an actual overlay is a matter of simply setting a few preferences in the Folio Overlays panel. You'll get a clearer picture of how all the pieces fit together as you proceed through the next several chapters. For now, let's start with an introduction to the types of overlays you can create.

The Folio Overlays panel enables you to define the parameters for your overlays.

Hyperlink(s and Buttons): For buttons and hyperlinks having Go To URL actions, the Folio Overlays panel allows you to choose whether the destination URL opens inside the app or in the device browser.

Slideshow: Slideshow overlays are created from multi-state objects that are built using the Object States panel. The individual states of a multi-state object can range in complexity from a single image to a collection of grouped elements, and can even include other overlays. The text and images in each slideshow state are resampled when output to a folio.

Image Sequence: Image Sequence overlays are typically used to simulate animation through a series of still images that portray a progression of incremental changes. Image sequences are perfect for 360° object rotations for example, but serve equally well for any subject that can be documented using a sequence of images—like a sunrise or sunset. The panel settings allow you to set the rate at which the images are played—to create a smooth animation or achieve more of a slideshow effect. You can also allow the viewer to move through the images manually. Assets used in an Image Sequence overlay are passed through to the final folio unchanged.

TIP: Multi-state objects—the foundation of DPS slideshows— can be exported to Flash as well as DPS. Unlike DPS slideshows, multi-state objects exported to .swf support complex InDesign animations.

Audio & Video: The Folio Overlays panel allows you to set play preferences for audio and video files placed in your InDesign document and to specify customized controller images for your audio files. The original controller images are passed through unchanged to the final folio. Learn to create custom controller images in Exercise 31.1: Creating Audio Controller Graphics, starting on page 472 .

Panorama: Panorama overlays are great for creating "virtual tours." The inside of a car, the rooms of a house, a scenic view—all are perfect subjects for a panorama overlay. The overlay is created from six source images, each representing the face of a cube. Creating the actual overlay in InDesign is effortless. Up-front however, you'll need some external resources and the investment of a substantial amount of prep time. Learn all about the prep process in Exercise 32.1: Preparing Panorama Overlay Images with Pano2VR, starting on page 485.

Web Content: How cool is it that you can embed actual web content directly in your app?! You can include Google Maps, YouTube videos and even HTML content of your own. If you need to find your way around the code, Chapter 24: HTML And CSS Fundamentals, starting on page 347 will help you to get off on the right foot. Check out Exercise 33.1: Creating Web Content Overlays, starting on page 494 to learn how to incorporate web content in your DPS folio.

Pan & Zoom: With a tap on an image to activate it, a pan & zoom overlay makes it possible to zoom in on and then pan around an image to better view its detail. The amount of zoom is determined by the amount the image has been scaled down to fit its frame—the larger the difference between the original image dimensions and its reduced size on the page, the greater the range of zoom in the overlay. Check out Exercise 32.3: Creating a Pan & Zoom Overlay, starting on page 489 to learn all about it.

Scrollable Frames: Scrollable frames are made of two parts, the content frame and the container frame into which the content is pasted. The Folio Overlays panel lets you choose the direction of the scroll (horizontal or vertical), whether to show or hide scrollbars, and how the content is initially positioned in the container. Scrollable frames can contain all kinds of content including other folio overlays and can be used to create draggable tabs—a very cool effect. To learn all sorts of ways to bring life to your folios with scrollable frames, check out Scrollable Frame Overlays, starting on page 460.

Overlay Structures

In order to decide how best to prepare your assets and choose the optimal folio format, it's important to understand the way DPS content and the various types of overlays translate to a compiled folio. Overlay content falls into three categories:

- **Static or background content:** Text and images on an article page that are not explicitly part of an overlay.

- **Resampled overlay content:** Overlay content that is resampled when converted to PDF or a compressed image format in the course of compiling a folio.

- **Pass-through overlay content:** Overlay content such as images, audio or video that is passed through unchanged to the final folio.

Static Content

Static content is either rasterized to JPEG or PNG format or converted to PDF, depending on the settings you define for your articles and folio. The PDF format provides several distinct advantages over the other rasterization options, particularly if you want your content to perform well on both standard definition (SD) and high definition (HD) iPads: With the PDF format:

1. Generally, the size of the resulting folio file is substantially smaller than a folio with contents rendered as JPEG or PNG.

2. Text and other vector objects remain resolution independent, producing a crisp and clear result on both SD and HD iPads.

3. Images exported to PDF are resampled with a resolution of 108 ppi instead of 72 ppi, so they perform well on both SD and HD devices.

4. In articles not set to be smooth-scrolling, PDF content allows for pinch and zoom of article pages.

The only downside to choosing PDF format for DPS folios and articles is that a slightly longer load time is required for vector content.

TIP: Multi-rendition articles automatically display standard definition assets on iPad 1 & 2 and HD assets on Retina display iPads. The articles and folio must be in PDF format, the SD and HD assets must have identical names, and the HD assets must be in subfolders named HD. The link from the overlay to its assets is made to the folder containing the SD content and the devices then display the appropriate assets automatically.

```
▼ 🗀 links                      --
  ▶ 🗀 audio_controllers        --
  ▼ 🗀 HD                        --
      pan_n_zoom.jpg      1.2 MB
      pan_n_zoom.jpg      1.2 MB
  ▼ 🗀 sandals_sequence          --
    ▼ 🗀 HD                       --
        sandals001.jpg    85 KB
        sandals002.jpg    70 KB
        sandals003.jpg    49 KB
        sandals004.jpg    56 KB
        sandals005.jpg    66 KB
        sandals006.jpg    69 KB
        sandals007.jpg    71 KB
        sandals008.jpg    70 KB
        sandals009.jpg    74 KB
        sandals010.jpg    75 KB
        sandals011.jpg    77 KB
        sandals012.jpg    73 KB
        sandals013.jpg    62 KB
        sandals014.jpg    65 KB
        sandals015.jpg    63 KB
        sandals016.jpg    68 KB
        sandals017.jpg    75 KB
      sandals001.jpg      31 KB
      sandals002.jpg      26 KB
      sandals003.jpg      23 KB
      sandals004.jpg      26 KB
      sandals005.jpg      31 KB
      sandals006.jpg      33 KB
      sandals007.jpg      33 KB
      sandals008.jpg      33 KB
      sandals009.jpg      35 KB
      sandals010.jpg      36 KB
      sandals011.jpg      36 KB
      sandals012.jpg      34 KB
      sandals013.jpg      30 KB
      sandals014.jpg      30 KB
      sandals015.jpg      29 KB
      sandals016.jpg      32 KB
      sandals017.jpg      35 KB
```

Resampled Overlays

Resampled overlay elements include buttons, slideshows, and the content in scrollable frames. DPS treats resampled overlays similarly to background content. If you choose PDF format for the article that contains them, slideshow and scrollable frame overlays can be rendered to either raster or vector. In a PDF article, by default, the frames of a slideshow are rasterized at 108 ppi, while scrollable frames are rendered by default to vector. Your choice of rendering mode should be based on the content in your overlay—when text predominates, choose vector; if your content is primarily images, raster is the better option. For articles that won't be converted to PDF, slideshow and scrollable frame content is rasterized to JPEG or PNG format at 72 ppi. Be aware that standard 72 ppi images may appear fuzzy on an HD iPad, especially when the content is text-heavy. PDF format is preferable since it works well for both SD and HD devices.

Pass-through Overlays

Pass-through overlays preserve and present your original source files in the finished folio, so it's important to optimize them for best performance. You have some choices to make when preparing pass-through overlay assets since the retina display iPad (iPad 3) has double the resolution of the iPad 1 and iPad 2. Your original assets for audio, video, panorama, image sequence, and pan & zoom overlays, as well as audio skins are all passed through to the final folio. The good news is that beginning with App Builder version 23, both standard and high-resolution assets can be included in your single edition folios to create what are called multi-rendition articles. As long as the file structure is properly defined, and PDF is chosen for the article and folio format, each version of the iPad will automatically display the folio content appropriate to its screen resolution. The trick is to nest a folder named "HD" inside the standard assets folder and put high-resolution versions of the standard-def images in it—with names that are identical to the SD asset names. When creating the overlay, you just link to the SD assets folder and leave it to the iPad to figure out where to retrieve the HD assets.

For pan & zoom, image sequence images, and audio skins, the dimensions of the high-resolution images must be exactly twice that of the SD images or InDesign will throw an error message when compiling the folio. If an SD image is 400 px square for example, the HD version of the image must be 800 x 800 px.

The high-resolution version of pan & zoom, image sequence, and audio skin images must be exactly two times the dimensions of the standard-resolution images or InDesign will produce the above alert.

Image sequences, panoramas and audio skins all require multiple files, so it's best to enclose those files in dedicated folders. Videos and pan & zoom overlays each require only one peripheral file, so there's no need to enclose them in their own folders. Place all the HD videos and pan & zoom images from the folio in a single HD folder that's nested in the links folder.

It's important to understand that the entire collection of SD and HD files are included in the folio and together contribute to its file size. As is the case with any digital project, you must continually be mindful of the tradeoff between file size and quality and the impact these factors have on the performance and download time of the final product. In the interests of minimizing file size, you might choose to use only one set of files for selected overlays rather than versions in both SD and HD. If you ensure that the resolution is right around 108 ppi, the images should perform well on both SD and HD devices. As always, testing is key to making this type of judgement call. For example, if you find that a high-resolution video plays successfully on an SD iPad, there is no reason to bloat the folio by including a low-resolution video as well.

Design Strategies

The creation of an interactive document—or the conversion of a print document to interactive—generally requires development or acquisition of additional assets. Potentially, you'll need additional images, additional written content, media files—if you want to include audio and/or video— and possibly HTML content; either external content that you embed from another site or web content of your own design. When scoping your project, be sure your budget of both time and money takes these additional requirements into consideration.

You'll also need to decide on the orientation you'd like to use for your publication—portrait, landscape or both—another determination best made in the early stages since your choice will most likely impact your asset requirements. A dual-orientation folio will undoubtedly require more time to create than one with a single orientation, but it can also open the door to vastly expanded creative options. Since the two layouts in a dual-orientation article are independent of one another, you could use them to serve separate functions, employing entirely different assets for each. You

> **TIP:** DPS portrait layouts support landscape-only viewing of full-screen video.

could reserve the landscape layout for slideshow and video content for example, while making the portrait layout more text-intensive—or, you could switch up the images between the horizontal and vertical orientations of the same article for variety. The possibilities are virtually endless if you have the flexibility to allocate the required time and resources for development.

TIP: In DPS Folios, Page flipping and smooth scrolling are determined on an article-by-article basis.

To reduce production time, some designers opt to use the same 700-pixel layout with smooth-scrolling articles for both portrait and landscape layouts. This approach also serves to minimize the transition between the horizontal and vertical positions of the device.

Limber Layout

Designing for multiple destinations used to be a pretty tedious task that relied on having multiple files open, lots of copying and pasting, and awful updates when it came to making across-the-board changes. Once again, it's InDesign to the rescue with a trio of features that make multi-destination, responsive design infinitely more efficient: alternate layout, liquid layout and the ability to link content between layouts for easy updates. In combination, these features make InDesign nothing short of a lean, mean, multi-layout machine.

Liquid Layout

TIP: Liquid layout and layout adjustment are mutually exclusive—enabling layout adjustment disables the Liquid Layout options.

Liquid Layout is a phenomenal tool for transforming documents/pages from one configuration to another—sizing and reorienting page content in the process. As is the case with nearly all things Adobe, there is more than one way to get from point A to point B, and with its five different flavors, liquid layout is no exception:

TIP: By default, liquid layout scales only the frame of an object and not its contents. Set your desired fitting options and enable Auto Fit to scale a frame and its contents together.

- **Scale:** Treats all objects on the page as a temporary group and scales them collectively as the page is scaled. Best used when the destination page matches or is similar in aspect ratio to the source.

- **Re-center:** Treats all objects on the page as a temporary group and re-centers them collectively—without scaling—as the page is re-sized. A good option for a layout of the same orientation and slightly different size.

- **Object-based:** Enables scaling rules to be set on an object-by-object basis with options to scale height, width or both. Objects can be individually anchored to the top, bottom, left and/or right of the page either through the Liquid Layout panel or directly on the document with the Page tool active. Object-based layout provides the greatest degree of control relative to individual objects on a page.

- **Guide-based:** Enables scaling of objects based on the placement of liquid guides on the page. Objects that touch or are intersected by vertical guides scale horizontally while objects interacting with horizontal guides scale vertically. Generally works best for simpler layouts.

- **Controlled by Master:** objects on the page scale based on the liquid layout rule applied to the master page—scale, re-center, object-based or guide-based.

Layout rules can be applied on a page-by-page basis and work best in conjunction with fitting rules and text frame options as you'll see in the next exercise.

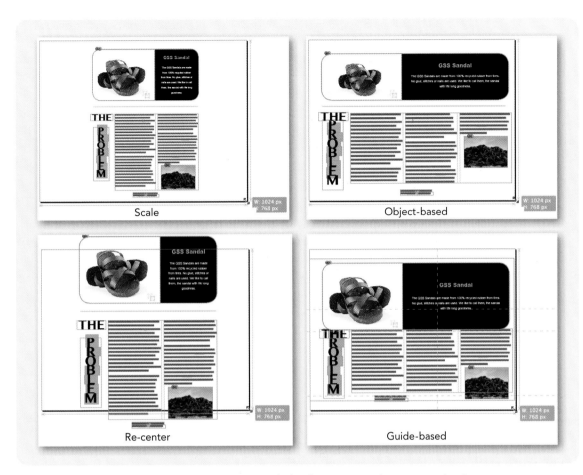

Scale	Object-based
Re-center	Guide-based

The four liquid layout options applied to the same example page. Note that the main content text frame is set to dynamically add and remove columns as seen in the object and guide-based examples.

Exercise 29.1: Working with Liquid Layout

In this exercise, you'll explore the various liquid layout options and how they affect objects on the page.

DOWNLOAD: Exercise files for this chapter can be downloaded from http://www.interactive-indesign.com.

1. Go to File > Open and navigate to the chapter_29_exercises folder. Double-Click **ex29_1_start.indd** to open it and save the file as ex29_1.indd. Go to View > Entire Pasteboard (Alt+Shift+Ctrl+0/Opt+Shift+Command+0) to make room around the page in the viewing window.

2. Select the Page tool and click anywhere on the document to activate the Page tool controls in the Control panel. If necessary, set the Liquid Page Rule dropdown to Off.

Click the document page with the Page tool to activate the Page tool controls on the Control panel.

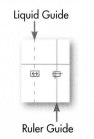
3. Position the Page tool cursor on the lower right corner of the page. When the cursor changes to a diagonal double arrow, click and hold and drag the mouse up and to the right. Use the smart guide dimensions that appear at the lower right of your cursor to approximate the target dimensions for the landscape version of the page—1024 x 768.

Note that when you resize the page with the Liquid Page Rule off, the page scales but the size and position of the objects on the page remain unchanged. Also note that the thumbnail for the page in the Pages panel changes dynamically as you drag the Page tool.

4. Release the mouse to allow the page to snap back to its original dimensions.

5. Choose Scale from the Liquid Page Rule dropdown, and once again, drag the lower right corner of the page to approximate the landscape page dimensions. Note that the page contents remain centered on the page and scale proportionally, maintaining their placement relative to one another. Release the mouse to revert to the original layout.

6. Choose Re-center from the Liquid Page Rule dropdown, and again, drag the lower right corner of the page to approximate a landscape layout. This time, observe that the page contents retain their original sizes and positions relative to one another but shift collectively to center themselves on the changing page. Release the mouse.

7. Choose Guide-based from the Liquid Page Rule dropdown and notice the one vertical and three horizontal guides on the page. Drag the page with the Page tool and notice that the content on the page is unaffected.

Despite the fact that you've selected the Guide-based liquid layout option, the page contents don't change when the page is resized. This is because the guides on the page are ruler guides, and they must be converted to liquid guides before they can help to reshape the page.

8. With the Page tool still active, hold the Ctrl/Command key to switch temporarily to the Selection tool and click to select one of the guides. Still holding the modifier key, mouse over the guide badge, wait until the comment box appears that says, "Ruler guide. Click to make a liquid guide." and click the badge to convert the guide.

Liquid guides are indicated by a dashed green line.

9. Select each remaining guide and click its badge to convert it to a liquid guide.

10. Drag the page with the Page tool again to see that, this time, the objects touching or intersected by the guides shift and change with the changing dimensions of the page. Pay particular attention to the changing column width in the two-column text frame located in the main content area. Release the mouse.

While the alternate layout would require some minor adjustments, overall, the reflow of the page contents presents a pretty good foundation for the landscape version of the page. The main content text might be easier to read, however, if there were three columns of text—rather than the wider columns needed to fill the expanded text frame. Well, it just so happens that InDesign has the intelligence to accomplish exactly that.

11. Switch to the Selection tool and select the two-column text frame in the bottom portion of the page. Press Ctrl+B/Command+B to open the Text Frame Options

dialog. With the General options pane active, choose Fixed Width from the Columns dropdown and click OK to close the dialog.

When you chose the Fixed Width option from the Columns dropdown in the Text Frame Options dialog, the Width and Maximum field values were automatically populated with the width of the columns in the existing text frame. The Fixed Width option enables InDesign to add or remove columns dynamically in response to changes in the width of the text frame.

Setting columns to a fixed width enables InDesign to dynamically add or remove columns in response to changes in the width of the text frame.

12. Once again, use the Page tool to preview the page at 1024 px by 768 px.

    This time, a third column is added to the main content text frame when you scale the page.

13. Choose Object-based from the Liquid Page Rule dropdown in the Control panel and go to Window > Interactive > Liquid Layout to open the Liquid Layout panel.

14. Using the Page tool, click the image of the shoes on the document, and note the dashed lines and the filled and hollow dots that appear around the image.

TIP: You can activate the Liquid Layout panel controls by clicking a document page using the Page tool.

You can apply an object-based liquid rule using the Liquid Layout panel or by setting constraints and pins directly on a selected object using the Page tool.

The shoes slideshow is pinned to the left and top edges of the page, which means that these edges will maintain their positions relative to the page edge when the page is scaled. The lock on the horizontal guide—the width constraint—indicates that the width of the object will remain constant when the size of the page is changed. The squiggle on the vertical guide indicates that the height of the object can change in response to a change in page size.

15. Drag the lower right page edge yet again, and observe the way the objects scale as you drag.

Object-based rules have been applied to a number of the objects on the page but there are a few that still require attention.

16. Click the word "Problem" with the Page tool to select it, and then click the hollow dot at its left edge to pin the object to the left edge of the page.

Click the outermost dots on an object to pin or unpin it from a page edge and the innermost dots to set width and height constraints. Alternatively, with the object selected, you can set all parameters in the Liquid Layout panel.

17. Pin the following:
    - The left edge of the word "The"
    - The left and right edges of the horizontal rule
    - The left and bottom edges of the main content text frame

18. Use the Page tool to preview the 1024 x 768 px layout and observe the scaling of the objects on the page.

Let's not forget Controlled by Master, the default liquid layout setting. With this option, the liquid rule applied to the master page is applied to the pages it governs. The Controlled by Master rule is the best option for documents with layouts dictated entirely by master pages.

19. With the Page tool still active, select Controlled by Master from the Liquid Page Rule dropdown in the Control panel. In the upper portion of the Pages panel, Double-Click A-Master to make it the active page in the document window. If necessary, press Shift+P to switch to the Page tool.

20. Choose Guide-based from the Liquid Page Rule dropdown on the Control panel and check the Show Master Page Overlay checkbox. Hold the Ctrl/Command key (to stretch your guide beyond the page into the pasteboard), and click and hold and drag a guide from the horizontal ruler to anywhere on the page. Drag a second guide from the vertical ruler to anywhere on the page.

21. Double-Click page 1 in the Pages panel to display it in the document window and drag the lower right corner of the document page with the Page tool to approximate a landscape layout. Note how the objects resize on the page.

22. Play with the placement of the guides on the master, adding and removing guides as desired. When you've finished experimenting, save and close the file to complete the exercise.

TIP: To remove a guide from your page, select the guide using the Selection tool and press the Delete key on your keyboard. Alternatively, click and hold and drag the guide off the page.

NOTE: To match the placement of the guides on the master to the liquid guides on page 1, position horizontal guides at 332 px, 521 px and 934 px, and a vertical guide at 464 px.

Alternate Layouts

Now that you've explored the liquid layout options, you're all set to put them to work creating an alternate layout. As you've already seen in the folio from the last chapter, alternate layouts make it possible for a single document to contain layouts in both portrait and landscape orientations. While a folio article can have at most two layouts, an InDesign file itself is not bound by such restrictions. In the context of digital publishing, you might include additional layouts in the same InDesign file for an Android device for example. In fact, the same techniques you use to create multiple layouts for digital publishing apply just as effectively to layout for print. Ideal for creating an assortment of display ads with varied dimensions for example, alternate layouts could also revolutionize your print workflow.

NOTE: Layouts targeted to different devices are called renditions.

You can access the Alternate Layout dialog from the Layout menu, the Pages panel menu, or the dropdown menu for an existing layout in the Pages panel. Alternate layouts can be based on a selected page, a specific liquid rule, or can preserve the rules applied on a page by page basis throughout the document.

The Create Alternate Layout Dialog

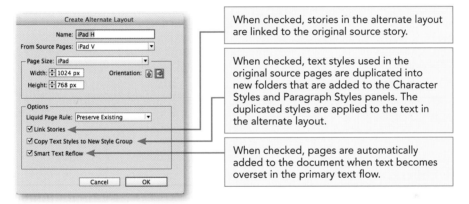

When checked, stories in the alternate layout are linked to the original source story.

When checked, text styles used in the original source pages are duplicated into new folders that are added to the Character Styles and Paragraph Styles panels. The duplicated styles are applied to the text in the alternate layout.

When checked, pages are automatically added to the document when text becomes overset in the primary text flow.

The Create Alternate Layout dialog

Whenever you create a new document, its layout is given a default name in the Pages panel that reflects the preset on which it is based—i.e., Letter, iPad, Custom, etc. The layout name is further characterized by the letter V or H to reflect the orientation of its pages (iPad V for example.) When an alternate layout is added, InDesign auto-populates the Name field with the original layout name appended by a space followed by either a V or H—whichever is not applied to the original layout name.

Like the layout name, InDesign auto-populates the page dimensions of an alternate layout based on the layout chosen as the layout source. Alternatively, page sizes can be selected from the presets in the Page Size dropdown or entered manually in the Width and Height fields. Manually entered page sizes change the base name of the alternate layout to Custom.

The From Source Pages option specifies the layout from which to generate the alternate layout. You can create an alternate layout for an individual page by specifying the name of the source layout followed by a colon and its page number; e.g., iPad H:2.

Choose Preserve Existing from the Liquid Page Rule options to apply the liquid rule specific to each page to the corresponding pages of the new layout. Optionally, you can designate a liquid rule to apply to the new layout as a whole.

Beyond its talent for creating new page configurations, the Create Alternate Layout dialog performs a few other nifty tricks that can work wonders for streamlining your workflow. Linked stories are particularly cool in that they dramatically reduce the headache of updating text content between layouts. When the Link Stories checkbox in the Create Alternate Layout dialog is checked, stories in the source layout become parent to their counterparts in the alternate layout. Thus, when an update is made to the parent, the child story displays an alert icon to inform you that a change has been made. Updating the child is as simple as Double-Clicking the alert—either on the story itself or in the Links panel.

When the Copy Text Styles to New Style Group checkbox is checked, InDesign replicates the styles from the original layout and puts them in the Paragraph Styles and Character Styles panels, in folders named after the new layout. The duplicated styles have the same names and definitions as the original styles, but you can change the style definitions in each group of styles independently. The best part is that you can update the original story content without sacrificing the stylistic differences between parent and child.

Last but not least is the Smart Text Reflow option, yet another great innovation in document transformation. The primary text frame that's included in the default Digital Publishing settings in the New Document dialog defines a text frame that can translate its content from one layout to another, adding pages as needed to ensure that your content doesn't become overset. Only one primary text frame is permitted per page but, particularly when reconfiguring text-heavy pages, it can be a wonderful tool to automatically flow text into your new layout.

Now that you've got the skinny on the alternate layout options, you're ready to create an alternate layout of your own.

Exercise 29.2 Working with Alternate Layouts

In this exercise, you'll create an alternate layout and discover the benefits of linked stories and mapped text styles.

1. Navigate to the chapter_29_exercises folder, Double-Click **ex29_2_start.indd** and when it opens, save it as ex29_2.indd.

2. Press Shift+P to switch to the Page tool and confirm that Object-based is the selected Liquid Page Rule in the Control panel. Drag the lower right corner of the document page up and to the right to preview the landscape layout and then release the mouse.

3. Expand the Paragraph Styles panel in the Panel Dock and notice that it contains three styles in addition to the default [Basic Paragraph] style. If necessary, expand the Pages panel in the Panel Dock, and notice that layout iPad V contains one page and that there is a single master page entitled A-Master.

4. Click the dropdown arrow to the right of iPad V at the top of the document pages section of the Pages panel and choose Create Alternate Layout.

5. When the dialog opens, keep the default settings. If necessary, check the Link Stories, Copy Text Styles to New Style Group, and Smart Text Reflow checkboxes. Click OK to create the new layout.

The Create Alternate Layout settings

6. Note in the Pages panel that InDesign generated a new layout named iPad H and a new master named B–Master iPad H.

7. Expand the Paragraph Styles panel and note that the original paragraph styles have been grouped in a folder named iPad V and the styles duplicated for the new layout have been grouped in a folder named iPad H.

8. Expand the Links panel in the Panel Dock and select the item with the name that begins with <The modern...) If the Link Info section of the panel is not visible, click the disclosure triangle at the lower left of the panel.

TIP: When developing styles intended for multiple layouts, ensure that the Based On setting in the General category of the text styles dialogs is set to [No Paragraph Style] in the Paragraph Styles panel or [None] for Character Styles. InDesign cannot create a mapped style when one of the source styles is based on another source style.

TIP: You can print/ export a single page, a single layout or all pages in a document. To specify a particular page in a layout for printing, enter the layout name followed by a colon followed by the page number. E.g., iPad H:2 targets page 2 in a layout called iPad H.

The Link Info section of the Links panel displays metadata for linked stories that includes but is not limited to: hyperlinks and page numbers for the linked stories, the layer on which the stories reside, and Story Status, which indicates whether edits have been made to the linked story content.

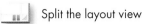 Split the layout view   Close the split layout view

Click the control at the lower right of the document window
to get a side by side view of your alternate layouts.

9. Locate and click the split layout view icon at the lower right of the document window and then click the rightmost page to activate it. Scroll to bring the landscape layout into view and press Ctrl+0/Command+0 to fit the page in the window.

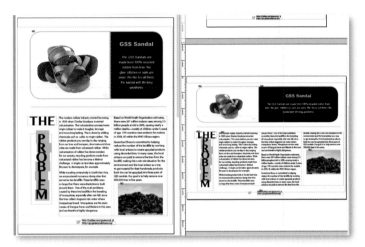

To view alternate layouts side by side, click the split layout view icon at the lower right of the document window or alternatively, go to Window > Arrange > Split Window.

10. Press T to switch to the Type tool, click to position the cursor in the main text frame and press Ctrl+A/Command+A to select the entire story.

11. Ensure that the Character Formatting controls are active in the Control panel and change the font size for the selected text to 14 pt. Expand the Paragraph Styles panel and choose Redefine Style from the panel menu.

12. Click and drag with the Type tool to select the white text in the black text frame. Note that the font size appears in the Control panel as 16 pt (15.04).

The strange font size with one of its values in parentheses is a result of the frame being scaled when the alternate layout was created.

13. Press Escape to select the text frame and to automatically switch to the Selection tool. Note that the Scale X and Scale Y Percentage values in the Control panel are both 94%.

14. Using the Selection tool, click and hold and drag from somewhere outside and above the image of the shoes, down and to the right to intersect and select both the shoes image and the black text frame. Open the Control panel menu from the menu icon at its far right, and choose Redefine Scaling as 100%. Click somewhere on the pasteboard to deselect the objects, and reselect the black text frame. Note that its Scale X and Scale Y Percentage values now both equal 100%.

15. Double-Click inside the black text frame, select the white text and note that the strange font value is gone. Set the font size on the Control panel to 17 pt, expand the Paragraph Styles panel, and choose Redefine style from the panel menu.

Now that each layout has distinct style definitions, you'll explore the benefits of linking stories between layouts.

16. Click back on the document window for the vertical layout to activate it. Click and drag the Type tool in the second paragraph of the main text frame to select the words "While traveling extensively." Type "During our extensive travels" to replace the selected text. Notice that an alert badge appears on the linked text frame in the landscape layout.

17. Click the alert badge on the landscape layout and note that the text frame content updates to match the parent frame and the alert badge disappears. Awesome! Save and close the file to complete the exercise.

When a parent story has been edited, an alert badge appears both on the linked story item in the Links panel and on each threaded text frame of the story in the document. To update the content of a linked story, you can either Click the alert badge on any of the story's text frames or Double-Click the alert badge in the Links panel.

While the changes made to the parent story can be conveyed to the child, the opposite does not hold true. Changes made to the child will be lost if the child is updated to match the parent. InDesign will, however, give you the courtesy of a warning before overwriting your linked story content.

Edits to linked story content go from parent to child only. Edits to the content in the child story get overwritten if the child is updated to match the parent.

The Content Collector and Placer Tools

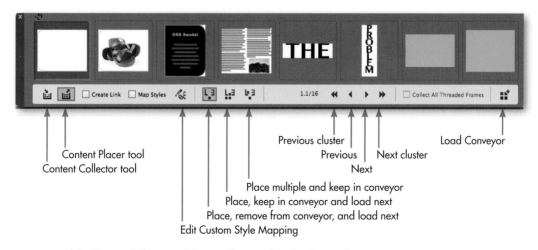

Content Placer tool
Content Collector tool

Edit Custom Style Mapping

Place, remove from conveyor, and load next
Place, keep in conveyor and load next
Place multiple and keep in conveyor

Previous cluster
Previous
Next
Next cluster

Load Conveyor

The Content Collector and Content Placer tools in the Content Conveyor enable you to link all manner of assets between layouts within a single document and between multiple documents as well.

As discussed earlier, duplication and updating of assets between layouts and between documents can present its own set of challenges. While the ability to link stories between alternate layouts is a start, the Content Collector and Content Placer tools go a step further to also enable linking of text and non-text assets both within and between documents.

Exercise 29.3: Using the Content Collector and Content Placer Tools

Before experimenting with the tools you'll set some link preferences so you can see the true versatility of InDesign's place and Link features.

1.   Navigate to the chapter_29_exercises folder and open **ex29_a.indd**, **ex29_b.indd** and **ex29_c.indd**. Choose 3-Up from the Arrange Documents dropdown on the Control panel or choose Window > Tile to display all three documents for comparison.

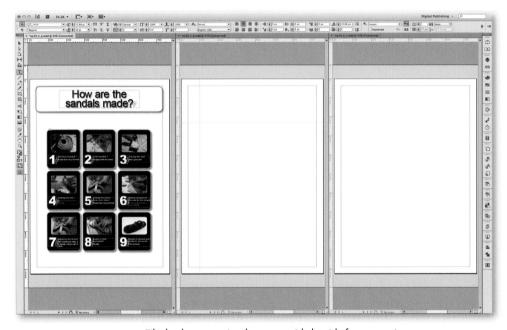

Tile the three exercise documents side by side for comparison.

2.   Make **ex29_4_a.indd** the active document and explore the style definitions in the Paragraph Styles, Character Styles, and Object Styles panels.

3.   Click **ex29_4_b.indd** to make it the active document and explore the Styles panels to confirm that they contain only the default style definitions.

4.   Explore the Styles panels for **ex29_4_c.indd** to find that the document already contains four paragraph styles, a single character style and two object styles. The style definitions for the object styles are different from those in the a-document and the banner and item paragraph styles replace the a-document's header and comment styles respectively.

     By setting a few linking preferences and mapping styles from one document to another, InDesign can selectively retain local changes to linked objects while also coordinating content updates.

5. Still in the c-document, expand the Links panel and choose Link Options from the panel menu. In the Link Options dialog, check the Appearance, Size and Shape, and Define Custom Style Mapping Checkboxes. Keep the dialog open.

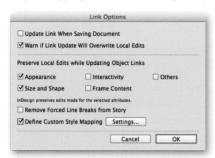

Through the Link Options dialog, you can instruct InDesign to preserve certain local edits to linked objects and still coordinate updates between documents.

6. Click the Settings button at the lower right of the Link Options dialog to open the Custom Style Mapping dialog. If necessary, select **ex29_4_a.indd** from the Source Document dropdown and choose Paragraph from the Style Type dropdown.

The Custom Style Mapping dialog.

7. Click the New Style Mapping button, click Select Source Style or Style Group and choose header from the style list. Click Select Mapped Style or Style Group and choose banner from the style list. Using the same procedure, map the number style from the a-document to the item style in the c-document. Click OK to close the dialog and then OK again to close the Link Options.

The Custom Style Mapping dialog showing two paragraph styles from the a-document mapped to paragraph styles in the c-document.

8. Click to activate the a-document in the document window and then press B to open the Content Conveyor. If the Content Collector is not the active tool (🖼) press B again to select it.

---

9. Mouse over the header at the top of the page and when a heavy blue outline appears around it, click once to add the header to the Content Conveyor. Click once on the group of numbered shoe production steps to add them to the conveyor as well.

10. With the Content Collector still selected, click and hold and drag the cursor to intersect both the header and the steps. Release the mouse to add both objects as a single cluster to the Content Conveyor.

    A cluster is a collection of objects added to the Content Conveyor as a divisible unit. You can use the Content Placer tool to place the entire cluster or to individually place the items it contains.

11. Click to activate **ex29_4_b.indd** in the document window and press B on your keyboard to switch from the Content Collector tool to the Content Placer tool. At the bottom of the Conveyor, check the Create Link and Map Styles checkboxes and the Place, keep in conveyor, and load next icon.

The Content Conveyor with the Content Placer tool active and the Place, keep in conveyor, and load next option active.

12. Ensure that the cursor is loaded with the single header object (![icon]). If it isn't, use the Right Arrow on your keyboard to cycle through the objects loaded into the Conveyor. Click with the Content Placer tool at the upper left margin of the page to place the header.

13. The numbered shoe production steps should now appear in the cursor. Click the Content Placer tool at the intersection of the horizontal and vertical ruler guides to place the steps.

14. Click to activate **ex29_4_c.indd** in the document window.

    The Content Placer tool should be loaded with the object cluster containing both the header and the production steps.

15. Click the Down Arrow on your keyboard to display the collected cluster items in the Conveyor If you chose to, from this view of the Conveyor, you could place any of the items in the cluster individually. Click the Up Arrow on your keyboard to reselect the cluster, and click at the upper left margin of the page with the Content Placer tool to place the cluster. Press V to switch to the Selection tool.

16. Expand the Links panel and click the hyperlink for each object. Note which object is selected on the page as you click through the links in the Links panel.

17. Click **ex29_4_a.indd** to activate it in the document window and Double-Click the image in step number 5 to select the step within the group. Double-Click the image again to select it within the step, and click the Relink button at the bottom of the Links panel. Navigate to chapter_29_exercises > links > sandal_steps and Double-Click **sandals_step5.png** to replace the image. Double-Click in the step instructions text field and when the cursor switches to the Type tool, select and delete the phrase "Rubber from recycled tires."

18. Press Escape four times to switch to the Selection tool and to select the group of production steps. Hold down Ctrl+Shift/Command+Shift and start dragging in from a corner of the group to resize it, and, optionally, add the Alt/Option key to the modifiers to scale the group from its center. Release the mouse and then release the modifier keys when you've scaled the group to about $2/3$ of its original size.

19. Activate **ex29_4_b.indd** and note that an alert icon appears at the upper left corner of its production step group. Mouse over the alert to see the list of applicable updates, and click the alert to implement the changes.

20. Switch to **ex29_4_c.indd,** and update its production step group as well.

    The production step group in ex29_4_b.indd updates to include the changes to both content and size that you made to the original object group. It does not, however, re-center itself on the page. Due to the Link and Style Mapping options you set for ex29_4_c.indd, only the content changes were implemented, leaving the appearance and size of the objects themselves unaffected.

21. Close all three files without saving to complete the exercise and the chapter.

CHAPTER SUMMARY

This chapter was all about setting the stage for your work with DPS and gaining an understanding of what's going on behind the scenes. You started out with an introduction to the players—learning about the different folio overlay types:

- Hyperlink(s and Buttons)
- Slideshow
- Image Sequence
- Audio & Video
- Panorama
- Web Content
- Pan & Zoom
- Scrollable Frames

In a further look behind the curtain you learned about:

- Static/background content
- Resampled overlay content
- Pass-through overlay content
- Export formats and resolution

A discussion of design strategies provided some creative direction and led to an exploration of the assortment of InDesign's responsive design tools and features:

- The Page tool and Liquid Layout with its five options:
  - Scale
  - Re-center
  - Object-based
  - Guide-based
  - Controlled by Master
- And tools and features for placing and linking content including:
  - Alternate layouts
  - Content Collector, Content Placer and Content Conveyor
  - Linking options
  - Custom Style Mapping
  - The Place and Link command

Now comes the part where you become the director, creating overlays and coaxing them into a splendid performance.

● Chapter 30

SCROLLABLE FRAME OVERLAYS

Extremely versatile, scrollable frame overlays can be used for a wide variety of cool effects from simple scrolling text frames to pull-out tabs and more. You can even use scrollable frames to contain other overlays. Starting with the basics, this chapter goes well beyond to provide a taste of what you can do with a little ingenuity.

Scrollable Frame Overlays

When you think of scrollable frames, most likely the first thing that comes to mind is a block of text that scrolls vertically within a frame to expose text that was hidden. While this is perhaps the most common way to employ them, scrollable frame overlays can also be used in other very clever ways to really spice up your apps. The next couple exercises will get you started, and, with the fundamentals under your belt, you can then let your imagination run wild with new possibilities.

Exercise 30.1: Basic Scrollable Frame Overlays

1. Navigate to the chapter_30_exercises folder and open **ex30_1_end.indd.**

2. Expand the Folio Overlays panel in the Panel Dock and click the Preview button at the bottom of the panel. When the Preview on Desktop button appears, click it to preview the document in Adobe Content Viewer.

3. When the document appears in Adobe Content Viewer, click and hold the arrow of the swipe icon and drag up to scroll through the text in the frame. Click and hold and drag down to scroll back to the top of the text. (You can actually click and drag anywhere in the body of the text to scroll the frame.) Return to InDesign when you're finished exploring.

4. Open **ex30_1_start.indd** from the chapter_30_exercises folder and save it as ex30_1.indd.

5. Expand the Layers panel in the Panel Dock, and, if necessary, click the disclosure triangle to the left of the scrollingText layer to show its object sublayers.

   Note that we've renamed each of the object layers according to the naming conventions outlined on page 172. The scrollableFrame object will become the container for the missionContent object. Both the content frame and the container frame in a scrollable frame overlay can be of any content type: text, graphic, unassigned or mixed. Both frames retain fill, stroke, corner options and transparency, as well as other assorted effects. While drop shadows are supported, layer blending modes are not.

6. Using the Selection tool, select the missionContent content frame on the pasteboard and press Ctrl+X/Command+X to cut it. Select the scrollableFrame container frame on the document page and go to Edit > Paste Into (Alt+Ctrl+V/Option+Command+V.)

   The pasted content is vertically centered and displayed inside the boundaries of the container frame.

7. With the container frame selected on the document, if necessary, expand the Folio Overlays panel in the Panel Dock. Scroll to the bottom of the panel and click Scrollable Frame to expose the overlay options.

   Scrollable frames can scroll vertically, horizontally or both. You can choose to hide or show scrollbars and whether to manually position the content in the container, or have InDesign align it automatically to the container's upper left corner. For PDF articles, you can choose to render the overlay content to vector or raster. (The best choice for text-heavy content is vector, while raster is best for images.)

8. Choose Vertical from the Scroll Direction dropdown and leave the Hide checkbox unchecked. If necessary, choose the Upper Left radio button and choose Vector from the Export Format in PDF Articles dropdown.

Settings for the scrollable frame overlay.

9. Click the Preview button at the bottom of the Folio Overlays panel. Pause until the Preview on Desktop option appears, and click it to display the document in Adobe Content Viewer.

   When the preview opens, notice that the top of the content frame is aligned with the top of the container frame. Note also that portions of the upper and lower left corners of the container frame are obscured by the edges of the content frame and that the left and right margins are unbalanced.

10. Click and hold and drag up on the scrollable frame content to test the overlay. When finished testing, return to InDesign.

NOTE: The scroll indicator used in the exercise is just one icon in the **icons.indl** library, which has been included with the exercise files for your use. Find it in the chapter_30_exercises folder.

When a content frame is selected inside its container, its entire bounding box is visible on the page, despite some content being masked by the container.

11. Switch to the Direct Selection tool (A) and click once on the text in the container to select the content frame. Either click and hold and drag or use your Arrow keys to reposition the content frame. Situate it in the container so the margins are balanced and the first line of text is visible at the top of the frame and has a little bit of white space above it. Adjust as necessary to ensure that the type in the last line of visible text doesn't get cut by the frame.

TIP: Hold the Shift key while pressing the Arrow keys on your keyboard to move objects ten times the distance they would move using the Arrow keys alone.

12. Select the overlay, and, in the Scrollable Frame pane of the Folio Overlays panel, select the Use Document Position radio button.

13. Preview the page again and note that the margins of the scrollable frame are balanced and the container corners are now fully visible when the text is scrolled.

14. Close Adobe Content Viewer and return to InDesign. Save and close all open files to complete the lesson.

Creating Pull-out Tabs

Scrollable frame overlays can be used to create a very cool pull-out tab effect. This outside-the-box approach to scrollable frames relies on three scrollable frame overlay features: the ability to set the initial position of the content frame within the container, the hide scrollbars option, and the ability to dictate the direction in which the content scrolls.

Exercise 30.2: Creating Pull-out Tabs

1. Navigate to the chapter_30_exercises folder and open **ex30_2_end.indd**.

2. If necessary, expand the Folio Overlays panel in the Panel Dock. Click the Preview button at the bottom of the panel, pause until the Preview on Desktop option appears, and click it to display the document in Adobe Content Viewer.

3. Click and hold and drag each of the tabs nested at the right edge of the page across to the left page edge and then back to their original positions.

   Notice that the scrolling content can be of any length and that it works equally well with both text and images.

4. When you're finished exploring, exit Adobe Content Viewer and return to InDesign.

NOTE: When viewed on the desktop version of Adobe Content Viewer, the tabs may behave erratically. They may jump, or pop fully open or collapse all at once to display only the tab. Don't let this concern you—when viewed on the iPad, the tabs scroll smoothly as intended.

TIP: For scrollable frame overlays that have stroked container frames, you can offset the content from the container by adding inset spacing in the Text Frame Options dialog (Ctrl+B/Command+B.) The inset is particularly useful in managing InDesign's automatic placement of the content frame in the container. Just remember that, in order to take advantage of the inset option, the containing frame must be for text rather than graphic content.

Pull-out tabs created using scrollable frame overlays.

5. Return to the chapter_30_exercises folder and open both **ex30.indl** and **ex30_2_start.indd**. Save the lesson file as ex30_2.indd.

   The guides were placed on the page to help you position the frames that will become the containers for the tab content frames. The first thing you'll do is create the container frames. Next, you'll position the frames from the library that contain the tab content, and then cut and paste them into the container frames.

6. Select the Rectangle Frame tool and click once where the uppermost of the three horizontal guides intersects the left page edge. When the Rectangle dialog opens, set Width to 767 px and Height to 440 px. In the Control panel, set the Fill and stroke to [None].

Clicking once on your document with any of the shape tools
opens a dialog where you can enter precise parameters.

7. Switch to the Selection tool, and, holding down the Alt/Option key, click and hold and drag the frame down to snap a duplicate frame to the second horizontal guide. With the new frame aligned to the guide, release the mouse and then the modifier key.

8. Holding down the Alt/Option key again, click and hold the second rectangle and drag down to snap a duplicate frame to the bottommost horizontal guide.

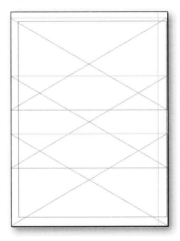

The appearance of the page after the three container
frames have been added and aligned to the guides.

With the container frames now in place, the next step is to add the content frames.

9. In the **ex30.indl** library, click the artisans library item, hold down the Shift key and click the shoes library item. With all three items selected, click and hold and drag them onto the page.

Using modifier keys, you can select multiple library items. Hold the
Shift key to select consecutive items and Ctrl-Click/Command-Click
to select items that are not contiguous.

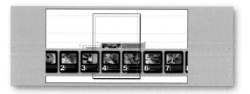

The process library item extends beyond the bounds of the pasteboard as indicated by the dotted lines in the gray area.

TIP: To view the entire pasteboard, go to View > Entire Pasteboard or press Alt+Shift+Ctrl+0/ Option+Shift+ Command+0.

NOTE: InDesign ensures that any placed object that extends beyond the pasteboard is selectable by positioning it so a portion of it overlaps a pasteboard edge.

While objects that extend beyond the bounds of the pasteboard are still selectable and their bounding boxes are visible, having to continually reposition them to access their content can become rather tedious. No problem! You can easily extend the pasteboard to make things easier to reach. The dimensions of the pasteboard are determined by adding the margins to the size of the page (which in this case is 1024 px by 768 px.) You'll resize the pasteboard to allow room to display the tab content and to properly position the process content in its text frame. The width of the process content frame is 3519 px and each of the tab content frames are 438 px in height.

10. Go to Edit > Preferences > Guides & Pasteboard/InDesign > Preferences > Guides & Pasteboard. In the Pasteboard Options section at the bottom of the Preferences dialog, enter 3500 px for Horizontal Margins and 500 px for Vertical Margins. Click OK to close the dialog.

In the Preferences panel, you can customize the size of the pasteboard by adjusting the margins surrounding the document page.

11. Go to View > Entire Pasteboard (Alt+Shift+Ctrl+0/Option+Shift+Command+0) and click somewhere on the empty pasteboard to deselect the library items.

12. Select the artisans content frame and align the leftmost edge of its tab to the vertical guide at the right of the page. Align the top of the frame to the topmost horizontal guide.

13. Press Ctrl+X/Command+X to cut the content frame. Select the topmost container frame and press Ctrl+Alt+V/Command+Option+V to paste the content into the container.

Only the tab of the artisans content frame should be visible in the container. The X that was in the container frame should have disappeared and the X from the middle container frame should show where the two frames overlap.

When the tab content is pasted into the container frame, only the tab remains visible. The X that was on the container frame disappears, while the X on the middle frame overlaps it and remains visible.

14. Position the shoes content frame with the left edge of its tab aligned to the vertical guide and the top of its frame aligned to the second horizontal guide. Cut the content frame and paste it into the middle container frame.

15. Position the process content frame with the left edge of its tab aligned to the vertical guide and the top of its frame aligned to the bottommost horizontal guide. Cut the content frame and paste it into the bottom container frame.

With all the content frames in their correct containers, you're ready to convert the tabs to scrollable frame overlays.

16. Using the Selection tool, select the artisans container, expand the Folio Overlays panel in the Panel Dock, scroll to the bottom of the panel if necessary, and click Scrollable Frame. Set Scroll Direction to Horizontal and check the Scroll Indicators Hide checkbox. Select the Use Document Position radio button and choose Vector from the Export Format in PDF Articles dropdown.

The settings for each of the three scrollable frame overlay tabs.

17. Apply the same settings to the shoes and process container frames.

To complete the creation of the scrolling tabs, you'll rename them in the Layers panel to avoid any possible name-related issues when the code is compiled.

18. Expand the Layers panel in the Panel Dock and click the disclosure triangle for the tabs layer to expose the object sublayers. Click the disclosure triangles for each of the object sublayers to see the names of the content frame objects.

Rename overlay objects in accordance with the proper naming
conventions to prevent possible code compiling errors.

19. Click, pause briefly, and then click again on the <sandal_ma...er-2.png> layer
    name to activate the name field. Rename the layer processFrame.

    It's important that object names contain no crazy characters and preferably
    no spaces.

20. Give the first <graphic frame> sublayer the name shoesFrame.

21. Give the second <graphic frame> sublayer the name artisansFrame.

22. Click the Preview button at the bottom of the Folio Overlays panel. Pause until the
    Preview on Desktop option appears and then click it to display the document in
    Adobe Content Viewer.

23. Click and hold and drag the tabs to test them and then pat yourself on the back.
    You've successfully created scrolling tabs! When you're done checking things out,
    close Adobe Content Viewer and return to InDesign.

24. Save the file and close all open documents to complete the exercise.

Editing Scrolling Frame Content

What happens if you've got your scrolling frame overlays all put together and then,
as you're previewing the file, you discover a change or correction that you just have
to make? How do you edit the overlays?

Well, there are basically two approaches to take. You can cut and either update
or replace the original content, or you can keep a version of your content on the
pasteboard for editing and paste a linked copy of it into the container frame.

You'll explore both options in the next exercise.

Exercise 30.3: Editing Scrolling Frame Content

1. Navigate to the chapter_30_exercises folder, open **ex30_3_start.indd** and save it
    as ex30_3.indd.

    Tab-style scrolling frame overlays pose a unique selection and editing
    challenge since most of their content is hidden. The Layers panel can be helpful
    in selecting hidden objects but the edits you can make to them are obviously
    quite limited. One way to edit the content of a scrolling frame is to extract it
    from the container.

2. Using the Selection tool, Double-Click anywhere in the scrollable frame overlay to
    select the content frame inside the container.

The selected content frame in the scrolling frame overlay is
indicated on the pasteboard by a dashed bounding box.

3. Press Ctrl+X/Command+X to cut the frame from the container and press Ctrl+V/
    Command+V to paste it back onto the document.

    When the tab content is pasted onto the page, an X reappears on the
    container frame. Using the Place and Link command, you'll create parent and
    child versions of the tab content. The content you just pasted will become the
    source file (parent) for the content in the container frame (child.)

NOTE: Learn more about the Content Collector tools and link options starting on page 453.

4. Position the tab content below the document page on the pasteboard, and, while
    it is still selected, go to Edit > Place and Link.

    The Content Conveyor appears at the bottom of the screen loaded with the tab
    content, and the cursor displays the loaded Content Placer tool ( )

TIP: The link on the loaded Content Placer cursor indicates that the object being placed will be linked to the item in the Content Conveyor.

The Content Conveyor loaded with the tab content and the loaded Content Placer.

5. Position the loaded cursor at the intersection of the top and right page margins,
    and click to place the tab content.

    Two versions of the content frame should now be visible: the parent
    frame positioned on the pasteboard below the page, and the child frame
    overlapping the container frame.

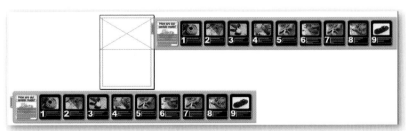

Use Place and Link or the Content Collector and Content Placer tools to establish
a parent/child relationship between assets in the same document or between files.

6. Press and hold Ctrl+Spacebar/Command+Spacebar and drag to draw a box
    surrounding steps 4, 5, and 6 of the parent content frame. Release the mouse and
    then the modifier keys to zoom in on the steps.

7. Press T to switch to the Type tool, and click and drag to select the orange text in step number four. Click the arrow to the right of the text Fill icon on the Control panel and choose RGB Red from the pop-up Swatches panel.

Changing the font color from the Control panel.

8. Hold down the Ctrl/Command key to switch temporarily to the Selection tool and click the star at the left of the now red text. Change its fill to RGB Red.

9. Change the fill color of the orange object and text in step six to RGB Red, and press Ctrl+S/Command+S to save the file.

10. Zoom in on the upper left corner of the child content frame to notice an alert icon. Click the alert icon to update the content, and, if necessary, scroll to the right to see that the orange objects and text in steps 4 and 6 have turned red to match the changes to the parent frame. Note that the alert has been replaced by a link icon.

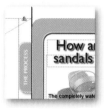

When changes are made to a parent object, an alert icon appears at the upper left of linked child objects indicating that an update is required.

11. Select the updated child content frame and press Ctrl+X/Command+X to cut it. Select the container frame and press Ctrl+Alt+V/Command+Alt+V to paste the child frame into it.

12. In the parent frame on the pasteboard, change the red objects and text back to orange. Alt+Click/Option+Click the alert icon that appears on the child tab in the overlay object to open the Links panel.

When a child object is selected, each of its elements is highlighted in the Links panel. Items that have been changed in the parent frame are indicated by an alert icon which, when Double-Clicked, updates the item in the child.

13. Scroll down in the Links panel if necessary to see the two items displaying the alert icon. Double-Click each alert icon to update the frame content. Note that the alert on the child frame is once again replaced by a link icon.

14. If you'd like to confirm that the child frame has indeed been updated, click the Preview button at the bottom of the Folio Overlays panel. Pause until the Preview on Desktop option appears, and click it to display the document in Adobe Content Viewer. Drag the tab contents across the screen to steps 4–6 to confirm that your changes have been implemented.

15. When you're finished exploring, close Adobe Content Viewer and return to InDesign. Save and close the open file to complete the exercise and the chapter.

CHAPTER SUMMARY

In this chapter you got to see how simple it is to create engaging interactive elements using scrollable frame overlays. Starting with a conventional scrolling text frame, you quickly jumped outside the box and, using the same technique in a novel way, transformed your scrollable frames into pull-out tabs.

In your work with scrollable frame overlays you:

- Distinguished between content frames and container frames
- Learned that the content frame and the container frame in a scrollable frame overlay can be of any content type: text, graphic, unassigned or mixed
- Learned that both content and container frames retain fill, stroke, corner options, transparency and drop shadows and that layer blending modes are not supported
- Learned that scrollable frame overlays can contain other overlays
- Learned that you can set scrollable frame options to:
  - Hide or show scrollbars
  - Manually position the content in the container or have InDesign align it automatically to the container's upper left corner
  - Render overlay content to vector or raster in PDF articles (The best choice for text-heavy content is vector, while raster is best for images.)

Along the way, you also picked up a few helpful tidbits including:

- The Edit > Paste Into command (Alt+Ctrl+V/Option+Command+V)
- How to select scrollable frame content within the container frame using the Direct Selection tool
- How to offset content from its container frame by ensuring that the container frame is a text frame and then applying inset spacing
- How to extend the pasteboard by going to Edit > Preferences > Guides & Pasteboard/InDesign > Preferences > Guides & Pasteboard
- The View > Entire Pasteboard command (Alt+Shift+Ctrl+0/ Option+Shift+Command+0)
- How to update linked content directly on the artboard or in the Links panel

Scrollable frame overlays are just the beginning of what overlays can do to enliven your DPS publications. There's much, much more to explore as you'll see in the coming chapters.

Chapter 31

AUDIO & VIDEO OVERLAYS

Adding audio and video overlays for DPS is as simple as placing a file and setting a couple preferences. Creating controller graphics for an audio overlay can become more of a challenge, however. This chapter walks you through the creation of both the overlays and progressive controller graphics—by way of a side trip to Photoshop and Bridge.

Audio & Video Overlays

TIP: While video overlays don't support streaming you can instead use Web Content overlays or HTML articles to add streaming content to your folios.

The overlay part of creating audio and video overlays is quite simple. As with most overlays, it's the pre-work that requires the effort. Audio and video files are passed through to the folio unchanged as are audio controller files. As is the case with any files destined for digital delivery, audio and video files should be optimized to achieve the best possible balance between quality and file size. For video, 10–12 MB per minute of film is a good starting point. The best format for audio files is MP3 and your best option for video is MP4 with h.264 encoding. iOS supports both inline and full-screen video which makes it a natural for inclusion in other overlays. Inline videos should be the exact dimensions desired for output, but, for video that will show full-screen, you may be able to get away with 1024 x 768 px across devices. If you find the quality of the 1024 x 768 px video to be unacceptable on an HD iPad, you could include a video as large as 1920 x 1080 px—the maximum allowed by Apple. A video of this size will of course substantially increase the size of your folio. If testing shows that your HD video plays successfully on an SD iPad, you could reduce the overall file size of your folio by omitting the SD video entirely.

TIP: Consider using video on the cover of your DPS publication to capture the attention of your audience at their very first glance.

Exercise 31.1: Creating Audio Controller Graphics

The toughest part of creating an audio overlay is creating the controller graphics, so we'll start by getting that handled. Of the three controller options—none, simple, and progressive—both the simple and progressive options require that you provide graphics. Creating sequenced graphics for a progressive controller would be a truly daunting task, but, with the rich video features in Photoshop and the batch renaming capabilities of Bridge, you can make the magic happen in fifteen minutes or less.

The steps to generating the graphics in Photoshop aren't all that intuitive so we've provided a source file for you to modify and reverse engineer if you wish. This exercise will take you on a brief side trip to Photoshop so you can learn your way around the audio controller file and then generate controller graphics of your own. If you'd rather skip the exercise, you'll still be able to create the audio overlay since a set of SD and HD controller graphics has already been included in the chapter_31_exercises folder.

Photoshop CC Essentials workspace on a Mac with Application frame enabled (Window > Application Frame) and the Timeline expanded.

1. Navigate to the chapter_31_exercises folder and open **audio-controller.psd** in Photoshop (CS6 or later.)

   When Photoshop opens, ensure that you're in the Essentials workspace (Window > Workspace > Essentials), and, if necessary, click the Timeline tab at the very bottom of the application window to expand the timeline. Don't be daunted by all the "layers" in the timeline—they represent the actual layers of the file as well as the properties of those layers that are, or can be, animated. The objects in this particular file are all vector objects so you can scale them however you like without losing fidelity. The object gradients are created using gradient overlays which makes them easy to edit. The idea was to make the file as adaptable as possible so you have the option to repurpose it as needed.

2. Click and hold and drag the blue playhead at the top of the timeline back and forth to see the animation of the progress indicator graphic moving across the controller track in the document window.

Drag the blue playhead right and left to scrub through the timeline.

3. In the Layers panel in the Panel Dock, click in the visibility column at the left of the panel to hide the play layer and show the pause layer. Scrub again through the timeline to see that the pause indicator has replaced the play indicator in the animation.

Switching between the play and pause animations is as simple as toggling the visibility of the indicator graphics in the Layers panel.

4. Click the pause layer in the Layers panel or the Timeline to select it. Press A to select the Path Selection tool and then click the Stroke color swatch on the Options Bar. Choose the Darker Magenta Red swatch—toward the bottom of the panel—to recolor the pause indicator.

Recolor the pause and play indicators to Darker Magenta Red.

5. Hide the pause layer in the Layers panel and show the play layer.

6. Select the play layer and then change its fill color to Darker Magenta Red.

7. Double-Click directly on the icon for the progressIndicatorGradient layer in the Layers panel to open the Gradient Fill dialog ( ).

NOTE: If you don't see all the layers in the timeline, mouse over the divider between the top of the timeline and the bottom of the document window. When the cursor changes to a double-sided arrow, click and hold and drag up to expand the panel and expose the layers.

NOTE: Drag the Control timeline magnification slider at the bottom left of the timeline panel to enlarge the view of the timeline for better control when dragging the playhead.

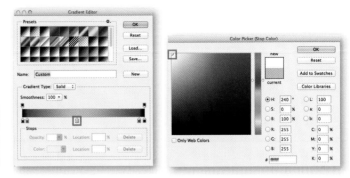

Gradient Fill Dialog ⟶ Gradient Editor ⟶ Color Picker (Stop Color)

8. Click once on the Gradient Fill gradient ramp to open the Gradient Editor.

9. Double-Click the gray color stop below the center of the Gradient Editor gradient ramp to open the Color Picker (Stop Color) dialog.

10. Choose White in the Color Picker and then click OK to close out of each of the open dialogs.

   Now that you've successfully changed the color of the progress indicators and their gradient background, it's time to export the new graphics.

TIP: In Photoshop, use the Path Selection tool to select vector objects and the Direct Selection tool to select individual object anchor points.

To set your objects to precise dimensions enter W (width) and H (height) values in the Options Bar.

11. Go to File > Export > Render Video. When the Render Video dialog opens, the name **audio_controller.mp4** appears in the Name field. Click the Select Folder button and navigate to the chapter_31_exercises folder. Create a new folder, name it **audio_controllers** and select it as the export destination folder.

The Photoshop Render Video options make it possible to export video content as a series of sequentially numbered images.

NOTE: Given that so many images are involved in creating the progressive audio controller, the optimization settings you choose can dramatically impact the size of your folio. As always, it's advised that you experiment to determine the best balance between quality and file size.

12. Choose Photoshop Image Sequence in the second section of the dialog, set the Format dropdown to PNG and click the Settings button. In the PNG Options dialog, choose the Smallest/Slow and None radio buttons if necessary, then click OK to close the dialog.

13. In the Render Video dialog, change Starting # to 1 and Digits to 3. Size should be set to Document Size and both Frame Rate and fps should be set to 15. Provided you haven't changed any of the timeline settings, it's OK for Range to be set to either All Frames or Work Area. Click the Render button to generate the sequence of 74 play images for the controller.

    To enable an audio overlay to distinguish between the play and pause versions of the controller images, you must add a _play or _pause suffix to each image in the sequence. With 74 images for the play controller state and another 74 for pause, not to mention a similar set of 148 images for the HD version, this could be a ridiculously time-consuming task. Thankfully, Bridge can dispatch with such a challenge in practically no time at all.

14. In Photoshop, go to File > Browse in Bridge. In Bridge, navigate to and open the audio_controllers folder you created.

15. Press Ctrl+A/Command+A to select all the controller images and go to Tools > Batch Rename.

Bridge is a tremendously efficient tool for renaming files such as the progressive controller files used in an audio overlay.

16. If necessary, choose the Rename in same folder radio button.

Bridge's Batch Rename feature enables you to customize and preview your new file names and choose from an assortment of file destinations.

17. In the New Filenames section of the dialog, choose Text from the first dropdown and enter audio_controller_ in the text field to its right.

18. If necessary, click the plus sign at the right of the text field to add a second naming parameter. Choose Sequence Number from the dropdown, enter 1 in the text field, and choose Three Digits from the second dropdown.

19. If necessary, click the plus sign again to add a third parameter to add the required _play suffix. Choose Text from the dropdown and enter _play in the text field.

Change the Sequence Number and the suffix text to
rename the "play" version of the controller images.

20. Confirm that the New filename preview at the very bottom of the dialog reads: audio_controller_001_play.png (New filename: **audio_controller_001_play.png**) and press the Rename button at the upper right of the dialog.

    Voilà! In barely a blink, all 74 play files are renamed and ready to go. Next you'll need to export the corresponding "pause" graphics from Photoshop.

21. Return to Photoshop. Hide the play layer and show the pause layer in the Layers panel.

22. Go to File > Export > Render Video. Leave all the settings as they are and click the Render Video button.

23. Return to Bridge and the _play files should still be selected in the audio_controllers folder. Click to select the first pause file which should be named **audio_controller001.png**. Scroll if necessary to see the last file in the folder, hold the Shift key and click to select it and all the files in between.

24. Go to Tools > Batch Rename. When the dialog opens, change Sequence Number to 1, replace _play with _pause and click the Rename button.

    Congratulations! You've created the play and pause images required for the SD version of your progressive audio controller. If you want to create an HD version, the HD images will need to be exactly double the SD image dimensions and must be named with the same names as their SD counterparts.

25. To double the dimensions of the controller images, return to Photoshop, go to Image > Image Size and ensure that the Constrain Proportions link is active. Choose Percent from the dropdowns to the right of the Width and Height measurements. Change the Percent value to 200 and click OK.

    Just that simply, Photoshop doubled the dimensions of the timeline graphics. Since the elements in the video are all vector shapes, you can scale the entire document up and down as much as you like without compromising the crispness of the exported images.

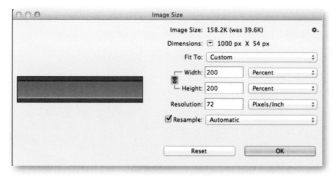

To have Photoshop calculate new document dimensions for you, go to Image > Image Size and choose Percent.

26. After you've is resized the video file, render and rename the HD images using the same process you used for the SD controller. (Refer to step 11 onward.) When choosing the destination folder in the Render Video dialog, create a subfolder inside your existing audio_controllers folder and name it **HD**.

TIP: While you can resize your image sequence images directly in Photoshop's Render Video dialog, the Image Size dialog produces better results—particularly if the file contains vector shapes.

In this exercise, you employed Photoshop's video features to generate a sequence of progressive audio controller images. Whether you opt for a simple controller that requires only one _play and one _pause image, or some version of a progressive audio controller as you did in the exercise, any controller images you create should be the exact dimensions you'd like them to be in your folio—in other words, the images should be used at 100% scale.

Now that you've created the controllers, next comes the easy part—creating the actual audio overlay.

Creating an Audio Overlay

You can set audio or video overlays to play automatically when the page or slideshow state that contains them is loaded. Since iOS can play only one media file at a time, only one auto play media overlay will play per page.

Exercise 31.2: Creating an Audio Overlay

1. Navigate to the chapter_31_exercises folder, open **ex31_2_start.indd,** and save it as ex31_2.indd.

2. Using the Selection tool, select the audio controller placeholder graphic and press Ctrl+D/Command+D. Navigate to chapter_31_exercises > links and Double-Click **alastair_interview.mp3** to replace the graphic with the audio file.

3. With the audio placeholder selected, expand the Folio Overlays panel in the Panel Dock and click Audio & Video.

4. Click the Controller Files folder icon (☐) and navigate to and select the chapter_31_exercises > links > audio_controllers folder.

5. Check the Show First Image Initially and Auto Play checkboxes and set Delay to 0.25 secs.

Audio overlay options

6. Save the file and click the Preview button at the bottom of the Folio Overlays panel. Pause until the Preview on Desktop option appears, and then click it to display the document in Adobe Content Viewer.

The audio file begins to play automatically after a quarter second delay. (The interview is just under a half hour long.) About 30 seconds in, the progress indicator jumps to the next graphic in the controller sequence.

7. Click the progress indicator to pause the audio and to display the play controller graphic. Click the indicator again to resume play and switch back to the pause controller graphic.

Unfortunately, despite the appearance of the controller and its implied functionality, audio overlays don't allow you to scrub through the audio timeline—you'd have to use a video overlay to provide that level of control. While you can't scrub through the audio in the folio, if you'd like to hear the interview, you can listen to it directly in the InDesign Media panel where you can jump through the timeline at your leisure.

8. With the audio overlay selected on the document, expand the Media panel in the Panel Dock (in the Digital Publishing workspace.) Click the play button and drag through the timeline as desired to listen to the interview.

InDesign's Media panel enables you to
"preview" placed audio and video files.

Exercise 31.3: Using Video for a Long Audio Clip

To provide your audience with the ability to navigate the timeline of a lengthy audio segment, an option worth entertaining is to use a video clip instead of an audio file. If you set the video overlay to play full-screen, users will be able to navigate the timeline using the default video controls.

1. Navigate to the chapter_31_exercises folder, open **ex31_3_start.indd**, and save it as ex31_3.indd.

2. Select the placeholder controller graphic and expand the Links panel in the Panel Dock. Click the Relink button at the bottom of the panel, navigate to the chapter_31_exercises > links folder, and Double-Click **alastair_interview_video.mp4** to replace the graphic with the video file.

Use the relink button at the bottom of the Links panel to
replace the controller graphic with the video file.

3. After replacing the graphic with the video, expand the Media Panel (▦) in the Panel Dock. Choose From Current Frame from the Poster dropdown.

You can choose a frame from the video to act as its poster or
you can specify a dedicated poster file. The poster you assign in
the Media panel gets carried over to the video overlay.

4. Expand the Folio Overlays panel and click Audio & Video. Check the Auto Play and Play Full Screen checkboxes and set the delay to 0.125 secs. Save the file.

> **TIP:** Looping of audio and video is currently unsupported in folio overlays.

5. If you have an iPad, connect it to your computer and start the Adobe Viewer app.

6. Return to InDesign and click the Preview button at the bottom of the Folio Overlays panel, pause until the Preview options appear and click the preview on iPad option. Otherwise, preview on the desktop.

Whether on the desktop or the iPad, the video version of the audio interview pops open in full screen mode with a black background and static title across the screen.

7. On the iPad, tap the video to toggle visibility of its controllers. Tap the X at the upper right of the video to close it. Tap the video poster to display the video again.

8. Close out of Adobe Viewer and return to InDesign. Save and close the file to complete the exercise.

Stopping Play of a Media Overlay

TIP: Video overlays don't support streaming but if you need to, you can stream video using Web Content overlays or HTML articles.

While you can have any number of media overlays on a page, iOS supports auto play for only one. Once begun, media will continue to play as long as the article containing it is being viewed, even after swiping to another page. In instances where this behavior is undesirable, there's a relatively easy, although not entirely perfect fix.

Swiping to an article page that contains an auto play media overlay automatically stops a media file from another page in the article from playing. If the first overlay is on page one for example, and there's a second auto play overlay on page two, swiping to page two effectively stops the media on page one from playing. If you can make the "stop" file short and sweet—it can be an itty bitty (16 x 16 px), black and white, one second long video with muted sound, or even a silent one-second audio file—it will stop any media that's playing including iPod music. Auto play media overlays play only once per article though—to reset the auto play, you must leave an article entirely and then return to it. Thus, if the original media overlay is played a second time during the same visit to an article, and if the overlay intended to stop the first overlay from playing has already played, the second overlay will be unable to stop the play of the first.

CHAPTER SUMMARY

Audio and video have an unrivaled ability to captivate your audience with a compelling narrative for your app. Content of course is king. That said, you discovered how simple it is to place audio and video files into InDesign and into audio and video overlays. Along the way, you learned some media file fundamentals including:

- The need for file optimization since audio & video assets are pass-through assets (Recommended: 10–12 MB per minute)
- Recommended file formats:
    - Audio: MP3
    - Video: MP4 with h.264 encoding
    - Recommended full screen video dimensions for SD and HD iPads: 1024 X 768 px or max 1920 X 1080 px

More challenging, you took some time to create customized progressive controller graphics using the Photoshop's video features coupled with its support for true vector graphics. In your foray into Photoshop you

- Became familiar with Photoshop's video timeline
- Learned how to hide and show layers in the Layers panel.
- Worked with vector graphics
    - Selecting vectors with the Path Selection tool
    - Assigning stroke and fill colors
    - Changing the colors of a gradient fill
    - Using Photoshop's calculation capabilities to resize graphics
- Used the Photoshop Image Sequence option to render out your video to a sequence of .png files

With your passel of Photoshop PNGs, you used the Tools > Batch Rename command in Bridge to prepare them for the progressive controller, customizing the file names as required.

In the process of creating the controller graphics, you made provisions for display on HD iPads, learning the proper file structure for HD pass through overlay assets and the requirement that HD assets be exactly two times the dimensions of their SD counterparts.

In creating the actual overlays you

- Learned the advantage of setting delay for better performance
- Used the Media panel to "preview" placed audio and video, and to set a media poster
- Employed video to deliver a long audio segment for easier navigation
- Learned how to use one media overlay to stop play of another

While audio and video overlays provide a powerful but passive entertainment experience, the next chapter introduces you to the panorama and pan & zoom overlays and the opportunity to actively engage your audience.

Chapter 32

PANORAMAS AND PAN & ZOOM

Perfect for a virtual tour or to share the wonders of a breathtaking view, panoramas provide your audience with an immersive 360° experience that can't help but impress. While panoramas provide a view from the inside out, pan & zoom overlays invite deeper discovery from the outside in. Detailed drawings, municipal maps, any content that contains more visual information than can be readily deciphered in the confines of a limited screen, are all perfect candidates for pan & zoom. In this chapter, not only will you learn how you can include these effects in your folios, but you'll learn all about the process of preparing the required resources as well.

Panorama Overlays

Panorama overlays are beyond cool, and creating the actual overlay in InDesign is surprisingly easy. Acquiring the source images to use in the overlay however, is an entirely different story, requiring four phases of preparation and some Photoshop skills before you can even think of starting with InDesign.

<u>PHASE 1</u> requires that you capture the images that you'll eventually stitch together to form the basis of your panorama. In a perfect world, you'd have a tripod that would enable you to rotate the camera at uniform increments—for example, you might shoot a sequence of ten images separated by increments of 36°. While nice to have, the tripod isn't an absolute requirement since Photoshop's truly awesome Photomerge function can piece things together quite nicely—even if your images aren't perfectly aligned. You also don't have to have a fancy camera. Case in point—the photos used in the panorama for the exercise were taken with a hand-held iPhone while standing in one spot and rotating 360°, for a total of three rotations. The first rotation included a series of about ten photos with the camera held perpendicular to the ground. The second and third rotations also included about ten photos each with the camera angled up slightly for the second rotation and angled down for the third.

<u>PHASE 2</u> takes you to Photoshop. Go to File > Automate > Photomerge. Click the Browse button, and choose the files you want to include in the panorama. Ensure that the Blend Images Together checkbox is checked, and, optionally, check Vignette Removal and Geometric Distortion Correction. For Layout, Cylindrical seems to be a good choice, but you'll want to do your own experimentation. When you're all set up, click OK and let Photoshop do its magic. If you're working with thirty or so sizeable files, it may take Photoshop quite some time to generate the masks it uses to blend the layers, so be patient and do something to take your mind off waiting.

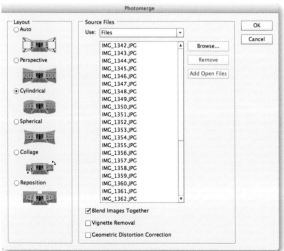

Photoshop does a masterful job of stitching many images together into a panorama using its Photomerge feature.

The resulting panorama combines all the images and leaves a lot of blank space which you can then fill using Photoshop's amazing tools like Content-Aware Fill and the Clone Stamp tool—or you can just crop the image to remove the empty areas.

Photoshop does a masterful job of adjusting color and aligning
numerous images to create spectacular panoramas.

Whichever approach you choose, you'll need to copy, paste and blend content
from the left and right edges of the image to create a seamless transition from one
edge of your image to the other. It's easiest to work with a flattened version of the
file since it will be dramatically smaller than the original and you won't have a
zillion masked layers to navigate. Be sure to save your original layered file though,
to save having to regenerate the whole thing should you run into trouble.

PHASE 3 calls for software that can convert your Photoshop panorama to
the series of six cube faces that you'll need for your panorama overlay in
InDesign. For about $100 you can buy Pano2VR which not only converts
your panorama to the images needed by InDesign, but which can also
generate virtual tours and more. The trial version is free and fully functional
(with watermarked output) for your experimentation. Check it out at:
http://gardengnomesoftware.com/pano2vr_download.php. If you'd like, you
can download it and take it for a test drive in the next exercise.

Exercise 32.1: Preparing Panorama Overlay Images with Pano2VR

This phase of pre-panorama prep is pretty straight forward.

1. Open Pano2VR. Navigate to chapter_32_exercises > links and drag the
   pano2vr.jpg file onto the placeholder diagram on the initial screen. Alternatively,
   click the Select Input button and navigate to and Double-Click the file to load it.
   When the Input window opens, leave the Type dropdown set to Auto.

When your panorama's been loaded you'll see a thumbnail of your file in the Pano2VR window.

2. Choose Transformation from the New Output Format dropdown at the right of the dialog and click the Add button at its right.

The Transformation/Thumbnail Output dialog opens and provides thumbnails to illustrate each of the many output options.

The Transformation/Thumbnail Output dialog options.

3. Choose Cube Faces from the Type dropdown and a naming format from the Face Names dropdown. For image size, we chose 1024 x 1024. (The Panorama overlay will display at full screen and since you can allow your audience to zoom in, you might consider using a larger image.) The default view settings are fine. Choose JPEG or PNG from the Format dropdown and play with the Image Quality settings as desired to find the right balance between quality and file size.

4. Click the Open button located to the right of the Output File field and navigate to the chapter_32_exercises folder. Create a new folder for your images, name it **panorama** and click Save.

5. Click OK, then click Yes in the confirmation alert dialog, and then click OK when you see the message "The project must be saved before exporting the first file. The project directory is used as the base for all exported files." Save the **pano2vr.p2vr** file in the chapter_32_exercises folder.

6. After the images have been generated, navigate to the chapter_32_exercises folder and preview them to see what they look like.

While the Pano2VR images will get you a good bit of the way there, there's still a substantial amount of Photoshop work to do (Phase 4.) If you want the panorama to rotate up or down, you'll need to add content to the top and bottom faces of the cube. It's likely that the other faces will need some touch-up as well. Once you have things looking the way you want them, you should optimize each of the six cube face files using Photoshop's Save for Web option or another image compression application. Remember, iTunes apps have a total file limit of 2 GB and a limit of 50 MB for download over a 3G—as opposed to Wi-Fi—connection.

Exercise 32.2: Creating a Panorama Overlay

Now that the pieces are properly prepared, at last you're ready to assemble the panorama in InDesign.

1. Go to File > Open and navigate to the chapter_32_exercises folder. Open **ex32_2_start.indd** and save it as ex32_2.indd.

   A placeholder frame into which you will place a poster image for the panorama is positioned in the center of the page. We've provided two versions of the cube face images generated by Pano2VR in subfolders named **panorama** and **panorama_ruled** located in the chapter_32_exercises > links folder. For the clickable panorama poster, you'll use a dedicated poster image rather than one of the cube faces.

NOTE: The cube faces for the exercise were generated by Pano2VR and then polished in Photoshop (but have not yet been optimized.)

2. Select the placeholder with the Selection tool and press Ctrl+D/Command+D to open the Place dialog. Navigate to the chapter_32_exercises > links folder, and Double-Click **panorama_poster.jpg** to place it in the document.

The poster for the panorama fills the placeholder frame.

NOTE: If you've previously made changes to the Digital Publishing workspace, choose Reset Digital Publishing from the Workspace Switcher to revert to the default setup.

3. With the poster frame still selected, expand the Folio Overlays panel in the Panel Dock and choose Panorama.

4. In the Panorama Overlay panel, click the Load Images folder icon. When the Browse for panorama folder dialog opens, navigate to chapter_32_exercises > links, select the **panorama_ruled** folder and click Open.

   Note that the Initial Zoom setting in the Panorama overlay panel is 70%, and the Field of View values are Min: 30 and Max: 80. Note also that the horizontal and vertical values are both 0 and that no limits are set to the horizontal or vertical pan.

NOTE: As an alternative to the customized poster image, you could instead check the Use First Image for Poster checkbox in the Panorama Overlay panel.

TIP: In a panorama overlay, a Vertical value of -90 includes the face at the top of the cube in the visible area of the panorama and a Vertical value of 90 includes the face at the bottom of the cube. For horizontal rotation only, set the Limit Vertical Tilt values to -1 and 1.

The default settings in the Panorama Overlay panel set the zoom range between 30% and 80% with an initial magnification of 70%. An unconstrained panorama can rotate a full 360°.

5. Leave the default Panorama panel settings unchanged, click the Preview button at the bottom of the panel, pause until the Preview options appear and choose Preview on Desktop.

   Each face of the cube constructing the panorama image has been marked with rectangles in 10% increments so you can clearly see how the Min and Max Field of View panel settings affect the magnification of the panorama

6. When the page opens in Adobe Content Viewer, click the panorama poster.

7. The panorama overlay pops up in its own full-screen window. Note that the initial zoom of the image is 70% as indicated by the 70% rectangle extending from the top to the bottom of the viewing area.

The concentric rectangles superimposed on the panorama faces help visualize the effect of the settings in the Panorama dialog.

8. Press and hold the + key on your keyboard to zoom in as much as the panorama will allow. Note that the zoom stops when the 30% rectangle stretches from the top to the bottom of the screen.

9. Press and hold the – key on your keyboard to zoom out as much as possible and note that the zoom stops at 80%, per the overlay panel settings.

10. Click and drag right and left and up and down to view the full 360° rotation that the default panorama settings permit.

NOTE: It's possible that Adobe Content Viewer may crash when you return to InDesign. Don't let it worry you. It should start right back up the next time you export.

11. When you've finished exploring, click the X at the upper right of the panorama overlay to close it, leave Adobe Content Viewer open, and return to InDesign.

12. In the Panorama Overlay panel, with the panorama poster selected, set Initial Zoom to 50 and Horizontal to 20. Check the Limit Vertical Pan checkbox and set Up to -10 and Down to 10. Select Preview on Desktop from the Preview dropdown.

    Notice that when the document opens in Adobe Content Viewer, the zoom is at 50% and the view is rotated 20°. When you click and drag up and down, the range of rotation on the vertical axis is constrained to 10° up and 10° down.

The Vertical and Horizontal Pan settings in the Panorama
Overlay panel constrain the rotation of the panorama.

13. When you've finished exploring, close out of Adobe Content Viewer and return to InDesign. Save and close the file to complete the exercise.

Pan & Zoom Overlays

Ideal for exploring the details of a map or diagram, pan & zoom overlays are a simple vehicle for providing your viewers with greater engagement.

The zoom in a pan & zoom overlay is determined by the relationship between the actual pixel dimensions of the image used in the overlay and the effective pixel dimensions of the scaled image in InDesign. To achieve a zoom of 200% for example, an image with original dimensions of 200 x 200 px must be scaled by 50% to a size of 100 px by 100 px on the page. Remember that the original image used in a pan & zoom overlay is passed through to the folio, so, in addition to being large enough to achieve the desired zoom amount, you'll want to prepare your files to accommodate both the SD and HD versions of the iPad. You can either create a single image with a resolution of somewhere around 108 ppi—which will zoom more on an SD iPad than it will for HD. Or, you can create two images: one for the SD iPad, and the other, an HD image of exactly double the dimensions of the SD version. Remember that if you choose the dual image option, the high-res image must be placed in an HD folder inside the folder where the SD image is located.

By default, the image used in the overlay also serves as its poster. You can however position an image that matches the overlay dimensions above it in InDesign to effectively replace the default poster. When the image is clicked in the folio, the overlay will pop above it. (If the zoomable overlay content contains transparency, a poster image positioned beneath it will show through when the overlay is active.)

Exercise 32.3: Creating a Pan & Zoom Overlay

1. Navigate to the chapter_32_exercises folder, open **ex32_3_start.indd** and save it as ex32_2.indd.

   The first thing you'll do is set up the foundation image for the overlay. To get the maximum pan & zoom effect, it's best to use an overlay frame that's the same aspect ratio as the image being zoomed.

---

2. Press Ctrl+D/Command+D and navigate to the chapter_32_exercises > links folder. Double-Click **childandtire_large.jpg** to load it in the Place Gun. Click once (without dragging) on the pasteboard to place the image at 100% magnification.

3. With the placed image selected, check the Auto-Fit checkbox on the Control panel.

4. Ensure that the Width and Height fields at the left of the Control panel are linked. Type a forward slash followed by the number 2 (/2) after the 900 px value in the Width field and press Enter/Return.

    You've let InDesign do the math to scale the image to half its original dimensions. This means that your overlay will be able to zoom in to a magnification of 200%.

5. Expand the Stroke panel in the Panel Dock, set the stroke of the frame to 19 px, and click the Align Stroke to Outside checkbox. Using the controls on the Control panel, set the stroke color to [Black]

    Align the stroke to the outside Align Stroke: so it will show when the object is converted to an overlay.

6. With the image still selected, choose Jump Object ( ) from the Text Wrap options, either on the Control panel or the Text Wrap panel (Ctrl+Alt+W/Command+Option+W, or Window > Text Wrap.)

7. Drag the image onto the document page and align its upper left corner to the intersection of the vertical and topmost horizontal guides. The text jumps beneath the image.

8. Drag the pan & zoom icon from the pasteboard and position it over the upper right corner of the stroke on the image frame.

9. Right-Click/Ctrl+Click the icon and choose Arrange > Bring to Front to reposition it on top of the image.

10. Select the image frame and expand the Folio Overlays panel in the Panel Dock. If necessary, scroll down in the panel to locate Pan & Zoom and select it. Click the On radio button in the overlay pane to enable the overlay.

Converting a properly prepared image to a pan & zoom overlay is as simple as clicking the On button.

11. Click the Preview button at the bottom of the Folio Overlays panel. Pause until the Preview on Desktop option appears and then click it to display the document in Adobe Content Viewer. Click the image to activate the overlay and use the + and – keys on your keyboard to zoom in and out. When zoomed in on the image, click and hold and drag to pan.

   This is an especially fun overlay to play with directly on an iPad so, if you have an iPad and haven't already done so, take a few minutes to download Adobe Content Viewer from the Apple App Store and install it.

   With a few simple steps, you can view your DPS content just as easily on your iPad as on the desktop.

12. Connect your iPad to your computer and start the Adobe Content Viewer app on your iPad. In InDesign, click the Preview button at the bottom of the Folio Overlays panel and pause until the Preview options appear. Choose Preview on <your name>'s iPad. When the preview appears on the iPad, tap the image once to activate the overlay, then drag your fingers apart from a pinch position to zoom in on the image. Once zoomed in, swipe the image or drag your finger around in the frame to pan it. Double-Tap the image to reset the overlay to its original magnification.

13. When you're finished exploring, close out of Adobe Content Viewer and return to InDesign. Save and close the file to complete the exercise and the chapter.

DOWNLOAD: Link to download Adobe Content Viewer from the iTunes App Store.

TIP: Once an overlay preview is loaded onto your iPad, you can disconnect the device from your computer and continue to interact with the preview. If it is not part of an actual folio however, the preview will not remain available on the iPad once you exit it.

CHAPTER SUMMARY

Once again, this chapter took you outside the confines of InDesign to discover additional tools and techniques. As part of creating a panorama overlay you learned:

- How to take a series of panorama photos
- How to use Photoshop to stitch panorama images together
- How to create cube faces for a panorama overlay with Pano2VR
- How to decipher panorama overlay preferences to control the viewing range and rotation of a panorama

In creating a pan & zoom overlay you

- Discovered the importance of including High Definition assets in your pan & zoom package in order to deliver a consistent experience across devices
- Learned how to create a pan & zoom poster image

Along the way you:

- (Hopefully) Downloaded Adobe Content Viewer and previewed your overlay on your iPad
- Learned about the Jump Object text wrap option
- Learned that a stroke aligned to the outside of an object will show when the overlay is active (while a stroke aligned to the inside will not)
- Learned how to make InDesign do math to scale things (InDesign's math skills can also be employed to position things perfectly)

The next chapter is all about web overlays and the ways you can use them to deliver dynamic content without direct updates to your apps.

Chapter 33

WEB CONTENT OVERLAYS & HYPERLINKS

Web content overlays are an ingenious way to incorporate changing content in your app even after it's been delivered. As long as the device being used by your viewers is connected to the internet, you can use online content to populate your articles on the fly. From YouTube to Google maps, Twitter, and beyond, web content overlays provide a means to populate your app dynamically. You can also include local web content—like HTML5 animation created with Edge Animate for example—that's delivered with your app and that will play with or without a connection to the web. Between hyperlinks and web content overlays, this chapter provides a potentially endless variety of ways to take your app outside the box. The question is, "Where will you take it from there?"

Web Content Overlays

TIP: Distinct from web content overlays, you can also include entire HTML articles in your DPS folios. To learn more, check out Colin Fleming's informative video at http://helpx.adobe.com/digital-publishing-suite/help/import-html-articles.html.

There are two types of web content you can include in a web content overlay: local content and online content. Local web content is literally a mini website—be it one page or many, with its html, css, script, and image files contained in a single folder—that is bundled into your folio just like any other pass-through asset. Since all its components are included in the published folio, web content overlays using local content can be viewed on an iPad whether or not the device is connected to the internet.

Online web content overlays utilize a link or embed code to populate the overlay frame with external content. At risk of stating the obvious, in order for an online web content overlay to appear on an iPad, the device must be connected to the internet. Since there are likely to be users of your app who view it offline, you'll want to provide a heads-up to inform them when your content requires an internet connection.

Exercise 33.1: Creating Web Content Overlays

You'll need to be connected to the internet to preview the results of this exercise. If you have the option, it's preferable to preview the files on an iPad since not all the functions available in the web content are fully supported by the desktop viewer.

Using URLs

DOWNLOAD: Exercise files for this chapter can be downloaded from http://www.interactive-indesign.com.

1. Navigate to the chapter_33_exercises folder and open **ex33_1_end.indd**. Expand the Folio Overlays panel in the Panel Dock and click the Preview button at the bottom of the panel. Pause until the Preview options appear and choose your preview preference.

    When the page opens in Adobe Content Viewer, depending on the speed of your internet connection, initially you should see an "internet connection required" notice on the page, and then after a brief load time, all three HTML web overlays should populate the page.

2. Interact with the web content on the page. When you're finished experimenting, return to InDesign, keep the file open for reference if you like, and open **ex33_1_start.indd**. Save the file as ex33_1.indd.

ALERT: If you view the exercise file on the desktop instead of an iPad, the YouTube video poster will appear but the video will not play and the links on the wikipedia page won't be functional.

A single page can contain multiple web content overlays as well as other overlay types.

The HTML code and links you'll need to create the web content overlays are available on the pasteboard to the left of the document page.

3. Using the Type tool, select the Wikipedia link in the text frame below the Wikipedia label on the pasteboard and press Ctrl+C/Command+C to copy it. Press and hold Ctrl/Command to switch temporarily to the Selection tool and click the rectangle below the page title on the document page to select it. (The rectangle has a blue bounding box.)

4. Expand the Folio Overlays panel and click Web Content. Position the Type cursor in the URL or File field and press Ctrl+V/Command+V to paste the copied URL. Check the Auto Play, Allow User Interaction, and Scale Content to Fit checkboxes. Set the delay to .125 secs.

TIP: Web Content overlays cannot redirect, so it's important to use the correct URL for your destination. For example, a Twitter URL needs to be directed to the URL for mobile devices: http://mobile.twitter.com.

The web content overlay settings for the wikipedia link.

5. Click the Preview button at the bottom of the Folio Overlays panel, pause until the Preview options appear, and choose a preview mode.

6. \When the document opens in Content Viewer and the web content populates the page, do some exploring. Return to InDesign when you've finished checking things out.

While entering a link in the URL or File field of the Folio Overlays panel is the simplest way to create a web content overlay, it has its limitations—only links to entire HTML pages are supported. The code required to include content excerpted from YouTube or Google Maps for example, is more involved than the Folio Overlays panel is equipped to handle. Fortunately, InDesign provides another means to include HTML in a web content overlay. But first, you must retrieve the necessary source code.

TIP: For Web Content overlays based on local HTML assets rather than URLs, make sure that the HTML file you specify is contained in its own folder and that you've entered the correct path. The entire HTML folder gets uploaded with the article, so the contents of the folder should be limited to the assets used in the HTML file(s).

Embedding YouTube Content

YouTube provides customizable code you can use to embed videos in a web content overlay or website.

DOWNLOAD: The direct link to the YouTube video is: http://www.youtube.com/watch?v=z-ueWwd9gUY

7. In InDesign, copy the URL under the YouTube label on the pasteboard, open your browser of choice, and paste the link into the browser address bar. Alternatively, go to youtube.com and search for "Manila's city of garbage."

8. Look below the YouTube video title to find and click the Share link. (It may appear grayed-out.) Below that, in the Share this video section, click Embed. Choose Custom size from the Video size dropdown and enter 400 in the width text field. The height value auto-populates with a height of 300.

9. Select the embed code, press Ctrl+C/Command+C to copy it, and return to InDesign.

ALERT: The Insert HTML menu option is grayed out when the Type tool is active in a text frame.

10. Switch to the Selection tool, and go to Object > Insert HTML. Delete the default code in the dialog, press Ctrl+V/Command+V to paste the embed code you copied from YouTube, and click OK.

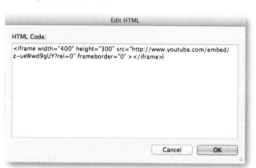

TIP: To access HTML code that was entered in InDesign's Edit HTML dialog, select and Right-Click/Ctrl+Click the generated HTML object and choose Edit HTML from the contextual menu.

You can write your own HTML or paste embed code from sites like YouTube and Google Maps into InDesign's Edit HTML window.

Initially, InDesign generates an HTML object that contains the message "This is arbitrary HTML." When you click OK to close the dialog, InDesign takes a few moments to parse the code and then a frame for the video appears that's sized according to the parameters in the pasted HTML.

TIP: If smart guides don't appear when aligning one object to another, you can use the keyboard command Ctrl+U/Command+U to toggle their visibility.

11. Drag the YouTube frame to center it in the video frame at the lower left of the document page. (A vertical green smart guide will appear when the video is centered in the frame.)

12. With the YouTube frame selected, expand the Folio Overlays panel in the Panel Dock—it should open automatically to the Web Content pane. (If not, click the Web Content selector.) Check the Auto Play and Allow User Interaction checkboxes, set Delay to .125 secs, and click the Preview button.

13. Preview the page, and, if previewing on an iPad, click to play the video. When finished previewing, return to InDesign.

Embedding Google Map Content

The process of embedding content from Google Maps is essentially the same as adding content from YouTube.

14. Open your browser of choice, navigate to http://maps.google.com and search for "Smokey Mountain Manila, Philippines."

15. Set the view of the map, and locate and click the link icon at the upper left of the screen—beneath the Google search field. A window pops up that contains the default embed code and a link to customization options.

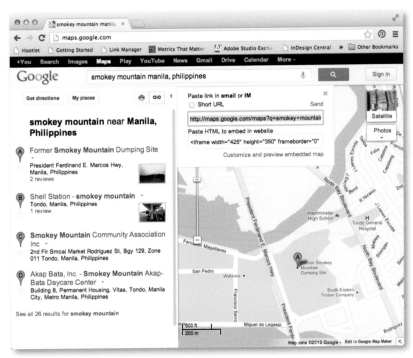

Like YouTube, Google Maps provides customizable HTML code that you can use to embed a map in your app (or website.)

16. To further refine the dimensions and display of the map, click the Customize and preview embedded map link at the bottom of the link pop-up window. When the customize window opens, select the Custom radio button, enter 254 in the Width field and 333 in the Height field. Use the navigation buttons at the upper left of the map to frame your desired view in the preview window. When you're satisfied with the map's appearance, select and copy the code and return to InDesign.

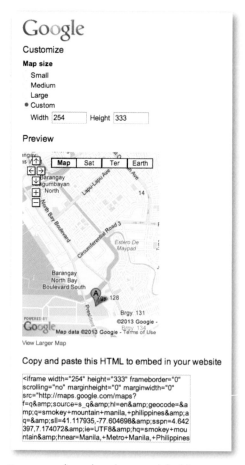

You can use the tools at the upper left of the map to customize the dimensions of the viewing window as well as the magnification and geographical area of focus.

17. Go to Object > Insert HTML, paste the embed code from Google Maps into the Edit HTML dialog, and click OK.

   InDesign generates a frame for your Google Map complete with a "poster image."

18. Using the Selection tool, drag the map to snap its upper left corner to the intersection of the vertical guide and the bottommost horizontal guide.

19. With the map frame still selected, expand the Folio Overlays panel in the Panel Dock and if necessary, click Web Content. Check the Auto Play and Allow User Interaction checkboxes, set delay to .125 secs, and click the Preview button.

20. Preview the page and test the map navigation buttons. When finished previewing, return to InDesign. Save and close all open files to complete the lesson.

Introduction to Adobe Edge Animate and HTML5 Animation

The fact that Flash animation is not supported on iOS devices raises the question of how you can include animation in your DPS apps. Until such time as we can export InDesign animation directly to DPS or HTML 5 (Adobe, hear our plea!) the best alternative is a very cool Creative Cloud application called Edge Animate.

Edge Animate provides a visual interface to develop HTML5 animation that can be viewed on iOS devices.

While it's a good bet that you already have a Creative Cloud subscription since this is a book about InDesign CC after all, you may not yet be taking advantage of all the benefits creative Cloud membership has to offer. Edge Animate is one of the many lesser-known but very cool goodies that Creative Cloud includes. Go to http://html.adobe.com/edge/animate/ to learn all about Animate and, in the off chance that you don't already have one, get a Creative Cloud membership. Just click the Get started button and complete the membership form to join.

NOTE: Creative Cloud provides both free and paid membership options. To learn more, go to http://www.adobe.com/products/creativecloud.html.

Joining Creative Cloud is as simple as filling out an online form.

Once registered, go to https://creative.adobe.com/, log in to Creative Cloud, and click the Apps link at the upper left of the page to get to the downloads.

NOTE: You may need to scroll down on the apps page to get to the Edge Animate download.

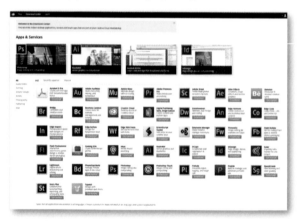

A free Creative Cloud membership includes Edge tools, 2GB of cloud storage, download of 30-day trial versions of the paid subscription applications, as well as a growing collection of other tools and services.

The initial screen of Adobe® Edge Animate provides easy to follow tutorials to get you started.

Exercise 33.2: Exporting for DPS from Edge Animate

Animations created in Edge Animate can be deployed in any environment that supports HTML5. This means that you can use the same animation on your website that you include in your iPad DPS publication. Before jumping into Animate, you've just got to take a look at this simple sample of what it can do.

A completed HTML5 animation generated by Edge Animate.

1. Navigate to the chapter_33_exercises > edge_animate folder. Locate and Right-Click/Ctrl+Click on **mission.html**. Select your browser of choice from the Open With option to preview the animation.

   Letters bounce onto the screen to compose the word "MISSION."

2. When you've finished viewing the animation, close the browser.

   We've provided an Animate source file for you to reverse engineer if you'd like—you'll export its animation following the steps in the exercise. If you'd rather not dig around in Animate at this point, skip to Exercise 33.3.

3. Navigate to the chapter_33_exercises > edge_animate folder, and Double-Click on **mission.an** to open the source file in Edge Animate.

4. Explore the file to your heart's content and when you're done, go to File > Publish Settings.

5. Select Animate Deployment Package at the left of the dialog, check its checkbox and deselect the Web checkbox if necessary. Leave the defaults for the Target Directory, Published name and Poster Image. Click the Publish button at the lower left of the screen.

To export an .oam file for import into InDesign, check the Animate Deployment Package checkbox in the Edge Animate Publish Settings dialog, choose a Target Directory, a name for the file (Published Name,) and a poster image.

6. Close Edge Animate and return to InDesign.

ALERT: In order to complete this exercise, you must first download and install Edge Animate from Creative Cloud.

TIP: To create a poster image directly in Edge Animate, drag the playhead through the timeline to display the desired view on the Stage. With the Stage selected, click the small camera icon in the Properties panel to the right of the Poster option at the left of the screen.

Poster: images/mission_poster.png

NOTE: Since the web content overlay that contains the animation will be set to Auto Play, and the animation begins with an empty stage, we captured an empty frame at the beginning of the animation to use as the poster image.

Exercise 33.3 : Adding an Edge Animate Web Content Overlay

Once the requisite .oam file has been exported from Edge Animate, creating a web content overlay with it is simply a matter of placing it as you would place any other page element.

TIP: When using an HTML animation in a Web Content overlay, set the overlay to Auto Play with a slight delay (such as 0.125 seconds.) Setting the delay allows time for the animation scripts to load, ensuring that the animation will play properly.

1. In InDesign, go to File > Open, navigate to the chapter_33_exercises folder, open **ex33_3_start.indd** and save it as **ex33_3.indd**.

2. Go to File > Place (Ctrl+D/Command+D,) navigate to the chapter_33_exercises > links folder and Double-Click **mission.oam** to load it into the place gun. Click once at the intersection of the horizontal and vertical guides to place the file.

   When you place the .oam file in InDesign, it is imported as a Web Content overlay.

3. With the .oam file selected, open the Folio Overlays panel. In the Web Content pane, check the Auto Play checkbox and set the Delay to .125 secs. If necessary, deselect Allow User Interaction.

4. Click the Preview button at the bottom of the panel and preview the page. When finished, save and close all open files to complete the exercise.

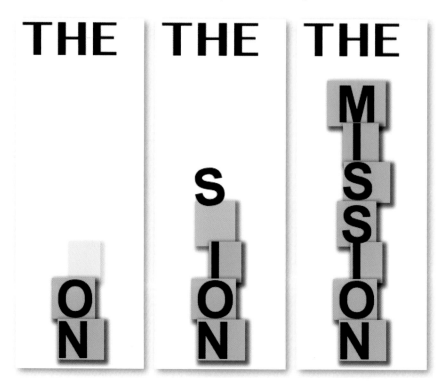

The progression of the Edge Animate animation.

Hyperlinks

You learned all about hyperlinks in Chapter 6, starting on page 99 and in Chapter 24 on page 356. There are a few things to add when it comes to linking between DPS articles however.

Links between DPS articles use navto:// instead of the familiar http:// employed in web URLS, and are targeted to the article name you assign when first adding the article to your folio. Be careful not to confuse the article name with the article title. The article name is an internal reference only and is not seen by the public, while the article title appears in the published folio.

NOTE: Of course, before you can link between DPS articles, you must first create them—and before you can create articles, you must create a folio to contain them. Check out Exercise 28.2: Creating a DPS Folio, starting on page 433 for a refresher on the process.

To link from one folio article to another, target the article name rather than the article title as the link destination.

Linking to a specific page in an article is similar to linking to an internal anchor in an HTML page—you employ the # sign followed by the index number of the link destination page. Article pages are indexed starting with 0 rather than 1, so if you want to link to page 5 of an article named "team" for example, you would write your link like this: navto://team#4. The same link format can also be used to create internal links between pages in a single article. Just be aware that in order for your internal navto links to work when tested, the article must be included in a folio and named.

For a more in-depth discussion of all types of links in DPS folios, check out Colin Fleming's very helpful tutorial at http://helpx.adobe.com/digital-publishing-suite/help/hyperlink-overlays.html.

For everything you could ever want to know about DPS email links, check out James Lockman's article: Sending email and email attachments from DPS Publications at http://blogs.adobe.com/jlockman/2012/09/26/sending-email-and-email-attachments-from-dps-publications/

To learn more about link formats for the iPad, check out the Apple URL Scheme Reference at: http://developer.apple.com/library/ios/#featuredarticles/iPhoneURLScheme_Reference/Introduction/Introduction.html.

Link to Colin Fleming's DPS Link tutorial

Link to James Lockman's tome on DPS email

Link to the Apple URL Scheme Reference

CHAPTER SUMMARY

A powerful addition to your repertoire, web overlays can be used to extend your apps to include the far reaches of the web. This chapter gave you a taste of what's possible including:

- Using URLs in web overlays to incorporate external websites

- Embedding selective content from external sites such as YouTube and Google Maps

- Incorporating local HTML content such as HTML5 animation generated by Adobe Edge Animate

In the course of your explorations, you got a further glimpse into Creative Cloud with a look at some of its benefits, including free access to Adobe Edge Animate. A quick side trip to Edge Animate provided an opportunity to experience its interface and export HTML5 animation for inclusion in a DPS folio.

You employed three different methods for adding HTML content to a DPS document: the Object > Insert HTML command, the Folio Overlays Web Content pane and placing an Edge Animate .oam file. Additionally, you learned how you can use links to access one folio article from another and even link to specific article pages.

Used creatively, web content overlays make it possible to push content updates to your app after it's been distributed, to include form and payment processing and anything else supported by an iOS browser. In other words, web content overlays can bring whole worlds of possibility right into your app!

Next up are slideshow overlays, another extremely versatile addition to your arsenal of overlays.

Chapter 34

SLIDESHOW OVERLAYS

Perhaps the most versatile type of overlay, slideshows can perform a panoply of functions—from serving up a simple slideshow to performing as a faux frame for other overlays, to providing a "package" for a PowerPoint-style presentation with other overlays nested inside. And that's just a taste of what they can do. This chapter will show you how to put slideshows through their paces to perform in ways no other type of overlay can.

Slideshow Overlays

Slideshow overlays start with multi-state objects (which can also be exported to Flash SWF.) Slideshows are special in that they can contain other overlays as well. Heck, with a little maneuvering, you can even nest one slideshow inside another as you'll learn in exercise 34.2.

Exercise 34.1: Creating a Slideshow Overlay

In this exercise, you'll compile nine sandal-making steps into a slideshow.

1. Navigate to the chapter_34_exercises folder and Double-Click **ex34_1_start.indd** to open it. Save the file as ex34_1.indd.

2. Using the Selection tool, position your cursor outside the upper left corner of the objects on the left side of the pasteboard. Click and hold and drag down and to the right to enclose the top two text frames and all nine production step frames to select them. Release the mouse.

TIP: For best results, the object or object group comprising each state of a multi-state object slideshow should be of approximately the same dimensions.

3. Click the step six frame to designate it as the key object and open the Align panel (Window > Object & Layout > Align.)

4. In the Align panel, click the Align right edges button and then the Align bottom edges button to align all the frames to the frame for step 6.

TIP: A multi-state object is identified by the [icon] icon at its lower right corner.

NOTE: MSO is an abbreviation for Multi-state Object.

Align the right and bottom edges of the of the slideshow state elements.

5. Open the Object States panel (Window > Interactive > Object States), and, with the eleven frames aligned and selected, click the Convert selection to multi-state object button at the bottom of the panel. Click each state of the MSO in the panel to see the content change on the document page.

TIP: When you create an alternate layout for a document containing interactive elements, InDesign automatically renames the elements in the new layout by appending a space and a number after the original name. For slideshows in a dual-orientation folio, be sure to rename both the object name and individual state names in the alternate layout slideshow to match the original in order to maintain continuity when the iPad is rotated.

Select and align multiple objects (or object groups) and click the Convert selection to multi-state object button at the bottom of the Object States panel to create multiple slideshow states with a single click.

6. Name the multi-state object msoSandals and expand the Folio Overlays panel. When the panel opens to the Slideshow properties, check the Swipe to Change

Image checkbox and ensure that the Cross Fade checkbox is checked. Leave the other default settings.

The Slideshow overlay converts a multi-state object to a slideshow that can play automatically, or that a user can tap to play and pause, and navigate by swiping from one state to another.

7. Using the Selection tool, drag the MSO to snap its upper right corner to the intersection of the vertical and horizontal ruler guides. Save the document.

8. Click the Preview button at the bottom of the Folio Overlays panel and choose whether to preview your overlay on your iPad (if it's connected and the Adobe Content Viewer app is installed and running) or on your desktop. When the preview opens, swipe through the slideshow to see each of the slides. (If you're previewing on your desktop, click and hold and drag your mouse from left to right or right to left on the slideshow.) When you've finished exploring, close out of the preview and return to InDesign. Save and close the file to complete the exercise.

Nested Overlays

The possible uses for slideshow overlays multiply exponentially when you take advantage of the ability to nest one overlay inside another. You can embed any type of overlay in a slideshow; however, to embed one slideshow inside another, the multi-state object that will become the nested slideshow must first be anchored in a text frame. The text frame containing the slideshow can then be incorporated in one of the "parent" slideshow states.

Exercise 34.2: Creating Nested Overlays

1. Navigate to the chapter_34_exercises folder and Double-Click **ex34_2_start.indd** to open it. Save the file as ex34_2.indd.

2. Using the Selection tool, click to select the msoSandals slideshow object in the lower right portion of the document page. Press Ctrl+X/Command+X to cut it.

3. Press T to switch to the Type tool and position the arrow at the upper left of the cursor at the intersection of the horizontal and vertical ruler guides. When the arrow turns white, click and hold and drag down and to the left—to the lower right corner of the frame containing the word Sandals—and release the mouse. With the blinking Type cursor active in the new text frame, press Ctrl+V/

Command+V to anchor the slideshow in the text frame. Press Shift+Ctrl+R/ Shift+Command+R to right-align the paragraph and thereby shift the slideshow to its original position at the right of the frame.

4. Press Escape to switch to the Selection tool and then position the cursor outside the upper left corner of the word "THE." Click and hold and drag down and to the right to select the slideshow and the frames containing the words "THE" and "SANDALS."

5. Press Ctrl+G/Command+G (Object > Group) to group the selected objects. Expand the Layers panel in the Panel Dock (❄), and click the disclosure triangle at the left of the content layer to show its sublayers. Click to select the <group> sublayer, then click its name to activate and select the text. Type "sandalsMain" and press Enter/Return to commit the new layer name.

6. In the Layers panel, with sandalsMain still selected, Shift-Click the selection square at the right of the impactMain, problemMain and missionMain sublayers to add the object groups to the selection. Click sandalsMain on the document page to designate it as the key object for alignment purposes.

A blue square appears in the selection column of the Layers panel for each of the selected layers.

7. If necessary, open the Align panel. Click the Align left edges button and then the Align top edges button to align the elements for the parent slideshow.

8. With the objects aligned and selected, if necessary, expand the Object States panel (Window > Interactive > Object States.) Click the Convert selection to multi-state object button at the bottom of the panel and name the MSO "msoMain."

9. Expand the Folio Overlays panel, and ensure that the Cross Fade checkbox is checked. Leave all the other checkboxes unchecked.

Since the viewer must swipe to navigate the slides of the msoSandals slideshow, you'll avoid confusion in the interface by setting up button actions—instead of swiping—to navigate the msoMain slideshow states.

10. Using the Selection tool, click the button bar on the document page to select it. In the Layers panel, twirl down the disclosure triangles for the content, <group>, and buttons layers. Click the selection square at the right of the sandalsBtn layer to select the button on the document.

NOTE: The existing actions on the button bar buttons navigate the states of the msoAbout slideshow at the top of the page. You'll add actions to the buttons to simultaneously show the corresponding states of the msoMain slideshow.

Using the Layers panel is the easiest way to select the sandalsBtn object which is nested within multiple sublayers.

11. With the sandalsBtn selected, expand the Buttons and Forms panel. Click the Add new action for selected event button (➕), and choose Go To State from the Actions dropdown. Choose msoMain from the Object dropdown and sandalsMain from the State dropdown.

Set a second action on the sandalsBtn to go to the sandalsMain state of the msoMain slideshow.

12. Similar to the process in steps 10 and 11, use the Layers panel to select each of the remaining button bar buttons and add Go to State actions to them as follows:

Button #	Button Name	Object	State
2	impactBtn	msoMain	impactMain
3	problemBtn	msoMain	problemMain
4	missionBtn	msoMain	missionMain

13. Save the document. Expand the Folio Overlays panel, click the Preview button at the bottom of the panel, and choose your preview mode. When your preview opens in Adobe Content Viewer, swipe through the states of the sandals slideshow and use the button bar buttons to navigate the main and about slideshows. When finished previewing and testing, return to InDesign. Close the file to complete the exercise.

Framing an Overlay

You may have noticed in previous exercises that, while the stroke surrounding the sandals image sequence was visible in InDesign, it disappeared when the overlay was previewed. When activated, overlays float above both the page and the InDesign object that contains them. In the case of the sandals sequence, the stroke on the object is aligned to the inside. When activated, the overlay fills the inside of its container and floats above it, thereby obscuring its stroke. Shifting the stroke to the outside of the object provides only a partial solution. Since the corners of the overlay frame are rounded and the sandal images are rectangular, when the overlay is active, the squared image corners float above the rounded corners of the frame and make them disappear. One way to correct this behavior is to employ a slideshow overlay in a rather unconventional way and position it above the image sequence overlay to act as a "frame."

As you are now well aware, at the heart of every slideshow overlay is a multi-state object. Multi-state objects must have a minimum of two states but there's no prohibition against having the same content in more than one state. The trick to framing an overlay—and this trick works to frame video overlays as well—is to create a "dummy" slideshow overlay from a multi-state object that has two identical states. The same "frame" graphic resides in both states of the MSO and the "frame" slideshow is positioned above the "framed" overlay in the document stacking order. Your audience can still click or tap to activate the content being framed and since the frame is also an overlay, as long as it's in the proper stacking order, it floats above the overlay it's framing—a quick and easy solution to what might otherwise present a maddening problem.

Exercise 34.3: Framing an Overlay

1. Navigate to the chapter_34_exercises folder, open **ex34_3_start.indd** and save it as ex34_3.indd.

2. Zoom out if necessary to see the "frame" object on the document pasteboard and expand the Layers panel (❁) in the Panel Dock.

    There are two layers in the Layers panel: the content layer and the frameSlideshow layer. The frameSlideshow layer contains the graphic that you'll use to create the "frame" slideshow overlay.

3. Using the Selection tool, select the frame graphic on the pasteboard. Press Ctrl+C/ Command+C to copy it and then go to Edit > Paste in Place (Alt+Shift+Ctrl+V/ Option+Shift+Command+V) to position the pasted graphic precisely atop the original.

4. In the Layers panel, click the disclosure triangle to the left of frameSlideshow to expand the layer. There should be a red square in the column to the right of the uppermost frame layer indicating that the duplicated frame is selected. Hold the Shift key and click in the selection column at the right of the bottom frame layer to add it to the selection.

5. With both frame graphics selected, click the double arrow at the upper right corner of the Layers panel to collapse the panel. Expand the Object States (🗔) panel in the Panel Dock and click the 🗔 button at the bottom of the panel to create a new multi-state object.

    The selected frame objects combine to create a new multi-state object with two identical states.

6. Still in the Object States panel, select the default Object Name, replace it with "frameMSO" and press Enter/Return to commit your change. Rename the object states "frame1" and "frame2."

The Object States panel showing the multi-state object (MSO) that forms the foundation of the "frame" slideshow overlay.

When you create or place objects in a document, the names InDesign assigns to the object layers in the Layers panel are typically enclosed by opening and closing chevrons like so: <rectangle>. As previously mentioned, these chevrons and other punctuation in object names can cause problems in the code that's generated when your folio is compiled. To avoid being plagued by name-related performance problems in your folios, rename the elements in your overlays, and the overlays themselves, with names that:

NOTE: In the exercise file, the frame graphic to which InDesign gave the default name of <rectangle> was renamed "frame" to avoid name-related code issues.

1. Begin with either a lower case letter or an underscore

2. Contain no spaces

3. Contain no characters other than lower case letters, numbers, hyphens or underscores.

7. With the MSO still selected, expand the Folio Overlays panel and the Slideshow pane should appear. Select the Auto Play checkbox and deselect Cross Fade and Loop. Check Stop at Last Image, and choose Vector from the Export Format in PDF Articles dropdown at the bottom of the panel. Leave the other default settings.

TIP: For best performance, disable looping and crossfade when using a slideshow to frame another overlay.

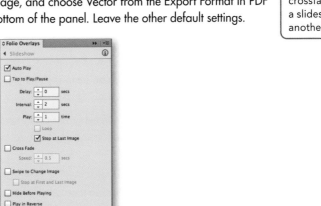

For a "frame" slideshow overlay, enable Auto Play and check the Stop at Last Image checkbox. Since the frame graphic is natively a vector object, choose Vector from the Export Format in PDF Articles dropdown.

8. Using the Selection tool and holding the Shift key to constrain motion, click and hold the stroke of the slideshow frame and drag to position it precisely over the sandals image sequence.

9. Click the Preview button at the bottom of the Folio Overlays panel. Pause until the Preview on Desktop option appears and then click it to display the document in Adobe Content Viewer.

The only difference between this file and the one from the previous exercise is that the green frame surrounding the sandal image sequence should be visible when previewed.

10. When you're finished exploring, return to InDesign. Save and close the file to complete the exercise.

Accessing Slideshow States for Editing

Let's say your slideshow is all ready to go and at the eleventh hour, you notice a typo. After getting past your self-recriminations for not religiously using spell check (been there, done that), you've got to get it fixed and get it out the door. But, the typo isn't in the state that's visible in your document. Now what?! The Object States and Layers panels to the rescue.

Exercise 34.4: Editing Slideshow States

In this exercise, you'll learn that it's not all that tough to dig down through multiple objects and layers to edit content in a nested slideshow.

1. Navigate to the chapter_34_exercises folder, Double-Click **ex34_4_start.indd** to open it, and save the file as ex34_4.indd.

2. Using the Selection tool, click the shoes at the bottom of the document page to select the msoMain slideshow. Expand the Object States panel in the Panel Dock (Window > Interactive > Object States) and notice that the sandalsMain state is highlighted in the panel.

3. Double-Click the text to the left of the shoes in the msoMain slideshow to drill down to the nested msoSandals multi-state object. Notice that the sandalsIntro state is highlighted in the Object States panel.

4. Scroll to the bottom of the Object States panel and select the state named "sandals09" to make it appear on the document page.

5. Switch to the Type tool and click to position the cursor after the "y" in the word "ready". Delete the "y" and type "ied" to compose the word "readied". Press Escape to switch to the Selection tool, scroll back to the top of the Object States panel and select the sandalsIntro state. Click on the pasteboard to deselect and then click the slideshow again to see the original msoMain states restored to the Object States panel.

6. Save and close the file to complete the exercise and the chapter.

CHAPTER SUMMARY

This chapter provided you with an introduction to slideshow overlays and several of the many ways you can put them to use.

You started with assembling a multi-state object by:

- Selecting multiple object groups of similar overall dimensions

- Aligning the object groups

- Using the button at the bottom of the Object States panel to create a multi-state object (MSO) in which each selected object group became a separate state.

Next, using the Folio Overlays panel, you converted your MSO to a slideshow overlay and became familiar with the various slideshow overlay options. You then learned how to nest one slideshow overlay inside another by anchoring the first slideshow in a text frame and then using the text frame as a state in the "parent" slideshow.

To edit a nested slideshow, you learned how to use the Object States and Layers panels to access hidden slideshow states. In the process you:

- Were reminded how to select an object on the document by clicking the square in the Layers panel selection column

- Renamed layers in the Layers panel to avoid performance issues in your folio that could result from InDesign's default object naming conventions

- Learned that the names for both slideshow overlays and each of their states need to be the same in both layouts of a dual-orientation folio in order to maintain continuity when the iPad is rotated

You also reviewed some other key skills including:

- Clicking one of multiple selected objects to designate it as a key object for alignment purposes

- Adding button actions through the Buttons and Forms panel

- Right-aligning a paragraph using the Shift+Ctrl+R/ Shift+Command+R keyboard shortcut.

And let's not forget that you learned how to use a slideshow overlay with two identical states to create a "frame" for another overlay.

Now that you know how to build the various DPS overlays and how to assemble your articles into a folio, you're ready to learn what it takes to get your app from InDesign to the App Store.

● Chapter 35

PUBLISHING TO DPS

You've made your documents more dynamic with the magic of interactive overlays, created a folio, and added articles and metadata. Now it's time to translate your travails into an awesome app. You'll learn how to collaborate and collect articles through shared folios, keep the content of your articles and folios current, learn about P12 certificates and provisioning files, and find your way around Folio Producer and DPS App Builder. Last but surely not least, we've provided two lengthy lists of reminders and resources to assist you in your further adventures into DPS and digital publishing.

Finishing Up with Folio Builder

Perhaps you're part of a team and need to conduct reviews and compile articles from other collaborators. Perhaps you've edited an article and need to update your folio to reflect the changes. The Folio Builder panel is the bridge to getting it all together and getting it done.

In Chapter 28: Intro to DPS, starting on page 427 you were introduced to the three faces of Folio Builder—the folios, articles and layouts panes. The panel menus are contextual with options that change depending on which screen is active and what's selected in the document. Regardless of the active screen, you can use the panel menu to sign in and out of DPS with a valid Adobe ID, a requirement for uploading local files to Folio Producer for sharing, and for finally converting your folio to an app.

Sharing Folios

You can share and unshare folios through the Folio Builder panel menu or the Folio Producer: Organizer.

TIP: To upload a folio to Folio Producer, select a local folio in the folio pane of the Folio Builder panel and choose Upload to Folio Producer from the panel menu options.

While InDesign affords you the option of creating a local folio, if you want to share it with others for collaboration or review, you must first sign in to DPS and upload the folio to Folio Producer. Once it's uploaded, select your folio in the folios pane of InDesign's Folio Builder panel, and choose Share from the panel menu. InDesign generates an email invitation with a link to your folio that you just address and send.

TIP: When you share a folio, the email addresses you use for the recipients of your invitation must be associated with valid Adobe IDs.

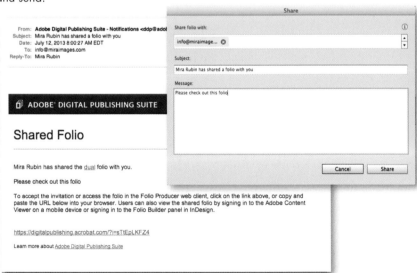

When you share a folio, InDesign generates an email invitation that contains a link to your folio in Folio Producer: Organizer.

Your recipients receive an email invitation from Adobe Digital Publishing Suite Notifications that contains instructions and a link to your folio in Folio Producer: Organizer. To accept the invitation, they must click the link and sign in with the Adobe ID that corresponds to the invitation email address. Once the invitation has been accepted, your recipients can download the free Adobe Content Viewer app, log in, and preview the folio. If the recipient signs in to DPS through the Folio Builder panel in InDesign, the shared folio appears in the Folios pane of the panel decorated with a badge that identifies it as a shared folio.

TIP: To create an Adobe ID, go to https://www. adobe.com/ account/sign-in. adobedotcom.html

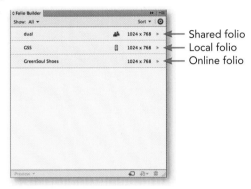

Shared and local folios are distinguished by
identifying badges in the Folio Builder panel.

Your recipient can then preview the shared content in Adobe Content Viewer—using the Preview button at the bottom of the Folio Builder panel to preview on the desktop or on a connected iPad.

The same shared folio badge appears in the Folio Builder panel for both the "sharer" and the "sharee." Article names of folios shared with you appear in the panel in gray, while those of folios you've shared with others appear in black. If you are not the owner/originator of the shared folio, you can't edit the original articles in InDesign, but you can rearrange the order in which they appear in the folio. You can also add articles, and the articles you add become available for editing through the Folio Builder panel to both you and the owner of the folio.

You can unshare a folio even more easily than sharing one. Simply select a shared folio in the Folio Builder panel, and choose Unshare from the panel menu. You can also easily remove a shared folio, or any folio for that matter, by selecting the target folio and choosing Delete from the panel menu. Deleting a folio deletes it permanently from the Folio Builder panel.

Updating Folios and Folio Articles

Throughout the process of developing your content, you'll be editing, adjusting, and testing, which, by definition, requires that you resave your content. If you've compiled your InDesign documents as articles in a folio, it's important to understand that changes saved to your InDesign documents don't always transfer automatically to the articles—particularly if you've added new overlays. To be on the safe side, you can explicitly update the compiled article in InDesign to ensure that your changes are implemented. Select the containing folio in the Folios pane of the Folio Builder panel and click the arrow to the right of the folio name to access the Articles pane. Select the article that requires updating and choose Update from the panel menu to recompile the article and implement your changes.

Once you've compiled a folio, to ensure that you're editing the right version of the right file, the Folio Builder panel is probably the best way to access the source files for your articles. From the Articles pane, select an article and click the arrow to the right of its name to display the article layouts. Double-Click a layout to open the source document in InDesign.

Updating Folio and Article Metadata

InDesign lets you compile a folio and its articles without requiring that you provide much of the metadata you'll need for final publication. Although you'll get yet one more chance in Folio Producer, for convenience sake, you might want to finish entering the necessary info in InDesign. The properties panels for both folios and articles are accessed from the Folio Builder panel menu when their respective panes are active in the panel.

NOTE: For a detailed explanation of article and folio metadata, see Chapter 28, starting on page 427.

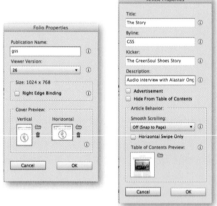

You can still update much of the metadata for folios and articles after they've been created through the Properties panels accessed from the Folio Builder panel menu.

Folio Producer

Much like Folio Builder in InDesign, the online Folio Producer Organizer and Editor provides access to all your folios—enabling you to view and edit folio and article metadata, and to add, arrange, and remove articles. It also enables you to share folios and copy articles from one folio to another—a great way both to replicate content without having to regenerate it and to share original InDesign source files. To access Folio Producer from InDesign, simply choose the Folio Producer option from the Folio Builder panel menu. To access Folio Producer online, go to https://digitalpublishing.acrobat.com/welcome and sign in with the Adobe ID for your folio.

Folio Producer: Organizer

When Folio Producer opens, you are presented with Organizer, a concentrated view of the metadata for all your folios. From Folio Producer: Organizer you can add and edit metadata, and share and remove folios. Select a folio and click the Open button at the top of the screen to access Folio Producer: Editor.

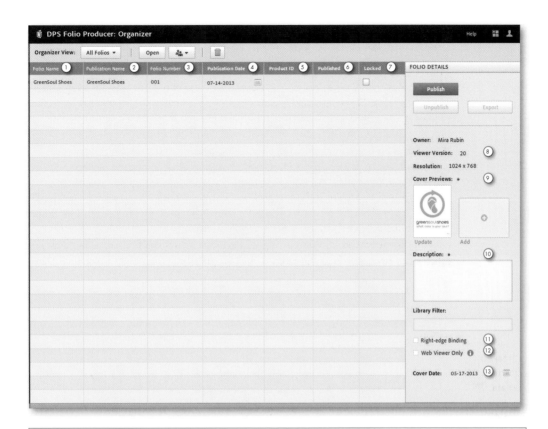

FOLIO PRODUCER: ORGANIZER

1. Folio Name: Different from the Publication Name that appears in the viewer, the Folio Name—maximum 60 characters—shows up in the Folio Producer and in the Folio Builder panel. Avoid crazy characters.

2. Publication Name: appears in the viewer library and in the viewer navigation bar.

3. Folio Number: can be a number or a description, such as "July, 2013."

4. Publication Date: Determines the order of folios in the library with the newest folios appearing at the top. Especially important for subscription viewers.

5. Product ID: The Product ID specified when you published the folio.

6. Published: Indicated by a check mark if the folio is published.

7. Locked: Prevents upload of a new version of the article or changing of article metadata. The Folio Builder panel displays a lock icon next to the article.

8. Viewer Version: Enables you to choose a viewer version for your folio and to ensure that the version you choose has already been approved by Apple. Version numbers can be updated but not rolled back. (Version 20 is the earliest viewer supported.)

9. Cover Previews: .png or .jpg images that appear in the viewer library.

10. Description: For internal use only and does not appear in the viewer.

11. Right Edge Binding: Displays articles from right to left rather than left to right in the viewer. Especially important for Asian languages.

12. Web Viewer Only: Does not apply to Single Edition apps.

13. Cover Date: A metadata control related to direct entitlements for Enterprise publishers.

Folio Producer: Editor

While Folio Producer: Organizer gives you access to folio metadata, Folio Producer: Editor gives you article-level access to both metadata and the actual articles.

To access Folio Producer: Editor, select a folio in Folio Producer: Organizer and click the Open button at the top of the screen. You can choose from two views of the Editor: a Thumbnail view for previewing articles and changing properties, and a List view for ordering, locking, and changing other metadata settings. Like the Organizer view, the Editor presents the metadata for all the articles in a unified view. Switch between the Editor views using the buttons at the upper left of the interface.

Folio Producer: Editor Thumbnail view.

Folio Producer: Editor List view,

List view active 

Thumbnail view active

Switch between the List and Thumbnail views of the Folio Producer:
Editor using the buttons located at the upper left of the screen.

At the time of this writing, Folio Producer: Editor cannot display thumbnails for
PDF articles. If you've exported your folio to PDF format, don't be alarmed if Folio
Producer: Editor displays only article names looking something like this:

Folio Producer: Editor displays only article names for articles exported to PDF format.

The Add Article feature of Folio Producer: Editor is pretty cool in that it allows you
to copy an article from one folio to another. The cool part is, if you copy the article
to a folio you own, you can access its source file in InDesign through the Folio
Builder panel, just as you would any other article—even if the article you copied is
from a folio that was shared with you. In Folio Producer: Editor, just select the folio
to which you want to add the article and click the Add button. In the Add Article
dialog, choose an existing folio from the From Another Folio dropdown, choose an
article, and click the Add button. The article is added to the folio in both the online
Folio Producer and the Folio Builder panel in InDesign.

A unique feature of the Folio Producer: Editor is that it allows you to
share articles between any of the folios to which you have access.

Switch from Folio Producer: Editor to Folio Producer Organizer view by clicking the
Folio Producer: Editor title at the top of the screen.

The Folio Producer: Editor title acts as a hyperlink to
navigate back to the Folio Producer: Organizer view.

TIP: In the Adobe
Content Viewer library
on an iPad, thumbnails
for folios hosted on
the Folio Producer
server display a blue
strip with a lightning
bolt. A blue strip with
a plug icon indicates a
folio loaded through
Preview on Device. No
icon indicates a folio
Published from the
Distribution service
A gray icon indicates
that a folio cover
hasn't been assigned.

TIP: To navigate
Adobe Content
Viewer: Tap the title in
the navigation bar to
return to the first stack
Double-tap the title to
toggle between the
title and the title plus
version display
Triple-tap the title to
reset the issue so that
each article starts at
the first page instead
of the page that was
previously viewed.

Updates to Folio Tools and Viewers

TIP: You'll want to confirm the version of Adobe Content Viewer available through the App store before publishing a folio to the newest Viewer version. At the moment, Neil Enns from Adobe seems be the one keeping folks up to date on Apple's approvals. To get the latest status, go to http://forums. adobe.com and do a search for Approval Status of Adobe Content Viewer.

With the only constant of digital publishing being change, it stands to reason that the DPS tools are subject to frequent updates. Since InDesign's Folio Builder panel must remain in sync with Folio Producer and DPS App Builder, and publishing a DPS Single Edition app requires coordination of Adobe and Apple technologies, there are times when things just get out of sync. With Adobe's release of a new set of DPS App Builder tools, an update of the viewer is often required, and there is frequently a lag time before that viewer is approved by Apple and made available through the App Store. It is for this reason that the Viewer Version you choose when creating your folio is so important. While you can update the properties of your folio to support a more current viewer, rolling a folio back to an earlier version is not an option. To roll back to an older viewer, you would need to recompile your folio and target it to an earlier version. Therefore, you'll want to confirm that the version of the Adobe Content Viewer app available through Apple's app store is no older than the Viewer version you choose for your folio.

As Adobe continues its development of DPS, you may receive notifications requiring that you update DPS components. The procedure is generally pretty straightforward and simple. In some cases InDesign won't let you proceed without making the updates. Just follow the instructions and, generally, you should be good to go. Of course, you'll want to first make backups of your work and then test extensively to ensure that everything is in good working order.

InDesign and DPS will require that you make periodic updates to DPS tools.

The DPS Status website http://status.adobedps.com/ is a valuable resource to help you stay on top of what's happening with the software updates, bugs, fixes, server maintenance and more.

Preparing to Build your App

While putting together your article content is certainly the most time-intensive part of creating your app, all your efforts will be for naught unless you take the essential steps required to get it to the app store. As emphasized in the beginning of this section, you'll need to register as an Apple iOS developer (a $99 annual fee), download and install Xcode, and it's a good idea to familiarize yourself with the App Store review guidelines. Next, you'll need to generate the required development and distribution p12 certificates.

You'll actually be creating two versions of your app—one for development and testing purposes, and the other, the final distribution version, that you'll submit to the iTunes App Store for approval. Apple requires that both versions have valid p12 certificates in order to run on an iPad. Once you've got your p12 certificates, you'll create an App ID and register each testing device you'll be using by providing Apple with its UDID (comparable to a serial number.) Next, you'll use your p12 certificates and app ID to create two mobileprovision files—one for development of your app and the other for its distribution. The development mobileprovision file includes the UDIDs for all the authorized testing devices—the only devices on which you'll be able to test your app. Unlike the p12 certificates, the mobileprovision files are app-specific and can only be used for the app for which they were created.

If you haven't already done so, here's yet another encouragement to download the Step-by-step guide to DPS Single Edition from the link in the sidebar. While it may seem somewhat overwhelming at first, the Step-by-step guide walks you through each and every detail of obtaining the necessary certificates as well as the rest of the publishing process. Just be meticulous about following the steps and you'll get through it without a hitch.

As part of your preparations you'll need to create anywhere between 12 and 16 icons as well as a series of screen shots to provide your audience with a taste of what they can expect from your app. The process of creating these images could easily add to your overwhelm so we've provided a template in this chapter's exercise folder (**dps_export_template.indd**) that contains a page the size of each of the required icons. To create the icon files, populate each of the pages with your icon art in InDesign, and then go to File > Export. Choose PNG as your format, and export All Pages as High Quality 72 ppi PNGs.

NOTE: If you have a valid Adobe ID, InDesign automatically signs in to DPS when you open the Folio Builder panel.

DOWNLOAD: Link to the Step-by-step guide to DPS Single Edition PDF:

http://help.adobe.com/en_US/ppcompdoc/Step_by_step_guide_to_dps_se.pdf.

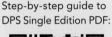

You can populate the pages of the template we've provided, and export the entire document to PNG to generate the many icons required for your app.

Since InDesign will generate a number of sequentially named images, it's a good idea to export your icons to a dedicated folder. While technically not necessary, you might find your icons easier to manage if you rename then according to their dimensions. Remember, it's best not to start the filename with a number—use an underscore or lower-case letter instead.

REQUIRED IPAD ICONS FOR RETINA DISPLAY AND IPAD 1 & 2		
	Retina Display iPad	iPad 1 & 2
App icon (required for all apps)	144 x 144	72 x 72
App icon for App Store (required for all apps)	1024 x 1024	512 x 512
Launch image (required for all apps)	1536 x 2048 (portrait) 2048 x 1536 (landscape)	768 x 1004 (portrait) 1024 x 748 (landscape)
Small icon for Spotlight search results (recommended)	100 x 100	50 x 50
Small icon for Settings	58 x 58	29 x 29
Toolbar and navigation bar icon (optional)	approx 40 x 40	approx 20 x 20
Tab bar icon (optional)	approx 60 x 60	approx 30 x 30

Once you've collected all your images, acquired your p12 certificates, Apple ID, and mobileprovision files, uploaded your folio to Folio Producer, and added all the necessary metadata to your articles and folios, you're finally ready to build your app.

DPS App Builder for Mac

DOWNLOAD: DPS App Builder for Mac: www.adobe.com/go/ digpubsuite_vb_mac

DPS App Builder (previously known as Viewer Builder) is a Mac-only tool you can use to compile your single-edition folio as a custom viewer app for submission to the Apple App Store. If necessary, you can download the newest version of DPS App Builder at www.adobe.com/go/digpubsuite_vb_mac.

Since Apple requires that all apps be submitted using a Mac, if you've been developing on Windows, this is the point where you need to switch platforms.

As long as you're on a Mac, you can initiate the app-building process directly in InDesign.

NOTE: The App Builder for Mac screenshots are from the version compatible with Viewer Version 26.

1. Expand the Folio Builder panel in InDesign, and, if necessary, sign in with the Adobe ID you want to use for your folio. Sign in and Sign Out (and, if applicable, Sign Up) options are available from the panel menu.

2. In the folio pane of the panel, select your folio and choose Create App from the panel menu. The DPS App Builder screen advises you of preliminary steps that must be completed prior to building your app. You may be required to sign in again, and then you will encounter a series of screens that should bear some resemblance to those that follow.

3. Complete the App Details screen with the appropriate information.

APP DETAILS SCREEN

1. The app name appears below the app icon. For best results, choose a name that has less than 14 characters. To preview an app name, open a website on your device, choose "Add to Home Screen" and type the desired name.

2. Specify the custom URL scheme that launches the viewer app from Safari and other apps. To ensure uniqueness, Apple recommends that you use the reverse-DNS format (com.publisher.publication.) For more information, see the Apple developer website.

3. Select this option to allow your users to pinch and zoom non-interactive pages. To enable pinch and zoom, make sure the format of the folio is PDF.

4. Select this option to allow your users to identify favorite articles within folios. Bookmarked articles appear in the favorites menu (star icon in the upper right corner of the viewer app.)

5. Select this option to hide folio scrollbars. Scrollbars are displayed by default.

6. Users tap on hot zones on either side of an article to navigate to next or previous.

7. You can enable a hot zone at the top and the bottom of a page to bring up the HUD, instead of having the whole page act as a trigger.

8. Enables rate app feature to help remind your users to rate your app on the App Store.

9. The Apple App ID is obtained from itunesconnect.apple.com via "Manage Your Applications." The Apple App ID is a unique nine-digit string of numbers assigned to your app by Apple; it is not the same as your application bundle ID.

10. By default, the rate the app dialog appears after two launches of the application but can be set to any value between 2 and 100. If the reader selects the Remind Me Later option in the dialog, the count will reset to zero.

11. Localized strings for selected languages are included in the viewer and will be listed as supported languages in the iTunes store.

4. If you've saved your icons to a folder, select all the images and drag them onto the Icons and Splash Screens panes, first for SD iPads and then for HD. Alternatively, you could click the folder icons to browse to the target images.

ICONS AND SPLASH SCREENS:

Use a 72 ppi, RGB, flattened, high-quality PNG file.
Apple rounds the corners automatically. Include the .png extension in your filename.

		iPad 1 & 2	Retina iPad
1	Icon will be used on the device Settings screen.	29 x 29	58 x 58
2	The 50 x 50 .png icon will be used in Spotlight search results.	50 x 50	100 x 100
3	The 72 x 72 .png icon will be used on the device Home screen.	72 x 72	144 x 144
4	The portrait splash screen is visible for 3 seconds when the viewer app is launched. For best results, your splash image should be different from the cover image. If the cover and the splash screen are identical, users may think the app is frozen when they first start it.	768 x 1024	1536 x 2048
5	The landscape splash screen is visible for 3 seconds when the viewer app is launched. For best results, your splash image should be different from the cover image. If the cover and the splash screen are identical, users may think the app is frozen when they first start it.	1024 x 768	2048 x 1536
6	The large app icon will be displayed on the desktop App Store and will be used to feature your app on the App Store. You can also specify a large app icon when submitting your app to the Apple Store.	512 x 512	1024 x 1024
7	The "Shine on app icon" indicates whether you want your app icons to include the "shine effect", which looks like a light is shining on the upper portion of the icon.		
8	You can include fonts in the HTML article or web view overlay in either the folio file or the viewer app. To include fonts in the viewer app, compress the fonts in a zip folder.		

TIP: To capture the UDID for an iPad
1) Attach the iPad to your Mac using a USB cable.
2) Launch iTunes on your computer.
3) Select your iPad either from the Devices section of the sidebar or by clicking the iPad button at the upper right of the iTunes window—whichever is available—to open the Summary screen.
4) In the Summary section, locate the serial number of your iPad.
5) Click the serial number, and it will change to the UDID.
6) Press Ctrl+C/Command+C to copy the UDID to the clipboard—no need to select the UDID before copying—and then paste the UDID into a text file for safekeeping.

5. Locate and load the .mobileprovision files you saved for development and distribution.

There's never a bad time for a little encouragement...

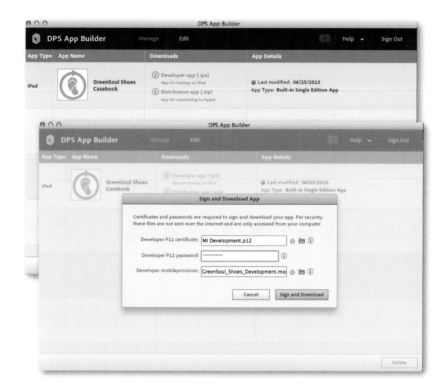

NOTE: P12 certificates are independent of an App ID and can be used for multiple apps. In contrast, the App ID is unique to the app for which it was created.

NOTE: For each P12 certificate you create you assign a password.

6. To download the Developer app (.ipa), locate and load your P12 certificate, enter your Developer P12 password and locate and load your developer mobileprovision file. Click the Sign and Download button to download your .ipa file.

7. Drag the .ipa file to iTunes.
8. Sync your iPad for testing.

To update the development version of your app after edits, simply choose Create App from the Folio Builder panel menu in InDesign and repeat the process. When you're ready to submit to Apple, you'll download the distribution .zip file, follow the submission process outlined in the Step-by-Step Guide, and wait for approval from Apple.

If you are a Creative Cloud subscriber you can make revisions to your published apps throughout the term of your subscription. You will of course then need to resubmit your apps to Apple for approval. Purchasers of a DPS Single Edition serial number can make revisions for a term of one year. Thankfully, creating revisions is much less taxing than your first build—in large part because you've already been through it once so it's not as scary. Secondly, most, if not all, of the peripheral files you'll need should already be place.

That pretty well completes the conversation about the mechanics of DPS, and you should definitely have enough information to be more than a little dangerous. There are of course other areas to explore if you're looking to gain broad distribution for your digital publication—keyword and metadata optimization, marketing strategies, and social media integration, for example. Apple has made lot's of support materials available on the developer site for these topics and more. Of course, the web is also teeming with marketing resources.

Don't Let the Gotchas Getcha

You've learned lots in the last few chapters, and a little review of some of the more salient points might serve as a helpful reminder. Here are some highlights.

Images

- For panoramas, 360° views, pan & zoom images, and audio controllers, use images with the exact pixel dimensions desired, at a resolution of 72 ppi. Exactly double the pixel dimensions for HD images.

- For images with large text, save to PNG or JPG format with medium-high compression. For images with small text, or icons with high detail, use PNG format.

- Create a 70 x 70 pixel PNG table of contents icon for your articles if you don't want to use the one InDesign generates automatically from the first page of the article.

- For panorama overlays, use an image of exactly the desired dimensions (JPEG recommended for best results) at a resolution of 72 px. (Maximum width and height of 2000 px with dimensions of no more than 1024 x 1024 px recommended.

Folios

- Maximum folio file size of 2GB.

- In laying out folio articles, designate a "safe area" of 44 px top and bottom for viewer navigation and menus.

- Files used in a folio can be different dimensions as long as they're the same aspect ratio. Apple iPad retina: 2048 x 1536, iPad 1 & 2: 1024 x 768, Aspect Ratio 16:9.5.

- Moving source documents to a new location can break the links in a folio. Use the Folio Overlays panel to relink your overlays to the correct file or folder and the Folio Builder panel to reconnected the folio articles to the proper source files. Test carefully to ensure that all necessary corrections were made and that everything works as intended.

- Despite being able to preview them through the articles pane of the Folio Builder panel, if all the articles in your folio do not have the same aspect ratio and layout orientation (vertical, horizontal, or both), the folio won't compile.

- Avoid using special characters in filenames and folders

- For slideshows in dual orientation folios, confirm that the same object and state names appear in the Object States panel for the multi-state objects in both the horizontal and vertical layouts to maintain a consistent user experience when the device is rotated.

- Don't run interactive elements into the document bleed area.

- To enable pinch & zoom, articles must be exported to PDF. Pinch & zoom works with static page content in snap-to-page articles only. Pinch & zoom is not applicable to smooth scrolling articles or pages with interactive content.

- Offline folios make it easy to preview your content on a tablet tethered to your computer via a USB cable. If you want to share a folio with others however, you must first upload it. An online folio cannot be reverted to an offline folio.

- You must provide both portrait and landscape cover images for your folio.

- There is often a lag time between Adobe's release of new Folio Producer tools and Apple's approval of the corresponding Content Viewer. When you create your folios, be sure to choose the appropriate Viewer Version.

- Article names are used as link references between articles and are not seen by your audience. They have a limit of 60 characters and should contain no crazy characters. Changing the name of an article breaks any links to that article.

- For best results, export to PDF format for folios meant to be viewed on both SD and HD iPads.

DPS Resources

Extensive but by no means exhaustive, we hope you'll find these resources helpful in your further engagement with DPS. We particularly recommend that you download Bob Bringhurst's DPS tips app from the Apple App Store, and check out Colin Fleming's extensive collection of video tutorials. The entire DPS section of this book wouldn't have been possible without knowledge gleaned from their collective wisdom.

Learning Resources

Step-by-Step Guide to DPS Single Edition
http://help.adobe.com/en_US/ppcompdoc/Step_by_step_guide_to_dps_se.pdf

Digital Publishing Suite Developer Center
http://www.adobe.com/devnet/digitalpublishingsuite.html

DPS HELP topics
http://help.adobe.com/en_US/digitalpubsuite/home

Learn Digital Publishing Suite: Single Edition
http://tv.adobe.com/show/learn-digital-publishing-suite-single-edition/

DPS Forum:
http://forums.adobe.com/community/dps

State of the Industry
http://blogs.adobe.com/digitalpublishing

Digital Publishing Gallery
http://blogs.adobe.com/digitalpublishinggallery

About Digital Publishing Suite, Single Edition:
http://www.adobe.com/products/digital-publishing-suite-single/buying-guide.html

Managing Article Metadata
http://helpx.adobe.com/digital-publishing-suite/help/create-articles.html

Guidelines for Creating Folios for iPad 3
http://blogs.adobe.com/indesigndocs/2012/03/guidelines-for-creating-folios-for-ipad-3.html

Creating HTML articles for DPS
http://helpx.adobe.com/digital-publishing-suite/help/import-html-articles.html

Building multi-rendition articles
http://www.adobe.com/devnet/digitalpublishingsuite/articles/building-multi-rendition-articles.html

Sending email and email attachments from DPS publications
http://blogs.adobe.com/jlockman/2012/09/26/sending-email-and-email-attachments-from-dps-publications/

DPS Downloads

DPS Tools Download
Mac: http://www.adobe.com/support/downloads/detail.jsp?ftpID=5377
Windows: http://www.adobe.com/support/downloads/detail.jsp?ftpID=5376

Pano2VR
http://gardengnomesoftware.com/pano2vr_license.php

Digital Publishing Suite Tips (App)
https://itunes.apple.com/us/artist/bringhurst-publishing-house/id397057892

Change Order of Articles with this sidecar.xml generator
http://digitalpublishing.tumblr.com/post/7042853716/change-order-of-articles-with-this-sidecar-xml

Websites

Digital Publishing Suite Dashboard
https://digitalpublishing.acrobat.com/app.html#x=dashboard

What's new in this release: Important to keep up to date on the latest DPS tool features
http://helpx.adobe.com/digital-publishing-suite/help/whats-new-release.html

Digital Publishing Suite Publisher Resources
https://digitalpublishing.acrobat.com/welcome.html

DPS Status page for scheduled maintenance: IMPORTANT site to track release of new tools, issues, etc.
http://status.adobedps.com/

Apple iOS Developer Program
https://developer.apple.com/programs/ios/

DPS Gurus (Alphabetical)

AdobeDigitalPub
@AdobeDigitalPub

Bob Bringhurst: @indesigndocs
http://blogs.adobe.com/indesigndocs/

Colin Fleming: @grayfive
http://tv.adobe.com/search/?q=Colin%20Fleming

Keith Gilbert: @gilbertconsult
http://blog.gilbertconsulting.com

Johannes Henseler (Secrets and Happiness of Digital Publishing)
http://digitalpublishing.tumblr.com

Bob Levine
http://boblevine.us

James Lockman: @jameslockman
http://blogs.adobe.com/jlockman/tag/dps/

Books

Digital Publishing with Adobe InDesign CS6
by Diane Burns and Sandee Cohen
http://indesigndigitalpublishing.com/category/dps/dps-new-releases/

ePublishing with InDesign
by Pariah Burke: @iampariah
http://iampariah.com/books

CHAPTER SUMMARY

This chapter was all about tying up loose ends and finalizing your folio. You picked up all kinds of pointers related to sharing folios for collaboration and content collection. Specifically, you learned that:

- You can't share a local folio—a folio must be uploaded to Folio Producer before the Share option even shows up in InDesign's Folio Builder panel menu. To upload a local folio, you must select it in the folio pane of the Folio Builder panel and choose Upload to Folio Producer from the panel menu.
- Once uploaded, you can share a folio from Folio Producer: Organizer online. Alternatively, you can share a folio from the Folio Builder panel in InDesign by selecting it in the folio pane and choosing Share from the panel menu.
- To access a shared folio, the person with whom you're sharing your folio must have a valid Adobe ID associated with the email address to which their invitation was sent.

You learned how to distinguish shared, local, and hosted folios based on their badges in the Folio Builder panel. Likewise, you learned to interpret the thumbnails in Adobe Content Viewer library:

- The blue band with the lightening bolt indicates folios hosted on Folio Producer.
- The blue band with a plug indicates a folio loaded through the Folio Builder panel Preview.
- No band at all indicates a folio loaded through the Distribution service.

You learned how to keep your folio and article content current, add articles and remove folios, and add and edit all manner of metadata in Folio Builder and Folio Producer—in both its Organizer and Editor views.

In preparing to publish your app, you started learning the language of an Apple developer with P12 certificates and mobileprovision files, developer and distribution versions of your app, and UDIDs to identify testing devices. You also came to understand the importance of choosing an appropriate version of the viewer for your folio, and stepped your way through App Builder for Mac to generate the .ipa file for testing on your iPad.

And that dear reader, brings us to the close of this chapter and of this book with our hopes and wishes that you've enjoyed the ride enough to continue the adventure. With Interactive PDF, Flash, EPUB and DPS as early signposts, you truly are at the edge of the rapidly emerging universe of interactive media. May you go forth boldly with inspired creative vision!

EXTRAS

As a parting gift, the next pages are packed with all manner of goodies: a collection of the tips that pepper the pages of the book, a compilation of keyboard shortcuts and a checklist of recommended preference settings. Enjoy!

TIPS

∙∙

TIP: To create a nested master, Right-Click/Ctrl-Click in the Master section at the top of the Pages panel and choose New Master from the contextual menu. When the dialog opens, name the new master and choose the desired parent master from the Based on Master dropdown. Click OK to create the master and close the dialog.
The new master appears in the document window and looks exactly like the first one. Try selecting any of the objects on the page, though, and you'll see that, like all master page items, the objects are locked by default.
When you base one master page on another, changes to the parent master update automatically in the children. 88

TIP: To change the name, number of pages or the Based On Master options for a master page, select Master Options for (Master Page Name) from the Pages panel menu. 88

TIP: To override and unlock a master page item on a document page, hold Ctrl+Shift/Command+Shift and click the item. 88

TIP: You can apply a master to document pages by dragging the master icon onto the page icon in the Pages panel or, with a master selected, you can use the Apply Master to Pages command from the Pages panel menu. 89

TIP: With the addition of modifier keys the Gap tool can perform all manner of manipulations:
Drag to move the gap and resize all the objects aligned to it.
Add the Shift key to any of its functions to affect only the two objects on either side of the gap.
Ctrl+Drag/Command+Drag to resize rather than move the gap.
Alt+Drag/Option+Drag to reposition rather than resize the gap and the objects aligned to it.
Ctrl+Alt+Drag/Command+Option+ Drag to resize the gap and move the objects without resizing them. 91

TIP: If a frame has no fill, clicking inside it will not select it. You must click the bounding box of an object that has no fill in order to select it. 92

TIP: If they aren't already showing, you can display the Distribute Spacing options in the Align panel by choosing Show Options from the panel menu.
To distribute space equally between selected objects, be sure to choose Align to Selection from the Align To dropdown. 93

TIP: When you drag multiple items from one layer to another in the Layers panel, InDesign reverses their stacking order. If the stacking order of the objects in the layer is important, you can drag to reorder them within the layer or drag them to the new layer individually. 93

TIP: To ensure that the hyperlinks you create are included in your exported files, select the Include All Interactivity and Media option when exporting to SWF, and All Forms and Media when exporting to PDF. 100

TIP: Hyperlinks can be applied to graphical elements as well as text. However, best practice dictates the use of buttons instead of hyperlinked graphics since buttons perform more reliably. 100

TIP: When you create a link to a URL, email address, or text anchor, the destination is recorded in InDesign as a named destination. You can modify the destination in the Hyperlink Destination Options dialog accessed through the Hyperlinks panel menu. The name of the destination is distinct from the destination definition, however, so changing one has no effect on the other. To change the name of a hyperlink destination, choose Rename Hyperlink from the Hyperlinks panel menu, enter a new name and then click OK. 104

TIP: You can import cross-reference formats from other documents. Choose Load Cross-Reference Formats from the Hyperlinks panel menu and then navigate to and select the file containing the desired formats. 105

TIP: Though technically it requires that you work with "code," InDesign makes the process of customizing Cross-reference Formats as painless as possible with a slew of built-in hints to help you craft your cross-reference code correctly.
Click the icons at the right of the Cross-Reference Formats dialog for help in formatting your cross-references. 106

TIP: Like paragraphs, text anchors too can be employed as cross-reference destinations. To create a text anchor, select the anchor text and choose New Hyperlink Destination from the Hyperlinks panel menu. The destination name will auto-populate with the selected text and the destination Type will be automatically set to Text Anchor. A cross-reference to a text anchor is created in the same way as a paragraph cross-reference, except you choose Text Anchor instead of Paragraph from the Link To dropdown. 108

TIP: The caret (^) shares the 6 key on your keyboard. The pipe (|) shares the backslash key. 114

TIP: If necessary, enter an appropriate number in the Start at field in the Numbering and Formatting pane of the Footnote Options dialog to continue footnote numbering across documents in an InDesign book. Otherwise, numbering of the footnotes will restart at 1 for each document in the book. 114

TIP: Space Before and Space After values in a footnote paragraph style only affect footnotes that contain multiple paragraphs. 114

TIP: Use the arrow keys on your keyboard to navigate from one footnote to another—even across pages. 115

TIP: To delete a footnote, delete the footnote reference number in the body of the document text. If you delete the actual footnote text, the structure of the footnote remains in the document. 115

TIP: If you accidentally delete the reference number in the footnote text, you can get it back—just place the Type tool cursor at the beginning of the footnote text, Right-Click/Control-Click, and choose Insert Special Character > Markers > Footnote Number from the contextual menu. 116

TIP: To make it possible for InDesign to generate PDF bookmarks for your TOC entries, be sure the Create PDF Bookmarks checkbox in the Options section of the Table of Contents dialog is checked. When exporting a PDF for print, you'll then need to check the Bookmarks checkbox in the Include section of the Export dialog. 122

TIP: To update the content of an existing TOC, position the type tool cursor in the TOC and go to Layout > Update Table of Contents. 122

TIP: As long as there's enough room for the Tab panel to fit above the active text frame, you can click the magnet icon (🧲) at the right of the panel to align and snap it to the top of the frame. 123

TIP: To remove a tab from the Tabs panel, click and drag it far up or far down and out of the panel. 123

TIP: If the Alignment tools aren't visible on the Control panel, go to Window > Object & Layout > Align to open the Align panel. 137

TIP To access Kuler, you must be connected to the internet. 139

TIP: The Effects controls are visible in the Control panel when the Type tool or the Note tool are not selected in the toolbar. If the Effects controls are not visible when they should be, choose Customize from the Control panel menu and ensure that the Effects checkbox is checked in the Object section of the dialog.
The Effects tool group on the Control Panel 155

TIP: Changes made to button instances in your document do not affect buttons in the Sample Buttons library. 157

TIP: At the right of the Find Font dialog is a More Info button that exposes a wealth of information about the selected font in the document including: PostScript name, font type and version, licensing restrictions, where the font file is located on your system, the number and names of styles using the font, a character count and the pages on which it occurs in the document. (The button caption changes to Less Info when pressed.) There is also a Reveal in Finder/Reveal in Explorer button that locates and selects the font file on your system. 159

TIP: Gradient stops look like little houses positioned below the gradient ramp. When a gradient stop is selected it's "roof" turns black. 160

TIP: For a linear gradient, the colors or transparency variations in the gradient are applied to an object sequentially, from left to right, as they appear on the gradient ramp.
While linear gradients go from left to right, the variations in a radial gradient radiate outward from the center. The leftmost gradient stop on the gradient ramp represents the center of the radial gradient and its origin, while the rightmost gradient stop represents the outermost edge of the gradient definition. 160

TIP: The lock icon at the upper left of the filmstrip graphic indicates that it is locked and cannot be selected or repositioned.
To lock an object, select it and click Ctrl+L/ Command+L or go to Object > Lock.
To unlock an object, click the lock icon on the locked object. 169

TIP: If Rulers are not visible, press Ctrl+R/ Command+R or go to View > Show Rulers. 169

TIP: Hold the Ctrl/Command key while you drag a guide to extend it across all pages of a multi-page spread. Dragging a guide from the ruler into the pasteboard rather than the page will also make the guide extend across the spread.
To switch the direction of a guide between horizontal and vertical, hold down Alt/Option while dragging. 169

TIP: InDesign enables you to place a wide variety of file formats including: native Illustrator, Photoshop, and InDesign files, multi-page PDFs, as well as TIFF, JPEG, GIF, EPS, BMP, PNG, DOC, DOCX, TXT, RTF, XLS, XLXS, FLV, F4V, SWF, MP4, and MP3 files. 169

TIP: InDesign's multiplace feature enables you to load the cursor with multiple files of any supported file type. You can place loaded files in a grid by using the arrow keys on your keyboard to add and remove columns and/or rows of frames. When you release the mouse, the loaded files are placed in the grid. 170

TIP: When a selected object or text has a style applied to it, that style is highlighted in the Styles panel. 170

TIP: The Auto-Fit feature enables you to scale the containing frame and its content as a unit, without the need to use modifier keys. Without Auto-Fit, you would need to hold Ctrl+Shift/Command+Shift while dragging in order to scale both the frame contents and the container frame together. 171

TIP: For the Show/Hide button Action, the X to the left of an object in the Visibility section of the Actions panel indicates that the object will retain its default visibility when the button is clicked. The 👁 icon indicates that the object will show and the 🚫 icon indicates that the object will be hidden. 175

TIP: Hold the Ctrl/Command key while any other tool is active to switch temporarily to the most recently selected Selection tool. 182

TIP: The Transform Sequence Again Individually command enables you to repeat and apply a sequence of transformations to multiple objects with only one click. 194

TIP: The Ellipse tool is hidden under the Rectangle tool (not the Rectangle Frame tool). Click and hold the Rectangle tool to expose the Ellipse tool so you can select it. 205

TIP: Easing: Transitions in animation speed are referred to as easing. InDesign has six easing options:
From Preset: Inherits easing from Preset.
None: No easing.
Ease In: Starts slowly and increases in speed to give the impression of acceleration.
Ease Out: Starts fast and slows down to give the impression of deceleration.
Ease In and Out: Starts fast, slows in the middle, and speeds up at the end. 205

TIP: To align objects to a key object, select the objects to be aligned and click the object against which you want to align them. A red bounding box appears around the object you clicked identifying it as the key object. When you align the objects, they will align relative to the position of the key object. 207

TIP: With your text or text frame selected, hold down the Shift+Ctrl/Shift+Command keys and press the > key to increase font size, or the < key to decrease it. 216

TIP: A triple click in the middle of a line of text with the loaded Eyedropper tool applies the formatting it's captured to the entire line. 216

TIP: When you click the Create Button Trigger button in the Animation panel, the cursor changes to a target until you click the button that you want to use to trigger the animation. 217

TIP: When attaching a custom motion path to an object, the path must be above the object in the layer stacking order. 222

TIP: To create a custom motion preset, select the animation you want to capture and then choose Save from the Animation panel menu. Enter a name for your preset and click OK. 223

TIP: To export a motion preset to share with other InDesign or Flash users, choose Manage Presets from the Animation panel menu. Select a Preset and click Save As. The Save dialog will appear with the preset name appended by the .xml extension. Browse to where you'd like to save the file and click Save. 223

TIP: Objects on hidden layers will not be visible when you preview the document or when it is exported. 226

TIP: If you ever want to turn off the target that selects the placed image inside a frame, go to View > Extras > Hide Content Grabber. 227

TIP: Motion paths snap to the center of the object being animated. Before connecting them, center the origin of the path on the object so when the motion path snaps to the object, the object maintains its position. 228

TIP: When exporting to SWF and Interactive PDF, buttons may break when they come in contact with transparency. If you encounter strange behavior in files containing buttons and objects with applied effects, removing the effects may effectively resolve the issue. 229

TIP: You can apply separate animations to a group and to the objects within that group. 232

TIP: To check out the page curl, mouse over a page corner. The page corner will automatically curl, just a little bit. When you see the curl, click and drag to begin turning the page. If you drag so that just over half the height of the page is curled, and then release, the page will flip as if you were turning a page in a book. 245

TIP: Depending on the version of Flash Player you are using, you may find that the Create Projector menu option is grayed out. So far, the only work-around we've been able to come up with is to use a different version of Flash Player. You can find archived versions of the player at http://helpx.adobe.com/flash-player/kb/archived-flash-player-versions.html#Flash%20Player%20archives 248

TIP: The bookmarks you create in InDesign export with navigational capabilities only but, you can modify them in Acrobat to add actions, set zoom levels and apply limited formatting. 254

TIP: If you have text selected when you create a bookmark, InDesign captures both the text and the document location in the bookmark definition. 257

TIP: An identifying badge appears at the lower right corner of every form field indicating the type of form field it is. 263

TIP: You can convert an object to a form field either through the Buttons and Forms panel or, go to Object > Interactive and choose from the available options. 263

TIP: Click and hold the Screen Mode icon on the Control panel or at the bottom of the Tool panel and choose from the options to change the screen display mode. Alternatively, press the letter "W" on your keyboard to toggle between Normal and Preview Mode. 265

TIP: Tables always reside in a text frame. If you want to have a stand-alone table, you must first create a text frame in which to insert it. 266

TIP: Using a Flush Space between entries on a line in a paragraph that has alignment set to "Justify all lines" distributes the entries evenly across the line. 267

TIP: Since buttons are only functional in the digital version of the document, there's no reason to include them in a printed version of a form. To prevent buttons from printing, deselect the Printable checkbox in the Buttons and Forms panel. 273

TIP: To clear all the page transitions from a document at once, choose Clear All from the Page Transitions panel menu. 284

TIP: When applying Security settings in PDF export, the passwords to open the document and to change permissions cannot be the same. 292

TIP: In Acrobat Professional, form fields can be sorted in the Fields pane alphabetically or based on tab order. 301

TIP: Although not recommended, you do have an option to include legacy media in your InDesign file for export to PDF. Legacy media that's supported includes MOV, AVI, MPG video, and AIFF and WAV audio files. Using legacy media requires that QuickTime be installed on the system, which could be problematic for Windows users. (If iTunes is installed, Quicktime is installed with it.) Since Flash

runtime is built into Acrobat XI and Reader XI, Flash Media, rather than legacy media, is the preferred, and more universal, option. 303

TIP: Though you may see it written in a variety of different ways, "EPUB" is preferred, per the IDPF. 310

TIP: Colophon: publisher's emblem or information related to the printing and publication of the book, including some or all of the following: date and place of publication/printing, name of the printer, name of the publisher, possibly name of a proof-reader or editor and other book- related references. 313

TIP: When publishing to EPUB, an InDesign story (including all its linked text frames) is treated as a single object, regardless of interspersed text or graphics or how many pages it may span. 322

TIP: Seeing frame edges makes it easier to anticipate the export order of objects in your EPUB. Go to View > Extras > Show Frame Edges to turn them on. 323

TIP: A change in metadata registers as a change to the related file. Such a change prompts the appearance of an out of date alert icon on the modified image on the page and to the right of the file name in the Links panel. Click the icon on the image or Double-Click the icon in the Links panel to update the link. 328

TIP: The backwards P symbol that indicates a paragraph is called a pilcrow. 331

TIP: In the EPUB Export Options dialog, the Settings Apply to Anchored Objects option applies only to Custom anchored objects. If you want spacing and/or page breaks before and/or after inline or above line anchored images, you must use the Object Export Options dialog. Spacing around inline anchored images will create a break in the paragraph at the point where the image is anchored. 332

TIP: Effective resolution is the resolution of an image after it's been scaled. If the image is scaled up, the effective ppi will be less than the actual ppi. If the image is scaled down, the effective ppi will be greater than the actual ppi. 334

TIP: InDesign uses the PNG format when rasterizing the first page of a document during EPUB export. 335

TIP: Multiply the pixel values for height and width to establish the total number of pixels in an image. 335

TIP: To remove a warning icon from a file listing in the Book panel, Double-Click the file to open it, then Save (or Save As if necessary), and close the file.
Alternatively, choose Update Numbering > Update All Numbers from the Book panel menu.   341

TIP: To replace a missing document in a book file, choose Replace Document from the Book panel menu and load the replacement file.   341

TIP: To create a style group, click the new style group button at the bottom of the styles panel and Double-Click the group name to enter a name of your choosing. To add a style to the group, drag it on top of the style group folder and release the mouse.   344

TIP: Check the Smart Match Style Groups checkbox in the book file Synchronize Options dialog to have InDesign detect styles of the same name and prevent duplication (regardless of whether a style resides inside a style group.)   344

TIP: Some of the commands in the Book panel menu are contextual and change based on which documents are selected. Commands for the entire book are available when all or none of the book files are selected. Otherwise, the available commands pertain to selected documents only.   344

TIP: For HTML tags with both an opening and closing tag, the closing tag is indicated by a forward slash preceding the closing HTML selector (</body>). In HTML tags without a separate closing tag, the tag is terminated by a space and a forward slash followed by a closing chevron (<br />).   350

TIP: The content of an HTML <em> tag generally appears italicized while the default appearance for the <strong> tag is bold.   351

TIP: Having InDesign export your EPUB with your custom stylesheet rather than adding it to your publication after the fact saves you the trouble of updating other files that itemize the EPUB contents.   364

TIP: To generate the cleanest possible code when exporting to EPUB, ALL your InDesign styling should ALWAYS be applied using saved styles.   366

TIP: The Split Document (EPUB only) checkbox in the Export Tagging category of the Paragraph Style Options dialog enables you to use the active paragraph style to split a single InDesign document into multiple HTML documents when you export to EPUB. Each new HTML document starts a new page in the EPUB. By splitting a document at its level one headers for example, you can ensure that each level one header in your EPUB begins a new page.   368

TIP: In Dreamweaver, selecting content in the design window selects the same content in the code window.   371

TIP: Press Ctrl+X/Command+X to cut selected text. This shortcut works across many applications including but not limited to Adobe and Microsoft programs.   372

TIP: To add space before to an HTML element, assign a value to the margin-top property in the appropriate CSS rule:
margin - top: .5em;
Likewise, to add space after, assign a value to the margin-bottom property
margin - bottom: .5em;   375

TIP: For a comprehensive list of iOS fonts, check out http://iosfonts.com.   377

TIP: Originally developed for the UNIX operating system, the term GREP comes from the command g/re/p
(global/regular expression/print) which would print all lines that matched a specified pattern.   380

TIP: Lost in space? Here's a key:
em space: fixed-width space equal to the size of the font. Often used to create a one-em indent at the beginning of a paragraph.
en space: fixed-width space that is half the width of an em space.
flush space: used at the end of a fully justified paragraph to position an end of story character flush right.
hair space: fixed-width space that is $1/24^{th}$ the width of an em space.
nonbreaking space: width of space created with the Spacebar, prevents a line break between words. Fixed width does not expand or compress with justified text.   380

Spaces continued:
thin space: fixed-width space that is $1/8^{th}$ the width of an em space.
figure space: a space the width of a figure in the given font.
punctuation space: a space the width of a period, colon, or exclamation point in the given font.
third space: fixed-width space that is $1/3^{rd}$ the width of an em space.
quarter space: fixed-width space that is $1/4^{th}$ the width of an em space.
sixth space: fixed-width space that is $1/6^{th}$ the width of an em space.   381

TIP: You can develop and test GREP expressions in the Find/Change dialog or in the GREP Style section of the Paragraph Styles panel. We prefer using the GREP Styles dialog because of the instant visual feedback you can receive using character styles to format the captured content.   381

TIP: To indicate a specific number of times a criterion should be met, enclose that number in curly braces. To indicate a repeat range, enter the minimum number followed by a comma, and then the maximum number. {2,5} means 2,3,4, or 5.   385

TIP: Enclosing code in parentheses isolates that code and creates what is called a "subexpression." Modularizing your code into subexpressions allows you to manipulate the captured content.   386

TIP: Surrounding GREP code with parentheses defines that code as a marked subexpression. You can reference marked subexpressions by number and use them to reorder document content.   389

TIP: To view two documents side-by-side, choose the first 2-up view from the Arrange Documents dropdown at the upper left of the InDesign interface.   391

TIP: To test GREP code that seems like it might not be performing properly, try starting your search from different locations in the document content. You'll note a pattern to what's targeted that could help you get on the right track.   392

TIP: Go to File > File Info and complete the Document Title metadata field on the Description tab to add a title to your document for export to EPUB.   400

TIP: Offline folios cannot be shared with others. An online folio cannot be reverted to an offline folio.434

TIP: If you have multiple documents open, the Add Open InDesign Document command adds the currently active document.   434

TIP: You can import an article or articles to your folios rather than adding an open document, however, the imported articles must reside in specially named folders that are structured in a very particular way. To learn more about structuring folders for article import see http://helpx.adobe.com/digital-publishing-suite/help/structuring-folders-imported-articles.html.
To learn about importing HTML articles, see http://helpx.adobe.com/digital-publishing-suite/help/import-html-articles.html.   434

TIP: The Article Name is used for creating links between articles and does not appear in the viewer. An Article Name can contain no more than 60 characters.   434

TIP: Smooth scrolling is only for DPS articles containing one long continuous page. (Pinch and zoom will not work with smooth scrolling articles and applies only to snap-to-page articles exported in PDF format that have no interactive elements.)   435

TIP: Multi-state objects—the foundation of DPS slideshows— can be exported to Flash as well as DPS. Unlike DPS slideshows, multi-state objects exported to .swf support complex InDesign animations.   440

TIP: Multi-rendition articles automatically display standard definition assets on iPad 1 & 2 and HD assets on Retina display iPads. The articles and folio must be in PDF format, the SD and HD assets must have identical names, and the HD assets must be in subfolders named HD. The link from the overlay to its assets is made to the folder containing the SD content and the devices then display the appropriate assets automatically.   442

TIP: DPS portrait layouts support landscape-only viewing of full-screen video.   443

TIP: In DPS Folios, Page flipping and smooth scrolling are determined on an article-by-article basis.   444

TIP: Liquid layout and layout adjustment are mutually exclusive—enabling layout adjustment disables the Liquid Layout options.   444

TIP: By default, liquid layout scales only the frame of an object and not its contents. Set your desired fitting options and enable Auto Fit to scale a frame and its contents together.   444

TIP: Hold the Alt/Option key while dragging with the Page tool to manually resize a page. (Be sure to release the mouse before releasing the modifier key.) To size a page more precisely, enter the desired page dimensions in the Control panel Page controls.   446

TIP: To position ruler guides or liquid guides precisely, select the guide using the Selection tool or Page tool and enter the desired coordinate in the X or Y field of the Control panel. Alternatively, enter the coordinate in the Transform panel (Window > Object & Layout > Transform.)   446

TIP: With the Guide-based option active in the Liquid Layout controls, you can click the badge on a guide with the Selection tool to convert it from a ruler guide to a liquid guide or vice versa.   446

TIP: You can activate the Liquid Layout panel controls by clicking a document page using the Page tool.   447

TIP: To remove a guide from your page, select the guide using the Selection tool and press the Delete key on your keyboard. Alternatively, click and hold and drag the guide off the page.   448

TIP: When developing styles intended for multiple layouts, ensure that the Based On setting in the General category of the text styles dialogs is set to [No Paragraph Style] in the Paragraph Styles panel or [None] for Character Styles. InDesign cannot create a mapped style when one of the source styles is based on another source style.   451

TIP: You can print/export a single page, a single layout or all pages in a document. To specify a particular page in a layout for printing, enter the layout name followed by a colon followed by the page number. E.g., iPad H:2 targets page 2 in a layout called iPad H.   451

TIP: One way to view alternate layouts side by side for comparison is to choose Split Window to Compare Layouts from the layout name dropdown at the top of the pages section of the Pages panel. 452

TIP: Deleting an alternate layout automatically deletes the text styles associated with it.   452

TIP: In addition to the Content Collector and Content Placer tools, you can use the Edit > Place and Link command to link content between layouts and documents.   454

TIP: Hold the Shift key while pressing the Arrow keys on your keyboard to move objects ten times the distance they would move using the Arrow keys alone.   461

TIP: For scrollable frame overlays that have stroked container frames, you can offset the content from the container by adding inset spacing in the Text Frame Options dialog (Ctrl+B/Command+B.) The inset is particularly useful in managing InDesign's automatic placement of the content frame in the container. Just remember that, in order to take advantage of the inset option, the containing frame must be for text rather than graphic content.   462

TIP: To view the entire pasteboard, go to View > Entire Pasteboard or press Alt+Shift+Ctrl+0/ Option+Shift+ Command+0.   464

TIP: The link on the loaded Content Placer cursor indicates that the object being placed will be linked to the item in the Content Conveyor.   467

TIP: While video overlays don't support streaming you can instead use Web Content overlays or HTML articles to add streaming content to your folios. 472

TIP: Consider using video on the cover of your DPS publication to capture the attention of your audience at their very first glance.   472

TIP: In Photoshop, use the Path Selection tool to select vector objects and the Direct Selection tool to select individual object anchor points.
To set your objects to precise dimensions enter W (width) and H (height) values in the Options Bar. 474

TIP: While you can resize your image sequence images directly in Photoshop's Render Video dialog, the Image Size dialog produces better results—particularly if the file contains vector shapes.   477

TIP: Looping of audio and video is currently unsupported in folio overlays.   479

TIP: Video overlays don't support streaming but if you need to, you can stream video using Web Content overlays or HTML articles.   480

TIP: In a panorama overlay, a Vertical value of -90 includes the face at the top of the cube in the visible area of the panorama and a Vertical value of 90 includes the face at the bottom of the cube. For horizontal rotation only, set the Limit Vertical Tilt values to -1 and 1.   487

TIP: If the Auto-Fit checkbox isn't visible in the Control panel, Right-Click/Command-Click on the image and choose Fitting > Frame Fitting Options from the contextual menu. When the dialog opens, check the Auto-Fit checkbox and then click OK to close the dialog.   490

TIP: In order to maintain a consistent experience across devices, it's best to create a dedicated HD version of your pan & zoom overlay images. If only one image is used, depending on its effective resolution in your layout, the initial pan & zoom image may appear at half its intended size on an HD iPad, or the image may shift suddenly when the overlay is activated. Additionally, the zoom range will be reduced.   490

TIP: Once an overlay preview is loaded onto your iPad, you can disconnect the device from your computer and continue to interact with the preview. If it is not part of an actual folio however, the preview will not remain available on the iPad once you exit it.   491

TIP: Distinct from web content overlays, you can also include entire HTML articles in your DPS folios. To learn more, check out Colin Fleming's informative video at http://helpx.adobe.com/digital-publishing-suite/help/import-html-articles.html   494

TIP: Web Content overlays cannot redirect, so it's important to use the correct URL for your destination. For example, a Twitter URL needs to be directed to the URL for mobile devices: http://mobile.twitter.com.   495

TIP: For Web Content overlays based on local HTML assets rather than URLs, make sure that the HTML file you specify is contained in its own folder and that you've entered the correct path. The entire HTML folder gets uploaded with the article, so the contents of the folder should be limited to the assets used in the HTML file(s). 495

TIP: To access HTML code that was entered in InDesign's Edit HTML dialog, select and Right-Click/Ctrl-Click the generated HTML object and choose Edit HTML from the contextual menu. 496

TIP: If smart guides don't appear when aligning one object to another, you can use the keyboard command Ctrl+U/Command+U to toggle their visibility. 496

TIP: To create a poster image directly in Edge Animate, drag the playhead through the timeline to display the desired view on the Stage. With the Stage selected, click the small camera icon in the Properties panel to the right of the Poster option at the left of the screen.

Poster: images/mission_poster.png 501

TIP: When using an HTML animation in a Web Content overlay, set the overlay to Auto Play with a slight delay (such as 0.125 seconds.) Setting the delay allows time for the animation scripts to load, ensuring that the animation will play properly. 502

TIP: For best results, the object or object group comprising each state of a multi-state object slideshow should be of approximately the same dimensions. 506

TIP: A multi-state object is identified by the icon at its lower right corner. 506

TIP: When you create an alternate layout for a document containing interactive elements, InDesign automatically renames the elements in the new layout by appending a space and a number after the original name. For slideshows in a dual-orientation folio, be sure to rename both the object name and individual state names in the alternate layout slideshow to match the original in order to maintain continuity when the iPad is rotated. 506

TIP: For best performance, disable looping and crossfade when using a slideshow to frame another overlay. 511

TIP: To upload a folio to Folio Producer, select a local folio in the folio pane of the Folio Builder panel and choose Upload to Folio Producer from the panel menu options. 516

TIP: When you share a folio, the email addresses you use for the recipients of your invitation must be associated with valid Adobe IDs. 516

TIP: To create an Adobe ID, go to https://www.adobe.com/account/sign-in.adobedotcom.html 517

TIP: In the Adobe Content Viewer library on an iPad, thumbnails for folios hosted on the Folio Producer server display a blue strip with a lightning bolt. A blue strip with a plug icon indicates a folio loaded through Preview on Device. No icon indicates a folio Published from the Distribution service A gray icon indicates that a folio cover hasn't been assigned. 521

TIP: To navigate Adobe Content Viewer: Tap the title in the navigation bar to return to the first stack
Double-tap the title to toggle between the title and the title plus version display
Triple-tap the title to reset the issue so that each article starts at the first page instead of the page that was previously viewed. 521

TIP: You'll want to confirm the version of Adobe Content Viewer available through the App store before publishing a folio to the newest Viewer version. At the moment, Neil Enns from Adobe seems be the one keeping folks up to date on Apple's approvals. To get the latest status, go to http://forums.adobe.com and do a search for Approval Status of Adobe Content Viewer. 522

TIP: To capture the UDID for an iPad
1) Attach the iPad to your Mac using a USB cable.
2) Launch iTunes on your computer.
3) Select your iPad either from the Devices section of the sidebar or by clicking the iPad button at the upper right of the iTunes window—whichever is available—to open the Summary screen.
4) In the Summary section, locate the serial number of your iPad.
5) Click the serial number, and it will change to the UDID.
6) Press Ctrl+C/Command+C to copy the UDID to the clipboard—no need to select the UDID before copying—and then paste the UDID into a text file for safekeeping. 527

DEFAULT KEYBOARD SHORTCUTS

File Menu
   Place... : Ctrl+D/Cmd+D
Edit Menu
   Copy: Ctrl+C/Cmd+C
   Cut: Ctrl+X/Cmd+X
   Deselect All: Shift+Ctrl+A /Shift+Cmd+A
   Find/Change...: Ctrl+F/Cmd+F
   Paste: Ctrl+V/Cmd+V
   Paste in Place: Alt+Shift+Ctrl+V/Opt+Shift+Cmd+V
   Redo: Shift+Ctrl+Z/Shift+Cmd+Z
   Select All: Ctrl+A/Cmd+A
   Step and Repeat...: Alt+Ctrl+U/Opt+Cmd+U
   Undo: Ctrl+Z/Cmd+Z

Layout Menu
   Go to Page...: Ctrl+J/Cmd+J
   Arrange: Bring Forward: Ctrl+]/Cmd+]
   Arrange: Bring to Front: Shift+Ctrl+]/Shift+Cmd+]
   Arrange: Send Backward: Ctrl+[/Cmd+[
   Arrange: Send to Back: Shift+Ctrl+[/Shift+Cmd+[
   Fitting: Fill Frame Proportionally: Alt+Shift+Ctrl+C/
      Opt+Shift+Cmd+C
   Fitting: Fit Content Proportionally: Alt+Shift+Ctrl+E/
      Opt+Shift+Cmd+E
   Group: Ctrl+G/Cmd+G
   Lock: Ctrl+L/Cmd+L
   Select: Container: Escape
   Select: Content: Shift+Escape
   Select: First Object Above: Alt+Shift+Ctrl+]/
      Opt+Shift+Cmd+]
   Select: Last Object Below: Alt+Shift+Ctrl+[/
      Opt+Shift+Cmd+[
   Select: Next Object Above: Alt+Ctrl+]/Opt+Cmd+]
   Select: Next Object Below : Alt+Ctrl+[/Opt+Cmd+[
   Text Frame Options...: Ctrl+B/Cmd+B
   Ungroup: Shift+Ctrl+G/Shift+Cmd+G

Product area : Tools
   Apply Color: ,
   Apply Gradient: .
   Apply None: /
   Apply default fill and stroke colors: D
   Direct Selection Tool: A
   Page Tool: Shift+P
   Gap Tool: U
   Content Placer Tool: B
   Ellipse Tool: L
   Hand Tool: H
   Line Tool: \
   Pen Tool: P
   Pencil Tool: N
   Rectangle Tool: M
   Rotate Tool: R
   Scale Tool: S
   Selection Tool: V, Text: Escape

Swap fill and stroke activation: X
Swap fill and stroke colors: Shift+X
Save all: Alt+Shift+Ctrl+S/Opt+Shift+Cmd+S
Toggle Character and Paragraph Modes in Control Panel:
   Alt+Ctrl+7 Opt+Cmd+7

Product area : View Menu
   Actual Size: Ctrl+1/Cmd+1
   Extras: Hide Text Threads: Alt+Ctrl+Y/Opt+Cmd+Y
   Fit Page in Window: Ctrl+0/Cmd+0
   Fit Spread in Window: Alt+Ctrl+0/Opt+Cmd+0
   Grids & Guides: Smart Guides: Ctrl+U/ Cmd+U
   Hide Rulers: Ctrl+R/Cmd+R

Screen Mode: Presentation
   Presentation Mode: Escape, Shift+W
   Set Presentation Background to Black
      (from within Presentation Mode) B
   Screen Mode: Set Presentation Background to Gray
      (from within Presentation Mode) G
   Screen Mode: Set Presentation Background to White
      (from within Presentation Mode) W

Product area : Window Menu
   Object & Layout: Align: Shift+F7
   Text Wrap: Alt+Ctrl+W/Opt+Cmd+W

Product area : Object Editing
   Decrease scale by 1%: Ctrl+,/Cmd+,
   Decrease scale by 5%: Alt+Ctrl+,/Opt+Cmd+,

Zoom
   Zoom In: Ctrl+/Cmd+
   Zoom Out: Ctrl–/Cmd–

Product area : Text and Tables
   Align center: Shift+Ctrl+C/Shift+Cmd+C
   Align force justify: Shift+Ctrl+F/Shift+Cmd+F
   Align justify: Shift+Ctrl+J/Shift+Cmd+J
   Align left: Shift+Ctrl+L/Shift+Cmd+L
   Align right:Shift+Ctrl+L/Shift+Cmd+L
   Apply bold: Shift+Ctrl+B/Shift+Cmd+B
   Apply italic: Shift+Ctrl+I/Shift+Cmd+I
   Apply normal: Shift+Ctrl+Y/Shift+Cmd+Y
   Decrease baseline shift: Alt+Shift+Down Arrow/
      Opt+Shift+Down Arrow
   Decrease kerning: Alt+Shift+Left Arrow/
      Opt+Shift+Left Arrow
   Decrease tracking: Alt+Left Arrow/Opt+Left Arrow
   Decrease leading: Alt+Up Arrow/Opt+Up Arrow
   Decrease point size: Shift+Ctrl+,/Shift+Cmd+,
   Increase baseline shift: Alt+Shift+Up Arrow/
      Opt+Shift+Up Arrow
   Increase kerning: Alt+Shift+Right Arrow/
      Opt+Shift+Right Arrow
   Increase tracking: Alt+Right Arrow/Opt+Right Arrow
   Increase leading: Alt+Down Arrow/
      Opt+Down Arrow
   Increase point size: Shift+Ctrl+./Shift+Cmd+.

RECOMMENDED PREFERENCE SETTINGS

··

With no document open:

1. Go to Preferences > Units & Increments and adjust the following:

   - Ruler Units: Pixels
   - Size/Leading: 1 pt
   - Baseline Shift: 1 pt
   - Kerning/Tracking: 10

2. Go to Preferences > Display Performance

   - Greek Type Below 0
   - Vector Graphics, slide to High Resolution

3. Go to Edit > Spelling > Dynamic Spelling

4. Go to Edit > Spelling > Autocorrect

5. Go to View > Extras > Show Text Threads

6. Change your default font: set font family, font size, paragraph formatting, etc.

7. Change the [Basic Paragraph] Paragraph style

   - Turn on Optical Kerning
   - Turn off Hyphenation

8. Choose Panel Options from the Pages panel menu. In the Panel Options dialog, uncheck Show Vertically in the Pages section at the top of the dialog

9. Add common colors to the Swatches panel

INDEX

Kuler panel 135

L

Layers panel 26, 32, 85
  adding new content 181
  collapsed 84
  content layer 510
  deconstructed 85
  dragging multiple items 93
  navigating 189
  non-appearance of Master pages
    86
  understanding 84
layout 22, 530
  DPS portrait layouts 443
  dual-orientation 6
  fixed 322
  form design 265–7, 269–70
  landscape orientation for the web
    21
  mobile devices and tablets 21
  multiple 451
  in PDFs 5
  portrait orientation for print 21
  screen display mode 265
Layout Adjustment 41, 42, 70
legacy media 303
  AIFF audio file 303
  AVI video 303
  MOV video 303
  MPG video 303
  WAV audio file 303
library
  adding items 192
  creation 192
  filter items 193
  saving items 272
  select multiple items 463
  snippets 193
LibreDigital 419
limber layout 444
Links
  absolute path 357
  foundation of HTML 356
  link and destination components
    356
  opening and closing anchor tag
    356–7

relative path 357
  see also HTML links; hyperlinks
Links panel 26, 30, 451
  customizing 47–8, 334
  out of date hazard icon 328
liquid layout
  alternate 446
  Controlled by Master 444, 448
  fitting options 444
  Fixed Width Columns 447
  guide-based 444, 447, 448
  match placement of guides 448
  object-based 444
  object-based rulers 448
  position ruler or liquid guides 446
  re-center 444
  remove guides 448
  resize page 446
  rules 444–5
  scale 444
  slideshow 447
  working with 445–8
  see also alternate layout
Liquid Layout panel 26, 28, 447
list boxes 263
lock icon 169
Lockman, James 503
looping 479, 511, 542
Lulu 419

M

Mac users
  Application Frame 33
  DPS App Builder 524–9
  EPUB Validation tool 419
  EPUBs 311, 316
  submitting apps to App Store 429
  zip/unzip scripts 419
margins 21, 401
  and bleeds 21
  defined in A-Master 70
Margins and Columns 37, 41, 42, 67
marquee selection 162, 163
marquee zoom 169
master pages 138
  A-Master 70, 90
  applying to document pages 89,
    341

objects on hidden layers 226
pop-ups 196
see also invisible buttons

W

W3C 355
web banners 42, 262-234
Web Content Overlays
   adding Adobe Edge Animate 502
   based on HTML assets 495
   creating 494–5
   embedding Google Map 497–8
   embedding YouTube content 496–7
   link or embed code 494
   local 494
   navto:// links 503
   online 494
   redirecting 495
   using URLs 494–5
websites 407, 419, 421, 531–2
Windows 26, 303, 311, 316
Workspaces, customizing 32–7
Workspace Switcher 36, 52, 54, 56, 150, 255, 431, 487
WYSIWG tools 374

X

XHTML 310, 313, 348, 349, 350, 355, 377
XHTML 1.1 (Document Type Definition) 355
XinXii 419
XML (Extensible Markup Language) 310, 311, 313, 322, 348, 355, 401
XML Structure panel 274
xmlns 355
XMP data 327, 328

Y

YouTube 32, 494, 496–7

Z

zoom 53, 72, 114, 169, 172, 212, 226, 242, 243, 254, 270, 442, 443
Zoom tool 169, 190, 248, 293